T&T CLARK HANDBOOK OF PNEUMATOLOGY

Forthcoming titles in this series include:

T&T Clark Handbook of Christology, *edited by Darren O. Sumner and Chris Tilling*

T&T Clark Handbook of Election, *edited by Edwin Chr. van Driel*

T&T Clark Handbook of Modern Theology, *edited by Philip G. Ziegler and R. David Nelson*

T&T Clark Handbook of the Doctrine of Creation, *edited by Jason Goroncy*

T&T Clark Handbook of Theology and the Arts, *edited by Imogen Adkins and Stephen M. Garrett*

T&T Clark Handbook of Intercultural Theology and Mission Studies, *edited by John G. Flett and Dorottya Nagy*

T&T Clark Handbook of Biblical Thomism, *edited by Matthew Levering, Piotr Roszak and Jörgen Vijgen*

Titles already published include:

T&T Clark Handbook of Christian Theology and Climate Change, *edited by Ernst M. Conradie and Hilda P. Koster*

T&T Clark Handbook of Political Theology, *edited by Rubén Rosario Rodríguez*

T&T Clark Handbook of Pneumatology, *edited by Daniel Castelo and Kenneth M. Loyer*

T&T Clark Handbook of Ecclesiology, *edited by Kimlyn J. Bender and D. Stephen Long*

T&T Clark Handbook of Christian Theology and the Modern Sciences, *edited by John P. Slattery*

T&T Clark Handbook of Christian Ethics, *edited by Tobias Winright*

T&T Clark Handbook of John Owen, *edited by Crawford Gribben and John W. Tweeddale*

T&T Clark Handbook of Theological Anthropology, *edited by Mary Ann Hinsdale and Stephen Okey*

T&T CLARK HANDBOOK OF PNEUMATOLOGY

Edited by
Daniel Castelo and Kenneth M. Loyer

LONDON • NEW YORK • OXFORD • NEW DELHI • SYDNEY

T&T CLARK
Bloomsbury Publishing Plc
50 Bedford Square, London, WC1B 3DP, UK
1385 Broadway, New York, NY 10018, USA
29 Earlsfort Terrace, Dublin 2, Ireland

BLOOMSBURY, T&T CLARK and the T&T Clark logo are trademarks of
Bloomsbury Publishing Plc

First published in Great Britain 2020
This paperback edition published 2022

Copyright © Daniel Castelo, Kenneth M. Loyer, and contributors, 2020

Daniel Castelo and Kenneth M. Loyer have asserted their right under the Copyright,
Designs and Patents Act, 1988, to be identified as Author of this work.

For legal purposes the Acknowledgments on p. viii constitute an extension
of this copyright page.

Cover design: Terry Woodley
Cover image © Chad Greiter/Unsplash

All rights reserved. No part of this publication may be reproduced or transmitted in any form
or by any means, electronic or mechanical, including photocopying, recording, or any information
storage or retrieval system, without prior permission in writing from the publishers.

Bloomsbury Publishing Plc does not have any control over, or responsibility for, any
third-party websites referred to or in this book. All internet addresses given in this book were
correct at the time of going to press. The author and publisher regret any inconvenience
caused if addresses have changed or sites have ceased to exist, but can accept no
responsibility for any such changes.

A catalogue record for this book is available from the British Library.

A catalog record for this book is available from the Library of Congress.

ISBN: HB: 978-0-5676-6741-0
PB: 978-1-3503-2036-9
ePDF: 978-0-5676-6742-7
eBook: 978-0-5676-6740-3

Typeset by Deanta Global Publishing Services, Chennai, India

To find out more about our authors and books visit www.bloomsbury.com and
sign up for our newsletters.

CONTENTS

ACKNOWLEDGMENTS   viii
LIST OF ABBREVIATIONS   ix

Introduction: Confessing the Holy Spirit   1
Daniel Castelo and Kenneth M. Loyer

1. The Holy Spirit in the Synoptic Gospels   7
Laura C. S. Holmes

2. The Lord the Spirit: Paul's Pneumatology   17
Nijay K. Gupta

3. The Role of the Acts of the Spirit within Scripture   25
Robert W. Wall

4. The Spirit in the Catholic Epistles   33
David R. Nienhuis

5. Pneumatology of the Johannine Corpus   41
Robert W. Wall

6. The Holy Spirit in the Work of Christ   55
D. Stephen Long

7. The Spirit-Infused Hope of Christ   65
Margaret B. Adam

8. The Spirit and the Old Testament   75
Lee Roy Martin

9. The Spirit and Learning in the Hebrew Scriptures   89
John R. (Jack) Levison

10. The Spirit, Mediation, and Sacramentality   103
Kenneth M. Loyer

11. The Spirit and Science   111
Wolfgang Vondey

12	The Spirit and Visions of Life: Seeing the World and Humanity Otherwise in the Light of God's Face *Daniela C. Augustine*	121
13	The Spirit and Ecology *J. J. Johnson Leese*	133
14	"The Giver of Life": The Spirit and Creation *Marc Cortez*	143
15	Pneumatological Development in Trinitarian Perspective *Jackson Lashier*	151
16	The *Filioque*: Theology and Controversy *Thomas G. Weinandy, O.F.M., Cap.*	165
17	"Who Together with the Father and Son Is Worshipped and Glorified": Roman Catholic Perspectives *Matthew Levering*	181
18	Eastern Orthodox Perspectives *Marcus Plested*	189
19	The Holy Spirit: Lutheran Perspectives *Cheryl M. Peterson*	197
20	Reformed Perspectives on the Holy Spirit *Shannon Nicole Smythe*	207
21	The Theology of the Holy Spirit in Anglicanism *Ephraim Radner*	215
22	The Holy Spirit in Wesleyan Perspective *Jason E. Vickers*	227
23	Quaker Pneumatology *Cherice Bock*	235
24	The Holy Spirit and Anticlericalism *J. Alexander Sider*	243
25	Pentecostal Perspectives in Pneumatology *Peter Althouse*	251
26	Charismatic Perspectives on the Holy Spirit *Andrew K. Gabriel*	261
27	Perspectives on the "Spirit" in Africa *Daniel K. Darko*	269

28 Toward an Asian Pneumatology: A Reflective Reading *David Sang-Ehil Han*	281
29 Spirit of Integration and Solidarity: Asian American Pneumatologies *Daniel D. Lee*	291
30 The Spirit in the Colonial Difference: A Story of Pneumatology in the American Global South *Oscar García-Johnson*	301
31 Black Theologians of the Spirit *Frederick L. Ware*	311
32 Latinx Perspectives *Daniel Castelo*	319
33 Where the Wind Blows: Pneumatology in Feminist Perspective *Lisa P. Stephenson*	327
34 Pneumatology and the Canonical Heritage *Mark E. Powell*	337
35 Discernment *Douglas M. Koskela*	345
36 Mysticism and Renewal *Daniel Castelo*	353
37 Anointing and Power *Chris E.W. Green*	361
LIST OF CONTRIBUTORS	369
AUTHOR INDEX	371
SCRIPTURE INDEX	379

ACKNOWLEDGMENTS

A book such as this one highlights the degree to which academic work is a collective enterprise. We the editors wish to extend our thanks to the contributors who made this volume possible. They are all busy professionals, yet they took time to offer their pneumatological reflections, and for that we are very grateful. We also would like to extend our gratitude to T & T Clark and in particular to Anna Turton, who resolutely supported this project over the several years that it required.

Scripture quotations in this volume are from the New Revised Standard Version Bible, copyright © 1989 National Council of the Churches of Christ in the United States of America. Used by permission. All rights reserved worldwide.

Daniel would like to thank his institution on a number of levels. The School of Theology within Seattle Pacific University and Seminary has been a wonderful setting in which to test and generate arguments. He is especially grateful that colleagues not only gave their verbal support but that some even contributed a number of chapters to the collection. Daniel was also supported with a Faculty Research and Scholarship Grant in 2017 that proved helpful in making this volume come to light. Ken wishes to thank his wife Molly for her encouragement as well as the congregation that he is privileged to serve as lead pastor, Spry Church (UMC) in York, Pennsylvania.

We would like to dedicate this volume in honor of one of our mentors who has recently passed, Geoffrey Wainwright (1939–2020). He truly was a doctor of and for the church. *Requiescat in pace.*

dc (Seattle, WA, USA)
kml (York, PA, USA)

ABBREVIATIONS

AB	Anchor Bible
ANF	Ante-Nicene Fathers
ANTC	Abingdon New Testament Commentaries
b. Ḥag	Babylonian Talmud *Ḥagigah*
BNTC	Black's New Testament Commentaries
BTNT	Biblical Theology of the New Testament
CCC	*Catechism of the Catholic Church*, 2nd ed.
CC	Continental Commentary
CD	Karl Barth, *The Church Dogmatics*, ed. Geoffrey W. Bromiley and Thomas F. Torrance, trans. Geoffrey W. Bromiley et al., 5 vols., 14 parts (Edinburgh: T & T Clark, 1936–1977)
De. cael.	Arisotle, *De caelo*
Ep. Mor.	Seneca, *Epistulae morales ad Lucilium*
Gen. Rab.	*Genesis Rabbah*
Int	Interpretation
Institutes	John Calvin, *The Institutes of the Christian Religion*, ed. John T. McNeill, trans. Ford Lewis Battles, 2 vols. (Louisville: Westminster John Knox, 1960)
Jub.	*Jubilees*
LNTS	Library of New Testament Studies
LW	*Luther's Works*
NAC	New American Commentary
NICNT	New International Commentary on the New Testament
NIDB	New Interpreter's Dictionary of the Bible
NIDPCM	New International Dictionary of Pentecostal and Charismatic Movements
NPNF1	Nicene and Post-Nicene Fathers, First Series
NPNF2	Nicene and Post-Nicene Fathers, Second Series

NT	New Testament
NTL	New Testament Library
NTT	New Testament Theology
OT	Old Testament
PG	Patrologia Graeca
Polyb.	Seneca, *de consolatione ad Polybium*
Pss. Sol.	*Psalms of Solomon*
SBLDS	Society of Biblical Literature Dissertation Series
SC	Sources Chrétiennes
SP	Sacra Pagina
ST	*Summa theologiae*, translation by the Fathers of the English Dominican Province
TDNT	Theological Dictionary of the New Testament
THNTC	Two Horizons New Testament Commentary
TOTC	Tyndale Old Testament Commentary
UBC	Understanding the Bible Commentary
WA	Weimarer Ausgabe (Weimar edition of Luther's works). 120 vols. Weimar: 1883–2009

Introduction

Confessing the Holy Spirit

DANIEL CASTELO AND KENNETH M. LOYER

There are not many sets of words that have been recited every day for nearly 2,000 years, but considering the development of Christianity over time and around the world, the universal church's emphasis on the worship of God, and the place of the creeds in its life and mission, the words of the Nicene Creed are likely among those that merit such a distinction.[1] That particular creed can provide a theological framework for a study of the third person of the Trinity, especially one that operates out of certain theological emphases we both share and wish to uphold. Whereas this entire volume reflects a creedal form, we will highlight the phrase "we believe in the Holy Spirit" here as a way of stating what these orienting emphases are.

"WE"

The Nicene Creed includes a small word of great significance, the second person plural pronoun "we." To declare that "we believe in the Holy Spirit" is to signal right away one's participation in the confessing community known as the Christian church. This gesture is simple enough to state but difficult to appreciate, given all the cultural forces in the modern West that register the primary social unit to be the individual person. While the personal element of faith is critical, the communal component is essential.

In the congregation one of us (Loyer) serves, the Nicene Creed is recited each week during worship. The gathered community stands together and in unison proclaims, "We believe." In its immediate context, the term "we" refers in one sense to those who are there in that place participating in the affirmation of our faith as a liturgical and doxological act. In a larger sense, that same word refers to much more: it is a vital expression of what the Creed goes on to describe as the one, holy, catholic, and apostolic church. The vast scope of that simple, tiny word spans a variety of locations—geographic, ecclesial, cultural, and more—for Christians around the world and throughout history. In short, the communal component represented by the "we" in the confession "we believe" finds expression on a number of levels, from the local to the global and even across time and space in the communion of saints and the kingdom of God.

Given these claims and convictions, we have chosen in this volume to emphasize traditions and communities and not individual persons per se. The reader will not find

---

[1] Jaroslav Pelikan has made this observation; see *Credo: Historical and Theological Guide to Creeds and Confessions of Faith in the Christian Tradition* (New Haven, CT: Yale University Press, 2005).

individual articles on Karl Barth or Yves Congar, as important as these and many more figures are to the field of Christian pneumatology. Oftentimes, when individuals are highlighted in collections such as this one, they are usually male, European, and privileged in a variety of ways. Additionally, their highlighting as individual voices reinforces the (often-implicit) argument that a person can pursue theology well on the basis of one's own creativity, industry, and skill. All these points are in tension with what we have articulated is at work with the creedal "we" of confessing, catholic Christianity. As a way of pushing against these tendencies, we the editors have made it a point to illustrate this communal and corporate dimension of theological reflection by highlighting various ecclesial/denominational traditions as well as a number of ethnic embodiments within Christianity. In these articles one will find references to figures like Barth and Congar, but only within the larger purview of their ecclesial and/or ethnic contexts. As editors, we tend to think that the form of this presentation is in keeping with the global patterns and shifts that Christianity is experiencing in the present day, ones that are impacting theology on a number of fronts, not the least of which would be the dogmatic locus of pneumatology.

"BELIEVE"

Confessing the Holy Spirit involves acknowledging a reality greater than oneself; that reality is the presence and power of the third person of the Trinity and, thereby, the *ecclesia* produced by the Spirit—the Christian community into which, through baptism and faith in Christ, the Spirit lovingly ushers Christ's followers and makes them participants in the life of God (cf. 2 Pet. 1:4). The Father calls and claims us through the Son and in the Holy Spirit. We respond in faith.

In its properly theological sense, to believe entails belonging. We are held in the grip of the One in whom we believe. One can distinguish between the faith by which one believes (*fides qua creditur*) and the faith that one believes (*fides quae creditur*). The faith by which one believes is the attitude and act of faith, and it involves a subjective element. The faith that one believes means the content of faith and is objective in shape. These two dimensions of faith must be coordinated. To say as in the Nicene Creed "we believe" not only implies the attitude and act of faith, but also reflects the content of faith.

These claims may be at times difficult to sustain within the theological academy. So many forces within the Western context work to divide the church and the academy, theology and belief. At some level, this development is understandable, especially if belief is understood to be a suspension of reason or an excuse not to reason. Those alternatives, however, are not the only ones available, and we would say they are not the proper ones for a vital Christian witness. Furthermore, "reason" is a context-specific matrix of judgments that only makes sense when others buy into those assumptions. Put another way, there are multiple accounts of belief and multiple rationalities, and some are mutually exclusive of others, given the baseline arguments at work. In our opinion, the theological academy would be best served were it to recognize these sundry possibilities, for in doing so, it would acknowledge that theology is a deeply internally contested discipline, in large part because its subject matter is a bewildering challenge to behold. The challenge is plainly available in the etymology of the word: theology is reasoning (*logos*) related to a god (*theos*). For Christians, both the reasoning and the god in question are inflected not simply by intellection but by confession. In fact, it is the latter that primarily grounds the former, otherwise the identity of "Christian" would make little difference in terms of the theology undertaken.

INTRODUCTION

For this volume, we have intentionally chosen contributors and topics that highlight the possibilities of bridging what we deem to be the problematic gap between theology and belief. Many of the contributors are active in ecclesial contexts, and some are even ordained. What they do in the parish connects with what they do on the bench and vice versa. This is the case because they have a pluriform identity: they belong to the church *and* to the academy. Whereas some say these identities are irreconcilable, through their lives these authors show that reconciliation of these identities is not only possible, but also that a dynamic and significant interaction between them can take place. To use a classic expression, they are doctors of and for the church.

Pneumatology not only benefits from this understanding; in some basic sense, pneumatology makes this understanding possible. The Spirit, who is closer to us than we are to ourselves, presses deeply into all our registers, including the intellective and the affective. The same Spirit who renews our minds is the One who kindles the proper loves of our hearts. The Spirit of truth is the One who engenders and prompts the knowledge of God, which is itself grounded in love and obedience. Put differently, the faith by which one believes (*fides qua creditur*) and the faith that one believes (*fides quae creditur*) are proper domains of the Spirit's capacitation and illumination. We cannot endeavor to reflect on faith apart from reference to the Spirit, in terms of both empowerment and content.

"THE HOLY SPIRIT"

The Nicene Creed clearly identifies the object of Christian faith as the triune God—Father, Son, and Holy Spirit. The name of the third person of the Trinity is theologically significant. "Holy Spirit" signifies the distinctiveness and full deity of this divine person. "Holy" refers to being set apart or distinct, and "Spirit" denotes (among other things) wind or breath. The Spirit of God is fully divine and so distinct from this world while being intimately involved in it. At the first moment of creation, the Spirit of God hovered over the waters (Gen. 1:2). In the closing pages of Scripture, we read the words of Jesus offering the invitation, "the Spirit and the bride say, 'Come'" (Rev. 22:17). What we have in the person of the Spirit is not an ancillary or incidental topic for our consideration; rather, we have the living God who is active and engaged with the world from its beginning on until its consummation.

In his 1749 "Letter to a Roman Catholic," which follows the Nicene Creed in basic structure, John Wesley describes the person of the Holy Spirit and the Spirit's work in believers this way:

> I believe the infinite and eternal Spirit of God, equal with the Father and the Son, to be not only perfectly holy in himself, but the immediate cause of all holiness in us: enlightening our understandings, rectifying our wills and affections, renewing our natures, uniting our persons to Christ, assuring us of the adoption of sons, leading us in our actions, purifying and sanctifying our souls and bodies to a full and eternal enjoyment of God.[2]

---

[2]Wesley, "Letter to a Roman Catholic," in *The Works of John Wesley*, ed. Thomas Jackson, 14 vols. (London: Wesleyan Conference Office, 1872; reprint, Grand Rapids, MI: Zondervan, 1958–1959), 10:82.

This work can be attributed especially to the Holy Spirit, whose indwelling presence within and among God's people yields ever-greater holiness and happiness in God. Whereas in the OT God is depicted as sending the Spirit upon specific people at specific times for specific tasks (for example, the leaders, prophets, and judges of Israel), in the NT the promise of God has been fulfilled at Pentecost with the outpouring of the Holy Spirit upon the church as a whole and its individual members as well (Acts 2; cf. Joel 2:28-32). The Spirit, who is the very essence of holiness, makes God's people holy. Since holiness is a characteristic and state of being defined by God, the designation of the Spirit as the Holy Spirit is itself a confession of the Spirit's divinity.

As pivotal as the Holy Spirit is for a Christian understanding of God and God's purposes in the world, the topic as a dogmatic locus is not without its challenges—ones that are reflected in the topic itself and that apply to those seeking to pursue the topic. For instance, talk of the Spirit bears into worldview matters. Language of "spirit" in certain contexts recalls a distinction between "spirit" and "matter"; the language may also beckon for the admission of a "spirit-world," which certain contexts deem "pre-modern," "mythological," or "un-Enlightened." Plenty of pressures exist within the north-transatlantic context to downplay spirit-talk, for it presses against the plausibility structures that many of us assume for understanding how our world works. This is in contradistinction to other regions of the world in which their view of reality is fundamentally constituted by a spirit-dimension. Therefore, every context has its orienting assumptions that complicate and make possible spirit-talk in unique ways. Aspiring pneumatologists would do well to take inventory of their own worldviews so as to see clearly how their biases would help or hinder the pursuit of Christian pneumatology.

Another challenge worth mentioning would be the way spirit-talk problematizes dyadic or binary presentations. This tendency is hinted at by Jesus when he remarks that the Spirit of truth abides *with* and *in* the disciples (Jn 14:17). Sometimes the Spirit is talked about in ontological, substance-oriented ways; at other times, the Spirit is spoken of in deeply personal ways. One notices these tendencies throughout Scripture as well as in the vast literature on pneumatology; the articles in this volume also show these tendencies. Readers should be mindful that this quality does not represent a lack of consistency on the part of these scholars; rather, it is a fixture of what is at play with the topic at hand. Just the wide range of connotative possibilities for the biblical terms *ruach* (Hebrew) and *pneuma* (Greek) should alert readers of the range of spirit-talk. This is a quality of the field that cannot be overcome; it must ultimately be accepted, as difficult as that may be.

When the Holy Spirit is consistently personalized, another challenge comes to the fore, especially for English speakers. This challenge has to do with gender specification, especially as it manifests itself in pronominal usage. Many other languages have grammatical conventions to turn to when specifying pronouns for the Holy Spirit. English speakers do not, thereby making the pronouns used for the Spirit ultimately a matter of choice. Unsurprisingly, this topic is one that is debated repeatedly in English-oriented pneumatology, and no simple answers present themselves. We the editors have our own assumptions about how to navigate this matter, and these are seen in our own chapters within this volume. However, given the broad range of commitments that exists on this score, we left this practice open-ended for all the authors, allowing each contributor to specify pronouns for the Spirit as each saw appropriate. Again, this matter is not something to rectify or correct in a project like this one but simply an issue to acknowledge as part of the terrain of pneumatology.

Although significant, these challenges are not overwhelming or debilitating. We can speak confidently of the Holy Spirit because of what we confess to be revealed and shared by the triune God to those who steadfastly worship and adore this One. The work may be difficult at times, but it can also be transformative and life-giving.

CONCLUDING REMARKS

Undoubtedly, this volume could have been significantly longer in that many more topics could have received article-length attention. As editors of this volume who have worked extensively in pneumatology prior to coming to this project, we have some understanding of the matters left untreated. At the same time, we wanted to produce a volume that was manageable both for ourselves and the reader.

We begin the volume with articles on the NT and Christology (Chapters 1 to 7), and the ensuing chapters work their way "backwards" to the OT and then "forwards" to the life of the church. We did this not to be implicitly supersessionist but to reckon seriously with the claim that the Spirit is "Lord" as attested by 2 Cor. 3:17 as well as the Creed itself. We believe the Spirit is both "Lord" and "Spirit of the Lord," both another Paraclete (Jn 14:16) and Spirit of the Paraclete (cf. 1 Jn 2:1). What we mean to say is that the way to reckon with the person, identity, and work of the Spirit is to do so in concert with the person, identity, and work of the Son. That is not to say we are allowing Christology to overdetermine pneumatology, a problem that has persisted unchecked in pneumatology for far too long. But we are attempting to wrestle with what makes pneumatology *Christian*, and doing so, we hold, involves at a primordial level accounting for the truly charismatic One—the One anointed with the Spirit so as to be Messiah and Christ. In order to behold faithfully the Holy Spirit, then, we believe one has to behold faithfully the Son.

The rest of the volume takes shape in the following way. After articles on the NT and Christology, we have included two devoted to the OT (Chapters 8 and 9), the first being largely a survey chapter and the second taking on a more focused approach on creativity, skill, and virtue. In the articles that follow (Chapters 10 to 14), special attention is placed on the Spirit as "the Giver of Life," meaning these articles highlight the presence and work of the Spirit at the creaturely, material level. These are followed by two chapters (Chapters 15 and 16) reflecting on the patristic development of pneumatological thought, coinciding with the phrase "who proceeds from the Father (and the Son)." The latter of these has within its purview the *filioque*, while the former is a bit broader in orientation. The last section of the volume, which was populated under the heading "who together with the Father and the Son is worshipped and glorified," highlights the embodiment of faith, the confession of the Spirit in a myriad of contexts and circumstances. Chapters 17 to 26 focus on different church traditions; Chapters 27 to 33 stress different kinds of ethnic, racial, and gender embodiment. Finally, Chapters 34 to 37 stress a Spirit-empowered and Spirit-expectant church. The Spirit "spoke through the prophets" in ages past and continues to speak to and through those who are willing to proclaim and embody the gospel in this eschatological "time between the times." This section—but really the volume as a whole—stresses that Christian confession is only possible through the sensed and witnessed presence of the Spirit. We the editors hope this volume resoundingly presses that point to those who come across its pages.

CHAPTER ONE

The Holy Spirit in the Synoptic Gospels

LAURA C. S. HOLMES

For those accustomed to reading about the role of the Holy Spirit as recorded in Acts and Paul's letters, the paucity of references to the Spirit in the Synoptic Gospels often comes as a surprise. Some interpreters claim that the few references to the Holy Spirit's work in the Synoptics are due to the Gospels' christological orientation, while others see a stronger connection between the church's experience and the work of the Spirit in the epistles.[1] Nevertheless, when considered together, the Synoptics bear witness to a consistent portrait of the Spirit drawn from the Old Testament.

The Synoptic Gospels share claims about the expected work of the Holy Spirit in the new age inaugurated by the Word's incarnation, particularly as it relates to creation, prophetic speech, and the relationship between the Father and the Son. Nevertheless, each narrative shows that the Spirit reveals distinctive christological portraits with unique implications for discipleship. In Matthew, the Spirit highlights the Son's faithfulness as he serves as a model for his disciples; in Mark, the Spirit plays a key role in anointing Jesus as the Messiah and in indicating the ways in which this unexpected messianic identity is connected to the OT; and in Luke, the Spirit empowers Jesus as a prophet who promises the Spirit's future work while underlining ways in which current faithful believers participate in this work.

In what follows, we consider the testimony of all the Synoptics together, and then conclude with observations about each Gospel. Fundamentally, the Holy Spirit enables

---

[1] In terms of Christology, some NT scholars follow C. K. Barrett, who claimed that the Spirit's role mirrored that of the Messiah's, as "spiritual power was both a revelation and a concealment." *The Holy Spirit and the Gospel Tradition* (London: SPCK, 1966), 68. Others follow James D. G. Dunn, highlighting exorcisms and miracles that Jesus did as a way of marking him as a charismatic figure; see *Jesus and the Spirit: A Study of the Religious and Charismatic Experience of Jesus and the First Christians as Reflected in the New Testament* (Philadelphia, PA: Westminster, 1975), 68. Anthony C. Thiselton argues that both perspectives are accurate when "qualified by the other." *The Holy Spirit—In Biblical Teaching, through the Centuries, and Today* (Grand Rapids, MI: Eerdmans, 2013), 39. George Lyons notes that it was the church's experience of the Spirit *as* the Spirit of Jesus, consistent with Scripture, that shaped the development of the church's worship, Acts and Letters, and later articulations of the Trinity; see "The Spirit in the Gospels," in *The Spirit and the New Age: An Inquiry from a Biblical Theological Perspective*, ed. R. Larry Shelton and Alex R. G. Deasley, Wesleyan Theological Perspectives 5 (Anderson, IN: Warner, 1986), 36.

Jesus's actions and ministry and, by doing so, empowers him to reveal God's incarnate presence in the world. In this way, chronicling the Spirit's work across the Gospels provides a revelatory narrative of God's presence in Jesus.

THE SYNOPTIC GOSPELS: AN OVERVIEW

The NT's opening narratives indicate that Jewish eschatological expectations of the Spirit's presence and action shift for those who believe Jesus is the Messiah. Expectations of the age to come are inaugurated in the present age.

While the term "spirit" (πνεῦμα) is attested seventy-six times in the Synoptic Gospels, most of those usages refer to "unclean spirit[s]" or the human spirit, meaning a person's character or life. If these uses are excluded, the primary texts under consideration are

Mt. 1:18, 20; 3:11, 16; 4:1; 10:20; 12:18, 28, 31-32; 22:43; 28:19

Mk 1:8, 10, 12; 3:29; 12:36; 13:11

Lk. 1:15, 35, 41, 67; 2:25-27; 3:16, 22; 4:1, 14, 18; 10:21; 11:13; 12:10; [24:49][2]

It is easiest to understand the role of the Spirit across the Synoptics in three general categories, all of which have precedence in the OT and early Jewish tradition. First, the presence of the Spirit at Jesus's birth highlights the continued role in bringing about new life. Second, the Spirit is associated with speech and Scripture, echoing how the Spirit was connected with Israel's law, prophets, and leaders in the Old Testament. Lastly, the Spirit is clearly the Spirit *of God* and therefore highlights the relationships of Father, Son, and Spirit. In the Synoptic Gospels, the presence of the Holy Spirit throughout the entirety of Jesus's life shows that the Spirit is consistently active in Jesus's ministry, just as Jesus promises his disciples that the Spirit will be active in their lives.

SIMILARITIES IN THE SYNOPTIC GOSPELS

New Life and Anointing

The first references to the Holy Spirit in the Synoptics are in the narratives of John the Baptist (Luke) and Jesus's conception (Matthew and Luke). Luke claims that John was "filled with the Holy Spirit" while he was in Elizabeth's womb (1:15). The full presence of the Spirit, as with his parents (1:41, 67), indicates that John's ministry is authorized and empowered by God.[3] He, like them, will be a prophet, but he is set apart even from birth. No part of John's life exists without the Holy Spirit.

Jesus's conception highlights the work of the Holy Spirit in a unique way in the New Testament. Matthew claims that Jesus is "conceived by the Holy Spirit" (γεννηθὲν ἐκ πνεύματός ἐστιν ἁγίου; 1:20) without providing more detail. However, in narrating Mary's encounter with Gabriel, Luke says that the Holy Spirit will come upon her and overshadow (ἐπισκιάσει) her (1:35). The same verb describes the coming of the Spirit upon the disciples (Acts 1:8) and the arrival of the cloud that veils God's presence at the transfiguration (Lk. 9:34, cf. Exod. 40:35, Ps. 90:4). These similar texts indicate that

---

[2]While Lk. 24:49 does not include the noun "spirit" (πνεῦμα), the "power from on high" Jesus refers to is the Holy Spirit, given the parallel with Acts 1:8.
[3]Joel B. Green, *The Gospel of Luke*, NICNT (Grand Rapids, MI: Eerdmans, 1997), 75.

while conception is a new kind of work, the Spirit's action has a precedent in God's care and providence for Israel.

Therefore, the Spirit's work in Jesus's conception illustrates three different points. First, the Spirit is at work creating new life, just as in Genesis (1:2, 2:7). This new life is unique: the Spirit here "acts creatively upon matter," producing something new rather than producing visible effects out of things that already exist.[4] Second, this work of the Spirit is consistent across Jesus's life: just as with John the Baptist, the Spirit's presence in Jesus's conception illustrates that there is never a moment of his life when Jesus is not directed and empowered by the Spirit.[5] Finally, because the "overshadowing" action of the Spirit is consistent throughout Scripture, it is clear that the Spirit plays a central role in tying together the ideas of new creation and redemption. Israel's new life—indeed, the church's new life—is integral to God's own life because it is breathed (Gen. 2:7) or overshadowed (Lk. 1:35, Acts 1:8) by God's Spirit (Ezek. 37:1-14).[6] This marks Jesus's birth as the beginning of the new age: just as God's Spirit was active at the beginning of the world, so God's Spirit is active at its renewal.[7]

The next event in the Gospels where the Spirit is associated with new life is at Jesus's baptism. There, newness means a new stage of life: Jesus is anointed in order to fulfill a particular purpose.[8] The narration of Jesus's baptism highlights how the dawning of the new age when the Spirit is tangibly present and active is bound together with the coming of the Messiah.[9] Only here in the Gospels is the Spirit described as having a visible form (Lk. 3:22) or as analogous to something visible (Mt. 3:16, Mk 1:12). This appearance links the work of the Spirit to the two aspects of new life we have already discussed: creation and empowerment through anointing. First, later Jewish rabbis used as an analogy to the Spirit's work at creation a dove hovering over the waters (Gen. 1:2).[10] Second, the Spirit is described as coming upon Jesus (Mt. 3:16) or descending upon him (Mk 1:10, Lk. 3:22, cf. *Pss. Sol.* 17:37). Furthermore, the Spirit's work is both unique and unifying. As at his birth, the Spirit's role in Jesus's baptism singles him out as God's uniquely beloved Son and Israel's Messiah. Yet, his participation in baptism unites him with Israel and his disciples to come.

Speech/Prophecy

The Spirit is associated with the inspiration of leaders and prophets in the OT (e.g., Exod. 31:3; Num. 11:25-29; Judg. 6:34, 11:29, 14:6; 1 Sam. 10:6, 16:13) and is the attributed source of prophecy and scriptural interpretation by some Jews in the first century (*Jub.* 31:12). The NT develops this connection between the Spirit and speech, particularly in the book of Acts. There, Peter (2:14-36, 4:8-12), the believers in general (4:31), Stephen (6:5, 10; 7:55), and Paul (13:9-12) are all described as speaking prophetically by means

---

[4]Barrett contrasts conception with exorcisms (*The Holy Spirit*, 17).
[5]Lyons, "The Spirit in the Gospels," 44.
[6]Barrett, *The Holy Spirit*, 20.
[7]Ibid., 23.
[8]John the Baptist prophesies that Jesus will baptize people with the Holy Spirit (Mk 1:8) and fire (Mt. 3:11, Lk. 3:16). See the section "Speech/Prophecy" in this chapter.
[9]Lyons, "The Spirit in the Gospels," 49.
[10]See *b. Ḥag.* 15a; *Gen. Rab.* 2.4; Morna D. Hooker, *The Gospel According to St. Mark*, BNTC 2 (Peabody, MA: Hendrickson, 1991), 45; Joel Marcus, *Mark 1–8: A New Translation with Introduction and Commentary*, AB 27 (New York: Doubleday, 2000), 160.

of the Spirit.[11] Therefore, it is unsurprising that the Synoptic Gospels also claim that the Holy Spirit inspires prophetic speech and provides truthful speech to Jesus's followers in times of crisis and temptation. Nevertheless, the Synoptics attest to the ability of humans to resist the Holy Spirit and the blaspheming consequences of doing so.

The Gospel of Luke highlights the Spirit's role in prophetic speech at the beginning of the narrative. As noted earlier, John and Jesus are described as being "full of the Holy Spirit," and they are joined by four others: Elizabeth, Zechariah, Mary, and Simeon. The experience of the Spirit elucidates inspired speech, whether blessings (1:41, 45), prophecy (1:67, 2:25-27, 3:16), or scriptural interpretation (4:1-13). At Jesus's baptism, Matthew and Mark join Luke's witness by narrating John's inspired word about Jesus's ministry (Mt. 3:16, Mk 1:8) and reiterating John's role as prophet (Mt. 11:13, 14:5, 21:26; Mk 8:28, 11:32; Lk. 1:76, 9:19, 16:16, 20:6).[12] The Spirit coming upon these individuals signals "God's perspective on [these] events" in the content of their proclamations.[13] Furthermore, the Spirit's action in these scenes is consistent with God's redemptive work in the OT, as the Spirit emphasizes social reversals: the first prophets in Luke are women, the old (Elizabeth and Simeon) bless the young, and God's favor is brought to those of low social and economic means (1:52-53, 2:24).[14]

Prophetic speech is integrally related to scriptural interpretation. However, even the biblical prophets did not commonly describe their prophecies as being made under the influence of the Spirit.[15] Instead, it is in later Jewish traditions that "rabbis link the Holy Spirit so strongly with prophecy that the two become virtually synonymous."[16] Aspects of this connection are evident in the Synoptics where the Spirit and Scripture are connected. This happens at Jesus's baptism, as the Spirit descends and the voice from heaven uses scriptural terminology (Ps. 2:7, Isa. 42:1) to profess favor and anointing on Jesus. It also happens during Jesus's temptation, as the Spirit drives or leads him out into the wilderness, and yet he responds to each temptation with Scripture (Mt. 4:1-11, Mk 1:12-13, Lk. 4:1-13). There is certainly power and authority in Jesus's words (Mk 1:21, 27), but those words are also grounded in Scripture. This provides a parallel between Jesus and those who believe in him, as Mary and Simeon have both used scriptural language as the basis of their prophecy. This is even more evident at one point in Matthew and Mark, where Jesus claims that David "spoke by the Spirit" (Δαυὶδ εἶπεν ἐν τῷ πνεύματι τῷ ἁγίῳ; Mk 12:36; cf. Mt. 22:43). This is not a claim of David's personal inspiration; rather, Jesus is saying that because David's psalm (Psalm 110) is Scripture, it is inspired.[17] Inversely, the prophetic speech of the characters in the Gospels, including Jesus, is grounded in Scripture. The overlap between prophecy and Scripture points to the Spirit's activity in their lives.

Prophetic speech is particularly valuable during times of crisis. The Synoptics attest to the Spirit granting believers the words to speak during these times. While this action

---

[11] Cornelis Bennema, "Spirit and Mission in the Bible: Toward a Dialogue between Biblical Studies and Missiology," *Trinity Journal* 32 (2011): 246.

[12] While Jesus certainly speaks in a manner inspired by the Spirit, the Gospels resist simply calling him a prophet without caveat (see Barrett, *The Holy Spirit*, 98).

[13] Green, *The Gospel of Luke*, 115.

[14] John T. Carroll, *Luke: A Commentary*, NTL (Louisville, KY: Westminster John Knox, 2012), 46.

[15] Barrett, *The Holy Spirit*, 147.

[16] Marcus, *Mark 1–8*, 152.

[17] Lyons, "The Spirit in the Gospels," 59–60; Barrett, *The Holy Spirit*, 108.

is present across the synoptic tradition, each evangelist describes it in a different way. Matthew 10:20 claims that "the Spirit of [their] Father speaks through" the disciples. Mark 13:11 claims that the disciples "will speak by the Holy Spirit." Finally, Lk. 12:12 says that the Holy Spirit "will teach [them] what [they] should say." Matthew and Mark emphasize the primary force of the Spirit. In Luke, the Spirit takes a secondary role as teacher. In Acts, Luke's readers see examples of the transformative power of the Spirit's teaching (4:1-22, 7:1-56).[18] In all these texts, the Spirit's activity brings comfort: the disciples are not alone.

Lastly, the Synoptics attest to the negative power of spiritual speech. In every Synoptic Gospel, Jesus uses his speech in order to cast out unclean spirits. However, some of the Jewish authorities claim that Jesus himself is able to perform exorcisms because he is possessed by an even stronger unclean spirit. In this context, Jesus claims that blasphemy against the Holy Spirit is an unforgiveable sin.[19] Essentially, blasphemy against the Holy Spirit means either confusing the Holy Spirit's work with Satan's work (Mt. 12:32, Mk 3:29-30) or deliberately lying to God (Lk. 12:10; cf. Acts 5:32, 7:51). In both contexts, confusion or lying is expressed through incorrect speech. The Holy Spirit's absence results in confusion or lying, while the Spirit's presence yields confident speech under trial.[20]

Relationships: Father, Son, and Spirit

The Synoptics do not have a developed trinitarian language or theology, yet they do attest to language and grammar that will influence the development of trinitarian theology through worship and reflection. Foundationally, the Synoptics identify interactive relationships involving the Father, Son, and Spirit. While only Matthew uses those names to bring all three together (28:19), all three Synoptics attest to the Spirit's consistent presence in the life of Jesus, again supporting the claim that all phases of Jesus's ministry are inspired and enabled by God's Spirit.[21]

As we have seen, the Spirit is active at Jesus's conception (Mt. 1:18, 20; Lk. 1:35) and baptism (Mt. 3:16, Mk 1:10, Lk. 3:22). Immediately following his baptism, the Spirit compels Jesus into the wilderness, where he is tempted (Mt. 4:1-11, Mk 1:12-13, Lk. 4:1-13). He resists temptation through the work of the Spirit (most clearly in Lk. 4:14) and begins his ministry by preaching via the Spirit's anointing (Lk. 4:16-19) or exorcising demons on the Spirit's behalf (Mk 1:21-27). While the language about the Spirit in Jesus's life is concentrated at the beginning of each Gospel's narrative, the implication is that the Spirit sanctifies all of Jesus's life. This is also his promise to his disciples post-resurrection (Mt. 10:20, Mk 13:11, Lk. 12:12). This constant presence of the Spirit indicates that Jesus's life and ministry are fully consistent with God's character and action.

---

[18]In Luke, Jesus also teaches the disciples what to say under trial (21:15), so the roles of Jesus and the Spirit are not vastly distinguished here, likely because the Spirit could easily be teaching or interpreting Jesus's life and message (see Jn 14:25-26).

[19]Mt. 12:32 and Lk. 12:10 differentiate between blasphemy against the Son of Man and blasphemy against the Holy Spirit: the former can be forgiven (as Peter and the disciples learned), while the latter cannot be.

[20]Luke puts this contrast side by side: those who stand with Jesus at trial will be rewarded and taught what to say by the Spirit (12:8, 11), while those who disown Jesus experience shame and those who blaspheme the Spirit are not forgiven (12:9-10).

[21]Green, *The Gospel of Luke*, 204–5; see the "New Life and Anointing" section above.

This consistency with God's character is evident in two particular contexts. The first is in Mt. 12:18, where Jesus quotes Isa. 42:1-4 as referring to himself. There he notes that God calls Jesus "my servant." God says, "I will put my Spirit on him, and he will proclaim justice to the nations" (Mt. 12:18, Isa. 42:1). God's Spirit is bestowed on Jesus through God's love and delight, and this granting of God's Spirit identifies him as God's servant. Second, it creates another parallel for the work of the Spirit in the lives of the disciples (cf. Mt. 28:19): one is only a servant of God if the Spirit of God dwells in that person.[22]

Being a servant of God also means that one acts how God acts: Jesus drives out unclean spirits and preaches for those who need justice (Mt. 12:18, 12:28; Lk. 4:16-19, 11:20). In this way, the "energizing power of God is given [to Jesus] not for himself but for others."[23] It is easy to see the Spirit enabling Jesus to accomplish powerful acts, like exorcisms. However, it is notable that when this occurs, the Gospels' emphasis is not that these miraculous actions bring glory to Jesus himself, but rather that they point to the reality of God's kingdom, which brings justice for the oppressed, deliverance for the captives, and salvation to the sinful and broken (Lk. 4:16-19). The Holy Spirit enables Jesus's ministry, thereby empowering him to reveal God's incarnate presence in the world. In this way, the Spirit's actions in the Gospels reveal God's presence in Jesus.

THE SPIRIT IN EACH SYNOPTIC GOSPEL

It is clear that there are significant similarities in the way the Synoptic Gospels present the Holy Spirit's work in Jesus's life. At the same time, each of the three Synoptic Gospels uniquely portrays the Spirit's encounters with Jesus and the ramifications for his disciples. As with most interpretative questions in the Gospels, this is a matter of emphasis rather than presence: every Gospel claims that Jesus is the Son of God, the Messiah, and a prophet; every Gospel also shows how the Spirit empowers him toward the cross that transforms God's communion with the world. Yet, each writer emphasizes these points differently.

Matthew: The Spirit Empowers Jesus as Son of God to Accomplish God's Purposes

All the Synoptics identify the Holy Spirit's presence at Jesus's baptism and resurrection,[24] but only in Matthew do all these events connect Jesus both to the Spirit and to the Father. At the announcement of Jesus's conception, the Father's presence is signaled by the angel of the Lord in a dream (cf. Gen. 31:11, 13), and the Son's conception is clearly "from the Holy Spirit" (Mt. 1:20). The Spirit creates new life as in Genesis 1–2, marking this point as the age of the Holy Spirit, a time of new creation. Similarly, at Jesus's baptism, with the Spirit's descent and the voice from heaven, readers understand that Jesus is empowered by the Spirit for his ministry. Specifically in Matthew, this empowerment emphasizes Jesus's divine sonship (3:17). Jesus is recognized as the Son of God by prophecy (2:15),

---

[22]R. T. France, *The Gospel of Matthew*, NICNT (Grand Rapids, MI: Eerdmans, 2007), 480.
[23]Jürgen Moltmann, *The Spirit of Life: A Universal Affirmation* (Minneapolis, MN: Fortress, 1992), 61.
[24]While Mark does not name the presence of the Spirit as a promise for the disciples in the post-resurrection appearances in the longer ending (16:9-20), the Spirit is promised to the disciples earlier in the Gospel (13:11), and the eschatological signs that are to accompany believers are often associated with the Spirit (16:17-18). Furthermore, both Gospels that describe Jesus's conception identify the presence of the Spirit (Mt. 1:20; Lk. 1:35).

divine voice (3:17, 17:5), demonic forces (4:3, 6; 8:29), the disciples (14:33, 16:16), and even his enemies (26:63; 27:40, 43, 54). His identity as Son of God is inextricably tied together with his identity as Emmanuel, God with us (1:23).

Uniquely in Matthew, at Jesus's baptism the Spirit not only descends but also "comes upon" (ἐρχόμενον) Jesus (3:16). In this way, Jesus becomes the model for how the Spirit will empower the lives of his disciples, as the Spirit will come on them in baptism as well (Mt. 28:19). Sonship language throughout the Gospel reiterates this. Jesus is God's faithful child, just as Israel is God's child to whom God is faithful (Hos. 11:1; cf. Mt. 2:15). By empowering Jesus to vanquish evil (4:1) and embody God's kingdom, the Spirit enables Jesus to accomplish God's purposes as the faithful Son.

Mark: The Spirit Anoints Jesus as Messiah, Acting Consistently with Scripture

Among the Synoptics, the Gospel of Mark has the fewest references to the Holy Spirit, and all of them overlap with references in the Gospel of Matthew. However, where Matthew closely connects the Holy Spirit to Jesus's identity as God's Son, and therefore as the model for his disciples, the Gospel of Mark highlights the role of the Holy Spirit as the one who anoints Jesus as Messiah. Given that the messianic age was connected to the age of the Spirit, this would have been anticipated in early Judaism.[25] Nevertheless, while earlier texts connected the identity of the Messiah with the empowerment of God's Spirit, Mark focuses the Messiah's role on the cross (e.g., 8:27–9:1). Therefore, the Holy Spirit anoints Jesus as Messiah at his baptism and then, through the rest of the Gospel, implicitly directs his way to the cross. The Spirit's actions run counter to expectations of the Messiah, but Mark demonstrates how they are grounded in Scripture.[26]

Most of the references to the Spirit's action in Mark have precedents in the OT. The descent of the Spirit through the open heavens alludes to Isa. 64:1, signaling new communication between God and humans.[27] When the Spirit drives Jesus into the wilderness, there is an echo of the Spirit carrying Elijah, the prophet of YHWH, away from Ahab's court and into the wilderness (1 Kgs 18:12). Lastly, Jesus's words in teaching, casting out demons, and healing individuals are attributed to the Spirit, just as inspired and transformative words were linked to the Spirit's work in the OT, whether at creation, exodus, or in the prophets.

Notably, the Holy Spirit in Mark acts in ways that the characters or Mark's readers perceive as violent. For example, in Mk 1:12 the Spirit drives (ἐκβάλλω) Jesus into the wilderness in the same way that Jesus drives unclean spirits out of people (Mk 1:34, 39; 3:15, 22; 6:13). In Matthew, however, the Spirit "leads" (ἀνάγω) Jesus into the wilderness (4:1). Mark's depiction of the violent, surprising, or disturbing action of the Spirit is consistent with OT expectation (1 Sam. 10:10, 1 Kgs 18:12, Ezek. 8:3). In this way, Mark highlights both the predicted and unexpected nature of the Spirit in parallel to the predicted and unexpected nature of the Messiah (Mk 8:27-39).

---

[25]See Marcus, *Mark 1–8*, 152; Barrett, *The Holy Spirit*, 21.
[26]This is implicit because Mark does not call attention to the Spirit's action very often. However, it is an easy conclusion that if the Spirit anoints Jesus to be the Messiah, and being the Messiah means that Jesus will die on the cross (8:31-32, 9:31, 10:33-34, 14:32-42), then the Spirit directs Jesus's way to the cross as the Messiah (cf. 14:38).
[27]C. Clifton Black, *Mark*, ANTC (Nashville, TN: Abingdon, 2011), 59.

Luke: The Spirit Inspires Jesus as Prophet and Works in the Lives of His Followers

More than any other Gospel, Luke highlights the prophetic nature of the Holy Spirit's presence. While we have seen that all the Synoptics connect the Spirit's inspiration to speech, Luke most clearly integrates the Spirit's power for speech with the prophetic nature of the Spirit in the OT and the eschatological promise for the Spirit's transformative arrival in the new age (Joel 2:28-29, Acts 2:17-21). This begins in Luke 1–2, where Elizabeth, Mary, Zechariah, and Simeon are all "filled with the Holy Spirit," which results in them prophesying about God's redemption of Israel and the nations through Jesus. In this way, the Spirit's presence signifies a "manifestation of eschatological blessing and empowering presence critical to God's redemptive mission."[28]

In Luke, the Holy Spirit takes on the role of guiding and sustaining Jesus through times of temptation (4:1-13) and in his ministry. Luke quotes Isa. 61:1 to indicate that God's Spirit has anointed Jesus in order to proclaim good news; in other words, the Spirit's anointing enables redemptive proclamation. Just as God's words created a new world in Genesis 1, now Jesus's words bring new life to dead places (Lk. 4:16-19). In this way, Luke affirms that Jesus's life and ministry are supported and enabled by the work of the Spirit.

By the end of the Gospel, it is clear that this same kind of presence of God's Spirit is promised to all (24:49, Acts 1:8). Like in Matthew, Jesus serves as the model for believers in Luke: as the Holy Spirit is present with Jesus, so the Spirit will be present with his followers. Yet, Luke contains several episodes that are not present in Matthew, which shift the former's point. For example, Luke records one of Jesus's prayers and introduces that prayer by claiming that "Jesus rejoiced in the Holy Spirit and said" (10:21). This connects prayer to the presence of the Spirit in addition to prophecy (cf. Acts 1:14). Furthermore, Jesus teaches that "the heavenly Father will give the Holy Spirit to those who ask him" (11:13), indicating the widely accessed presence of the Spirit to come. These episodes show it is not just in Jesus's life that the Spirit is at work, but that Jesus expects believers to experience the same kind of communion with God that he does.

The character of Simeon reiterates this continuity at the beginning of the Gospel. While a very brief episode in the narrative, Simeon's description is rich with references to the Holy Spirit: the Spirit is mentioned three times in three verses. Luke's audience is told that the Holy Spirit was "upon" Simeon (πνεῦμα ἦν ἅγιον ἐπ' αὐτόν), that the Holy Spirit had revealed (κεχρηματισμένον) that he would not die before he had seen the Lord's Messiah, and that he was "in the Spirit" (ἐν τῷ πνεύματι) when he came into the temple and saw Jesus (2:25-27). His response, informed by Scripture, was to prophesy.[29] In this way, Simeon serves as a model for how the Spirit engages with believers after Jesus's resurrection. The Spirit interacts with believers and uses Scripture in order to reveal and accomplish God's purposes. This modeling of the Spirit's work in the lives of Jesus's followers is unique among the Synoptics and, for readers of the Fourfold Gospel, prepares the way for the Gospel of John's focus on the Paraclete.

The Spirit's work in Luke focuses on inspired, prophetic speech and centralizes the importance of that speech in Jesus's ministry: the proclamation of the good news is part of why Jesus is anointed by the Spirit (4:16). Yet, this prophetic nature of the Spirit is not

---

[28] Green, *The Gospel of Luke*, 181.
[29] John R. Levison, *Inspired: The Holy Spirit and the Mind of Faith* (Grand Rapids, MI: Eerdmans, 2013), 148.

limited to Jesus but is carried on to his followers, modeled both by him and by Simeon, who, through the Spirit, bore witness to the Lord's Messiah, just as the disciples do.

CONCLUSION

The Synoptic Gospels do not offer a comprehensive pneumatology; however, they do reveal ways in which the Holy Spirit is active in Jesus's ministry, with hints and promises about how the Spirit will continue to be active in the church. These activities focus on the Spirit's continued work in sustaining and transforming creation, the Spirit's role in speech, and the Spirit's relationship with the Father and the Son. Furthermore, since each Gospel offers its own portrait of the interaction between Jesus and the Spirit, we have seen how Matthew's description of the Spirit highlights Jesus's identity as God's faithful Son, Mark's emphasizes Jesus's identity as an unexpected Messiah, and Luke's highlights how Jesus functions as a prophet for both Israel and the gentiles. These "two hands of God"[30] interact in mutually beneficial ways to reveal God's kingdom and to empower Jesus's followers to work toward it. Whether Jesus serves as a model for believers, Jesus teaches how to rightly interpret Scripture, or Jesus and other followers embody the prophetic empowerment of the Spirit, these three Gospels attest to a Spirit who is essential for understanding the character of God and the role of the church.

FOR FURTHER READING

Gathercole, Simon J. "The Trinity in the Synoptic Gospels and Acts." In *The Oxford Handbook on the Trinity*, edited by Gilles Emery, O. P. and Matthew Levering, 55–68. Oxford: Oxford University Press, 2011.

Lyons, George. "The Spirit in the Gospels." In *The Spirit and the New Age: An Inquiry from a Biblical Theological Perspective*, edited by R. Larry Shelton and Alex R. G. Deasley, 33–87. Wesleyan Theological Perspectives 5. Anderson, IN: Warner, 1986.

Thiselton, Anthony C. *The Holy Spirit—In Biblical Teaching, through the Centuries, and Today*. Grand Rapids, MI: Eerdmans, 2013.

---

[30]Irenaeus, *Against Heresies*, 3.24.2.

CHAPTER TWO

The Lord the Spirit

Paul's Pneumatology

NIJAY K. GUPTA

For the Apostle Paul, the presence and work of the Holy Spirit were central to the Christian life, from initial faith, to growth in righteousness, and beyond death. He could refer to mature believers as *pneumatikoi*, "spiritual ones," or "Spirit-people" (Gal. 6:1). Before we address Paul's understanding of the person and work of the Spirit, it behooves us to set "spirit" terminology in its ancient context, especially the understanding of Spirit and spirituality from the Jewish scriptures and tradition.

In the Greco-Roman world, the Greek word *pneuma* commonly referred to wind or the breath of humans or animals. It was also considered the animating power of life (see *Polyb*. 31.10.4). In the Greek concept of divination, *pneuma* could produce ecstatic experiences in seers and priests (see Plutarch, *The Obsolence of Oracles*).[1] The NT offers an example of this in the slave girl who was possessed by a "spirit of divination" (Acts 16:16). Roman Stoic Seneca wrote about the existence of a "holy spirit" (Latin: *sacer spiritus*) within, an entity that guides reason and conscience and is integrally related to the divine spirit (see *Ep. Mor.* 41.8).[2]

As for Jews, in the OT we see only brief and rare attestation of "spirit" language in relation to divine activity and human anthropology. In Gen. 1:2, we are told the *ruach* (spirit) of God was involved in creation. In most cases in the OT, the "spirit of God" is the living power of the one God that can act, equip, and enlighten (e.g., Judg. 14:6).[3] God could also send an influence that is referred to as a "spirit," like a "spirit of confusion" (Isa. 19:14; cf. Isa. 29:10). In early Jewish literature, we see spirit-language used more frequently and consistently in reference to spiritual beings (e.g., "spirits of Belial"; see 4Q117 4.14; cf. Tob. 6:8). In the NT in general, we can detect evidence of strong Jewish influence on the use of spirit-language. The NT writers' attitude toward spiritual entities by and large follows Jewish concerns over evil and unclean influences and beings.

---

[1] We can mistakenly assume that Greeks thought of "spirit/s" as immaterial and intangible, for Aristotle believed that the stars were comprised in part of a hot ether known as *pneuma* (see *De. cael*. 1.2.269a).
[2] See Rick Stelan, "What Might a Pagan Have Understood by 'Holy Spirit?'" *Colloquium* 42, no. 2 (2010): 151–72.
[3] For an incredibly insightful and rewarding study of spirit-language in ancient Judaism and early Christianity, see John R. Levison, *Filled with the Spirit* (Grand Rapids, MI: Eerdmans, 2009); on the OT and early Judaism specifically, see pages 1–217.

SPIRIT TERMINOLOGY IN PAUL

Before investigating in depth Paul's thoughts on the divine Spirit, it is helpful to outline the manner in which he (like other NT writers) used spirit terminology. Paul could use *pneuma* in reference to the person in general (Gal. 6:18, Phil. 4:18). Sometimes Paul's anthropological use of *pneuma* involved the soul or heart (Rom. 1:8, 1 Cor. 16:18, 2 Cor. 2:13).[4] In 2 Corinthians, he refers to being "refreshed" in spirit through fellowship (7:13). Paul also appears to make a distinction between the human spirit (*pneuma*) and the human body (*soma*; cf. 1 Cor. 7:34; 2 Cor. 7:1), though it is open to debate whether this was conceived of as ontological or rhetorical.[5]

Aside from discourse about the human *pneuma*, Paul also attributed to the world its own *pneuma* (1 Cor. 2:12). Furthermore, as with many in his culture, he warned of evil spirits (Rom. 8:15, 1 Cor. 12:10) and described attitudes or dispositions as "spirits" (cf. "spirit of gentleness," 1 Cor. 4:21). It is precisely this complex range of usage that makes an examination of his divine pneumatology so challenging. Even when it comes to titles, Paul showed remarkable variance in his expressions for the divine Spirit: "Holy Spirit" (Rom. 5:5, 9:1, 14:17, 15:13, 16; 1 Cor. 6:19, 12:3; 2 Cor. 13:13; 1 Thess. 1:5-6, 4:18; cf. Eph. 1:13, 4:30), "Spirit of holiness" (Rom. 1:4), "Spirit" (e.g., Rom. 7:6, 8:2-9; 1 Cor. 2:10; 2 Cor. 3:17), "Spirit of God" (Rom. 8:9, 14; 15:19; 1 Cor. 2:11; Phil. 3:3), "Spirit of Christ" (Rom. 8:9), and "Spirit of the Living God" (2 Cor. 3:3). And there are a number of occasions where it is unclear whether Paul was referring to the human or divine Spirit (e.g., 2 Cor. 6:6, Phil. 1:27). While the precise nuancing of how Paul used *pneuma* remains elusive, it does appear that the Apostle had a conception that the human *pneuma* was that part of the person connected to the Spirit of God. Hence, in Romans he writes, "For you did not receive a spirit (*pneuma*) of slavery to fall back into fear, but you have received a spirit of adoption. When we cry, 'Abba! Father!' it is that very Spirit (*pneuma*) bearing witness with our spirit (*pneuma*) that we are children of God" (Rom. 8:15-16). I liken this to how digital devices today go through a process of "pairing," whereby they link up in such a way that they are able to communicate on an ongoing basis with a direct connection—often in a "language" that is imperceptible to our external senses (cf. Rom. 8:26-27, 1 Cor. 2:13).

THE AGE OF THE SPIRIT

Before engaging directly with Paul's theology of the Spirit, it is helpful to establish the backdrop for the Apostle's understanding of the Spirit's coming, influence, and operations. Because Paul was convinced that he was living in a new age of the Spirit, we ought to look back to relevant biblical promises. In the prophetic literature especially, we catch glimpses of Jewish anticipation of pneumatological endowment offering restoration, renewal, wisdom, empowerment, and covenantal reconciliation and unity.

---

[4] Paul could, though, distinguish human *pneuma* (spirit) from human *nous* (mind); see 1 Cor. 14:14-15.

[5] It is at least safe to say that spirit/*pneuma* involves for Paul "the dimension of human existence in and through which God is encountered"; see James D. G. Dunn, "Towards the Spirit of Christ: The Emergence of Distinctive Features of Christian Pneumatology," in *The Work of the Spirit*, ed. Michael Welker (Grand Rapids, MI: Eerdmans, 2006), 6. For a more detailed treatment of Paul's pneumatology, see Dunn, *Theology of Paul the Apostle* (Grand Rapids, MI: Eerdmans, 1998), 413–41.

> For I will pour water on the thirsty land, and streams on the dry ground; I will pour my spirit upon your descendants, and my blessing on your offspring. (Isa. 44:3)

> and I will never hide my face from them, for I will pour out my spirit upon the house of Israel, says the Lord God. (Ezek. 39:29)

> Then after I will pour out my spirit on all flesh; your sons and your daughters shall prophesy, your old men shall dream dreams, and your young men will see visions. Even on the male and female slaves, in those days, I will pour out my spirit. (Joel 2:28-29)[6]

While Paul did not quote any of these texts explicitly, it is clear he believed that the presence and empowerment of the Spirit experienced by the earliest Christians (including himself) were signs of the dawning of a new era.[7] He writes to the Galatians that the Abrahamic blessing for gentiles is signaled by the reception of the promised *pneuma* (Gal. 3:14). Indeed, a major part of this epistle involves Paul's appeal to the initiating and confirming work of the Spirit in the lives of the Galatians. When they came to believe in Jesus Christ, they received the Spirit (3:2), and at least part of this involved inexplicable, miraculous activity (3:5).[8] In Romans, Paul makes reference to the "new life of the Spirit" (7:6) and the "law of the Spirit of life," which set them free from "the law of sin and death" (8:2)—that is, a new aeon of the Spirit has arrived to abolish the powers of evil. So central was the Spirit to Paul's eschatological conception of the kingdom of God that he could define it as "righteousness and peace and joy in the Holy Spirit" (14:17).

The focal point of the Spirit's activity for Paul involves indwelling the person and community. As the Spirit comes to live inside, it actualizes the presence of Christ and brings new resurrection life (Rom. 8:10-11). The indwelling Spirit gives life but also re-identifies the person as a true member of God's family through Jesus the Son of God and brother of believers, so that they receive a "spirit of adoption" and can cry out "Abba! Father!" in prayer (Rom. 8:15). In one sense, then, the Spirit helps the sin-tainted human to become restored to his or her true self; but in another sense, the believer must be reminded that if the Spirit lives within, that person belongs to God and the body becomes a holy temple and vessel dedicated for worship (1 Cor. 6:19).

Here, too, we can mention the role for Paul that the Holy Spirit plays in testifying to the broader acceptance of gentiles into the people of God. These former outsiders to the covenant are accepted through Jesus Christ and confirmed and made holy by God's Spirit (Rom. 15:16). Given the natural controversy within the early Jewish Jesus-following community about the status of gentiles, special signs were needed to help signal their full inclusion (cf. Rom. 15:18-21).[9]

THE SPIRIT SANCTIFIES AND TRANSFORMS

According to Paul, the Spirit serves as a sign of the eschatological age of God's redemption and lives inside the believer to testify to this truth. But the Spirit is also active in the work

---

[6]These references are registered in Dunn, "Towards the Spirit of Christ," 7.
[7]This is a central point made by Gordon D. Fee in his classic work *God's Empowering Presence* (Peabody, MA: Hendrickson, 1994), esp. 803–25.
[8]See Graham H. Twelftree, *Paul and the Miraculous* (Grand Rapids, MI: Baker, 2013).
[9]See T. David Beck, *The Holy Spirit and the Renewal of All Things* (Cambridge: James Clarke, 2007), 54–5.

of transformation.[10] The first thing to observe is Paul's preferred descriptor—more than any other adjective, Paul preferred to call the Spirit "holy."[11] In fact, it should not be ignored that if 1 Thessalonians is the earliest extant piece of "Christian literature," his reference to the "Holy Spirit" precedes any other Christian writer (1 Thess. 1:5).[12] What did it mean when Paul referred to the divine *pneuma* as "holy"? Part of this involves the unique, "numinous" quality of this *pneuma* associated with the divine realm that is wholly unlike the many kinds of evil and unclean "spirits" that existed on earth and in the heavenlies. This "holiness" includes the *consecrating* work of the Spirit, initiating believers into the family of God and qualifying them to be called "saints" or "holy ones" (*hagioi*; see 1 Cor. 1:2). Through the self-offering of Christ and the purifying power of the Spirit, Paul reminds the Corinthians how they were washed, sanctified (or consecrated), and justified, such that they ought to live into that new identity, status, and life (1 Cor. 6:11).

The "holy" Spirit not only initiates through cleansing, but also transforms and purifies toward a more complete sanctification (Rom. 15:16, 1 Thess. 5:23). Paul did not conceive of this work as autonomous but rather a process into which believers must participate and "cooperate" with the Spirit. Paul uses a wide variety of terminology to express this ongoing formative work of the Spirit. In 2 Corinthians he describes this as like a radiating energy or light that imprints upon the believer while increasing the movement toward glorification (2 Cor. 3:18). With the Galatians he talks about alignment by "walking" by the Spirit (Gal. 5:16; cf. Rom. 8:4) as well as being "led" (Rom. 8:14, Gal. 5:18), bearing "fruit" (Gal. 5:22), and "living by" and "keeping in step" with the Spirit (Gal. 5:25).

The reason why Paul was so emphatic about this commitment to following the Spirit attentively is because he viewed the world as a great conflict between flesh (*sarks*) and Spirit (*pneuma*). The flesh pursues an agenda of tempting mortals to give in to their worst vices and pleasures, but the Spirit militates against this to free believers from oppression (see Rom. 8:5-6, Gal. 5:17-18).

THE SPIRIT INSPIRES AND EMPOWERS

Another set of responsibilities that Paul attributes to the Spirit involves inspiration and empowerment for wise living and community upbuilding. That is, the Spirit, present in the community, operates in such a way as to enhance human life together to strengthen persons and relationships and to counteract the negative effects of ongoing problems with sin and human weakness.[13]

The first thing we can say from Paul's perspective is that the Spirit inspires *faith*. Paul wrote his second letter to the Corinthians with a specific concern that some of them were focusing on the external rather than the heart of the matter, even when it came to Paul's own ministry. He appeared to them and others to be a suspicious, weak, and incompetent failure, yet he directed their attention to the hidden *treasure* within the unassuming vessel of his body (2 Cor. 4:7). Quoting Ps. 116:10 from the Septuagint, he exclaims, "I believed; therefore I spoke" (2 Cor. 4:13)—that is, his (foolish) proclamation came from a place of conviction based on divine revelation. He explains how he shares with the psalmist "the same *pneuma*

---

[10] See Fee, *God's Empowering Presence*, 846–69.
[11] Rom. 5:5; 9:1; 14:17; 15:13, 16; 1 Cor. 6:19, 12:3; 2 Cor. 13:13; 1 Thess. 1:5-6; 4:8.
[12] But, of course, Jews and Israelites before Paul had used this language as well (e.g., Ps. 51:11, Isa. 63:10-11, Wis. 9:17, *Pss. Sol.* 17:37).
[13] See Fee, *God's Empowering Presence*, 870–95.

of faith" that professes from a vision of reality determined by the resurrection of the crucified Christ (2 Cor. 4:14). Furthermore, in 1 Corinthians, Paul explains how the truth he conveys is not taught in philosophy books, but rather via wisdom generated by the Spirit that is able to offer a unique and higher form of knowledge (1 Cor. 2:13; cf. Eph. 1:17).

This is also the category where we can place the so-called "spiritual gifts"—a subject in the NT unique to Paul's letters. Paul explains in 1 Corinthians that there is one Spirit that endows believers with different gifts (12:1-11). These facilitate the express purpose of service within the community (and not, for example, flamboyant self-promotion; 12:4, 7). Several of the gifts that Paul mentions relate to cognitive enhancement (e.g., utterance of wisdom and utterance of knowledge), which appear to be similar to concepts of spirit-ecstasy and inspiration that would have been familiar in Greco-Roman culture. Paul mentions other gifts, including healing, miracle-working, prophecy, discernment of spirits, tongues, and tongues-interpretation. The distribution of gifts is not about the capacity or status of the person, but each is given special abilities for the purpose of contributing to the whole (12:12). Paul is implying in this passage that believers are not endowed by competing spirits to one-up the other; rather, *one Spirit* generously distributes these gifts to bring individuals together to help them become a healthy whole.

THE SPIRIT GUARANTEES ESCHATOLOGICAL HOPE

We have brought attention to the Spirit's relationship to the "past" (the Spirit renews and consecrates) and the "present" (the Spirit inspires and empowers), but for Paul, the Spirit also points believers toward "future" hope of final redemption, sanctification, and righteousness. Twice Paul mentions how the Spirit was given as a deposit (or down payment) in view of a full payment to come (1 Cor. 1:22, 2 Cor. 5:5). This is part of the already/not yet tension of Paul's eschatology.[14] The Spirit has brought vitality and joy in terms of a foretaste, with the promise and hope of completeness ahead. It is as if the Spirit is a companion sent from the future to journey with the believer through life, all the while "representing," so to speak, the heavenly commonwealth and acting as an ambassador and cultural coach preparing believers for transmigration.[15]

One should not underestimate the importance of "hope" for Paul: as believers faced sometimes severe persecution in the first century, they clung to the apostolic and divine promises of ultimate deliverance and restoration in spite of present opprobrium and even the grim reality of death (see 1 Thess. 4:13–5:11). Thus, Paul could pray for his friends like this: "May the God of hope fill you with all joy and peace in believing, so that you may abound in hope by the power of the Holy Spirit" (Rom. 15:13).

THE LORD IS THE SPIRIT

In the end, though, we are left with the question—What exactly *is* the Spirit according to Paul?[16] On some occasions, we see an overlap between Paul's descriptions and teachings

---

[14] Fee, *God's Empowering Presence*, 846–7.

[15] I am reminded of the angelic companion who accompanies Tobias, the young man unaware that this disguised heavenly being was sent to assist him on his journey (see Tob. 5:1–12:22). But for Paul, believers *are* aware of this holy presence.

[16] J. Christiaan Beker is right to talk about the "hidden character" of the Spirit, which makes Pauline pneumatology so difficult to explain: "the Spirit grasps hold of us . . . and in so doing hides itself from our analysis. . . . It points

and how pagans viewed the mystical and ethereal nature of "spirits" (1 Cor. 12:8). But it is clear that Paul treated this inimitable *pneuma* with absolute authority and also with thorough (for lack of a better word) "personhood."[17] On the first matter, we might point to 1 Thessalonians, where Paul warns these believers that anyone who rejects apostolic teaching in fact rejects the ultimate authority of the Holy Spirit (4:8). On the second matter (personhood), Paul portrays the Spirit as having very human-like qualities and skills, such as "pleading" with the Father on behalf of believers (Rom. 8:26-27) and having the kind of interpersonal interaction that assumes thoughtful relationship (cf. 1 Cor. 2:11). At the same time, the Spirit is portrayed as an influential *agent* always working on behalf of *another*. The Spirit acts as the power of God that brings life and vitality and operates as a sort of "host" that facilitates relationship and community (e.g., Phil. 1:27, 2:1). We will consider further now the nature of the Spirit in view of three questions.

What Did Paul Mean When He Wrote, "The Lord is the Spirit" (2 Cor. 3:17)?

The third chapter of 2 Corinthians compares the "new covenant" of the Spirit with the former covenant (3:6). Paul engages Exod. 34:29-35, where Moses had to wear a veil to dim the shining glory from his face when he left the presence of God and went back to the people. Paul points to his ministry as having a greater glory because of the power of the Spirit at work (2 Cor. 3:8). He reappropriates the "veil" language to talk about those who are shrouded with a spiritual "veil" that darkens their understanding when "Moses is read" (3:15). But the veil is removed whenever someone turns to the Lord, and here Paul interjects that "the Lord is the Spirit" and that this Spirit brings freedom (3:17). It is unclear precisely how Paul relates the Holy Spirit here to the reference to Moses and the Lord in view of Exodus 34. But at the most basic level, Paul was affirming that the figure that "powers" divine glory and transforms believers is none other than the Spirit.

The idea that "God is spirit" is found in Jn 4:24, but something similar is communicated in Phil. 3:3, where Paul explains that gentile Christians can identify as "the circumcision" (in a sense, those especially dedicated to God) but that their worship is "in the Spirit of God" and they put no confidence in the flesh. To worship in the Spirit has something to do with living and honoring God in ways that are not easy to discern by outside observation. Again, in John, Jesus tried to explain to Nicodemus the strange workings of the Spirit (cf. Jn 3:1-21, esp. 3:8), and no doubt Paul would have agreed. One must engage spiritual perception to "see" the true work of the Spirit of God (cf. 1 Cor. 2:11).

How Do Christ and the Spirit Relate?

For Paul, Jesus Christ and the Spirit were separate persons, yet we find them connected and paired in unique ways. Sometimes Paul paired them as dual agents: "I appeal to you, brothers and sisters, by our Lord Jesus Christ and by the love of the Spirit, to join me in earnest prayer to God on my behalf" (Rom. 15:30). Perhaps more perplexing is when Paul refers to "the Spirit of Christ" (Rom. 8:9; cf. 1 Pet. 1:11) or "the Spirit of Jesus Christ" (Phil. 1:19; cf. Acts 16:7). Here the reference is clearly to the Spirit, but somehow this *pneuma* recognizes or mediates the ministry of Christ. The matter is well articulated by James Dunn when he talks about the sense in Paul that "Jesus did not absorb the role of the Spirit and that *there was still a role for the Spirit not restricted to Christ*, and yet

---

away from itself." "Aspects of the Holy Spirit in Paul," *Union Seminary Quarterly* 14 (1958): 3.
[17]See Fee, *God's Empowering Presence*, 5–9.

the Spirit was recognized now as *the Spirit of Jesus*, as the Spirit bearing and generating the character of Christ."[18]

Was Paul (proto-)trinitarian?

It is rather obvious that it is anachronistic to assume a full-fledged "trinitarian" theology for Paul, if by that we imagine three persons (as is sometimes portrayed in art) sitting at a table communing and inviting the believer to fellowship. Neither should we ignore the fact that Paul uniquely ascribes ultimate authority to each of these persons and especially pairs Christ and Spirit together on occasion (see earlier in this chapter). And, at least in one case, we find a benediction that includes all three: "The grace of the Lord Jesus Christ, the love of God, and the communion of the Holy Spirit be with all of you" (2 Cor. 13:13). According to Paul, to call each of these a "person" seems appropriate, and to ascribe to each the word "divine" is also fitting. But it ultimately comes down to the *way* these relate, and at least with respect to Paul, it is no good to parcel out systematically discrete activities among Father, Son, and Spirit or to establish a rigid and consistent hierarchy. Paul was clearly *not* a modalist, but neither did he seem to believe these to be three completely separate deities. They appear to relate and interact dynamically, such that they are in some way different and in another way unified.[19] All these have some connection to the word "lord" (*kyrios*); all play some central part in salvation and redemption; all test and judge mortals; and all move in compassion and love. What can be said about the unique role of the Spirit in Paul's thought is the way the Spirit empowers, inspires, gives life, equips, and trains. The Spirit behaves as a supporter, coach, and sustainer. While Christ is also described as present and active, as noted earlier, the Spirit pervasively operates in a more hidden way, always pointing both away from itself and to Christ.

CONCLUSION

The study of Pauline pneumatology has flowered over the last few decades, marked by numerous monographs, articles, and even the development of a specialized periodical (the *Journal of Biblical and Pneumatological Research*). Gordon Fee wrote one of the most important academic volumes on Paul's pneumatology in 1994, and his book title captures well the heart of this topic: *God's Empowering Presence*. For the Apostle, the dawning of a new era involves the ushering in of the age of the Spirit—the Spirit that comes and lives inside the believer and the community of Jesus; the Spirit that washes them clean and transforms them into Christ's likeness; the Spirit that "powers" belief, inspires wisdom, and dispenses to each spiritual gifts of service to build up the body of Christ; and the Spirit that serves as a deposit, guarantee, and foretaste of a yet unrealized kingdom of joy and peace.

FOR FURTHER READING

Dunn, James D. G. *Theology of Paul the Apostle*. Grand Rapids, MI: Eerdmans, 1998.
Fee, Gordon D. *God's Empowering Presence*. Peabody, MA: Hendrickson, 1994.

---

[18]Dunn, "Towards the Spirit of Christ," 25. Beker describes the matter as "the living presence of the Lord Jesus Christ" and therefore "power-Spirit-Christ belong inseparably together" ("Aspects of the Holy Spirit in Paul," 4).
[19]See the trenchant study by Wesley Hill, *Paul and the Trinity: Persons, Relations, and the Pauline Letters* (Grand Rapids, MI: Eerdmans, 2015).

CHAPTER THREE

The Role of the Acts of the Spirit within Scripture

ROBERT W. WALL

John Chrysostom introduced his homilies on Acts by implying that it is "the gospel of the Holy Spirit."[1] His naming of this book simply recognized that there is much at stake in the church's discussion of God's Spirit according to Acts.

THE STRATEGIC ROLE OF ACTS

Any of the core narrative themes of Acts must be given serious attention by its Christian readers. Especially after finishing the Fourfold Gospel's narrative of Jesus's life, interested readers will naturally want to know what became of the messianic movement now cued by his resurrection. Did his followers, some of whom still doubted him (cf. Mt. 28:17), follow his parting instructions to proclaim God's gospel of forgiveness to the nations (cf. Lk. 24:44-49)? Was Jesus yet another done-and-gone pretender to the messianic office God had promised Israel according to its scripture? Likewise, readers will also want to know what became of John the Baptizer's prophecy that Jesus would baptize his followers "with the Holy Spirit and with fire" (Mt. 3:11, Lk. 3:16). Acts picks up this prophecy to set the stage for the story that follows, thereby anticipating the fulfillment of this very promise as decisive to the story's plotline.

The "great commission" of Luke's Jesus, which directed his followers to proclaim his messianic mission to the nations, predicted they would do so with the heavenly "power" this same Spirit would supply (Lk. 24:49, Acts 1:8)—a prophecy fulfilled on the Day of Pentecost, according to Acts 2. The book of Acts may be read, then, as a narrative of fulfillment in which the community's baptism into the Spirit's power yields charismatic utterances and performances that continued to implicate Jesus's messianic mission to an international, global audience.

---

[1] This title for Acts is F. F. Bruce's, who rightly infers it from Chrysostom's first homily on Acts. *NPNF1*, 11:1-10; see "Luke's Presentation of the Spirit in Acts," *Criswell Theological Review* 5, no. 1 (1990): 18. Chrysostom interprets the prefatory of Acts as stipulating the direct continuity between the gospel disclosed in what Jesus "began to do and to say" according to Luke's Gospel and the gospel proclaimed by his apostles following their baptism with the Spirit according to Acts. In this sense, then, what the apostles continue "to do and to say" in the power of God's Spirit constitutes the same gospel incarnate in God's Son; hence, in this sense the Acts narrative is a post-ascension version of "the gospel of the Holy Spirit."

Both the title of this narrative, "The Acts of the Apostles," and its final placement within the biblical canon, between the Fourfold Gospel and the two Letter Collections (Pauline and Catholic), commend the strategic importance of this book. Each is a postbiblical property of the canonical process during which the Spirit signaled those sanctified writings intended for inclusion in the church's scripture. Each aspect is suggestive of the church's approach in using Acts as Scripture in worship and catechesis. In the first place, the title given to this canonical narrative is *not* "The Acts of the Spirit," as preferred by some who contend—not without good reason—that God's Spirit is the narrative's central character and that its various performances in guiding the *missio Dei* plot its storyline. But the title given when the church received Acts as canonical toward the end of the second century alerts readers that its narrative's storyline should focus on the "acts" the apostles perform as testaments to their divine authorization and the importance of remembering their witness, now canonized, for guiding the church's future. We are put on notice in the story's preface that their acts, whether performed as charismatic speeches (e.g., Acts 4:8-12) or as miraculous "signs and wonders" (e.g., Acts 5:12-16), are enabled by the Spirit's filling to demonstrate the inauguration of God's reign because of Jesus.

Moreover, the title concentrates the community's attention on those apostolic figures whose memory continues to delineate the theological and missional boundaries of its public identity as "one, holy, catholic, *and apostolic*" church. Reading Acts not only informs the church what its confession of faith implies about its public identity in and for the world, but also secures the apostolate as the normative source of its self-understanding: even as the apostles continued to do and say what the risen One had begun according to the gospel, so also must today's church imitate the patterns and personae of the Lord's apostles.[2]

Just as critical is the placement of Acts within the biblical canon, which was probably finalized toward the end of the fourth century as an element of the ecclesial process that shaped the final form of the NT canon. There is some manuscript evidence that evinces Acts circulated early on with a second collection of letters, first called the "Catholic Epistles" by Eusebius, in what was called "*The Apostolos*." The actual reasons for this remain unclear from the extant historical record. What seems clearer, however, is that Acts is placed between the Fourfold Gospel on the one hand and the two Letter Collections on the other to provide faithful readers with a canonical narrative that would help contextualize their effective use of the NT in at least three different ways.

Biographies of Key Apostolic Figures

The memories Luke receives and uses to draw his portraits have already been refined to reflect the enduring or canonical character of their witness.[3] The relationship between the Spirit's filling and the persuasive effect of the apostles' missionary speeches (e.g.,

---

[2] David P. Moessner argues that the role of Paul's biography in Acts is to underscore the importance of continuity between the future church (= us), for whom the Paul of Acts has supreme importance, and the original apostles, whose example he imitates. "Luke's 'Witness and Witnesses': Paul as Definer and Defender of the Tradition of the Apostles—'from the Beginning,'" in *Paul and the Heritage of Israel*, ed. David P. Moessner et al., LNTS 452 (London: T&T Clark, 2014), 117–47.

[3] Whether the narrator was an associate of Paul who traveled with him and took notes of his urban missions reported in the second half of Acts, cued by the use of the first-person plural "we" (the first of which is 16:10), remains contested among Acts scholars.

4:8, 31; 13:9) and authorizing miracles (e.g., 5:12; 9:34-35, 41-42; 14:3) underscores the necessity of the Spirit's power to continue the risen Lord's mission to the ends of the earth (cf. 1:8).

Similar to Paul's conception of Timothy's Spirit-ordained leadership, which he sets out in 1–2 Timothy, the emphasis of Acts is not on an ecclesiastical office. Acts profiles the church's charismatic leadership in practical ways, ever adaptable to the changing landscape of the church's mission. The similarity between Peter (see 4:32–5:16) and Paul (see 20:18-35) is that the exercise of their religious authority is not that of an ecclesial office—since Paul did not meet the criteria of apostleship according to Acts 1:21-22—but of prophetic vocation, which is confirmed and enabled by the Holy Spirit rather than based on individual talent or education (see 4:13).

These various apostolic leaders stand out as virtuous individuals; they are moral exemplars for the whole church to imitate (cf. 1 Cor. 11:1). Even though nowhere is the Spirit presented as the agent of their moral formation as in the Pauline Letters, their exemplary personal portraits in Acts orients readers to this feature of Pauline pneumatology. Perhaps this is the idea that secures the apostles' unsettling rebuke of Jerusalem's religious elite when they predicate their Spirit-enabled witness to the risen Jesus on their acts of obedience (rather than professions of faith; so 5:32). The apostles embody characteristics that are critical markers of a congregation's moral practices: their courageous and costly obedience to their calling, their handling of possessions, their theological perspicuity, their religious practices, and their personal piety—all target the holy ends of a covenant-keeping people (cf. 20:18-35).

Normative Patterns of Ecclesial Community and Mission

The implied connection between the repentant community's reception of the gift of the Holy Spirit (2:38) and the pattern of its Christ-centered formation set out in Acts 2:42 is subsequently made clearer by the Spirit's indispensable role in enabling the apostles' effective teaching of Scripture and forming a people of one heart and soul by conflict resolution and the practice of sharing common goods. That is, the community's baptism into the Holy Spirit marks also the initiation into a particular kind of community of practice.

Those who consider Pentecost in some sense an initial work of the Spirit—for example, never before had the Spirit filled the household of rank-and-file believers—tend to find more discontinuity between the Spirit of the OT and of the NT than exists.[4] For example, Stephen's prophetic critique of Jerusalem's religious elite (cf. 7:51-53) would rather imply continuity between the Spirit of Israel and the Spirit of the church. According to Stephen, Israel's resistance of the Spirit is a common feature of those who oppose both prophets and apostles throughout the history of God's people (7:51). What is new about the acts of the Spirit in Acts is not its empowerment for prophecy or even the international scope of the Spirit's activity. The antecedent of both ideas is found in Israel's scripture. What is clearly new is the referent of the Spirit's activity: the risen Jesus. The messianic event, glossed by Pentecost, transforms how we think about the acts of the Spirit.

The church of Acts is a community of goods. Its united witness to the Messiah's resurrection is not only proclaimed but also embodied in its common life under the aegis

---

[4]Thomas R. Schreiner, *New Testament Theology* (Grand Rapids, MI: Baker Academic, 2008), 454–5.

of the Holy Spirit. The community's "resurrection praxis" includes four discrete elements: economic, spiritual, religious, and social. First, as economic *koinōnia*, the community reorders its possessions according to the principle of Jubilee (cf. Lk. 4:16-18) so that its generosity toward the needy reciprocates God's generosity in the gift of salvation (see 2:44-45, 4:32-35, 4:36–5:11, 6:1-6, 11:27-30). Second, the gift of God's salvation is embodied as the gift of God's Spirit. As with material possessions, the Holy Spirit is the common property of an inclusive community so that its pentecostal coming upon repentant Jews is repeated on repentant Samaritans (see 8:14-16) and gentiles (see 10:44; cf. 11:17, 15:9). Living boldly under its powerful influence is a second resurrection practice of those who follow Jesus. Third, the religious dimension of the community's solidarity is expressed most profoundly by a prohibition: "abstain from things polluted by idols" (15:20; see 15:29, 21:25). And finally, the sociopolitical concern of Acts is not so much the inward, spiritual purification of individual believers but the political purity of a community's public identity. The sin of idolatry undermines Scripture's legacy in giving shape to a people's worship of and allegiance to God (see 7:38-44). Those who practice idolatry—who substitute alternative deities for worship of Israel's God, the only God—demonstrate their ignorance of God's redemptive purpose (14:14-18; 17:22, 24-29; 19:26). A prophetic community is a counterculture that lives in tension with the surrounding order. A sociology of external conflict requires all the more a sociology of internal unity. This is possible to maintain only by a carefully managed protocol of conciliation that forges unity between its disparate groups (see 6:1-6, 14:27–15:29). The solidarity of believers is emphatic within Acts: believers are "together" when at worship and in mission.

Scripture as a Principal Revelatory Medium of God's Plan of Salvation

What also is clear in Acts is the necessity of the Spirit's illuminating presence to illumine a messianic reading of Scripture. The Spirit's principal role in the divine economy according to Acts is as witness to God's redemptive plan (5:32). Primarily, the Spirit's witness is effected through Scripture's production (1:16, 4:25, 28:25) or its messianic interpretation (8:32, 35) but also more directly through speech (e.g., 8:29, 10:19, 13:2, 20:23, 21:11) or some other media (e.g., 16:6-7).

In any case, Israel is divided over the apostles' messianic reading of its scripture (e.g., 17:1-9), even if not over its authority as God's word. The conflict provoked over the apostolic proclamation of Jesus is grounded in a battle for a messianic reading of the Bible. Among the various points Luke's gospel implicates in its distinctive narrative of Jesus's post-resurrection appearances is the importance of the right biblical hermeneutic in completely "opening" (διανοίγω) both eyes (24:31-32) and minds (24:45) to his messianic mission. Luke's version of the "great commission" (Lk. 24:44-49) stipulates that the risen One's instruction of Scripture forges the apostles' witness of his messianic work and that the repentance of the nations turns on their reception of this rightly interpreted holy text.

To this crucial point is added the implied necessity of Jesus's promise of heavenly "power," mediated by the Spirit's baptism (so Acts 1:5-8), that enables this witness. The pairing of Scripture's interpretation and proclamation and the empowering Spirit in Acts is a central element of its narrative of the *missio Dei* from Jerusalem to Rome. There is hardly a better example of this than the eunuch's programmatic question of Philip about a right reading of Scripture: "About whom is the prophet [Isaiah] saying this [LXX Isa. 53:7; cf. 8:32-33]—himself or someone else?" (8:34). The peculiar expression used of

Philip's verbal response—that his mouth "was opened" (the verb, ἀνοίγω, is expressed in the passive voice)—suggests that his messianic interpretation of Scripture is effected by another: namely, it is the Spirit of the resurrected Jesus (cf. Acts 16:7) that guides his reading of Scripture. Elsewhere in Acts, the Spirit's "filling" enables those it fills to render Israel's scripture in a way that cues a decision about Jesus that occasions repentance but just as often provokes conflict (cf. 2:4; 4:8, 31; 6:4, 5; 7:55; 9:17; 11:24; 13:9).

Jacob Jervell is right in concluding, then, that "the church does not lead and guide itself: God does through the Spirit."[5] It is the Spirit who sanctifies the succession of figures who continue Jesus's messianic mission to save the world (cf. 8:14-19), who illumines Scripture's messianic argot, who enables the untrained to speak the word of God persuasively (cf. 4:8) and boldly (see 4:29-31; 9:27, 29; 19:8; 28:31; cf. 18:26), and who performs mighty "signs and wonders" (see 5:12-16, 8:13, 14:3, 15:11) to insure the forward movement of salvation to the ends of the earth. It is the public experience of the Spirit's reception that marks out the gift of God's forgiveness (2:38; 8:14-17, 39-40; 9:17; 10:34-44; 15:7-11; 19:5-6).

THE ROLE OF THE SPIRIT OF ACTS WITHIN THE CHURCH

The study of Acts generally and its conception of the Holy Spirit in particular remain crucial for revitalizing today's Christian congregations for several reasons.

The Pentecostal Communion's Identity in Acts

For Pentecostals, Acts remains its canon within the Canon. Perhaps more importantly, the stories of Spirit-filling in Acts shape a particular way of thinking about reality.[6] Different from Anselm's rubric of a thoughtful faith that seeks after theological understanding—which is often reduced to a sectarian grammar of core beliefs—a Pentecostal approach may be characterized as an affective faith that seeks after real experiences of the divine—those material or embodied phenomena that disclose God in stunning, fresh ways.

Pentecostals typically locate the pivot point on which the Acts narrative turns in Peter's peculiar reading of his community's baptism of the Spirit (at least to his Torah-believing audience), which drew upon Joel's prophecy of those eschatological "signs and wonders" the Spirit outpours upon the entire household of Israel (cf. 2:5) as Scripture's commentary on its experience of Pentecost—it is a light-and-sound show of God's revelatory day when all who call upon the risen Lord (cf. 2:36) for deliverance will be saved from their sins (cf. 2:38). What becomes clear only as the narrative unfolds is that the redemptive implications of the Spirit's "signs and wonders" extend to the entire world and anticipate a great reversal that will "turn the world upside down" (17:6). They heal, persuade, disrupt, and generally expand a people's understanding of how God acts within the world to lean it toward new creation.

---

[5]*The Theology of the Acts of the Apostles*, NTT (Cambridge: Cambridge University Press, 1996), 51.
[6]For works that take this Pentecostal approach to reality, see James K. A. Smith, *Thinking in Tongues: Pentecostal Contributions to Christian Philosophy* (Grand Rapids, MI: Eerdmans, 2010); Steven J. Land, *Pentecostal Spirituality: A Passion for the Kingdom* (Sheffield: Sheffield Academic Press, 1993); Daniel Castelo, *Pneumatology: A Guide for the Perplexed* (London: Bloomsbury T & T Clark, 2015), chap. 4; and Douglas Jacobsen, *Thinking in the Spirit: Theologies of the Early Pentecostal Movement* (Bloomington, IN: Indiana University Press, 2003), chap. 1.

An Acts-shaped understanding of Christian existence, then, not only concentrates on the person and work of the Holy Spirit but also is expectant of the Spirit's continuing charismatic presence and dynamic participation in the church's mission and life together. In particular, the evident effects of the Spirit's material "signs and wonders" within a charismatic congregation (e.g., healing, prophecy, and social activism) forge an optimistic practice of faith that presumes God is at work globally, holistically, and concretely, often in surprising ways to transform bad news into good news. In addition, Acts 4:23-31 is an apt template of Pentecostal worship, which includes the practices of public testimony, Scripture reading and figural interpretation, prayer and pastoral exhortation for prophetic boldness, and petitions for renewed experiences of Spirit-filling. The apostolic expectation of "signs and wonders" (4:30) reclaims Joel's prophecy of the Spirit's outpouring (see 2:19) as a normative, ongoing experience of "the last days" of salvation's history (2:17).

Lectionary Readings

The most prominent way Christian congregations, both ancient and contemporary, have ordered their public reading of Scripture in worship is by the lectionary. Today, the most commonly used lectionary among Protestant traditions is the Revised Common Lectionary, which itself is based upon Roman Catholicism's post-Vatican II's *Ordo Lectionum Missae*. Even though their selection of passages from Acts differs significantly, both substitute passages from Acts for OT lessons during Eastertide. These passages come from the first half of Acts, but the chosen passages used in each lectionary effect different emphases. In the Protestant lectionary, the emphasis is on the apostolic proclamation of the church's Christ-centered gospel. In the Roman lectionary, emphasis is rather placed on the global scope of the church's mission and the inclusive character of its membership—that is, the "catholicity" of the Roman church is underlined by its Acts readings. In each lectionary, however, the seminal passages that target the activities of the Spirit, with the exception of Acts 19, are covered.

Ecclesial Practices

The heavenly power mediated by the Spirit facilitates a range of ecclesial practices. Spirit-filling enables persuasive speech and healing signs and wonders that testify to the apocalypse of God's salvation because of the risen Jesus whom God has made both Messiah and Lord (2:36). In this sense, the ecclesial practices effected by the Spirit's filling are missional in purpose. Moreover, the practices of Spirit-filling (πλήθω; 2:4; 4:31; cf. 6:8) are embodied in those who are "full of the Spirit" (πλήρης; 6:3, 8). If Stephen personifies this dynamic, the power the messianic community receives with the Spirit of Jesus as the gift of salvation is never disembodied from its membership: those full of the Spirit are enabled by the filling of the Spirit to practice its heavenly powers. The message and messenger are of a piece.

Craig Keener distinguishes the Spirit's powerful performances within and upon the church into two instantiations: purification and prophetic.[7] The Spirit of holiness (rather

---

[7] Craig Keener, *Acts: An Exegetical Commentary*, 4 vols. (Grand Rapids, MI: Baker, 2012), 1:532–7. Keener distinguishes "Holy Spirit" in which "holy" designates an eternal attribute of the Third Person (i.e., what the Spirit is) from a "Spirit (or spirit) of holiness" in which "holiness" is an activity of the Spirit (i.e., what the Spirit does).

than "Holy Spirit") is God's purifying agent whose baptism cleanses the heart in a way that draws the repentant to God while consecrating them for God's service. This seems to be the subtext of the Jerusalem Council and makes sense, then, of James's report to Antioch that the decisions achieved by the church's episcopacy in response to the Pharisees' concerns about the purity of repentant gentiles were "good to the Holy Spirit and to us" (15:28). Indeed, while Peter stresses inward (and individual) purity (15:9), James goes on to stress a complement of outward (and communal) purity practices (15:20).

Transformative Knowledge

In my estimation, the principal theological problem addressed by the apostolic mission according to Acts is a people's ignorance about God's way of salvation (3:17, 17:30). The variety of practices enabled by the Spirit according to Acts addresses this problem as a central feature of the *missio Dei*. This emphasis in Acts, especially when coupled with the importance of the Spirit's empowerment for interpreting Scripture and the apostles' prophetic ministry (2:42, 6:2), underlines that knowing and communicating God's redemptive plan is an indispensable element of the gospel. Repentance (μετανοέω) is the proper response to ignorance (so 3:19, 17:30) and envisages a transformation of the mind.

If the Spirit is divine agent of those experiences that recognize, even if unknowingly, the apocalypse of God's salvation in human history and is also the agent of Scripture's messianic exegesis and proclamation, then readers should expect a mutually glossing dialogue between the two. Nowhere in Acts is the human capacity to know God's will through experiences of God's redemptive activities in history marginalized, either because of the supposed depravity that subverts our sense reception of God's truth or because of the inherent inadequacy of natural revelation when compared to Scripture. In Acts, the Spirit directs both our experiences of God's reign and our reading of Scripture toward the same target: the resurrected Jesus who is Lord and Christ (2:36).

While it is true that the Pauline witness makes emphatic the Spirit's effective agency in transforming human character and social relationships while Acts concentrates on the Spirit's equally effective agency in enabling the church's witness to the risen One, I would insist that the two are not mutually exclusive. The common ground between both canonical witnesses, Paul and Acts, is the Spirit's work in transforming the human intellect.

The story of Apollos in Acts 18, especially when paired with the following conversion story of the so-called "Ephesian Twelve" (19:1-7), is a case in point.

This element of the Spirit's portrait in Acts is also introduced by the gospel's concluding story in which the risen Jesus commissions his disciples to give witness of his messianic mission to the nations. Two interpenetrating kinds of epistemic practices are noted in Luke's edition of this story, each cued in turn by the evocative verb "to open" (see earlier in the chapter). Together, they describe a pattern of the Lord's response to "troubled hearts" and lingering "doubts" he observes in them (Lk. 24:38). The evocative use of δια λογισμός often envisages a line of reasoning that results in "doubt." Luke's point is to characterize the mindset of the Lord's disciples following the resurrection, which then requires him to stay with them and teach them as their risen Christ in order to persuade them that Scripture's promised salvation is fulfilled because of him. The narrative says that sharing a couple of meals with the flesh-and-blood Jesus occasions his exhortation to "see my hands and feet . . . handle me" (24:39), which results in their "recognition" of him (24:31). Luke's strategic use of the catchword ἐπιγινώσκω (cf. 24:16; Acts 3:10, 4:13, 12:14, 28:1) envisages that one's realization of God's saving activity is based on physical evidence, sometimes produced by the Spirit's power in Acts (3:10, 4:13).

Perhaps more important than the opening of the disciples' eyes to eyewitness the resurrected Jesus who stands before them—an eyewitness that provides a central element of their subsequent *apologia* for Messiah Jesus in Acts—is the opening of their minds (Lk. 24:45) that enables them to interpret and then proclaim Israel's scripture as a textual witness to Messiah Jesus. This too supplies their missionary speeches, especially for a Jewish audience, with another line of evidence. This witness in particular requires them to be "clothed with heaven's power" (24:49)—that is, an intellectual acuity that results not only from their memory of Jesus's instruction (24:45; cf. Acts 1:3), but also from their baptism into the Spirit, who aids their recall of the Lord's instruction (so Jn 14:26) but then also enables them to present it with persuasive speech (cf. Acts 4:5-13).

The Spirit's use of Scripture as a sanctified auxiliary of God's word when considered with the Spirit's filling of Jesus's apostolic successors underwrites the practice of the nations' theological catechesis as an indispensable feature of the *missio Dei* in the world. In fact, the "witness" to which the church is called *includes* Scripture's witness to Jesus's messianic work. This vocation is not abandoned by the church when it enters the public square or when it testifies to God's salvation in the midst of a non-believing, hostile setting. Paul did not do so at Mars Hill or in Lystra where he proclaimed the gospel in the shadow of the town's temple of Zeus. Rather, the theological catechesis of the nations requires the translation of the gospel into an idiom that communicates its theological goods. Only then can a choice be made for or against God's Christ based upon reason and understanding. A leap of faith based upon ignorance is not an option. Repentance—a change of intellectual orientation—requires evidence supplied by witnesses, whether apostolic or scriptural. This is what the missional practices of the Spirit-filled church provide the nations according to Acts.

FOR FURTHER READING

Bonnah, George Kwame Agyei. *The Holy Spirit: A Narrative Factor in the Acts of the Apostles*. Stuttgart: Katholisches Bibelwerk, 2007.

Gaventa, Beverly Roberts. *The Acts of the Apostles*. ANTC. Nashville, TN: Abingdon, 2003.

Jervell, Jacob. *The Theology of the Acts of the Apostles*. NTT. Cambridge: Cambridge University Press, 1996.

Johnson, Luke Timothy. *The Acts of the Apostles*. SP. Collegeville, MN: Liturgical, 1992.

Levison, John R. *Filled with the Spirit*. Grand Rapids, MI: Eerdmans, 2009.

Shepherd, William H. *The Narrative Function of the Holy Spirit as a Character in Luke–Acts*. SBLDS 147. Atlanta, GA: Scholars, 1994.

Stronstad, Roger. *The Charismatic Theology of St. Luke*. Peabody, MA: Hendrickson, 1984.

Wall, Robert W. "The Acts of the Apostles." In *New Interpreter's Bible*. 12 vols. 10:1–368. Nashville, TN: Abingdon, 2002.

CHAPTER FOUR

The Spirit in the Catholic Epistles

DAVID R. NIENHUIS

A study of the witness to the Spirit in the collection of NT letters traditionally identified as the "Catholic Epistles" (CE) must necessarily begin with a clarification of the range of texts under consideration. In fact, to even speak of the CE is to enter contested ground, as modern biblical scholarship is not in full agreement as to the number of letters involved (apart from the rather obvious fact that they are not part of the larger Pauline literary inheritance) and indeed to whether or not they actually form anything like a coherent collection at all. As we will see, however, the decision we make in this regard will have a profound effect on our reception of this collection's witness to the Spirit.

The most common contemporary approach promotes a five-letter collection typically called "the General Letters," which would include Hebrews, James, 1–2 Peter, and Jude. This interpretative decision is consistent with modern historical-critical concerns to reorganize the biblical canon according to presumed authorship and provenance. Hebrews is therefore typically included because it is not written by Paul, and the Letters of John are removed to be treated alongside the Gospel of John. The relatively recent collapse of historical-critical methodological hegemony and the concomitant rise of literary and theological approaches to Scripture have had the effect of increasing our appreciation of the commonly accepted final form of the NT canon. When these "non-Pauline" letters are viewed through a more canonical lens, one finds multiple reasons to embrace the traditional content and boundaries of the seven-letter CE collection of James, Peter, John, and Jude.

To begin, the canonical titles of the NT letter collection underscore the distinction between those belonging to the Pauline canon, which are titled according to the recipient(s) (*pros*, "to ____"), and the CE, which are titled according to the author (*epistole*, "the letter of ____"). Thus, a canonical boundary is marked not between the letters "to Philemon" and "to the Hebrews," but between the Letter to the Hebrews and the Letter of James, the latter set off to function as the introductory letter for a new collection.

Second, the letter sequence of James–Peter–John, which does not follow the Pauline convention of organizing letters by length from longest to shortest, recalls Paul's own designation of the "acknowledged pillars" of Jerusalem in Gal. 2:9, conveying the sense that the CE collection was intended to be received as the witness of the ancient Jerusalem apostolate in contrast to the Pauline witness to the early mission to the gentiles. The shape of the canon thereby suggests that we receive the CE collection as a kerygmatic counterpoint of sorts to the Pauline collection.

Related to this observation is the fact that the collection closes with a letter from a person named "Judas" (traditionally rendered "Jude" to distinguish him from the betrayer) whose only identifying feature is that he is "the brother of James" (Jude 1). The close association of the names "James" and "Jude" recalls the scene in Matthew and Mark where the residents of Nazareth are offended by Jesus because they know the facts of his humble origins, which include his mother Mary and his brothers "James and Joses and Judas and Simon" (Mt.13:55, Mk 6:3). A collection that begins with a letter from Jesus's brother James and closes with one from his brother Jude suggests that these seven letters, which witness to the Jerusalem apostolate, are handed down to us in the embrace of the Holy Family. In this respect, the notion that the CE is a kerygmatic counterpoint to Paul is strengthened, for unlike Paul, these four traditional authors were eyewitnesses to the pre-Easter Jesus. Thus, in the CE we encounter a witness to the Lord who not only died for our sins and rose again in power (so prominent in the Pauline kerygma), but who also lived a Spirit-empowered human life and instructed his disciples to follow him on that path.

In sum, if we want to receive the witness to the Spirit in the CE, we should do so according to the canonical framework which was, according to Christian confession, bestowed upon us by the work of that same Spirit. Thus, we will trace the CE's witness to the Spirit according to its canonical presentation, reading in succession the introductory Letter of James, followed by the Letters of Peter and John, and concluding with the Letter of Jude. Doing so will provide us with a unique witness designed to shape our overall reception of the person and work of the Spirit in the Christian life.

THE SPIRIT IN THE LETTER OF JAMES

Our appreciation of the distinctiveness of the CE's witness to the Spirit is marked by the striking fact that the collection begins with a letter that offers no overt mention of the Spirit of God at all. This apparent absence makes sense in light of the implied recipients of the letter, who are said to reside "in the dispersion" (Jas 1:1). This "geo-theological" designation recalls the OT story of God's people Israel, who were "scattered" away from their homeland to live as exiles in foreign lands because of their unfaithfulness to God's will and ways (e.g., 2 Kings 17–25). But it also recalls that story's redemption in the Acts of the Apostles, where faithful believers are painfully "scattered" away from Jerusalem through a persecution which has the counter-intuitive effect of bringing growth to the church, spreading the gospel to Judea, Samaria, and ultimately to the ends of the earth (Acts 8:1b; cf. 1:8).

Therefore, James sets the tone of the CE by locating readers as a displaced people, residing away from their homeland, having been scattered abroad in a hostile world which troubles their faith and tests their allegiance to God. The letter describes a community that includes the poor and powerless (1:9-11, 27; 5:1-6), those who are mistreated by the wealthy (2:2-7), and those who are tempted by worldly desire for goods and services that bring comfort to the flesh (1:14-15, 4:1) but lead only to conflict and competition (3:14-16, 4:2-3). The result is double-mindedness within (1:8, 4:8), a duplicitous prayer life (4:3), and disregard for the vulnerable in the community who are beloved of God (2:5). Those who wish to remain faithful to God in such a context will experience many trials of faith (1:2-4): they will feel the absence of God's guiding Spirit, wondering if indeed God is out to destroy them (1:13), and they will be tempted to minimize the effects of their spiritual and cultural alienation by compromising with the ways of the world (4:4).

Those who have attended to Israel's experience of life in the diaspora, however, will know that the Spirit of God is still present even when appearing to be absent (e.g., Ps. 139:7-8). In this light, an intuition honed by the whole of Scripture helps the reader discern the hidden presence and work of the Spirit in the Letter of James, which utilizes familiar tropes for the Spirit found elsewhere in the New Testament. For example, James describes a "wisdom" which "comes down from above" (3:17) from the God who gives perfect gifts "from above" (1:17); this wisdom produces the same sort of virtues that Paul identifies as the fruit of the Spirit (Gal. 5:22-23) and easily brings to mind Paul's many discussions of gifts of the Spirit (Rom. 12:6-8, 1 Cor. 12:4-11, Eph. 4:7-13).

Indeed, the repetition of "from above" inevitably brings to mind Jesus's words to Nicodemus that those who wish to see the kingdom of God must be born "from above" (Jn 3:3). In response to Nicodemus's confusion, Jesus insists, "Very truly, I tell you, no one can enter the kingdom of God without being born of water and Spirit. What is born of the flesh is flesh, and what is born of the Spirit is spirit" (Jn 3:5-6). In similar fashion, James describes God's gift "from above" as a "birth by a word of truth" (1:18), a phrase found in Pauline tradition to describe the gospel (Eph. 1:13, Col. 1:5, 2 Tim. 2:15). This word, which is "implanted" within believers and has the power to save souls (Jas 1:21), must be "done" and not merely "heard" (1:22-25), for only by following a distinctive pattern of holiness will believers avoid self-deception (1:16, 26), endure temptation, pass the tests of faith, and ultimately "receive the crown of life that the Lord has promised to those who love him" (1:12).

Thus, James directs readers who suffer spiritual crisis to seek the wisdom of God as it is found in the scriptural way of obedience. They should abide long before the word until they come to know themselves anew as God's blessed people (1:22-25). There they will find exemplars of faith who passed tests of their own, heroes of old like Abraham (2:21), Rahab (2:25), Job (5:11), and Elijah (5:17); there they will learn how to draw close to God (4:8) by controlling their speech practices (1:19, 26; 3:1-12; 4:11-17; 5:9), by learning from the community to pray with the right spirit (1:5-8, 4:2-3, 5:13-18), and by caring properly for the vulnerable in their midst (1:27, 2:1-26), who are rich in the very faith in God the letter's recipients seek for themselves (2:8).

THE SPIRIT IN THE FIRST LETTER OF PETER

If one is left confused by James's more obscure presentation of the Spirit, 1 Peter immediately follows to clear things up. As before, readers find themselves addressed as believers dwelling in the diaspora of spiritual trials (1:1), but now the tone is far more celebratory and worshipful (1:3). It is as though 1 Peter continues the story where James left off: in 1 Peter, believers *have* avoided the worldly compromise James warned against, and they *have* kept themselves holy in the midst of a hostile world; as a result, they now live as "aliens and exiles" who suffer harassment and intimidation from outsiders who malign them as evildoers for their refusal to accommodate to the ways of the world (2:11-12). In 1 Peter, then, the trial being faced is not that of *worldly temptation* as in James, but *persecution from the world* resulting from Christian commitment to follow the Spirit of holiness.

First Peter's response offers an exhortation to build the sort of hope (1:13) that will sustain believers through the trials of faith they experience until Christ returns to reward their faithful endurance (1:6-9). This hope is grounded in the recognition that what the exiled Christians suffer is the determinative element of their vocation in the world. Believers have been specifically elected to this task, "destined by God the Father and sanctified by the Spirit to be obedient to Jesus Christ" (1:2). This Holy Spirit, explicitly identified as "the Spirit of Christ," has spoken through the prophets of old and now comes afresh in and through the proclamation of the gospel (1:10-12), which gives believers a new birth (1:23-25) in order to discipline them for holy conduct in imitation of a Holy God (1:13-16). In this way, the Christian community will be transformed into "a spiritual house, to be a holy priesthood, to offer spiritual sacrifices acceptable to God through Jesus Christ" (2:5); in so doing, the Spirit will fulfill the charge laid on God's people long ago to perform their ministry in the world as "a chosen race, a royal priesthood, a holy nation, God's own people, in order that you may proclaim the mighty acts of him who called you out of darkness into his marvelous light" (2:9).

In 1 Peter, this ministry is conducted by the reception of spiritual empowerment (1:2) to follow the explicit pattern of Jesus's suffering obedience. Indeed, believers should not be surprised by the suffering they experience in the world (4:12), for this has been part of God's plan all along. The Spirit, who testified to the prophets of ancient Israel concerning "the sufferings destined for Christ and the subsequent glory" (1:11), has sanctified believers that they may imitate Jesus's model of suffering love for others (1:2), which God provided as an example for them to follow in the world (2:21).

Thus, believers experiencing sociocultural alienation are told to "rejoice insofar as you are sharing Christ's sufferings, so that you may also be glad and shout for joy when his glory is revealed" (4:13). Indeed, those who are reviled for their holy lifestyle are in fact blessed "because the spirit of glory, which is the Spirit of God, is resting on you" (4:14). This "spirit of glory" made manifest in the faithful endurance of suffering is the clear sign that believers are spiritually empowered, for just as God "raised Jesus from the dead and gave him glory" (1:21), so also God will lead believers down that same path, which leads "after a little while" (1:6, 5:10) to "praise and glory and honor when Jesus Christ is revealed" (1:7).

THE SPIRIT IN THE SECOND LETTER OF PETER

The Letter of James opened the CE by warning readers of the temptation to compromise with the world in order to alleviate the suffering and alienation associated with the life of faith. First Peter followed on this with a worshipful exhortation to those who have succeeded in holding fast to their identity as aliens and exiles in the world, encouraging them to continue to follow the distinctive pattern of faith until Christ returns in glory. By the time we get to 2 Peter, the implied situation has progressed: the struggle no longer involves worldly people who abuse followers for being different; now, some fellow believers have taken up the ways of the world as their own and are promulgating a new and dangerous teaching in the Christian community (2:1-3). This new teaching insists that certain aspects of the proclamation handed down by apostles like Peter were in fact "cleverly devised myths" (1:16) that need no longer be heeded by believers. The author writes to express his concern that these teachers will deceive naïve believers, with the result that "many will follow their licentious ways" and "the way of truth will be maligned" (2:2-3). Thus, 2 Peter witnesses to an epistemic crisis wherein believers must struggle to discern which leader in their midst is spiritually inspired to speak for God.

In response to this situation, the author follows the pattern established by James and 1 Peter, directing readers to "remember the words spoken in the past by the holy prophets, and the commandment of the Lord and Savior spoken through your apostles" (3:2).

Believers can be kept safe from these dangers because they have access to authoritative Scripture, which mediates the trustworthy words of the prophets who, when "moved by the Holy Spirit, spoke from God" (1:21). Scripture tells the story of Israel, which not only warns of the advent of false prophets, (2:1), but also provides readers with multiple analogous accounts of those who "left the straight road and have gone astray" (2:4-10, 15-16) right alongside accounts of God's power to intervene and judge (3:5-7). Finally, they have the testimony of Jesus's apostles, who "were with him" to witness his words and deeds (1:18), along with a collection of Paul's letters, even though the latter are especially "hard to understand" and are susceptible to misinterpretation by those who twist Scripture to their own destruction (3:16). In short, 2 Peter insists that Christians must not automatically accord prophetic authority to teachers who claim the inspiration of the Spirit, but they must hold fast to the established authorities passed down by their apostolic representatives.

At the core of the apostolic witness is the communication of God's "precious and very great promises" by which believers "may escape from the corruption that is in the world because of lust, and may become participants of the divine nature" (1:4). Those promises communicate "holy commandments" of God that direct believers along a "way of righteousness" (2:21). This path leads them beyond the beginning point of their faith in Christ through the inculcation of Christian virtues that will keep them "from being ineffective and unfruitful in the knowledge of our Lord Jesus Christ" (1:8). Those who follow this path, leading lives of holiness and godliness (3:11), will find that "entry into the eternal kingdom of our Lord and Savior Jesus Christ will be richly provided" for them (1:11). Those who rely on "destructive opinions" (2:1) which allow them to "indulge their flesh in depraved lust" and to "despise authority" (2:10) will face judgment and destruction. Those who follow the apostolic tradition of holiness, by contrast, will remember the words spoken in the past by the Spirit which are now enshrined in Scripture's witness of prophets and apostles, for they "wait for new heavens and a new earth, where righteousness is at home" (3:13).

THE SPIRIT IN THE LETTERS OF JOHN

Reading in canonical sequence helps us discover that 1 John begins precisely where 2 Peter left off, with continued insistence on the priority of the historic apostolic tradition: "We declare to you what was from the beginning, what we have heard, what we have seen with our eyes, what we have looked at and touched with our hands, concerning the word of life" (1:1). As in 2 Peter, so also in John's letters: believers face an epistemic crisis of faith initiated by the presence of rival teacher-prophets. But as we have come to expect with the CE, a progression is once again detected: where in 2 Peter the rival teachers have risen up within the community (2 Pet. 2:1), in the Johannine letters the worldly Christians have split off to form a separate, rival community (1 Jn 2:19, 4:1-6).

The Letters of John are written to encourage and empower those believers to keep clinging to the historic apostolic inheritance of faith. These believers are told they have nothing to fear, for they "have been anointed by the Holy One" (2:20), who "abides" in them such that they do not need to listen to any novel teaching (2:27). It is not immediately clear whether the "Holy One" is the Spirit, whom Jesus prophesied would lead them into truth (John 14–16), Jesus himself (as he is explicitly titled in Jn 6:69), or perhaps an actual communal rite of initiation whereby the truth of Christ and the Spirit was somehow directly communicated to the believer. Indeed, all three may well be in mind. Regardless, the author insists, "Let what you heard from the beginning abide in you. If what you heard from the beginning abides in you, then you will abide in the Son and in the Father" (1 Jn 2:24; cf. 2 Jn 9).

What the community has had "from the beginning" is the commandment to love one another as the defining hallmark of Jesus's teaching (1 Jn 3:11, 2 Jn 5–6). Indeed, "we know that we have passed from death to life because we love one another" (1 Jn 3:14); this is the "Spirit that he has given us" by which "we know that he abides in us" (3:24, 4:13). Those who do not follow this love command, who do not care for the needy (3:17), and who do not practice hospitality with Christian brothers and sisters (3 Jn 5–10) are liars (1 Jn 2:4-6) who do not actually know God at all (4:7-8).

It is therefore not enough to simply claim an experience of the Spirit as an authoritative source of truth. Believers must "test the spirits to see whether they are from God" because, as 2 Peter also warned, "many false prophets have gone out into the world" (1 Jn 4:1; cf. 2 Pet. 2:1). The true test of spiritual authority, it turns out, is this: "Every spirit that confesses that Jesus Christ has come in the flesh is from God, and every spirit that does not confess Jesus is not from God" (1 Jn 4:2; cf. 2 Jn 7). Given 1 John's close connection between right confession, right action, and the historic apostolic tradition, it would be a mistake to imagine that this spiritual test targets an esoteric debate over the two natures of the second person of the Trinity. No, these "Christians" may confess a Christ of some sort, but they apparently do not confess Jesus of Nazareth, the one in whom God took flesh at a specific point in history, who was clearly seen and physically touched by those who both heard his actual commandments and passed them down for the benefit and correction of the Christian churches.

This historical Jesus "is the one who came by water and blood . . . not with the water only but with the water and the blood. And the Spirit is the one that testifies, for the Spirit is the truth. There are three that testify: the Spirit and the water and the blood, and these three agree" (1 Jn 5:6-8). Whether the water and blood spoken of here refer to the water and blood that burst from Jesus's side at his death (Jn 19:34-35) or the water of Jesus's baptism and the blood of his death, the impact is the same: whatever the Spirit says today will conform to what Jesus said and did in his life and teaching, as recorded by his authoritative apostolic witnesses: "Whoever says 'I abide in him' ought to walk just as he walked" (1 Jn 2:6). No supposed experience of the Spirit can be allowed to undermine this basic fact (2 Jn 9). Hence, the author can say without hesitation, "Whoever knows God listens to us, and whoever is not from God does not listen to us. From this we know the spirit of truth and the spirit of error" (1 Jn 4:6). Those identified as "us" are not just another partisan faction arbitrarily claiming divine authority based on a particular spiritual experience; they are the representatives of historic Christian faith making a reasoned case for testing all spiritual experience against the standard of basic Christian orthodoxy handed down by the eyewitnesses to Jesus's life and work.

THE SPIRIT IN THE LETTER OF JUDE

The short letter of Jude draws the CE to a close by referring back to the opening letter of his brother James (1:1) and epitomizing the more important themes of the collection as a whole. Jude joins the other CE authors by insisting that while there is one "salvation we share" that was "once for all entrusted to the saints" (3), some who claim to be Christian "pervert the grace of God into licentiousness and deny our only Master and Lord, Jesus Christ" (4). These false Christians, whose advent was already predicted by the apostles of Jesus (17), are labeled "dreamers" (8), a common OT designation for false prophets who imagine they speak by the Spirit of God (e.g., Deut.13:1-5, Jer. 23:25-28, Zech. 10:2). These "worldly people" are revealed to be "devoid of the Spirit" by the very fact that they are "causing divisions" (19) among God's people, chiefly by rejecting apostolic authority, which provides them license to misuse their own bodies and arrogantly claim authority over the things of God (8). The elaborate description of their identity and behavior (10-16), which echoes so much of the parallel description of false teachers in 2 Peter (2:10-22), describes ignorant and boastful people driven into patterns of ungodliness by unchecked desires and unholy appetites.

What must those Christians who wish to keep from falling do in response to this threat? The letter began with an appeal for believers to "contend for the faith that was entrusted once for all to the saints" (3), but how does that struggle actually play out? It apparently does not involve the rejection and removal of the false Christians, for they are to be treated with mercy (22-23). Instead, believers must do the opposite of those whose actions divide the community: they must work to build themselves up in the historic faith they share (20). This work of building up is elaborated in trinitarian terms: believers are told to "pray in the Holy Spirit; keep yourselves in the love of God; [and] look forward to the mercy of our Lord Jesus Christ that leads to eternal life" (20-21). By rooting themselves in the faith, hope, and love of the living God, they will be kept by the one who can keep them from falling as they walk the path to stand before the divine presence (24).

CONCLUSION: THE SPIRIT IN THE CE

When read in sequence, the CE collection unfolds dramatically to cast a distinctive vision of Christian existence. Believers are depicted as dwelling in a diaspora of trials and temptations (James), where they live as aliens and exiles harassed for their holy lifestyle (1 Peter). Some believers abandon this holy calling and take up the ways of the world while retaining the name Christian, thus posing a threat to those who seek to follow the way of righteousness (2 Peter). Others split off to form new communities that will be more at home in the world, and in so doing, they become the antithesis of what Christ has called them to be (1–3 John). Those who wish to remain in the love of God will therefore have to "contend for the faith that was once for all entrusted to the saints" (Jude 3).

This struggle for faithfulness is described throughout the CE in terms of varying spiritual crises. Faithful Christians who dwell in the diaspora will experience trials and temptations that may leave them feeling the absence of the Spirit (James). Others will strive to follow the way of the Spirit and will suffer persecution as a result (1 Peter). Still others will make the mistake of associating the work of the Spirit with their experiences in the world, such that they will wander away from the one true God and birth an epistemic crisis of authority within the Christian community (2 Peter, Jude), which will result in a divided church (1–3 John).

Taken as a whole, the CE warn against according authority to spiritual experiences without first testing those experiences against the testimony of the apostolic leaders who were eyewitnesses to the earthly sojourn of Jesus Christ. Paul had to do the same thing, of course: he was well aware of his status as a latecomer in the earliest Christian mission (1 Cor. 15:8-9, Eph. 3:8), and though he had experienced the risen Lord, he was not personally acquainted with the Jesus who walked the way of faithful obedience and taught others to follow in his steps. Paul knew he needed to check his experience of the Spirit against the apostolic tradition of the pillar apostles who knew Jesus from the beginning in order to be certain that he "was not running, or had not run, in vain" (Gal. 2:2).

The structure of the NT canon replicates the Pauline pattern, inviting us to check our reading of Paul against the testimony of the Pillars. The result is a canonical counterbalance that must be maintained if believers are to keep from falling on the difficult path that leads to eternal life. The Pauline witness authorizes the contemporary experience of the Spirit, who speaks in us (1 Cor. 12:3), works through us (Gal. 5:22-25) and teaches us the deep things of God (1 Cor. 2:6-16); who comes upon us unexpectedly (Acts 9:1-19) to pour God's love into our hearts (Rom. 5:5) and sets us free from bondage to sin and death (Rom. 8:1-5); and who provides gifts for the building up of Christian community (1 Cor. 12:4-11) and establishes the unity in Christ (Eph. 4:3-6, Phil. 2:1) on which Christian witness to the world depends. But the CE collection follows that of Paul to remind us of the many risks an experience-based Christianity holds for life in a world that does not honor God. Each in their own way insists that the only way to be certain that it really is the Spirit of Christ we are experiencing is to check our experience of the Spirit against the historic witness of God's word and work handed down through historic apostolic tradition and enshrined in Scripture.

FOR FURTHER READING

Niebuhr, Karl-Wilhelm, and Robert W. Wall, eds. *The Catholic Epistles and Apostolic Tradition: A New Perspective on James to Jude*. Waco, TX: Baylor University Press, 2009.

Nienhuis, David R., and Robert W. Wall. *Reading the Epistles of James, Peter, John and Jude as Scripture: The Shaping and Shape of a Canonical Collection*. Grand Rapids, MI: Eerdmans, 2013.

Schlosser, Jacques. *The Catholic Epistles and the Tradition*. Leuven: Peeters, 2004.

Scott, Ian W. *Paul's Way of Knowing: Story, Experience, and the Spirit*. Grand Rapids, MI: Baker Academic, 2009.

CHAPTER FIVE

Pneumatology of the Johannine Corpus

ROBERT W. WALL

TWO INTERPRETATIVE CUES

The postbiblical reception of the canonical writings produced by the "community of the beloved disciple"—the Fourth Gospel, the Letters of John, and the Apocalypse of John—provides two indispensable cues for their present interpretation as Christian scripture. *The first cue* follows from the manuscript evidence of the second century, which suggests the existence and circulation of such a corpus. The use of this pre-canonical collection by the church's most important teachers (such as Irenaeus, Clement of Alexandria, and Tertullian) to recall and vocalize John's apostolic witness commends an awareness that during an early stage of the canonical process a coherent theological deposit proved useful in the formation of Christian faith.

In fact, as Charles Hill points out, the intertextual dialogue between the Fourth Gospel and 1 John carried on by these teachers in the few writings we still possess from the second century commends the existence and circulation of a codex of Johannine writings, even though there is no manuscript evidence to support it.[1] This seems especially the case since, with the exception of John's apocalypse, these writings are anonymous and written in different literary genre. It seems likely that the Fourth Gospel, Letters, and Apocalypse were bound together because of their theological agreements and connection to a common apostolic tradition. For this reason, the defense of John's authorship of the Fourth Gospel and Letters in antiquity is less about the modern apologetics of their apostolic origins as about the coherence of their theological conception and idiom. The implication of this conclusion for the present study is that we can speak of an overarching "Johannine pneumatology" that not only draws from the entire corpus but also presumes an origin in a community shaped by John's apostolic tradition.

The precise nature of this community is contested by Johannine scholars even though a consensus has emerged in support of its existence. Most agree that (a) the Johannine community consisted of a network of congregations (cf. 3 John) grounded in a particular apostolic tradition linked to the Lord's "beloved disciple," John (cf. Jn 21:24); and (b) the essential formative task of this community's elders, much like the schools of antiquity, was the catechesis of its membership, often to the exclusion of any outsider (cf. 2 John).

---

[1] Charles E. Hill, *The Johannine Corpus in the Early Church* (Oxford: Oxford University Press, 2006), 451–2.

Teaching and learning were the community's principal activities. The central figure of the school was its founder, in this case the Apostle John, whose memories of Jesus cultivated a sectarian way of life and witness.

Suffice it to say, then, that the implied author of the anonymous Fourth Gospel and the three "Johannine" letters (as well as the presumed identity of the "John" who wrote the Apocalypse) is the Apostle John as profiled in the New Testament. The author's identity (likely there were several authors of the Johannine writings) is indeterminate in any case and is secured by church tradition for theological reasons. The deposit of an apostolic eyewitness of the incarnate One grounds this corpus and justifies any claim of its overall theological coherence. The theological agreement regarding its distinctive witness to the Holy Spirit is introduced by the *Paraclete* sayings of the Fourth Gospel. The memory of Jesus's promised role of this "other *Paraclete*" during his temporary absence from the disciples was not publicly disclosed but given to an intimate group of "friends" that included his "beloved disciple." His earwitness of this "farewell speech" (cf. John 14–17) is the implied source of this familiar identification of the Holy Spirit as *Paraclete* who assumes the responsibility as the divine catechist during the time of the risen Jesus's personal absence from the disciples until his future return to earth to complete his messianic mission.

A second cue tracks the developing canon lists and manuscripts from a subsequent stage of the canonical process beginning already in the second century and continuing through the fourth, which left this Johannine corpus divided: John's gospel is placed with three others to form a fourfold canonical gospel while John's apocalypse is finally placed at the end of the NT canon to conclude Scripture's story of redemption. Beginning sometime during the third century, the three Johannine epistles are gathered together in due time and placed in a second collection of apostolic letters, named "catholic" by the church because of their broad usefulness and also because of their defense of apostolic or "catholic" Christianity. That is, the corpus is divided along the lines of the NT's final redaction, with each writing lending support to the intended roles of different canonical collections within the New Testament.

Suffice it to say that the historical record is silent about the church's intentions for subdividing this Johannine corpus. Although surely evident differences of literary genre and practical uses may have led the church to reposition each text with others of a similar role, a canonical approach understands the deep logic of the church's canonical process in theological terms, including the repositioning of the Fourth Gospel with the Synoptics to complete the Fourfold Gospel's witness to the risen Jesus, the Johannine epistles with other Catholic Epistles to provide a sevenfold counterbalance to the Pauline epistles, and the placement of the Apocalypse at the end of the church's two-testament Bible to provide a fitting conclusion to its self-presentation of the triune God. Moreover, titling of the anonymous Fourth Gospel, Letters, and Apocalypse as from "John" not only secures their witness to an authoritative apostolate that is formative of a genuine Christianity (versus non-apostolic Christianities), but does so in a way that safeguards the full cohort of Jerusalem pillars (cf. Gal. 2:7-9). Their collective testimony, reified and recalled by this canonical deposit, is set next to the Pauline testimony within the NT canon to engender a conversation that makes a distinctive contribution to Scripture's pluriform witness to God's Spirit in the work of salvation.

If interpreters approach the different Johannine writings according to their purposeful placement within the NT, then they are prompted to compare the remarkably different presentation of the Spirit in the Fourth Gospel with the preceding Synoptics as though completing the full gospel's witness to the Spirit. The same may be said of the role performed by the Spirit of truth in the Johannine letters within the Catholic Epistles collection and also of the sevenfold Spirit of the Apocalypse as the Bible's concluding testimony of God's Holy Spirit. A canonical approach to this topic recognizes that a Johannine-shaped pneumatology is apprehended differently according to genre of expression (gospel, letter, and apocalypse) and especially according to the roles given to the canonical collection in which each is finally placed.

A JOHANNINE PNEUMATOLOGY

The Fourth Gospel

The Spirit is introduced in the Fourth Gospel's opening narrative by John the Baptizer, who testifies to the Spirit's baptism of "the Chosen One of God" (1:34b)[2] who has come to "baptize with the holy Spirit" (1:32). While the Baptizer did not at first recognize "this man" whom he confesses as the "Lamb of God who takes away the sin of the world" (1:29), the Spirit's "descending and remaining" on him occasions his recognition of Jesus as the "Chosen One of God" (= Messiah; cf. Lk. 9:20). Significantly, then, the Spirit's primary role according to John's gospel is made clear through the Baptizer's experience: the Spirit's role is to disclose publicly (in this case, in a form "like a dove") the messianic identity of Jesus to those who do not otherwise know him. Equally important is the Baptizer's response once the Spirit's baptism of Jesus makes his identity clear: he "testifies" (μαρτυρέω) to Jesus, which is a thematic of John's gospel as a definitive accounting of what is true based upon what is known from experience (see 21:24).

The Spirit is subsequently mentioned in several sayings during Jesus's public ministry. Best known is his schooling of Nicodemus, himself a teacher, that citizenship in God's kingdom is restricted only to those who have been reborn by the Spirit (Jn 3:5-8). Jesus's pairing of water and Spirit may suggest that the believer's rebirth is a purifying, restoring activity—a point underscored by the narrator's subsequent interpretation that the flow of "rivers of life-giving water" is regulated by the Spirit (7:38-39). In fact, this seems the point of the elaboration of Jesus's claim in 1 Jn 2:28–3:10 where spiritual rebirth takes a practical direction by contending that the test of the Spirit's recreation of God's children is whether or not they continue to sin. In his encounter with Nicodemus, however, Jesus testifies to knowledge learned from his unique experience of "heavenly things" (3:11-12) as God's Son (3:13-21)—a divine knowledge that one can learn only through rebirth and by abiding in him.

Jesus seems to elaborate on the Spirit's teaching role in this catechesis of the reborn in the episode's conclusion in John 3:31-36. Jesus not only claims that his messianic vocation as God's Son is to speak the "words of God," but infers that his instruction is made intelligible to the believer by the Spirit. This idea of a teaching or illuminating Spirit is crucial to Jesus's next encounter with the Samaritan woman as well. In this case, Jesus claims that "true" worship of God is grounded in "spirit and truth" (4:23-24), an allusion to the community's experience of "the Spirit of truth" (14:17, 15:26, 16:13; cf. 1

---

[2]The Baptizer's affirmation of Jesus in Jn 1:34 is corrupted, and critics disagree how it should be read, whether "the Chosen One of God" or "this is the Son of God," which enjoys broad manuscript support. I prefer the first reading, which is also the earliest, simply because it is easier to explain a scribal redaction from the first to the second than the reverse; see Raymond E. Brown, *John*, 2 vols., AB (Garden City, NY: Doubleday, 1966–1970), 1:57.

Jn 4:6) who not only witnesses to Jesus as "the way, truth, and life" (14:6), but who will then teach and guide Jesus's disciples into "all the truth" (16:13) following his departure.

Without question and with considerable irony, the most important claim about the Spirit during the public ministry of John's Jesus is by the narrator, not Jesus, who interprets Jesus's famous "life-giving water" saying (7:37-38) for his readers as a reference to the Spirit. He then adds this pregnant aside: "there was no Spirit yet (οὔπω γὰρ ἦν πνεῦμα) because Jesus was not yet glorified" (7:39). What are we to make of this cryptic commentary within the narrative world of the Fourth Gospel? At the very least, we are to understand that the Spirit's role in dispensing "life-giving water" is delayed to a future following Jesus's glorification. We further are to understand this ministry as restricted to Jesus's followers: the river's flow is "from within him" (literally "from his digestive track"). Although the referent of "him" is ambiguous, it likely refers to the believer whose faith in Jesus issues in an inward transformation, the result of "digesting" the Spirit in the believer's rebirth (see earlier and Jn 3:5-8).

But what are we to make of the narrator's final statement that "there was no Spirit yet"? Clearly, the Spirit has been active in Jesus's ministry, having testified to him at his baptism. Moreover, the narrator, who is in constant dialogue with Israel's scripture, must be aware of the Spirit's vitalizing role within Israel's history. We should not presume, then, that the narrator is claiming the Spirit has a future without a past in the divine economy. Rather, he is pointing readers ahead to a future, inaugurated by Jesus's glorification, when the Spirit will be poured out afresh upon Jesus's disciples as a "river of life-giving water."

The prospect of Jesus's future glorification is thematic of John's gospel. The "hour" of his glorification of God begins with the passion (12:23), when "the son of man" is "lifted up" on the cross to complete the messianic task given to him (cf. 17:4). At least initially, however, it is the very idea of Jesus's departure and not his death that provokes a crisis among his disciples. They are disturbed by the unhappy prospect of following after someone who is headed for a place where they no longer will be his followers (13:31-33)—that is, the effective end of their discipleship. With the link the narrator makes between the Spirit's future ministry and the hour of Jesus's glorification, readers are already put on alert for Jesus's explanation in his farewell speech (John 13–17) of the nature and scope of the Spirit's ministry following his passion.

Jesus's explanation comes in five *Paraclete* sayings, which fund the core of a Johannine pneumatology (Jn 14:16-17, 25-26; 15:26-27; 16:7-11, 12-15). The first (14:16-17) and last (16:12-15) sayings bracket the résumé of the Spirit's post-passion mission in response to the disciples' bewilderment as to how they can continue to follow "the way, truth, and life" if he is absent from them. Here, then, are the details of Jesus's answer to the barrage of questions his disciples register about their future with him, as framed by Thomas's unvarnished "How can we know the way?" (14:5): First, in response to the Son's request for "another *Paraclete* (παράκλητος)" (14:16)—a request that is likely motivated as an act of friendship for his disciples (15:13-15)—the Father will send them the "Spirit of truth" (14:17). A Johannine catchword, παράκλητος envisions the Holy Spirit's vocation of being "called" (-κλητος) by God to come "alongside" (παρά-) Jesus's disciples. But for what holy ends? Second, Jesus's repeated naming of the Spirit as the bringer of truth[3]

---

[3] The genitive construction of this phrase, "Spirit of truth," is objective; that is, the Spirit is the one who reveals God's truth to the disciples.

(14:17, 15:26, 16:13; cf. 1 Jn 4:6, 5:6) underscores a vocation that somehow concerns the dissemination of God's truth disclosed in and through Jesus Christ (1:14, 17). Third, it is a mission that targets disciples with whom the Spirit will "abide forever" (14:16-17)—a sure note of permanence that no doubt corrects his disciples' mistaken concern that the truth brought by a soon departed Jesus is transient. Fourth, in contrast to the community of Jesus-followers who know the Spirit because it abides in them, the "world is unable to receive" (οὐ δύναται λαβεῖν) the Spirit's truth because they neither see nor know it (14:17). Lastly, in the conduct of the Spirit's vocation as the bringer of truth, the Spirit functions as the community's pedagogue and guides its learning (ὁδηγέω) of God's truth (i.e., "all truth," because all truth is God's truth) within this world of conflict (16:13).

The Lord's petition for "another *Paraclete*" who is the bringer of truth to the community of disciples is predicated on the experiences of the first *Paraclete*, Jesus Christ, who exemplified and taught his followers the truth he received from God (Jn 3:32-35; 7:16-18; 8:26-29, 42-43; 12:47-50). The intertextuality of the Johannine corpus allows us to read the Fourth Gospel's identity of "another *Paraclete*" by 1 John's affirmation of "Jesus Christ, the Righteous One" as the community's first παράκλητος (1 Jn 2:1), whose principal work is to atone for the sins of the world (1 Jn 2:2). This act of self-sacrificial love for his friends is the essence of God's truth, which the Spirit now communicates to Jesus's disciples (cf. 14:15 in relationship to 14:16-17). This distinction between their two interdependent roles is already indicated by the testimony of the Baptizer, who in observing the Spirit's baptism of Jesus recognized and testified to him as the "Lamb of God who takes away the sin of the world" (1:29-34). The primary role performed by the Spirit during the last days is to resolve the epistemic crisis occasioned by Jesus's departure when his disciples who do not know him in the flesh will come to know him in the Spirit. In this sense, the Spirit is "with the disciples forever" as their teacher. In doing so, the Spirit completes an epistemological circle in a trinitarian manner: the truth God discloses to/in Jesus as God's word witnessed by his disciples is then digested by his future disciples through the abiding Spirit, but only during the Lord's temporary absence "in a little while when you will see me no longer until you will see me again" (16:16; cf. 14:18-21).

As an interpretative aside, let me add that the Fourth Gospel's very different narrative of the Pentecost of the *Paraclete* in Jn 20:19-23 (when compared with the Pentecost of Acts 1–2) agrees with Jesus's prophecy of its timing: following Jesus's glorification (i.e., death) but *not* his departure (as in Acts) according to Jn 7:39. Moreover, the image of the glorified Jesus's breathing the Spirit into the disciples (20:22) recalls the creation narrative when God breathed life into Adam (Gen. 2:7). This creational intertext recalls Jesus's prophecy that from the Spirit would "flow rivers of life-giving water" (Jn 7:38). This prophecy is realized in "the Johannine Pentecost." Rather than playing one Pentecost against the other, the canonical witness includes both, presuming that only by reading them together do we better approximate the fullness of the church's reception of the Spirit on Pentecost: empowering (Acts) *and* life-giving (John).

Jesus suggests that the Spirit's post-passion curriculum is delimited by two contrary claims. On the one hand, the naming of the Spirit as "the Spirit of truth" indicates lesson plans that set out the full truth ("everything"; 14:26) of God's sanctifying word (17:17), which was incarnate in Jesus (1:14, 17) and witnessed by the Spirit within the community of disciples. The "world" that opposes God does so in large part because its citizens have no access to this truth since they have no access to the Spirit whom they are unable to receive and learn from because they are without the requisite faith in Jesus.

On the other hand, the Spirit is hardly excluded from operating within the world as its teacher. If God loves the world (3:16) and Jesus has taken the sin of the world off the table (1:29), then we should presume God's desire to communicate God's truth to the world. Yet, the learning goals of the Spirit's catechesis of the world is very different than they are for the community of disciples: it seeks to persuade (ἐλέγχω) the world (16:8) of its "sinfulness" (16:9), of God's "righteousness" made clearer by Jesus's physical absence from the world (16:10), and of its inevitable "judgment" following after the destiny of its ruler who "has already been tried and condemned" (perfect passive of κρίνω) because of Jesus (16:11). I would argue that the Spirit's future (now present) role as pedagogue during this interim period of Jesus's physical absence from this world is to help both believer and nonbeliever envision the real world, which is the kingdom of God.

This is no modalism in which the departure of Jesus ends his role and the Pentecost of the Spirit succeeds him to begin a new and different period in the history of God's salvation. Nonetheless, to this point in John's gospel, Jesus has indicated that he alone is the recipient and dispenser of liberating truth from Father to Son (cf. Jn 8:31-32). With his imminent departure precipitated by the world's rejection of God's Son, however, the Spirit must assume a different—although integral—role than the Son assumed as Messiah: its arrival intends to continue what Jesus began to teach the disciples (cf. Acts 1:1) by reminding them of "everything he said to them" (Jn 14:26) during this interim period between his going and returning (16:16).

The interplay between "teaching" and "reminding" in the Spirit's job description may suggest that it will not teach a brand-new truth but rather will remind the disciples of what they already have witnessed in God's incarnate word. This interplay between teaching and reminding is not unlike the narrator's commentary when he notes in parenthetical asides following a saying or action of Jesus that its real meaning is allusive of Scripture's prophecy or what the disciples would eventually come to realize as true during their post-passion existence.[4]

The problem remains, however, to know something of the phenomenology the Spirit employs to teach and remind the disciples of what Jesus had said. The problem becomes more pressing for a postbiblical community of disciples without a memory of the historical Jesus. What will test or regulate those who claim to have been reminded by the Spirit that Jesus had said this or that, especially when it seems to part ways from the apostolic witness? In fact, this epistemic crisis may be in view in 1 John in the contest between the apostolic word and the experience of "anointing" that confirms it (1 Jn 2:20, 27) and the secessionists led by "anti-christs" whose Christology is contrary to what the apostles had seen "from the beginning" and now proclaim (1 Jn 1:1-4). In a later day, Montanism believed the *Paraclete* of John's gospel inspired "new oracles" for a new day, which Eusebius reported departed from the apostolic rule of faith, even though his report was based on the polemics of anti-Montanists who considered the movement a heresy rather than the substantive writings of the great Tertullian. In any case, many historians think the Montanist controversy, which took place during an early stage of the canonical process (late second, early third century), likely confirmed the need for a "fixed" biblical

---

[4] John R. Levison nicely describes this kind of recollection in which the narrator adds parenthetical comments that help readers understand the theological meaning of certain events or sayings of Jesus's life as analogous to the Spirit's inward recall of the meaning of Jesus's instruction; see "Holy Spirit," in *NIDB*, 2:877-8.

canon that delimited the scope of inspired texts—especially the Fourfold Gospel—during the canonical process.

The connection between the Spirit's role as the community's pedagogue and Scripture is implicit but crucial in John's gospel. An element of concern registered about Montanism was the ecstatic experiences of the movement's prophets who claimed to have new revelation from the Spirit. The conclusion of John's gospel underscores the *written* or fixed form of truth to which the apostles witness in Jesus (Jn 21:24-25), a point repeated and emphasized in 1 John both to teach the community and to correct its opponents (see the adumbration of γράφω beginning with 1:4). The Spirit's teaching role is facilitated and contextualized by its use of Scripture in the catechesis of disciples. Moreover, the Spirit's use of Scripture is the mode of its witness to the glorified Son (cf. Jn 15:26, 21:24), which agrees in different words with Jesus's parting remarks to his disciples according to Lk. 24:44-49 (presuming his prophecy about coming "power from on high" in 24:49b is allusive of the pentecostal coming of the Spirit of prophecy; cf. Acts 1:8). The image of the evangelist's selection of what stories about Jesus to tell, which purposes to secure belief in Jesus (20:31), is of a piece with the Spirit's role as the community's (perhaps also the world's) inspiring pedagogue.

A final question remains of this survey of the Spirit in the Fourth Gospel: How does Jesus's portrait of "another Paraclete" complete the Fourfold Gospel's witness of the Holy Spirit? Interpretation from Augustine forward has noted that the theological and linguistic differences between the Fourth Gospel and the Synoptics fill in theological gaps or complete the full gospel's authorized biography of Jesus. The gospel's pneumatology is a case in point. Not only does the Jesus of the Synoptic Gospels rarely mention the Holy Spirit, but only in John's "farewell" does Jesus speak of a future when he will be absent from them but present in a fresh way through the abiding, teaching *Paraclete*. If the Synoptic Gospels allude to this period as a time of the church's persecution and suffering—something the synoptic Jesus takes for granted—John's Jesus who speaks of a hostile world also speaks of the presence of a Holy Spirit who comes alongside the disciples, not only to remind them of what Jesus had taught as God's revelatory word but also to comfort them, which many scholars and translators think is the sense of παράκλητος in 14:26. Given the fuller sense of the Spirit that emerges in reading the Fourfold Gospel from beginning to end, in particular how the Fourth Gospel fills in the pneumatological gap, it is difficult to imagine a robust discipleship without these *Paraclete* sayings. That is, the departure of the exalted Son does not leave his followers in a lurch; rather, they are now able to remember and experience him afresh because the Holy Spirit has drawn alongside them, especially in their encounters with a hostile world.

The Letters

The precise relationship between the Fourth Gospel and Letters remains a contested topic among biblical scholars. Quite apart from historical considerations, however, if one allows that the sequence of the NT's canonical collections envisages a "canon logic," then Jesus's prophecy of the *Paraclete*'s post-passion portfolio finds resonance in the Johannine letters that follow it in a way that elaborates Scripture's theology of a *Paraclete*-enabled discipleship within the bounds of particular Christian congregations. In particular, 1 Jn 4:1-6 is decisive, for it places a process of Spirit-led discernment at the center of forming disciples who are shaped by the gospel's truth to become sin-free practitioners of Christ-like love for one another.

Despite the speculations about the person of Jesus that characterize modern biblical criticism, the memories of eyewitnesses to his historical particularity that guide the telling of his story in the canonical gospels make it exceedingly difficult to fictionalize his life. But the Spirit is like the wind (cf. Jn 3:5-8, Gen. 1:2), vaguer and more pliable. Frank D. Macchia admits that this makes the Spirit more susceptible to "being hijacked in the contemporary context of self-serving and destructive forces." He goes on to observe that a veneer of pious "spirit" language often hides "deeply entrenched and competing public interests that often discriminate and oppress."[5] This is especially true when a transcendent yet holy "Spirit" is applied to justify uncritically various public programs, whether religious, social, political, or economic, whose purposes are often detached from the particularity of Jesus, who alone is the criterion of truth.

Even though 1 John is occasioned by a battle over Christology, 1 Jn 4:1-6 speaks of a contest between two rival spirits: one demonic and the other the Spirit of truth. The *Paraclete*'s post-passion reception and ministry as pedagogue is challenged by the rival "spirits" of "false prophets" that deceive and seek to subvert the community's apostolic teaching about Christ (4:1). J. C. Thomas rightly notes that 1 John's opening exhortation "not to trust every spirit" (4:1a) is not an abrupt transition to a new topic as some commentators suggest, but it continues to unpack the prior claim that God's abiding Spirit forges both a belief in Christ and the practice of self-sacrificial love embodied by him (3:23-24). Thomas notes the linguistic links that suggest this claim draw upon 1 John's earlier warning of the arrival of "antichrists" (= "false prophets") in 2:18-27, whose christological error (i.e., teaching that is contrary to the apostolic witness of the incarnate "word of life"; 1 Jn 1:1) is exposed by a charismatic "anointing" that "teaches (the apostolic community) about everything" (2:27; cf. 2:20).[6]

Against this backdrop, then, the ensuing battle between rival spirits is instantiated in the teachers of competing Christian congregations who disagree over Jesus. The *Paraclete* reminds disciples of the historical Jesus not only by the *written* works of eyewitnesses that stabilize what is remembered and taught about him—a point made in concluding the Fourth Gospel and made emphatic in 1 John by the constant repetition of γράφω—but also *by Christian teachers* who are faithful to the apostolic tradition and who have not "gone out into the world" as false prophets (= antichrists) who spread lies and falsehoods about Jesus (4:1b; 2:19, 22). Both Scripture and its faithful interpreters are the media of the *Paraclete*'s teaching ministry while Jesus is absent from his people until his return.

I mentioned earlier a third, more mysterious auxiliary of the Spirit's post-passion catechesis of believers: the "anointing." The community knows the truth because they possess written traditions of Jesus and are led by faithful interpreters of these eyewitness records. But 1 John presses the point that the "Spirit of truth" (4:6) indwells its faithful membership (3:24) and presumably is the source of its charismatic experiences of "anointing" that confirm (but not expand) the apostolic instruction about Christ (cf. 2:20, 27). Written texts about Jesus, teachers who are faithful to the apostolic traditions of Jesus, and charismatic experiences of the Spirit's truth-telling instruction are the instruments that forge a congregation's unyielding loyalty to the risen One during the present season of his personal absence from them.

---

[5] John Christopher Thomas and Frank D. Macchia, *Revelation*, THNTC (Grand Rapids, MI: Eerdmans, 2016), 485–9. Frank Macchia works with the theme of "pneumatic discernment" in his theological reflections on Revelation's Spirit of prophecy.

[6] John Christopher Thomas, *1 John, 2 John, 3 John*, Pentecostal Commentary (London: T & T Clark, 2004), 197–98.

The epistemic confusion over "the spirits" occasioned by the presence of "many false prophets in the world" (1 Jn 4:1), whose "spirit of antichrist" engenders a confession of faith contrary to the apostolic testimony, now resolves to the community's public confession that "Jesus, Christ in the flesh, has come from God" (4:2; cf. 3:23; 4:9-10, 14-15; 5:13). The "test" or metric of faith is whether or not the *content* of any prophetic speech that claims its divine origin or is grounded in trustworthy knowledge of the historical Jesus or promises a redemptive result agrees with 1 John's apostolic summary, which has its origins from God (4:14-15), is grounded in ear/eyewitness of the historical Jesus (1:1), and results in forgiveness of sins (4:9-10). As Paul put it in responding to a battle over competing spirits in his Corinthian congregation according to 1 Cor. 12:3b: "No one can say, 'Jesus is Lord,' except by the Holy Spirit."

Finally, the *Paraclete*'s abiding presence within a Christian congregation after Jesus's departure is detected not only by the content of what is taught, whether it aligns with the apostolic eyewitness and interpretation of Jesus, but also by the manner of its life together, whether it practices love for one another. The Johannine gospel never detaches the truth of what is confessed—"we believe in the name of God's Son Jesus Christ" (3:23a)—from the moral conduct of life—"and we love one another just as he gave us the commandment" (3:23b). It is the ministry of the *Paraclete*-in-residence (3:24b: καὶ ἐν τούτῳ γινώσκομεν ὅτι μένει ἐν ἡμῖν, ἐκ τοῦ πνεύματος οὗ ἡμῖν ἔδωκεν), then, to secure this connection for all the world to observe and know that God is love (cf. Jn 17:23).

A canonical approach to the Johannine letters raises an additional question regarding how this distinctively Johannine conception of the spiritual warfare is received within the Catholic Epistles collection to which it belongs in the church's scripture.[7] In many ways, the collection's Johannine deposit continues and develops what James already has introduced as rival mindsets between friendship with the world or friendship with God (Jas 4:1-10). This conflict over materialism is also spiritual and internal (Jas 4:5-7). Second Peter continues this sense of spiritual struggle but locates it within the community rather than within its individual members. As with 1 John, false prophets are denying the truth of the apostolic word, which is received and understood in the company of the Holy Spirit (2 Pet. 1:21). To deny this word is to deny the powerful impress of God's Spirit in guiding the community's formation and, indeed, its destiny with God forever. First John continues to develop this same thematic. God's Spirit is given to the community (3:24) to lead its members to discriminate between error and truth, between false prophets and those whose teaching agrees with the apostles (4:1-6). The members of a community, who embrace the truth (2:12-28) and experience new birth (2:29–3:1), purify themselves of sin to practice not sinning (3:3-10). The Spirit-led transformation of moral life and formation of a confident faith heralds God's victory over sin and death (2:28, 5:1-5).

It strikes me, however, that the impress of the Johannine witness within this collection settles on the idea of a congregation's liturgy that "tests the spirits to determine whether they are from God" (4:1). First, what is assumed by 1 John is that the activities of the *Paraclete* in the present age are experienced and will always lead a community into deeper devotion of Jesus. It is a deception to teach a community that the presence and performances of the Spirit purpose any other result than this. It is also misplaced to focus the manner of this test only on charismatic performances—which are routinely

---

[7] See David Nienhuis's article "The Spirit in the Catholic Epistles" in this volume.

mimicked—rather than on the spiritual byproducts of the indwelling Spirit of prophecy, who cultivates the community's life with Christ and love for one another.

Second, the exhortation for a community to "test the spirits" is applied to individual teachers who claim to have the charism of prophecy. In fact, 1 John's instruction is occasioned by the pastor's awareness that particular Christian teachers are actively engaged in self-promoting "prophetic" ministries that subvert the apostolic traditions about Jesus received in the canonical gospel. It is within those local congregations of saints (see, e.g., 3 John) that the spirit of deception is afoot, sometimes embodied in those who present themselves as their spiritual leaders. It is there that the "test of spirits" must be conducted—whether by their worship, catechesis, public witness, or personal devotion—so that they draw their congregations into deeper communion with the exalted Lamb.

The Apocalypse

Richard Bauckham argues with good reason that John's apocalypse presents the most fully trinitarian theology of any NT writing.[8] Following other uses of "seven" within this book's visionary world, the naming of the Spirit as "sevenfold" symbolizes its work in establishing God's rule on earth. The repeated use of the catchphrase "in the Spirit," which introduces each of four visionary blocks (1:10, 4:2, 17:3, 21:10) of this remarkable composition, underscores the Spirit's importance in producing and shaping the prophet's vision of the last days (see the following paragraphs).

But perhaps it is the title given to this book, "Apocalypse of John," that cues its most distinctive contribution to the Johannine depiction of the holy *Paraclete* as divine pedagogue. The title is puzzling since the book's prefatory sentence clearly claims it is an "apocalypse of Jesus Christ," not of John. Why exchange John for Jesus in the book's title? The interpreter should suppose the paratextual features of any canonical writing, including book titles and their final placement within the Bible, are deliberate markers added during the canonical process that purpose to guide the community's practice of Scripture in worship and instruction. In this case, the church exchanges John for Jesus in the title to guide the church's recognition of John's importance as a true prophet with whom the Spirit does business to help secure the future of the church.

In fact, unlike the NT's other Johannine writings, this author is named and introduced, not as an apostle but as a prophet who received Jesus Christ's apocalypse "in the Spirit" (1:10) and was then commissioned by Jesus, envisioned as Daniel's "son of man" (1:13, Dan. 7:13), to write his apocalypse down and deliver it to the sevenfold church (1:4; cf. Revelation 2–3). If the Johannine letters underscore the importance of apostolic *texts* that are written down for and received by Christian congregations as a normative auxiliary of the *Paraclete*'s teaching ministry, then the Apocalypse continues this core thematic to underscore the importance of apostolic *teachers*, exemplified by John, who receive God's revelatory word (1:2) "in the Spirit" and faithfully communicate it to all the disciples so that they "may give ear to what the Spirit says to the churches" (2:7, 11, 17, 29; 3:6, 13, 22). That is, both texts *and* teachers are the indispensable media in a catechism of the

---

[8]Richard Bauckham, *The Theology of the Book of Revelation*, NTT (Cambridge: Cambridge University Press, 1993), 164.

Paraclete that continues effectively to teach and comfort those disciples of the present age with ears to hear what the risen Lord says through them.

Not surprisingly, then, the essential characteristic of true prophets exemplified by John is their reception of God's word "in the Spirit" and their distribution of it so that the disciples of Jesus may "give ear to what the Spirit" teaches them. As Bauckham notes, every reference to the Spirit in the Apocalypse (apart from references to the "sevenfold Spirit"—see later in the chapter) refers to the "Spirit's inspiration of John's prophecy, the book of Revelation itself."[9] The Spirit's role in the production of biblical texts, subsequently canonized, is distinct from its role in sanctifying ecclesial performances of these same texts when rightly used in Christian worship and instruction. Yet the role of one Spirit in every stage of production and performance maintains a coherent line between a text's origins as composition and canon and its ongoing use for Christian formation.

Since the *Paraclete*'s responsibility in the present age is to remind/teach disciples of what Jesus said and did prior to his departure, we should expect that what the Spirit says to the churches comes directly from a script of Jesus-sayings. Yes and no. Clearly, when the Spirit speaks, it trades on what Jesus/the Lamb says in the vision (e.g., his addresses to the seven churches in Revelation 2–3) and also according to the Fourfold Gospel traditions (cf. Rev. 1:2). But the Spirit's speech-acts are not verbatim transcripts of Jesus-sayings but midrash—that is, contemporary applications of what Jesus has said that the Spirit then translates as God's word on target for a new setting. The Spirit tells all the truth but tells it slant!

The repeated use of the catchphrase "in the Spirit" to introduce the four blocks of the prophet's visionary experiences at the very least indicates the Spirit's agency (perhaps by prophetic ecstasy) in the writing of the entire text. Thomas argues on this basis that the phrase also cues the Spirit's active involvement in the community's reception of the entire text as Scripture for a season of spiritual discernment.[10]

The vision of a third beast who envisions the work and influence of a charismatic "false prophet" (13:11-18, 16:13) is a rarely noted irony of the Apocalypse's depiction of the Spirit. The machinations of an unholy trinity of three beasts are initiated by the victory of God's exalted Son and the defeat of the beastly dragon who "now has come down to the earth" (Rev. 12:12). John does not envision a future battle between forces of good and evil on "the great day of God the Almighty" at Armageddon (cf. Rev. 16:12-16) but a battle already engaged. In large part, the pneumatic discernment called for by the exhortation is for the embattled saints of the present age to endure and remain faithful; this is not a spiritual struggle delayed to an indeterminate future, but it is upon us right now.

The choices facing embattled saints are not always obvious or easy. The beast's imitation of the Spirit of prophecy presumes a subtlety that requires mature pneumatic discernment shaped by Christian worship and catechesis, both activities that are emphasized in the Johannine tradition.[11] In particular, John's allusive use of apostolic traditions of the Spirit, both Johannine and Lukan (i.e., Pentecost), to envision

---

[9] Ibid., 115.
[10] Thomas and Macchia, *Revelation*, 80–1.
[11] See John R. Levison, *Filled with the Spirit* (Grand Rapids, MI: Eerdmans, 2009), 232–5, for the widespread connection in earliest Christianity between Spirit and true/false prophecy. I take it that John drinks deeply from this well when trying to make sense of this vision.

Spirit-practices that the beast imitates underscores this very subtlety—a sleight of hand that intends to "deceive" (πλανάω) people away from Christ to antichrist (13:14).

For example, much like the Spirit-traditions Luke appropriates in Acts, the beast "speaks" with prophetic authority to draw people into worship of the risen beast (13:11b-12; cf. Acts 4:23-31).[12] Significantly, its performances of "signs" and "fire" (13:13; cf. 11:5) echo the Spirit's Pentecost (cf. Acts 2:19).[13] Nonetheless, the beast mimics the Spirit's performance of "great signs" (13:13a; Acts 6:8), including Pentecost-like "fire from heaven" visible to human sight (13:13b; cf. Acts 2:3, 19), and the use of "the name" of the second beast in the distribution of goods (13:17, 14:1-2) seems similar to the apostles' use of "the name" of the risen Jesus in their distribution of goods (e.g., Acts 3:6, 16; 4:7, 10-12). The echo of God's life-giving breath in the creation narrative (Gen. 2:7) in observing the beast's *pneuma* to animate the beast's image—and so its mission of deception—may draw upon a different Spirit-tradition similar to the *pneuma* of the so-called Johannine Pentecost when John's Jesus breathes the Spirit upon the disciples to enliven their mission of forgiveness (Jn 20:21-23). Finally, the act of making impressions upon the people of the beast to divide the world into two groups, one given the death sentence and the other a reprieve, is strikingly similar to the Pauline idea that those belonging to Christ are "marked" by their reception of the Spirit for "the day of redemption" (Eph. 1:13, 4:30; 2 Cor. 1:22). Of course, the effects of the demonic spirit, even though similar in performance, are the exact opposite of the community's baptism in the Spirit. The pneumatic discernment of a people of the Spirit would make truth the clear option.

The intertextuality between 1 Jn 4:1-6's admonition to engage in a process of spiritual discernment to "test rival spirits" (see earlier in this chapter) helps thicken the importance of John's vision of a third beast who arose from the land as a "false prophet" to peddle influence on behalf of the antichrist by imitating the Spirit. The repetition of the prophetic formula, Ὧδέ ἐστιν (13:10b, 18a) forms a rhetorical *inclusio* to bracket off this vision as a call for pneumatic discernment to cipher the meaning of the number 666 to learn the identity of a human who personifies the first beast who arose from the sea (13:1-8). It is this Spirit-led process of discernment that is challenged by the spirit that emanates from the false prophet whose Pentecost-like performances intend to deceive the world, if not also the true followers of the Lamb. The beast's imitation of God's Spirit effects more than a disguise that may confuse the immature or uncertain; its Pentecost-performances that mimic the sending of the Spirit of life intend the opposite fate: certain death or imprisonment for those whose names are written in the Lamb's book of life and whose public mark is their fearless opposition to this unholy trinity. From the book's opening address of the sevenfold church, this pastoral concern regards the community's capacity to cipher the wily deceptions of the evil one in order to choose to "follow the Lamb wherever he goes" (14:4).

This intertext reminds us that the *Paraclete*'s ongoing catechesis of the disciples during this present moment when their exalted Lord is absent on earth is not located out of

---

[12] For this connection, see Jacob Jervell, *Theology of the Acts of the Apostles*, NTT (Cambridge: Cambridge University Press, 1996), 43–54.

[13] See Enrique Treiyer, "Fuego del cielo y marca de la bestia: Un estudio exegético de Apo 13:11-18," *Theologika* 19 (2004): 78–101, who observes that an elaborate chiastic structure centers Rev. 13:11-18 on 13:13 and the false prophet's pentecostal signs as the primary means of deceiving the world.

public viewing in the sanitized environs of a civil society but is smack in the mess and muck of a hostile world. Deception is a very real present danger in a world of competing and powerful spirits. The capacity of the community to navigate its life with God requires not only attentiveness of the Spirit's instruction mediated through sacred texts and true prophets, but also the congregation's participation in a Spirit-led process of discernment that carefully measures the truth of what is said and done when making decisions.

The Apocalypse's placement at the end of the biblical canon is indicative of its role as the normative conclusion to the Bible's metanarrative of God's salvation. Appropriately, the final note of this stunning vision of God's victory over death sounds the flow of living water pouring down from the throne of God through the city's main street (Rev. 22:1-2). It is the Spirit who invites the thirsty to come and drink the water of life from this river for it is "free of charge" (22:17). This too is the final note sounded by Scripture. The Spirit's invitation is apropos given its role as *Paraclete* since it reminds readers of Jesus's promise of life-giving water (Jn 7:37-38), which is here received as Scripture's concluding and perhaps most essential promise with the Spirit's assurance that it is forever and freely realized within all those who trust in the triune God.

FOR FURTHER READING

Bauckham, Richard. *Gospel of Glory: Major Themes in Johannine Theology*. Grand Rapids, MI: Baker Academic, 2015.

Köstenberger, Andreas J. *A Theology of John's Gospel and Letters*. BTNT. Grand Rapids, MI: Zondervan, 2009.

Lieu, Judith M., and Martinus C. de Boer, eds. *The Oxford Handbook of Johannine Studies*. Oxford: Oxford University Press, 2018.

Rainbow, Paul A. *Johannine Theology: The Gospel, the Epistles and the Apocalypse*. Downers Grove, IL: InterVarsity, 2014.

Thomas, John Christopher, and Frank D. Macchia. *Revelation*. THNTC. Grand Rapids, MI: Eerdmans, 2016.

CHAPTER SIX

The Holy Spirit in the Work of Christ

D. STEPHEN LONG

Christology is the theological study of the work and person of Christ. Both aspects are central for a proper understanding of Jesus. His *work* tells us what he has done. His *person* tells us who has done this work, but we would not know or understand his person without the work, nor the work without the person. For simplicity's sake, who he is and what he has done can be distilled into five themes: (a) his birth, including the doctrine of the incarnation; (b) his life and mission, including his teachings; (c) his betrayal, arrest, and crucifixion; (d) his resurrection; and (e) his ascension and promised return. These five themes have been well-discussed in systematic theology. What I do that is different in this essay is relate these five themes to the work of the Holy Spirit. I do so by focusing on Scripture and tradition.

Let me begin with a brief statement relating the Holy Spirit to Jesus that will then be elaborated in what follows. The Holy Spirit makes possible the conditions by which the second person of the Trinity, the Son, is incarnate in Jesus of Nazareth. These conditions reflect OT signs where God dwells with God's creatures, especially in the tabernacle and temple. The NT manifests the Spirit's presence inaugurating Jesus's mission and guiding him through its various stages. The one noticeable place where the Spirit appears to be absent is in his crucifixion and death, although there are indicators of the Spirit's work implicitly in the haunting stories of Christ's death. The Spirit returns in the resurrection and ascension, first by being the tacit agent in Jesus's resurrection, and then by being subject to Jesus's agency when he pours the Spirit on his followers. As the Spirit makes possible the conditions for Jesus's person and work, so Jesus in turn sends the Spirit upon his disciples and the world, creating a trinitarian symmetry of divine agency and establishing the time of the Spirit's work of witness in the church and creation.

BIRTH AND INCARNATION

The fullest biblical account of Jesus's birth is found in the Gospel of Luke. The first reference to the Holy Spirit is Lk. 1:15 when the angel tells Zechariah that his wife, Elizabeth, will have a son who will be "filled with the Holy Spirit." The word used for "filled" here is a synonym for the opening sentence to the gospel, Lk. 1:1, when Luke explains to "Theophilus," to whom the gospel is written, that his purpose is to give a "narrative of the things which have been fulfilled among us." This word "fulfill," from the Greek verb *plêrô*, has an important role in Luke's gospel. It can mean "fulfill," "accomplish," "complete," or "finish." What is fulfilled are the deeds found in previous prophets such as Elijah and Elisha, who received the prophetic spirit so that they could do such deeds. Elizabeth is part of that fulfillment, for she gives birth to John the Baptist, who points the way for Jesus.

The second reference to the Spirit is found in Lk. 1:17 when the angel tells Zechariah that his son John will "go before the Lord with the spirit and power of Elijah, to turn fathers' hearts toward their children, and faithless people to the perceptions of the righteous, in order to make ready a people prepared for the Lord."[1] The "spirit of Elijah" may be a reference to 2 Kgs 2:9 when Elijah is departing from the prophet Elisha and he asks for a "double share of your spirit." What is the "spirit" of Elijah in this second reference, and how is it related to the "Holy Spirit" in the first? The "spirit of Elijah" is the spirit that comes upon the prophets in Israel. As the Elijah-Elisha story shows, it can be passed on, but it is not up to the prophet to give it. When Elisha asks Elijah for a "double share" of his spirit, Elijah cannot guarantee that he will receive it; it is not his possession to pass on like some inheritance. It is not the prophet, but the Holy Spirit who gives the prophetic spirit.

John the Baptist receives the prophetic spirit of Elijah that his father, Zechariah the priest, is promised to his son as Zechariah served in the temple. The location and characters that begin Luke's gospel are important: there are times when theologians set the prophetic and priestly offices against each other, but in these stories, they come together. Zechariah the priest in the temple and John the Baptist the prophet in the wilderness witness to Jesus who, as we shall see, not only receives the spirit of Elijah but also sends the Spirit on his apostles to be witnesses. That Jesus sends the Spirit identifies him as more than a prophet.

The next reference to the Spirit in Luke's gospel is when the angel Gabriel announces to Mary that she will conceive a child even though she is a virgin. She wonders how this will be, and the angel says, "The Holy Spirit will come upon you and the power of the Most High will overshadow you" (Lk. 1:35). Notice the similarity and difference with the angel's announcement to Zechariah about John. He inherits "the spirit and power of Elijah" and is promised to be filled with the Holy Spirit, but the Holy Spirit is not the cause of John's conception. Jesus not only inherits the prophetic spirit but is also conceived by "the Holy Spirit . . . and the power of the Most High." The Holy Spirit inaugurates his conception and birth.

Matthew makes the same claim in a less dramatic form. We are simply told that Mary "was found to be with child of the Holy Spirit" (Mt. 1:18). When this news alarmed her husband, Joseph, an angel announced to him not to be fearful because "that which is conceived in her is of the Holy Spirit" (Mt. 1:21). Both in Luke and Matthew, the Spirit makes possible Jesus's conception: Matthew with the more straightforward and passive, "she was found," and Luke with the significant phrase that the Spirit "overshadows" or "fills" Mary.

What does it mean that Jesus's conception occurs by the Holy Spirit's "overshadowing" Mary? Tradition has repeatedly insisted that the Spirit's agency should not be understood in any sexual sense. In fact, the key to interpreting it is found in its allusion to the temple

---

[1] The translation comes from Luke Timothy Johnson, *The Gospel of Luke*, SP 3 (Collegeville, MN: Liturgical, 1991), 31.

that once again, as in the announcement to Zechariah in the temple, unites the prophetic and priestly. "Overshadow" is the same term used to describe God's glory as it descends upon the tabernacle, the place where God dwells with creatures. In Exod. 40:34-35 after Moses made all the preparations for God's dwelling place in the tabernacle, we are told according to the Septuagint (the Greek OT) that the glory of God filled the tabernacle (*skênê*) and that Moses could not "enter the tent of meeting because the cloud filled [or overshadowed—*episkiazô*] the tabernacle." The same verb *episkiazô* is used both in Exod. 40:35 as a reference to the tabernacle and in Lk. 1:35 in reference to Mary's womb. Both have become the place where God dwells with creatures. In Luke's gospel, however, the cloud and glory that fill the tabernacle have become the Holy Spirit and the power of the Most High that "overshadows" Mary's womb. John the Baptist is promised the prophetic "spirit and power" of Elijah. Jesus is conceived in the Spirit and power of God.

A similar allusion is present in the Gospel of John without the explicit reference to the Spirit. John does not have the story of the virgin birth, but like Luke, John records that John the Baptist was sent as a witness to Jesus. John 1:14 also refers to the tabernacle in explaining who Jesus is and what he has done—"the Word became flesh and dwelt among us." The verb translated "dwelt" in Jn 1:14 is *skênoô*, which is related to the word for tabernacle also found in Exod. 40:35 and noted earlier—*skênê*. This verse could be translated as "the Word became flesh and tabernacled among us."

Raymond Brown relates Jn 1:14 to Exod. 25:8-9, where Israel is told to make a "dwelling" or "pitch a tent" that will serve as "the site of God's localized presence on earth." The tabernacle becomes the temple, which is destroyed when Israel is taken into exile. A longing for restoration requires remembering Jerusalem (Psalm 137) and hoping that God and God's people will return to it. In prophecies such as Ezek. 43:7, Joel 3:17, and Zech. 2:10, God promises to "make his dwelling in Zion," or in Israel's midst. The Ezekiel passage states, "My name shall dwell in the midst of the house of God forever."[2] The prophets hold forth the expectation of return. God will once again dwell with God's people, and the expectation is centered on the temple because it has been the site in which God and creatures have lived together. In John's gospel, this expectation gets transferred to Jesus's body. Brown states, "When the Prologue proclaims that the Word made his dwelling among men, we are being told that the flesh of Jesus Christ is the new localization of God's presence on earth, and that Jesus is the replacement of the ancient Tabernacle. The Gospel [of John] will present Jesus as the replacement of the Temple."[3]

Unlike Luke's gospel, John does not give an explicit role to the Holy Spirit in his opening prologue, but there may be an indirect reference. He refers to "grace and truth" that come from Jesus (Jn 1:18), and in Jn 15:26, Jesus promises that he will send the "Spirit of truth" who will witness to him. Perhaps, then, we could see a proleptic reference to the Spirit in John 1:18. Whether that is the case or not, both Luke and John witness to God's unique presence in Jesus and do so by referring to the Holy Spirit. Luke is explicit that this presence is possible because of the Holy Spirit's work in "overshadowing" Mary as God's glory overshadowed the tabernacle.

John's prologue and Luke's birth narratives show the inseparable unity between who Jesus is, what he does, and the Holy Spirit's agency. Jesus is the expected restoration of God to the temple—the fulfillment of God's promise to dwell with creatures. The work

---

[2]Raymond Brown, *The Gospel According to John*, 2 vols., AB (New York: Doubleday, 1966–1970), 1:32–3.
[3]Ibid., 33.

of the Holy Spirit is (a) to prepare Jesus's way by giving the prophetic spirit to John the Baptist who witnesses to him, (b) to transform Mary's womb into the tabernacle that unites divinity and humanity, and (c) to conceive the one person Jesus who has two natures, divinity and humanity, in her womb. This miraculous action of the Spirit is a new work of creation similar to the Spirit's work in Genesis 1, which is why John 1 repeats the creation story of Genesis 1.

The Nicene-Constantinopolitan Creed (325 and 381) and Chalcedonian definition (451) gave expression to the unity of God and humanity in Jesus. The Creed establishes that the "one Lord, Jesus Christ" is the "only begotten of the Father" and is of "one essence" (*homoousion*) with the Father. The Spirit is also the "Lord" who proceeds from the Father. The Western tradition of Christianity, following St. Augustine, later added that the Spirit proceeds from the Father "and the Son" (*filioque*). This addition has created a long-standing controversy between the Western and Eastern churches that has not been resolved until this day. The Chalcedonian definition is a fuller articulation of the Son that emphasizes three things: Christ's full divinity, Christ's full humanity, and the inseparable unity of these two natures in his one person. It is the person, Jesus Christ, who acts. This one person who acts always acts according to both natures, revealing that God and creatures dwell together. This defines who he is, but it also tells us what he has done. His being is at the same time the work of God's restoration in which God and creatures dwell in unity.

The unity of humanity and God in Jesus is not only about who Jesus is; it is also about what he accomplishes. Saint Augustine emphasized both the action of the Holy Spirit and the Virgin Mary in Jesus's birth. He stated, "Born by the power of the Holy Spirit and from the Virgin Mary; that's how he came, and to whom he came: from the Virgin Mary in whom the Holy Spirit, and not a human husband acted; he made the chaste one fecund, conserving her intact." He then related Mary's work to the church, for it too is the body of Christ. He stated, "The Holy Church is virgin and gives birth. She imitates Mary who delivered the Lord. . . . And if you think about it, she gives birth to Christ himself, as it is the members of Christ that are baptized. . . . If, therefore, the Church gives birth to Christ's member, that means she is very similar to Mary."[4] The correlation between the Spirit, Jesus, and the church takes us into the next point: Jesus's life and mission.

JESUS'S LIFE AND MISSION

The Spirit, the glory and power of God, overshadows the tabernacle and the womb of Mary, making God present in the world. In the work of the incarnation, the Spirit sends the Son into the world. Once the Son is incarnate, the Spirit also leads him in his mission. The Holy Spirit descends upon him at his baptism (Mt. 3:16, Mk 1:10, Lk. 3:22, Jn 1:32). This work of the Spirit empowers Jesus for his mission. It does not make him divine. As we saw above in Luke's birth narratives, Jesus's conception as divinity and humanity occurs in Mary's womb, which is why in giving birth to him it is appropriate to say that she gives birth to God. She has been given the title *theotokos* (God-bearer) to mark this extraordinary act. When the Spirit descends upon Jesus at his baptism, then, it is not another conception of his divinity but his empowerment for mission that is consistent with his conception in Mary's womb. The doctrine of the incarnation is not only about Jesus's conception and

---

[4]Cited in Raniero Cantalamessa, *Mary: Mirror of the Church* (Collegeville, MN: Liturgical, 1992), 179–80.

birth; it is also about his mission. Jesus performs the perfect unity of divinity and humanity in creation, restoring the latter to the Father's intentions. Another work of the Spirit is to guide Jesus for, and strengthen him in, the work that lies before him.

The first place the Spirit guides Jesus is the wilderness where he will face the same temptations Israel faced when they wandered in the wilderness (Mt. 4:1, Mk 1:12, Lk. 4:1). Jesus faces three temptations—first an economic, second a religious, and third a political one. He has learned Moses's teaching well, for he repeats Moses's words in response to each of the devil's temptations. In response to the economic temptation, Jesus cites Moses, "one does not live on bread alone" (Deut. 8:3); in response to the religious, he quotes Moses, "worship and serve only God" (Deut. 6:13); and in response to the political temptation when the devil tells him he will be given all the kingdoms of the world, he speaks Moses's words, "do not put God to the test" (Deut. 6:16). Led by the Spirit, Jesus is strengthened by the Spirit to resist the temptations that come from the principalities and powers of the world. Throughout his mission, those powers are dethroned.

The Spirit who filled him at his baptism (Lk. 4:1a) and led him into the wilderness (Lk. 4:1b) now guides him in his teaching: "Then Jesus, filled with the power of the Spirit, returned to Galilee.... He began to teach in their synagogue" (Lk. 4:14). His first sermon has as its text Isa. 61:1: "the Spirit of the Lord is upon me." This prophecy promises restoration for Israel, and Jesus tells his hometown people that he is the one who will bring it about. He also proclaims that it will be widely available. For some reason, the latter seems to have provoked the people of his own hometown, and after he preaches his first sermon, he is exiled. His exile becomes the basis for his ongoing mission. He gathers twelve disciples and heads for Jerusalem. The twelve disciples represent the twelve tribes of Israel that had been dispersed in exile. The journey to Jerusalem signifies God's presence returning to the temple, but there is a twist. When they arrive in Jerusalem, Jesus enters the temple and casts out those who are in it. Jesus announces that he will destroy the temple and rebuild it in three days (Jn 2:19), an announcement that is placed on the lips of his accusers (Mk 14:58). John tells us that his disciples remember this crucial announcement after his resurrection.

Jesus's mission, then, consists of being guided and empowered by the Spirit for each of its specific works: gathering the twelve, casting out demons, healing, giving his disciples commands and instructions, and heading toward Jerusalem. In the Synoptic Gospels (Matthew, Mark, and Luke), once it has been established that Jesus begins his mission full of the Spirit and that the Spirit is leading him and anointing him for his work, explicit references to the Spirit become rare. John's gospel, however, has explicit references to the Spirit's role in the "farewell discourses" (John 14–17). First, Jesus tells them that he must go away, but he promises to send the "Spirit of truth" who will "remain with them" (Jn 14:15). The Spirit, who is sent by the Father in Jesus's name, will also "teach" and "bring to remembrance" everything that Jesus has taught and told them (Jn 14:26). As the Spirit of truth, the Spirit bears witness to Jesus and enables the disciples to do so as well (Jn 15:26-27). A central passage that relates Jesus and the Spirit is John 16:5-15. In it, Jesus tells his disciples what the work of the Spirit is: (a) "convince the world concerning sin and righteousness and judgment," (b) "guide you into all truth," and (c) "glorify" the Son.[5] The Spirit is divine agency manifesting truth and glory.

---

[5] For an excellent introduction to the doctrine of the Holy Spirit, see Geoffrey Wainwright, "The Holy Spirit," in *The Cambridge Companion to Christian Doctrine*, ed. Colin Gunton (Cambridge: Cambridge University Press,

BETRAYAL, ARREST, AND CRUCIFIXION

Explicit references to the Holy Spirit are conspicuously absent in the story of Jesus's betrayal, arrest, and crucifixion. This absence is conspicuous because Jesus comforted his disciples in each of the four gospels by telling them that when they are "delivered up" or "brought before the synagogue," they should not be "anxious" about what to say, for the Holy Spirit or the "Spirit of your Father" will speak through them (Mt. 19:19-20, Mk 13:11, Lk. 12:11-12, Jn 14:26). Yet during Jesus's own arrest, we are not explicitly told if, or what, the Spirit spoke through him. Perhaps we should consider what occurred in his betrayal, arrest, and trial as the Spirit speaking even in the silence. John's gospel suggests as much when the high priest states, "it is expedient for you that one man should die for the people," and the narrator informs us, "He did not say this of his own accord, but being high priest that year he prophesied that Jesus should die for the nation" (Jn 11:50-51). The Spirit works even through those conspiring against him.

Prior to his arrest, however, there is an implicit but crucial work of the Holy Spirit in Jesus's transfiguration. In Luke's gospel, prior to Jesus setting "his face to go to Jerusalem," he went up the mountain to pray with Peter, John, and James. A cloud "overshadowed" them, using the same verb we saw above—*episkiazô* (Mt. 17:5, Mk 9:7, Lk. 9:35). Luke then states that "his face changed and his clothes became dazzling white." The disciples who are with him see Moses and Elijah, who appear "in glory" and are speaking with him about what was to be "accomplished" in Jerusalem. The verb "accomplished" is from the same verb used in Lk. 1:1 that was translated "fulfilled"—*plêrô*. Here we have the prophet and the law (Elijah and Moses, respectively) witnessing to God's presence in the radiant Christ. Words similar to those the Father pronounced at Jesus's baptism are pronounced once again, "This is my Son, my Chosen," now with the additional command "listen to him" (Lk. 9:33). Peter's response is to build three "tents," *skênas*, the word also used for the tabernacle. Peter understands what is going on—God's presence is on this mountain as it was in Exodus. Janet Soskice, a contemporary theologian, offers a compelling interpretation of the transfiguration, relating it to God's glory (the Shekinah) present in the holy of holies in the temple and Jesus's baptism. She writes, "The dove is not present, but instead Jesus and his garments shine with an uncreated light, the very Shekinah of God."[6] For the Eastern church, as Soskice notes, the transfiguration is an important sign of biblical trinitarianism. Moses and Elijah "experienced theophanies on Mount Sinai: Moses in the burning bush (Exodus 3.1-15) and Elijah in the whispered voice (I Kings 19.8-13)." Jesus is the theophany of God, illumined by God's Spirit. His face having been transfigured, he now heads to Jerusalem.

There may also be a tacit reference to the Spirit in the anointing Jesus receives in the house of Simon the leper when the unnamed woman (Martha's sister, Mary, in John's gospel) anoints him with "expensive ointment" (Mt. 26:7, Mk 14:3, Lk. 7:38, Jn 12:3). This pouring out prepares his body for burial (Mt. 26:12, Mk 14:8), an action that the women who arrive at the tomb intended to do but were incapable of performing because his body was not present. The work of the Holy Spirit becomes associated with "pouring out" in the tradition, which makes it all the more important that it is the unnamed woman

---

1997), 273-95 (and especially p. 278 on the importance of Jn 16:5-15).
[6]Janet Soskice, "Biblical Trinitarianism," in *Heresies and How to Avoid Them: Why It Matters What Christians Believe*, ed. Ben Quash and Michael Ward (London: SPCK, 2007), 129.

who anoints Jesus for his burial, a liturgical act of preparation. In turn, Jesus will pour out water and blood in the two scenes that follow this one in the gospels—Jesus washing his disciples' feet (Jn 13:1-20) and the Lord's Supper (Mt. 26:26-29, Mk 14:22-25, Lk. 22:15-20). The pouring out of water and blood from his side in the crucifixion becomes the fount of the sacraments—baptism and the Lord's Supper. Although there are other scenes in which Jesus gives or pours the Spirit on his disciples, the blood and water that come from his side pour the Spirit upon the world.

John's gospel, as I noted earlier, has the most explicit references to the giving of the Spirit to the disciples in the farewell discourses that arise between the Lord's Supper and Jesus's arrest. After his high priestly prayer in John 17 in which he asks the Father to let his disciples share in the "glory" that they share, Jesus speaks very little. During his arrest, when Peter attempts to defend him with the sword, he gives the command, "No more of this." Then Jesus asks why they come to arrest him in "the power of darkness" when he was present daily in the temple (Lk. 22:53). What is striking is that even though he had told his disciples the Spirit would give them words to say when they are arrested and prosecuted, the words Jesus is given to say are either non-defensive—"I have said nothing secretly. . . . Ask those who have heard me, what I said to them; they know what I said" (Jn 18:21)—or he is silent, refusing to answer the questions posed. His life is the words the Spirit speaks. His coronation as King of the Jews is intended as mockery, but like the high priest's words, it speaks the truth. Even the taunts that echo the devil's temptation to throw himself down from the cross are met with silence. Darkness follows, and Jesus cries out in abandonment.

RESURRECTION

The silence of God turns to joyful speech—speech that has continued to this day through proclamation and witness—when the women who were prepared to anoint Jesus's body find the stone rolled away and the tomb empty. Biblical scholars refer to two traditions of the resurrection accounts. One is the empty tomb, the only tradition present in Mark's gospel. The other are the appearances. Few explicit references to the Holy Spirit are present in the synoptic accounts of the resurrection. The "Great Commission" at the end of Matthew makes explicit reference to the Holy Spirit: "Go therefore and make disciples of all nations, baptizing them in the name of the Father and the Son and the Holy Spirit" (Mt. 28:19). There is also an implicit reference in Jesus's final words, "And remember, I am with you always, to the end of the age" (Mt. 28:20). He does not identify the Spirit as the one who makes him present until the end of the age, but the interpretation of Mark in terms of John has led the tradition to make this claim.

The work of the Spirit also makes sense of the inscrutable agential mystery that the gospel never resolves. Jesus, the one person in two natures, divine and human, really dies. As the Creed puts it, "he suffered under Pontius Pilate, was crucified, died and was buried." God gives God's self over in human flesh in the incarnation, trusting Mary and Joseph to feed and care for him. Joseph is the patron saint of workers for this very reason. Jesus does not feed and clothe himself. This "giving over" continues throughout his life, including at the time of his betrayal, arrest, and crucifixion. Others commit these acts against him, and he suffers them. His is a "passive" obedience. After his death, his dead body is taken by others and laid in the tomb, which is then sealed. All these are acts of human agents that Jesus's body depends upon. He does not do them himself. Then comes this moment of mystery. Who is the agent rolling back the stone, raising Jesus from the dead, and empowering him with new life? If we read these mysterious events within the narrative whole of the gospels and remember that the Spirit was present in his conception, empowered him for ministry, and was promised to guide him and those who followed him, then it is best to think of the Spirit as the agential power who as "Lord and Giver of life" gives life not only in creation but also in the new creation. Perhaps this is why it is only now with this powerful and glorious act of new creation that Jesus can say to the disciples, "Receive the Holy Spirit" (Jn 20:22).

ASCENSION AND PROMISED RETURN

Why did the story not end with the resurrection? If, as Luke's gospel suggests, things have been fulfilled and completed, then why should history continue? Jesus's odd coronation as not only King of the Jews but also as the ruler of the universe has been established. What began with his coronation in his crucifixion culminates in his ascension to the right hand of the Father. Not all things are yet placed in subjection to him, as Hebrews reminds us (2:5-9), but we see him enthroned at the right hand of God, the rightful ruler and heir of all creation. Why not establish his rule at this moment? His disciples ask this question prior to his ascension.

Luke continues the story in his second work, *The Acts of the Apostles*. He begins by reminding Theophilus what he presented to him in the first book, "I wrote about all that Jesus did and taught from the beginning until the day when he was taken up to heaven, after giving instructions through the Holy Spirit to the apostles whom he had chosen" (Acts 1:1-2). The Holy Spirit instructs his disciples what they are to do next. They ask the question, "Lord, is this the time when you will restore the kingdom to Israel?" Jesus tells them that when this restoration occurs is not for them to know, but they are to "receive power when the Holy Spirit has come upon" them, and then they will be witnesses. The Spirit's work is now to make them witnesses; the time between Christ's ascension and the restoration of heavenly rule is the time of witness. The disciples receive the Spirit at Pentecost, and the church is born, reversing the curse of Babel. The time of witness is a time of unifying the nations in peace and justice through communion.

CONCLUSION

Jesus repeats a similar scene in both Lk. 24:50-53 and Acts 1:8-11.[7] In the latter verses, Jesus promises his disciples not a share of his spirit as with the Elijah and Elisha cycle, but that they "will receive power when the Holy Spirit has come upon" them; the result is that they will be "witnesses." Unlike Elijah, Jesus gives the Spirit to whom he chooses. Having given it to his disciples, he then ascends. His work is completed, and yet it continues. The Spirit who inaugurated it in Jesus's conception and mission, completed it in his resurrection and ascension and now continues it in the time of witness. Jesus sends the Spirit upon his disciples to empower them as witnesses, overcoming the judgment at Babel by the pentecostal mystery. It is not so much ecstatic utterances and manifestations, as important as they are, but the new life of communion identified in Acts 2:37-47 and 4:32-37. When those who hear the witness are baptized, they receive the "gift of the

---

[7] See Johnson, *The Gospel of Luke*, 13.

Holy Spirit" and participate in the Spirit's slow, patient work of restoration through forgiveness of sins and economic sharing. "Communion," "the Lord's Supper," or the "Holy Eucharist" will be the central symbol of the Spirit's work, pouring out her life upon the gifts of everyday existence to make us one with the body of Christ. The work of the Spirit in Christ's work never comes to an end. Much as the Trinity is the eternal gift and reception of God within God's own being, so the work of the Spirit in Christ and the work of Christ in the Spirit are the taking up of creation into that eternal gift. The two acts that bookend Luke's orderly account of what has been fulfilled—the Holy Spirit conceives and guides Jesus so that he may fulfill his work, and Jesus sends the Spirit so that she may fulfill his work—invite all creation to dwell with God as God dwells with us. Both acts, of course, are one with the Father, who sends the Son and Spirit to complete, fulfill, and perfect all creation.

FOR FURTHER READING

Barbeau, Jeffrey W., and Beth Felker Jones, eds. *Spirit of God: Christian Renewal in the Community of Faith*. Downers Grove, IL: InterVarsity, 2015.

St. Basil the Great. *On the Holy Spirit*. Crestwood, NY: St. Vladimir's Seminary Press, 1980.

Congar, Yves. *I Believe in the Holy Spirit*. Translated by David Smith. 3 vols. New York: Crossroad Herder, 1997.

Del Colle, Ralph. *Christ and the Spirit: Spirit-Christology in Trinitarian Perspective*. Oxford: Oxford University Press, 1994.

Felker Jones, Beth. *God the Spirit: Introducing Pneumatology in Wesleyan and Ecumenical Perspective*. Eugene, OR: Cascade, 2014.

Hauerwas, Stanley, and William Willimon. *The Holy Spirit*. Nashville, TN: Abingdon, 2015.

Wainwright, Geoffrey. "The Holy Spirit." In *The Cambridge Companion to Christian Doctrine*, edited by Colin Gunton, 273–95. Cambridge: Cambridge University Press, 1997.

CHAPTER SEVEN

The Spirit-Infused Hope of Christ

MARGARET B. ADAM

The hope of Christ is the hope for Christ's presence now and in everlasting life. It is the hope for Christ's justice, mercy, and cosmic reconciliation. To hope for Christ's redemption is to hope for Christ as the ultimate hope. The hope that is Christ, the hope of Christ, exceeds the limitations of human finitude and frailty. Human beings lack the expanse of imagination and the perfection of desire to approach the hope of Christ. The Holy Spirit provides the necessary supplementation of grace that grants both the means with which to hope for the presence of Christ and the possibility of attaining the presence of Christ.

HOPE *WITHOUT* THE SPIRIT'S INFUSION OF DIVINE GRACE

Hope *without* the Spirit's assistance—that is, human hope—is an expectant desire for and reaching toward something good. The good is absent, but it is potentially obtainable. One might hope for the good that is the restoration of a broken friendship. The aim of this hope is almost entirely absent; perhaps only the memories of happier days remain. The restoration will be difficult to obtain, but it is possible to attain within the resources of creation. Hope, in this context, describes the aim (reconciliation), the emotion (the feeling of hope), and the activity of achieving (reaching toward and attaining) the good end.

Human hope is the *aim* that is desired and anticipated, not yet attained, and at least possible to attain. "Your hope is a healed relationship with your friend." "My hope is a raise." "*Obi Wan Kenobi* is our only hope." The renewed friendship, the raise, and Obi Wan Kenobi are all mostly absent; there is no need to hope for what is already fully present. These aims are at the same time somewhat present as a hint, a memory, or a promise. The faint suggestion of the good aim, in its absence, informs and directs the emotion and activity of hope.

Human hope is the *emotion* of hope. "I am feeling hopeful that I may grow in wisdom." "We are experiencing hopeful feelings that justice is possible." This feeling of hope shifts and changes, as do all human emotions. We can feel hopeful or hopeless; we can grow or falter in hope; and we can hope to feel more hope.

Human hope, as an *activity*, is to desire and anticipate the attainment of a hoped-for good. It is the expression of the emotion and the reaching toward the aim. It is to strive for and wait for something that has not yet arrived. "I hoped to find you." "They are hoping to win the race." "All we can do is hope for the best." To hope is to direct one's imagination, abilities, and efforts toward the achievement of what is longed for, toward the presence of what is (mostly) absent and can potentially be rendered fully present by human endeavor.

At its best, human hope can identify good aims, provoke hopeful feelings, and motivate hopeful activities toward aims. At the same time, it is always vulnerable to disordered desires and the limits of human finitude. Hope without the Spirit's assistance cannot become the hope of Christ or attain everlasting life in Christ.

HOPE *WITH* THE SPIRIT'S INFUSION OF DIVINE GRACE

Hope *with* the assistance of the Holy Spirit—that is, theological hope—is the eschatological hope of life fulfilled in Christ. It is not a practical goal, a human emotion, or a matter of human effort. This hope exceeds the limitations of human capacity and possibility. The Holy Spirit transforms merely human hope into theological hope, the hope of Christ. The presence of Christ is impossible to attain without the Holy Spirit's infusion of grace. The Spirit gives the means with which to hope for Christ, and it makes possible the achievement of that hope of Christ. Theological hope is one of the three theological virtues, along with faith and love, because the Holy Spirit directs it toward the ultimate good, which is the attainment of eternal life with God. Thomas Aquinas explains: "Wherefore, in so far as we hope for anything as being possible to us by means of the Divine assistance, our hope attains God Himself, on Whose help it leans. It is therefore evident that hope is a virtue, since it causes a human act to be good and to attain its due rule."[1] Like merely human hope, theological hope can describe the desired good itself, the desire to attain the not-yet attained good, and the activity of reaching for that good. Unlike human hope, theological hope is empowered by the Holy Spirit and specifically focused on Christ, encompassing and directing all other hopes.

The *aim* of theological hope, that which is desired and anticipated, is *the* good: Christ who grants resurrected life in the presence of God. "My hope is in my baptism into the death and life of Christ." "Her hope is the fulfillment of healing in Christ." "Our only hope is Jesus Christ, our savior." Christ, the aim of theological hope, is absent (we do not hope for what we already have). The Holy Spirit makes Christ present-in-absence now, in hope. The Holy Spirit makes Christ known in Scripture, the saints, the church, the sacraments, and in inspired memory, imagination, and reason. The hope of Christ is a specific and all-encompassing hope in the salvation that is already and not yet accomplished in Jesus Christ's life, death, resurrection, and ascension. It is the ultimate hope of everlasting life after death with God.

The hope of Christ is more than a feeling. It is a *Spirit-inspired, internal, motivating drive* that provokes, strengthens, and renders possible that which would otherwise be impossible to imagine, sustain, or achieve. "I have a hope that I will become Christ-like." "We have a hope that we will gain new life in the presence of Christ." "They have a hope in the salvation of all creation." Left to our own devices, we might never grasp the hope of Christ. The infusion of the Spirit's grace generates and empowers hope that can aspire for and attain life in Christ, death with Christ, and eternal life in Christ.

---

[1] Thomas Aquinas, *ST*, II-II, q. 17, a. 1c.

Theological hope is the *activity* of anticipating the coming of Christ. It is the inspired striving and waiting for Christ. To hope for Christ is to direct one's imagination, abilities, and efforts toward eternal life in Christ *and* to receive the Holy Spirit's gift of the grace necessary for that hope to attain Christ. Christians live out this theological virtue of hope through the practices of discipleship developed in the context of the church. "We are hoping to see Christ in the eyes of the enemy we are trying to love." "We are hoping to give glory to Christ as we sing the Psalms." "We hope to be of one mind—the mind of Christ—in our community of believers." Prayer and the imitation of Christ are the explicit expressions of the Holy Spirit's gift of the hope of Christ. Charles Pinches writes that the virtue of hope

> is in it for the long haul. It equips our hearts for an extended journey on which we both deeply long for but also patiently await the dawning of a new day when every tear shall be wiped away, and all things made new (Rev. 21:4-5). To walk in the light of this day, leaning on Christ whose love and companionship opens our hope to cover those many others who walk with us, is to work and act and live in a Christian hope that does not disappoint.[2]

The Holy Spirit expands the human hope for good things into this long-haul, grace-infused human theological virtue of hope, the hope of Christ. The Holy Spirit gives the divine assistance of infused grace that informs, nurtures, and fulfills eschatological hope. It reveals the object of this hope, which is the subject of all hope: Christ who grants eternal life with God. The Holy Spirit sparks and sustains the hope of Christ in believers who are the body of Christ as they wait for the fulfillment of Christ's cosmic reconciliation.

THE SPIRIT *EFFECTS* THE PRESENCE OF CHRIST THROUGH THEOLOGICAL HOPE

Christ is eternal, unlimited by time and space. Creation, which is neither divine nor eternal, exists within the boundaries of time and space. Jesus Christ, God incarnate, submitted to created time and space in the life of Jesus, as fully human and fully divine. We would experience this lack of contact with Jesus as Christ's absence, if not for the Holy Spirit's extension throughout time of the presence of the eternal Christ. The Spirit *effects*, makes happen, the presence-in-absence of Christ through theological hope.

The Spirit breathes life into creation, thereby filling human beings, animals, earth, wind, and seas with the hope of Christ their creator and their savior. Scripture makes it clear that all creation is God's, that Christ's incarnation is the divine presence for the cosmos, and that human beings are accompanied by the rest of creation in hoping for ultimate reconciliation through Christ. We do not know much about the specifics of Christ's relationship with nonhuman animal species or with plants, rocks, sea, and sky, except that all creation is created by God to be good, and that God's love and mercy are sure and constant. Presumably, species-specific hope and grace pertain to nonhuman creatures also, as God cares for them all according to their kind. The hope of Christ received and practiced by humans plays out in the biblical narrative of a particular group of people, their descendants, their messiah, and their extending families in faith and adoption.

---

[2]Charles Pinches, "On Hope," in *Virtues and Their Vices*, ed. Kevin Timpe and Craig Boyd (Oxford: Oxford University Press, 2016), 367.

The Holy Spirit effects the presence of Christ in God's chosen people. Long before the incarnation, the Holy Spirit effects the presence of Christ in the people of God as a messianic hope, through promises and prophecy, and through the heroes of the faith. The Spirit nurtures and sustains the hope of Christ in God's covenant people through slavery and exile, freedom, and abundance; this hope perseveres through loss, lament, and praise.

The Holy Spirit reveals the fully divine nature of Christ in the fully human body of Jesus. Christ becomes present in created time and space by the Holy Spirit with Mary, the Mother of God. The Holy Spirit reveals Jesus's identity as Christ at his baptism and in the signs and wonders of Jesus's preaching, teaching, and healing. It stirs Jesus's followers to recognize him as the Messiah, the Son of God, and moves them to place their hope in him for life beyond their understanding and for transformation.

The Holy Spirit renders Christ present, even in death, by nurturing the hope that nothing can separate us from the love of Christ. Jesus Christ dies both as a creature and as the begotten, not created, Son of God. The Holy Spirit inhabits both the presence and the absence of Christ, such that the hope of Christ does not end with the crucifixion. The resurrected Jesus Christ affirms this Spirit-filled hope when he promises his followers that he will send the Spirit to them when he is gone. The Holy Spirit effects the presence of Christ after the ascension, when he is absent as a particular body in a particular time and place. At Pentecost, the Holy Spirit, which has no body, fills many bodies with the hope of Christ; the new church extends that hope as the new body of Christ enlivened and sustained by the Spirit.

THE HOLY SPIRIT PRESENTS CHRIST IN HOPE

The Holy Spirit grants the presence of Christ as hope by eternally *presenting* in time. The Spirit does not come and go as creatures do or as Jesus did. It is not finite and so does not alternate presence and absence as we do in birth and death, existing only in one body and in one place at a time. The Holy Spirit—like Christ—is not born and does not die. It is always active in creation, and that activity is one of *arrival*. Some people slip in and out of a crowd, without notice. Others enter with a flourish that changes the atmosphere in the room. The Holy Spirit makes an entrance. It arrives, and it is always arriving. It *presents* in a way that does not require preceding absence, but it does transform the bodies it enlivens. The Spirit's entrance might cause a quiet, barely discernible change of heart. And it might set hearts on fire and call whole communities to mission.

> The Spirit's testimony does not supply new evidence of the truth of the Gospel: rather, it illumines or shows to be convincing evidence that is already there. It is not a question of brainwashing or propaganda or making feeble evidence appear strong. It is a question of removing blinders and helping people to grasp the epistemic situation correctly. It is not a process of reasoning or weighing evidence, but a direct intuition of truth. It is like the opening of blind eyes, the unplugging of deaf ears, the removal of a veil. "And by this we know that [Christ] abides in us, by the Spirit that he has given us" (1 Jn 3:24; cf. 4:13; Eph. 1:13).[3]

---

[3]Stephen T. Davis, "An Ontology of the Spirit," in *The Testimony of the Spirit: New Essays*, ed. R. Douglas Geivett and Paul K. Moser (Oxford: Oxford University Press, 2017), 59.

The Spirit arrives to reveal the hope of Christ: life everlasting with Christ, beyond the human lifespan of Jesus, and beyond the finitude of creation. The Holy Spirit incorporates us into previous and future time and by doing so reveals Christ who is present to all times. It reveals and instills the promise of Christ; it saturates creation with the hope of Christ. That saturation of hope fuels creaturely responses to the resurrection that reflect and anticipate the consummation of creation.

The dramatic, public arrival of the Holy Spirit at Pentecost intensifies the absence and presence of the Lord. Jesus's body is not there. The apostles no longer have him to follow, and they do not know what to do. The Spirit presents the absent Christ to them, and they are changed from the condition of overwhelming loss to the life of hope. The Holy Spirit fills them so that they make Christ known to all the gathered people. The apostles gain a new agency in the Spirit, in a hope that is no longer simply human hope, but eternal, graced hope.

> It is true that [Pentecost] involves the future of Christ, what Tennyson called "the Christ that is to be." It initiates "Christ in the future," but that Christ is still Christ. The Spirit displays something that is new, in the novelty of history and the variety of cultures, but it is a new thing that comes from the fullness that has been given once for all by God in Christ.[4]

In the Spirit, the apostles perform the gospel in teaching and preaching, in caring for the needy, and in living together as Christ's present-in-absence body. The Spirit has not stopped arriving. The church is still called to welcome the arriving and presenting Spirit.

ONE HOPE IN TWO PERSONS

The hope of Christ is one hope. The hope of Christ does not jockey for position with the hope of the Spirit. The Holy Spirit is one with Christ in the Trinity and presents the hope of Christ, with Christ. The Holy Spirit and Christ are two distinct persons of the Trinity, but there is no competition between them. It is not that one is inadequate and needs the other to be whole. These two persons are still the same God, both of and one with the Father, both eternal and in time and space.

> Paul (in 1 Cor. 12:3) and John (in 1 Jn 4:2) make the testimony borne to the Lord Jesus a criterion of the activity of the Spirit. He brings something new into the course of history, but that novelty is not something vague and imprecise. . . . The Word may be permeated with the Spirit, but the Spirit is also permeated with the Word. The two are inseparable. They both proceed from the Father.[5]

They do not fight for power, nor does one eclipse the other. The Holy Spirit does not stand in for Christ before the incarnation, leave the scene during the incarnation, or replace Christ after the ascension. The Spirit of Christ and the Holy Spirit are not two different Spirits. Christ and the Spirit are unified, together revealing God's accomplished and coming salvation. The Spirit gives incarnate life to Jesus Christ, who gives the Spirit to his followers as promised, after his ascension, at Pentecost, and ever since. The Son and

---

[4]Yves Congar, *The Word and the Spirit*, trans. David Smith (San Francisco, CA: Harper and Row, 1986), 71.
[5]Ibid., 71.

the Spirit perform and make known the love of God, as particular persons of the Trinity and as one. They establish the reign of God, now and coming.

ONE HOPE, DIVINE AND HUMAN

The Spirit's infusion of grace does not pit individual human hope against the imposition of superhuman hope. The Spirit gives theological hope that inspires and becomes one with human hope. The Holy Spirit transforms merely human hope into graced theological hope by empowering and enlivening—not overpowering and conquering—human will, agency, and desire. The Holy Spirit supplies the material of faith that makes hope possible. It invigorates faith that can support and launch hope that reaches beyond faith. "It is *that influence of the Holy Spirit on the minds of believers that causes them to believe firmly that the Christian message, or some aspect of it, is true.*"[6] It does not impose an external hope; it implants hope as an organic recognition of the potential presence-in-absence of Christ. It works within creatures as "the Beyond who is within."[7] It supplies truth internally that might be experienced as new cognitive knowledge or as a more affective awareness of the Good. This intuition heightens the yearning for Christ and affirms the possibility of attaining in full the presence of Christ.

The hope of Christ forms what to do, how to do it, and the motivation to do it. Believers who receive the presence of Christ through the Holy Spirit in hope cannot separate their grace-infused hope from their independent, personal hope. In this way, "the work of the Holy Spirit [is] always preceding any human work," and "any movement humans make toward God is in fact initiated by God, who endeavors to draw people to himself. This includes the Christian's efforts—which are prompted by the Holy Spirit—to help lead others to Christ."[8] There is no more distinction; the gift of hope now springs from within, and with that hope comes the motivation to act toward its fulfillment.

The Holy Spirit promotes the hope of Christ by inspiring the prophecy, teaching, and witness that rehearses Christ's presence-in-absence. "Hope is the theological virtue by which we desire the kingdom of heaven and eternal life as our happiness, placing our trust in Christ's promises and relying not on our own strength, but on the help of the grace of the Holy Spirit."[9]

The Spirit gives hope by revealing the work of Christ in glimpses of the promised redemption: unexpected forgiveness, generous patience, a moment of calm, an argument ended. It gives hope by sustaining the life in Christ of the gathered community. It communicates Christ's love, truth, justice, and mercy. It gives hope by moving hearts, minds, and bodies to desire and cling to Christ, who is not fully present.

The Holy Spirit does not require a particular level of human cognition in order to reveal to creatures the hope of Christ. If hope were solely a matter of human capacity and agency, then perhaps only some human beings would be able to hope, and only those who were able to master a certain level of reasoned knowledge about Christ would receive the

---

[6] Stephen T. Davis, *Christian Philosophical Theology* (Oxford: Oxford University Press, 2006), 17 (italics original).
[7] Anthony C. Thiselton, *The Holy Spirit—In Biblical Teaching, through the Centuries and Today* (Grand Rapids, MI: Eerdmans, 2013), 470.
[8] Kevin Kinghorn and Jerry L. Walls, "The Spirit and the Bride Say 'Come': Apologetics and the Witness of the Holy Spirit," in Geivett and Moser, *The Testimony of the Spirit*, 225.
[9] CCC, §1817.

Holy Spirit's gift of hope, the presence and promise of Christ. This is not the case. Neither does the Holy Spirit supplant common sense with a fanciful, irrational, insupportable hope. The hope is *of Christ*, whose reconciliation of the world is not constrained by creaturely reason or limited imagination. The hope is given by the Spirit, whose identity with Christ as creator is not dependent on creation for divine giving.

In the hope of Christ, the Holy Spirit gives both the presence-in-absence of Christ and the means with which to know and hope for Christ. "To come to know God—the true God—means to receive hope."[10] The Holy Spirit pours the perfect life of Christ into created lives as the gift of love, and in so doing it orders hearts to recognize, desire, and receive that gift as the fulfillment of hope.[11] The hope of Christ, the faith of Christ, and the love of Christ—all three infused and cultivated by the Holy Spirit—are "the pledge of the presence and action of the Holy Spirit in the faculties of the human being."[12]

ONE HOPE, ON EARTH AND IN HEAVEN

The hope of Christ embraces immanent and transcendent hope in the fully human and fully divine Christ incarnate. There is no competition between a hope for here and now and the eschatological hope for eternal life in the peaceable kingdom. The hope of Christ is both present and future. The Holy Spirit's instigation of the hope of Christ is not eschatological apart from the created world and its past, present, and future in time and space. This hope encompasses, holds together the apparently tenuous, apparently impossible connection between the hopes we yearn for and struggle to make happen now, and the fullest completion of those hopes in the life, death, and resurrection of Jesus Christ.

The Holy Spirit does not separate the grace-assisted eschatological virtue of hope from the more immediate hope for deliverance now. There is no competition between the eschatological hope of creation's consummation and the hope for justice, freedom, peace, and comfort today. Rather, the Holy Spirit displays disordered, distracted hopes as sinful and redirects disparate hopes toward the one hope of Christ, which embraces created life now and to come. The incarnation performs the unification of those hopes, as the human life of Jesus Christ is one and the same as the eternal, death-of-death, life-for-our-lives life of Jesus Christ. The Holy Spirit presents that one hope by enlivening hearts and bodies in Christ's body. Hopes for the end of oppression and deprivation now reflect and anticipate the once-for-all cosmic end of oppression and deprivation to come. Christ sets the goal and end of hope: full participation in the reconciliation of all creation in the merciful love of Christ. All hopes in Christ reflect that hope of Christ.

The activities of virtue are small, habituated practices of Christ-like character. Many of these can be learned from Jesus's life and teaching, the Acts of the Apostles, the Epistles, the saints, and one another. To live well in the hope of Christ is to share resources, with special attention to the needs of the poor, the lonely, the sick, and those in prison. Living in the hope of Christ is to strive for peace—even when it seems impractical—by

---

[10] Benedict XVI, *Spe salvi* (San Francisco, CA: Ignatius, 2008), 3.
[11] Christopher A. Beeley, "Christ and Human Flourishing in Patristic Theology," paper prepared for the Yale Center for Faith & Culture consultation on "Christ and Human Flourishing" (December 2014), 12.
[12] CCC, §1813.

exercising fidelity to Christ's coming kingdom over conflicting earthly powers and by conforming to the body of Christ in the face of death.

> To live the good life now—to flourish as human beings by dwelling in the grace of Christ—means to undertake the hard work of seeking Christ's peace in oneself and among one's neighbors, whatever the circumstances may be. For now we love God and our neighbors in Christ with a trust that is based on faith, seeking to benefit them as far as it lies in our power as we look in hope to the perfect peace promised in Christ's resurrection.[13]

To live in hope is to develop and sustain constancy in friendship, to praise together, and to try to be of the same mind as Christ together.

Living into the hope of Christ promises no visible success. Receiving and embracing the hope of Christ is not likely to make much of a difference in the world or to bring on the new kingdom in a blaze of glory. It is likely to be misunderstood and unappreciated. This is because receiving the presence-in-absence of Christ in hope means living into the cruciform body of Jesus Christ, who died a sociopolitical failure. In the hope of Christ, the church reaches through failure, loss, and death to resurrection life, by the grace of the Holy Spirit, until attaining the true presence of Christ.

> We are not optimists; we do not present a lovely vision of the world which everyone is expected to fall in love with. We simply have, wherever we are, some small local task to do, on the side of justice, for the poor. This, in the power of the Spirit, we will try to do, and we know that to do it is to risk hostility and persecution as Jesus risked crucifixion. It is to risk defeat. And this is what we mean by hope. For our hope is the kind that goes through defeat and crucifixion to resurrection. We know that we shall sometimes have to fail rather than betray the very justice that we struggle for; we shall have to fail rather than use the weapons of the oppressor against him, but we can do this because we have hope, because we know that God will bring life out of such defeat and failure as he brought life out of the tomb of Jesus.[14]

The church often leans toward the pre-resurrection side of the narrative; where loss and failure abound, it is far easier to apprehend the absence than the presence of Christ. The theological virtue of hope reflects the confidence of faith and the constancy of love, but it is still a dangerous and uncertain stretch toward the currently invisible and inaccessible Christ. When that reach seems too risky and implausible, the temptation is to divide the hope of Christ into two conflicting hopes: the ultimate, eschatological hope and the apparently more urgent, day-to-day earthly hopes. To set here-and-now hopes against consummation hopes is to deny the Christ presented by the Holy Spirit in Scripture and in the lives of the faithful. Human work for justice, righteousness, and the coming of the kingdom in hope reflects the work of the Holy Spirit already begun.

The hope of Christ is not merely a matter of time (waiting now for what will come in the future); it is also a matter of space and place. The Holy Spirit keeps the presence of Christ with human bodies now in suffering and injustice. The Holy Spirit does not reserve eschatological hope for those who are feeling relatively comfortable and who dole out earthly hope to those who are struggling to survive in the face of catastrophic

---

[13] Beeley, "Christ and Human Flourishing," 18–19.
[14] Herbert McCabe, O.P., *God, Christ and Us*, ed. Brian Davies, O.P. (London: Continuum, 2003), 14–15.

circumstances. The hope of Christ is one, and the Holy Spirit presents Christ to all bodies, in all places. The challenge to Christians is to receive the Holy Spirit's gift of hope, to receive and claim the hope that we cannot desire and attain on our own. This is the hope of Christ: to live as if the one who seems absent is here and as if the kingdom to come is at hand, through the power of the Holy Spirit.

FOR FURTHER READING

Thomas Aquinas. *Summa Theologiae*. 2nd and rev. ed. Translated by the Fathers of the English Dominican Province. 1920. Online ed., 2016.

Benedict XVI. *Spe salvi*. San Francisco, CA: Ignatius, 2008.

Catechism of the Catholic Church. 2nd ed. New York: Doubleday, 1995.

Pinches, Charles. "On Hope." In *Virtues and Their Vices*, edited by Kevin Timpe and Craig Boyd, 350–68. Oxford: Oxford University Press, 2016.

CHAPTER EIGHT

The Spirit and the Old Testament

LEE ROY MARTIN

The OT does not express its theology in a topical and systematic fashion. Instead, its portrait of God emerges from narratives of God's activity, prophetic oracles, and the psalms. God creates the universe, makes promises to Abraham, delivers Israel from Egypt, makes covenant, defeats enemies, disciplines Israel, raises up kings, speaks through prophets, rules over the nations, exiles Israel, and brings them back again. Embedded within the stories, prophecies, and songs are metaphors and adjectives that further clarify the portrait of Yahweh, the God of Israel. Yahweh is savior, king, shepherd, rock, warrior, and spouse. Yahweh is holy, eternal, good, righteous, compassionate, just, great, mighty, wise, and faithful.

Although the OT describes God in some detail, there remains an element of mystery and ambiguity, and the nature of the Spirit of God is certainly one aspect of that mystery. Identifying the activity of the Holy Spirit in the OT is not always easy because even the word "spirit" (Hebrew רוּחַ) itself is sometimes ambiguous. It can signify "air in motion, a blowing, breeze, wind, nothingness, spirit, sense."[1] Wilf Hildebrandt determines that of its 389 occurrences in the OT,[2] רוּחַ refers to the divine Spirit 107 times.[3] Adding to the difficulty of identifying the Spirit in the text, the Hebrew term נשׁמה ("breath"), which is found twenty-four times in the OT, can also refer to the Spirit of God (e.g., Job 32:8, Isa. 30:33). Moreover, other terms such as the "face of God,"[4] "hand of God,"[5] and "finger of God"[6] may serve as metaphors of the Spirit.

---

[1] Ludwig Köhler and Walter Baumgartner, *The Hebrew and Aramaic Lexicon of the Old Testament*, study ed., 2 vols. (Leiden: Brill, 2001), 2:1197.
[2] It appears 378 times in Hebrew and 11 times in Aramaic. Abraham Even-Shoshan, ed., *A New Concordance of the Old Testament* (Grand Rapids, MI: Baker, 1989), 1063–6. Cf. F. W. Horn, "Holy Spirit," in *The Anchor Yale Bible Dictionary*, ed. David N. Freedman, 6 vols. (New York: Doubleday, 1992), 2:262.
[3] Wilf Hildebrandt, *An Old Testament Theology of the Spirit of God* (Peabody, MA: Hendrickson, 1995), 1.
[4] See Scott A. Ellington, "The Face of God as His Creating Spirit: The Interplay of Yahweh's *Panim* and *Ruach* in Psalm 104:29-30," in *Spirit Renews the Face of the Earth*, ed. Amos Yong (Eugene, OR: Pickwick, 2009), 3–16.
[5] R. Albertz and C. Westermann, "רוח," in *Theological Lexicon of the Old Testament*, ed. E. Jenni and C. Westermann, 3 vols. (Peabody, MA: Hendrickson, 1997), 2:1215.
[6] For example, Exod. 8:15, Deut. 9:10, and Ps. 8:8. Jean Leclercq asserts, "That the Holy Spirit is the finger of God is unanimously affirmed by the Fathers of the Church." "The Finger of God," *Worship* 36, no. 7 (1962): 429. Cf. Larry Perkins, "Why the 'Finger of God' in Luke 11:20," *The Expository Times* 115, no. 8 (2004): 261–2 and David T. Williams, "Why the Finger?" *The Expository Times* 115, no. 2 (2003): 45–9.

The OT texts regarding the Spirit are diverse, and they defy simple categorization. The difficulty of producing an OT pneumatology has led to a number of approaches to the task, each one categorizing the biblical material in different ways. Lloyd Neve organizes the OT texts according to their date and so produces a chronological development of the OT teaching on the Spirit.[7] Christopher Wright uses a topical approach, describing the Spirit with the modifiers "creating," "empowering," "prophetic," "anointing," and "coming."[8] John Rea and others have discussed the texts in canonical order.[9] Each of these approaches has its strengths and weaknesses. I would prefer to study the texts in their canonical order, with a concluding synthesis of results—an approach that appreciates both the diversity and unity of Scripture. However, the brief nature of this chapter precludes such a lengthy method. The chronological/developmental approach is based on too much speculative historical reconstruction; therefore, I am left with the topical approach, which seems to be the only efficient method for a brief survey like this one. In order to avoid duplicating the work of other scholars, to organize the material theologically, and to offer a study that is more consistent with my interpretative context, I have chosen to read the OT texts through a five-part scheme that highlights Yahweh as savior, sanctifier, Spirit-baptizer, healer, and soon-coming king.[10]

THE SPIRIT AND SALVATION

The Spirit and Salvation in Exodus

It should not be surprising that the Spirit would be associated with salvation, inasmuch as Yahweh is described throughout the OT as Israel's savior (e.g., Exod. 15:2, Ps. 106:21, Isa. 43:3, Jer. 14:8, Hos. 13:4). Israel's primal and paradigmatic salvation narrative is the exodus,[11] which is effected by Yahweh's direct intervention, an intervention that sometimes comes through the agency of the mysterious and powerful רוּחַ. Yahweh uses an

---

[7]Lloyd Neve, *The Spirit of God in the Old Testament* (Cleveland, TN: CPT, 2011). See also George T. Montague, *The Holy Spirit: Growth of a Biblical Tradition* (New York: Paulist, 1976), 3–126 and Dale Moody, *Spirit of the Living God* (Philadelphia, PA: Westminster, 1968), 11–32.

[8]Christopher J. H. Wright, *Knowing the Holy Spirit through the Old Testament* (Downers Grove, IL: IVP Academic, 2006). David G. Firth and Paul D. Wegner have arranged their volume to address the Spirit in relation to "Creation," "Wisdom," "Creativity," "Prophecy," "Leadership," and "Future." *Presence, Power, and Promise: The Role of the Spirit of God in the Old Testament* (Downers Grove, IL: IVP Academic, 2011). Others who use a topical arrangement include Anthony C. Thiselton, *The Holy Spirit—In Biblical Teaching, through the Centuries, and Today* (Grand Rapids, MI: Eerdmans, 2013), 3–21; Hildebrandt, *An Old Testament Theology of the Spirit of God*; French L. Arrington, *Encountering the Holy Spirit* (Cleveland, TN: Pathway, 2003), 25–52; William H. Griffith Thomas, *The Holy Spirit of God*, 5th ed. (Grand Rapids, MI: Eerdmans, 1964), 9–17; and Michael Green, *I Believe in the Holy Spirit* (Grand Rapids, MI: Eerdmans, 1975), 18–31.

[9]John Rea, *The Holy Spirit in the Bible* (Lake Mary, FL: Creation, 1990), 27–116; Trevor J. Burke and Keith Warrington, *A Biblical Theology of the Holy Spirit* (Eugene, OR: Cascade, 2014); and Stanley M. Horton, *What the Bible Says about the Holy Spirit* (Springfield, IL: Gospel, 1976), 17–78.

[10]This scheme is sometimes called the "Fivefold Gospel," and it is a feature of Wesleyan-Pentecostal soteriology. Although used originally in terms of Jesus, my theological—particularly trinitarian—commitments allow me to generalize the model to Yahweh. As such, this Christian theological approach represents one of many constructive ways of organizing the vastness of materials related to the Spirit in the Old Testament.

[11]John Goldingay writes, "Israel's deliverance from Egypt is the real beginning and essential content of the First Testament Gospel." *Old Testament Theology: Israel's Gospel* (Downers Grove, IL: InterVarsity, 2003), 288–9. Cf. Ernest W. Nicholson, *Exodus and Sinai in History and Tradition* (Richmond, VA: John Knox, 1973), 56–7; and Walter Brueggemann, *Theology of the Old Testament* (Minneapolis, MN: Fortress, 1997), 177–81.

east wind (רוּחַ) to bring the locust plague against the Egyptians and a west wind to drive them into the sea (Exod. 10:13, 19). Yahweh uses the wind (רוּחַ) to divide the waters of the Red Sea, allowing the Israelites to pass over on dry ground (14:21). A number of OT texts, when reflecting on the exodus tradition, make clear that this רוּחַ is God's Spirit. David sings, "Then the channels of the sea were seen, the foundations of the world were laid bare, at the rebuke of the LORD, at the blast of the breath of his nostrils" (2 Sam. 22:16).[12] The "breath" of the LORD refers to the Spirit/wind (רוּחַ) that divided the Red Sea in Exod. 14:21.[13]

Furthermore, after the people came up out of the Red Sea, Yahweh "put his Holy Spirit in their midst" (Isa. 63:11), apparently in the form of the pillar of cloud and the pillar of fire that were given to the Israelites to "guide them" (Neh. 9:19). In his prayer, Nehemiah recounts Yahweh's care of the exodus generation, saying, "You gave your good Spirit to instruct them. You did not withhold your manna from them, and you gave them water for their thirst" (9:20). According to Isaiah, the goal of the Spirit's leading was to bring the people out of Egypt and into the promised land: "Like cattle that go down into the valley, the Spirit of the LORD gave them rest. So you led your people, to make for yourself a glorious name" (Isa. 63:14). Haggai insists that the Spirit remained among the Israelites from the exodus even through the exile: "According to the word that I covenanted with you when you came out of Egypt, so my Spirit remains among you; do not fear" (Hag. 2:5).

Not only did the Spirit divide the Red Sea and lead the Israelites through the wilderness, but the Spirit also prepared and strengthened Moses for the task of leading God's people into salvation, to "deliver them from the power of the Egyptians" (Exod. 3:8). Yahweh appears to Moses in the burning bush and promises to "be with" Moses (3:12). We learn later that Yahweh's promised presence comes in the form of the Spirit. In Numbers 11, the Spirit that was upon Moses is shared with seventy elders, who are enabled to prophesy and to assist Moses in leading the people through the wilderness (vv. 17-25).

In light of these OT texts, Dale Moody contends that "the primacy of the exodus in Israel's faith promoted *ruach* as the metaphor for God's direct action in nature and history."[14] I would add that the work of the Spirit in the exodus is more specifically a work of salvation.

The Spirit and Salvation in the Judges

The saving work of the Spirit is also evident in the book of Judges. The Israelites violate their covenant with Yahweh by pursuing other gods, thereby provoking the wrath of Yahweh, who gives his people over to an enemy power (Judg. 2:11-19). Once in bondage to oppressive forces, they "cannot evade the superior power."[15] The Israelites, therefore, require a deliverer who is empowered by the Spirit of Yahweh and who will restore hope,

---

[12] Extended quotes of the Bible are my translations.
[13] While the trinitarian nature of the Spirit is not a concern of these texts, it has been noted that Yahweh is the only ancient Near Eastern deity who has a spirit. Other gods may control the רוּחַ (wind), but they have no רוּחַ (spirit). See Neve, *The Spirit of God in the Old Testament*, 1 and Hildebrandt, *An Old Testament Theology of the Spirit of God*, 5. Goldingay contends that the רוּחַ indicates that Yahweh is present "in part, but not in whole" (*Israel's Gospel*, 541).
[14] Moody, *Spirit of the Living God*, 13–14.
[15] Michael Welker, *God the Spirit* (Philadelphia, PA: Fortress, 1994), 52.

build unanimity, and lead them to salvation. Regarding the first of the judges, Othniel, the text states, "When the Israelites cried out to the LORD, the LORD raised up a savior for the children of Israel, who saved them: Othniel the son of Kenaz, Caleb's younger brother. The Spirit of the LORD came upon him, and he judged Israel" (3:9-10). Othniel led the people in battle, and God gave them the victory. We read that the Spirit "came upon" Othniel, and the phrase "came upon him" is suggestive of several points: First, the Spirit is the active subject of the verb, and Othniel is a recipient of the action; second, the Spirit is not a part of Othniel either physically or psychologically but comes to him from outside; third, the Spirit's action registers Yahweh's movement from perceived absence to perceived presence;[16] and fourth, the phrase "came upon" is a vivid figure of speech that signifies a theological concept in phenomenological terms. The theological concept is that the Spirit of Yahweh empowers, energizes, and equips Othniel for the task of saving the Israelites.

The Spirit is said to have come upon not only Othniel but also Gideon (6:34), Jephthah (11:29), and Samson (13:25; 14:6, 19; 15:14). In each case, the Spirit enables the judge to defeat Israel's enemy. The work of the Spirit in the book of Judges is often categorized as enablement for "leadership,"[17] and so it is, but it is leadership for the purpose of salvation (as in the case of Moses). The judges are called "saviors" (מושיע—3:9, 15; 12:3), and their work is to "save" Israel (ישע—2:16, 18; 3:9, 31; etc.). The Israelites are saved from both the physical/political bondage to Canaanite oppressors and from the spiritual bondage to Baal or Asherah, the gods of Canaan. At the end of the Samson saga, Yahweh strengthens Samson so that he might win both a physical and spiritual victory by destroying the temple of the Philistine god Dagon. Furthermore, Frederick Greenspahn has shown that salvation in Judges is based upon the theology of the exodus.[18] Israel's cry in Judges is reminiscent of the exodus (Judg. 3:9/Exod. 2:23), and the framework of Judges "perceives the period of judges as continuing the process initiated by the exodus in which Israel's suffering is dealt with by divine salvation."[19] Even after their dramatic deliverance from Egypt, the Israelites continue to be tempted and seduced by outside forces, and once they have yielded to those forces, the seducing powers control and threaten to destroy the community. Yahweh's saving power, exercised in the giving of his Spirit to the judges, rescues the community of faith from complete ruin. Yahweh, the God who had saved Israel from the servitude of Egypt, now hears their cries and saves them from the servitude of tyrannical Canaanite rulers.

The Spirit of Yahweh in the book of Judges authorizes and equips God's chosen leaders to effect salvation, even if, as in the case of Samson, it is only the inception of salvation (13:5). The judges' encounter with the Spirit "is not for its own sake—it is for the sake of

---

[16] Cf. Stanley M. Horton, "The Holy Spirit in the Book of Judges," *Paraclete* 3, no. 2 (1969): 9–14, who writes that the Spirit is not "a mere influence coming from a God who is far away" (14).
[17] For example, David G. Firth, "The Spirit and Leadership: Testimony, Empowerment and Purpose," in Firth and Wegner, *Presence, Power, and Purpose*, 259–80; Hildebrandt, *An Old Testament Theology of the Spirit of God*, 112–50; Keith Warrington, *The Message of the Holy Spirit* (Downers Grove, IL: InterVarsity, 2009), 42–8; and Rea, *The Holy Spirit in the Bible*, 43–70.
[18] Frederick E. Greenspahn, "The Theology of the Framework of Judges," *Vetus Testamentum* 36 (1986): 385–96.
[19] Greenspahn, "Framework of Judges," 395. Goldingay writes that the Spirit comes on a leader and "he or she is inspired to undertake extraordinary ventures for the sake of the people's freedom and well-being" (*Israel's Gospel*, 541).

the community."²⁰ Clearly, the Spirit proceeds from Yahweh, represents the interests of Yahweh, and serves to highlight the role of Yahweh as savior.²¹

The Spirit and Salvation in the Prophets

The prophetic oracles of salvation often associate the Spirit with future salvific blessings. For example, the prophet Isaiah declares, "The Spirit of the LORD God is upon me, because the LORD has anointed me to bring good news to the afflicted; he has sent me to bind up the brokenhearted, to proclaim liberty to the captives, and the opening of the prison to those who are bound" (61:1). In this important text, the Spirit empowers the LORD's messenger to bring salvation through the proclamation of good news, freedom, and release from bondage.

Salvation is also in view in Zechariah's prophetic word to post-exilic Israel. The LORD promises to "save" Jerusalem, to "destroy all the nations that come against Jerusalem," and to "pour out on the house of David and on the inhabitants of Jerusalem the Spirit of grace and of mercy" (12:7-10). Then, a "fountain will be opened" to cleanse Israel from "sin and uncleanness" (13:1). For Zechariah, the רוּחַ is the soteriological Spirit of grace (חֵן) and mercy (תַּחֲנוּן), which signals God's renewed favor toward his people.

However, in the OT prophets, salvation is paired with judgment as surely as God's compassion is paired with his justice (Exod. 34:6-7). Therefore, the Spirit of salvation is also the Spirit of judgment. Through the Spirit, God will "destroy" Israel's enemies (Zech. 12:9); through the Spirit, Israel is judged and then saved (Isa. 40:7-10);²² and through the Spirit, the coming Messiah will "slay the wicked" (11:4).

A third important OT text links the Spirit to God's eschatological plan of salvation. Joel proclaims

> And it will come about after this, that I will pour out my Spirit on all flesh; and your sons and daughters will prophesy, your old men will dream dreams, your young men will see visions, and even on the male and female servants I will pour out my Spirit in those days.... And it will come about that whoever calls on the name of the LORD will be saved. (Joel 2:28-32)

Pentecostals have observed the importance of Joel's prophecy in relation to the democratization of the Spirit—and rightly so. The Spirit will be poured out even on the lowly slaves. However, we should not overlook the fact that this text is in the midst of an oracle that proclaims destruction for Israel's enemies and salvation for the remnant who escape the exile (3:1-19). The oracle concludes with a final word of salvation: "Judah shall abide forever, and Jerusalem from generation to generation, and I will forgive their bloodguilt, whom I had not forgiven" (3:20-21).²³ The outpouring of the Spirit is accompanied by restoration, deliverance from enemies, and forgiveness of sin.

---

²⁰Brueggemann, *Theology of the Old Testament*, 571. Cf. Welker, *God the Spirit*, who insists, "in no instance is the descent of the Spirit merely a private affair" (75); Alphonsus Benson, "The Spirit of God in the Didactic Books of the Old Testament" (STD Diss., Catholic University of America, 1949), 72.

²¹For a more complete study of the Spirit in the book of Judges, see Lee Roy Martin, "Power to Save!? The Role of the Spirit of the Lord in the Book of Judges," *Journal of Pentecostal Theology* 16, no. 2 (2008): 21–50.

²²Cf. John Goldingay, "The Breath of Yahweh Scorching, Confounding, Anointing: The Message of Isaiah 40–42," *Journal of Pentecostal Theology* 11 (1997): 3–34.

²³Regarding this translation of נקה in v. 21, see for example Hans Walter Wolff, *Joel and Amos*, Hermeneia (Philadelphia, PA: Fortress, 1977), 84.

THE SPIRIT AND SANCTIFICATION

It has been asserted almost universally that the work of the Spirit in the OT is primarily a work of power and does not include sanctification or transformation of character.[24] While I would agree that an inward transforming work of the Spirit is not the main concern of most OT texts, several texts point in that direction. A few texts about the Spirit even make sanctification the primary concern. First of all, the naming of the Spirit as the "Holy Spirit" indicates that holiness is an attribute of the Spirit (Ps. 51:11; Isa. 63:10-11). Inasmuch as holiness is essential to God and to the Spirit of God, the sanctification of God's people is a crucial work of the Spirit. The Spirit originates from outside the OT characters but produces effects within them.[25] For example, the spirit is "upon" Moses, but his journey of faith bears the marks of genuine spiritual formation under the continuing influence of the Holy Spirit. The narratives of Joseph and Joshua—both of whom were endowed with the Spirit—record a similar depth of spiritual growth. Gideon also experiences the transformative effect of the coming of the Spirit. J. Paul Tanner argues that the Gideon narrative is structured to highlight Gideon's fear and to show the change that transpired in Gideon as God crafted the circumstances in such a way that Gideon moves from fear to faith.[26]

Moreover, we must beware of constructing a purity and power dichotomy that distorts the message of the Old Testament. The perspective on sin and idolatry in the OT is more communal than what we find in contemporary views of soteriology. The sanctifying work of the Spirit in the life of the individual is not a dominant concern of the OT; rather, the sanctification of the community in covenant takes precedence over the sanctification of the individual. The holiness of the community is the dominant theme of the book of Leviticus, and Yahweh declares to the Israelites, "And you shall keep my statutes and practice them; I am the LORD who sanctifies you" (Lev. 20:8). The pronoun "you" is plural, pointing to the entire community of faith.

Yahweh first saved Israel from Egyptian bondage and then he met with them at Mt. Sinai to make a covenant with them, through which Israel was sanctified as Yahweh's own special people. The covenant included the commandments written on two stone tablets, "inscribed with the finger of God" (Exod. 31:18, Deut. 9:10). As noted above, the "finger of God" is a metaphor that most likely stands for the Spirit. Furthermore, as a prophet, Moses was given the task of teaching his people to serve the LORD in faithfulness and holiness, a task that was accomplished through the ministry of the Spirit (cf. Num. 11:17).

This sanctification of the community is ultimately dependent upon its full reception of the Spirit, a process that is described by the prophet Ezekiel. Ezekiel points out that Judah had "defiled" the land by their "uncleanness" (36:17), and they had "polluted" the holy name of Yahweh (36:20). Uncleanness and pollution are the opposite of holiness,

---

[24] Gordon D. Fee, *God's Empowering Presence* (Peabody, MA: Hendrickson, 1994), 8. In contrast to Fee, see Max Turner, *The Holy Spirit and Spiritual Gifts*, rev. ed. (Peabody, MA: Hendrickson, 1998), 18.

[25] For a discussion of the inward work of the Spirit in the OT, see Gary Fredericks, "Rethinking the Role of the Holy Spirit in the Lives of Old Testament Believers," *Trinity Journal* 9, no. 1 (1988): 81–104; and E. John Hamlin, *At Risk in the Promised Land: A Commentary on the Book of Judges* (Grand Rapids, MI: Eerdmans, 1990), 95.

[26] J. Paul Tanner, "The Gideon Narrative as the Focal Point of Judges," *Bibliotheca Sacra* 149 (1992): 146–61.

but Yahweh is determined to "sanctify" his name again (36:23), and he will do so through the agency of his Spirit.[27] The LORD explains:

> I will give you a new heart and put a new spirit within you; I will take the heart of stone out of your flesh and give you a heart of flesh. I will put my Spirit within you and cause you to walk in my statutes, and you will observe my ordinances and do them. . . . I will save you from all your uncleanness . . . Then you will remember your evil ways and your deeds that were not good; and you will loathe yourselves in your own sight, for your iniquities and your abominations. (Ezek. 36:26-31)

The Spirit of Yahweh will transform God's people, giving them a "new heart" and "new spirit." This transformation has implications for two elements of sanctification. The Spirit will enable them to live in positive obedience, to "walk" in God's statutes, to "keep" his ordinances, and to "do" them. The Spirit will also deliver them from their previous bondage to "uncleanness," which is another term for their habitual idolatry. Therefore, the Spirit will free the people of God from sin and unto righteousness in the same way that their initial salvation had freed them from Pharaoh to serve Yahweh.

In addition to the profound eschatological promise of sanctification found in Ezekiel, two other OT texts point to the ongoing work of the Spirit in the sanctifying of God's people. First, we read in the book of Isaiah, "But they rebelled and grieved his Holy Spirit; therefore, he turned to be their enemy, and he himself fought against them" (63:10). It appears from this text that the Holy Spirit acts as a guide to God's people, perhaps working through what we call the conscience. If rebellion is tantamount to resisting the Holy Spirit, as this text seems to say, then the Spirit must be a force for holiness and faithfulness.

The second text that demonstrates the Spirit's ongoing work in the life of the OT believer is David's prayer in Psalm 51: "Create in me a clean heart, O God, and put a new and right spirit within me. Cast me not away from your presence, and take not your Holy Spirit from me" (v. 10). David confesses his sin (vv. 1-5) and pleads for forgiveness, cleansing, and a renewal of joy. The presence of sin in his life, however, causes David to fear the loss of the Holy Spirit, apparently because he views the Spirit's presence as incompatible with the presence of sin. At the initial anointing of David, the Spirit had come upon him "from that day forward" (1 Sam. 16:13), that is, as a permanent endowment. However, in light of the Spirit's departure from King Saul (1 Sam. 16:14, 18:12), it appears that the Spirit can be lost. Commenting on David's prayer, Leonard Maré writes, "He acknowledges that only the Spirit of God can effect the inner transformation, the new heart, the steadfast spirit that is needed to live a life dedicated to Yahweh."[28] Erich Zenger adds, "And when God causes the divine '*holy spirit*' (v. 13b) to work in him, he can live a 'holy' life: that is, such an intensive community of life with the holy God that sin becomes impossible."[29]

THE SPIRIT AND CHARISMATIC GIFTS

The charismatic work of the Spirit corresponds broadly to the NT concept of Spirit baptism and Spirit fullness, and a large number of OT texts fit into this category—so

---

[27]Horn, "Holy Spirit," 263.
[28]L. P. Maré, "Psalm 51: 'Take Not Your Spirit Away from Me,'" *Acta Theologica* 28, no. 1 (2008): 99.
[29]Erich Zenger, "Psalm 51," in *Psalms 2: A Commentary on Psalms 51–100*, ed. Erich Zenger and Frank Lother Hossfeld, Hermeneia (Minneapolis, MN: Fortress, 2005), 21 (emphasis original).

many in fact, that we cannot discuss all of them in this brief foray into OT pneumatology. Charismatic gifts include any kind of divine enablement that either adds to a person's abilities or grants them new abilities. Most of the Spirit's endowments in the OT can be located under the headings of wisdom and prophecy.[30]

The Gift of Wisdom

Joseph is the first person in the OT who is said to have the Spirit of God. Through the Spirit, Joseph experienced his own dreams along with their interpretations, and he was able to interpret the dreams of his fellow prisoners and the Egyptian Pharaoh. In the ancient Near East, the ability to interpret dreams was considered a characteristic of the wise; therefore, the Pharaoh describes Joseph as "discerning and wise" (Gen. 41:39). Furthermore, the source of Joseph's wisdom is declared to be the "Spirit of God" (41:38). Joseph's wisdom was confirmed when he quickly devised a plan to deal with the famine that Pharaoh had foreseen in his dreams.

Like Joseph, Daniel found himself in the court of a foreign ruler, and he was exalted because of his Spirit-inspired ability to interpret dreams. We read that the "Spirit of the Holy God" was in him, and he had "light and understanding and wisdom, like the wisdom of the gods" (Dan. 5:11). Therefore, Daniel's wisdom—distinguished by his ability to interpret dreams—was attributed to the Spirit.

In the OT, wisdom is also known as skill and creativity. It is the Spirit who enables artisans to construct priestly garments (Exod. 28:3) and the tabernacle (Exod. 31:3, 35:31, 36:1-2). Bezalel was filled

> with the Spirit of God, in wisdom, in understanding and in knowledge and in all craftsmanship; to make designs for working in gold and in silver and in bronze, and in the cutting of stones for settings, and in the carving of wood, so as to perform in every inventive work . . . and of a designer and of an embroiderer, in blue and in purple and in scarlet, and in fine linen, and of a weaver, as performers of every work and makers of designs. (Exod. 35:30-35)

The gift of wisdom is also given to leaders and rulers. Near the end of the wilderness wanderings, the LORD directs Moses to prepare for a transition in leadership. He says to Moses, "Take Joshua and the son of Nun with you, a man in whom is the Spirit, and lay your hand on him" (Num. 27:18). The result of Joshua's inauguration was that Joshua "was filled with the spirit of wisdom, for Moses had laid his hands on him" (Deut. 34:9). Wisdom was considered an important characteristic of anyone who served as a leader in Israel (Deut. 1:13-15, 16:18-19; Prov. 20:26).

The role of the Spirit in the lives of the judges and kings is not altogether clear. Apparently, the Spirit was given to them first as a sign, authorization, or confirmation of their divine appointment that caused the people to follow their leadership. Second, the Spirit imparted courage and decisiveness (especially in regard to military affairs). Third, the Spirit gave them the wisdom that was needed to rule. In the case of the judges, the text emphasizes their role as saviors, but it also indicates that the judges ruled for many years in peace (Judg. 3:11, 30; 5:31; 8:28; 12:7; 16:31) during which time they would serve the community and settle disputes (4:5).

---

[30] Similarly, the NT gifts of the Spirit are mostly associated with wisdom or speech.

The first and second of the kings (Saul and David) were charismatic leaders who had the Spirit upon them. Both received the Spirit at their inauguration when they were anointed by the prophet Samuel. They were authorized and empowered by the Spirit, and at times they demonstrated great wisdom (although the text never states that Saul or David possessed wisdom). The stories of judges, Saul, and David demonstrate that the Spirit enhances the human volition but does not displace it. Gideon, Jephthah, Samson, Saul, and David committed grave errors and sins while the Spirit was upon them.

In the case of King Solomon, the text repeatedly emphasizes his great wisdom, but that wisdom is never attributed directly to the Spirit. In a dream, the LORD offers to give Solomon any request, and Solomon asks, "give to your servant an understanding heart to judge your people, that I may discern between good and evil." The LORD replies, "Because you have asked . . . for yourself understanding to discern justice, behold, I have done according to your words; see, I have given you a wise and discerning heart" (2 Kgs 3:9-12). Although the Spirit is not mentioned, the terminology of "gift" suggests that the wisdom given to Solomon was, in fact, a bestowal of the Spirit.

The final ruler that I will mention here is Zerubbabel, who was governor of Judah after the exile. He had undertaken the task of rebuilding the temple, but the work had stalled soon after the foundation was laid (Ezra 5:2, Hag. 2:2-13). The prophet Zechariah received a vision that included a divine message for Zerubbabel: "This is the word of the LORD to Zerubbabel: Not by might, not by power, but by my Spirit, says the LORD of hosts. . . . The hands of Zerubbabel have laid the foundation of this temple; his hands shall also finish it" (Zech. 4:6-9). The exact nature of the Spirit's gift is not stated, but given the nature of the task, we may infer that it included determination, wisdom, and faith.

The Spirit of Prophecy

While it could be said that the prophets often displayed wisdom, the OT characterizes the prophets as recipients of divine revelation in the form of dreams, visions, and "the word of the LORD." The prophet Zechariah declares that the Spirit is the source of prophetic revelation. He writes in regard to pre-exilic times, "They made their hearts hard as stone lest they should hear the law and the words which the LORD of hosts had sent by his Spirit through the former prophets" (Zech. 7:12). Yahweh's Spirit is upon the prophet Moses and is given to seventy elders who prophesy and who then serve as assistants to Moses (Num. 11:17-29). The Spirit of God "came upon" the non-Israelite soothsayer Balaam and inspired him to prophesy a blessing upon the Israelites (24:2-9). The works of Elijah and Elisha are attributed to the influence of the Spirit (1 Kgs 18:12; 2 Kgs 2:9, 15-16). Several other OT prophets are mentioned who prophesied when the Spirit came upon them; these include Amasai (1 Chron. 12:18), Jahaziel (2 Chron. 20:14), and Zechariah (2 Chron. 24:20). The prophet Micah seems to attribute his prophetic abilities to the Spirit when he says, "But as for me, I am filled with power, with the Spirit of the LORD, and with justice and might, to declare to Jacob his transgression and to Israel his sin" (Mic. 3:8). The prophet Isaiah declares that he is sent by Yahweh and by Yahweh's "Spirit" (Isa. 48:16); moreover, he views the Spirit as the authorizing power for salvific proclamation, as we have already noted in Isa. 61:1. More than any other prophet, Ezekiel might be understood as the prophet of the Spirit. From his call narrative in the first chapter to his vision of the eschatological temple in Ezek. 43, the Spirit is active in Ezekiel's life. The Spirit "entered" him (2:2), "lifted him up" (3:14), and "fell upon him"

(11:5). Altogether, רוח is mentioned fifty-two times in the book of Ezekiel. Finally, Joel expands the prophetic ministry to include the entire people of God in a passage already cited, Joel 2:28-29. Joel explains that every category of society will receive the Spirit, and by receiving the Spirit, they will become prophets.[31]

THE SPIRIT OF HEALING

Yahweh declares himself to be Israel's healer (Exod. 15:26), and in a number of OT texts the Spirit is involved in the process of healing.[32] The Spirit was upon Moses, and he prayed effectively for Miriam's healing (Num. 12:13). The Spirit was upon Elijah and Elisha, and their narratives include a variety of healings and other miracles. However, the texts that most clearly connect the Spirit to healing occur in Isaiah and Ezekiel, who envision the Spirit as healing at the eschaton and restoring water that is poured out on the dry desert land. Isaiah anticipates the following: "Until the Spirit is poured out upon us from on high, and the wilderness becomes a fertile field, and the fertile field is considered as a forest" (32:15); and Yahweh promises, "For I will pour out water on the thirsty and streams on the dry ground; I will pour out my Spirit on your offspring and my blessing on your descendants; and they will spring up among the grass like poplars by streams of water" (44:3-4). The result of the Spirit's outpouring is symbolized by the transformation of the wilderness into a fertile field and the springing up of lush grass. Death is transformed into life.

Similarly, Ezekiel sees a river of living water flowing out of the restored temple in Jerusalem. The healing river grows deeper and wider as it flows farther from the temple. Ezekiel describes "the miraculous effect of this river which emerges from the sanctuary and grows into a mighty force"[33] this way: "And it shall be that every living thing that moves, wherever the rivers go, will live. There will be a very great multitude of fish, because these waters go there; for they will be healed, and everything will live wherever the river goes" (47:9). Cooper exclaims, "Everything in Ezekiel's description presents a picture of the life-giving, healing, and life-sustaining properties of the water from the sanctuary."[34] Although the word "Spirit" is not found in the text, interpreters agree that the river represents the life-giving presence of God that goes forth into the world.[35] I would argue that the "presence of God in the world" would be expressed theologically as the "Spirit of God in the world." The similarities to Isa. 32:15 and 44:3, mentioned earlier, also suggest that the water is a metaphor for the Spirit. Furthermore, in Ezekiel the power of life resides in the Spirit (37:6, 9-10, 14).[36] Walther Zimmerli observes,

---

[31] For the expansion of this idea into the NT, see Roger Stronstad, *The Prophethood of All Believers* (Cleveland, TN: CPT, 2010).

[32] Healing is one of the NT charismata (1 Cor. 12:9); therefore, it could have been included in the section on charismatic gifts. Obviously, some overlap of categories is unavoidable. Healing also overlaps with prophetic ministry, especially in regard to Elijah, Elisha, and Isaiah.

[33] Walther Zimmerli, Paul D. Hanson, and Leonard Jay Greenspoon, *Ezekiel 2: A Commentary on the Book of the Prophet Ezekiel, Chapters 25–48*, Hermeneia (Philadelphia, PA: Fortress, 1983), 513.

[34] Lamar Eugene Cooper, *Ezekiel*, NAC (Nashville, TN: Broadman & Holman, 1994), 413.

[35] John B. Taylor, *Ezekiel: An Introduction and Commentary*, TOTC (Downers Grove, IL: InterVarsity, 1969), 270; Joseph Blenkinsopp, *Ezekiel*, Int (Louisville, KY: John Knox, 1990), 231–2; Zimmerli, Hanson, and Greenspoon, *Ezekiel 2*, 511; Steven Shawn Tuell, *Ezekiel*, UBC (Grand Rapids, MI: Baker, 2012), 330.

[36] If resurrection is a type of healing, then Ezek. 37:1-14 could also be included in this section as a healing text.

"What he is proclaiming is not far removed from that message of new life which was expressed in 37:1-14."[37] Also, water as a symbol of the Spirit is utilized later in the Fourth Gospel when Jesus says, "He who believes in me let him drink, as the Scripture has said, out of his heart will flow rivers of living water. But this he spoke concerning the Spirit" (Jn 7:38-39).

Finally, the role of the Spirit in healing is attested by Isa. 61:1, a text referenced earlier. The Hebrew word in this passage לַחֲבֹשׁ, "to bind up," suggests to Gary Smith "the purpose of restoration to physical and or spiritual health."[38] Calvin agrees that it "means nothing else than 'healing'" (cf. Ps. 147:3).[39] The "brokenhearted" are those who are "demoralized, crushed in mind and spirit."[40] Therefore, the anointing with the Spirit grants the recipient power to preach and heal.

THE SPIRIT AND ESCHATOLOGY

The Spirit and the Messiah

The OT prophets speak of God's coming kingdom in terms of a descendant of David who will reign on the throne of Israel. Based partly upon Isa. 61:1, this Davidic king came to be known as the Messiah ("anointed one"), and the character of his eschatological rule is known in large part from the prophecies of Isaiah.

> Then a shoot will spring from the stump of Jesse, and a branch from his roots will bear fruit. And the Spirit of the LORD will rest on him, the Spirit of wisdom and understanding, the Spirit of counsel and strength, the Spirit of knowledge and the fear of the LORD. And he will . . . decide with fairness for the afflicted of the earth; and he will strike the earth with the rod of his mouth, and with the breath (רוּחַ) of his lips he will kill the wicked. (Isa. 11:1-5; cf. Isa. 42:1)

Isaiah insists that the coming kingdom will be ruled by a son of David, "a shoot . . . from the stump of Jesse."[41] The attributes of the Messiah and the character of his reign will be determined by the "seven-fold Spirit" that rests upon him. That the Spirit "rests" upon him suggests permanence. The Spirit is the Spirit of Yahweh, Israel's covenant God. "Wisdom" is the most fundamental quality necessary for a just and effective ruler, for the "ideal king."[42] "Understanding" is the ability to discern and judge righteously—it "refers to knowledge which is superior to the mere gathering of data."[43] "Counsel" is "the ability to devise a right course of action,"[44] and "strength" is the power to carry through with that course of action. "Knowledge" and "fear of Yahweh" speak of "experiential knowledge of God that will be characterized by a fear of God. These two factors,

---

[37]Zimmerli, Hanson, and Greenspoon, *Ezekiel 2*, 516.
[38]Gary V. Smith, *Isaiah 40–66*, NAC (Nashville: Broadman & Holman, 2009), 635.
[39]John Calvin, *Commentary on the Book of the Prophet Isaiah*, 4 vols. (Bellingham, WA: Logos Bible Software, 2010), 4:305.
[40]John Goldingay, *Isaiah*, UBC (Grand Rapids, MI: Baker, 2012), 347.
[41]Cf. Isa. 9:7, 22:22, 55:3; Jer. 23:5, 30:9, 33:15-22; Ezek. 34:23-24, 37:24-28; Hos. 3:5; Amos 9:11.
[42]Hans Wildberger, *Isaiah 1–12*, CC (Minneapolis, MN: Fortress, 1991), 471.
[43]L. Goldberg, "בִּין," in *Theological Wordbook of the Old Testament*, ed. R. L. Harris, G. L. Archer, Jr., and B. K. Waltke, 2 vols. (Chicago: Moody, 1999), 1:103.
[44]J. Alec Motyer, *Isaiah: An Introduction and Commentary*, TOTC (Downers Grove, IL: InterVarsity, 1999), 117.

knowledge and fear, point to an intimate relationship between this rule and God."[45] The symbolism of the number seven expresses the perfect anointing of the Messiah. They are personal qualities, not the characteristics of an impersonal force, and they show powers of thought and volition. These show that it is in the power of the Holy Spirit that the Messiah fulfills the glorious reign that is described in the rest of Isaiah 11.

The Spirit and the People of God

The OT portrayal of God's kinship contains elements from the past, present, and future. Much of what the OT has to say about the Spirit points forward rather than backward. The future reign of God is the same in character as his reign in the past and present, but it is broader in scope and intensity. That is, just as the Spirit was present in the nation of Israel, the Spirit will be present universally. Just as the Spirit rested upon a few chosen individuals, the Spirit will be poured out "upon all flesh" (Joel 2:28). Isaiah foresees a day when the Spirit will be given to "the whole people"[46] and will remain permanently with the people of God: "And as for me, this is my covenant with them, says the LORD: my Spirit which is upon you, and my words which I have put in your mouth, shall not depart out of your mouth, or out of the mouth of your children, or out of the mouth of your children's children, says the LORD, from this time forth and for evermore" (59:21). Ezekiel recognizes that the giving of the Spirit will guarantee immediate access to the presence of God;[47] the LORD says, "And I will not hide my face from them any longer, for I shall have poured out my Spirit on the house of Israel, declares the LORD God" (Ezek. 39:28-29).

THE SPIRIT OF LIFE

Jürgen Moltmann is not far from the truth when he observes that the Spirit's nature and attributes may be summarized in the phrase "the Spirit of life."[48] The Nicene Creed affirms that the Holy Spirit is "the Giver of life" (τὸ ζῳοποιόν), and the OT supports that affirmation. This examination of the Spirit in the OT through the lens of soteriology has made clear that the Spirit gives, affirms, enriches, and restores life. However, we have yet to explore a number of texts that speak directly to the Spirit as the Giver of Life.

Whatever lives has spirit; whatever is dead does not have spirit, and the life-giving spirit is derived from God. The Holy Spirit moved on the face of the waters in the process of creation: "And the earth was formless and void; and darkness was on the face of the deep. And the Spirit of God was moving over the surface of the waters" (Gen. 1:2). The Spirit acts not just upon humans but upon the whole creation. The Spirit gives life to humanity at the time of creation: "the LORD God formed the human from the dust of the earth and breathed into his nostrils the breath of life, and the human became a living soul" (Gen. 2:7; cf. Gen. 7:22, Job 33:4). Karl Barth writes, "It is His, the Lord's breath, by which the creature is created and without which it would inevitably vanish away at once."[49] Thus, it is the Spirit that continues to give life to humanity: "Thus says God, the

---

[45] Gary V. Smith, *Isaiah 1–39*, NAC (Nashville, TN: Broadman and Holman, 2007), 272.
[46] Horn, "Holy Spirit," 263.
[47] Ibid.
[48] Jürgen Moltmann, *The Spirit of Life* (Minneapolis, MN: Fortress, 1992).
[49] *CD*, I/1:472.

Lord, who created the heavens and stretched them out, who spread forth the earth and what comes from it, who gives breath to the people upon it and spirit to those who walk in it" (Isa. 42:5). This is the continuing work of the Holy Spirit. Every human life is the product of the work of the divine Spirit; therefore, every life is sacred to God as the work of the Holy Spirit. Psalm 104:28-30 associates the creating spirit with the presence of God and accents even more sharply the complete dependence of all creatures upon the Spirit: "When you hide your face, they are dismayed; when you take away their breath, they die and return to dust. When you send forth your Spirit, they are created, and you renew the face of the ground."[50]

Because of human corruption, the LORD decided to shorten the human lifespan; and because the removal of the Spirit causes life to cease, the shortening of life is accomplished by removing the Spirit. "Then the LORD said, My Spirit will not remain in humans forever, for they are flesh, but their days shall be a hundred and twenty years" (Gen. 6:3). The removal of the Spirit continues to be the cause of death for all living things. "If he should gather to himself his Spirit and his breath, all flesh would perish together, and humans would return to dust" (Job 34:14-15; cf. Job 27:3).

The importance of the Spirit for the life of God's people is highlighted by the prophet Ezekiel. The exiled Israelites had lamented, "Our bones are withered and our hope has vanished" (37:11); therefore, the Spirit brought Ezekiel to a valley full of dried bones. Then the LORD instructed Ezekiel, saying, "Prophesy to the breath (רוּחַ), prophesy, son of man, and say to the breath, Thus says the LORD God, Come from the four winds (רוּחוֹת), O breath, and breathe on these slain, that they come to life" (37:9). When Ezekiel obeyed God's command, "the breath came into them, and they came to life, and stood on their feet, an exceedingly great army" (37:10). The message to Israel was that Yahweh would bring them out of the exile and restore life to them. The LORD explains, "And I will put my Spirit within you, and you will come to life, and I will place you on your own land. Then you will know that I, the LORD, have spoken and done it, declares the LORD" (37:14).

"To the extent that Ezek now describes the reversal of the distress with unusual realism as the revival of the dry bones, he transfers *rûaḥ* to a new plane of meaning: In analogy to the creation of humanity, the returning life-force becomes the breath of life that blows on the dead (*nph* as in Gen. 2:7) and enlivens them (*ḥyh* pi. vv. 5ff., 9ff., 14)."[51]

To Ezekiel, the Spirit is indeed the Spirit of life.

CONCLUSION

In the OT, the Spirit registers divine mystery and transcendence, but the Spirit also signifies divine immanence as an expression of God's power. The Spirit creates, sustains, saves, heals, restores, empowers, guides, fills, completes, and perfects. Essentially, the Spirit accomplishes the works of God in all creation, in the covenant community, and in the individual believer. While contemporary popular theology gives priority to the work of the Spirit in the individual, the OT shows that even when the Spirit is working within an individual, the Spirit's goal is to benefit the covenant community and the world.

---

[50] On Ps. 104:29-30, see Ellington, "The Face of God as His Creating Spirit," 3–16.
[51] Albertz and Westermann, "רוח," 1209.

FOR FURTHER READING

Firth, David G., and Paul D. Wegner. *Presence, Power, and Promise: The Role of the Spirit of God in the Old Testament*. Downers Grove, IL: IVP Academic, 2011.

Green, Michael. *I Believe in the Holy Spirit*. Grand Rapids, MI: Eerdmans, 1975.

Hildebrandt, Wilf. *An Old Testament Theology of the Spirit of God*. Peabody, MA: Hendrickson, 1995.

Horton, Michael. *Rediscovering the Holy Spirit: God's Perfecting Presence in Creation, Redemption, and Everyday Life*. Grand Rapids, MI: Zondervan, 2017.

Horton, Stanley M. *What the Bible Says about the Holy Spirit*. Springfield, IL: Gospel, 1976.

Montague, George T. *The Holy Spirit: Growth of a Biblical Tradition*. New York: Paulist, 1976.

Moody, Dale. *Spirit of the Living God: The Biblical Concepts Interpreted in Context*. Philadelphia, PA: Westminster, 1968.

Neve, Lloyd R. *The Spirit of God in the Old Testament*. Edited by John Christopher Thomas and Lee Roy Martin. Cleveland, TN: CPT, 2011.

Rea, John. *The Holy Spirit in the Bible: All the Major Passages about the Spirit, A Commentary*. Lake Mary, FL: Creation, 1990.

Thiselton, Anthony C. *The Holy Spirit—In Biblical Teaching, through the Centuries, and Today*. Grand Rapids, MI: Eerdmans, 2013.

Wright, Christopher J. H. *Knowing the Holy Spirit through the Old Testament*. Downers Grove, IL: IVP Academic, 2006.

CHAPTER NINE

The Spirit and Learning in the Hebrew Scriptures

JOHN R. (JACK) LEVISON

Leaping from the pages of the Hebrew scriptures comes Saul, Israel's first king—not so much leaping as flailing, writhing in ecstasy. The image is unforgettable: approached by a band of prophets, who are fortified with musical instruments rather than weapons of war, Saul succumbs to their sphere of influence, falls to the ground, and prophesies. As Samuel had predicted, Saul is transformed into another sort of person during this experience, when the spirit comes upon him (1 Sam. 10:1-13). No longer the ass-led farmer, Saul is born to be king.

Then, of course, there is the indomitable, if fickle, Samson. When the spirit rushes upon him, Samson tears a lion apart (Judg. 14:6) or kills thirty men in hot anger (14:16) or slays a thousand with the blood-drenched jawbone of an ass (15:13). No flailing here—but plenty of rope-melting (knee-melting too, for the women of Philistia apparently), muscle, spontaneous force, and superhuman power.

Time and again, it seems, the Hebrew scriptures are rife with ecstasy, peppered by spontaneity and dripping in dumbfoundedness, at least when the spirit shows up. But this is a false impression, fueled perhaps by the cinematic nature of larger-than-life figures such as Saul and Samson. In fact, of the nearly 400 references to *rûaḥ* in the Jewish scriptures, only a smattering thrum with untrammeled impulse. More pervasive is an association of the spirit with the cultivation of learning. It is this neglected dimension of the spirit in the Hebrew scriptures that this essay explores.

In the Hebrew scriptures, the spirit enters the domain of history in a variety of ways. It comes or rushes upon, rests upon, is distributed upon, is poured out over, cleanses, fills, and stands. These are many and manifold modes of the spirit's presence, which, often enough, have little to do with one another except for the recurrence of the word *rûaḥ*—Spirit, spirit, wind, or breath.[1] By studying three modes of the presence of *rûaḥ*—coming upon, resting upon, and filling—it is possible to gather how the spirit is joined at the hip to a life of learning. The coherence of this commitment is particularly evident in light of

---

[1] Throughout this study, I do not capitalize the word "spirit" so as not to drive a wedge between the divine and human spirits. My rationale for this decision is explained in *Filled with the Spirit* (Grand Rapids, MI: Eerdmans, 2009), 3–13 and "Filled with the Spirit: A Conversation with Pentecostal and Charismatic Scholars," *Journal of Pentecostal Theology* 20 (2012): 220–2.

how different these modes of the spirit's presence are from one another. Three modes, one association: whether rushing, resting, or filling, the spirit is tethered to learning.

THE SPIRIT COMING UPON

Among the oldest memories of the spirit in the Jewish Bible are those of the judges, upon whom the spirit came in power so that they could liberate Israel.[2] The fleeting presence of the spirit on Israel's judges occurs a half dozen times. The paradigm for their liberation is depicted in a brief sketch of the first judge.

> But when the Israelites cried out to the LORD, the LORD raised up a deliverer for the Israelites, who delivered them, Othniel son of Kenaz, Caleb's younger brother. The spirit of the LORD came upon him, and he judged Israel; he went out to war, and the LORD gave King Cushan-rishathaim of Aram into his hand; and his hand prevailed over Cushan-rishathaim. So the land had rest forty years. Then Othniel son of Kenaz died. The Israelites again did what was evil in the sight of the LORD; and the LORD strengthened King Eglon of Moab against Israel, because they had done what was evil in the sight of the LORD." (Judg. 3:9-12)[3]

This sketch sets the pattern for many of the judges to come: Israel cries out; a deliverer-judge arises; the spirit comes upon the deliverer-judge; the judge delivers Israel; Israel has peace; Israel sins and is again oppressed, which begins the cycle afresh. Slight variations characterize this pattern. The spirit *is upon* Othniel and Jephthah in Judg. 3:10 and 11:29. The spirit *clothes* Gideon (6:34). The spirit *rushes upon* Samson (14:6, 19; 15:14).

Michael Welker attempts to avoid the impression that the spirit inspires violence in the book of Judges. He discerns instead an exclusive association of the spirit with solidarity of the oppressed—certainly an element of inspiration in the book of Judges. Still, the spirit is tied perilously close to war.[4] Further, there is a decidedly overwhelming element in the spirit's onslaught.

This element comes to the fore in the story of Saul, not only in his experience with the prophets, but also after he became king, when he operated with the same power that the spirit had unleashed in the judges before him. When he was told of a plot that would lead to the gouging out of Israel's eyes,

> the spirit of God came upon Saul in power when he heard these words, and his anger was greatly kindled. He took a yoke of oxen, and cut them in pieces and sent them throughout all the territory of Israel by messengers, saying, "Whoever does not come out after Saul and Samuel, so shall it be done to his oxen!" Then the dread of the LORD fell upon the people, and they came out as one. (1 Sam. 11:6-7)

---

[2] The first person on whom the spirit comes is not Israelite at all but Mesopotamian seer Balaam (Num. 24:1-3).
[3] As with other pieces in this volume, English translations are from the New Revised Standard Version. At times, however, I modify this translation; at others, I offer my own.
[4] Michael Welker writes, "Even the early experiences of God's Spirit are *experiences of how a new beginning is made toward restoring the community of God's people. They are experiences of the forgiveness of sins, of the raising up of the 'crushed and oppressed,' and of the renewal of the forces of life*." *God the Spirit* (Minneapolis, MN: Fortress, 1994), 65 (emphases original).

Empowered by the spirit, Saul issued an ultimatum, to which 370,000 troops responded by gathering for battle.

The image of the spirit coming as an onslaught of power, though vivid and memorable, lay dormant until the Persian era, when it emerged, surprisingly enough, in books whose very names testify to an eye for detail and a penchant for order. The books of 1–2 Chronicles resurrect the image of the spirit's coming or rushing—but with a twist. In four references to the spirit, a new pattern emerges vis-à-vis the spirit, in which there is a taut connection between the spirit and learning.

The first of these concerns "Amasai, chief of the Thirty," a group of legendary warriors (1 Chron. 12:18 [Hebrew 12:19]). When the spirit clothed[5] Amasai, as it had Gideon, Amasai did not prepare for battle, as Gideon had in Judges. Instead, the warrior-turned-poet remarked:

We are yours, O David;
and with you, O son of Jesse!
Peace, peace to you,
and peace to the one who helps you!
For your God is the one who helps you.

Success was immediate: "David received them, and made them officers of his troops" (1 Chron. 12:16-18 [Hebrew 12:17-19]).

Amasai's poetry is not the product of spontaneous inspiration; it is hard-won political poetry that subtly but unmistakably represents a pledge of loyalty to David. Just the pair "David" and "son of Jesse" recall Nabal's refusal to give food to David's men (1 Sam. 25:10). Amasai too pairs "David" with "son of Jesse," but he erases any hint of disloyalty. Amasai then picks up the word "peace" from David's initial response, "if you have come to me in peace." Three times he pronounces "peace" upon David and the one who helps him. Amasai continues, "For your God is the one who helps you." His choice of the words "your God" rather than the traditional "God of our ancestors" is a rhetorical bow to David (1 Chron. 12:17 [Hebrew 12:18]).

In this poetic snippet, Amasai topples an anti-Davidic sentiment in Israel's sacred tradition, dispels the suspense prompted by David's ambivalence, exudes the obligatory tenor of deference, and acknowledges that David's God is the source of victory. At the end of the day, the warrior-poet is *both* inspired and shrewd.

Much later, "the spirit was upon Azariah son of Oded" (2 Chron. 15:1; my translation). Like Amasai, Azariah delivered a speech rife with both allusions to Israel's traditions and support for the king. His words, in fact, are referred to as a prophecy (15:8).

The association of the spirit with inspired learning comes to full flower in the story of Jahaziel. The author, in typically formulaic language, notes that "the spirit of the LORD was upon Jahaziel" (20:14, my translation), but the speech that follows is anything but formulaic. What Jahaziel says when the spirit is upon him is a nuanced combination of precise military strategy and the sort of encouragement a priest would give to troops before battle. Jahaziel's speech gives clear military direction. He says,

---

[5]The translation of the root *labash* in the NRSV is puzzling. In Judg. 6:34 and 2 Chron. 24:20, the translators choose "took possession of." Here, in 1 Chron. 12:18, they choose "came upon." Neither is adequate. The first conjures images of spirit, even demon, possession; the second is the translation of a different verb entirely, *to be*, as in 2 Chron. 15:1.

> Listen, all Judah and inhabitants of Jerusalem, and King Jehoshaphat: Thus says the LORD to you: "Do not fear or be dismayed at this great multitude; for the battle is not yours but God's. Tomorrow go down against them; they will come up by the ascent of Ziz; you will find them at the end of the valley, before the wilderness of Jeruel. This battle is not for you to fight; take your position, stand still, and see the victory of the LORD on your behalf, O Judah and Jerusalem." Do not fear or be dismayed; tomorrow go out against them, and the LORD will be with you. (2 Chron. 20:15-17)

The precision in this speech is noteworthy, including the precise location of the enemy: the ascent of Ziz.

Yet this speech does not exclusively consist of strategy. The encouragement not to fear, the promise of victory, the realization that the battle is not Judah's to fight but God's—these are *priestly* instructions. According to Deuteronomy, the priest is to speak to the troops prior to battle against superior armies:

> Before you engage in battle, the priest shall come forward and speak to the troops, and shall say to them: "Hear, O Israel! Today you are drawing near to do battle against your enemies. Do not lose heart, or be afraid, or panic, or be in dread of them; for it is the LORD your God who goes with you, to fight for you against your enemies, to give you victory." (Deut. 20:2-4)

When the spirit comes upon Jahaziel, he speaks in the role of Deuteronomic priest by gathering the essential ingredients of the priestly instructions, which must be delivered prior to battle. He is the inspired keeper of the priestly tradition, and he does so by integrating the prescribed priestly speech, to be delivered prior to battle, into his own speech prior to battle.

The speech also contains distinct allusions to Israelite texts. The words "the battle is not yours but God's" recall David's final words to Goliath before he kills the giant: "the battle is the LORD's" (1 Sam. 17:47). The command "Fear not. . . . This battle is not for you to fight; take your position, stand still, and see the victory of the LORD on your behalf" recollects Moses's monumental words to Israel on the cusp of the sea, with Egyptian horses and chariots in hot pursuit: "But Moses said to the people, 'Do not be afraid, stand firm, and see the deliverance that the LORD will accomplish for you today'" (Exod. 14:13).

Jahaziel is also identified as a member of the levitic line, the sons of Asaph: "David and the officers of the army also set apart for the service the sons of Asaph, and of Heman, and of Jeduthun, who should prophesy with lyres, harps, and cymbals" (1 Chron. 25:1). Jahaziel was, in short, one of Israel's trained musicians.[6] Because of Jahaziel's advice, the people of Judah did not need to do a thing; they simply looked on and sang praises while their enemies ambushed one another (2 Chron. 20:20-23). Afterwards, the victors, who had lifted voices rather than a finger against the enemy, returned to the temple, laden with the spoils and weapons of war—harps, lyres, and trumpets, "for the LORD had enabled them to rejoice over their enemies" (20:27-28).

---

[6]What follows musician Jahaziel's speech is not surprising. The king bowed down, face to the ground, with all Judah, worshipping. The Levites and others stood "to praise the LORD, the God of Israel, with a very loud voice" (2 Chron. 20:18-19).

This speech emblematizes the relationship between the spirit and learning. On the one hand, prophesying in the context of a community of musicians is reminiscent of the community of prophets to whose ecstatic state Saul and his emissaries succumbed. On the other hand, the precision of Jahaziel's speech contains clear allusions to Israel's literature. Two ends of the spectrum fuse in this speech.

The fourth and final inspired figure in 1–2 Chron. is a priest, though his words sting with prophetic venom and lead directly to his death—ironically on the temple mount. "The spirit of God clothed Zechariah son of the priest Jehoiada," so "he stood above the people and said to them, 'Thus says God: Why do you transgress the commandments of the LORD, so that you cannot prosper? Because you have forsaken the LORD, he has also forsaken you.'" While being stoned in the temple court, he cried, "May the LORD see and avenge!" (2 Chron. 24:20-22).

The Persian-era iteration of the rushing, coming, or clothing of the spirit gives testimony to the power of the relationship between the spirit and learning. Though the impetus of the spirit's onrushing lay principally in the stories of Israel's early judges, the impact of the spirit's onrush, according to Persian-era texts, lay elsewhere: in the book of Judges, the spirit inspired acts of liberation through figures such as Othniel, Gideon, Jephthah, and Samson; in 1–2 Chronicles, the spirit inspired a prophet to compel the people of Judah, through highly persuasive speech, *not* to fight; in the book of Judges, the spirit was associated with action; in 1–2 Chronicles, the spirit inspired only speech—political, prophetic, priestly speech—rife with tradition and marked by precision. This swing from the judges to the prophet-priests of the Persian era underscores again the symbiosis that existed between the spirit and learning.

THE SPIRIT RESTING UPON

In the Isaiah corpus, during a politically unstable era prior to the annihilation of the Northern Kingdom in 722 BCE, Isaiah imagined that a root would emerge from Jesse's stump.

> A shoot shall come out from the stump of Jesse,
> and a branch shall grow out of his roots.
> The spirit of the LORD shall rest on him,
> the spirit of wisdom and understanding,
> the spirit of counsel and might,
> the spirit of knowledge and the fear of the LORD.
> His delight shall be in the fear of the LORD.
> He shall not judge by what his eyes see,
> or decide by what his ears hear;
> but with justice he shall judge the poor,
> and decide with equity for the meek of the earth;
> he shall strike the earth with the rod of his mouth,
> and with the breath of his lips he shall kill the wicked.
> Justice shall be the belt around his waist,
> and faithfulness the belt around his loins. (Isa. 11:1-5)

This is not a simplistic utopian vision. God has lopped off geopolitical boughs and hacked down forests with an axe (Isa. 10:33-34). Out of this destruction comes, not a cedar, but a stump. Yet he will be a remarkable ruler, not because he is David's descendant or Solomon's heir, but because the spirit of the LORD rests upon him, inspiring him with (a) intellectual and practical skills needed for peacetime leadership (understanding and wisdom); (b) the skills of developing various strategies and perhaps leading in battle (counsel and courage), though in Prov. 8:14 this pair is used of peacetime leadership as well; and (c) devotion to God, presumably through participation in worship (knowledge and fear of God).

These are precisely the qualities that human beings can only make a pretense of possessing. Assyria's arrogance impels it to make an ill-advised claim to wisdom and understanding (Isa. 10:13). Judah's counsel (8:10) comes to nothing, and its mighty warriors fall in battle (3:25). As a consequence, Judah is void of knowledge (5:13) and full of misguided fear (7:4, 8:12-13, 10:24). This ruler, on whom the spirit rests, embodies what other nations, and Judah too, lack.

Essential to this vision of inspired leadership are wisdom,[7] understanding,[8] counsel,[9] and knowledge,[10] which together yield a just rule—a rule driven by justice rather than perception, tempered by equity rather than hearsay.[11] At the heart of this ruler's vocation is justice—judging on behalf of the poor. Clothed with justice as his belt and faithfulness as his undergarment, he will bring about justice, not with violence, but with the rod of his mouth; his inspired words alone will destroy the wicked.

It is difficult to miss the point that the work of the spirit is tied to learning, given the preponderance of words such as understanding, wisdom, counsel, and knowledge, coupled with a keen commitment to justice. These are not charismatic endowments in the sense of gifts that come without preparation to the ruler. It would be better to say that the ruler comes to the spirit with a predisposition for justice. On this ruler, a spirit with the qualities of a just reign rests. It is not either-or. It is not a charismatic gift *or* human preparation. Where the spirit's work ends and the human begins, where human effort ends and inspiration begins, is not possible to pinpoint.

During the exile to Babylon, sometime after 587 BCE, a prophetic heir of Isaiah of Jerusalem picked up the themes of Isa. 11:1-9. The key figure is not now a ruler but a servant, about whom God says,

> Here is my servant, whom I uphold, my chosen, in whom my soul delights; I have put my spirit upon him; he will bring forth justice to the nations. He will not cry or lift up his voice, or make it heard in the street; a bruised reed he will not break, and a dimly burning wick he will not quench; he will faithfully bring forth justice. He will not grow faint or be crushed until he has established justice in the earth; and the coastlands wait for his teaching [*torah*]. (Isa. 42:1-4)[12]

---

[7]Typically, human wisdom does not benefit in Isaiah 1–39 (10:3, 29:14).
[8]This word occurs elsewhere in Isaiah 1–39 only once, of the wisdom of the wise that will perish (29:14).
[9]The Hebrew word for counsel occurs thirteen times in Isaiah 1–39, of bad counsel, good counsel, and God's own counsel. In Isa. 16:3, it is linked to justice, as in this description of an inspired ruler.
[10]In Isa. 5:11-13, those who get up to drink and finish their day drunk, who feast but ignore God's handiwork, "go into exile without knowledge."
[11]In Isa. 33:5-6, similar attributes are ascribed to "the LORD," who "is exalted, he dwells on high; he filled Zion with justice and righteousness; he will be the stability of your times, abundance of salvation, wisdom, and knowledge; the fear of the LORD is Zion's treasure."
[12]It is difficult to identify this servant. For an introduction to the so-called Servant Songs in Isaiah 40–55, see Raymond Collins's entry, "Servant of the LORD, the," in *NIDB*, 5:192–5.

The servant's message is characterized as *torah*, "teaching," for which the coastlands wait. The basis of such teaching becomes evident in a later depiction of the servant.

> The Lord GOD has given me the tongue of a teacher, that I may know how to sustain the weary with a word. Morning by morning he wakens—wakens my ear to listen as those who are taught. The Lord GOD has opened my ear, and I was not rebellious, I did not turn backward. (Isa. 50:4-5)

The pervasiveness of teaching and learning in this autobiographical snippet is conspicuous. The Hebrew verb *lamadh*, "to teach" and "to learn," occurs in the *piel* stem frequently to describe teaching and training on various topics, such as God's statutes and ordinances (Deut. 4:1, 5), about which parents are commanded, "Teach them to your children, talking about them when you are at home and when you are away, when you lie down and when you rise" (11:19).[13] Teaching—learning too—is a matter of repetition, recurrence, and recitation. Learning—teaching too—takes place morning by morning rather than through the spontaneous combustion of charisma. Again, the border between discipline and inspiration is diaphanous.

The servant's teaching, though positive and perfectly aligned with God, leads to suffering and pain. The seeds of suffering are muted in the first description of the servant. The verb translated as *cry* in the line "he will not cry or lift up his voice" (Isa. 42:2) refers throughout the Isaiah corpus to cries of anguish (19:20, 33:7, 46:7, 65:14). The servant will not cry in anguish publicly. The servant will not grow weary or be crushed until after his task of bringing justice to the earth is successfully completed and his teaching reaches the coastlands.

Once again, leading and inspiration coexist in the presence of the spirit. From a position without privilege, so unlike the inspired ruler of Isaiah 11, the servant proclaims a destiny of light for the very nations who, decades earlier, had destroyed Judah. He does this, like the inspired ruler, with the temperate breath of his lips, with a keen commitment to justice, and with a message that, with evocative resonance and without a moment's hesitation, the prophet of the exile calls *torah*.

Later still, a prophet of the exile or restoration claims:

> The spirit of the Lord GOD is upon me, because the LORD has anointed me; he has sent me to bring good news to the oppressed, to bind up the brokenhearted, to proclaim liberty to the captives, and release to the prisoners; to proclaim the year of the LORD's favor, and the day of vengeance of our God; to comfort all who mourn; to provide for those who mourn in Zion—to give them a garland instead of ashes, the oil of gladness instead of mourning, the mantle of praise instead of a faint spirit. (Isa. 61:1-3)

This mission is rooted in the understanding and wisdom of the inspired messiah (Isa. 11:1-4) and the justice for the nations that lies at the core of the exilic servant's teaching (42:1-7). Now, however, it is not the place of Israel among the nations or the nations themselves that are pre-eminent but the demand to liberate the poor *within* Israel: the

---

[13] The *piel* stem is used for teaching songs (2 Sam. 1:18), training soldiers for war (2 Sam. 22:35, Ps. 18:35 [Hebrew]), and, in the related *pual* stem, skilled singers (1 Chron. 25:7). Such teaching is also aligned with study in Ezra 7:10: "For Ezra had set his heart to study the law of the LORD, and to do it, and to teach the statutes and ordinances in Israel."

prophet preaches good news to the oppressed, release to prisoners, and comfort for those who weep in Jerusalem.

This prophet is capable of painting with words a palette vivid with the hues of justice. This is no empty speech in light of the powerful images of inclusion that saturate Isaiah 56–59, with its intense image of eunuchs at worship (Isa. 56:3-5), foreigners in the temple (56:3, 6-7), and outcasts gathered (56:8). This prophet is able with language to create a new heaven (65:17), though not without a new earth that quakes with a shift in social templates: eunuchs embrace the promise to Abraham and Sarah, foreigners lead worship, and the debt-poor have the good news preached to them.

The spirit rests, in summary, upon a messianic ruler (Isaiah 11), a suffering servant (Isaiah 42), and a prophetic champion of the oppressed (Isaiah 61). As political angst (Isaiah 11) turned to Babylonian exile (Isaiah 42) and perhaps the vagaries of rebuilding during the Persian era (Isaiah 61), the universal tendency that is hinted at in Isaiah 11 swelled to encompass proselytes from distant coastlands (Isaiah 42) and then narrowed, though not in any sort of parochial way, to an intense preoccupation with the debt-poor in Israel (Isaiah 61). At the heart of each of these figures is the warrant of justice. To engender justice, the only weapon he or she wields is the spoken word—the rod of the ideal ruler (Isaiah 11), the sharp sword of the servant (Isaiah 50), and the speech of the anointed prophet (Isaiah 61). Once again, then, inspiration is not just the source but the product of the right commitments. The ruler's penchant for justice makes him the right recipient of the spirit of understanding, wisdom, counsel, and knowledge. The servant's light to the nations is none other than *torah*—the sort of learning that comes through discipline. The prophet's anointing hinges upon a wholehearted commitment to a vision fueled perhaps, probably even, by the year of jubilee, when the captives would be liberated and prisoners released, as well as earlier visions of justice in the Isaiah corpus. Inspiration and tradition combine in fantastic, though not fanciful, images of a nation whose oppressed know finally the meaning of good news.

THE SPIRIT-FILLING[14]

From the story of Joseph—perhaps one of the oldest in the Jewish Bible—to one of the latest, the story of Daniel, which dates from approximately 160 BCE, various Israelite and Jewish authors expressed their belief that human beings could be filled with the spirit from God. This, one of the most enduring of many long-standing trajectories related to the spirit in the Hebrew scriptures, also offers something fresh: not so much the advent of the spirit as the stirring of the spirit-breath.

In the tale of Joseph, who interprets a cryptic dream, an Egyptian Pharaoh asks the question, "Can we find anyone else like this—one in whom is the spirit of God?" (Gen. 41:38). Pharaoh, as rulers are wont to do, answers his own question: "Since God is making known all of this to you, there is no one discerning and wise like you" (41:39). Even an outsider to Israel is able to discern the connection between the spirit and wisdom. This is hardly surprising, since Joseph has honed his skills at dream interpretation from his youth. He dreamt—and interpreted, to his brothers' chagrin—dreams in which sheaves and stars

---

[14]For detailed analyses of these texts, see my *Filled with the Spirit*, 34–86. This section complements Lee Roy Martin's discussion of "The Spirit and Charismatic Gifts" in his entry for this volume, "The Spirit and the Old Testament."

bow down to one in particular: Joseph (37:5-11). In Egyptian prison, he interpreted the dreams of the cupbearer and the butler with acuity (40:1-23). Joseph's ability to interpret dreams is hard won. Joseph, further, does more than interpret dreams; he also instructs Pharaoh to prepare in practical ways for famine. Joseph has honed his administrative skills over both Potiphar's house and in prison (39:6, 23). When, therefore, the Pharaoh affirms both the presence of the spirit in Joseph and his remarkable wisdom, he draws the first indisputable connection between the spirit and learning—what might be called inspired learning—in the Hebrew scriptures.

If the story of Joseph furnishes one of the earliest prose instances of the association of the spirit and wisdom, the book of Micah, written as early as the eighth century BCE, supplies the earliest prophetic oracle. The Judean prophet rails against his prophetic opponents, laying claim instead to the spirit. He excoriates them for prophesying for profit and forecasts that they will be "without vision" and "without revelation." These "seers" and "diviners," who discern direction in various signs, like wisps of sacrificial smoke, shall have nothing to say. "But as for me," claims Micah,

> I am filled with power,
> with the spirit of the LORD,
> and with justice and might,
> to declare to Jacob his transgression and to Israel his sin. (Mic. 3:5-8)

As in the oracles of the Isaiah corpus, the spirit is joined at the hip to justice, as well as power and capability. Yet this is not the whole picture. Micah's claim leads to still further insight into the nature of *rûaḥ*: the perception of the spirit as a permanent endowment within Micah that inspires him to live justly and to speak powerfully.

The linchpin of this realization is that Micah is filled with three permanent qualities: strength, justice, and might. These qualities are not charismatic endowments. Justice, for example, is so essential that Micah begins his cross-examination of the leaders with the rhetorical question, "Should you not know justice?" (Mic. 3:1). Of course, they should! Justice is so axiomatic, in fact, that Micah can indict his people for failing to know what everyone should know: "God has told you, O mortal, what is good; and what does the LORD require of you but to do justice, and to love kindness, and to walk humbly with your God?" (6:8). The justice with which Micah is filled, like the spirit with which he is filled, is a permanent part of his character, not a transitory or late-on-the-scene endowment. *Everyone* should know what justice is. Micah certainly does. He is not filled with justice conveniently or occasionally; nor is he filled with the spirit sporadically or expediently.

Another clue to the association of the spirit with learning is Micah's indictment of other prophets. False prophets look for inspiration in visions, revelations, and divinations—short-lived modes of divine presence. Micah's message to Judah, in contrast, arises from his always being filled with power, justice, the LORD's spirit, and might.

Micah's claim to the spirit reverberates with his contemporary, Isaiah of Jerusalem (Isaiah 1–39). Although Micah was rural and Isaiah urban, and Micah criticized Jerusalem and Isaiah floated comfortably in its corridors of power, both prophets affirmed the relationship between the spirit and justice, the character of which must—and should—be learned. The ruler on whom the spirit rests is known especially for justice (Isa. 11:3-5); Micah, filled with the spirit, is known for his relentless commitment to justice (Mic. 3:5-8).

The association between the spirit and learning crescendos in the unlikeliest of places—in a putatively Persian-era story that communicates meticulous information on the construction of the tabernacle (Exod. 25:1–31:11, 35:4-33). An inventory of material dimensions, this story nonetheless describes a moment of sumptuous giving. In the context, *rûaḥ* plays a pivotal role.

God tells Moses, "And you shall speak to all the wise of heart whom I have filled with a spirit of wisdom, and they will make Aaron's vestments" (Exod. 28:3, my translation). The association of the spirit with learning—God fills artisans with a spirit of wisdom—is incontestable in this bit of instruction. Yet something more is discernible: God selects these skilled laborers, not so that they may receive a charismatic endowment of the spirit, but because they have *already* demonstrated their skill.[15] The skilled, the wise-of-heart, are to be filled with the spirit of wisdom.

The roadblock in this interpretation appears to be the verb *fill*—but only at first blush. On the one hand, the verb *fill* can point to an initial filling, what looks like a charismatic endowment: a skin is filled with water (Gen. 21:19), a bag with grain (42:25), and a horn with oil (1 Sam. 16:1).[16] It can also refer less to initial filling than to completeness, topping up, or fulfilling. A pregnancy comes to term—*is filled* (Gen. 25:24). A period of purification is completed—*filled* (Lev. 12:4, 6).[17] Spaces, too, are filled. When Egyptian houses are filled with swarms of flies, more than a few flies can be expected (Exod. 8:17 [Hebrew]). When the hem of God's robe fills the temple, more than a tip of the garment occupies the inner sanctum (Isa. 6:1). When Jeremiah protests that the land is filled with idols, he refers to more than a few idols (Jer. 16:18). When the Jordan fills its banks, the river floods those banks (Josh. 3:15).[18] From this perspective, the simple phrase "whom I have filled with spirit of wisdom" suggests something like full-filling—fruition, sapiential wholeness, and fullness of skill.

In a lavish scene, in which the hues and textures of the priestly garments are vivid, the artisans who produce such splendid garments are depicted in equally lavish terms as "the wise of heart whom I filled with spirit of wisdom." There is now more than enough spirit within these gifted laborers to complete the daunting task that lies before them. The artisans are not moderately well-equipped. They are full to the brim with spirit and wisdom. Their hearts, in short, are full of wisdom, flooded with the skills that will create a tent for God's presence in the wilderness.[19]

The artisans' leaders are especially full of the spirit. Of Bezalel and Oholiab, God says to Moses:

> See, I have called by name Bezalel son of Uri son of Hur, of the tribe of Judah: and I have filled him with spirit of God, with wisdom, intelligence, and knowledge in every kind of craft, to devise artistic designs, to work in gold, silver, and bronze, in cutting stones for setting, and in carving wood, in every kind of craft. Moreover, I

---

[15]Throughout this story (e.g., Exod. 36:8), the phrase "wise of heart" refers to skilled laborers in contrast to unskilled. See Levison, *Filled with the Spirit*, 51–65.

[16]A charismatic endowment could have been communicated by any number of other verbs, such as *put upon* (Num. 11:29), *come or be upon* (e.g., Num. 24:2; Judg. 3:10; 1 Sam. 10:6, 16:13), *clothe* (Judg. 6:34), *rush upon* (Judg. 14:6), *rest upon* (Isa. 11:2), and *give* (Ezek. 36:26-27).

[17]Jacob's wait for Rachel was over—*filled* (Gen. 29:21). A vow is *fulfilled* (Num. 6:5). Banquets end—*are filled* (Est. 1:5). Babylonian exile ends—*is filled* (Jer. 25:12).

[18]For similar understandings of filling, see Jer. 23:24, 44:25; Hab. 2:14; Ezek. 40:34-35, 44:4; 1 Kgs 8:10, 15; 2 Chron. 6:4.

[19]For slightly more analysis, including the adjective "full" and the noun "fullness," see Levison, *Filled with the Spirit*, 52–8.

have appointed with him Oholiab son of Ahisamach, of the tribe of Dan; and I have given wisdom in the heart of all the wise of heart, so that they may make all that I have commanded you. (Exod. 31:2-6, my translation)

Bezalel resurfaces when Moses says:

> See, the LORD has called by name Bezalel son of Uri son of Hur, of the tribe of Judah; he has filled him with spirit of God, with wisdom, intelligence, and knowledge in every kind of craft, to devise artistic designs, to work in gold, silver, and bronze, in cutting stones for setting, and in carving wood, in every kind of craft. And he put into his heart to teach, both him and Oholiab son of Ahisamach, of the tribe of Dan. He has filled them with wisdom of heart to do every kind of work done by an artisan or by a designer or by an embroiderer in blue, purple, and crimson yarns, and in fine linen, or by a weaver—by any sort of artisan or skilled designer. (Exod. 35:30-35, my translation)

In these dual depictions, the correspondence between spirit and heart, which described the artisans in Exod. 28:3, occurs with utter precision. In 28:3, artisans are the *"wise of heart,"* whom *"I have filled with spirit of wisdom."* A similar parallel occurs in Exod. 35:30-35:

> 35:31: [God] *has filled him* [Bezalel] *with spirit of God, with wisdom . . . for every craft*

> 35:35: [God] *filled them* [Bezalel and Oholiab] *with wisdom of heart . . . to do every craft*

Alongside wisdom of heart, God's filling with "spirit of God, wisdom" solidifies the relationship between the spirit and learning. These are skilled artisans, who will now construct the tabernacle. They are selected because of their skill. Yet there is, as in Micah's oracle, something more here. This text, like Micah's claim, does not communicate a fresh influx, a charismatic endowment, of the spirit. The heart is not something that comes and goes. Nor is the spirit. The mirror images of heart and spirit suggest rather that filling with *rûaḥ* ought to be understood as a filling full of a lifelong spirit that is the locus of learning.

Although there is no new heart or spirit in this narrative, there is something new here: at this point in Israel's history, the spirit of God, with which God had filled Bezalel and the artisans from the start, was made even fuller with wisdom, insight, and intelligence at this unique moment in Israel's history. These artisans, and their capable leaders, are full to the brim with God's Spirit and, consequently, are capable of constructing a sacred tent in a godforsaken wilderness.

It is essential not to let all this talk of inspiration obfuscate the centrality of learning in this description of Bezalel and Oholiab. What they did with their own inspired learning is telling: "And [God] gave in his heart to teach, both him and Oholiab son of Ahisamach, of the tribe of Dan" (Exod. 35:34).[20] This discreet line suggests a good deal about how the artisans were "filled with spirit of wisdom." While the image of filling with the spirit may evoke images of direct, divine intervention—a charismatic endowment—this role of

---

[20] The translation of the NRSV, with the verb "inspire," is too evocative of a charismatic endowment: "And he has inspired him to teach, both him and Oholiab son of Ahisamach, of the tribe of Dan." It is better to translate the Hebrew verb *give* as "gave," following the lead of the Septuagint. God *gave* into his heart to teach.

teaching suggests otherwise. The artisans were filled with a spirit of wisdom and were given wisdom in their heart because they learned from extraordinary teachers, who had mastered every craft.

The latest exemplar of the association of the spirit with learning is probably the product of the Maccabean era (ca. 167–160 BCE). Set in the context of exile, the story of Daniel spans three generations.

During the first generation, after Daniel interprets his dream, King Nebuchadnezzar of Babylon claims three times that Daniel has *"a spirit of a/the holy God(s) in him"* (Dan. 4:8, 9, 18 English; 4:5, 6, 15 Aramaic; my translation).[21] However the Aramaic is translated, the presence of a noteworthy spirit in Daniel is central to this text.

During the second generation, Nebuchadnezzar's daughter-in-law, after hearing about the baffling writing that appears during Belshazzar's party, recalls, "There is a man in your kingdom who is endowed with a spirit of the holy gods. In the days of your father he was found to have enlightenment, understanding, and wisdom like the wisdom of the gods." She recalls that "an excellent spirit, knowledge, and understanding to interpret dreams, explain riddles, and solve problems were found in this Daniel" (Dan. 5:11-12). Her husband, Nebuchadnezzar's son Belshazzar, is also aware of Daniel's *spirit of God* (5:14) and *excellent wisdom*.

During the third generation, Darius of Media plans to appoint Daniel to the heights of imperial power after he translates the mysterious handwriting on the wall because "an excellent spirit is in him" (Dan. 6:3 English; 6:4 Aramaic). This is a reiteration of what was said during the prior generation.

In over half a dozen references to the spirit in close sequence, the spirit is associated with Daniel's wisdom. In the second story, an especially conspicuous verbal correspondence between the spirit and wisdom rises to the surface:

rûaḥ yattîrāh . . . in him (5:12);

ḥāḵᵉmāh yattîrāh . . . in him (5:14).

This correspondence is compelling, but it begs the question of the source of Daniel's wisdom. It is possible that this wisdom is a charismatic gift—though this interpretation falters on a couple of fronts. The first is that Daniel, like Joseph, on whom the figure of Daniel is modeled, gains this wisdom first through discipline. While eating only vegetables and drinking only water, to Daniel and his companions "God gave knowledge and skill in every aspect of literature and wisdom; Daniel also had insight into all visions and dreams" (Dan. 1:17). At the end of this period, "in every matter of wisdom and understanding concerning which the king inquired of them, he found them ten times better than all the magicians and enchanters in his whole kingdom" (1:20). These descriptions, of course, could be interpreted to mean that God gave Daniel and his companions knowledge, wisdom, and understanding as charismatic gifts—except for an earlier detail that this entire group of young men, who were taken into exile, were "young men without physical defect and handsome, versed in every branch of wisdom, endowed with knowledge and insight, and competent to serve in the king's palace; they were to be taught the literature and language of the Chaldeans" (1:4). In short, Daniel and his companions, who resisted royal rations, *learned better* than the others. They excelled in their education. Inspiration

---

[21] This translation reflects the ambiguity of the Aramaic text.

in this story is the product of a rich symbiosis between human fidelity, learning, and the gift of divine wisdom. Through this symbiosis, Daniel came first to interpret dreams—a skill that would, later in life, be attributed to the *rûaḥ* in him.

Something else to note is that the spirit and wisdom within Daniel are described as *yattîrāh rûaḥ* (or *rûaḥ yattîrāh*) in the book of Daniel (5:14, 6:3-4). The NRSV translation of this word as "excellent" is deceptive; the Aramaic and Hebrew communicate something else: extreme degree. The brilliance of Nebuchadnezzar's statue was *extreme* (2:31). The fiery furnace, into which Shadrach, Meshach, and Abednego were cast, was *extremely* hot (3:22). A beast in Daniel's visions was *extremely* terrifying" (7:19). This word communicates something other than excellence. It communicates sheer brilliance, sheer heat, sheer terror—*and sheer spirit*, spirit so perfectly spirit that it is clearly a spirit from God.

The stories about Daniel from the world of early Judaism accentuate the association of spirit and learning. Like Joseph, in much older stories, Daniel is an interpreter of the inscrutable and an administrator of the routine because in him is sheer divine *rûaḥ*— an extraordinary share of the divine vitality that, when cultivated through simplicity and skill, becomes the source of knowledge and wisdom. This is not an intermittent experience, the advent of the spirit for a particular purpose at a particular time. It is the product of alchemy between the spirit within a human being and lifelong learning.

The portrait of Daniel, filled with sheer spirit, sheer wisdom, for a full three generations shares a core conviction with the stories of Joseph, the artisans who engineered the tabernacle, and the men who resurrected their tradition to effective political and military ends in 1–2 Chronicles. It is of a piece, too, with the image of the inspired ruler of Isaiah 11 and the conviction of Micah. This conviction has to do with the integral relationship between the spirit and learning. To say this, however, is not to say enough, because it allows for the possibility that the spirit gives knowledge without human effort, without the lifelong pursuit of learning. This is not the case.

In the stories of Joseph and Daniel, arguably among the earliest and latest in the Hebrew scriptures, both men interpret the inscrutable and ably administrate great empires because they labored earlier in their lives to learn—Joseph in prison and Potiphar's house, Daniel in early exile. If Joseph and Daniel possess extraordinary knowledge, it is not because they receive a charismatic endowment of the spirit of God, but because the spirit within them is the perpetual source of enlightenment, wisdom, and prescience. This wisdom is the product of a mysterious association of inspiration and education; both are essential to what distinguishes these men, whose early labors come to fruition later, when they become apparent to foreign rulers, all of whom recognize that the source of their wisdom is the spirit within them. Not a come-lately spirit but a spirit within, a spirit recognizable, in Daniel's case, at least, for three generations.

Daniel's knowledge is reminiscent, too, of the story of desert artisans, who were filled with *rûaḥ*—spirit of wisdom—because they had honed their skill under the capable direction of Bezalel and Oholiab, their inspired teachers, who themselves were filled "with spirit of God, with wisdom, intelligence, and knowledge in every kind of craft." Daniel's wisdom mirrors Micah's as well; Micah claimed to be filled, unlike other prophets, whose revelation came by fits and starts, with God's lifelong spirit in him, along with power, might, and justice. Justice, Micah knows, is learned; it requires no special endowment.

For Joseph, the artisans, Micah, and Daniel, the spirit is a lifelong presence within, a perennial source of wisdom. This conception of inspiration is probably different from

Isaiah's inspired messiah, upon whom the spirit rests. The association of the spirit with knowledge, wisdom, and justice is no different at all. A single, seamless association lies at the base of these two quite different modes of the spirit's presence.

The scenario in the story of Daniel is different as well from the book of Chronicles, where the spirit comes upon key figures, who speak to Israel and its leaders. Men like Azariah and Jahaziel presumably receive the spirit temporarily, yet what they say reflects a lifetime of learning, as they take up ancient traditions for new ends. The spirit, in short, inspires them to speak from a life of learning; there is an undeniable symbiosis between learning and inspiration. In what they have to say, there is certainly no disparity between life in the spirit and a lifetime of learning.

SPIRIT AND LEARNING REPRISED

The association between the spirit and learning did not evaporate with the rise of the Hasmoneans or the death of Jesus or the fall of Jerusalem to Rome. A discreet story tucked into the earliest chapters of Luke's gospel attests to its perseverance (Lk. 2:25-35). Jesus and Mary, while bringing Jesus to the temple for his dedication, are met by an old man, who, Luke tells his readers, is inspired by the spirit: the spirit rests on him; the spirit reveals to him; the spirit guides him into the temple. Simeon is genuinely inspired. And in this inspired state, he utters a prayer that has reverberated in liturgies over the centuries:

> Lord, now lettest thou thy servant depart in peace according to thy word.
> For mine eyes have seen thy salvation,
> Which thou hast prepared before the face of all people;
> To be a light to lighten the Gentiles and the glory of thy people Israel. (Lk. 2:28-32)[22]

As he gathers the baby in his arms, Simeon gathers up words he has long since memorized. His simple prayer is drenched in the language of Isa. 40–55: "a light for revelation to the nations" (Isa. 42:6, 49:6) and "glory to your people Israel" (46:13). Even when he stage-whispers to Mary, "This child is destined for the falling and the rising of many in Israel, and to be a sign that will be opposed," Simeon imagines afresh the suffering servant, whose uncompromising expansion of God's reign to all nations would lead to rejection and death (53:3).

Simeon has waited, prayed, and studied. He has immersed himself in prophetic texts, memorizing Scripture with an eye to that single significant inspired moment when all that he has studied will combust. And that moment arrives when, under the inspiration of the spirit, he recognizes the inclusive, expansive, and perilous salvation of God in the baby carried to the temple by a pair of peasants.

FOR FURTHER READING

Levison, John R. *Filled with the Spirit*. Grand Rapids, MI: Eerdmans, 2009.
Welker, Michael. *God the Spirit*. Minneapolis, MN: Fortress, 1994.

---

[22] I opt to use the traditional language of the liturgy here rather than the NRSV translation.

CHAPTER TEN

The Spirit, Mediation, and Sacramentality

KENNETH M. LOYER

Under the broad heading of the Spirit and creation, two related themes emerge: mediation and sacramentality. This article focuses on the nature and purpose of each in relationship to the Holy Spirit. The Spirit's role in mediation and sacramentality takes shape in the context of the dynamic unfolding of the saving purposes of the triune God from creation to covenant, fulfilled in the incarnation and at Pentecost, and finally brought to eschatological completion in God's promised new creation.

THE SPIRIT AND MEDIATION

From the beginning of creation, the Holy Spirit has been at work mediating God's presence and power in and for the world. "In the beginning when God created the heavens and the earth, the earth was a formless void and darkness covered the face of the deep, while a wind from God swept over the face of the waters" (Gen. 1:1-2). The phrase *ruach Elohim*, translated above as "wind from God," could also read "the Spirit of God," and in a Christian understanding, it refers to the third person of the Trinity. With God's Spirit moving over the face of the waters, God speaks creation into existence. The result of God's creative, Spirit-infused speech is repeatedly called "good" (1:4, 10, 12, 18, 21, 25). Then, after the creation of human beings, God saw all that he had made and it was "very good" (1:31).

As the biblical saga continues, however, a force opposed to God is quickly introduced. Just a few chapters later, in Genesis 3, that force is represented by the first sin, a stark rejection of God (vv. 1-12), with deleterious consequences for humankind and all of creation (vv. 13-24). In words made famous by John Milton's epic poem, paradise was lost.

Mediation is necessary because of the scandal of sin and its disastrous effects. Farther along in the history of salvation, following the call of Abram (Gen. 12:1-3) and the covenantal formation of the people of Israel as God's "treasured possession" (Exod. 19:5), Isaiah describes the need for mediation in clear and memorable terms: "See, the Lord's hand is not too short to save, nor his ear too dull to hear. Rather, your iniquities have been barriers between you and your God, and your sins have hidden his face from you so that he does not hear" (Isa. 59:1-2). By separating the people from God, sin has deeply damaged their relationship with God. Sin not only is an affront to the holiness of God but also denies the divine principle of justice.

> For our transgressions before you are many, and our sins testify against us. Our transgressions indeed are with us, and we know our iniquities: transgressing, and denying the Lord, and turning away from following our God, talking oppression and revolt, conceiving lying words and uttering them from the heart. Justice is turned back, and righteousness stands at a distance; for truth stumbles in the public square, and uprightness cannot enter. Truth is lacking, and whoever turns from evil is despoiled. The Lord saw it, and it displeased him that there was no justice. He saw that there was no one, and was appalled that there was no one to intervene; so his own arm brought him victory, and his righteousness upheld him. (Isa. 59:12-16)

Sin is an active force that wreaks havoc and denies truth and justice. It alienates human beings from God and from one another, resulting in thoughts of iniquity (Isa. 59:7), words of wickedness (59:3), deeds of violence (59:6), and crooked paths devoid of justice and peace (59:8)—in short, leading far from salvation (59:11). In turning away from God, human beings have created and propagated a problem that they cannot solve. Intervention is desperately needed. Yet who is there to intervene (59:16), and who but God actually can?

In one form of intervention, the Spirit of God would come upon individuals like Isaiah so that, as the Lord's prophets, they could proclaim the word of God to his people. Other biblical prophets spoke of the time when God would pour out his Spirit on all the people and not just certain individuals. For example, Ezekiel relayed God's promise to gather the people from exile in these terms: "I will leave none of them behind; and I will never again hide my face from them, when I pour out my Spirit upon the house of Israel, says the Lord God" (Ezek. 39:28-29, author's own translation). The principle is expressed most clearly in Joel, in words that Peter later quotes on the Day of Pentecost: "Then I will pour out my Spirit on all flesh; your sons and your daughters will prophesy, your old men will dream dreams, and your young men will see visions. Even on the male and female servants, in those days, I will pour out my Spirit" (Joel 2:28-29, author's own translation). Here and elsewhere, the words of the prophets provide glimpses of the ultimate solution that would come in the outpouring of the Spirit for the redemption and renewal of God's world.

The NT further diagnoses the dilemma of sin and points toward both the need for and the provision of saving mediation. The Apostle Paul, commenting on the universality of sin, explains that "all have sinned and fall short of the glory of God" (Rom. 3:23). Yet God, refusing to abandon his people, has made a way for there to be restoration and healing, both vertically in their relationship with God and horizontally in relation to other people and creation. "For there is one God; there is also one mediator between God and humankind, Christ Jesus, himself human, who gave himself as a ransom for all" (1 Tim. 2:5-6). The vertical and horizontal dimensions intersect to form a cross, the decisive sign of God's reconciling love. The mediation necessary to bring healing, hope, and wholeness to both God's people and the wider world comes in the incarnation of Jesus Christ. As fully divine and fully human, he is uniquely able to overcome the barriers between God and his people created by sin. Sent by the Father for the redemption of the world, Jesus performed mighty acts, taught the truth about God, and ultimately suffered, died, and was resurrected in the power of the Holy Spirit—the same Spirit who, as promised, descended upon the early followers of Jesus to create a new community of God's people, the church (Acts 2:1-41), and still guides the church today.

Christ's saving work has healed and restored the capacity for human relationship with God through the Holy Spirit, the gift through whom "God's love has been poured into our hearts" (Rom. 5:5).[1] The theme of the Spirit's role in mediation figures with particular prominence in John 14–16, part of what is known as Jesus's farewell discourse. Jesus promises the gift of the Spirit to his disciples:

> If you love me, you will keep my commandments. And I will ask the Father, and he will give you another Advocate, to be with you forever. This is the Spirit of truth, whom the world cannot receive, because it neither sees him nor knows him. You know him, because he abides with you, and he will be in you. (Jn 14:15-17)

Jesus declares to his followers that the Father will send the Holy Spirit in the name of Jesus, and the Spirit "will teach you everything, and remind you of all that I have said to you" (14:26). Then the Lord gives them his peace (14:27); it is fitting that news of the Spirit brings the peace of Jesus, because peace is a fruit of the Holy Spirit (Gal. 5:22). Jesus says that the Spirit will also testify about him (15:26); reveal to the world the truth about sin, righteousness, and judgment (16:8); guide the disciples into all the truth (16:13); declare what is to come (16:13); and glorify Jesus by taking what is his and declaring it to his followers (16:15). Since the gift of the Holy Spirit draws God's people into the life of the Trinity, the activity of the Spirit is the key to a restored relationship with God and to transformational knowledge of God.

In order to continue the mission and work of Jesus, the Spirit is active in mediation to and for the church and through the church to the world. Having reconciled the world to himself in Christ, God has entrusted to the church the ministry of reconciliation (2 Cor. 5:17-21). The church, by the aid of the Spirit, is the witness to the incarnate Lord, Jesus Christ, in whom all things hold together—although the church bears such witness imperfectly, given the realities of human frailty and sin. For example, the scandal of Christian disunity must be taken seriously because it denies the gospel and limits the church's ability to provide an alternative to the world's division and violence.[2] Nevertheless, the church is, and uniquely remains, divinely called to be a sign, instrument, and foretaste of the kingdom of God through the mediating power of the Holy Spirit.[3]

THE SPIRIT AND SACRAMENTALITY

Such ecclesiological descriptions allude to the concept of sacramentality and therefore invite consideration of the Spirit's role in relation to the sacraments. Additional evidence of Christian disunity is the lack of consensus about the number and even nature of

---

[1] For further reflection on this theme and its implications for Christian living, see Kenneth M. Loyer, *God's Love through the Spirit: The Holy Spirit in Thomas Aquinas and John Wesley* (Washington DC: The Catholic University of America Press, 2014).
[2] The failure of the church, and so of Christians, to live up to this high calling poses enormous problems theologically as well as practically, as shown by Ephraim Radner's stunning analysis in *A Brutal Unity: The Spiritual Politics of the Christian Church* (Waco, TX: Baylor University Press, 2012).
[3] The phrase identifying the church as "sign, instrument, and foretaste of the kingdom of God" is commonly used in ecumenical texts, such as *Called to Witness and Service: The Reuilly Common Statement with Essays on Church, Eucharist and Ministry* (London: Church House Publishing, 1999), §16–18; *On the Way to Visible Unity: The Meissen Common Statement* (London: Church House Publishing, 1988), §1–3; and *The Niagara Report: Report of the Anglican-Lutheran Consultation on Episcope 1987* (London: Church House Publishing, 1988), §67.

the sacraments as well as differences in sacramental practice that continue to separate certain Christian traditions from one another and, for example, prevent a joint sharing of the eucharist. Yet ecumenical efforts over the last century have given rise to a notable convergence, to a large degree across the ecclesial spectrum, concerning the dominical sacraments of baptism and the eucharist, the two sacraments that are most widely recognized and practiced by churches both historically and still today.[4] In baptism, God incorporates persons into the body of Christ, the church, and gives them new birth through water and the Spirit. The Holy Spirit works through the eucharist to make the gifts of bread and wine be for God's people the body and blood of Christ, that they might be for the world the body of Christ redeemed by his blood. God gathers up from the earth some of its most basic elements and products—water, bread (made primarily from flour, yeast, salt, and water), and the fruit of the vine—and, through the Spirit, transforms them into channels of the presence and power of the risen Christ for the sake of building up the church and advancing God's kingdom. The water of baptism and the bread and wine of the eucharist are outward signs of the Spirit's inward work. They derive their spiritual efficacy from the enlivening agency of the Spirit, making sacramentality a profoundly pneumatological matter.

The connection between the Holy Spirit and the sacraments is rooted in Scripture and bears fruit in the church and the life of faith. While Paul describes baptism in terms of dying and rising with Christ, he does not explicitly name the Spirit, but surely the Spirit's vivifying influence is implied: "Do you not know that all of us who have been baptized into Christ Jesus were baptized into his death? Therefore we have been buried with him by baptism into death, so that, just as Christ was raised from the dead by the glory of the Father, so we too might walk in newness of life" (Rom. 6:3-4). Not only has God raised Christ from the dead through the power of the Holy Spirit, but also the same Spirit now dwells in God's people and leads them from death to new life in the crucified and resurrected Jesus. Likewise, Paul's teaching about the Lord's Supper highlights a dynamic participatory element, which is again made possible through the life-giving Spirit:

> For I received from the Lord what I also handed on to you, that the Lord Jesus on the night when he was betrayed took a loaf of bread, and when he had given thanks, he broke it and said, "This is my body that is for you. Do this in remembrance of me." In the same way he took the cup also, after supper, saying, "This cup is the new covenant in my blood. Do this, as often as you drink it, in remembrance of me. For as often as you eat this bread and drink the cup, you proclaim the Lord's death until he comes." (1 Cor. 11:23-26)

The Spirit both aids in remembering the past events of Christ's meal with his original disciples and imparts its ongoing significance and benefits, here and now and looking ahead to the return of the Lord. By eating this bread and drinking the cup, the church, enlivened by the Spirit, proclaims and actually inhabits the mystery of faith: Christ has died, Christ is risen, and Christ will come again.

Earlier it was noted that there is a development in the Bible concerning the idea of the outpouring of the Spirit: what was once, by and large, an occurrence involving specific individuals at specific times for specific purposes—prophets raised up by God to proclaim

---

[4] See, for example, the influential document *Baptism, Eucharist, and Ministry*, Faith and Order Paper No. 111 (Geneva: World Council of Churches, 1982).

the word of the Lord—eventually leads to the promise that the day is coming when the Spirit will abide in all of God's people. A similar broadening in perspective takes place with regard to certain key concepts throughout the canonical witness. Specifically, the NT employs a figural reading of key OT themes in order to demonstrate how they point beyond their original context to a deeper sacramental reality disclosed in Christ and through the Spirit. For example, addressing the topic of suffering for doing good, 1 Peter 3 suggests a connection between the ark and the sacrament of baptism:

> For Christ also suffered for sins once for all, the righteous for the unrighteous, in order to bring you to God. He was put to death in the flesh, but made alive in the Spirit, in which also he went and preached to the spirits in prison, who in former times did not obey, when God waited patiently in the days of Noah, during the building of the ark, in which a few, that is, eight persons, were saved through water. And baptism, which this prefigured, now saves you—not as a removal of dirt from the body, but as an appeal to God for a good conscience, through the resurrection of Jesus Christ, who has gone into heaven and is at the right hand of God, with angels, authorities, and powers made subject to him. (1 Pet. 3:18-22, author's own translation)

Seen through the lens of the sweeping narrative of salvation history, the account of Noah's ark is found to prefigure the age of the Holy Spirit, foreshadowing the salvation of God's people through faith in Christ and through baptism into the death and resurrection of the one who is Lord of all. Likewise, the entire sacrificial system is a shadow of what would come in Christ, who fulfilled the law perfectly and completely through his one-time sacrifice of himself as both priest and offering. The book of Hebrews says this about Jesus: "Unlike the other high priests, he has no need to offer sacrifices day after day, first for his own sins, and then for those of the people. He sacrificed for their sins once for all when he offered himself" (Heb. 7:27, author's own translation). In the eucharist, the church re-presents the one-time offering of Christ to the Father through the Spirit. The schema of promise and fulfillment demonstrates Scripture's overall coherence, which is itself a work of the Holy Spirit.

Each of these two sacraments also has a deeply communal nature, as baptism marks initiation into the church, for whom a constitutive liturgical act is the celebration of the eucharist. The church does each not on the basis of mere human ingenuity, but at the command of Christ himself (Mt. 28:18-20, 26:26-29; Mk 14:22-25; Lk. 22:14-20). Given this specifically ecclesial form and shape, the question of the sacramentality of the church arises. How, if at all, is the church itself like a sacrament, conveying the presence of Christ by the inspiration of the Holy Spirit?

In response, a concept that figures prominently in Anglican and Methodist traditions can be instructive, namely, the means of grace. John Wesley, Anglican priest and founder of Methodism, described "means of grace" as "outward signs, words, or actions, ordained of God, and appointed for this end—to be the *ordinary* channels whereby he might convey to men, preventing, justifying, or sanctifying grace."[5] Wesley identified these three as chief means: "prayer, whether in secret or with the great congregation; searching the Scriptures (which implies reading, hearing, and meditating thereon) and receiving the Lord's Supper, eating bread and drinking wine in remembrance of him; and these we

---

[5] John Wesley, "The Means of Grace," in *The Works of John Wesley*, ed. Albert C. Outler et al. (Nashville, TN: Abingdon, 1984–), 1:381.

believe to be ordained of God, as the ordinary channels of conveying his grace to the souls of men."[6] Presumably, Wesley did not include baptism in this list because unlike the others, baptism is not a repeatable act, though it functions similarly as a channel of God's grace through the Holy Spirit. Clearly, however, Wesley insisted that the value of the means depends on their connection to the end, which is the knowledge and love of God.

The Holy Spirit establishes that vital connection. As Wesley stated, "all outward means whatever, if separate from the Spirit of God, cannot profit at all, cannot conduce, in any degree, either to the knowledge or love of God."[7] No intrinsic power can be found in any such means—not "in the words that are spoken in prayer, in the letter of Scripture read, the sound thereof heard, or the bread and wine received in the Lord's Supper"—but only in God: "the whole power is of him, whereby through any of these there is any blessing conveyed to our soul."[8] Wesley stressed that God remains above the means and is not limited by them, but in grace God has chosen these appointed means and works faithfully through them by the Holy Spirit.

This logic can also be extended to the church, as that community of God's people entrusted to practice the means of grace. Christ cannot be reduced to the church, but God's work through the church is an expression of grace. Scripture repeatedly designates the church as the body of Christ (e.g., Rom. 12:5, 1 Cor. 12:27). Scripture is also clear that Christ is the head of the body (Eph. 5:23, Col. 1:18), which is a critical distinction. The church is not the presence in the world of an otherwise absent Christ. Through the Spirit, Christ is already at work in the world, drawing all things unto himself. Christians are called to point to the living presence of Jesus Christ, the Savior and hope of the world. God has graciously conferred on the church the identity of the body of Christ, and the church is of the Holy Spirit through sheer gift. God's activity through the church by the Holy Spirit is reliable and trustworthy, not because of the church per se, but simply because of God's mercy. That the power comes from God's agency through the Holy Spirit, and not from the outward sign itself, is true of the means of grace and the church as a whole.

The Spirit of God actively imparts the presence of the risen Christ to his people and to this world through the sacraments and, given their necessarily ecclesial context, through the church itself. The Spirit's activity endows the church with a kind of sacramental character, a sacramentality that is utterly dependent on and revealing of the Spirit's ongoing activity to make Christ known to the glory of the Father.

CONCLUSION

The role of the Holy Spirit in mediation and sacramentality is vital. These related topics depend on and reflect a pneumatological dynamism that is crucial not only simply to understand but also to encounter and indeed experience. Through the saving work of the triune God, the Holy Spirit mediates grace to establish, heal, confirm, and strengthen God's relationship with his people. That same Spirit faithfully conveys the presence and power of Jesus Christ, crucified and risen from the dead, in the sacraments and in sacramental-like practices so that the Father's good purposes from creation to new

---

[6]Ibid.
[7]Ibid., 382.
[8]Ibid.

creation—and everything in between—will be fulfilled. Ultimately, the Spirit's activity in each respect is taken up in doxology, all to the praise of the one God who is Father, Son, and Holy Spirit.

FOR FURTHER READING

Baptism, Eucharist, and Ministry. Faith and Order Paper No. 111. Geneva: World Council of Churches, 1982.

Boersma, Hans. *Sacramental Preaching: Sermons on the Hidden Presence of Christ*. Grand Rapids, MI: Baker Academic, 2016.

Radner, Ephraim. *A Brutal Unity: The Spiritual Politics of the Christian Church*. Waco, TX: Baylor University Press, 2012.

Schillebeeckx, Edward. *Christ the Sacrament of the Encounter with God*. New York: Sheed & Ward, 1963.

Schmemann, Alexander. *For the Life of the World: Sacraments and Orthodoxy*. 2nd rev. and exp. ed. Crestwood, NY: St Vladimir's Seminary Press, 2002.

CHAPTER ELEVEN

The Spirit and Science

WOLFGANG VONDEY

Pneumatology and modern science share a complex history, albeit little cooperation. If by pneumatology is meant more broadly the study of spirit, then we can find a pneumatological interest implicit in contemporary physics, cosmology, astrology, and the natural sciences, although without direct recourse to theological inquiry. Likewise, the theological notion of pneumatology as the pursuit of the Spirit of God shares many of the pneumatological concerns of the sciences but has traditionally not engaged scientific methodology and associated empirical discoveries. This chapter attempts to bring out joint pneumatological concerns, including potential divergence and benefits of mutual inquiry. The essay traces both scientific and theological developments in order to highlight opportunities for further engagement of shared pneumatological interests. The starting point for this investigation is a placement of the notion of "spirit" in the science-religion conversation in order to suggest a general typology of pneumatological engagement. On this basis, the remainder of the chapter looks at pneumatological approaches to nature and the cosmos and concludes with an assessment of the role of the Spirit in contemporary theological dialogue with the sciences.

SPIRIT IN THE SCIENCE-RELIGION DIALOGUE

A metaphysical theological reading of Scripture shows two central pneumatological commitments: (a) the ontological statement that God is spirit (e.g., Jn 4:24) and (b) the experiential dimension of existence cannot escape the encounter with this divine spirit (e.g., Psalm 139). Christian pneumatology has struggled to reconcile these commitments with the scientific observations of matter and nature, primarily because of the difficulties surrounding the notion of "spirit." The theological difficulty concerns in particular the question whether to identify with "spirit" either the divine nature or a divine person, that is, to endorse either a pneumatology from the metaphysical perspective of spirit or a pneumatology from the theological perspective of the Spirit.[1] The blurring of distinctions between divine Spirit and human spirit have further expanded the scope of Christian pneumatology to include also in the notion of "spirit" concerns for the soul, mind,

---

[1] Wolfgang Vondey, "Pneumatology from the Perspective of the Spirit: A Historical and Theological Assessment," in *Third Article Theology: A Pneumatological Dogmatics*, ed. Myk Habets (Minneapolis, MN: Fortress, 2016), 77–96.

and human consciousness.[2] The difficulties become particularly evident in attempts to find a shared approach to the notion of "spirit," and the numerous, often ambiguous, ways in which the term has been used in the relationship between science and religion suggests the need for either a very broad understanding of pneumatology or a very particular definition that is likely restricting the possibility of mutual engagement.[3] Recent developments on both sides raise questions about the significance of the term "spirit" for mutual rapprochement.

The notion of "spirit" finds significant use in the science-religion conversation. On the theological side, the term appears (a) in the adoption of "spirit" from the theosophical tradition; (b) as a philosophical category (borrowed from philosophy of law, political philosophy, or philosophy of culture); (c) derived from the understanding of "spirit" in cultural anthropology or religious naturalism; (d) in the foundational role of the Spirit in spirituality, sometimes identified with the idea of religion; (e) in pastoral care and the psychological sciences; (f) in the discussions of systematic theology and pneumatological theology, including recent conversations in feminist and ecofeminist discourse; and (g) in the experiential identification of "spirit" in Pentecostal, charismatic, evangelical, and conservative Protestantism. In the sciences, approaches to "spirit" include (a) interest in the relationship of pneumatology to field theory in contemporary physics, (b) the concept of emergence in the biological sciences, (c) consciousness in the cognitive sciences, (d) advances in the discussions of "spirit" in information theory, (e) "spirit" as relationality and relatedness in the psychological and behavioral sciences, and (f) the developing connections between "spirit" and science in interfaith conversations. Despite the obvious ubiquity of terminology, the diversity of interests invested in the various approaches to pneumatology warrant further investigation of the role of "spirit" in the conversation.

In his widely known typology of options for relating science and religion, Ian Barbour suggests four different views: conflict, independence, dialogue, and integration.[4] Although these classifications and suggested modifications have made no significant use of the notion of "spirit,"[5] and historical introductions to the debate generally ignore the role of pneumatology, the broad significance of ambiguous and overlapping definitions raises the question where a pneumatological approach fits the typology. Recent developments in religious and theological studies, in particular, have significantly advanced insights into a shared pneumatological approach.[6] The success of such attempts depends not entirely on the room each view allows for the notion of spirit, but rather on the plausibility of each view in light of the multifarious identities of the pneumatological quest.

---

[2] Cf. Paul S. MacDonald, *History of the Concept of Mind: Speculations about Soul, Mind and Spirit from Homer to Hume* (Aldershot: Ashgate, 2003).

[3] See Amos Yong, "Discerning the Spirit(s) in the Natural World: Toward a Typology of 'Spirit' in the Religion and Science Conversation," *Theology and Science* 3, no. 3 (2005): 315–29.

[4] See Ian G. Barbour, *When Science Meets Religion: Enemies, Strangers, or Partners?* (San Francisco, CA: HarperSanFrancisco, 2000); Barbour, *Religion and Science: Historical and Contemporary Issues* (San Francisco, CA: HarperSanFrancisco, 1997).

[5] See James E. Hutchingson, ed., *Religion and the Natural Sciences: The Range of Engagement* (Eugene, OR: Wipf & Stock, 2005); Mikael Stenmark, *How to Relate Science and Religion* (Grand Rapids, MI: Eerdmans, 2004); John F. Haught, *Science and Religion: From Conflict to Conversation* (New York: Paulist, 1995).

[6] Bradley Shavit Artson, *Renewing the Process of Creation: A Jewish Integration of Science and Spirit* (Woodstock, VT: Jewish Lights, 2015); Michael Welker, ed., *The Spirit in Creation and New Creation: Science and Theology in Western and Orthodox Realms* (Grand Rapids, MI: Eerdmans, 2012); Diarmuid O'Murchu, *In the Beginning Was the Spirit: Science, Religion and Indigenous Spirituality* (Maryknoll, NY: Orbis, 2012).

The conflict model asserts that science and religion are incompatible and irreconcilable. They not only exist in competition but have fundamentally opposed ontological commitments and methodological convictions so that one cannot stand on both grounds. Consequently, the notion of "spirit" is either reserved for only one of the two (generally, religion) or the identity of "spirit" in each field is unrelated and incompatible with the other. Even if unintended, the conflict view takes on an explicit pneumatological position, namely the rejection of the ubiquitous theological notion of "spirit" as a resource for scientific inquiry. This position is effectively a rejection of the notion of "spirit" altogether, since the same term cannot be used in theology and science without indicating similarity. At the very least, the conflict model reduces pneumatology to a particular discipline and segregates pneumatological (and disciplinary) realms. If the conflict view allows for some sort of pneumatological orientation in the sciences, its presupposition is that despite the empirically verifiable quality of observations, the identical notion of "spirit" (whatever its term and definition in the sciences) cannot be appropriated for use in theology.

The independence model asserts that science and religion are unrelated and thus non-conflicting domains. Each discipline possesses a unique language designed to answer different questions, which may also be complementary, as long as the distinctive domains are observed. The ontological commitments of the natural sciences can identify with "spirit" only empirically verifiable, material or immaterial, substance without immediate recourse to theological claims of divinity. Any identification of a scientific notion of "spirit" with the presence and experience of God is the task of the theological enterprise. Nonetheless, because independence does not preclude compatibility, the theological notion of the Spirit and a scientific concept of "spirit" can offer legitimate insights into different dimensions of pneumatology. The independence view effectively divides pneumatology into (at least) two assessable disciplines and suggests that this division is justified by the existence of two (or more) quantifiable realms of spirit. While the latter distinction is readily confirmed by a typology of spirit,[7] the independence view, like the conflict view, radically alters the pursuit of pneumatology and denies the notion of "spirit" the ubiquitous quality foundational to theology.

The dialogue model presupposes similarities between science and religion that warrant communication. While respecting the integrity of each discipline, dialogue invites mutual and critical interpretation of one realm in terms of the other. Scientific concepts may yield information on empirical observations which clarify the theological imagination of "spirit" (and vice versa, although the influence of theological ideas on the hard sciences is difficult to show). Dialogue forms the presupposition for engaging the conceptual ubiquity of the notion of "spirit" and the hospitality of a shared pneumatological quest. This model also allows for the possibility of conflict albeit not at the cost of irreconcilability. Rather, the dialogue model forms the basis for the multidisciplinary pursuit of pneumatology by expanding and modifying the notion of "spirit" in one discipline in light of the discoveries made by the other.[8] In this sense, pneumatology is, in a foundational sense, the dialogical pursuit of spirit.

---

[7] See Amos Yong, "The Spirit Hovers over the World," *Metanexus* (October 26, 2004), available at http://www.metanexus.net/essay/spirit-hovers-over-world.

[8] Cf. Wolfgang Vondey, "The Presence of the Spirit in the Academy: Pentecostal and Charismatic Studies as an Interdisciplinary Concern," *PentecoStudies: Interdisciplinary Journal for Research on the Pentecostal and Charismatic Movements* 16, no. 1 (2017): 85–116.

The integration model extends the assertions of the dialogue view by seeking support for one discipline in the arguments of the other. Science and religion are mutually compatible and complementary domains that allow for instruction, vindication, and even correction of independently held ideas.[9] Integration is not simply a strong version of the dialogue position but espouses a radical pneumatology which sees a harmonious understanding of spirit resulting from a unified pursuit of all disciplines. Knowledge of what is "spirit" cannot be claimed by either science or religion independently, and the theological assertions that God is a ubiquitous Spirit must both find reflection in the sciences and cannot be understood without recourse to scientific disciplines. The ultimate consequence of this view is that integration itself is based on the same "spirit" who is both the object and subject of pneumatology. How the different methodological commitments of science and theology affect the dialogue forms the heart of both critical responses and interdisciplinary collaborations.

The remainder of this essay details the history of these approaches to pneumatology. The traditional fields for dialogue between theology and science have undoubtedly been shared concerns for cosmology, the origins of the universe (cosmogony), a theology of nature, and anthropology.[10] Nonetheless, whether the scientific revolution and the emergence of modern science has opened the doors for further engagement with scientific observations in the attempt to clarify in particular how the divine, as spirit, can be manifested in the world, has not been widely explored.[11] The modest goal for the remaining chapter is to indicate the place of "spirit" in the theological engagement with the history of modern science in order to assess the role of pneumatology for the relating of science and theology.

SPIRIT IN THE HISTORY OF MODERN SCIENCE

Isaac Newton's monumental work *The Principia* signaled a dramatic change in the history of the natural sciences toward developing a philosophy of nature based on universal mathematical principles.[12] Yet, Newton's continuing interest in alchemy also signaled the importance of finding an empirical link between material and immaterial substances in the increasing dominance of quantitative scientific experimentation.[13] In principle, Newton proposed that matter was infused with a force that could be understood as the origin of all activity.[14] He ended *The Principia* with reference to a "spirit" pervading the natural world and indicated its correspondence to this force, although its exact nature had remained undefined.[15] For Newton, the chief scientific task was finding an explanation for this

---

[9] Barbour, *When Science Meets Religion*, 3–4; Haught, *Science and Religion*, 3–4.
[10] Cyril Hovorum, "Convergence between Theology and Science: Patterns from the Early Christian Era," in Welker, *The Spirit in Creation*, 111–19; Andrew Louth, "The Holy Spirit in Creation and Re-Creation: The Byzantine Fathers," in Welker, *The Spirit in Creation*, 171–8.
[11] Cf. Wolfgang Vondey, "The Holy Spirit and the Physical Universe: The Impact of Scientific Paradigm Shifts on Contemporary Pneumatology," *Theological Studies* 70, no. 1 (2009): 3–36.
[12] Isaac Newton, *The Principia: Mathematical Principles of Natural Philosophy*, trans. I. Bernard Cohen and Anne Whitman (Berkeley, CA: University of California Press, 1999).
[13] See, for example, Betty Jo Teeter Dobbs, *The Foundations of Newton's Alchemy or "The Hunting of the Greene Lyon"* (Cambridge: Cambridge University Press, 1975).
[14] Ernan McMullin, *Newton on Matter and Activity* (Notre Dame, IN: University of Notre Dame Press, 1978), 54.
[15] Ibid., 94.

"spirit" as substantially present in the cosmos without being corporeally manifested in the natural world. Although Newton did not make any particularly theological claims in his scientific studies, his perspective has provided a succinct framework for modern theology.[16]

Newton's work highlights the difficulties in defining the properties of a spirit that has not been verified experimentally. Since Newton considered God to be both radically transcendent and the ultimate cause of all natural phenomena, his scientific pneumatology pursued in principle the existence of an intermediary agent between God and the world.[17] His imagination with regard to this idea of spirit surfaced initially in the alchemical concept of a universal, vital aether and eventually in the scientific notion of "force." The former had already found entrance into Christian thought through the influence of Stoic philosophy.[18] Yet, it is the latter approach which has become the most enduring concept for the Christian understanding of the Spirit. While Newton's insistence that all forces can be quantified by natural phenomena effectively established the roots of modern science, the spiritual status he attributed to nonmaterial forces also provided a framework for the development of modern Protestant and Catholic theology. The impact of Newton's ideas can be observed in the thought of such influential thinkers as Karl Barth, Karl Rahner, Wolfhart Pannenberg, and Jürgen Moltmann.[19] Nonetheless, the understanding of "spirit" as "force" remains highly dependent on the material dimensions of space and time which govern the Newtonian universe in an absolute sense. The main obstacle for a theological engagement with the concept of force is its apparent material limitation placed on the divine Spirit—a concern inherited from patristic engagement with Stoic philosophy.[20] The scientific advances of the concept of force and the eventual replacement of Newtonian mechanics in the twentieth century with the theories of relativity and quantum physics have radically altered the possible convergence of scientific and theological pneumatology.

SPIRIT AND NATURE

The physical dimensions of nature are the primary building blocks of pneumatology in a Newtonian universe. Theological attempts to identify the presence of God in the world have aimed primarily at understanding the character of divine action embodied in the Christ-event.[21] However, the renaissance of pneumatology in the twentieth century has raised questions about the possibility of the embodiment of the Spirit in, and also apart from, the incarnation. Two dominant approaches are the identification of divine action through the Spirit conceived, on the one hand, as intellect or, on the other, as force. The interpretation of the Spirit as "mind" or "intellect" has dominated Christian pneumatology since the

---

[16]Thomas F. Torrance, "Newton, Einstein and Scientific Theology," *Religious Studies* 8 (1972): 239.
[17]Betty Jo Teeter Dobbs, *The Janus Faces of Genius* (Cambridge: Cambridge University Press, 1991), 36–7.
[18]See Betty Jo Teeter Dobbs, "Newton's Rejection of the Mechanical Aether: Empirical Difficulties and Guiding Assumptions," in *Scrutinizing Science: Empirical Studies of Scientific Change*, ed. Arthur Donovan et al. (Baltimore, MD: The Johns Hopkins University Press, 1988), 69–83.
[19]Cf. Wolfgang Vondey, "The Holy Spirit and Time in Contemporary Catholic and Protestant Theology," *Scottish Journal of Theology* 58, no. 4 (2005): 393–409.
[20]See Samuel Sambursky, *Physics of the Stoics* (London: Routledge & Paul, 1959). Cf. Theodore James Whapham, "Spirit as Field of Force," *Scottish Journal of Theology* 67, no. 1 (2014): 15–32.
[21]See Denis Edwards, *How God Acts: Creation, Redemption, and Special Divine Action* (Minneapolis, MN: Fortress, 2010).

patristic age and likely also influenced Newton's thought. As intellect or information, the Spirit does not possess physical dimensions but is distributed spatially in a way that determines the very nature of physical reality.[22] In this manner, God as spirit can be seen as both present and active in creation: God's Spirit as the mind of the universe is essentially identical with the laws of nature, although no direct causal relationship can be established between the divine action and the natural and material spheres.[23]

In contrast, the modern development of physics has moved the idea of force away from the dynamics of a mechanical universe and the strict confines of space and matter toward independent qualities of reality.[24] Michael Faraday's reintroduction of ancient field theory, with its origins in the Stoic notion of *pneuma*, opened the doors for further development of the idea of an immaterial force to both scientific and theological ontology. Faraday's experiments in electromagnetism improved the understanding of an immaterial force's effect from a distance through the energy of a field. James Clerk Maxwell's demonstration of gravity as a field of force further helped integrate Newton's work with Faraday's by loosening strict geometric interpretations of space and matter. Wolfhart Pannenberg has most widely engaged these two developments in their direct implications for a theological understanding of the Spirit.[25] In his opinion, the identification of "spirit" with scientific notions of "force" and "field" has directed theology away from a reductionist identification of "spirit" and "mind." Further developments in gravitational theory and quantum mechanics allow the field to be conceived beyond matter and only in relation to space-time corresponding to the theological notions of divine omnipresence and eternity.[26] Pannenberg proposes that the Holy Spirit can "be understood . . . as a unique manifestation (singularity) of the field of the divine essentiality."[27] According to Pannenberg, by insisting on the personhood of the Spirit, and thus on the importance of the doctrine of the Trinity, the theological perception of the Spirit in creation as a dynamic operation of the Father and the Son must also reflect on the scientific use of field theory.[28] The Spirit as field of force can be understood as the actual principle of movement (omnipotence) and unity of the divine essence (omnipresence) in the physical universe.[29] Although Pannenberg interprets the metaphysical statement that "God is Spirit" in terms of the field concept and directs this interpretation ultimately toward the traditional theological statement that "God is love," there has been little wider theological engagement with Pannenberg's proposal.[30]

SPIRIT AND THE COSMOS

A major criticism of Pannenberg's idea comes from Anglican priest and theoretical physicist John Polkinghorne, who faults the theological use of field theory as failing to recognize

---

[22] John Polkinghorne, *Belief in God in an Age of Science* (New Haven, CT: Yale University Press, 1998), 63.
[23] Nicholas Saunders, *Divine Action and Modern Science* (Cambridge: Cambridge University Press, 2002), 17–47.
[24] Max Jammer, *Concepts of Force* (Cambridge, MA: Harvard University Press, 1957).
[25] Wolfhart Pannenberg, *Systematic Theology*, 3 vols. (Grand Rapids, MI: Eerdmans, 1991), 1:370–83; 2:76–115. See Whapham, "Spirit as Field of Force," 16–27.
[26] Pannenberg, *Systematic Theology*, 1:382; 2:84–102.
[27] Ibid., 2:83.
[28] Ibid., 84.
[29] Ibid., 1:397–421.
[30] Whapham, "Spirit as Field of Force," 30–1.

that fields "are carriers of energy and momentum . . . as rigidly deterministic as those of Newtonian particle dynamics."[31] Polkinghorne laments the widespread theological neglect of Einstein's paradigm shift, and indeed, Pannenberg (as much as others) continues to speak of space and time in dominantly Newtonian ideas virtually indistinguishable from the notion of the universal aether.[32] In contrast, insisting that the properties of nature are invariant to a particular frame of reference, the theory of relativity postulates that the properties of space and time are codependent in the material universe.[33] With space and time no longer independent and absolute, no symmetry can be assumed with regard to universal and instantaneously acting forces, and if field theory replaces the Newtonian concept of force, then the entire cosmos can be considered subject to motion and extension.[34] The notion of "spirit" can therefore be defined only relative to the symmetry of the space-time continuum and possesses no material qualities literally composed of the entities in nature. If the metaphysical claim that "God is spirit" is to be located in the physical universe, post-Newtonian physics locates "spirit" most clearly as the universal principle and rational order of the cosmos.[35] Cosmic pneumatology, whether ancient or modern, continues to make use of the classical identification of "spirit" and "mind," albeit now within a relative frame of reference dominated by pantheistic or panentheistic notions of the divine presence.

The development of quantum physics and chaos theory since Einstein has directed the focus further into the micro-level of elementary physical processes. Arthur Peacocke, in particular, has called for further developing our understanding of quantum divine action, downward causation, and emergence.[36] Of pneumatological interest in these recent scientific developments is the place of "spirit" in understanding God's immanence in nature in a way that not only may not be analogous to the classical laws of physics, but also may be more complex than the inherent structures of the universe. Pneumatology offers a theological account of complexity corresponding to scientific observations. The prospect of allocating God's action pneumatologically at the quantum mechanical level allows for affirmation of God's presence in all quantum events, although God may choose to influence only some, which effectively makes the Spirit a potential constant variable in the processes of nature.[37] Others have pointed to the potential impact of chaotic unpredictability that opens room for a theology of the Spirit less dependent on the determinism of Newtonian laws of physics.[38] Ontological commitments of Christian theology do not readily find a correspondence in the empirical world of contemporary physics, chemistry, or biology.

---

[31]John Polkinghorne, "The Hidden Work of the Spirit in Creation," in Welker, *The Spirit in Creation*, 4; John Polkinghorne, "Fields and Theology: A Response to Wolfhart Pannenberg," *Zygon* 36, no. 4 (2001): 795–7.
[32]Cf. Vondey, "The Holy Spirit and the Physical Universe," 25.
[33]See Michio Kaku, *Einstein's Cosmos: How Albert Einstein's Vision Transformed Our Understanding of Space and Time* (New York: Norton, 2004).
[34]See Albert Einstein, *Relativity: The Special and the General Theory* (New York: Random House, 1961).
[35]Cf. Vondey, "The Holy Spirit and the Physical Universe," 26.
[36]See Arthur Peacocke, *Theology for a Scientific Age: Being and Becoming—Natural, Divine and Human*, 2nd ed. (Minneapolis, MN: Fortress, 1993).
[37]See the essays in Robert John Russell, Nancey Murphy, and Arthur R. Peacocke, eds., *Chaos and Complexity: Scientific Perspectives on Divine Action* (Vatican City State: Vatican Observatory; Berkeley, CA: Center for Theology and the Natural Sciences, 1998).
[38]John Jefferson Davis, *The Frontiers of Science and Faith: Examining Questions from the Big Bang to the End of the Universe* (Downers Grove, IL: InterVarsity, 2002).

In response, recent attempts suggest a theological approach which envisions God as spirit as an emergent form of complexity rather than a fundamental ontological category inherent to nature.[39] In contrast to classical evolutionary theory, which explains the development of nature from a causal relation to preceding forms of species, the focus of emergence is on the teleological prospect of arriving at something new that may not be directly derived from previous states of nature. The notion of "spirit" is in this view the result of a correspondence of the divine Spirit to a natural process of emergent complexity.[40] The eternally existing Spirit is also in the process of becoming spirit amidst the material permutations of the physical world. Pneumatology must therefore negotiate a more complex and relational account of the fit of the classical metaphysical presuppositions of Christianity in the scientific projections of an ever-changing universe.

SPIRIT AND SCIENCE IN CONTEMPORARY THEOLOGY

Theological attempts to come to terms with the development of scientific pneumatology and the role of the Spirit in the cosmos reflect a widespread concern for both methodological concerns of how to relate science and religion and the relating of traditional theological themes to the discoveries of the modern sciences. The initial methodological challenge inherited from classical theism remains the reconciliation of scientific accounts of the cosmos with the traditional reading of Scripture.[41] Whether a pneumatological reading of divine activity in the world can be traced in the creation narratives of the OT remains widely debated. The primary difficulty is not only a "scientific" reading that may appear forced on the biblical texts but also, more importantly, a solution to the question how a scientific pneumatology can integrate the biblical material, considering the often weak pneumatological reading of Scripture in the first place.[42] Pneumatology with its hospitality to interdisciplinary inquiry offers room for discussion on the convergence of scientific method and theological method rooted in a shared interest in the nature of spirit rather than the exclusive commitments of each discipline. Nonetheless, pneumatology has generally found greater interest in the "soft" sciences, whereas the "hard" sciences have typically remained inaccessible to most Christian thinkers.

Traditional themes of classical theism engage the scientific conversation typically on the premises of existing, dominant theological loci. A prominent line of discussion has been the anthropological question of how the Spirit features in the formation of human beings and society. How the Spirit of God can be seen in the human spirit, as image of God, in relation to body and soul, and in human personhood remains among the most dominant enquiries.[43] A second area of focus has been eschatological questions

---

[39]Philip Clayton, *Mind and Emergence: From Quantum to Consciousness* (Oxford: Oxford University Press, 2004).

[40]Philip Clayton, *Adventures in the Spirit: God, World, Divine Action*, ed. Zachary Simpson (Minneapolis, MN: Fortress, 2008), 110–11.

[41]See Jeffrey Schloss, "Hovering over the Waters: Spirit and the Ordering of Creation," in Welker, *The Spirit in Creation*, 26–49.

[42]See Vern S. Poythress, *Science and Hermeneutics*, Foundations of Contemporary Interpretation 6 (Grand Rapids, MI: Zondervan, 1988).

[43]See Michael Welker, ed., *The Depth of the Human Person: A Multidisciplinary Approach* (Grand Rapids, MI: Eerdmans, 2014), 79–146.

arising with the revival of eschatology in the twentieth century. Of chief concern have been the Spirit's teleological role in the material destiny of the universe and related questions of divine providence and the interpretation of history in light of the physicality of God's kingdom.[44] Another dominant perspective of traditional theism confronting pneumatology are christological questions engaging the philosophy of science. The traditionally strong anthropological concerns of Christology, but also its eschatological emphasis, engage well with the cosmic scope of pneumatological concerns in the sciences, while pneumatology benefits from the metaphysical and incarnational depth of traditional Christology.[45] A final prominent approach is the revival of trinitarian contributions to the science and theology conversation. The doctrine of the Trinity has served both methodological approaches and specific attempts to rethink the nature of scientific discoveries.[46] A pneumatological focus has contributed particularly to trinitarian theologies of creation, nature, and the environment emerging from the Spirit's personal activity in the world.[47]

A most recent development is the rise of Pentecostal and charismatic Christianity and its engagement with the sciences. The material and experiential concerns of Pentecostals and the strong influence of pneumatology on the theology of the movement have led to significant questions about the involvement of God as spirit (and of Christianity as a movement of the Spirit) in the renewal of creation, the relation of the natural and the supernatural, the theory of evolution, the link of anthropology and spirituality, the medical and behavioral sciences, human empowerment and flourishing, and a pneumatological ecology.[48] The historical ambivalence of Pentecostals to the sciences has made room for dialogue with a more scientifically informed metaphysics of "spirit" engaging the divine, human, natural, and demonic realms of creation.[49] This variegated pneumatological approach has led Pentecostal theology both to constructive engagement with scientific disciplines and to critical response to scientific reductionism and its prominent pneumatological deficit. The charismatic emphasis encourages a re-enchanted vision of nature through a pneumatological cosmology which envisions the world as an enspirited creation in which the Spirit of God takes center stage.[50] The future of relating science and the Spirit lies therefore perhaps in redressing the concerns of classical theism (e.g., the Holy Spirit as person) and classical physics (e.g., the laws of nature) in light of experiential and embodied forms of encountering the Spirit that are both empirically verifiable and theologically fruitful.

---

[44]See Jürgen Moltmann, *God in Creation: A New Theology of Creation and the Spirit of God* (Minneapolis, MN: Fortress, 1993).
[45]See F. LeRon Shults, *Christology and Science* (Aldershot: Ashgate, 2008).
[46]See John Polkinghonrne, *Science and the Trinity: The Christian Encounter with Reality* (New Haven, CT: Yale University Press, 2004).
[47]See Denis Edwards, *Breath of Life: A Theology of the Creator Spirit* (Maryknoll, NY: Orbis, 2004); Mark I. Wallace, *Fragments of the Spirit: Nature, Violence, and the Renewal of Creation* (Harrisburg, PA: Trinity, 2002).
[48]See James K. A. Smith and Amos Yong, eds., *Science and the Spirit: A Pentecostal Engagement with the Sciences* (Bloomington, IN: Indiana University Press, 2010); Amos Yong, ed., *The Spirit Renews the Face of the Earth: Pentecostal Forays in Science and Theology of Creation* (Eugene, OR: Wipf & Stock, 2009).
[49]Amos Yong, *The Spirit of Creation: Modern Science and Divine Action in the Pentecostal-Charismatic Imagination*, Pentecostal Manifestos 6 (Grand Rapids, MI: Eerdmans, 2011).
[50]Ibid., 173–225.

FOR FURTHER READING

Clayton, Philip. *Adventures in the Spirit: God, World, Divine Action.* Edited by Zachary Simpson. Minneapolis, MN: Fortress, 2008.

Pannenberg, Wolfhart. *Systematic Theology.* 3 vols. Grand Rapids, MI: Eerdmans, 1991.

Peacocke, Arthur. *Theology for a Scientific Age: Being and Becoming—Natural, Divine and Human.* 2nd edn. Minneapolis, MN: Fortress, 1993.

Smith, James K. A., and Amos Yong, eds. *Science and the Spirit: A Pentecostal Engagement with the Sciences.* Bloomington, IN: Indiana University Press, 2010.

Welker, Michael, ed. *The Spirit in Creation and New Creation: Science and Theology in Western and Orthodox Realms.* Grand Rapids, MI: Eerdmans, 2012.

CHAPTER TWELVE

The Spirit and Visions of Life

Seeing the World and Humanity Otherwise in the Light of God's Face

DANIELA C. AUGUSTINE

Orthodox Christianity understands theology not as a solitary intellectual enterprise, but as a charismatic gift given to the community of faith by the Holy Spirit,[1] the One who grants humanity the vision of its origin and *telos*—the vision of the trinitarian proto-community—and incarnates it into the redeemed human *socium* as the life of the new creation. Consistent with this understanding, John Meyendorff describes theology as "internal vision," which requires both personal and communal "ascetic effort"—"an effort made within the community of saints."[2] Thus, theology is "an act of the Church"[3] summoned in/by the Spirit to discern the vision and to become what she beholds as the visible, in-Spirit-ed image of the invisible divine communal presence within the material creation. It is not accidental, then, that, in the words of St. Seraphim of Sarov, the aim of the Christian life is "the acquisition of the Holy Spirit."[4]

The breathtaking prologue of the Fourth Gospel, presenting John's christological commentary on the act of creation, is translucent with this Spirit-breathed, theological vision. It is paradigmatic for the Christ-filtered hermeneutical lenses of the post-resurrection, post-Pentecost faith community. The prologue's theological poetry, however, elucidates also the Spirit's redemptive transformation of the believer's perception of the world—its origin, essence, and eschatological destiny. It articulates the story of cosmic becoming in terms of a communal conversation—a loving, perichoretic trialogue in interface with the other. The text depicts the Word speaking forth the world

---

[1] H. A. H. Bartholomew I, *Encountering the Mystery* (New York: Doubleday 2008), 42–3. Reflecting on humanity's intellectual limitations in defining and describing adequately God, Patriarch Bartholomew I asserts that "all theology is made possible exclusively through the gift of the Holy Spirit. It is the divine Spirit that allows us to approach and encounter the mystery of theology in a manner that is worthy of God" (ibid.).
[2] "Doing Theology in an Eastern Orthodox Perspective," in *Eastern Orthodox Theology: A Contemporary Reader*, ed. Daniel B. Clendenin (Grand Rapids, MI: Baker, 1995), 87.
[3] Bartholomew I, *Encountering the Mystery*, 44.
[4] St. Seraphim of Sarov, *On Acquisition of the Holy Spirit* (Louisville, KY: CreateSpace, 2014), 9.

while being turned toward God (*pros ton theon*) (Jn 1:1).[5] The creative speech is not directed outside the divine communal reality but rather remains in the inner communion of the Trinity itself. The prologue raptures the theological imagination into a mesmerizing vision of the Trinity as a tri-directional discourse of harmonious, perichoretic beauty that sings forth the cosmos into existence within its own communal reality. Creation comes forth as the visible poetry and triune song of Love itself, for Love cannot help but make place (or rather present itself as a sanctuary) for the other. Thus, in the act of creation, we see the Trinity as an *ascetic* (self-respacing) and *kenotic* (self-sharing) community—a communal life of radical hospitality (*philoxenia*) marked by unconditional love for the other and the different, all the while sustaining their uncompromised otherness.

In the first chapter of Genesis, the Spirit-illuminated eyes of faith see a vision of God creating the other and building for them a home within the divine communal self.[6] Yet, God creates within himself the world as humanity's home so that, in turn, humanity may learn to image the trinitarian communal life by welcoming God within itself as a home/sanctuary for the divine presence. This cosmic home-building is the work of the Spirit in the human community, guiding, indwelling, and carving it into its *telos*—the last Adam in his communal form, the church—until the entire cosmos becomes one grand, pneumatic, ecclesial *anthropos*.[7] Since, from the beginning, the last Adam is the ontological *telos* of the first Adam and of all creation (1 Cor. 15:28), and his communal body is to circumscribe all existence (both terrestrial and celestial) into union with the Creator, then not the first Adam but the church as cosmic, charismatic, christoformed community is the crown of creation—the christified destiny of all existence. To paraphrase *The Shepherd of Hermas*, the church is the goal for which the world exists[8]—the embodied eschatological vision of the Spirit-saturated cosmos. Therefore, from the beginning, creation is spoken into existence in anticipation of Pentecost.

Pentecost unveils the church as both the *telos* of the cosmos and the incarnate hope for its mending. It offers a tangible vision of the *eschaton* embodied in the pneumatized human community whose eyes have been opened by the Spirit to see the world, oneself, and the fellow human, and to discern God's face in the face of the other, mirroring it back

---

[5] On the significance of the preposition *pros*, see, D. A. Carson, *The Gospel According to John* (Grand Rapids, MI: Eerdmans, 1991), 116 and Francis J. Moloney, S.D.B., *The Gospel of John*, ed. Daniel J. Harrington, S.J., SP 4 (Collegeville, MN: Liturgical, 1998), 35.

[6] For an exposition on God as an architect who is building and furnishing a house, see John Dominic Crossan, *God and Empire: Jesus Against Rome, Then and Now* (New York: Harper One, 2007), 51–2.

[7] For Vladimir Lossky, the church (as the communal body of Christ) is destined to engulf the cosmos, reuniting it with God. Lossky states, "The Church is the center of the universe, the sphere in which its destinies are determined. All are called to enter into the Church, for if man is a microcosm, the Church is a *macro-anthropos*, as St. Maximus says. It increases and is compounded in history, bringing the elect into its bosom and uniting them to God. The world grows old and falls into decay, while the Church is constantly rejuvenated and renewed by the Holy Spirit who is the source of its life. At a given moment, when the Church has attained to the fullness of growth determined by the will of God, the external world, having used up its vital resources, will perish. As for the Church, it will appear in its eternal glory as the Kingdom of God." *The Mystical Theology of the Eastern Church* (Crestwood, NY: St. Vladimir's Seminary Press, 2002), 178. Dimitru Staniloae, also utilizing the language of St. Maximus the Confessor (*Mystagogy*, chap. 7, PG 91.684C-685A), depicts the human being as a *microcosm* and the world as a *macro-anthropos* and emphasizes human agency in the process of gathering all creation into union with God; see *The Experience of God: Orthodox Dogmatic Theology*, vol. 1 (Brookline, MA: Holy Cross Orthodox Press, 2005), 4–6.

[8] *The Shepherd of Hermas*, vision II, chap. 4; available at http://www.earlychristianwritings.com/text/shepherd.html.

for all to see until everything becomes illuminated by its light. In view of this assertion, the present chapter offers a theological reflection on the Spirit's vision of the world as sacrament unfolding within the divine presence. It further highlights the theology of the face articulated through Orthodox iconography[9] and its pneumatic vision of human ontology and vocation as well as their redemptive renewal in the event of Pentecost. The chapter concludes by uplifting the Spirit's vision of the Beautiful (the triune life) inscribed through the liturgy's pneumatic movement upon Christ's communal body on earth.

SEEING THE WORLD OTHERWISE: THE SPIRIT'S VISION OF CREATION AS A EUCHARISTIC SACRAMENT

The book of Job offers a brief glimpse of creation's unfolding as a joyous divine liturgy performed by God himself before heaven's worshipping host in the cathedral of the universe (Job 38:4-7). Illuminated by the Spirit, the eyes of faith discern the trinitarian liturgical movement also in the account of Genesis, seeing each creature coming forth as a communal/congregational response to the summoning self-proclamation of the uncreated, eternal Word. Therefore, in the act of creation, the world unfolds as an exquisitely choreographed eucharistic liturgy, an *epicletic* sacramental act during which matter comes forth as means of communion between the human being and its creator toward the actualization of humanity's pneumatic ontological *telos* in *theosis*.

As a teleological eucharistic element, the world cannot be kept for oneself—it is made to be shared with the other. By participating in it, human beings have to learn solidarity with others in the shared cosmic nature that each one of them hypostatizes and yet all have in common. As Staniloae insightfully suggests, "A separation of cosmic nature taken to the limit between human individuals is impossible."[10] Therefore, the God-given limitations of the material world are part of the intentional pedagogy on becoming like him—they press humanity to share life and to grow spiritually out of self-centeredness toward communal solidarity with others, realizing that the only way matter can meet all existential needs is in the generosity of the Spirit. This is a mark of eucharistic existence that provides an antidote to unrestrained, self-indulgent consumerism, which commodifies the world, distorting its sacramental purpose alongside the vision of the other from a co-celebrant in the cosmic liturgy[11] to a competitor for ever-shrinking material resources.[12]

Indeed, in the act of creation, God gives the world to humanity in self-sharing as a gift of life so that humanity may, in turn, learn to share it with the other and the different.

---

[9]Some of the thoughts in this section were explored first in "Image, Spirit and *Theosis*: Imaging God in an Image-distorting World," in *The Image of God in an Image Driven Age: Explorations in Christian Anthropology*, ed. Beth Felker Jones and Jeff Barbeau (Downers Grove, IL: InterVarsity, 2016), 173–88. An extensively edited and much expounded version of this section can be found in Daniela C. Augustine, *The Spirit and the Common Good* (Grand Rapids, MI: Eerdmans, 2019).
[10]Dimitru Staniloae, *The Experience of God: Orthodox Dogmatic Theology*, vol. 2 (Brookline, MA: Holy Cross Orthodox Press, 2005), 2.
[11]Alexander Schmemann, *For the Life of the World* (Crestwood, NY: St Vladimir's Seminary, 1983), 17.
[12]In the wise and righteous structure of the universe are "the checks and balances" also visible of divinely established limitations/boundaries that are not to be transgressed. Thus, as Moltmann points out, ecological limits are placed on economic growth, which in turn makes terminal to both society and nature the unrestrained exploitation of one human being by another; see Jürgen Moltmann, *Ethics of Hope* (Minneapolis, MN: Fortress, 2012), 221.

The world is a gift with a pedagogical purpose—helping humanity "to grow spiritually"[13] in the likeness of its Creator. According to Staniloae, this pedagogy develops through the "dialogue of the gift" between the recipient and the giver in which the world is to be continually received with gratitude and offered back to God in an act of self-giving.[14] However, the gift's christoforming pedagogy teaches giving to the other more than one has received from them (cf. Mt. 25:14-30). One adds to the gift one's very life in the form of creative labor before offering it back to God (thus, grain and grapes are transformed through the *askesis* of human work into bread and wine before being offered to God).[15] Ultimately, the eucharistic nature of the cosmos is to transform everyday work of world-making into a liturgical act of home-building for the other.

If the creation of the world is an outcome of a loving communal conversation made visible in the divine creative act, then the world's transformation into a sanctuary for God's presence via in-Spirit-ed human agency cannot be accomplished through other means but by reflecting the Trinity's way of world-making. It takes an intentionally dialogical human community, bringing together its polyphonic cultural and ethnographic diversity into a constructive conversational unison, imaging the divine life in active, creative consensus of world-making as sanctuary-carving for the other—for the flourishing of all God's creatures.

REMEMBERING THE DIVINE FACE IN THE FACE OF THE FELLOW HUMAN: THE SPIRIT'S VISION OF THE OTHER

Human beings are homesick creatures, haunted by the primordial memory of Eden as their lost home—a living sanctuary, illuminated by the divine countenance and actualized in communion with the One in the image and for the likeness of whom they are created. This haunting memory of *shalom* amidst cosmic flourishing articulates life as shaped by seeing God's face and recognizing it in the face of the other as in oneself—a tri-directional, mirroring of the meaning and destiny of being human. It expresses the longing for a different world—one in which humanity stands without fear before the eyes of God and neighbor in transparent openness toward the other. This openness is built within the very fibers of human ontology's communal reality as sacramental imaging of the trinitarian life. While church liturgy, as choreographed theology, visibly expresses this evanescent knowing of and longing for home in and with God, its anamnetic structure does not center on lament for the loss but bridges origin and *eschaton* in hopeful reorientation

---

[13]Staniloae, *The Experience of God*, 2:22.

[14]"The paradox [of the return of the gift] is explained by the fact that the gift received and returned draws the persons close to one another to such an extent that the object of the gift becomes something common and comes to be the transparent means for the fullest communion between persons. And not only is the gift something common, but it is also increased through the life that the persons communicate to one another through the love manifested in the gift they make; in this way the persons give themselves as a gift, and through this giving they grow spiritually" (ibid.). Staniloae goes on to say, "The dialogue of the gift between God and the human person lies in the fact that each bestows himself upon the other" (ibid., 23).

[15]For more on the liturgical nature of human creativity, see James K. A. Smith, *Desiring the Kingdom: Worship, Worldview, and Cultural Formation* (Grand Rapids, MI: Baker Academic, 2009), 199 and Daniela C. Augustine, "The Liturgical Teleology of Human Creativity and the City of God as *Theosis* of Culture," *Cultural Encounters: A Journal for the Theology of Culture* 10, no. 2 (2015): 3–26.

from the tragic irreversibility of the past to the welcoming embrace of the adventing future. As an event in, with, and through the Spirit, the liturgy becomes a passage from the old into the new creation[16] and an *epicletic* time-travel from the present age to the age to come—a homecoming in the Christ-shaped eschatological future of the world where he is all in all.

Iconography (as theology in images) is a powerful medium in this process of anamnetic reorientation, allowing the viewer to remember not only the world but also oneself and the other otherwise—a remembering illuminated by the *eschaton*. The icon is a depiction of the renewed creation summoned in the last Adam and made once again luminous with the beauty of restored communion between heaven and earth.[17] The significance of the theology of the face (the all-summoning divine countenance imprinted upon the human community) is elucidated by Orthodox iconography. The faces of the saints, while being distinctly different, are all intentionally reminiscent of the face of Christ—the one fully pneumatic, eucharistic human being—the prototype and *telos* of humanity. The icons depict humanity transfigured in *theosis* together with all creation. The recapturing of the divine face in the faces of the saints articulates holiness as the visible and tangible life of God in a human life that has been united to and transfigured by the Holy Spirit in Christ-likeness. Therefore, the liturgical incorporation of the saints' icons could be understood not merely as recognizing the presence of and communing with the "great cloud of witnesses" (Heb. 12:1), but also as being summoned by the divine face into an encounter with one's *telos* and vocation within the cosmos—Christ Himself in his mystical communal body. Standing face to face with the icon one is faced with one's true, healed human ontology and so with the meaning and purpose of being human. Looking at the icon becomes pedagogy on discerning the face of God in the fellow human that, in turn, humanizes the beholder.

Perhaps no other icon offers a more insightful hermeneutical key to this theology of the face than the icon of the creation of humanity. In its eloquent narration, humanity's creaturely essence exhibits the communion of matter and spirit in a *perichoretic* movement of love toward God and neighbor. The icon emphatically states that the human being does not image the Trinity on its own, nor just within the parameters of one's relationship with the fellow human; rather, God appears as the third (or rather the first) person of the communal dynamic that sustains the essence of authentically human ontology. The relationship with the Creator is depicted as preceding that with the fellow human and the rest of creation. Therefore, as the icon points out, the very first face that humanity sees while coming forth from the earth through the divine creative agency is the face of its maker. Through the theology of the icon, the beholder understands that together with Adam one is beholding the face of God, which (in a perspective illuminated by revelation) one has come to recognize as the face of Christ—the only face of the Creator that humanity has seen in the face of the last Adam (1 Cor. 15:45). Indeed, as in a mirror, the first Adam sees his face in the countenance of the last Adam. The icon asserts its theological point: God and humanity have something in common, something expressed in the theological symbolism of the divine face. The uncreated, eternal God shares His

---

[16]The articulation of sacrament as "passage" from "the old" into "the new" is proposed and extensively developed in the works of Alexander Schmemann; see for example, *Of Water and Spirit: A Liturgical Study of Baptism* (Crestwood, NY: St. Vladimir's Seminary Press, 1974), 35.

[17]Leonid Ouspensky, "The Meaning and Content of the Icon," in Clendenin, *Eastern Orthodox Theology*, 58.

face with the created, finite human being. He gives his face to Adam and Eve so that they may become his icon within the cosmos. Thus, the depositing of the divine image within the human being becomes the mystical mark of both humanity's priming for communion and community with God and with one another—a communion that, through the agency of the Holy Spirit, makes one a partaker in the divine communal life and nature.

The progression of the image emerges from the fundamental interface with God toward turning one's face to the fellow human by following God's own example in movement and orientation. The human being realizes that it is to be a *prosopon* (face/countenance) turned toward the other in the freedom of encounter.[18] It realizes its social nature by following God who turns his face toward the other in willingness to share himself with the other in communal life. God shares himself with humanity by raising it to his own image. Now in turn humanity is to learn to share itself with the other, for the image is social and visibly manifested in the communal encounter. When humanity learns to share the face of God and live out its embodied openness and vulnerability in orientation toward and for the other, the human being becomes like him in its relation to all of the created cosmos, treating it with the loving care of nurture and protection. In that communal imaging of the divine face, humanity lives the life of the Spirit as life to the fullest, for to be in the Spirit is to be in communion/community of love with the other—God and neighbor. Therefore, the icon depicts humanity's fall as turning away from both the face of the Creator and from the fellow human and moving toward the world, making it an end in itself. The icon makes the theological assertion that all sin is, in a way, a form of idolatry and that idolatry is an outcome of misplaced/misdirected love that sabotages humanity's theotic, christified destiny. In the icon, humanity opens its eyes to behold the vision of life itself in the countenance of the other—the vision of life that starts with the divine face, which is to be stewarded, shared, and turned toward the other. The icon's summary is that to be human is to be Christ with and for the other.

THE ANOINTED HOMO *ADORANS*: CHRIST AS THE SPIRIT'S VISION OF HUMAN ONTOLOGY AND VOCATION

If Christ is humanity's prototype and *telos*, then he is paradigmatic also for understanding human vocation. As Schmemann asserts, the triadic royal, priestly, and prophetic dimensions of the christic vocation are ontological categories—inherent characteristics of humanity in its pre-lapsarian state. He states that one of the Bible's unique revelations about human ontology is that before the royal, priestly, and prophetic offices became associated with a particular human being, they belonged to the very reality of being human as humanity's distinct "calling and dignity."[19] According to Schmemann, Scripture's anthropological account depicts humanity's kingship, priesthood, and prophethood as created, fallen, and, finally, redeemed in Christ. The author asserts that Christ's kingship, priesthood, and prophetic office are "rooted above all in His human nature"; they are not exceptions but an "integral part" of his humanity. Indeed, he is the last Adam, the perfect

---

[18] Bartholomew I, *Encountering the Mystery*, 132.
[19] Schmemann, *Of Water and Spirit*, 82, 95, 100. On this foundation, Schmemann argues for the priesthood, prophethood, and kingship of all believers as redeemed vocational dimensions of human ontology.

human being, the redeemer and restorer of humanity to its "wholeness and totality." Thus, the soteriological meaning of these three offices is found in their "ontological character," in their "belonging" to the very nature of humanity "assumed by Christ for its salvation."[20]

The ontological human vocation in the cosmos is to mirror this triadic christic vocation. This is why, amidst the Divine Liturgy performed by God in the act of creation, humanity is summoned into existence as the special creature made to hear the Word and respond to it in prayer. As Schmemann states, humanity is first and foremost *homo adorans*, a worshipping creature, *the priest* ministering before God on behalf of the entire creation.[21] Humanity's ontological actualization is to be attained through partaking (via priestly intersession) within God's communal discourse, carrying the world in itself (in its body, mind/thoughts, and heart/affections) before God, making it "spoken of" within the trinitarian liturgy of world-making and (in post-lapsarian conditions) world-mending.[22]

The Word addresses humanity not only as a summoning to priestly intercession, but also ultimately as a call to its prophetic hearing, proclamation, and embodiment/incarnation in the human community. Actualizing its prophetic calling, the human being is not just to hear the Word but to enact it as a free-willed doer of the divine will, thus becoming the Word's living epistle (cf. 2 Cor. 3:2)—its embodied extension amidst the created order (Jas 1:22). In light of this assertion, Schmemann describes humanity's priestly and prophetic vocation as inscribed from *the beginning* within human ontology alongside the royal mandate for just stewardship of all creation.[23] Scripture, however, articulates the essence of all three ontological dimensions of human vocation (the royal, priestly, and prophetic) as *charisms* of the Holy Spirit—as the Spirit's movement within the world in enactment (and embodiment) of the divine will through consecrated/anointed human agency. Therefore, from the beginning, humanity is created to move in and with the Spirit and to be an in-Spirit-ed, pneumatized sanctuary of God's breath (his living and enlivening presence) within the cosmos (Gen. 2:7).

Often theologies that justify greedy, unrestrained exploitation and destruction of nature perceive the first human beings as the perfect, complete project (the very crown of creation) for whom all exists, thereby having irrevocable, royal dominion over the created world. In contrast, Orthodox Christianity views the first Adam as a good but still unfolding creation—an ongoing project whose *telos* is the last Adam—Jesus Christ—the visible icon of the invisible God and, therefore, the one fully human, pneumatized, and eucharistic being. Therefore, creation is a movement toward christoformation in and through the sanctifying/christifying agency of the Holy Spirit. Life in the Spirit is growing in the freedom of divine, cruciform love toward all that exists[24]—that is, the totality of the cosmos; it is the free-willed journey into the likeness of God, in which humanity

---

[20] Ibid., 95.
[21] Schmemann, *For the Life of the World*, 15.
[22] For more on the actualization of human vocation in prayer, see Daniela C. Augustine, "Creation as a Perichoretic Trinitarian Conversation: Reflections on World-Making with Robert W. Jenson," in *The Promise of Robert W. Jenson's Theology: Constructive Engagements*, ed. Stephen John Wright and Chris E. W. Green (Minneapolis, MN: Fortress, 2017), 99–114, esp. 108–11.
[23] Schmemann, *Of Water and Spirit*, 95.
[24] Echoing St. Isaac the Syrian, Patriarch Bartholomew I discusses sanctification in terms of "love for the whole of creation," seeing the world as a "'cosmic liturgy' or celebration of the essential interconnection and interdependence of all things" (*Encountering the Mystery*, 94).

is transfigured by the Spirit "from glory to glory" (2 Cor. 3:18) in a perpetual ascent toward Christ-likeness. In the words of Schmemann, it is "the very communion with the Holy Spirit that enables us to love the world with the love of Christ," and the joy of the kingdom (as life in the Spirit) "makes us remember the world and pray for it."[25]

If Christ represents redeemed humanness in union with the Spirit, then we can understand the true original meaning and teleological intent of the triadic human vocation only in light of its fulfillment in and through him—his life, character, and mission amidst and on behalf of all creation.[26] Therefore, while violent consumerism has become the mark of fallen humanity's dominion over creation, Christ's dominion is one of self-giving to the other so that they may live life to the fullest. Beholding the life of Christ as the Spirit's vision of the anointed *homo adorans*, we realize that there is "not kingship alone and not priesthood alone"; they belong together "as fulfillment of one in the other," thus a "royal priesthood."[27] The power of humanity over creation is "fulfilled in *sacrifice*" and in "*sanctifying* the world, by 'making' it into communion with God"[28] as the Holy Spirit transforms human life itself into "a 'liturgy,' a service to God and communion with Him."[29] In light of this pneumatic anthropology, to be human is *to be for others*, living out the life of the Spirit so that they may flourish.

PENTECOST AS THE SPIRIT'S VISION OF THE WORLD'S ESCHATOLOGICAL FUTURE

Echoing St. Athanasius, Vladimir Lossky asserts that God became flesh so that humanity may receive the Holy Spirit,[30] that is, become pneumatized. Therefore, Pentecost should not be understood as a continuation of the incarnation or its sequel but as its result and purpose—as the inaugural event of the Spirit's christoforming work in humanity.[31] Pentecost is the beginning of the "last things," for it unveils the church—the goal of creation.[32] Pentecost is, indeed, the end of the divine creative act and as such is (according to Bulgakov) "anticipated and prepared from the foundations of the world which has always been vivified by the Holy Spirit.'"[33] Therefore, Bulgakov draws a breathtaking cosmic vision of Pentecost that stretches from the beginning of creation on to the Upper Room as the internal teleological movement of God's world-making. The vision starts with the Spirit's life-giving, incubating hovering over the surface of the waters (cf. Gen. 1:2) as "the first *cosmic* Pentecost by anticipation" passes through to the second, this time "*human* Pentecost" of God breathing within humanity's "nostrils the breath of life"

---

[25] Schmemann, *For the Life of the World*, 44.
[26] Schmemann, *Of Water and Spirit*, 95–6.
[27] Ibid., 95.
[28] Ibid., 96.
[29] Ibid., 97.
[30] See Lossky, *The Mystical Theology*, 179.
[31] Vladimir Lossky, *Orthodox Theology: An Introduction* (Crestwood, NY: St. Vladimir's Seminary Press, 2001), 85.
[32] As Sergius Bulgakov states, the "descent of the Holy Spirit is the fulfilment of Christ's work and the realization of God's conception of man, since man was created to be the temple of the Holy Spirit together with the world of nature of which he is meant to be the head and the soul." "Pentecost and the Descent of the Spirit," in *A Bulgakov Anthology*, ed. Nicolas Zernov and James Palin (Eugene, OR: Wipf & Stock, 2012), 184.
[33] Ibid.

(Gen. 2:7); it crescendos into the incarnation, articulated by Bulgakov as the "Pentecost of the Virgin Mary," and later saturates the "human nature of Christ" in the Spirit's descending upon the last Adam during his baptism in the waters of Jordan—an event that for Bulgakov "already contained the substance of the universal Pentecost to come."[34]

The event of Pentecost could be understood as constituting and revealing the last Adam's incarnation through the agency of the Holy Spirit within the (illuminated by faith) communal body of the first Adam.[35] In what Bulgakov terms "the Pentecost of the Virgin,"[36] the Holy Spirit descends upon Mary in response to her free-willed self-giving (Lk. 1:38) and transforms her into an instrument of God's Word, becoming flesh amidst the human *socium* (Jn 1:14). In the vision of the incarnation's mystery, as depicted by the words of the Resurrection Dismissal *Theotokion*, Mary's womb "became more spacious than the heavens," for she welcomed in it her Creator—the One who hosts and sustains the cosmos. In a similar manner, as the Spirit descends upon the disciples, Christ is conceived in them and they are empowered (Acts 1:8) toward Christ-likeness. Through the agency of the Holy Spirit, they become *theophorous* (God-bearing) and enlarged with the divine spaciousness as a renewed image of the Trinity's all-circumscribing love and unconditional hospitality. Therefore, if Babel is exclusion and alienation of the other—refusal to welcome them in communion—the event of Pentecost constitutes its redemptive overturning. Pentecost is the antidote to the age-old temptation to employ Babel's blueprint in human world-making. It offers a paradigmatic vision of the incarnation of God's self-giving hospitality in the community of the believers through the outpouring of the Spirit, manifesting God's ascetic respacing and kenotic self-sharing in welcoming all nations under heaven (Acts 2:5) through submitting his Word to the form and sound of their ethnic tongues (v. 6). On the Day of Pentecost, the proclamation speech of the faith community embraces the language of the other in a gift of divine hospitality as the Spirit invites all humanity to make its habitat in the inter-sociality of the Trinity. The Spirit brings about the inclusion of restored communion with the other in a gesture of welcoming all foreigners, aliens, and strangers, literally *in* their own terms.

As marking creation's ontological renewal and completion, Pentecost represents also the transference of the messianic anointing from Christ to his communal body—the church—and the renewal of humanity's triadic vocation.[37] In a manner similar to that in the narrative of Jesus's inauguration (Lk. 3:21-22), the Spirit descends upon his own—the incarnated Christ in his communal form—empowering the church as his living extension in the cosmos. Therefore, the prophetic, royal, and priestly dimensions of Christ's life become an inseparable part of his communal body's charismatic reality, transformed into a royal priesthood and prophethood of all believers, living the life of Christ for the life of the world.[38]

---

[34]Ibid., 184–5.
[35]For more on the ecclesiological significance of the event of Pentecost, see Daniela C. Augustine, *Pentecost, Hospitality and Transfiguration: Towards a Spirit-inspired Social Transformation* (Cleveland, TN: CPT, 2012).
[36]Sergius Bulgakov, "The Virgin and the Saints in Orthodoxy," in Clendenin, *Eastern Orthodox Theology*, 67.
[37]Rodger Stronstad draws the parallel between Pentecost and the transfer of the Spirit from Moses to the seventy elders (Num. 11:10-30). *The Charismatic Theology of St. Luke* (Peabody, MA: Hendrickson, 1989). As Stronstad notes: "Both narratives record the transfer of a leadership from a single individual to a group.... In both cases the transfer of the Spirit results in an outburst of prophecy" (59).
[38]On the prophethood of the Pentecost community, see Roger Stronstad, *The Prophethood of All Believers*, JPTSup 16 (Sheffield: Sheffield Academic Press, 1999), 65–70.

CONCLUDING THOUGHTS: THE SPIRIT'S VISION OF THE BEAUTIFUL

Returning to the opening thought of the present chapter (and echoing John Meyendorff), one can think of theology as a vision of the triune God, and of the liturgy as the vehicle for the believers' incorporation through the Spirit's agency into that vision.[39] In the liturgy, the Spirit inscribes this vision upon believers, forming and shaping them into what they behold: the trinitarian communal life as *the* vision of truth, goodness, and beauty. Therefore, the liturgy is the consecrated *synaxis*[40] of time and space in which the Spirit makes *lex orandi* into *lex corporalis*, inscribing our faith (*lex credendi*) on our very being in virtually inerasable ways.[41] It is not just an icon of humanity's eschatological future, but also the iconographic process itself in which the Spirit (the great iconographer) makes believers living icons of Christ[42] so that the world can behold the One who is truly human and (by mirroring him) become re-humanized. This vision points to the pneumatic, participatory, communal reality of truth, goodness, and beauty as harmonious life in the Spirit with the other and the different—the life of the kingdom conceived by the Spirit's indwelling presence within redeemed humanity. It also illuminates the theological synthesis between dogmatics, ethics, and aesthetics within the liturgy as a christoforming communal dance in and with the Spirit. This is the vision of the holy, articulating truth, goodness, and beauty as love for the other[43]—an invitation for partaking and imaging the triune life as the freedom to be oneself in communion with others through the Spirit's sanctifying movement of nurturing and sustaining diversity in the unity of love. The liturgy as corporal, communal movement in and with the Spirit "re-trains" the believers' affections, teaching them to love and be loved rightly. It molds them into the likeness of the Lover of humanity and the world (Jn 3:16), making them lovers of God and neighbor and of all creation. They become "people in love" (and a living extension of God as love—of the active, creative, generous spaciousness and unconditional hospitality of divine love). Embodying this love transfigures the totality of one's life into an act of worship to the Creator, making it *ars liturgica* and, therefore, *ars amatoria*.[44] Thus, as liturgical/worshipping creatures, the faith community performs the liturgy as the

---

[39] John Meyendorff describes Orthodox theology "as internal vision, which requires personal, ascetic effort." It requires not only an individual but also a communal effort, "an effort made within the community of saints." "Doing Theology in an Eastern Orthodox Perspective," in Clendenin, *Eastern Orthodox Theology*, 87.

[40] Bishop Maxim Vasilijevic discusses the Divine Liturgy as the representative icon of the synaxis of time—past, present, and future—in the mystery of Christ. *History, Truth, Holiness: Studies in Orthodoxy and Epistemology* (Alhambra: Sebastian, 2011), 166.

[41] Edward Foley, "Re-attaching Tongue to Body: The Aesthetics of Liturgical Performance," in *Ars Liturgiae: Worship, Aesthetics and Praxis—Essays in Honor of Nathan D. Mitchell*, ed. Clare V. Johnson (Chicago: Liturgy Training, 2003), 105–6. James K. A. Smith articulates the foundations of liturgical anthropology as residing in the understanding of human beings as liturgical, sacramental, story-telling, and story-incorporated animals and builds the case for perceiving liturgies "as compressed, repeated, performed narratives that, over time, conscript us into the stories they 'tell,' by showing, by performing." *Imagining the Kingdom: How Worship Works* (Grand Rapids, MI: Baker Academic, 2013), 109.

[42] Bishop Maxim Vasilijevic describes the church in terms of the eucharistic gathering of living icons. He asserts that God's mandate for humanity issued in the summoning of Lev. 11:44-45 ("be holy, for I am holy") is "the most perfect invitation . . . because it enables the acquisition of true hypostatic existence for every participant." *History, Truth, Holiness*, xxi.

[43] Ibid., 3.

[44] See Gilbert Ostdiek's inspiring essay, "Let the Poet Speak," in Johnson, *Ars Liturgiae*, 115–33.

Spirit-filled and inspired art of true love and lives its christoforming *telos* in its daily life as incarnate love—love as self-giving for the life and flourishing of others, love as the essential, embodied form of holiness—living out what is true, good, and beautiful with and for others.

If in worship, believers become what they behold, then both the iconic representation of "the great cloud of witnesses" as well as the living icons (fellow believers) who surround them are essential for the cultivation of right understanding of truth, goodness, and beauty. Eastern Orthodox iconography teaches the beholder to discern the rapturous beauty of the body of Christ with its radical racial, ethnic, gender, age, and class inclusivity as a visible celebration of in-Spirit-ed diversity in unity. The iconography brings before one's eyes the human face of the holy, which comes in all skin-colors, in different ethnic attires, as both male and female, young and old, rich and poor. In a world plagued by anxiety at the sight of the other, this vision teaches that the segregation or marginalization of the racial, ethnic, and gendered other (as well as that of the handicapped, the homeless, and the poor) from the church, as the gathering of living icons (or of the human community created to become a living icon of God) is a form of iconoclasm—a violence against the bearer of the divine face, against the temple/home of God on earth. In contrast, love as the ultimate act of freedom has, in the words of Hannah Arendt, the capacity to "insert a new world into the existing world"[45]—a world of fusion of the self with the other, a world in which the good is what we have in common—the common good. We know this love as the beginning and end of creation—the love that hosts the world, sustaining its very breath in unconditional hospitality toward the other—that same love that through the Spirit finds residence within humanity and renews the world, carving space for the other, and refusing to see one's well-being and future without them.

As H. A. H. Bartholomew I asserts, "Beauty is a call, beyond the here and now, to the original principle and purpose of the world."[46] Beholding the Beautiful One, the church's liturgical anamnesis commits to the Spirit what is still being perfected in order for it to be enabled to articulate perfection. The Spirit takes what is and makes it what is to come before the spiritual eyes of the beholder, who sees the advent of the *eschata* in the midst of the present until the now is transfigured into its future form. Thus, the *epiclesis* of the Spirit is a conditioning for a new way of seeing the world—a new worldview as an outcome of liturgical (trans-)formation.[47] The world is seen bathed in the brilliant light of Mt. Tabor's transfigured and transfiguring Christ as a gift of grace, beauty, and goodness that reflects the glory of God. Such a vision mandates a different way of relating to the world—not as to a disposable commodity but as to a sacrament of social transformation into the likeness of God. Such a vision makes the life of the Trinity the aesthetic and ethical "social program" of humanity,[48] and the Spirit crafts its living icon, the church, so that the world can behold and become the Community of the Beautiful.

---

[45] Hannah Arendt, *The Human Condition* (Chicago: University of Chicago Press, 1998), 242.
[46] Bartholomew, *Encountering the Mystery*, 28.
[47] For a compelling articulation of the dialectic of the movement from worship/liturgy to worldview, see Smith, *Desiring the Kingdom*, 133–54.
[48] Bartholomew, *Encountering the Mystery*, 133. "Every form of community—the work-place, the school, the city, even a nation—has as its vocation to become, each in its own way, a living icon of the Trinity. Nations are called to be transparent to one another, just as the three persons of the Trinity are transparent to one another. Such is surely part of the role of religion in a changing world—namely, to promote freedom among human beings as the basis of encounter and communion" (ibid.).

FOR FURTHER READING

Augustine, Daniela C. *Pentecost, Hospitality, and Transfiguration: Toward a Spirit-Inspired Vision of Social Transformation.* Cleveland, TN: CPT, 2012.

Moltmann, Jürgen. *The Living God and the Fullness of Life.* Translated by Margaret Kohl. Geneva: World Council of Churches, 2016.

Yong, Amos. *In the Days of Caesar: Pentecostalism and Political Theology.* Grand Rapids, MI: Eerdmans, 2010.

CHAPTER THIRTEEN

The Spirit and Ecology

J. J. JOHNSON LEESE

Particularly within the Western Christian tradition, Christians and professional theologians have often conceptualized the Spirit as primarily engaged in human transformation and building the Christian community. Influenced in part by a dualism between spirit and matter, this perspective views the Spirit as less involved with or even completely detached from the other-than-human created order. The combination of ecology with Spirit, "ecopneumatology," provides one example of contemporary scholarship challenging such conventional approaches as impoverished and unnecessarily anthropocentric. Throughout the past four decades, ecopneumatology has emerged as a vibrant corollary discipline of pneumatology classified within the broader and relatively new field of ecological theology (ecotheology). Although ecotheology remains a relatively unknown term for many today, Jürgen Moltmann's magisterial study *God in Creation* inspired a renewed interest in pneumatology, particularly the relationship of the Spirit with the tripartite concept of creation—*creatio originalis*, *creatio continua*, and *creatio nova*.[1] Burgeoning ecotheological scholarship demonstrates how the current global ecological crisis is transforming our reading of biblical texts, helping to construct a new set of theological questions, and contributing to the reimagining of pneumatological paradigms. In order to situate this relatively new academic development within the current context, this article will clarify terminology, outline the historical and cultural factors reshaping the study of ecology and the Spirit, and then outline four paradigms representative of historic and emerging ecopneumatological trajectories.

TERMINOLOGY

As a foundation for the discussion that follows, three terms—Spirit, ecology, and ecopneumatology—need to be clarified. The Spirit, *ruach* in Hebrew and *pneuma* in Greek, is variously identified through metaphors and descriptors in Scripture. In the OT, the Spirit is typically not described through anthropomorphic terms but rather by nature metaphors paired with maternal, life-giving descriptors. In the NT, a sense of personhood emerges when the Spirit is referred to with the more personal title of "Paraclete." The Creator Spirit hovers/moves over primordial chaos (Gen. 1:1, *creatio originalis*); through animated breath brings life to humanity (Gen. 2:7); is essential to continuous life (e.g.,

---

[1] Jürgen Moltmann, *God in Creation: A New Theology of Creation and the Spirit of God* (San Francisco, CA: Harper & Row, 1985), 206–8.

Job 33:4, 34:13-15; Ps. 104:29-30; Wis. 1:7, 12:1, *creatio continua*); indwells with and in (1 Cor. 6:19); searches all things, even the depths of God (1 Cor. 2:10); and fills and holds all things together (Wis. 1:7). Nature metaphors include the Spirit as living water that refreshes (e.g., Jer. 2:13, 17:13; Jn 4:14, 7:37-39), the healing wind (e.g., Judg. 6:34, Jn 3:6-8, Acts 2:1-4), the divine dove (e.g., Gen. 8:11, Mt. 3:16), and the cleansing fire that ignites the mission of the church (Mt. 3:11-12, Acts 2:1-4).

Ecology, a term coined by Ernst Haeckel in the late nineteenth century, refers to the scientific study concerned with the dynamic interrelationship of diverse organisms and their ability to coexist within a given environment. Ecology derives meaning from the Greek term *oikos*, meaning "house" or "household," and the related term *oikonomia*, understood as "stewardship," "plan," or "management." These Greek terms are used theologically to describe the divine economy of the triune God in relationship to the creation (e.g., Eph. 1:10). By combining ecology with pneumatology, theologians address the Spirit's relationship to the "household of earth" inclusive of all its complex components of life. Scripture employs the terms "earth" (*ge*), "nature" (*physis*), and "creation" (*ktisis*) differently, determined by the broader symbiotic field and context—often inclusively of all living organisms, including humanity, yet at other times limited to the other-than-human community. While acknowledging that humanity is part of the household of the earth community, within the parameters of this essay, I primarily employ "earth," "nature," and "creation" to refer to other-than-human creation.

FACTORS CONTRIBUTING TO THE STUDY OF SPIRIT AND ECOLOGY

Thomas Aquinas's insight that any error about creation leads to an error about God[2] anticipates one of the key factors contributing to the emergence of ecopneumatology. The multitude of voices warning of the threat of environmental crisis (sometimes referred to as ecocide), confirmed through scientific studies and compounded through human behavior, has challenged scholars and practitioners alike to re-examine historic theological teaching that may have contributed adversely to this situation. One impetus for this reassessment resulted from the influential article of Lynn White published in 1967. White identifies the roots of the environmental crises in two broad categories: the secular progress resulting from the Industrial Revolution and the Judeo-Christian theology that considers the natural world as "explicitly for man's benefit and rule; no item in the physical creation had any purpose save to serve man's purposes.... Christianity is the most anthropocentric religion the world has seen ... and thus bears a huge burden of guilt [for the ecological crisis]."[3] White's critique, although oversimplified, prompted a generation of biblical and theological scholars to acknowledge that anthropocentric readings of biblical texts, at least since the post-Reformation and Enlightenment periods, have contributed to an "error about creation"—and ultimately "an error about God."

To be sure, from the earliest days of Christian thinking, patristic writers discussed and debated the relationship of God to creation and, more specifically, the role and

---

[2] Saint Thomas Aquinas, *Summa Contra Gentiles*, 5 vols. (Notre Dame: University of Notre Dame, 1975), 2:32–4 (II.3).
[3] J. L. White, "The Historical Roots of Our Ecological Crisis," *Science* 155 (1967): 1203–7.

function of the Spirit to other-than-human nature. Ecotheologians have identified the contributions of historic voices such as Irenaeus, Basil, Gregory, Hildegard, and Francis of Assisi with fruitful results. Each of these theological thinkers, albeit to differing degrees, reflects on the Spirit in relationship to the triune God, humanity, and creation. Based on the questions emerging out of their historical, cultural, and religious contexts, these pneumatological discussions were mainly focused either on the Spirit's role in the Trinity or the Spirit's soteriological function of human conversion and sanctification. The twenty-first-century context, however, has a vastly different set of theological questions shaped both by a different understanding of the world and by a set of challenges foreign to those of the patristic or medieval periods. Within the contemporary global context, the impending ecological crisis has contributed significantly toward a fresh reconsideration of the relationship of the Spirit to creation.

The heightened awareness of the ecological crisis combined with a critical reassessment of how anthropocentric readings of biblical texts have exacerbated the problem has subsequently led many scholars to rethink the place of creation in biblical theology. Covenant themes, once prominent in OT theology, have been increasingly overshadowed by studies that deem creation themes and motifs as central to the overall substratum of biblical thought and theology. Numerous scholars affirm this trajectory. For example, Rolf Knierim writes, "Yahweh is not the God of creation because He is the God of the humans or of human history. He is God of the humans and of human history because He is the God of creation. . . .The most universal aspect of Yahweh's dominion is not human history. It is the creation and sustenance of the world."[4] Likewise, Terence Fretheim emphasizes the theological importance of canonical starting points that "the Bible begins with Genesis, not Exodus, with creation, not redemption, is of immeasurable importance for understanding all that follows."[5]

Another factor contributing significantly toward a robust ecotheology is the increased acknowledgement by theologians of the need for an interdisciplinary approach to Scripture, one that particularly engages the sciences. In spite of periods of rejecting scientific developments (e.g., the church's censure of Galileo), many Christians today reflect openness to scientific findings. For example, statements of the Second Vatican Council and more recently the publication of the encyclical *Laudato si'* by Pope Francis demonstrate shifts within the Catholic tradition. Increasingly, theologians condemn the bifurcation of theology and the sciences. Intentional dialogue with experts in genetics, evolutionary biology, molecular biology, cosmology, ecology, and environmental science has prompted new theological consideration about the nearly incomprehensible age and size of the cosmos and the dynamic and organically complex nature of the world. The convergence of scientific discoveries, technological advancements, and global urbanization has given rise to deep reflection on the symbiotic and organic relationship of humanity with creation. Humans share DNA with other-than-human life forms, are completely dependent on the natural elements for life, and through exploitation are responsible for the depletion of natural resources. All these factors have likewise prompted scholars to consider how the trinitarian interrelationship of God as *communio* relates to complex

---

[4]Rolf Knierim, *The Task of Old Testament Theology: Substance, Method and Cases* (Grand Rapids, MI: Eerdmans, 1995), 40.
[5]Terence Fretheim, *God and World in the Old Testament: A Relational Theology of Creation* (Nashville, TN: Abingdon, 2005), xiv.

creaturely life forms and the evolutionary process from which they came. It is within these discussions that a profusion of ecotheological studies, constructive and practical, is exploring theological questions of the relationship of the Spirit with ecology, such as the following: Where is the Spirit of God in an evolving universe? Is the Spirit of God breathing life into the natural world? Is the trinitarian God present in the natural world? Within such a vibrant theological discussion, this article lays out four models or paradigms that inform the ecopneumatological discussion. The first model has influenced Christians ever since first-century gnosticism, and its dualism continues to have impact on Christians today. The second through fourth models provide a hopeful trajectory of thought and action for God's people to live faithfully with a "new creation" perspective on this beautiful planet we call home.

PARADIGM ONE: SPIRIT AND NATURE DUALISM

Throughout history, many segments of Christian tradition have maintained a hierarchical Spirit-nature dualism. This framework was present in the earliest centuries through gnostic teaching that was influenced by Greco-Roman philosophy. The material realm, including the earth as a whole and the human body, was understood as provisional and less valuable than the spiritual realms.[6] Although Irenaeus and others effectively countered gnostic teaching, remnants have remained. This paradigm generally reflects an anti-world impulse, with the earth variously understood as the space where pagan deities reign, an object of conquest, and more recently a commodity for consumption. Genesis 1 has become a prime text to support this approach. Select readings of Genesis emphasize God as creating through the spoken word distant from created matter and humanity as set apart from earthly matter by being created in the image and likeness of God (Gen. 1:26-28). Early Christian thinkers pondered what the *imago Dei* implied about the nature of human beings and by extension the nature of God. In Augustine's influential study *On the Trinity*, he concludes that the qualities of will, memory, and understanding represent the *imago Dei* within humanity. It is of note that *none* of these qualities emerged from the material realm. Such inferences drawn by Augustine and others led to perceptions of God in strictly otherworldly categories. By extension, assumptions about humans as the *imago Dei* were articulated through spiritual categories that distanced them from the material world of nature.

These early dualistic formulations reemerged in later periods within Christian theology and practice with catastrophic results. The spirit realm was further bifurcated from the material, with humanity, as ensouled creatures, elevated *above* and *over* nature. The material realm was perceived as merely a backdrop overshadowed by the main biblical story of the salvation of humanity. Salvation was envisioned as a spiritual ascent from human bodies, materiality, and nature. Some strands of Protestant theology influenced by the Industrial Revolution, the promise of technological advancements, and the early modern scientific objectification of nature resulted in an intensely anthropocentric theology. Texts such as Gen. 1:26-28 and Psalm 8 were interpreted to justify human unfettered domination and rule over the creation. A hierarchy of relationships resulted,

---

[6] For an important work outlining the history of this theological paradigm within Christianity, see Paul Santmire, *The Travail of Nature: The Ambiguous Ecological Promise of Christian Theology* (Minneapolis, MN: Fortress, 1985).

with God as the creator of all things, humanity as the subject/ruler of all things, and creation relegated to the realm of temporal and profane. Francis Bacon and René Descartes represent scholars who espoused philosophical frameworks that further divided the Spirit from ecology. Within the search for a positive expression of Christian stewardship of the created realm, a sharp division between the Spirit and the creation has sparked interest in alternative perspectives. Paradigm Two considers more closely the biblical witness to revelation of God in and through nature itself.

PARADIGM TWO: ECOLOGY AS REVELATION OF THE TRIUNE GOD

Do animals, birds, plants, and fish *teach, tell,* and *declare* the works of God (Job 12:7-9)? Within Christian history, there has been a long, diverse tradition that affirms that somehow the other-than-human world mediates knowledge about the nature of the triune God. Referred to as "natural knowledge" or "natural revelation," this knowledge is understood as distinct from revelation through Scripture.[7] Drawing upon texts such as Ps. 19:1 ("The Heavens are telling the glory of God and the firmament proclaims his handiwork") and Rom. 1:20 ("Ever since the creation of the world his eternal power and divine nature, invisible though they are, have been understood and seen through the things he has made"), Augustine declares nature as a book of revelation.

> Others, in order to find God, will read a book. Well, as a matter of fact there is a certain great big book, the book of created nature. Look carefully at it top and bottom, observe it, read it. God did not make letters of ink for you to recognize him in; he set before your eyes all these things he has made. Why look for a louder voice? Heaven and earth cries out to you, 'God made me.' . . . Observe heaven and earth in a religious spirit.[8]

Basil of Caesarea reflects a similar sentiment when he writes, "I want creation to awaken such a profound admiration in you, that in every place, whatever plants you may contemplate, you are overcome by a living remembrance of the Creator."[9] These types of theological insight about the connection of nature to revelation have informed Christian doctrinal and moral reflection for most of the history of Christianity. The biblical texts referenced to support general revelation of God through nature are typically the creation psalms (e.g., Psalms 8, 19, 29, 65, 104) and the Apostle Paul's engagement with Athenian philosophers at the Areopagus (Acts 17:16-34). In the latter, Paul establishes the truth of Christ by appealing to the natural order. During the Protestant Reformation, natural revelation of God was debated, with growing disagreement about its validity. John Calvin remained convinced of its value, as demonstrated, for example, in his reflections on Psalm 19 and Romans 1:19-20. Commenting on the latter, Calvin writes, "God is in himself invisible; but as his majesty shines forth in his works and in his creatures everywhere, men

---

[7] I am not developing the topic of natural theology in this discussion. For perspectives on natural theology, see *The Oxford Handbook of Natural Theology*, ed. Russell Re Manning (Oxford: Oxford University Press, 2013).
[8] Augustine, "Sermon 68," in *Sermons III (51-94)*, trans. Edmund Hill, O.P.; ed. John E. Rotelle, O.S.A. (Brooklyn, NY: New City, 1991), 225 (68.6).
[9] Basil, *Hexaemeron* 5.2 (SC 26:284).

ought in these to acknowledge him, for they clearly set forth their Maker."[10] Eventually, the objection to natural revelation found favor within Christian history. Many factors contributed toward this development. Certainly, the Reformation emphasis on *sola Scriptura* combined with increased literacy rates gave priority to the written word. Industrial progress and scientific discoveries amplified the progress of humanity, which downplayed the value of natural revelation.

The pendulum is now swinging back with an emerging contemporary interest in the knowledge of God revealed in the natural world, particularly as the dialogue between scientists and theologians increases. Ecotheologians have contributed toward this renewal as they seek to listen to the natural world through the expert voices of our day—scientists, cosmologists, agrarians, historians, and ecologists. The findings of such experts are affirming a world that is marked by complexity, a cosmos that is incomprehensibly old and expansive in size, and a planet that is unparalleled in life forms and fecundity—dynamic, interrelated, organic, boundless, ever-expanding, biologically diverse, and extraordinarily beautiful and intricate. These experts are also listening to a creation that is groaning under intense distress.

These staggering scientific revelations in dialogue with Christian theologians are challenging former dualistic paradigms and displacing fanciful notions of humanity as the center of the universe. They are also challenging contemporary theologians to consider pneumatology as a promising theological resource for bridging the divide between the triune God and ecology. In this context, two particular ecopneumatological frameworks are developed in what follows to further the discussion.

PARADIGM THREE: CREATOR SPIRIT AS BREATH OF LIFE AND CONSTANT COMPANION FOR ALL CREATION

The third framework focuses on the creative and perfective function of the Spirit in light of modern scientific discoveries and through the lens of a trinitarian theology of mutual relations. Central to this pneumatological framework is a universal, cosmic interpretation of the Spirit's dynamic presence at every stage of creation's origin and existence—*creatio originalis*, *creatio continua*, and *creatio nova*. This framework identifies the Spirit that drove Jesus into the wilderness (Mk 1:12) and the Spirit that poured down on humanity at Pentecost (Acts 1:1-3) as the same Spirit that millions of years earlier ignited the evolutionary process resulting in the cosmos (Gen. 1:1-3, 2:7). The vivifying breath of the Spirit is not limited to a particular event nor exclusive to human salvation or piety. Rather, the Spirit is divine life-giver ("It is the spirit that gives life" Jn 6:63) and universal divine presence ("Where can I go from your spirit?" Ps. 139:7).

Theologians articulating this framework often find inspiration in Irenaeus of Lyon, who famously envisioned the creative and redemptive work of God through the image of a Father creating with his two hands, the Son and the Spirit.[11] Irenaeus differentiates the creative function of the triune God: the Father "plans and gives commands," the

---

[10] John Calvin, *Calvin's Commentaries*, ed. and trans. John Owen, 22 vols. (Grand Rapids, MI: Baker, 2009), 22:70.
[11] "As if [God] did not possess His own hands. For with Him were always present the Word and Wisdom, the Son and the Spirit, by whom and in whom, freely and spontaneously, He made all things." Irenaeus, *Against Heresies* 4.20; *ANF*, 1:487–8.

Son "performs and creates," and the Spirit "nourishes and increases."[12] This analogy is interpreted in helpful ways through contemporary scientific understandings of the world. For example, theologian and biochemist Christopher Southgate uses the language of evolutionary biology to conceptualize Irenaeus's analogy: "The work of the 'two hands' of the Father in creation both draws onward the ever-shifting distribution of peaks in the fitness landscape, through the unfolding creative work of the Logos, and encourages organisms, through the power of the Spirit, in their exploration of that landscape, giving rise to new possibilities of being a self."[13] Similarly, John Polkinghorne, a physicist-theologian, suggests the following contemporary interpretation:

> The Father is the fundamental ground of creation's being, while the Word is the source of creation's deep order and the Spirit is ceaselessly at work within the contingencies of open history. The fertile interplay of order and openness, operating at the edge of chaos, can be seen to reflect the activities of the Word and Spirit, the two divine Persons that Irenaeus called "the hands of God."[14]

As the Creator declares the creation "good . . . very good" (Gen. 1:10, 12, 18, 21, 25, 31), this framework affirms the integrity and value of the other-than-human creation apart from any relationship to humanity. Unlike the dualistic framework where the relationship between humanity and creation is modeled as subject-to-object, here the interrelationship is framed as subject-to-subject. The creation narrative in Gen. 2:4b–3:24 supports the immanence and closeness of God with all creation and humanity in an organic, symbiotic, kinship relationship to the earth and animals. Both Adam (*'adam*) and the living animals and birds have their source of being from the earth/soil (*ha'adam*; Gen. 2:7, 19). These texts and others align with the modern study of ecology, which affirms the interconnected web of life that humanity shares with other organisms and ecosystems.

Creation texts such as Psalms 104 and Job 38–41 explode with imagery of a playful God who delights in, provides for, and engages with the plethora of creaturely diversity. The psalmist poetically images creatures in relationship with their Creator:

> These [animals] all look to you to give them their food in due season; when you give to them, they gather it up; when you open your hand, they are filled with good things. When you hide your face, and they are dismayed; when you take away their breath [*ruach*], they die and return to their dust. When you send forth your breath [*ruach*], they are created and you renew the face of the ground. (Ps. 104:27-30; cf. Gen. 1:2)

All creatures, both human and nonhuman, are recipients of divine care and are invited to rejoice in God's works. The Spirit, as a rejuvenating energy, enables the creation to relate to its Creator.

In a helpful analogy, Clark H. Pinnock outlines how the Spirit embraces the relatively autonomous creation and opens up space for new creation to occur:

> History is not the playing out of a timelessly fixed decree, but a theater where the divine purposes are being worked out. . . . History is neither random nor predetermined. The

---

[12]Ibid., 4.38.3; *ANF*, 1:521–2).
[13]Christopher Southgate, *The Groaning of Creation: God, Evolution, and the Problem of Evil* (Louisville, KY: Westminster John Knox, 2008), 61.
[14]John Polkinghorne, *Science and the Trinity: The Christian Encounter with Reality* (New Haven, CT: Yale University Press, 2009), 1.

Spirit is active in everything but in ways that are respectful of the dignity of creation. One might think of Spirit as choreographing the dance of creation by analogy to what he does in the fellowship of the sublime Trinity.[15]

Similarly, Denis Edwards provides analogies of the Spirit as both midwife and companion to the creation.[16] These analogies testify to the Spirit, who in self-limiting love and compassion comes alongside the creation that is waiting and groaning as in birth pangs, anticipating an eschatological freedom from bondage and death (Rom. 8:19-23). These analogies portray the immanent presence of God through the Spirit, who works to transform, renew, and make space for each creature to evolve within the mysterious cosmos that is coming into being.

PARADIGM FOUR: SPIRIT IN COMMUNION WITH ECOLOGY

The fourth pneumatological framework extends Irenaeus's analogy of God's creative embrace to the imagery of God's Spirit making room within the divine nature for the cosmos to dwell, while paradoxically the Spirit dwells in the creation. Central to this thinking is that the Spirit's indwelling animates nature, permeating it with sacred presence—without making it ontologically divine. Jürgen Moltmann's work set the stage for subsequent thoughtful endeavoring, particularly among ecofeminists. Differentiating his theology from pantheism and animism, Moltmann develops an ecological theology of creation utilizing the philosophical term "panentheism." This word constructed of three Greek terms literally means "all-in-God" and is increasingly used in ecopneumatology to describe the immanence and transcendence of God with nature through the Spirit. Moltmann draws upon the biblical concept of *shekinah*, God's dwelling among the people and creation, and pairs it with the theological term *perichoresis*, which refers to the mutual indwelling of the persons of the Trinity and is also used to describe the intermingling of human and divine natures in the incarnation. These concepts shape Moltmann's pneumatology, for he states, "Through his cosmic Spirit, God the Creator of heaven and earth is present *in* each of his creatures and *in* the fellowship of creation which they share.... Through the powers and potentialities of the Spirit, the Creator indwells the creatures he has made, animates them, holds them in life, and leads them into the future of his kingdom."[17] More recently, Edwards utilizes evolutionary science to affirm a form of trinitarian panentheism where the Spirit makes space for the processes of the emerging and evolving universe to take place and move forward toward the eschatological new creation.[18] Cosmology and ecology affirm a planet of constitutive relationships. This provides a useful point of discussion of the mutual relations and communion within the Divine and of what constitutes the relationship of the Spirit's cooperative work with the laws of nature drawing creatures and the universe toward communion with God so

---

[15] Clark H. Pinnock, *Flame of Love: A Theology of the Holy Spirit* (Downers Grove, IL: InterVarsity, 1996), 56.
[16] Denis Edwards, *Breath of Life: A Theology of the Creator Spirit* (Maryknoll, NY: Orbis, 2004). This work offers a helpful overview of this framework.
[17] Moltmann, *God in Creation*, 14.
[18] Edwards, *Breath of Life*, 130–42.

that "God may be all in all" (1 Cor. 15:28). Elizabeth Johnson suggests that the Trinity as divine communion "epitomizes the connectedness of all that exists in the universe."[19]

Although the term has been popularized in modern times, panentheism as a concept, as applied to the relationship of the Spirit with ecology, was present in earlier theologians. For example, the abbess and mystic Hildegard of Bingen (1098–1179) had a deep sense of the interconnectedness of nature and God. She identifies the Spirit's vitality as *viriditas*, a Latin term meaning "greening energy." She envisioned nature as the space where the divine and the earthly partner for holistic wellness, and via these encounters in nature she developed her understanding of divine presence. She had a vision of the world as God's body and the Spirit as present within: "You [Spirit] are the mighty way in which everything that is in the heavens, on the earth, and under the earth, is penetrated with connectedness, penetrated with relatedness."[20]

Martin Luther certainly did not equate God as identical to nature, yet he was able to use the concept of panentheism to communicate the mystery and paradox of God's immanence and transcendence in creation—the apophatic and kataphatic. While debating the presence of God in the sacraments, he used the prepositions "in," "with," and "under" to capture the mystery of God's presence in relationship to the elements of bread, wine, and water. He argued for the real presence of Christ in the eucharist with the phrase "the finite is capable of the infinite" (*Finitum capax infinitis*).[21] Luther maintained this paradoxical notion of the presence of God to nature as well.

> God is substantially present everywhere, in and through all creatures, in all their parts and places, so that the world is full of God and He fills all, but without being encompassed and surrounded by it. . . . For how can reason tolerate it that the Divine Majesty is so small that it can be substantially present in a grain, on a grain, through a grain, within and without, and that, although this is a single Majesty, it nevertheless is entirely in each grain separately, no matter how immeasurably numerous those grains may be?[22]

Historic voices such as these provide trajectories for contemporary thought. Ecofeminists have explored the panentheistic framework by drawing upon the maternal imagery of God having room within God's life for the cosmos. Johnson, for example, writes that "to be structured so that you have room inside yourself for another to dwell is quintessentially a female experience."[23] The analogy of God's womb as the space for the Spirit's guided process of sustaining an expanding universe in love, while remaining distinct and separate from the universe, provides possibilities for consideration. In a similar metaphor, Sallie McFague articulates the image of the world as God's body, an image that reflects God's total self-giving to the cosmos.[24] This intermingling portrays the creation in sacramental ways, with the Spirit bringing healing and restoration to the brokenness of relationships.

---

[19] Elizabeth Johnson, *She Who Is* (New York: Crossroad Publishing, 1992), 222–3.
[20] Gabrielle Uhlein, *Meditations with Hildegard of Bingen* (Santa Fe, NM: Bear and Company, 1983), 41.
[21] See Kurt Hendel, "'*Finitum capax infinitis*': Luther's Radical Incarnational Perspective," *Currents in Theology and Mission* 35, no. 6 (December 2008): 420–33.
[22] Martin Luther, WA, 23:134–6, cited by Henrich Bornkamm, *Luther's World of Thought*, trans. Marten Bertram (St Louis, MO: Concordia, 1958), 189.
[23] Johnson, *She Who Is*, 234.
[24] Sallie McFague, *The Body of God: An Ecological Theology* (Minneapolis, MN: Fortress, 1993).

CONCLUSION

Attention given to the relationship of the Spirit with ecology is one of the most promising and important areas of inquiry for pneumatology today. The models suggested here are representative of a larger corpus of pneumatological scholarship that has collectively elevated the integrity and value of the natural world within a dynamic and immanent relationship to the Spirit. These discussions are prompting people of faith to consider environmental care as a new context of ethical imperative for faith and practice, while revising traditional pneumatological frameworks most often with an anthropocentric focus. One of the most promising features of this work is the vibrant interdisciplinary discussions taking place. These broaden the epistemological horizon from which to consider the Spirit's relationship to ecology while opening up new perspectives for reading texts—readings that seek to engage Christian theology with the social, moral and political challenges of our day. When ancient texts such as Rom. 8:18-23 are read in light of scientific findings, these texts have a contemporary ring. In this example, Paul presents a symbiotic interrelationship of humanity, the Spirit, and nature: "Creation waits in eager longing. . . . We know that the whole creation has been groaning in labor pains until now; and not only the creation, but we ourselves who have the first fruits of the Spirit, groan inwardly while we wait for adoption, the redemption of our bodies" (vv. 19, 22, 23). Yet in the midst of this eschatological vision, Paul expresses "hope that the creation itself will be set free from its bondage to decay and will obtain the freedom of the glory of the children of God" (v. 21). Creation is a gift of God and is the *oikos*, our home or household, in which our lives are embedded and upon which we are completely dependent. The Spirit is likewise a gift of God, the source of continuous life on this planet. Ecopneumatological studies provide an area of theological discourse with both academic appeal and practical relevance for the church, contributing to the ongoing conversation of the trinitarian relationship of God through the Spirit to the creation.

FOR FURTHER READING

Bergmann, Sigurd. *Creation Set Free: The Spirit as Liberator of Nature*. Grand Rapids, MI: Eerdmans, 2005.

Buxton, Graham, and Norman Habel, eds. *The Nature of Things: Rediscovering the Spiritual in God's Creation*. Eugene, OR: Pickwick, 2016.

Edwards, Denis. *Breath of Life: A Theology of the Creator Spirit*. Maryknoll, NY: Orbis, 2004.

McFague, Sallie. *The Body of God: An Ecological Theology*. Minneapolis, MN: Fortress, 1993.

Moltmann, Jürgen. *God in Creation: A New Theology of Creation and the Spirit of God*. San Francisco, CA: Harper & Row, 1985.

CHAPTER FOURTEEN

"The Giver of Life"

The Spirit and Creation

MARC CORTEZ

The Nicene Creed famously identified the Holy Spirit as "the Lord and Giver of life," seemingly giving theologians a firm basis upon which to emphasize the significance of the Spirit's work in the doctrine of creation. This commitment flows at the very least from a recognition of the doctrine of inseparable operations, which requires us to affirm that all three persons of the Trinity are inseparably involved in any work of the Trinity *ad extra*. Consequently, we must acknowledge that the Spirit was somehow involved in the work of creation. Additionally, quite a number of biblical texts explicitly connect the Spirit and the giving of life in creation. Genesis itself begins with a reference to the *ruach* of God (Gen. 1:2), though some question whether we should interpret this as an explicit reference to the Holy Spirit. The Spirit's work in creation comes out most clearly in the Wisdom literature, with the psalmist declaring, "By the word of the LORD the heavens were made, their starry host by the breath (*ruach*) of his mouth" (Ps. 33:6). Another psalm similarly states, "When you send your Spirit, they are created, and you renew the face of the ground" (Ps. 104:30). And in the book of Job, Elihu maintains that if God were to withdraw his Spirit, "all flesh would perish together" (Job 34:14-15). For both exegetical and theological reasons, then, it would seem to be relatively simple to affirm that the Spirit has an intrinsic role to play in the creation of the world as the Giver of Life.

Yet contemporary theologians often lament an apparent neglect of the Spirit's work in creation, contending that many earlier theologians focused primarily on the Spirit's redemptive work to the neglect of his creational work.[1] While these earlier theologians would never *deny* that the Spirit is involved in creation in *some* way, this critique suggests that they left the Spirit's creational work largely unexplored for at least two reasons. First, the creation narratives in Genesis seem almost entirely silent about the work of the Spirit in creation. Although we should not build our theologies of creation on the Genesis narratives alone, the lack of clear reference to the Spirit in these central narratives has undoubtedly influenced later formulations of the doctrine. Second, when the biblical authors do address the relationship between the Spirit and creation, they frequently focus primarily on the Spirit's eschatological work of bringing creation to its eschatological

---

[1] See for example David T. Williams, "The Spirit in Creation," *Scottish Journal of Theology* 67, no. 1 (2014): 2 and Colin E. Gunton, *The Triune Creator: A Historical and Systematic Study* (Grand Rapids, MI: Eerdmans, 1998), 196.

telos (e.g., Joel 2:29-31, Rom. 8:22-23, Rev. 21:10). Although this is a clear biblical emphasis that must be addressed in any comprehensive view of the Spirit's relationship to creation, such biblical verses may have distracted many theologians from considering legitimate questions about the Spirit's role in the act of creation itself.

We can see both factors at work in Augustine's interpretation of Gen. 2:7. Despite the fact that Augustine offers a relatively robust understanding of the Spirit's role in human life as a whole, Augustine argues that we should not understand the "breath of life" in this passage as a reference to the Holy Spirit. I will suggest in this essay that Augustine's interpretation here is overly restricted by the twofold dynamic mentioned earlier: (a) an overemphasis on the need for explicit references to the Spirit in the creation narratives and (b) a tendency to allow later biblical concerns about the Spirit's eschatological work to distract from legitimate questions about the Spirit's role in creation. Although this essay will focus rather narrowly on the interpretation of a single text, which itself focuses specifically on the creation of the human person, I will suggest that this discussion can serve as a case study that offers resources for appreciating the Spirit's role in creation more broadly. Without dismissing the legitimate concerns raised by Augustine and others—in particular the strong biblical emphasis on the Spirit's eschatological work of bringing creation to completion—a discussion like this helps us appreciate the Spirit's fundamental and pervasive role in creation as the Giver of Life.

THE "BREATH OF LIFE" IN *CITY OF GOD*

We begin with Augustine's interpretation of the text in question: "Then the LORD God formed a man from the dust of the ground and breathed into his nostrils the breath of life [*nishmat hayyim*], and the man became a living being" (Gen. 2:7). Viewed from the perspective of his overall theology, we might reasonably expect Augustine to argue that the "breath of life" here refers to the Spirit of God. After all, Augustine's theology offers a robust pneumatology in which the Spirit is actively at work in all human persons.[2]

Nonetheless, when Augustine focuses specifically on the meaning of this verse in the thirteenth book of *City of God*, he rejects the idea that it refers to the Holy Spirit.[3] Augustine is countering here the suggestion that this verse depicts God as first creating a complete human person ("formed a man"), which would include both the body and the soul, and then breathed into this human person the Holy Spirit ("breath of life"). According to Augustine, we should read the two stages of Gen. 2:7 as referring first to the creation of the human body ("formed a man") and then to the infusion of the human soul into that material body ("breath of life").[4] Consequently, Gen. 2:7 refers simply to the fact that the *adam* has now become a living/breathing creature.

Augustine supports this reading of the text with both exegetical and theological arguments. Exegetically, Augustine points out that the text makes no explicit reference

---

[2] See Chad Tyler Gerber, *The Spirit of Augustine's Early Theology: Contextualizing Augustine's Pneumatology* (Farnham: Routledge, 2016); Joseph Ratzinger, "The Holy Spirit as Communio: Concerning the Relationship of Pneumatology and Spirituality in Augustine," *Communio* 25, no. 2 (1998): 324–39; and Kathryn L. Reinhard, "Somebody to Love?: The Proprium of the Holy Spirit in Augustine's Trinity," *Augustinian Studies* 41, no. 2 (2010): 351–73.
[3] Augustine, *City of God*, trans. Henry Bettenson (London: Penguin, 1972), 536–46.
[4] Ibid., 540–2.

to the Spirit and that the terms used in this verse denote creaturely realities rather than the divine Spirit.[5] If the author wanted us to hear Gen. 2:7 as a reference to the Spirit, Augustine argues that he would have used the same terminology consistently used elsewhere to denote the Spirit (*ruach/pneuma/spiritus*).[6] Yet Gen. 2:7 uses a different term entirely (*neshama/pnoê/flatus*). According to Augustine, this term is used frequently in Scripture to denote no more than the mere fact that humans are the kinds of creatures that breathe. Ancient thinkers commonly used breath as a way of differentiating living and nonliving creatures, so the presence of breath in the human creature serves to categorize them among the "living" class of creatures. Augustine thus points out that the language of this verse is often applied to other living creatures as well. Humans, cows, and porcupines are all distinct from rocks and tables in that they all breathe and thus have *neshama*. A similar argument can be made from the reference to *adam* becoming a "living creature" (*nephesh hayya*) when he received the breath of life. The creation account itself uses this same phrase to denote nonhuman creatures (Gen. 1:20, 24), reinforcing the idea that the "breath of life" is something possessed by all living creatures and that it does not refer to the Spirit in his unique relationship to human persons.[7]

In addition to these exegetical considerations, Augustine also offers an important theological argument for rejecting the idea that the "breath of life" refers to the Spirit. According to Augustine, Jn 20:22 and 1 Cor. 15:45 both point to the radical newness of the gift of the Spirit, something that is only true of humans in Christ and not merely in virtue of their existence as living creatures. Augustine discusses the Pauline text at some length, noting the distinction Paul makes between first-Adam humanity, in which we have "animal bodies" and "living souls," and second-Adam humanity, which is shaped by the presence of the Spirit.[8] Augustine thus argues that the giving of the Spirit in Christ is not something done merely to restore that which was lost in the fall. Instead, he contends that Paul contrasts the Spirit-formed humanity that we have in Christ with the prelapsarian humanity we received in Adam. This provides the theological framework for Augustine's reading of Jn 20:22. When Jesus breathes upon the disciples in order that they might receive the Spirit, he is not merely restoring them to the condition of humanity in the Garden. Instead, by this act Jesus is inaugurating a radically new form of humanity, one only made possible by the reception of the Spirit.

Having said all of this, it is important to emphasize two things about Augustine's argument. First, as I mentioned earlier, none of this entails that Augustine downplayed the role of the Spirit in creation. Since Augustine viewed creation as an act of the triune God, he maintained that the Spirit was necessarily and inseparably involved in every act of creation. Similarly, Augustine also recognized the importance of the Spirit's role in human life even before the giving of the Spirit through the ministry of Christ.[9] Augustine's argument does not require him to deny that the Spirit had *any* role to play in creating humanity, only that whatever we think about the role of the Spirit in creation, we must still be able to affirm the radical newness of the Spirit-empowered humanity we receive

---

[5] Ibid., 542–3.
[6] Augustine also argues that even using a term like *pneuma* in this text would not have resolved the question since the biblical authors occasionally use this to denote creaturely realities as well.
[7] Augustine still interpreted this text as affirming human uniqueness, but he did so on the basis of the unique human *anima* (soul) that God breathed into the *adam* rather than the presence of the Spirit.
[8] Augustine, *City of God*, 536–40.
[9] Augustine, "Letter 11," in *Letters 1–99* (Brooklyn, NY: New City, 2001), 37.

in Christ. Despite these two clarifications, however, Augustine's argument does require him to reject any suggestion that the "breath of life" in Gen. 2:7 refers to the Holy Spirit in any direct way.[10]

THE *IMAGO DEI* AND THE "BREATH OF LIFE"

Despite the cogency of Augustine's arguments on this point, we have good reasons for reading this verse with more pneumatological depth than he allowed. We begin with Augustine's exegetical arguments. As we have seen, much of Augustine's argument depends on the fact that Gen. 2:7 makes no explicit reference to the Spirit, and that the terms it does use are frequently used elsewhere to denote creaturely life/breath. One way of responding to Augustine's argument would be to contend that the Spirit is often depicted as the "breath" of God by which he creates the universe.[11] Thus, for example, Ps. 33:6 declares, "By the word of the LORD the heavens were made, their starry host by the breath (*ruach*) of his mouth." And Job explicitly relates this motif to the creation of human persons: "The Spirit of God has made me, the breath (*nishmat*) of God gives me life" (Job 33:4). This motif occurs frequently enough that Frank Macchia identifies the "breath" of God as "the chief metaphor for the Spirit of God in the Bible."[12] If this is the case, then maybe we have a more explicit link between the Spirit and Gen. 2:7 than Augustine thought.

As Lyle Dabney rightly points out, the biblical authors often use various terms and concepts (e.g., glory or power) as "circumlocutions for the Spirit," allowing us to see the Spirit at work in texts even when he is not specifically named.[13] Consequently, it remains entirely possible that the text hints at a pneumatological connection even if we remain unconvinced by the connection between the Spirit, the breath of God, and creation. I suggest that we can hear such a circumlocution in the idea of the *imago Dei* as it is developed in Genesis 1–2. We can see this most clearly if we pay attention to important developments in OT studies with regard to the *imago Dei*.

Fortunately, for our purposes, we do not need to address all the complex issues involved in understanding this fraught theological concept. Instead, we merely need to recognize the significance of the growing consensus among biblical scholars that we must view the *imago Dei* at least partly against the background of the ancient Near Eastern conception of cultic images (e.g., idols). As many have pointed out, the relevant terms, "image" (*selem*) and "likeness" (*demut*), should be understood as operating within the broad range of terms the biblical authors used to describe cultic images.[14] James Barr thus concludes: "There is

---

[10]Augustine is not alone in drawing this conclusion, as seen by the number of contemporary commentators who likewise reject the idea that the Spirit of God is in view in this text; see G. Ch. Aalders, *Genesis*, trans. William Heynen, 2 vols. (Grand Rapids, MI: Zondervan, 1981), 1:85; Victor P. Hamilton, *The Book of Genesis: Chapters 1–17* (Grand Rapids, MI: Eerdmans, 1990), 159; Robert Davidson, *Genesis 1–11* (Cambridge: Cambridge University Press, 1973), 31.

[11]See, for example, Williams, "The Spirit in Creation," 2; Daniel Castelo, *Pneumatology: A Guide for the Perplexed* (London: Bloomsbury, 2015), 66; Frank D. Macchia, "The Spirit of Life: Toward a Creation Pneumatology," in *Third Article Theology: A Pneumatological Dogmatics*, ed. Myk Habets (Minneapolis, MN: Fortress, 2016), 113.

[12]Macchia, "The Spirit of Life: Toward a Creation Pneumatology," 113.

[13]D. Lyle Dabney, "The Justification of the Spirit: Soteriological Reflections on the Resurrection," in *Starting with the Spirit*, ed. Stephen Pickard and Gordon Preece (Hindmarsh: Australian Theological Forum, 2001), 63.

[14]For example, James Barr, "The Image of God in the Book of Genesis—A Study of Terminology," *Bulletin of the John Rylands Library* 51, no. 1 (1968): 11–26; David J. A. Clines, "The Image of God in Man," *Tyndale Bulletin* 19 (1968): 53–103; Edward Mason Curtis, "Man as the Image of God in Genesis in the Light of Ancient Near

an antecedent probability that the term 'image of God' might suggest, and might therefore require some delimitation against, the then familiar use of images or idols of the divine."[15] Consequently, even if we maintain, as we should, that there may be important conceptual differences between the *imago Dei* and common notions of what constituted an idol in the ancient Near East, the latter is at least relevant for understanding the former.

Central to the idea of such cultic images is that they served as a locus of divine presence in the world. Although we often use the language of the symbolic to describe ancient idols, as though they merely represent or direct our attention toward divine beings, it is more accurate to say that cultic images were understood as involving "a *physical, living manifestation* of an otherwise invisible reality."[16] When a statue became an idol, it was understood to be infused with the divine presence such that it was now a truly living thing, capable of eating, drinking, talking, and so forth.[17] This close link between the presence of the divine and its cultic image explains the common practice in which vanquished cities would have their idols removed by the victors. In doing so, the victors are literally removing their gods' presence from the vanquished.

This leads directly to the importance of the Spirit for the *imago Dei*. If it is the case that we need to hear the language of the *imago Dei* against the background of these cultic images, and if such images necessarily involve the idea of divine presence, then a proper understanding of the *imago Dei* will be inherently pneumatological, given that the biblical authors frequently identify the Spirit as the one who manifests divine presence in the world. Although the reference to *ruach* in Gen. 1:2 is debated, Richard Middleton speaks for many when he describes it as "God's creative presence."[18] Throughout the OT, wherever the Spirit goes, there God is for blessing or judgment. We see this most clearly in the psalms where, for example, the psalmist asks, "Where can I go from your Spirit? Where can I flee from your presence?" (Ps. 139:7). And again, "Do not cast me from your presence or take your Holy Spirit from me" (Ps. 51:11). Elsewhere, God assures Israel of his covenantal faithfulness by promising that his Spirit will remain among them (Hag. 2:5). God routinely "sends" his Spirit into the world as an expression of his presence (e.g., Ps. 104:30). This consistent emphasis on the Spirit as the manifestation of divine presence requires that we take seriously the pneumatological foundation of the *imago Dei*.

At this point, one might legitimately begin to wonder whether this discussion of the *imago Dei* has begun to wander rather far from our discussion of Gen. 2:7. However, a number of scholars have recently argued that the second creation narrative is itself

---

Eastern Parallels" (PhD diss., University of Pennsylvania, 1984); John F. Kutsko, *Between Heaven and Earth: Divine Presence and Absence in the Book of Ezekiel* (Winona Lake, IN: Eisenbrauns, 2000); J. Richard Middleton, *The Liberating Image: The Imago Dei in Genesis 1* (Grand Rapids, MI: Brazos, 2005); Richard Lints, "Imaging and Idolatry: The Sociality of Personhood in the Canon," in *Personal Identity in Theological Perspective*, ed. Richard Lints, Michael S. Horton, and Mark R. Talbot (Grand Rapids, MI: Eerdmans, 2006), 204–25; Stephen L. Herring, *Divine Substitution: Humanity as the Manifestation of Deity in the Hebrew Bible and the Ancient Near East* (Göttingen: Vandenhoeck & Ruprecht, 2013); Catherine L. McDowell, *The Image of God in the Garden of Eden: The Creation of Humankind in Genesis 2:5–3:24 in Light of the Mīs Pî Pīt Pî and Wpt-R Rituals of Mesopotamia and Ancient Egypt* (Winona Lake, IN: Eisenbrauns, 2015).

[15] Barr, "The Image of God," 15.

[16] McDowell, *The Image of God in the Garden of Eden*, 3 (emphasis original). For more on this, see especially Herring, *Divine Substitution*, 26–9.

[17] Herring, *Divine Substitution*, 29.

[18] Middleton, *The Liberating Image*, 86.

modeled on cultic rituals surrounding the creation of idols that were widely practiced in the ancient world.[19] The *mīs pî* ("mouth washing") and *pīt pî* ("mouth opening") ceremonies were the specific rituals in which a divine being was understood to breathe its own life into the cultic image so that it could become a "living idol."[20] According to these scholars, Genesis 2 echoes many of the specific details of these rituals, suggesting that we are to see the creation of the *adam* as at least analogous to the creation of such cultic images. Andreas Schüle helpfully summarizes some of the main points of comparison between Genesis 2 and these cultic rituals:

> Similarities occur in the general pattern—the material shaping of a body, its being brought to life, the change of environment from some desert place to the garden—but also in details like the furnishing of the garden with plants and animals and the fact that God himself is present there and joins with Adam and Eve in the early evening hours when there is a nice breeze coming in from the Mediterranean sea.[21]

More recently, Stephen Herring has convincingly demonstrated the significance of the *mīs pî/pīt pî* rituals for understanding the *imago Dei*,[22] and Catherine McDowell has provided an even deeper treatment of the connections between these rituals and the second creation narrative.[23] We thus have a growing body of literature establishing the connection between divine presence, the *imago Dei*, and the Spirit in both of the creation narratives in Genesis.[24]

Most important for our purposes is the significance of the "breath of life" in this context. Even if we accept Augustine's argument that there is no explicit, linguistic connection between this phrase and the Spirit of God, the background material we have just discussed strongly suggests that we should hear such a claim against the background of a deity "breathing" its divine presence into a physical object such that the object becomes a "living being," the living manifestation of divine presence. If this is the case, then we have good reasons for hearing "breath of life" as emphasizing that these creatures have now become living beings in virtue of the Spirit's presence.

Although this argument allows us to respond to the specifically exegetical concerns raised by Augustine's arguments, we still need to address the more theological arguments. If we maintain that humans have been constituted pneumatologically from the very beginning, what are we to make of texts like Jn 20:22 and 1 Cor. 15:45? Does the interpretation we have been exploring require us to say that these texts point to nothing more than a restoration of the state of humanity in the Garden, as if the Spirit-empowered new humanity was no more than a repetition of adamic humanity? Surely not. Paul clearly portrays Jesus as the second Adam who inaugurates the transformation of humanity into its eschatological state. That is the significance of the

---

[19] Michael B. Dick, *Born in Heaven, Made on Earth: The Making of the Cult Image in the Ancient Near East* (Winona Lake, IN: Eisenbrauns, 1999).
[20] José Faur, "The Biblical Idea of Idolatry," *Jewish Quarterly Review* 69, no. 1 (1978): 1–15.
[21] Andreas Schüle, "Made in The 'Image of God': The Concepts of Divine Images in Gen 1–3," *Zeitschrift für die Alttestamentliche Wissenschaft* 117, no. 1 (2005): 13.
[22] Herring, *Divine Substitution*.
[23] McDowell, *The Image of God in the Garden of Eden*.
[24] This does not mean, of course, that biblical readers would have thought the text was saying that humans were exactly like these cultic images in every way. But the metaphor would have resonated with readers in a cultural context thoroughly familiar with the use of such cultic images.

contrasting images Paul uses to describe modes of human existence: spiritual/natural, earthly/heavenly, and perishable/imperishable. And although it would take too long to establish the point here, many have argued that John uses new creation motifs to establish the epochal significance of Jesus as the new Adam who leads humanity—indeed, creation as a whole—into an even higher state.[25] Yet nothing about the interpretation suggested here requires us to deny the climactic nature of the outpouring of the Spirit that comes through the person and work of Jesus Christ. It is entirely possible to maintain both that human persons were pneumatologically constituted in the beginning and that this creational reality is transformed and/or heightened in some meaningful way in the new creation. Indeed, something like this seems necessary if we are going to maintain both the continuity and the discontinuity of creational and eschatological humanity.

CONCLUSION

Augustine is rightly cautious about over-interpreting a text, even when the interpretation being proposed would have fit well with pneumatological emphases he has developed elsewhere. And his argument also displays considerable sensitivity toward the eschatological focus that guides how many biblical authors locate the Spirit in relation to creation. Nonetheless, I think we have seen that it is possible to maintain both of these emphases while still recognizing the ways in which the Genesis narratives themselves identify the Spirit as absolutely fundamental to the creation of the human person. These points alone would give us resources for emphasizing the Spirit's role in creation to a greater degree than has often been the case. By helping us see some of the ways in which the Spirit is present throughout the Genesis narratives, even when he is not explicitly named, this case study should also provide an impetus for reflecting more broadly on the Spirit's role in creation, both in Genesis and in other biblical creation accounts. In so doing, we can only grow in our awe and wonder of the One who is the Lord and Giver of Life.

FOR FURTHER READING

Bergmann, Sigurd. *Creation Set Free: The Spirit as Liberator of Nature*. Grand Rapids, MI: Eerdmans, 2005.

Gunton, Colin E. "The Spirit Moved over the Face of the Waters: The Holy Spirit and Created Order." *International Journal of Systematic Theology* 4, no. 2 (2002): 190–204.

Macchia, Frank D. "The Spirit of Life: Toward a Creation Pneumatology." In *Third Article Theology: A Pneumatological Dogmatics*, edited by Myk Habets, 113–30. Minneapolis, MN: Fortress, 2016.

Williams, David T. "The Spirit in Creation." *Scottish Journal of Theology* 67, no. 1 (2014): 1–14.

---

[25] For a more extended discussion of both these passages, see Marc Cortez, *ReSourcing Theological Anthropology* (Grand Rapids, MI: Zondervan, 2018).

CHAPTER FIFTEEN

Pneumatological Development in Trinitarian Perspective

JACKSON LASHIER

The Council of Nicaea in 325 was notoriously brief in its assessment of the Holy Spirit. After a detailed paragraph on the relationship of the Father and the Son, the original Nicene Creed includes, almost as an afterthought, the statement "and [we believe] in the Holy Spirit."[1] The Council of Constantinople, meeting in 381, is much more detailed on the subject: "And [we believe] in the Holy Spirit, the Lord and life-giver, Who proceeds from the Father, Who with the Father and the Son is together worshipped and together glorified, Who spoke through the prophets."[2] The discrepancy in the two creeds on this point suggests a good deal of pneumatological development and innovation in the fifty-six years between the councils, to which the primary texts bear witness. Nevertheless, it is inaccurate to assume that prior to 325 there was little written about the nature and work of the Spirit.[3] Indeed, the second century witnessed a "high" pneumatology in several writers.[4] The question that arises from this observation is why the Council of Nicaea did not make use of this earlier high pneumatology. Related to this question is a second, namely, what changed to allow for the stunning pneumatological advancements in the latter half of the fourth century, which resulted in the robust trinitarian theology at Constantinople?

In this essay, I will explore these two questions, first, by examining the high pneumatology of the second century through the works of Irenaeus of Lyons to discern both the factors that qualify it as high and the gaps that led to its demise in later centuries.[5] Second, I will

---

[1] J. N. D. Kelly, *Early Christian Creeds*, 3rd ed. (London: Continuum, 2006), 216.
[2] Ibid., 298.
[3] As, for example, R. P. C. Hanson concluded in what was at one point the definitive account of the era. He writes of Nicaea, "The surprising thing is, not that more attention was not paid to the Spirit, but that the theologians continued to include the Spirit in the framework of their theology." *The Search for the Christian Doctrine of God: The Arian Controversy, 318–381* (1998; repr., Grand Rapids, MI: Baker Academic, 2005), 739.
[4] "High" in this context refers to the divinity of the Spirit and to his participation with the Father and Son in the divine work in the economy.
[5] Irenaeus is not the only second-century figure with a high pneumatology. The writings of Theophilus of Antioch, for example, also evince these characteristics. Nevertheless, Irenaeus's pneumatology is the high point of this early trajectory of thought and, therefore, engagement with his pneumatology will suffice for the present essay.

explore the scriptural ambiguities related to the Holy Spirit, first encountered in Irenaeus's work, through the lens of Spirit Christology that dominated the writings of the third century and hastened the neglect of the Spirit. Finally, I will focus on the resurgence of pneumatology in the later fourth century through close readings of the pneumatologies of five figures—Athanasius and Didymus from Alexandria, and Basil, Gregory of Nazianzus, and Gregory of Nyssa from Cappadocia—to discern why they recovered the earlier high pneumatology. The result will be a better understanding of the nonlinear development of pneumatology as it relates to the trinitarian controversies culminating at Constantinople in 381.

SECOND-CENTURY HIGH PNEUMATOLOGY

The theological challenges facing the emerging church of the second century converged on a division within the Godhead. Marcion held that the god revealed by Jesus was different from the ontologically inferior creator god revealed in the Jewish scriptures, while the various theological communities known to history as Gnostics believed the divine nature was constituted by a series of thirty spiritual beings. Writing in the last decades of the second century, Irenaeus countered these dualist theologies by focusing on the unity of the Godhead as revealed through both the Jewish scriptures and the writings of the apostles. Irenaeus's reading of these scriptures, however, shows the Godhead as a unity not just of Father and Son, as was standard in the second century, but of Father, Son, and Spirit. Irenaeus shows this unity in two primary ways, both of which are Jewish in origin.[6] First, he includes the Spirit with the Father and the Son, over against the creation, by referring to him as the Wisdom (*Sophia* or *Sapientia*) of God. Second, he understands the Spirit, as God's Wisdom, to be involved in the properly divine work of creating. I will examine these related aspects in turn.

Irenaeus's identification of the Spirit as the Wisdom of God corresponds to the more traditional identification of the Son as the Word of God. According to Irenaeus, these titles demonstrate that the Son and the Spirit are both with God eternally (as God's own Word and Wisdom) and are themselves God. For example, he writes, "And that the Word, that is the Son, was always with the Father, we have demonstrated many times. And that also Wisdom which is the Spirit was with him before the whole creation."[7] The inclusion of the Spirit with the Father and Son is noteworthy because Irenaeus maintains everywhere a strict ontological distinction between the Creator and what is created.[8] This

---

[6] See Michel R. Barnes, "The Beginning and End of Early Christian Pneumatology," *Augustinian Studies* 39, no. 2 (2008): 169–86. Irenaeus is likely acquainted with Jewish pneumatology through his early years in Smyrna, which is then reinforced, as Anthony Briggman has shown, through his reading of Theophilus at some point in the midst of writing *Against Heresies*. Briggman, *Irenaeus of Lyons and the Theology of the Holy Spirit*, Oxford Early Christian Studies (Oxford: Oxford University Press, 2012), 97–103.

[7] *Against Heresies*, 4.20.3. Where not noted, translations of Irenaeus are mine. I am relying on the following critical editions of Irenaeus's Latin text (and Greek where we have fragments) for the quotations I have made in this article: *Contre les Hérésies* 2.1 and 2, trans., intro., and notes Adelin Rousseau and Louis Doutreleau, SC 293 and 294 (Paris: Éditions du Cerf, 1982); *Contre les Hérésies* 3.1 and 2, trans., intro., and notes Rousseau and Doutreleau, SC 210 and 211 (Paris: Éditions du Cerf, 1974); and *Contre les Hérésies* 4.1 and 2, trans., intro., and notes Rousseau, et al., SC 100.1 and 100.2 (Paris: Éditions du Cerf, 1965).

[8] "And in this God differs from man, since God indeed makes, but man is made. And indeed he who makes is always the same, but what is made must receive both a beginning and a middle, as well as an addition and an increase" (ibid., 4.11.2).

constitutes, therefore, a clear affirmation of the Spirit's divinity, a conviction nowhere allayed by either a subordination of the Spirit to the Son and Father or a causal link between the distinct existence of the Spirit and his work in creation, which would have rendered the Spirit's existence as merely functional. Rather, for Irenaeus, the Spirit, like the Son and the Father, is eternal and fully divine.

This leads to the second, related aspect of Irenaeus's pneumatology, namely, the Spirit as co-creator with the Father and the Son. He writes, for example, "We should know that he who made and formed and breathed in them the breath of life and nourishes us by creation, establishing all things by his Word, and binding them together by his Wisdom—this is he who is the only true God."[9] The "binding together" work of the Spirit is indicative of a wider field of verbs Irenaeus uses that describes the creative work of the Spirit as a completing or perfecting of the work, which has its source in the Father and takes its form from the Son. In his most mature statement of this cooperative work, he writes:

> In this way, then, it is demonstrated [that there is] One God, [the] Father.... And as God is verbal, therefore he made created things by the Word; and God is Spirit, so that He adorned all things by the Spirit, as the prophet also says, "By the Word of the Lord were the heavens established, and all their power by His Spirit."[10]

Irenaeus here shows that the Spirit is not incidental to the work of creating nor that his creative function can be subsumed into the general creative work of the Son. Rather, the Spirit *as Spirit* is necessary to the completion of God's creative work.

Irenaeus's high pneumatology at this early date is remarkable, given its source in Scripture as read through Jewish traditions of thought.[11] Against the common modern assumption that the development of high pneumatology is subsequent to and dependent upon similar developments in Christology, Irenaeus shows a simultaneous recognition of the divinity of Son and Spirit precisely because Scripture reveals the divine work of the economy to be the product of *three* divine actors.

Nevertheless, two related gaps remain in Irenaeus's pneumatology that help explain, beyond the loss of the "Jewish theological superstructure," why it is not more influential to third and early fourth-century theologians.[12] First, while Irenaeus includes the Spirit with the Father and the Son on the Creator side of the ontological distinction between Creator and created, he never develops a clear category to distinguish among the three within the unified Godhead. Second, nowhere does Irenaeus provide an aetiological account of the Spirit, which, given Irenaeus's strict adherence to Scripture, might be a gap attributable to Scripture itself. At the very least, it is clear that Irenaeus did not perceive

---

[9]Ibid., 3.24.2. See also ibid., 4.20.2, 4 and 4.38.2.

[10]*Proof*, 5. *On the Apostolic Preaching*, trans. John Behr (Crestwood, NY: St. Vladimir's Seminary Press, 1997), 43. The scriptural passage Irenaeus quotes here is Ps. 33/2:6, the central passage from which Irenaeus develops a two-agent theory of creation.

[11]Per the strictures of his anti-gnostic polemic, Irenaeus confines himself to Scripture because, as he explains, speculative theology that moves beyond what is revealed in Scripture is one of the sources of his opponents' errors. See *Against Heresies*, 2.28.2-3.

[12]Barnes, "Beginning and End," 170. Barnes explains the neglect of this early high pneumatology by the loss of the Jewish theological superstructure that supported it. While this loss certainly factors into the equation, one suspects that had Irenaeus's pneumatology provided the necessary resources for the theological exigencies of the third century, his pneumatology would have been more influential regardless of whether its Jewish roots were known or retained.

a scriptural term for the Spirit's eternal relation to and derivation from the Father to correspond to the begetting of the Son. These oversights, coupled with Irenaeus's strong insistence on the simplicity of the divine nature,[13] make a so-called "modalist" reading of Irenaeus plausible, wherein, for reasons I will demonstrate presently, the distinct existence of the Spirit becomes particularly vulnerable.[14] While such a reading is ultimately inaccurate, its mere plausibility makes Irenaeus's pneumatology unhelpful when the theological crises shift at the beginning of the third century.

THIRD-CENTURY SPIRIT CHRISTOLOGY AND THE AMBIGUITY OF SCRIPTURE

The new challenge facing the church at the beginning of the third century came from a system of thought that focused on the unity of the Godhead to the exclusion of real distinctions among the Father, Son, and Spirit. According to this system, Father, Son, and Spirit are not real persons or relations, but are masks or modes in which the one God works and appears.[15] As Tertullian describes the thought of his opponent Praxeas, "the Father himself came down into the virgin, himself was born of her, himself suffered, in short himself is Jesus Christ."[16] Tertullian identifies Asia Minor as the birthplace of this thought, though it comes into focus in Rome where it gained a strong following. By the mid-third century, figures from North Africa to Rome to Alexandria were confronting it.

Third-century writers countered modalism by emphasizing the scriptural account of the Son's begetting from the Father, for this showed their real distinction, not simply in name but in person (*hypostasis/persona*). Tertullian, for example, wryly states, "the Father said to the Son, 'Thou art my Son, this day have I begotten thee': if you will have me believe that the Father himself is also the Son, show me that it is stated elsewhere in this form, The Lord said to himself, I am my son, today I have begotten myself."[17] Origen uses Wis. 7:25-26, which speaks of Wisdom as a breath of the power of God, to write of the Son, "there comes into existence, therefore, another power, subsisting in its own proper nature, a kind of breath, as the passage of Scripture calls it, of the first and unbegotten power of God, drawing from this source whatever existence it has."[18] Perhaps clearest of all, Novatian can summarize the entirety of Scripture's support of a distinct Son by writing, "Since the divine Scripture, not so much of the Old as also of the New Testament, everywhere shows

---

[13] *Against Heresies*, 2.13.3, 8.

[14] Behr, for example, has suggested that Zephrinus and Callistus, labeled by one ancient author as the source of modalistic thought for their failure to engage the history of Christ behind the incarnation, "were maintaining the style of theology developed by Irenaeus." *The Way to Nicaea* (Crestwood, NY: St. Vladimir's Seminary Press, 2001), 141.

[15] Hence the modern designation "modalism." Writers contemporary to the events refer to this thought as Monarchianism (for its emphasis on the Monarchy or unity of the Godhead), Patripassianism (for its belief that the Father is the one crucified), or, most commonly in later years, Sabellianism (after an early figure associated with such thought). For ease of reference, I will refer to this trajectory of thought by its modern designation of modalism.

[16] *Against Praxeas*, 1. *Tertullian's Treatise against Praxeas*, trans. Ernest Evans (1948; repr., Eugene, OR: Wipf & Stock, 2011), 170.

[17] Ibid., 11 in *Tertullian's Treatise*, 143. The scripture quoted here is Ps. 2:7.

[18] *On First Principles*, 1.2.9. Translation by G. W. Butterworth (1936; repr., Notre Dame, IN: Christian Classics, 2013), 30–1.

Him to be born of the Father ... what can be so evident proof that this is not the Father, but the Son?"[19]

The upshot of this approach, and likely the reason for its popularity, is that accounts of the Son's begetting from the Father showed not only their real distinction but also their sameness, for if the Son came from the Father, then the two must in some way be similar. For example, Tertullian writes, "Therefore according to the precedent of these examples, I profess that I say that God and his Word, the Father and his Son, are two: for the root and the shoot are *two things, but conjoined*; and the spring and the river are *two manifestations, but undivided*; and the sun and its beams are *two aspects, but they cohere*."[20] Similarly, Hippolytus writes:

> But when I say another, I do not mean that there are two Gods, but that it is only as light of light, or as water from a fountain, or as a ray from the sun. For there is but one power, which is from the All; and the Father is the All from whom comes this Power, the Word. And this is the mind which came forth into the world, and was manifested as the Son of God.[21]

Other methods for demonstrating their distinction, such as passages where the Father and the Son speak to one another, failed to show their sameness.

This approach to establishing the real distinction of the Father and the Son clearly reveals why the high pneumatology of Irenaeus does not factor into these later discussions. For all its richness, Irenaeus's pneumatology is missing the one aspect that would have provided the resources to challenge modalism, namely, an aetiological account of the Spirit.

This observation, in turn, explains the third-century focus on the relationship of the Father and Son to the exclusion of the Spirit (which was not a characteristic of theology in a pre-Monarchian context). In relation to the Spirit, Scripture does not further the anti-Monarchian polemic. Accordingly, scriptural passages that Irenaeus had interpreted pneumatologically are now shifted to the Son as a way to bolster the scriptural argument of an eternal distinction between the Father and Son. This includes not only Wisdom passages, as we saw above with Origen,[22] but even spirit (*pneuma/spiritus*) passages. Indeed, Scripture uses "spirit" to refer both to a distinct Holy Spirit and to the Godhead as a whole, an ambiguity that makes the Holy Spirit vulnerable to assimilation into one or both of the other divine figures.[23] Consequently, in the so-called "Spirit Christology" that emerged and dominated in the third century, the Spirit is identified as the pre-existent Son. Hippolytus is a prime example of such thinking, writing, "Now what subject is meant in this sentence, 'I came forth from the Father,' but just the Word? And what is

---

[19]*Treatise on the Trinity*, 26 (ANF, 5:637).
[20]*Against Praxeas*, 8 in *Tertullian's Treatise*, 39 (italics added).
[21]*Against Noetus*, 11 (ANF, 5:227). Although Origen is clear that the distinction between the three *hypostases* results in a subordination of the Son and Spirit to the Father (see, for example, *On First Principles*, 1.3.7), even he is concerned to demonstrate a sameness of the three, though his answer is much more complex; claims he used the definition *homoousios* of Father and Son are almost certainly incorrect. See Lewis Ayres, *Nicaea and Its Legacy: An Approach to Fourth-Century Trinitarian Theology* (Oxford: Oxford University Press, 2004), 20–8.
[22]Wisdom as a christological title is the older model, going back to Paul in 1 Cor. 1:24 and witnessed in second-century writers such as Justin and Athenagoras. It remains a title for the Son throughout the third and fourth centuries.
[23]See, for example, John 4:24.

it that is begotten of Him, but just the Spirit, that is to say, the Word?"[24] Tertullian also demonstrates this tendency, interpreting John 1 as follows: "For as, when John says 'The Word was made flesh,' we understand also the Spirit at the mention of the Word, so also here we recognise also the Word under the name of the Spirit. For spirit is the substance of the Word, and word is an operation of the Spirit, and the two are one [thing]."[25]

With the loss of the eternal distinctiveness of the Spirit, so too goes any clear concept of the Spirit's distinct function in the economy as we saw with Irenaeus's understanding of the Spirit as co-Creator. Tertullian's interpretation of Ps. 33/2:6 demonstrates this loss. He writes,

> "By the Word of the Lord were the heavens confirmed, and all their hosts by his Spirit"—that Spirit of course which was present in Word—it is clear that it is one and the same function, now under the name Wisdom, now under the designation of Word which received the beginning of ways for God's works' sake, which confirmed the heaven, by which all things were made and without which nothing was made.[26]

For Irenaeus, Ps. 33/2:6 supported the creative work of the Spirit alongside the Word, but Tertullian has collapsed the Word and the Spirit into one being and, using Jn 1:3 as his proof, argues for a one-agent understanding of creation. This interpretation becomes standard throughout the third and early fourth centuries.

The theological exigencies of the third century and the lack of scriptural resources in reference to the Spirit to meet these exigencies thus retard the development of pneumatology from its promising start at the end of the second century. While writers continue to mention the Spirit as the third article of faith behind the Father and Son, they fail to expand on the Spirit's eternal relationship with the Father and Son or on the Spirit's work in the economy. This is, essentially, the pneumatology that appears in the 325 Creed of Nicaea.

FOURTH-CENTURY RECOVERY[27]

The general neglect of pneumatology that characterized the third century is initially exacerbated by the trinitarian controversies at the beginning of the fourth century. The theology of Arius, Eusebius of Nicomedia, and others dictated the terms of the debate, which meant an almost exclusive focus on the relationship of the Father and Son.[28] This is true both of the writings leading up to Nicaea[29] and, with one notable exception, those from the two decades following the Council.[30] Athanasius's three *Orations*, written in the

---

[24]*Against Noetus*, 16 (ANF, 5:229).
[25]*Against Praxeas*, 26 in *Tertullian's Treatise*, 170–1.
[26]Ibid., 7 in *Tertullian's Treatise*, 137. See also *Against Praxeas*, 7, 19.
[27]"Recovery" as a description of the pneumatologies of the latter fourth century comes from Ayres, "Innovation and Ressourcement in Pro-Nicene Pneumatology," *Augustinian Studies* 39, no. 2 (2008): 187–205.
[28]Numerous accounts of Arius's theology exist, and these are helpful for understanding why the initial trinitarian controversies had to focus on Father and Son. Unparalleled in this aspect is Rowan Williams, *Arius: Heresy and Tradition*, rev. ed. (Grand Rapids, MI: Eerdmans, 2001).
[29]The letters of Alexander and Arius, for example, are fairly silent on the Spirit.
[30]Cyril of Jerusalem devoted two of his *Catechetical Lectures*, delivered at the end of the 340s, to the Holy Spirit. The nature of these lectures as interpretations of the various articles of the baptismal creed used at his church, explains his unique ability to break out of the period's tendency to focus on the Father and Son. Like Irenaeus,

330s–340s, are indicative of the concerns of this time period among the emerging pro-Nicene consensus. Against Arius and later figures like Asterius, Athanasius identifies the Son with the Father and, against the modalistic interpretation of Nicaea's *homoousios* in the writings of Marcellus of Ancyra, he distinguishes the Son from the Father.[31] Like the anti-Monarchian writers of the third century, Athanasius relies on the scriptural account of the Son's begetting to meet both objectives. The Son, as begotten from the Father's essence, is "proper (*idios*) to the Father's essence"[32] but, precisely as offspring, is eternally distinct from the Father.[33] Athanasius refers to the Spirit as an entity distinct from the Father and Son in places throughout the *Orations*, and he refers to the work of the Spirit primarily as that of sanctifying.[34] However, he has no concern to include the Spirit with the Father and Son or to unite the Spirit's sanctifying work with the divine work of the Godhead.

A striking change in Athanasius's interest in the Spirit appears in the late 350s. In a series of letters he writes to his fellow Egyptian bishop Serapion, Athanasius discusses the Spirit at length and in a manner that both recalls the high pneumatology of the second century and anticipates later developments. The letters engage a faction within Serapion's church, called the *Tropikoi* by Athanasius,[35] who affirmed the full divinity of the Son but believed the Holy Spirit was "a creature [and] one of the ministering spirits . . . different from the angels only in degree."[36] Their position rests on the ambiguity of Scripture's use of *pneuma* as demonstrated in their interpretation of Amos 4:13 ("He who forms the mountains and creates the spirit [*pneuma*]") as referring to the Holy Spirit.[37] As we have seen, this pneumatology fits quite well within a third-century context and is, arguably, a valid interpretation of the 325 Creed.

Athanasius rejects this position, however, because he has come to see, in a way not clearly articulated just a decade before, that the Spirit and Son are interconnected, such that what is affirmed of one must be affirmed of the other. Put differently, the Spirit corresponds to the Son as the Son corresponds to the Father.[38] This means that the Spirit,

---

he sees the centrality of the Spirit to the divine work apart from a dependence upon Christology. Cyril, thus, is an anomaly who revealed the importance of the curious retention of the Spirit in the creedal statements even when no developed pneumatology supported its presence. I will note below two places where his pneumatology anticipates later developments.

[31]Marcellus's modalistic interpretation of Nicaea explains why Athanasius does not rely on *homoousios* to make his arguments at this early stage and why the Council of Nicaea did not fully solve the questions raised by Arius. See Ayres, *Nicaea and Its Legacy*, 62–76, 105–17. On Marcellus, see Joseph T. Lienhard, *Contra Marcellum: Marcellus of Ancyra and Fourth-Century Theology* (Washington DC: Catholic University of America Press, 1999).

[32]See *Oration*, 1.29. Athanasius likely acquired *idios* as a technical term from Alexander who used it in his *Letter to Alexander of Thessalonica* (32). For a study on the significance of the term in Alexandrian theology more generally, see Andrew Louth, "The Use of the Term *idios* in Alexandrian Theology from Alexander to Cyril," *Studia Patristica* 19 (Louvain: Peeters, 1989), 198–202.

[33]*Oration*, 3.4.

[34]Ibid., 1.12.47.

[35]This title, a play on the term *tropos*, is a polemical device Athanasius uses to refer to his opponents' idiosyncratic way of reading Scripture. Thus, it does not necessarily indicate a well-organized or even self-aware community based on this pneumatology. See the introduction to *Works on the Spirit*, trans. Mark DelCogliano, Andrew Radde-Gallwitz, and Lewis Ayres (Yonkers, NY: St. Vladimir's Seminary Press, 2011), 20–2.

[36]*Letters*, 1.1.2 in *Works*, 53.

[37]According to Athanasius, they also used 1 Tim. 5:12, which names the angels behind Father and Son, as a reference to the Holy Spirit.

[38]See, for example, *Letters*, 1.21.1.

like the Son, is proper (*idios*) to the divine essence.[39] Whereas a decade before, Athanasius had used *idios* only in reference to the Son, he now expands this crucial definition to the Spirit. Because of this correspondence of Spirit to Son, Athanasius now sees the former as integral to the Godhead in a manner not witnessed since Irenaeus.

The justification of the Son and Spirit's correspondence and the subsequent connection of the Spirit to the Godhead come from Scripture's account of the work of the Spirit, which Athanasius now sees as unified with that of the Father and Son. Nevertheless, unlike Irenaeus, who had used the title "Wisdom" to refer to the Spirit's divine work, Athanasius focuses solely on Scripture's *pneuma* language. To make this argument, he has to provide a rule to clarify Scripture's ambiguous use of *pneuma*. Thus, he writes, "if 'spirit' is said without the definite article or without one of the aforementioned modifiers, it cannot be the Holy Spirit who is signified."[40] When applied to the *pneuma* passages of Scripture, this rule offers Athanasius a plethora of passages that demonstrate a living and active Holy Spirit who corresponds to the divine Son. For example, he interprets Ps. 103:30 ("You send forth your Spirit, and they are created, and you renew the face of the earth") by writing, "if you rightly think that the Son is not a creature because all things came into existence through the Word, how is it not blasphemous for you to call the Spirit a creature, in whom the Father through the Word perfects and renews all things?"[41] Elsewhere, he writes of the same psalm, "if the Father creates and renews all things through the Word in the Holy Spirit, what sort of likeness or kinship could the Creator have with creatures? How could the one in whom he creates all things possibly be a creature?"[42] The same conclusion can be drawn from the Spirit's work in redemption as shown, for example, in his interpretation of Heb. 6:4, which says that enlightened humans become partakers of the Holy Spirit. Athanasius writes, "But if he is always the same and participated in, and creatures participate in him, the Holy Spirit can be neither an angel nor a creature in any way, but must be proper to the Word."[43] The Spirit is proper to God's essence, then, precisely because Father, Son, and Spirit share in the same divine work.[44]

We have seen, however, that such a definition renders the Spirit's distinct existence vulnerable due to the lack of an aetiological account of the Spirit. Using the correspondence argument, Athanasius demonstrates that the Spirit, like the Son, is an "offspring" of the Father.[45] In the course of that argument, Athanasius identifies a scriptural word for the origin of the Spirit from the Father to correspond to the "begetting" of the Son, namely,

---

[39]Ibid., 1.12.5 in *Works*, 73. In *Letters* 1.27.4 (*Works*, 96), Athanasius equates the phrase to *homoousios*, the only time he applies the term to the Spirit.

[40]Ibid., 1.4.2 in *Works*, 58. In addition to the modifier "holy," those others he mentions are "of God," "of the Father," "my," "his," "of Christ," "of the Son," "from me," and "of Truth." Cyril of Jerusalem anticipates Athanasius in this need for clarity, although his method is not as substantive and did not produce the same clear results. *Catechetical Lectures*, 16.3.

[41]*Letters*, 1.9.7 in *Works*, 67.

[42]Ibid., 1.24.5-6 in *Works*, 91. Athanasius also uses Ps. 33/2:6, which, as we have seen, had been similarly used by Irenaeus before falling victim to the Spirit Christology of the third century.

[43]*Letters*, 1.27.2 in *Works*, 95.

[44]See ibid., 1.14.6, 1.20.4, and 1.31.2. Cyril of Jerusalem makes a similar argument in *Catechetical Lectures*, 16.13. It should be noted that Athanasius also refers to the Spirit as a "power" of God. *Letters*, 1.20.5. This line of argumentation will be explicitly rejected in later writers with the maturation of the "one power" argument for the unity of the Father, Son, and Spirit.

[45]*Letters*, 1.20.5.

"procession" (*ekporeuomai*). This word comes from Jn 15:26 ("the Spirit of Truth who proceeds from the Father"), which Athanasius interprets to mean that "the Spirit shines forth, and is sent, and is given from the Word, who is confessed to be from the Father."[46] Although this account remains underutilized in his thought, Athanasius's identification of Jn 15:26 is a crucial development, absent, as we have seen, from second-century pneumatologies.

Writing around the same time from Alexandria is the somewhat lesser known figure, Didymus the Blind.[47] In his short treatise *On the Holy Spirit*, which likely responds to the same current of thought represented by the *Tropikoi*, Didymus reflects similar emphases as Athanasius's *Letters*. Like Athanasius, Didymus bases his pneumatology on the *pneuma* passages of Scripture gleaned through his own, similarly stated, rule for identifying the referent of every occurrence of *pneuma*.[48] Likewise, Didymus groups the Spirit with the Father and Son, contrasting their uncreated natures to the created nature of every other thing.[49] And his scriptural proof of this distinction is the Spirit's activity, which Didymus understands to be unified with the activity of the Father and the Son.

In many respects, however, Didymus's pneumatology surpasses that of his more celebrated contemporary. Notably, Didymus is clearer about the inclusion of the Holy Spirit into the divine essence shared by Father and Son, writing in one place, "the fact that there is a single grace of the Father and the Son perfected by the activity of the Holy Spirit demonstrates that the Trinity is of one substance."[50] Elsewhere he writes,

> On the basis of all these passages it is proved that the activity of the Father and the Son and the Holy Spirit is the same. But those who have a single activity also have a single substance. For things of the same substance (*homoousios*) have the same activities, and things of a different substance have discordant and distinct activities.[51]

At a time when the word *homoousios* was still suspect for its modalistic implications, and Athanasius was sparing in its application to the Spirit, Didymus does not hesitate to use it of the Spirit. This could simply reflect Didymus's ignorance of the problems associated with *homoousios*, but that is doubtful, considering he writes from Alexandria and is also highly influenced by Origen. More likely, Didymus understood the implications of the one activity argument for the one essence of Father, Son, and Spirit.

More significantly, and perhaps owing to his unqualified use of *homoousios*, Didymus has a more developed aetiological account of the Spirit. Like Athanasius, he takes the "procession" of Jn 15:26 as a reference to the Spirit's origin from the Father, which, he says, corresponds to the begetting of the Son. Unlike Athanasius, however, Didymus spells out this correspondence to the Son's eternal begetting through a clever juxtaposition of christological passages. Instead of using the begetting passages, such as Psalm 2 or John 1,

---

[46]Ibid., 1.20.5 in *Works*, 85. See also ibid., 1.2.5.
[47]In older scholarship, Didymus's work was dated to the 370s, primarily because of the developed pneumatology and the presumption that he was dependent upon Basil's work. More recent scholarship argues for an earlier date, perhaps only a few years after Athanasius's *Letters to Serapion*. See Mark DelCogliano, "Basil of Caesarea, Didymus the Blind, and the Anti-Pneumatomachian Exegesis of Amos 4:14 and John 1:3," *Journal of Theological Studies* 61 (2010): 644–58.
[48]*On the Holy Spirit*, 73, 237–56.
[49]Ibid., 10, 26, 29, 34.
[50]Ibid., 76 in *Works*, 167.
[51]Ibid., 81 in *Works*, 168.

to refer to the Son's aetiology, Didymus emphasizes Jn 8:42, where Jesus says of himself, "I proceeded forth (*exerchomai*) and have come from God." This is the same general idea (although with a different Greek verb) that Jn 15:26 highlights of the Spirit, which gives a scriptural precedent for the correspondence argument in relation to the respective aetiologies of Son and Spirit. He writes, "we ought to understand that the Holy Spirit goes out from the Father as the Savior himself goes out from God."[52] This account, thus, shows the distinction of Spirit (and Son) from Father, for only the Father is the source as this is "the distinctive feature of the Father and the concept of Fatherhood."[53] Surprisingly, however, Didymus, like those before him, did not employ a term to name this distinct entity within the oneness of the divine essence. This final piece of the pneumatological puzzle, as it were, would be left to three theologians from Cappadocia, writing on the eve of the Council of Constantinople.[54]

In their polemic against opponents of the same trajectory as Athanasius's *Tropikoi*,[55] the Cappadocian Fathers classify the Spirit with the Father and the Son over against creatures by attention to the Spirit's divine works, such as creation and redemption. Although they draw on many of the same exegetical arguments we have seen, their focus is more philosophical regarding the implications of a simple divine nature.[56] As Gregory of Nyssa writes:

> But in a Divine nature, as such, when once we have believed in it, we can recognize no distinctions suggested either by the Scripture teaching or by our own common sense; distinctions that is that would divide that Divine and transcendent nature within itself by any degrees of intensity and remission, so as to be altered from itself by being more or less. . . . If, then, the Holy Spirit is truly, and not in name only, called Divine both by the Scripture and by our Fathers, what ground is left for those who oppose the glory of the Spirit?[57]

---

[52]Ibid., 113 in *Works*, 179.

[53]Ibid., 114 in *Works*, 180. In support of this assertion, Didymus notes the use of "Father" instead of "God" in Jn 15:26, for presumably God would name both Father and Spirit. However, he is curiously silent on the fact that in Jn 8:42 Jesus says he comes forth from God.

[54]Basil, Gregory Nazianzus, and Gregory of Nyssa traditionally have been treated as a unified group, an approach which neglects the differences and development discernable within the three figures. Recent scholarship has rightly moved to considering these figures in their own right. See, for example, Ayres's treatment in *Nicaea and Its Legacy*, 211–21, 244–51, 344–63 and Christopher A. Beeley, "The Holy Spirit in the Cappadocians: Past and Present," *Modern Theology* 26, no. 1 (2010): 90–119. Nevertheless, inasmuch as their contributions to pneumatology align (though more clearly present in the Gregorys), it will suffice for the purposes of this essay to treat them as a whole. For the purposes of brevity, I will consider Basil's *On the Holy Spirit* (c. 375), Gregory of Nazianzus's *Oration*, 31 (c. 380), and Gregory of Nyssa's *On the Holy Spirit: Against Macedonius* and *To Ablabius: On Not Three Gods* (both c. 380).

[55]Basil calls this group the *Pneumatomachians* or "Spirit-Fighters" for their classifying of the Spirit with creatures. *On the Holy Spirit*, 11.27.

[56]This is particularly the case with Gregory of Nyssa. For him, as for Nazianzen, the exegetical support is often assumed. Nazianzen specifically notes this when he writes, "We leave to others a careful, critical analysis of the many different senses in which 'spirit' and 'holy' are used in Scripture, with the texts that bear upon the enquiry. . . . We, though, shall now turn to a further stage in the discussion." *Oration*, 31.2. *On God and Christ: The Five Theological Orations and the Two Letters to Cledonius*, trans. Frederick Williams (Crestwood, NY: St. Vladimir's Seminary Press, 2002), 139. This statement demonstrates the gains of the exegetical arguments of the Alexandrians and Basil as well as the extent to which these arguments in favor of the divinity of the Spirit had become standard by 380.

[57]*On the Holy Spirit: Against Macedonius*. NPNF2, 5:316.

If the Spirit is included with Father and Son by his names and by his works, as Scripture suggests, then the simplicity of the divine nature means a divine unity of the Spirit with the Father and Son.

This unity is confirmed by Scripture's account of the Spirit's work. Thus, Basil can refer to "the unity and indivisibility in every work of the Holy Spirit from the Father and the Son,"[58] and Gregory of Nazianzus can ask, "Is there any significant function belonging to God, which cannot apply to him except 'ingenerate' and 'begotten?'"[59] However, the unity of the works cannot simply be a matter of cooperation, as was the case with Irenaeus and, to a lesser extent, Athanasius, but rather of the simplicity of the divine nature constituting a singularity of function. This is most clearly articulated by Nyssen who writes, for example, of the work of creation:

> In the case of the Divine nature we do not similarly learn that the Father does anything by Himself in which the Son does not work conjointly, or again that the Son has any special operation apart from the Holy Spirit; but every operation which extends from God to the Creation . . . has its origin from the Father, and proceeds through the Son, and is perfected in the Holy Spirit . . . yet what does come to pass is not three things.[60]

In all previous pneumatologies, the Son and Spirit are creative and salvific agents of God, which is what Athanasius meant when he referred to the Spirit as a power of God. In contrast, Nyssen maintains that the Father does not use the Son and Spirit because he needs them; rather, God creates with one divine power that is possessed by the three. This is the clearest articulation of divine unity of the Father, Son, and Spirit we have seen.

The Cappadocians famously differ on how this argument relates to the one essence language of Nicaea. Basil was hesitant to use one essence language of the Spirit, whereas Nazianzen states in the clearest terms possible: "Is [the Spirit] consubstantial? Yes, he is God."[61] Nyssen's clear articulation of the divine simplicity, likewise, implies a unity of essence. He writes, "we acknowledge [the Spirit's] inseparable union with [Father and Son]; both in nature, in honour, in godhead, and glory, and majesty, and almighty power, and in all devout belief."[62] While the logic of the two conceptions of divine unity (one power and one essence) differed, by the Council of Constantinople they were largely viewed as compatible and so, despite all of the problems *homoousios* caused the early Nicenes, this definition would be retained in the expanded creed. While the term expressly defines the relationship of Father and Son alone, the Creed of 381 implies the Spirit's inclusion in this one essence through its inclusion of the Spirit in the worship of the Father and the Son.

Nevertheless, essence language still carried with it the specter of modalism. Aware of this danger in discussions of the divine unity, the Cappadocians continue to develop the term "procession" of Jn 15:26 as a means of discussing the Spirit's origin from the Father. Unlike Didymus, however, they have no interest in the correspondence between the respective origins of the Son and the Spirit. To the contrary, they emphasize the distinction

---

[58]*On the Holy Spirit*, 16.37. Translation by Stephen Hildebrand (Yonkers, NY: St. Vladimir's Seminary Press, 2011), 70.
[59]*Oration*, 31.29 in *On God and Christ*, 139.
[60]*To Abablius, On Not Three Gods*, NPNF2, 5:334. See also Basil, *On the Holy Spirit*, 16.38.
[61]*Oration*, 31.10 in *On God and Christ*, 123.
[62]*On the Holy Spirit: Against the Macedonians*, NPNF2, 5:320.

of the origin words precisely as a means of eternally distinguishing Spirit from Son. Thus, Basil writes, "[the Spirit] is said to be from God, not as all things are from God, but insofar as he comes forth from God, not begottenly as the Son does, but as the breath of his mouth."[63] Likewise, Nyssen writes, "the Holy Spirit is indeed from God, and of the Christ, but that, while not to be confounded with the Father in being never originated, nor with the Son in being the Only-begotten, and while to be regarded separately in certain distinctive properties, He has in all else, as I have just said, an exact identity."[64]

Of the three, Gregory of Nazianzus is the clearest in his articulation of the Spirit's procession. In developing his argument, he is responding to his opponents who had used aetiological language to deny the Spirit's place in the Godhead. He quotes them as saying, "The Holy Spirit must either be ingenerate or begotten. If he is ingenerate, there are two unoriginate beings. If he is begotten . . . there will be two sons who are brothers."[65] In response, Nazianzen rejects the premise that ingenerate and begotten are the only options for understanding the Spirit's aetiology. He writes that procession is "a mean term between alternatives. . . . Insofar as [the Spirit] proceeds from the Father, he is no creature; inasmuch as he is not begotten, he is no Son; and to the extent that procession is the mean between ingeneracy and generacy, he is God."[66] Thus, the concept of procession, introduced by Christ himself in Jn 15:26, allows Nazianzen to include the Spirit in the eternal Godhead without fear of his assimilation into the Son. Furthermore, these aetiologies, as we saw with Basil and Nyssen, are for Nazianzen the defining and distinguishing characteristic of the three members of the Godhead who, in all other aspects, are one:

> The very fact of not being begotten, of being begotten and of proceeding, give them whatever names are applied to them—Father, Son, and Holy Spirit respectively. The aim is to safeguard the distinctness of the three *hypostases* within the single nature and quality of the Godhead. . . . The three are a single whole in their Godhead and the single whole is three in personalities. Thus there will be no Sabellian "One," no three to be mischievously divided by our contemporaries.[67]

Nazianzen admits that "procession" as such really reveals nothing about the nature of the Spirit's origin. This is not, however, a problem for the Spirit alone, but, given the nature of theological language, applies to the Father and Son as well. He writes, "What, then, is 'proceeding'? You explain the ingeneracy of the Father and I will give you a biological account of the Son's begetting and the Spirit's proceeding—and let us go mad the pair of us for prying into God's secrets."[68] The point of procession, then, is not to understand the details of the Spirit's origin. Rather, the point of the aetiologies is to demonstrate, as they did in the third century, both the distinction of the three and their unity as one Godhead, inasmuch as the Son and Spirit's respective origins in the Father make them like

---

[63] *On the Holy Spirit*, 18.46 in *Holy Spirit*, 81.
[64] *On the Holy Spirit: Against the Macedonians*, NPNF2, 5:315.
[65] *Oration*, 31.7 in *On God and Christ*, 121. Although there is no textual evidence to suggest Nazianzen's opponents knew Didymus's work, the latter part of this statement could be directed toward the Alexandrian's argument from correspondence. The point they are making, which Nazianzen tacitly accepts, is that a shared aetiology of Son and Spirit, such as Didymus proposed, would result in a lack of distinction between Son and Spirit.
[66] Ibid., 31.8 in *On God and Christ*, 122.
[67] Ibid., 31.9 in *On God and Christ*, 123.
[68] Ibid., 31.8 in *On God and Christ*, 122.

the Father. The only difference is that Gregory can now affirm of the Spirit what third-century writers could only affirm of the Son.

Nazianzen's thoughts on the Spirit's procession are intricately connected to the final pneumatological development discernable in the Creed of 381, namely, the identification of Father, Son, and Spirit as *hypostases* or persons. The Cappadocians are, of course, not the first to use this term of the three. Notably, Origen had done so a century and a half before. The problem was that for much of the third and fourth centuries, it was associated most closely with Arius, who, like Origen, had used the word to affirm a distinction *in essence* of Father and Son. The Council of Nicaea, thus, promptly rejected it in an anathema statement that made clear the synonymous meanings of *ousia* and *hypostasis*. But, as with the absence of an aetiological account of the Spirit, the lack of a term to distinguish the three within the unified essence ultimately produced Marcellus's modalism.

For all the pneumatological developments of the fourth century, by the 360s, theologians still lacked such a term. Many prior attempts at constructing this meaningful distinction were made,[69] but it is the Cappadocians who provide the term and the systematic arguments that underlie the pneumatology of Constantinople. Basil is the source of this idea within the Cappadocians; he writes, "There is one God and Father and one Only-begotten and one Holy Spirit. We proclaim each of the persons (*hypostases*) singly."[70] Elsewhere, while referring to Father and Son, he is clear that this distinction of personhood does not jeopardize the essential unity: "They have unity in the fact that the latter is whatever the former is and the former is whatever the latter is. And so, with regard to the particularity of the persons, they are one and one, but with regard to the common nature, both are one thing."[71] This parallels Nazianzen's statement:

> The aim is to safeguard the distinctiveness of the three *hypostases* within the single nature and quality of the Godhead. The Son is not the Father; there is *one* Father, yet he is whatever the Father is. The Spirit is not the Son because he is from God; there is *one* Only-begotten. Yet whatever the Son is, he is. The three are a single whole in their Godhead and the single whole is in three persons.[72]

Nyssen, like Nazianzen, also stresses the unity of the three, admitting only a distinction of person with its "peculiar attributes," by which he means the distinct origins, as we saw earlier.[73]

Although the terminology of "person" is not expressed in the Creed of 381, it is almost certainly assumed in both the titles and the closely corresponding aetiological statements of Son and Spirit. Thus the Cappadocians provide the logic by which the Creed of 381 is no longer open to a modalist reading, even though statements of one essence remain. This conclusion is confirmed by a letter written in 382 by many of the bishops who were

---

[69]Ayres posits five possible sources of this thought, although the terms used differ. Ayres, *Nicaea and Its Legacy*, 202–4. Basil himself credits Dionysius of Alexandria in a work against the Sabellians for his use of "persons." *On the Holy Spirit*, 29.72.
[70]*On the Holy Spirit*, 18.44 in *Holy Spirit*, 80.
[71]Ibid., 18.45 in *Holy Spirit*, 80. Basil includes the Spirit in this definition in the next passage.
[72]*Oration*, 31.9 in *On God and Christ*, 123.
[73]*On the Holy Spirit: Against Macedonius*, NPNF2, 5:315.

present at Constantinople.[74] The letter makes clear how important the development of the language of *hypostasis* was for maintaining the distinction of Father, Son, and Spirit within the one Godhead. It reads, in part: "There is one Godhead, Power, and Substance of the Father and of the Son and of the Holy Spirit; the dignity being equal, and the majesty being equal in three perfect *hypostases*."[75] This important letter reveals, then, that the Cappadocians, inheritors of both an early high pneumatology and an Alexandrian resurgence in the decades prior, provided the final pneumatological developments whereby the Spirit is seen to be, in the words of Constantinople, "the Lord and life-giver, Who proceeds from the Father, Who with the Father and the Son is together worshipped and together glorified."

CONCLUSION

Returning now to the two questions with which this essay started, we can say that the Alexandrians and Cappadocians recovered the high pneumatology of the second century through their collective insight that the exegetical arguments that demonstrated the equality of the Father and Son also applied to the Holy Spirit. This conclusion was a recovery inasmuch as Irenaeus had already demonstrated the pneumatological fruits of similar readings of Scripture. Nevertheless, he lacked the crucial aspects—namely, an aetiological account of the Spirit and a term by which to distinguish the divine persons within the one Godhead—to sustain this pneumatology against the Monarchianism that developed in his wake. The limited pneumatology of the Council of Nicaea, then, reflects the regressions of the third century more than the traditional pneumatology present in Scripture and fleshed out by Irenaeus. Conversely, the pneumatology of the Council of Constantinople, made possible by the exegetical arguments of the latter half of the fourth century, better reflects the content of Scripture. The church, in her wisdom, has rightly endorsed the Creed of 381, and not the Creed of 325, as the traditional teaching of Scripture.

FOR FURTHER READING

Anatolios, Khaled. *Retrieving Nicaea: The Development and Meaning of Trinitarian Doctrine*. Grand Rapids, MI: Baker Academic, 2011.
Ayres, Lewis. *Nicaea and Its Legacy: An Approach to Fourth-Century Trinitarian Theology*. Oxford: Oxford University Press, 2004.
Barnes, Michel René. *The Power of God*: Dunamis *in Gregory of Nyssa's Trinitarian Theology*. Washington DC: The Catholic University of America Press, 2001.
Briggman, Anthony. *Irenaeus of Lyons and the Theology of the Holy Spirit*. Oxford Early Christian Studies. Oxford: Oxford University Press, 2012.
Burns, J. Patout, and Gerald M. Fagin. *The Holy Spirit*. Eugene, OR: Wipf & Stock, 2002.

---

[74] This letter survives in Theodoret's *Ecclesiastical History*, 5.9. I follow Ayres's translation. Ayres, *Nicaea and Its Legacy*, 258.
[75] As quoted in Ayres, *Nicaea and Its Legacy*, 258.

CHAPTER SIXTEEN

The *Filioque*

Theology and Controversy

THOMAS G. WEINANDY, O.F.M., CAP.

This essay explores the Holy Spirit's relationship to the Father and the Son, specifically the controversy over whether the Spirit proceeds from the Father alone or from the Father and the Son (*filioque*).[1] Given the space allowed, it is not possible to delve into the biblical revelation concerning the Holy Spirit, though pertinent passages will be noted as we examine the pneumatology of various theologians.[2] By way of introduction, we will begin by summarizing briefly the pre-Nicene theology on the Holy Spirit.

A theology of the Holy Spirit arose gradually. This delayed growth was partially due to the questions that confronted the early Apologists. Because they combated the philosophical thought of their time, they dealt with issues concerning the Logos/Word, for Platonism and other philosophical schools already spoke of a Logos within their own teaching. Although all human beings possess a spark or seed of the Logos (*logos spermatikos*), only Christians possess the fullness of God's divine Word, for that Word became flesh in Jesus. Since pagan philosophy concerned itself principally with ignorance and not with sin, it did not treat of the need for a divine principle that would ensure one's holiness. Thus, the Apologists, in refuting them, had little opportunity to consider the person and role of the Holy Spirit. Nonetheless, they did speak of the Trinity and the Holy Spirit being the Wisdom of God who spoke to the prophets of old.

Irenaeus (c. 130–200) provided a more robust understanding of the Trinity than his predecessors and saw the Son and the Holy Spirit, who eternally came forth from the Father, as the Father's hands acting within the economy of salvation. The fruit of the saving work of the incarnate Son was the Holy Spirit who transformed believers into the image of the Son and so allowed them to share in the holy life of God as the Father's

---

[1] Since this essay is an introductory theological summary of the *filioque* controversy, many aspects of this issue—historical, theological, and ecclesial—cannot be treated fully. For more inclusive presentations of all the issues treated in this essay, see especially Boris Bobrinskoy, *The Mystery of the Trinity: Trinitarian Experience and Vision in the Biblical and Patristic Tradition* (Crestwood, NY: St. Vladimir's Seminary Press, 1999), 261–316; Yves Congar, *I Believe in the Holy Spirit*, 3 vols. (New York: Crossroad, 1997), vol. 3. See also A. Edward Siecienski, *The Filioque: History of a Doctrinal Controversy* (Oxford: Oxford University Press, 2010). While I would hold, for the most part, the Western view that the Holy Spirit proceeds from the Father and the Son, I hope that my exposition of the issues involved is fair and that my theological judgments are correct.

[2] For a good summary of the biblical revelation of the Holy Spirit, see Bobrinskoy, *The Mystery of the Trinity*, 13–153, and Congar, *I Believe in the Holy Spirit*, vol. 1.

children. Tertullian (c. 160–c. 220) spoke of the Holy Spirit proceeding from the Father through the Son and so ranked third within the Trinity. While this may imply a divine hierarchy, Tertullian insists that the persons of the Trinity (a termed he coined—*Trinitas*) share in the one divine substance (*substantia*) as three distinct persons (*personae*). Origen (c. 185–254), schooled in Middle-Platonism, argued that since the Father was eternally the Father, the Son and the Holy Spirit were equally eternal, for they eternally proceeded from him. However, like most of his antecedents, Origen held that the Father as *ho Theos* possessed the fullness of divinity, with the Son being *deuteros theos*, that is, ranking in second place, with the Holy Spirit ranking third within the divine hierarchy. Origen, nonetheless, spoke of all the persons (*hypostases*) as *homoousion* (of one substance) in that they all shared in the same divine nature. While Jesus stated that the Spirit proceeds from the Father, Origen notes that Jesus adds that the Holy Spirit will take all that the Father has given to him (Jn 12:16), and, therefore, the Spirit is dependent upon the Son for who he is.[3] Origen speculates that this is why the Spirit differs from the Son. In Origen we begin to see clearly an attempt to distinguish and unite the persons of the Trinity and particularly the relationship that both unites and distinguishes the Son and the Holy Spirit. Although Origen, in accord with biblical revelation and the church's belief, clearly held that all three persons of the Trinity were truly divine, with each possessing distinct identities, his hierarchical conception unintentionally fostered Arianism—the view that the Son was not divine but the first and most divine-like of all creatures.[4]

The Council of Nicaea (325) declared, contrary to Arius and his supporters, that "the Son of God was begotten from the Father, only-begotten, that is, from the substance of the Father, God from God, light from light, true God from true God, begotten not made, of the same substance (*homoousion*) with the Father."[5] Things that are made always differ in kind from their maker—ants make anthills. That which is begotten is always of the same nature as the begetter—ants beget ants. Thus, the only-begotten Son, not being made, but eternally begotten of the Father, possesses one and the same nature as the Father. Moreover, for Nicaea, the fullness of divinity does not reside, as supposed by many earlier theologians, in the Father alone. Rather, the Father's begetting of the Son defines and constitutes the one divine nature. The Council simply adds, after defining the Son's full divinity and his becoming man for humankind's salvation, that the church also believes "in the Holy Spirit." This appears a meager acknowledgement of the Holy Spirit, yet even its scantiness does place the Holy Spirit in communion with the Father and Son as one of the three persons in whom the church believes, thus implying his equal divinity with them.

The Arian controversy would continue to rage for another forty years, but in the course of its resolution, the issue of the Holy Spirit's divinity rose to the fore. The question was not simply whether or not the Holy Spirit is God, but also, if he is God, how does he differ from the Son? Since both the Son and the Holy Spirit come from the Father, what differentiates the Spirit's coming from the Father from that of the Son's being begotten

---

[3] See Origen, *Commentary on Romans*, 6.13.3. Interestingly, Origen here employed the same passage from the Gospel of John as Augustine and Aquinas (and therefore the whole Western tradition) would use to argue that the Holy Spirit proceeds from the Father and the Son.

[4] For a summary of the development of trinitarian thought prior to the Council of Nicaea, see J. N. D. Kelly, *Early Christian Doctrines* (London: Adam & Charles Black, 1968), chaps. 4 and 5.

[5] Heinrich Denzinger and Peter Hünermann, eds., *Enchiridion Symbolorum*, 43rd ed. (San Francisco, CA: Ignatius, 2012), §125 (translation slightly altered).

of the Father? Similarly, if the Spirit proceeds from the Father through the Son, does that make the Holy Spirit the Father's grandson? Moreover, while it may be understandable that the Father, being the Father, begets a Son, what is it about the Father's fatherhood that would necessitate that he spirate a Holy Spirit? These are the questions that arose subsequent to the Council of Nicaea, and they are questions and issues that continue to confront theology today. Furthermore, the controversy surrounding the *filioque* first surfaced in the course of addressing these questions.

THE PROCESSION OF THE HOLY SPIRIT— THE EARLY EASTERN FATHERS

The first focused theology concerning the Holy Spirit was undertaken by the Eastern or Greek Church Fathers—Athanasius of Alexandria (c. 296–373), Basil the Great (c. 330–79), Gregory of Nyssa (c. 330–c.395), Gregory of Nazianzus (329/30–389/90), and Cyril of Alexandria (d. 444). Each will be briefly treated in turn.

Although Athanasius spent almost his entire episcopal career defending the creed of the Council of Nicaea, toward the end of his life he undertook a defense of the Holy Spirit's divinity. In his *Letters to Serapion*, Athanasius marshalled a host of biblical passages that reveal and confirm that the Holy Spirit is God. He is called the Spirit of holiness and life through whom the faithful are divinized. The faithful are baptized in the name of the entire Triad, and thus, if the Father and the Son are divine, so too must be the Holy Spirit, for through him they are conformed into the Son's divine likeness and become children of the Father. Moreover, the Spirit always works in communion with Jesus, the incarnated Son and anointed Christ, and so is divine as the Son is divine. Athanasius's governing theological principle with regard to the Holy Spirit's divinity is that since the Son is truly divine because he is begotten of the Father and so shares in the Father's divine nature, so the Holy Spirit must also be divine because he proceeds from the Father and is always related to the divine Son. "Because the Spirit is one, and still more, because he is proper to the Word who is one, he is proper to God who is one, and one in essence (*homoousion*) with him."[6] "The Spirit is in the Son, and the Son in him."[7] Athanasius's pneumatology is, then, thoroughly christological, for the Holy Spirit's divine identity and salvific work are always in relation to the Son's divine identity and saving work. "And so, as the Lord is Son, the Spirit is called Spirit of Sonship. Again, as the Son is wisdom and truth, the Spirit is described as Spirit of wisdom and truth. Again, the Son is the power of God and Lord of glory, and the Spirit is called Spirit of power and glory."[8]

For Athanasius, the Holy Spirit is intimately aligned to the Son, for as the Son is the image of the Father, so the Spirit is the image of the Son. "The Spirit bears the same relation to the Son as the Son to the Father."[9] "The Spirit has to the Son the same proper relationship as we know the Son to have with the Father. And as the Son says, 'All things whatsoever the Father has are mine' (Jn 16:15), so we shall find that through the Son

---

[6]Athanasius, *Ad Serapionem*, 1.27; see also 3.3. Translation from *The Letters of Saint Athanasius Concerning the Holy Spirit*, trans. G. R. B. Shapland (New York: Philosophical Library, 1951).
[7]Ibid., 1.21.
[8]Ibid., 1.25. See also 4.4.
[9]Ibid., 1.21.

all these things are in the Spirit also."¹⁰ The Spirit is "the image of the Son. . . . For as the image is, so also must be that who is the image."¹¹ For Athanasius, while the Spirit proceeds from the Father, it is the Son who bestows his divinity upon him, and so the Spirit is the Spirit of the Son as well as the Spirit of the Father. Essential to Athanasius's defense of the Holy Spirit's divinity is not only the Spirit's relationship to the Father but also to the Son. All three persons must be ontologically related to one another if all three are to be fully divine.

Although Athanasius does not specifically say that the Spirit proceeds from the Father and the Son, his thought is not averse to that concept. Actually, he is on the cusp of articulating such an understanding. However, his argument contains one significant flaw. The Son is the image of the Father both as to sharing his Father's divinity as well as constituting his personal identity as Son. The Spirit, on the other hand, is the image of the Son only as to partaking of the Son's divinity and not as to his personal divine identity. If the latter were the case, the Holy Spirit would be the Father's grandson, which Athanasius vigorously denies.[12] The flaw is, as explained, that if the Holy Spirit is the image of the Son as to his personal identity as Holy Spirit, he would be the grandson of the Father, which is ridiculous. The way to resolve it is simply to say that the Holy Spirit is not the image of the Son.

Basil the Great followed Athanasius's lead, though unlike his predecessor, Basil, in accordance with Scripture, never explicitly called the Holy Spirit God, nor did he state that the Holy Spirit, like the Son, was *homoousion* with the Father. Nonetheless, the Holy Spirit must be divine because the church's faith resides within the triune God, and into that divine triune life Christians are baptized. Thus, "if the Spirit is ranked with the Son and the Son with the Father, then the Spirit is obviously ranked with the Father also."[13] Similar to Athanasius as well, Basil argues that while the monarchy of the Father must be maintained, "the Holy Spirit is one, and we speak of him as unique, since through the one Son he is joined to the Father."[14] "Likewise, natural goodness, inherent holiness and royal dignity reaches from the Father through the only-begotten to the Spirit."[15] Because Basil is similar to Athanasius, Latin theologians past and present have argued that his theology also possesses a latent expression of the *filioque*. However, while he does sustain an intrinsic relationship of the Spirit to the Son, Basil clearly maintains that the Spirit proceeds from the Father in accordance with Jn 15:26. For Basil this "proceeding" (*ekporeuetai*) from the Father is what distinguishes the Holy Spirit from the Son who is begotten of the Father. Beginning with Basil, the East will insist that the term *ekporeuetai* pertains uniquely to the Holy Spirit as well as to his singular relationship to the Father,

---

[10] Ibid., 3.1. In *Contra Arianos*, 3.24, Athanasius writes that "the Spirit receives from the Word . . . for he, as has been said, gives to the Spirit, and whatever the Spirit has he has from the Word." As with Origen, Athanasius employs the same passage from John as the Latin tradition uses to argue that the Holy Spirit proceeds from the Father and the Son.

[11] *Ad Serapionem*, 1.24; see also 4.3.

[12] For a more complete study of Athanasius's theology of the Holy Spirit, see Thomas G. Weinandy, *Athanasius: A Theological Introduction* (Aldershot: Ashgate, 2007; repr. Washington DC: Catholic University of America Press, 2018), 103–19.

[13] Basil the Great, *De Spiritu Sancto*, 18.47. Translation from Basil the Great, *On the Holy Spirit*, trans. D. Anderson (Crestwood, NY: St. Vladimir's Seminary Press, 2001), 74–5.

[14] Ibid., 18.45 (72).

[15] Ibid., 18.47 (75).

and so it defines his distinctive personhood in contrast to the Son. This understanding will be the principle foundational argument against the West's claim that the Spirit proceeds from the Father and the Son. To assert that the Spirit proceeds from the Son would destroy the inherent meaning encompassed within the term *ekporeuetai*. As we will see, the problem is that while the East will ardently insist—down to the present—that the *ekporeuetai* defines the Spirit's coming forth from the Father and so differentiates him from the Son, it has never been able to articulate positively the actual theological content of that term other than that it does not mean "begotten." Its distinguishing noetic characteristic remains hidden.

Gregory of Nyssa continued in the tradition of Athanasius and his brother Basil. Founded upon the baptismal formula, the full divinity of the Spirit was upheld by Gregory, for in the Spirit the faithful are divinized. Unlike Basil but like Athanasius, Gregory professed that the Holy Spirit was one in substance (*homoousion*) with the Father and the Son. Gregory, being more speculative than his brother and following upon the principle that the economy of salvation reveals the inner life of the Trinity, states that "the Holy Spirit is indeed from God, and of the Christ" and so "the Father is always Father, and in him the Son, and with the Son the Holy Spirit."[16] For Gregory, the Son always resides within the proper understanding of the Father, and the Holy Spirit always resides within a proper understanding of the Son, for the Holy Spirit is from the Father of the Son.

> The Holy Spirit, from whom all the abundance of good things gushes up to creation, depends on the Son, with whom he is indivisibly apprehended, and has his being attached to the Father as a cause, from whom he also proceeds, he has the identifying sign of the particularity with respect to the *hypostasis*, to be made known after the Son and with him, and to subsist from the Father.[17]

While the Spirit's identity depends in some manner on the Son, in that he is made known after and so through the Son, his causal divine existence is determined by the Father. Causality for Gregory is the hermeneutical tool for distinguishing the persons.

The Father is the cause of the Son and the Holy Spirit and within that causality the difference between the Son and the Spirit is made.

> For one [the Son] is directly from the first Cause [the Father], and another [the Spirit] by that which [the Son] is directly from the first Cause; so that the attribute of being Only-begotten abides without doubt in the Son, and the interposition of the Son . . . does not shut out the Spirit from His relation by way of nature to the Father.[18]

For Gregory, there is a trinitarian order: The Father begets the Son, and the Spirit proceeds from the Father by way of the Son. This proceeding through the Son distinguishes the Spirit from the Son, for he eternally proceeds from the Father of the Son. "For as the Son is bound to the Father, and, while deriving existence from Him, is not substantially after Him, so again the Holy Spirit is in touch with the Only-begotten, Who is conceived of as before the Spirit's subsistence only in the theoretical light of a cause."[19] Gregory wants to ensure, despite the sequential causal ordering, that the Son and the Holy Spirit exist

---

[16] Gregory of Nyssa, *Adversus Macedonianos* in NPNF2, 5:315, 319.
[17] *Letter to Peter*, 4. Translation from John Behr, *The Nicene Faith* (Crestwood, NY: St. Vladimir's Seminary Press, 2004), 419.
[18] *Ad Ablabium* in NPNF2, 5:336.
[19] Gregory of Nyssa, *Adversus Eunomium*, 1.42 in NPNF2, 5:100.

eternally from the Father. The manner in which they exist from the Father differs and this difference distinguishes them. The difference is that, while both are caused by the Father, the Spirit's divinity is mediated through the only-begotten Son.

Because Gregory never explicitly stated that the Father and the Son together were causal agents in the procession of the Holy Spirit, Eastern theologians have consistently argued that he did not intend and, therefore, would not have embraced the Western *filioque*. To hypothesize on Gregory's judgment of the *filioque* is pointless speculation. What we do know is that, similar to Athanasius and Basil, his pneumatology gravitates toward that concept.[20]

Basil's friend Gregory of Nazianzus greatly influenced the subsequent Orthodox theology concerning the procession of the Holy Spirit. Frustrated with Basil's reluctance to simply call the Holy Spirit God and as such *homoousion* with the Father and the Son, Gregory proclaims: "What then? Is the Spirit God? Certainly. Is he consubstantial? Yes, if he is God."[21] To a greater extent than even Gregory of Nyssa, Gregory perceives the notion of causality as the key for discerning the unity and distinctions within the Trinity. The Father, the uncaused cause, is the source of both unity and distinction among the persons. The Father in begetting his Son distinguishes himself from his Son in that the Son possesses all that the Father is except that of being unbegotten. The Spirit cannot be begotten of the Father, for then there would be two Sons; nor can he be begotten of the Son for then he would be the Father's grandson. Both alternatives, for Gregory, are ludicrous.

For Gregory, the Spirit, in keeping with Jn 15:26, proceeds from the Father, yet he cautions against thinking that such revelation can be fully grasped by the human mind. "The Holy Spirit is truly Spirit, coming forth from the Father, but not in the manner of a Son or by generation but by procession (*ekporeusis*), if one must create new terminology for the sake of clarity."[22] Thus, Gregory wishes to employ *ekporeusis* specifically to the manner in which the Holy Spirit comes forth from the Father. "Procession," in this new specific singular sense, is in contrast to the begetting of the Son and is what distinguishes the Spirit from the Son and so what identifies him as the Spirit. However, Gregory asks frustratingly and rhetorically: "What, then, is 'proceeding'? You explain the ingeneracy of the Father and I will give you a biological account of the Son's begetting and the Spirit's proceeding—and let us go mad the pair of us for prying into God's secrets."[23] While Gregory's reverence for the triune mystery is admirable, his irritatingly throwing-up-his-arms argument is hardly theologically adequate. Although it is impossible to comprehend fully the mystery of the Trinity, it is possible to know what the mystery is. Thus, it is imperative that we possess some knowledge concerning the nature of the Holy Spirit's procession from the Father such that it illumines the nature of the Father's fatherhood; it differentiates itself from the begetting of the Son and so distinguishes the Holy Spirit from the Son. Nonetheless, Gregory of Nazianzus especially, along with his

---

[20]For a more complete study of Gregory of Nyssa's views, see Michel R. Barnes, *The Power of God: Dynamics in Gregory of Nyssa's Trinitarian Thought* (Washington DC: Catholic University of America Press, 2001).
[21]Gregory of Nazianzus, *Oration* 31.10. Translation from Gregory of Nazianzus, *On God and Christ: The Five Theological Orations and Two Letters to Cledonius*, ed. and trans. Lionel Wickham and Frederick Williams (Crestwood, NY: St. Vladimir's Seminary Press, 2002), 123.
[22]Gregory of Nazianzus, *Oration* 39.12. Translation from *Gregory of Nazianzus*, trans. Brian Daley (New York: Routledge, 2006), 133.
[23]Gregory of Nazianzus, *Oration* 31.8 in *On God and Christ*, 122.

Cappadocian cohorts, Basil and Gregory of Nyssa, established the theological character for the subsequent Orthodox insistence that the Holy Spirit proceeds solely from the Father.[24] This theological resolve assumes further ecclesial and doctrinal significance at the First Council of Constantinople.

THE FIRST COUNCIL OF CONSTANTINOPLE

The issue of the Holy Spirit's divinity was dogmatically settled at the First Council of Constantinople (381), and the pneumatology of the Cappadocian Fathers exerted the decisive influence. The Council declared: "We believe in the Holy Spirit, the Lord and Giver of life, who proceeds from the Father, who together with the Father and the Son is worshiped and glorified, who has spoken through the prophets."[25] Notably, the Council neither said that the Spirit is God nor did it declare that the Holy Spirit is *homoousion* with the Father and the Son. After having endured a decades-long battle over the term *homoousion*, the Council decided not to initiate another fracas over its appropriate use in defining the divinity of the Holy Spirit. Moreover, influenced by Basil's reverence toward Scripture, the Council did not explicitly declare that the Holy Spirit is "God." Nonetheless, the Council did employ Scripture to define doctrinally the Spirit's full divinity. In accordance with 2 Cor. 3:17, the Council declared the Spirit to be "Lord," a divine title equally used for the Father and the Son. The Spirit is the Giver of Life and as such must be divine, for only God is the source of life. Appropriately, the divinity of the Holy Spirit is defined in accord with Christian worship where his divine identity was traditionally most clearly seen and expressed, for he is worshipped and adored together with the Father and Son, both of whom are fully divine. That he spoke through the prophets accentuates that he is eternal with the Father and the Son.

For our purposes the crucial phrase, quoting Jn 15:26, is "he proceeds from the Father." As the Son is God because he is begotten of the Father, so the Spirit is God because he proceeds from the Father. Within such a declaration, the Council is not commenting upon or judging the Spirit's relationship to the Son and so is neither condemning nor affirming any theological variation of the *filioque*. It simply wanted to profess that he is divine as the Father, from whom he proceeds, is divine. Nonetheless, this creedal declaration will become a theological and ecclesial flashpoint within the subsequent conflict over the theological legitimacy of the *filioque* and its insertion into the Western Creed.

CYRIL OF ALEXANDRIA

With Cyril one once more resides in the theological home of Athanasius. Not only does Cyril endorse and advance Athanasius's Christology, as witnessed in his clash with Nestorius, but he also develops Athanasius's pneumatology, particularly concerning the nature of the Spirit's procession. Cyril argues that, since the Holy Spirit is consubstantial with the Father and the Son, the Spirit is the Spirit of the Father and of the Son and comes

---

[24]For a more complete study of Gregory of Nazianzus, see Christopher A. Beeley, *Gregory of Nazianzus on the Trinity and the Knowledge of God: In Your Light We Shall See Light* (Oxford: Oxford University Press, 2008).
[25]Denzinger and Hünermann, *Enchiridion Symbolorum*, §150.

forth from both.[26] Jesus, the Son, calls the Spirit "another paraclete" "who is from the essence of the Father and from his own essence," and so "the Spirit is of the Father and of the Son."[27] Because the Father, in his begetting of his Son, has given him all things, when the Spirit of truth comes he will take from what has been given to Jesus, the Son, and declare it to all. The reason is that "the Holy Spirit is not understood to be foreign to the essence of the Only-Begotten, but he proceeds naturally from that essence and is not something else beside him."[28] Jesus, the Son, can send "the Spirit to sanctify his holy disciples because the Spirit belongs to him, just as the Spirit certainly belongs to God the Father."[29]

The logic of Cyril's argument is founded upon Jesus, the Son, pouring out the Holy Spirit upon the faithful. In order for Jesus to do this, he, as Son, must by nature possess the Spirit. The reason he naturally possesses the Spirit is that the Father, in begetting him, gives to him the fullness of his divinity which includes the fullness of the Spirit's divinity; thus, the Spirit, by nature, proceeds from both the Father and the Son—the Spirit proceeds from the Father and from the Father's Son. Therefore, in the economy of salvation the Spirit, who proceeds from the Father, can rightly sanctify the faithful, for the Spirit comes from the Father through the Son.

Cyril perceives, similar to Athanasius and to a lesser extent the Cappadocians, the ontological relational communion between the persons of the Trinity, and thus he has accentuated the Spirit's relation to the Son, for the Spirit in proceeding from the Father also proceeds from the Father's Son. From this perspective, his pneumatology, like Athanasius's, can be interpreted as verging on the *filioque*. However, the concerns he was addressing were not the same as those addressed by Augustine (354–430). Cyril was more simply attempting to confirm that the Holy Spirit was truly divine. To assure this, he rightly argued that the Spirit proceeds from the Father of the only-begotten Son and, therefore, he proceeds from and is one in essence with the Son and so one in essence with the Father. Augustine, and subsequently the West, wanted to achieve the same theological truth, but he did so by arguing that the Spirit proceeds as the Father's love for the Son and, thenceforth, proceeds as the Son's love for the Father—thus, he proceeds from the Father and the Son (*filioque*).[30] So to Augustine, we must now turn.

THE PROCESSION OF THE HOLY SPIRIT—AUGUSTINE

Earlier we saw that Tertullian spoke of the Holy Spirit proceeding from the Father through the Son, and it is this formulation that gave rise to the Western tradition that the Holy Spirit proceeds from the Father and the Son (*filioque*). "The Spirit, then, is third

---

[26]See Cyril of Alexandria, *Commentary on John*, 15:26. Translation can be found in *Commentary on John*, trans. David R. Maxwell and ed. Joel C. Elowsky, 2 vols. (Downers Grove, IL: InterVarsity, 2015), 2:246.
[27]Ibid., 14:26-27 in 2:178.
[28]Ibid., 16:12-13 in 2:256.
[29]Ibid., 15:26 in 2:246.
[30]For further studies on Cyril's pneumatology, see George C. Berthold, "Cyril of Alexandria and the *Filioque*," *Studia Patristica* 19 (1989): 143–7; Marie-Odile Boulnois, "The Mystery of the Trinity according to Cyril of Alexandria: Deployment of the Triad and Its Recapitulation into Unity of Divinity," in *The Theology of Cyril of Alexandria: A Critical Appreciation*, ed. Thomas G. Weinandy and Daniel A. Keating (London: T & T Clark, 2003), 75–111; A. Manzone, *La Dottrina Dello Spirito Santo Nell' In Joannem di San Cirillo D'Alessandria* (Rome: Pontificia Universitas Gregoriana, 1972), 1–68.

from God and the Son, just as the third from the root is the fruit from the stem, and third from the fountain is the stream from the river, and third from the sun is the apex of the ray."[31] Employing these various analogies, we see that, for Tertullian, the Holy Spirit comes forth from the Father through the Son as the fruit/stream/apex proceeds from the root/fountain/sun (the Father) through the stem/river/ray (the Son), and so his divinity is mediated through the Father's Son. Similarly, Hilary of Poitiers (d. 367) likewise holds that the Holy Spirit proceeds from the Father through the Son in that he receives his divinity from the Father through the Son.[32] Ambrose of Milan (d. 397), in his attempt to ensure the full divinity of the Holy Spirit, is the first Western Father to state explicitly that the Holy Spirit proceeds from the Father and the Son and so is fully divine as they are divine.[33] Significantly, when translating the Bible into Latin, Jerome used *procedere* (proceed) to translate not only *ekporeuetai* with regard to the manner of the Holy Spirit coming from the Father, but also other notions of proceeding as well. Thus, while the East was advocating that *ekporeuetai* possessed a singular meaning when applied to the Holy Spirit, Jerome translated it in a more general manner that could be applied more broadly, and thus both the Son and the Holy Spirit could be said to proceed from the Father. This will cause confusion and become contentious within the later *filioque* controversy.

Scholars in the past have often criticized Augustine and the West for taking as their starting point the unity of God and only then considering the distinctiveness of the three persons. This is in contrast to the more positive assessment of the Eastern Fathers who, scholars claim, began with the dynamic relational unity of the persons.[34] Such a characterization is not true. Augustine's concern was not how the one God could be three persons, but rather how three persons could be one God. This is why he was constantly attempting to demonstrate that their distinct interrelated subjectivities constitute the one being of God.

For Augustine, the manner in which the persons of the Trinity manifest themselves within the economy of salvation reveals the manner in which they exist eternally as the one God. Moreover, the Father and the Son are relational terms, thus as the Father reveals the Son and the Son reveals the Father within divine economy, so they are dynamically related as Father and Son from all eternity. The Father is Father in relation to the Son, and the Son is Son in relation to the Father, for the Father eternally begets his Son as his perfect image. What then, for Augustine, distinguishes the Holy Spirit's proceeding from the Father from that of the Son's being begotten of the Father? Equally, what is it about the Father's fatherhood that demands that he not only begets a Son but also spirates a Holy Spirit? In considering these questions, Augustine conceives and articulates his understanding of the Holy Spirit proceeding from the Father and the Son (*filioque*).

Augustine perceives that within Scripture the Holy Spirit is called the Spirit of the Father (Mt. 10:20, Jn 15:26) and the Spirit of the Son (Lk. 6:19; Jn 14:26, 20:22; Rom. 8:15; Gal. 4:6). Since the Spirit is both the Spirit of the Father and the Son, Augustine concludes that he must proceed from both.[35] This is in keeping with Jesus's statement

---

[31]Tertullian, *Ad Praxeam*, 8; see also 4. Translation taken from Henry Bettenson, *The Early Christian Fathers* (Oxford: Oxford University Press, 1956), 120–1 (translation slightly altered).
[32]See *De Trinitate*, 8.20.
[33]See *De Spiritu Sancto*, 1.11.120.
[34]This false characterization was initiated by Theodore de Régnon, *Etudes de théologie positive sure la Saite Trinité*, 4 vols. (Paris, 1892–1898). For a discussion of this, see Congar, *I Believe in the Holy Spirit*, 3:xvi–xvii.
[35]See *De Trinitate*, 4.29; 5.12, 15.

that the Father has given everything to the Son (Jn 3:35). Although Augustine stresses that the Father is the principle source from which the Spirit proceeds, the Holy Spirit also proceeds from the Son.[36]

> It is not without point that in this triad only the Son is called the Word of God, and only the Holy Spirit is called the gift of God, and only the Father is called the one from whom the Word is born and from whom the Holy Spirit principally proceeds. I added "principally," because we have found that the Holy Spirit also proceeds from the Son. But this too was given the Son by the Father—not given to him when he already existed and did not yet have it; but whatever the Father gave to his only-begotten Word he gave by begetting him. He so begot him then that their common gift would proceed from him too, and the Holy Spirit would be the Spirit of them both.[37]

For Augustine—referring to Jn 4:10; Acts 2:37, 8:20; and Rom. 5:5—the Holy Spirit is the supreme "gift" given by the Father and the Son, for he is the consummate gift that they give to one another, that is, the gift of love. God is love (1 Jn 4:16) precisely because the Father fully loves the Son, and the Son fully loves the Father, and the Holy Spirit is that substantial and personal love that the Father and the Son share with one another.[38] Thus, the Holy Spirit proceeds from the Father as the Father's love for the Son and proceeds from the Son (*filioque*) as the Son's love for the Father.

> Therefore the Holy Spirit too takes his place in the unity and equality of substance. For whether he is the unity of both the others or their holiness or their charity, whether he is their unity because of their charity, and their charity because of their holiness, it is clear that he is not one of the two, since he is that which the two are joined each to the other, by which the begotten is loved by the one who begets him and in turn loves the begetter. . . . So the Holy Spirit is something common to Father and Son, whatever it is. . . . Call this friendship, if it helps, but a better word for it is charity.[39]

Thus, what distinguished the Holy Spirit from the Son, and so the begetting from the proceeding, is that the Holy Spirit proceeds from the Father and Son as their mutual love for one another. Moreover, the Father is the primary principle of this Spirit-filled love, for he first loves the Son in the Holy Spirit, who then loves the Father in the same Holy Spirit. Unlike the Eastern Fathers, Augustine, by conceiving the Holy Spirit as the substantial gift of love between the Father and the Son, provides positive noetic content to the manner of the Spirit's proceeding. In so doing he articulates both why the Holy Spirit possesses a distinct identity from the Son as well as why the Father not only begets a Son but also spirates a Holy Spirit. Following upon Augustine's trinitarian theology, subsequent Western pneumatology will profess and advocate that the Holy Spirit proceeds from the Father and the Son (*filioque*).[40]

---

[36] See ibid., 15.19 and 47.
[37] Ibid., 15.29. Translation from *St. Augustine: The Trinity*, trans. Edmund Hill (Hyde Park, NY: New City Press, 1991), 419.
[38] See ibid., 15.27, 31 and 35–7.
[39] Ibid., 6.7 (209).
[40] For a more complete study of Augustine, see Lewis Ayres, *Augustine on the Trinity* (Cambridge: Cambridge University Press, 2010). For a classic study of the Holy Spirit within the patristic period, see Henry B. Swete, *The Holy Spirit in the Ancient Church* (London: Macmillan, 1912).

THOMAS AQUINAS (c. 1225–1274)

Space demands that we forgo treating Anselm, Richard of St. Victor, Bonaventure, and other medievals and move directly to Thomas Aquinas. Following upon Gregory of Nazianzus and Augustine, Aquinas emphasizes that the persons of the Trinity exist in relation to one another. They are "subsistent relations," that is, they subsist or exist as who they are only in relation to one another. The Father only subsists as Father in relation to the Son and the Holy Spirit, and the Son only subsists as Son in relation to the Father and the Holy Spirit, and the Holy Spirit only subsists as Holy Spirit in relation to the Father and the Son.[41] For Aquinas, the persons are distinguished in relational opposition to one another—for example, the opposing relation of Father to Son and vice versa. In order for the Holy Spirit to have an opposing relationship, he must not only proceed from the Father, but he must proceed from the Father in a manner that differs from the Son's begetting. For Aquinas, following Augustine, the Holy Spirit "proceeds by way of love."[42]

> The Holy Spirit is said to be the bond of the Father and Son, inasmuch as he is Love; because since the Father loves himself and the Son with one Love, and conversely, there is expressed in the Holy Spirit, as Love, the relation of the Father and the Son, and conversely, as that of lover to the beloved. But from the fact that the Father and the Son mutually love one another, it necessarily follows that this mutual Love, the Holy Spirit, proceeds from both.[43]

This is what differentiates the Holy Spirit, and so accounts for his distinct identity from the Father and the Son. This differentiation demands that the Holy Spirit proceeds from the Father and the Son. "It must be said that the Holy Spirit is from the Son. For if he were not from him, he could in no wise be personally distinguished from him."[44] Thus, the Holy Spirit proceeds from the Father and Son as their mutual love for one another. In being begotten from the Father, "the Son receives from the Father that the Holy Spirit proceeds from him." This is what it means for the Spirit to proceed from the Father through the Son.[45] Thus, the Holy Spirit proceeds principally from the Father for only in begetting his Son does he give to the Son the ability to have the Holy Spirit proceed from him as well. Aquinas, nonetheless, also perceives the procession of the Holy Spirit as from one principle in that he proceeds simultaneously from both.[46] Eastern theologians, not recognizing the distinction Aquinas is attempting to make, accuse him of undermining the monarchy of the Father, that is, that he is no longer the one source from whom the Spirit proceeds.

---

[41]*ST*, I, q. 28–29.
[42]Ibid., I, q. 36, a. 1.
[43]Ibid., I, q. 37, a. 1 ad 3. Aquinas, as did Augustine, also sees the Holy Spirit as Gift. See ibid., I, q. 38.
[44]Ibid., I, q. 36, a. 2.
[45]Ibid., I, q. 36. a. 3. Aquinas believes this is in keeping with the authentic Greek understanding of the Holy Spirit proceeding through the Son.
[46]Ibid., I, q. 36, a. 4. For more complete studies of Thomas Aquinas's trinitarian thought, see Gilles Emery, *The Trinity in Aquinas* (Ave Maria, FL: Sapientia, 2003); idem, *The Trinitarian Theology of St. Thomas Aquinas* (Oxford: Oxford University Press, 2010); William J. Hill, *The Three-Personed God: The Trinity as a Mystery of Salvation* (Washington DC: Catholic University of America Press, 1982); and Matthew Levering, *Engaging the Doctrine of the Holy Spirit* (Grand Rapids, MI: Baker Academic, 2016).

THE RISE OF THE CONTROVERSY

Maximus the Confessor (c. 580–662) held, along with the East, that the Spirit proceeds (*ekporeuetai*) from the Father through the Son and so exists in communion with them. He gave an irenic interpretation to the Western understanding of the *filioque*. Commenting upon the Western Fathers he wrote: "They showed that they themselves do not make the Son the cause of the Spirit for they know that the Father is the one cause of the Son and the Spirit, one by begetting and the other by procession, but they show the progression through him and thus the unity of essence."[47] Thus, for Maximus, the Western tradition did not violate the primacy of the Father and, similar to the East, acknowledges that the Spirit proceeds from the Father through the Son and so shares in the Son's divinity. Following upon Maximus, the question of the Spirit's procession lay, for the most part, dormant until the outbreak of the *filioque* controversy in the late 700s.

In response to the Arianism of the Visigoths, the Third Council of Toledo (589) demanded that King Reccard profess what all believed was the Creed of the Council of Constantinople. The version that Reccard professed contained the declaration "in equal degree must the Holy Spirit be confessed by us and we must preach that he proceeds from the Father and the Son (*a Patre et a Filio*) and is one substance with Father and Son."[48] The Council wanted to ensure that the Son and Spirit were truly God, and by having the Holy Spirit proceed from the Father and the Son assured both the Son's and the Spirit's divinity. Although it is unknown when this phrasing was added to the Creed, it nonetheless became the common profession within the Western church. The actual use of the term *"filioque"* was added to the Nicene-Constantinopolitan Creed during this time frame. Alcuin brought this Spanish tradition, via England, to the court of Charlemagne in 782 along with the now traditional recital of the Creed during Mass. In 787 the Second Council of Nicaea approved the veneration of icons and also professed that the Holy Spirit proceeded from the Father through the Son. Upon receiving the Council's results, Charlemagne protested to Pope Hadrian I, who in turn replied that the Creed was in conformity with church tradition. Charlemagne convened a council in Frankfurt (794), which demanded that the *filioque* be professed. Pope Leo III upheld the Council of Nicaea and condemned the Council of Frankfurt. At this time, on the Mount of Olives in Jerusalem, Frankish monks were reciting the Creed with the *filioque*. Their Greek neighbors condemned such usage as heresy. Charlemagne defended the monks and convoked another council at Aix-la-Chapelle (809) which declared that the *filioque* was a doctrine of the church and must be retained in the Creed when sung at Mass. Leo III agreed that the *filioque* was sound doctrine but refused to change the Creed, engraving it in Latin and Greek and placing the engravings in St. Peter's. These events, nonetheless, precipitated what is known as the Photian Schism.

Photius of Constantinople (d. 895) attacked the West's theology of the *filioque*, arguing that if the Holy Spirit proceeds from the Son as well as from the Father, this would destroy the monarchy of the Father. The Holy Spirit must proceed from the Father alone, for if the Son participated in the procession of the Holy Spirit, not only would the distinctiveness of the Father be lost but also the distinctiveness of the Son. The Son would take on the attribute of fatherhood, which would undermine the integrity of both

---

[47] Maximus the Confessor, *Letter to Marinus*, Opusculum, 10. Translation taken from Siecienski, *The Filioque*, 80–1.

[48] Translation taken from J. N. D. Kelly, *Early Christian Creeds* (London: Longmans, Green and Co., 1950), 361.

the Father and the Son.[49] These arguments, along with the West's illegitimately adding to and so changing a conciliar creed, became the Greek's foundational arguments against the Western tradition of the *filioque*. This controversy climaxed when Cardinal Humbert charged the Greeks (1054) with suppressing the *filioque*, and so accused them of heresy. Thus, the schism between the Eastern Orthodox Churches and the Roman Catholic Church, founded upon the *filioque* controversy, persists to this day.

ATTEMPTS AT RECONCILIATION

In subsequent centuries to the present, there have been various attempts at reconciliation between the East and West over the issue of the *filioque*. Here we can only comment briefly on some of the most significant. The Second Council of Lyons (1274) was the first major attempt at reunion. Various popes and the Byzantine Emperor Michael VIII corresponded over a number of years prior to the Council. At the onset of the Council, before the Greek delegation arrived, the Latin bishops already confirmed a profession of faith in which the *filioque* was declared to be a doctrine of the faith. Upon the arrival of the Emperor and his delegation, they agreed to make such a profession of faith but asked that the Eastern church not be required to include the *filioque* within their creed. They knew that such a requirement would be soundly rejected by their clergy and faithful. While this request was rejected, the Greek delegation pledged their support of the doctrinal statement and so to the union between the East and the West, thus supposedly ending the schism. While the end of the schism was celebrated in Constantinople, the creed professed at the liturgical celebration did not include the *filioque*. In reality the schism remained.

Another reconciliatory attempt was made at the Council of Ferrara-Florence (1438–39). Here there was much theological debate between the East, especially in the person of Mark Eugenicus of Ephesus, and the West. After agonizing negotiations, there appeared to be an agreed statement:

> The Holy Spirit is eternally from the Father and the Son, and he has his essence and his subsistent being at once from the Father and the Son, and he proceeds eternally from both as one principle and one spiration [*cf. Council of Lyon II:* § 850]. We declare that when the Holy Doctors and Fathers say that the Holy Spirit proceeds from the Father through the Son, this tends toward that understanding which signifies that the Son, like the Father, is also what the Greeks call "cause" and the Latins "principle" of subsistence of the Holy Spirit.

This is in keeping with the trinitarian principle that the Father, in begetting his Son, gave all to his Son, such that the Holy Spirit proceeds from him as well. Moreover, the Council stated: "We define also that the explanation of those words 'Filioque' have been added to the Creed legitimately and with good reason for the sake of clarifying the truth and under the impact of a real need at the time."[50] Mark Eugenicus was notably absent when this agreement was made and, as seen from the text, it was a complete victory for the Latin West. In the end, the Greeks felt that they had betrayed

---

[49]See Photius, "Encyclical Letter to the Bishops of the East," in *Creeds and Confessions of Faith in the Christian Tradition*, ed. Jaroslav Pelikan and Valerie Hotchkiss, 4 vols. (New Haven, CT: Yale University Press, 2003), 1:298–308.

[50]All of the above quotations taken from *Laetentur Caeli* in Denzinger and Hünermann, *Enchiridion Symbolorum*, §1300–2.

their tradition and their faith, and so by the time they reached Constantinople, they had completely rejected the Council of Ferrara-Florence. Reunion was not achieved, and the *filioque* conflict persisted.

Although the Union of Brest (1596) reconciled the Ruthenian or Ukrainian Church with the Catholic Church, and while other churches later entered into communion with the Catholic Church—the Syrian Church in 1662, the Antiochene Church in 1724, and the Armenian Catholic Church in 1742—this served to antagonize the other Orthodox Churches on the whole. Thus, relations between the East and West remained distant until the post-Vatican II era. All post-Vatican II popes have attempted, in various ways, to foster fraternal relations with the Orthodox. When, for example, the Nicene-Constantinopolitan Creed is now proclaimed between popes and various Eastern patriarchs, the *filioque* is removed. At the instigation of Pope John Paul II, the Congregation for the Doctrine of the Faith in union with the Orthodox issued a statement (1995) entitled *The Greek and the Latin Traditions Regarding the Procession of the Holy Spirit*. This document stated that all Christians must believe that the Latin teaching regarding the *filioque* "does not concern the *ekporeusis* of the Spirit issuing from the Father as source of the Trinity, but manifests his *proienai* [*processio*] in the consubstantial communion of the Father and the Son." The East states this in holding that "the spiration of the Spirit from the Father takes place by and through . . . the generation of the Son." Thus, the document acknowledges that there is a complementarity between the Eastern and Western traditions.[51] Both Catholics and Orthodox were, on the whole, pleased with this ecumenical statement, for it clarified the history of both theological traditions and sought to elucidate their difference and commonality. Following upon this Vatican and Orthodox endeavor, the North American Orthodox-Catholic Theological Consultation began a dialogue in 1999 concerning the *filioque* and issued a document in 2003, *The Filioque: A Church Dividing Issue? An Agreed Statement*. As with the Vatican/Orthodox statement, this document provides a summary of the theological development in the East and West as well as that of the ensuing controversy. Both dialogue partners agreed "that the Father is the primordial source and ultimate cause of the divine being . . . [and] that the three hypostases or persons in God are constituted in their hypostatic existence and distinguished from one another solely by their relationships of origin."[52] They acknowledged the unique term *ekporeuetai* as applying solely to the coming forth of the Holy Spirit and that the term "procession" contains a broader meaning. Yet both sides recognized that they could not reach a mutual agreement on the *filioque*. Nor could they resolve the ecclesial issue of the Latin church inserting the *filioque* into the Creed. What is evident within all these recent statements and dialogues is that both the Orthodox Churches and the Roman Catholic Church are willing, on the whole, to ponder together the theological issues involved and hopefully to resolve them amicably.[53]

---

[51]All the above quotes are taken from *The Greek and Latin Traditions regarding the procession of the Holy Spirit*, https://www.ewtn.com/catholicism/library/greek-and-latin-traditions-regarding-the-procession-of-the-holy-spirit-2349.

[52]*The Filioque: A Church-Dividing Issue? An Agreed Statement of the North American Orthodox-Catholic Theological Consultation*, available at http://www.usccb.org/beliefs-and-teachings/ecumenical-and-interreligious/ecumenical/orthodox/filioque-church-dividing-issue-english.cfm.

[53]For a recent theological and ecumenical discussion, see Myk Habets, ed., *Ecumenical Perspectives on the Filioque for the 21st Century* (London: Bloomsbury, 2014).

SOME UNRESOLVED ISSUES

By way of concluding, it would be good to address some unresolved issues.

First, as seen within recent ecumenical statements, both parties agree that the term *ekporeuetai* applies, in a singular manner, to the procession of the Holy Spirit (Jn 15:26) and so is different from the begetting of the Son. However, the exact conceptual positive meaning of that term remains ambiguous, particularly with regard to the East. The Latin tradition differentiates the proceeding from the begetting by perceiving the Holy Spirit as the gift of love that proceeds from the Father to the Son and from the Son to the Father. The East has no such alternative conception.

Second, all parties agree that it is proper to speak of the Holy Spirit proceeding from the Father through the Son. Such an understanding follows upon the economy of salvation where the Spirit proceeds from the Father and is given to the faithful through the Son. However, to subsume these trinitarian actions within the Trinity itself demands one to ask: How does the procession through the Son effect both the Spirit and the Son? The Son cannot simply be a conduit through which the Spirit passes, effecting no constitutive change either in the Spirit or the Son. In some manner the procession must constitutively define the Spirit and the Son.

Third, within the Eastern tradition, the Father is constitutively defined as Father because he is the sole cause of the Son and the Holy Spirit. However, while the Son and the Holy Spirit are active within the economy of salvation, they are not defined by any inherent act that constitutes and so defines them as Son and Spirit within the Trinity. Within the Trinity, they are passive. Within the Western tradition, the Father and Son are defined by specific acts that define them. The Father is the Father because he begets the Son and spirates the Spirit. Although begotten, the Son acts in that the Spirit proceeds from him as his filial love of the Father. However, within the Western tradition the Spirit is purely passive. He is simply the mutual Love that the Father and the Son share. If the Spirit is active within the economy of salvation, this demands that he be active within the Trinity itself.

Fourth, in both the East and the West there is a sequentialism. For the East, the Father begets the Son and *then* the Spirit proceeds from the Father through the Son. For the West, the Father begets the Son and *then* the Father and the Son together spirate the Spirit as their mutually binding love. While this is not a temporal but a logical progression, this sequence, nonetheless, undermines the eternal simultaneity of the Father begetting the Son and of the Father and Son spirating the Holy Spirit.

I have attempted to address all these issues. All the aforementioned concerns can be addressed if one simply recognizes that the Father begets the Son in the love of the Holy Spirit, and that the Son, in turn, loves his Father in the same Spirit-filled love in which he was begotten.[54] For the Spirit, then, to proceed from the Father through the Son means that the Spirit, through his proceeding from the Father, conforms the Father into the loving Father of his Son and, in the same proceeding from the Son, conforms the Son into the loving Son of his Father.[55] The Holy Spirit now possesses a defining act. While he proceeds from the Father

---

[54] This is in keeping with the Spirit's actions within the economy of salvation. The Father conforms the faithful into the likeness of his Son through the Holy Spirit (see Rom. 8:14-16 and Gal. 4:6-7). Also, the Father sends his Son into the world, and he is conceived as the incarnate Son through the power of the Holy Spirit. The Father declares him to be his beloved Messianic Son through the outpouring of the Holy Spirit at his baptism. The Father makes him the glorious incarnate Son by raising him from the death by the power of the Holy Spirit. Thus, the Father begets his eternal Son in his proceeding love of the Holy Spirit.

[55] By way of analogy, when a man begets a son in love, this loving act conforms him into a loving father. Equally, when the son comes to love his father, that love conforms him into a loving son. Although the father and the son

and the Son, the Spirit does so in a manner that he imbues the Father and Son with love such that they mutually love one another. The proceeding from the Father and the Son does not simply constitute the Holy Spirit, but the proceeding of the Holy Spirit is also constitutive of the Father being the loving Father of the Son and the Son being the loving Son of the Father. The Holy Spirit, the Spirit of Love, acts such that he imbues the Father with paternal love and imbues the Son with filial love. Thus, within the Trinity all three persons—logically and ontologically—spring forth in one simultaneous, non-sequential, eternal act in which each person of the Trinity subsistently defines, and equally is subsistently defined by, the other persons. This is why they are subsistent relations fully in act. They are constitutively fully in act in relation to one another because each person is who he is only in his fully giving himself to the others. The Father gives himself fully in begetting his Son in the full love of the Holy Spirit. The Son gives himself fully to his Father in the full love of the Holy Spirit. The Holy Spirit gives himself fully both in the Father giving himself fully in love to his Son and in the Son in giving himself fully in love to his Father. The Holy Spirit is the immediate active agent of love between the Father and the Son.

Such a reconception of the Trinity accentuates, in conformity with the East, the monarchy of the Father, for the Son and Holy Spirit simultaneously come forth from him as the principal agent of both. It also defines the *ekporeuetai*, for the Spirit principally proceeds from the Father as the Father's paternal begetting-love for his Son. Likewise, it upholds, in an innovative and proper manner, the Western conception that the Spirit proceeds from the Father and the Son, for he proceeds as the Spirit informed filial-love of the Son for his Father. Moreover, it overcomes the weakness of both traditions in that it attributes to the Holy Spirit a proper, non-sequential, active, and constitutive role within the Trinity itself.[56]

Although a great deal more could be addressed concerning the history and theology of the *filioque*, it is hoped that this as an adequate introduction to such a long, but important, controverted issue.

FOR FURTHER READING

Congregation for the Doctrine of the Faith. *The Greek and the Latin Traditions Regarding the Procession of the Holy Spirit*. Vatican Publication, 1995.

Habets, Myk. *Ecumenical Perspectives on the Filioque for the 21st Century*. London: Bloomsbury, 2014.

Habets, Myk, ed. *Third Article Theology: A Pneumatological Dogmatics*. Minneapolis, MN: Fortress Press, 2016.

Siecienski, A. Edward. *The Filioque: History of a Doctrinal Controversy*. Oxford: Oxford University Press, 2010.

---

initiate the love, that love, nonetheless, actively makes them loving. Within the Trinity, this conforming love is the substantial person of the Holy Spirit.

[56] For a fuller exposition of my position, see *The Father's Spirit of Sonship: Reconceiving the Trinity* (Edinburgh: T & T Clark, 1995); "Clarifying the *filioque*: The Catholic-Orthodox Dialogue," *Communio* 33, no. 2 (1996): 355–67; "The *Filioque*: Beyond Athanasius and Thomas Aquinas," in Habets, *Ecumenical Perspectives on the Filioque for the 21st Century*, 185–97. Myk Habets also takes up my reconception of the Trinity in "Getting Beyond the *Filioque* with Third Article Theology," in ibid., 211–30. For an interesting and important collection of essays on contemporary pneumatology, see Myk Habets, ed., *Third Article Theology: A Pneumatological Dogmatics* (Minneapolis, MN: Fortress Press, 2016).

CHAPTER SEVENTEEN

"Who Together with the Father and Son Is Worshipped and Glorified"

Roman Catholic Perspectives

MATTHEW LEVERING

The purpose of this essay is to introduce Roman Catholic perspectives on the divinity of the Holy Spirit. To accomplish this task, one has to start in the patristic period, since to do otherwise would be to leave out the fundamental building blocks of Catholic reflection on the Spirit. A longer essay would canvass the patristic debates over the key biblical texts about the Spirit, but I cannot do this here. Introducing Catholic perspectives on the Spirit also requires passing through the medieval period, as well as touching upon post-Tridentine theology, before connecting with Vatican II and contemporary Catholic theology. In this essay, I can only treat a very few authors as a starting point for further research. If one wished to address this topic in a fuller way, the best place to start would be the Catholic theologian Yves Congar's *I Believe in the Holy Spirit*.

In introducing Catholic perspectives on the divinity of the Holy Spirit, I focus on the Creed's phrase "who together with the Father and Son is worshipped and glorified." In contemporary theology, we spend so much time discussing what the Spirit does in creation and redemption that we sometimes fail to attend to the most important theological task with regard to the Spirit: namely, fostering the worship and glorification of the Spirit, with the Father and Son. In what follows, therefore, I will also address the question of whether it is desirable, or even possible, to worship and glorify one divine Person (the Holy Spirit) without excluding the other two divine persons.

THE COUNCIL OF CONSTANTINOPLE (381): EAST AND WEST IN CATHOLIC UNITY

In a letter written by the bishops gathered at Constantinople in 382 to their fellow bishops who were gathering at the Council of Rome (including Pope Damasus and Ambrose of Milan), the bishops at Constantinople explain that while they are unable to travel to Rome, they will send three bishops as representatives to the Roman council. The Eastern bishops complain that even now, "we are oppressed by wolves who even after expulsion from the fold go on ravaging the flocks up and down dale, making so bold as to hold rival assemblies, activating popular uprisings and stopping at nothing which might harm the churches."[1] Writing a year after the Council of Constantinople of 381, the Eastern bishops reaffirm its tenets and urge approval of the Niceno-Constantinopolitan Creed. As they say,

> It is the most ancient and is consistent with our baptism. It tells us how to believe in the name of the Father and of the Son and of the Holy Spirit: believing also, of course, that the Father, the Son and the Holy Spirit have a single Godhead and power and substance, a dignity deserving the same honour and a co-eternal sovereignty.[2]

Fortunately, there was no difference on this matter between the Catholic bishops East and West. In 380, Bishop Ambrose had attended a council convened by Pope Damasus in Rome, whose topic was the question of the divinity of the Holy Spirit. The council condemned the Macedonians, who denied the divinity of the Spirit. In 381, Ambrose published *The Holy Spirit*, which aimed to refute the Macedonians (named after Macedonius, an earlier, semi-Arian bishop of Constantinople). Far from advocating a Western position over against an Eastern one, Bishop Ambrose used his excellent knowledge of Greek and the availability of manuscripts to draw upon Bishop Basil of Caesarea, Didymus the Blind, and others. His work, like theirs, is charged through and through with biblical exegesis, as we would expect. He begins with an extended reflection on the story of Gideon (Judges 6), and he makes ample use of Genesis, the Psalms, Isaiah, Joel, Romans, 1 Corinthians, the Gospel of John, the Gospel of Matthew, the Gospel of Luke, Acts, Hebrews, Colossians, Ephesians, Galatians, and so on. Ambrose's purpose is to confute anyone who might "dare to say that the substance of the Holy Spirit is created."[3] Like Bishop Basil, Bishop Ambrose emphasizes that as Matthew 28 makes clear, "in baptism is the operation of the Father and the Son and the Holy Spirit"—and he notes that since baptism forgives sins, and only God can forgive sins (Mk 2:7), the Holy Spirit must be God. Having shown that the Holy Spirit is the Creator, he states that Christians must adore and worship the Spirit, who "is one with the Father and the Son."[4]

In Book I of his *The Trinity*, Bishop Ambrose's erstwhile parishioner, Bishop Augustine of Hippo, describes the indebtedness of his project to earlier Catholic authors:

> The purpose of all the Catholic commentators I have been able to read on the divine books of both testaments, who have written before me on the trinity which God is, has been to teach that according to the scriptures Father and Son and Holy Spirit in the inseparable equality of one substance present a divine unity; and therefore there are not three gods but one God.[5]

---

[1]"Epistua Constantinopolitani concilii ad papam Damasum et occidentales episcopos," in *Decrees of the Ecumenical Councils*, ed. Norman P. Tanner, S.J., 2 vols. (Washington DC: Georgetown University Press, 1990), 1:26.
[2]Ibid., 1:28.
[3]Ambrose, *The Holy Spirit*, I.8 in Saint Ambrose, *Theological and Dogmatic Works*, trans. Roy J. Deferrari (Washington DC: Catholic University of America Press, 1963), 68.
[4]Ibid., III.19 (205).
[5]Augustine, *The Trinity*, trans. Edmund Hill, O.P. (Brooklyn, NY: New City, 1991), I.ii.7 (69).

Indeed, the very same thing is taught almost sixteen centuries later by the *Catechism of the Catholic Church*. There we read that "we must believe in no one but God: the Father, the Son, and the Holy Spirit."[6] In its exposition of trinitarian faith, the *Catechism* cites multiple church councils, but gives pride of place to a lengthy passage from Bishop Gregory of Nazianzus's *Oratio* 40.

THOMAS AQUINAS AND THE WORSHIP AND GLORIFICATION OF THE HOLY SPIRIT

If the Holy Spirit is truly a distinct divine person without compromising the divine unity, can we worship and glorify the Holy Spirit distinctively? Must our worship and adoration be directed always to the three persons together, in a manner that does not accord with worshipping the Holy Spirit distinctly? Put another way, how might the personal distinctiveness of the Holy Spirit affect our worship of God?

Certainly, when we worship one divine person, we worship the other two divine persons. This is so both because of the unity of the Godhead, which means that the divine persons perfectly indwell each other, but also because each person implies the others. As Thomas Aquinas says, indebted to Augustine, it is "relative opposition" in the order of origin that distinguishes the divine persons.[7] The Father is Father in relation to the Son; the Spirit is Spirit in relation to the Father and Son. Thus we cannot worship one person without worshipping the other two. Lest this emphasis on "relative opposition" seem a Western innovation, the Catholic theologian Gilles Emery points out that it was Basil of Caesarea, in his *Contra Eunomius* II.22, who developed "the first speculative theory of relation within Trinitarian theology."[8] Again citing Basil, Emery observes that not only the grounding of the distinction of persons in relative opposition but also the unity of the Godhead ensure that worshipping one divine person entails worshipping the other two. He states that "the Spirit is adored 'together with' the Father and the Son, because he possesses the same creative and salvific power, the same divine dignity as the Father and the Son."[9] For his part, articulating the mutual indwelling of the persons (*perichoresis* or circumincession), Aquinas comments that this indwelling is total due to "the essence, the relation, and the origin."[10]

It may seem, then, that there is no distinctive worship or glorification of the Holy Spirit possible for the Christian, since in every act of worshipping the Spirit, the believer worships the whole Trinity. Aquinas points out that in the liturgy of his day, believers on Good Friday were expected to "genuflect at each separate invocation" of each divine person; but he emphasizes that "since there is one excellence of the three divine persons, one honor and reverence is due to them and consequently one adoration."[11] By this he means that we do not worship one person rather than, or more than, another; nor is any

---

[6] CCC, §178.
[7] See Thomas Aquinas, *ST*, I, q. 30, a. 2 (and ad 1); see also ibid., I, q. 40, aa. 2-3.
[8] Gilles Emery, O.P., *The Trinitarian Theology of Saint Thomas Aquinas*, trans. Francesca Aran Murphy (Oxford: Oxford University Press, 2007), 80.
[9] Gilles Emery, O.P., *The Trinity: An Introduction to Catholic Doctrine on the Triune God*, trans. Matthew Levering (Washington DC: Catholic University of America Press, 2011), 76.
[10] *ST*, I, q. 42, a. 5.
[11] Ibid., II-II, q. 84, a. 1, obj. 3 and ad 3.

worship appropriate that breaks the unity of the Trinity. In the liturgy, too, "we beseech the Blessed Trinity to *have mercy on us*."[12] But for Aquinas, it is an act of worship to praise God's name. As he says, "divine praise is part of divine worship, for it is an act of religion."[13] He quotes Ps. 34:1, "I will bless the Lord at all times; his praise shall continually be in my mouth."[14] He appreciatively cites the Syriac Father Pseudo-Dionysius's *Divine Names*, in which the author, while granting that God is unnamable, affirms that when "we offer worship to that which lies hidden beyond thought and beyond being" we do so through names revealed in the "holy words of scripture," including the names by which we praise and worship the persons of the Trinity (although Pseudo-Dionysius focuses on the naming of God in his unity).[15]

Aquinas devotes painstaking attention to the names that distinguish the divine persons, for example Father, Son, Word, Image, Holy Spirit, Love, and Gift. In fact, it is in knowing the proper name of each divine person—a name that truly distinguishes the person from the other two by expressing the relative opposition in the order of origin—that we are able to worship the Trinity. We worship the Holy Spirit distinctively, then, when we adore and glorify him as Holy Spirit, Love, and Gift. These names express personal properties that distinguish the Spirit from the Father and the Son, though always in a way that relationally links the Spirit with the Father and the Son. When we proclaim the name of the Spirit—divine Love and Gift—we praise and glorify him in his distinctiveness.

At the same time, however, we never give the Holy Spirit a worship that we do not also and equally give the Father and the Son. This is because the worship that we owe to the Father, Son, and Spirit is one worship—a worship that is due to them because they are God. We worship them because they are God, and we do not reserve a different worship for the Son than we have for the Spirit. Aquinas explains that "in the Trinity there are three who are honored, but only one cause of honor."[16] The cause of honor is that the three persons are God.

Yet, when we worship Christ, we truly worship the person of the Son, since Christ is the incarnate Son. In worshipping the Son as God, we of course worship the Father and the Spirit who are God. But the worship of the Son in his distinctiveness remains perfectly appropriate, so long as we worship him because he is God, which is the same reason why we equally worship the Father and the Spirit. Canon 9 of the Second Council of Constantinople, cited by Aquinas, teaches that we should indeed worship Christ as "God the Word in human flesh."[17] In worshipping God the Word—or God the Holy Spirit—we affirm at the same time that "there is a consubstantial Trinity, one Deity to be adored in three subsistences or persons."[18]

---

[12]Ibid., q. 83, a. 4.
[13]Ibid., q. 91, a. 1, obj. 2.
[14]Ibid., q. 91, a. 1.
[15]Ibid., q. 91, a. 1, ad 1. See *The Divine Names* in Pseudo-Dionysius, *The Complete Works*, trans. C. E. Rolt and J. Jones (New York: Paulist, 1987), 589B, 592A (50–1).
[16]*ST*, III, q. 25, a. 1, ad 1.
[17]Second Council of Constantinople (553), "Anathemas against the 'Three Chapters'," canon 9, in *Decrees of the Ecumenical Councils*, 1:118, cited by Aquinas in *ST*, III, q. 25, a. 1, *sed contra*.
[18]Second Council of Constantinople, "Anathemas against the 'Three Chapters'," canon 1, in *Decrees of the Ecumenical Councils*, 1:114.

YVES CONGAR, THE *CATECHISM OF THE CATHOLIC CHURCH*, MATTHIAS SCHEEBEN ET AL.

In his magisterial collection *I Believe in the Holy Spirit*, Yves Congar comments that in fourth-century Jerusalem, at the Feast of Pentecost, "The mysteries of the Word made man were celebrated and the divine persons were not isolated—the Spirit was 'coadored and conglorified with the Father and the Son.'"[19] But Congar immediately adds a clarification: "This does not mean that Christians did not pray to him as a separate Person, in the same way that they prayed to Christ. According to J. A. Jungmann, this practice was favored by reaction against the Arians."[20] Indeed, praying to the Spirit as God is central to recognizing the Spirit's divinity and to worshipping and glorifying him together with the Father and Son. Admittedly, he goes on to say that "prayer to the Holy Spirit was relatively uncommon in the early Church," even though it was practiced.[21] Most commonly, prayer to the Holy Spirit as a distinct person exhorted him to "come" into believers, into the world, and into the church. Congar gives a beautiful example of such prayer to the Spirit in the writings of Symeon the New Theologian. Congar explains that the purpose of such prayer is to call for—and to rejoice in—"the divine missions and particularly . . . the sending of the Spirit by the Father and the Son, with a shade of meaning that points to the procession of the Spirit in love."[22] In addressing the Spirit as a distinctive divine person, such prayer articulates the believer's worship and glorification of the Spirit.

The *Catechism of the Catholic Church* describes trinitarian prayer toward the end of its catechetical survey of Catholic doctrine and practice. It notes that "there is no other way of Christian prayer than Christ. Whether our prayer is communal or personal, vocal or interior, it has access to the Father only if we pray 'in the name' of Jesus. The sacred humanity of Jesus is therefore the way by which the Holy Spirit teaches us to pray to God our Father."[23] This sounds as though trinitarian prayer must be directed to the Father, in the Son, and through the Spirit. But the *Catechism* goes on to approve prayer "to the Lord Jesus," even though prayer is normally addressed to the Father.[24] The *Catechism* appreciates that Christians often simply pray the name "Jesus," or, as frequently in the East, ground their prayer in the repeated invocation "Lord Jesus Christ, Son of God, have mercy on us sinners." And the *Catechism* observes that, since the Holy Spirit teaches us to pray (1 Cor. 12:3), "how could we not pray to the Spirit too?"[25] As a divine person, the Spirit leads us to the Son who leads us to the Father. Therefore, it makes sense for us to pray to the divine Holy Spirit. The *Catechism* encourages believers "to call upon the Holy Spirit every day, especially at the beginning and the end of every important action."[26] The form of this prayer, as we have seen is already the case in the early church, will often take the form of "Come, Holy Spirit."[27]

---

[19] Yves Congar, O.P., *I Believe in the Holy Spirit*, trans. David Smith, 3 vols. (New York: Crossroad, 1997), 1:76.
[20] Ibid.
[21] Ibid., 2:112.
[22] Ibid.
[23] CCC, §2664.
[24] Ibid., §2665.
[25] Ibid., §2670.
[26] Ibid.
[27] Ibid., §2671.

When we recognize the Holy Spirit as God and pray to him as God—one with the Father and Son—we enter into a relationship with the Spirit, though never with him alone. The nineteenth-century Catholic theologian Matthias Joseph Scheeben describes how grace gives us this experience: by making us adopted sons of the Father in the incarnate Son. We are changed and transformed by the triune God's indwelling. Scheeben describes not simply how we are changed, but also the worship and glorification that we now direct toward the Holy Spirit whose indwelling presence unites us to the Father in the Son (who likewise indwell us, as distinctive persons in the one God). He states that "when we for our own part know and love the Holy Spirit thus dwelling within us in His own character," we "rejoice at our possession of Him," and "we return God's kiss and taste His ineffable sweetness."[28] We never love or rejoice solely in the Spirit, because the Spirit leads us at the same time to the Father and the Son. But we do distinctively experience the Spirit in accord with his personal property, due to our intimate communion with him in faith and charity. Scheeben repeats that "our love regales itself and rejoices in the possession of Him," and he remarks that "the Holy Spirit Himself, now clasped by us in loving embrace, is according to the Apostle the earnest of Himself and the other two persons, inasmuch as they are to be ours entirely in eternity."[29] With the Father and the Son, the Holy Spirit is God; and as we embrace and rejoice in the Father and the Son, we lovingly embrace the distinctive person of the Spirit and rejoice in our communion with him.

For his part, the early twentieth-century Catholic theologian Réginald Garrigou-Lagrange comments that "Philip of the Blessed Trinity and Anthony of the Holy Ghost state very clearly: 'All ought to aspire to supernatural contemplation. All, and especially souls consecrated to God, ought to aspire and to tend to the actual union of enjoyment with God.'"[30] Such supernatural union with God pertains to "mystical" experience, and thus goes beyond simple worship of the Trinity, but as Garrigou-Lagrange points out, all Christians are called by God to this "actual union of enjoyment with God." Garrigou-Lagrange grants, "The Blessed Trinity dwells in the just soul as in a living temple which knows and loves in varying degrees."[31] Indwelling the soul of the believer—and thus indwelling the entirety of the church as the Mystical Body of Christ—the Holy Spirit prompts us to worship and glorify the Trinity: "The stream of grace, which comes from the Holy Ghost, unceasingly reascends toward God under the form of adoration, prayer, merit, and sacrifice."[32]

Less we instrumentalize the Spirit, we need to recognize that our primary relationship to the Spirit in faith and charity is that he is God and he is worthy of all our worship and glorification. The Holy Spirit's greatest work is raising our hearts and minds to worship the Creator rather than the creature. It can seem that time spent worshipping God is wasted time, or at least one should do it only a little. But in fact, while we must prudently attend to worldly matters, time spent adoring and glorifying God is time where we attain our greatest good. Liturgically raising our hearts and minds to the living God, which we do in Christ and through the Spirit, is—as teaches Vatican II's Constitution on the Sacred

---

[28]Matthias Joseph Scheeben, *The Mysteries of Christianity*, trans. Cyril J. Vollert, S.J. (New York: Crossroad, 2006), 160.
[29]Ibid., 164.
[30]Réginald Garrigou-Lagrange, O.P., *The Three Ages of the Interior Life*, trans. M. Timothea Doyle, O.P., 2 vols. (St. Louis, MO: Herder, 1947), 1:87.
[31]Ibid., 1:104.
[32]Ibid., 1:108.

Liturgy, *Sacrosanctum Concilium*—"the high point towards which the activity of the church is directed, and, simultaneously, the source from which all its power flows out."[33] Along this line, Bishop Francis de Sales comments after citing the Shema of Deuteronomy 6: "For as God is the only Lord, his goodness is infinitely above all goodness, and he is to be loved with a love which is eminent, excellent, and mighty beyond all comparison."[34]

None of this, of course, is to minimize the praise that we owe the Spirit for the whole range of works that, in union with the Father and Son, he performs in the creation and redemption of the world, and which show themselves to be expressive of his distinctive personal property in the Trinity even while arising from all three persons in the unity of the Godhead.[35] In his 1986 encyclical on the Holy Spirit, *Dominum et Vivificantem*, Pope John Paul II draws particular attention to the Creed's affirmation that the Holy Spirit is "Giver of life" in creation and in redemption. John Paul II affirms that the Holy Spirit "is at the center of the Christian faith and is the source and dynamic power of the Church's renewal."[36] In his encyclical, John Paul II examines at some length the Holy Spirit in relation to the Father and Son, and the Spirit in relation to Christ's humanity. Discussing the Spirit's outpouring at Pentecost and the establishment of the church, John Paul II treats the Spirit's indwelling in believers, the Spirit's unifying and guiding the church in truth and charity, the Spirit's gifts to the church, and the Spirit's building up of the church. John Paul II also gives lengthy attention to the fact that the Spirit, in accord with Jesus's promise, convicts the world "of sin and of righteousness and of judgment" (Jn 16:7).

The Catholic theologian Jean Corbon has observed that the "basic question that holds men in its grip" and that is "the only really important question" is the question of human death.[37] Given that we are to die, what is the meaning of our lives, and do we have a real future? No wonder, then, that a central part of the good news is the truth enunciated in the Creed and highlighted by John Paul II, namely that the Holy Spirit is the "Lord and Giver of life." The Spirit acts in the economy of creation and the economy of salvation to give us life—a life that consists in sharing in Christ and in the trinitarian communion whose ultimate source is the Father. Indeed, the Catholic theologian Hans Urs von Balthasar, indebted to Louis Bouyer and others, argues that "the Spirit cannot be objectivized: he is not only the fruit but always the ever-new source of the love between Father and Son, and he will always attain his greatest manifestation or personalization where he is able to manifest this ineffable unity in the most profound way."[38] The point is that, although we should indeed worship and glorify the Holy Spirit, we will always find that to know the Holy Spirit means to be led in Christ to the love of the Father and the Son, and to discern in an ever greater way the wondrous unity in love of the three divine persons.

"The Spirit and the bride say 'Come.' And let him who hears say, 'Come'" (Rev. 22:17).

---

[33]*Sacrosanctum Concilium* §10, in *Decrees of the Ecumenical Councils*, 2:823.
[34]Francis de Sales, *Treatise on the Love of God*, trans. Henry Benedict Mackey, O.S.B. (Rockford, IL: TAN, 1997), 426.
[35]See my *Engaging the Doctrine of the Holy Spirit: Love and Gift in the Trinity and the Church* (Grand Rapids, MI: Baker Academic, 2016), chaps. 5–7.
[36]Pope John Paul II, *Dominum et Vivificantem*, §2, in *The Encyclicals of John Paul II*, ed. J. Michael Miller, C.S.B. (Huntington, IN: Our Sunday Visitor, 2001), 245.
[37]Jean Corbon, *The Wellspring of Worship*, trans. Matthew J. O'Connell, 2nd ed. (San Francisco, CA: Ignatius, 2005), 45.
[38]Hans Urs von Balthasar, *Theo-Logic*, trans. Graham Harrison, 3 vols. (San Francisco, CA: Ignatius, 2005), 3:51.

FOR FURTHER READING

Catechism of the Catholic Church. 2nd ed. Vatican City: Libreria Editrice Vaticana, 2000.

Congar, Yves, O.P. *I Believe in the Holy Spirit*. Translated by David Smith. 3 vols. New York: Crossroad, 1997.

Emery, Gilles, O.P. *The Trinity: An Introduction to Catholic Doctrine on the Triune God*. Translated by Matthew Levering. Washington DC: Catholic University of America Press, 2011.

Levering, Matthew. *Engaging the Doctrine of the Holy Spirit: Love and Gift in the Trinity and the Church*. Grand Rapids, MI: Baker Academic, 2016.

CHAPTER EIGHTEEN

Eastern Orthodox Perspectives

MARCUS PLESTED

The Eastern Orthodox tradition has consistently been particularly alive and responsive to the distinct person and ministry of the Holy Spirit. A typical instance of its distinctive pneumatology may be seen in the life and teaching of the early nineteenth-century Russian hermit St. Seraphim of Sarov. In conversation with his spiritual child Nikolai Motovilov, Seraphim declared that the summit and purpose of the Christian life is the acquisition of the Holy Spirit: "in this consists the true aim of our Christian life, while prayer, vigil, fasting, almsgiving and other good works done for Christ's sake are merely means for acquiring the Spirit of God." Seraphim delves deep into Scripture and the church fathers to convince his disciple that the indwelling of the Spirit in the human heart is indeed the utmost fulfillment of the promises made by the Savior. Motovilov remains unsure what this all means in practice and so Seraphim, in a striking and almost unparalleled move, quite literally extends the mystical experience of the Holy Spirit to his disciple, enveloping both in an overwhelming vision of God as light.[1]

In claiming the acquisition of the Spirit to be the goal and apex of the Christian life, Seraphim was consciously echoing a call made some 1,400 years earlier by the author of the Macarian homilies. These homilies, dating to the late fourth century, constitute one of the fullest ever explorations and expressions of the role of the Holy Spirit in the life of the baptized Christian and have remained a constant source of inspiration ever since—even through all the centuries of seemingly interminable debate about the *filioque*. In what follows, I shall attempt a survey of some of the distinctive emphases and insights of Orthodox pneumatology going back in the first instance to the fourth century and the Macarian Homilies. This chronological framework is of course somewhat arbitrary in that Orthodoxy traces its pneumatology back not to the fourth but to the first century and indeed well beyond that (cf. Gen. 1:2). But the fourth century has the advantage of serving not only as the time in which the divinity of the Spirit was formally proclaimed, but also as a period in which we can begin with some caution to speak of a distinctive and profoundly experiential pneumatology emerging within the Greek East. It is this experiential tradition of pneumatology that I shall focus on in what follows.

---

[1] "Conversation of St. Seraphim with Nicholas Motovilov," in *A Treasury of Russian Spirituality*, ed. Georgy Fedotov (London: Sheed and Ward, 1948), 273–5.

The Macarian Homilies have traditionally been ascribed to St. Macarius the Great of Egypt, the disciple of St. Anthony and the founder of the famed monastic community at Scetis. This ascription has since been shown to be mistaken. The actual author was, rather, the leader and spiritual guide of a network of monastic communities located in south-eastern Asia Minor or northern Mesopotamia, who wrote and preached between roughly 370 and 390 AD. The author (known as pseudo-Macarius or Macarius-Symeon, hereafter simply Macarius) composed a monumental collection of works addressed to an ascetic audience preoccupied with the pursuit of the vision and experience of God. Indeed, the master theme of his work is precisely the quest for the perfecting and deifying experience of the Holy Spirit. Macarius speaks with unprecedented precision, poetry, and power of operation of the Holy Spirit.

Macarius stands very much betwixt and between the Greek and Syriac thought-worlds. Although a Greek author, Macarius is manifestly closely connected with the world of St. Ephrem the Syrian. He displays the same symbolic apprehension of the cosmos and hymns the Spirit in very similar terms.[2] But Macarius, unlike Ephrem, was able to translate much of the poetic and pneumatic tradition of the Syriac Orient into the language and thought-forms of the Greek East. This double inheritance gives his writing much of its potency and goes some way to explaining his extraordinary and timeless appeal to Christians of both East and West alike.[3]

The divine status of the Spirit is not in any doubt for Macarius (unlike for many of his contemporaries). The Spirit is "uncreated," for only the divine can deify created beings (I 50.1.7-8).[4] This is a very similar argument to that found in St. Gregory the Theologian's *Fifth Theological Oration (On the Holy Spirit)*. Indeed, Macarius is demonstrably connected with the Cappadocian Fathers in their struggle against the so-called *Pneumatomachi*, the "Spirit-fighters" who refused to accept the divinity of the Holy Spirit. Saint Gregory of Nyssa re-worked portions of Macarius's *Epistola magna* as his own *De instituto christiano*, and he may very plausibly have had Macarius and his circle in mind when lauding certain Spirit-filled Mesopotamians in his *In Gregorii ordinationem* (or *In suam ordinationem*).[5] This praise came in the context of the Ecumenical Council of Constantinople (381) and the ongoing controversy over the divinity of the Holy Spirit. Gregory credits these Mesopotamians with renewing the gifts of the Spirit vouchsafed to

---

[2]It is no coincidence that substantial chunks of the Greek Ephrem are, in fact, Macarius. See Werner Strothmann, *Schriften des Makarios/Symeon unter dem Namen des Ephraem*, Göttinger Orientforschungen I, Reihe Syriaca 22 (Wiesbaden: Harrassowitz, 1981).

[3]Speaking only of the West, we may mention as legatees the Spiritual Franciscans, the Jesuits, the Wesleys, and contemporary Pentecostalism. Macarius also has the distinction of having been condemned four times by the Spanish Inquisition. Doubtless he had not expected this. See further Marcus Plested, *The Macarian Legacy* (Oxford: Oxford University Press, 2004), 1–2.

[4]Note on references to works of Macarius: I = *Makarios/Symeon: Reden und Briefe*, ed. Heinz Berthold (Berlin: Akademie Verlag, 1973); II = *Die 50 Geistliche Homilien des Makarios*, ed. Hermann Dörries, Erich Klostermann, and Matthias Kroeger (Berlin: De Gruyter, 1964); II:51–7= *Macarii Anecdota: Seven Unpublished Homilies of Macarius*, ed. George L. Marriott (Cambridge, MA: Harvard University Press, 1918); III = *Pseudo-Macaire: Oeuvres spirituelles I: Homélies propres à la Collection III*, ed. Vincent Desprez, SC 275 (Paris: Éditions du Cerf, 1980); EM = *Makarios-Symeon: Epistola Magna*, ed. Reinhart Staats (Göttingen: Vandenhoeck & Ruprecht, 1984).

[5]*Gregorii Nysseni Opera* 9.1, ed. Ernestus Gebhardt (Leiden: Brill, 1967), 331–41. See further Reinhart Staats, "Die Asketen aus Mesopotamien in der Rede des Gregor von Nyssa 'In suam ordinationem,'" *Vigiliae Christianae* 21 (1967): 165–79.

the early church and thereby providing experiential confirmation of the divinity of the Holy Spirit.

For Macarius, the whole purpose of the economy of salvation is not only that man might be wrenched from the grip of evil but that he might come to participate in the gift of the Holy Spirit (I 22.2.1). This gift of the Spirit is a gift beyond simple restoration of the paradisiacal state of Adam and Eve. The Incarnation "has restored to humankind the original nature of Adam and in addition bestowed upon it the heavenly inheritance of the Holy Spirit" (I 61.1.1). Drawing on a metaphor derived from Plato's *Phaedrus* in which the perfect soul is described as "winged," Macarius speaks of this inheritance as the granting of "wings" to the soul by the Spirit.[6]

> When he created Adam, God did not give him bodily wings, as he gave to the birds. His intention rather was to give the wings of the Spirit to him at the resurrection, so that he might be lifted up by them and carried wherever the Spirit wished. Such spiritual wings are given to the souls of the saints even in this life, raising their intellects up to the heavenly mind. (I 48.6.9)

With these wings, man is able to live and fly in "the air of the divinity" (III 4.2.2). It is precisely this capacity of the Holy Spirit to incorporate us into the life of the Trinity—to deify us—that lies at the heart of Macarius's recognition of the Spirit's divinity.

Participation in the Holy Spirit is described with a stunning range of images and metaphors. This poetic repertoire is very much Macarius's calling card. One should note that one of the key features of Macarius's pneumatology, and an unmistakable sign of his Syriac connections, is his interest in the theme of the motherhood of the Spirit.[7] Souls still in this world should call upon the "heavenly mother," the Holy Spirit, in order that she might

> come to the souls that seek her and take them in her arms of life, warm them with the spiritual and heavenly food of the delicious, desirable, holy, rational and pure milk so that day by day they might grow in spiritual maturity and increase in knowledge and perception of the heavenly Father. (III 27.4.2)

The Holy Spirit is also spoken of as, *inter alia*, dew, wine, rain, seed, sea, spring, food, fire, air, farmer, and bridegroom—nuptial imagery being something of a distinguishing marker of Macarian pneumatology. But for all his abundant and colourful imagery, Macarius never forgets the insufficiency of symbolic language.

> Whenever you hear about the communion [of bride and bridegroom], about spiritual dances and feasts, do not understand these things in a material or worldly manner. They are spoken of simply as shadows and illustrations since otherwise we would be unable to grasp them. For these realities are spiritual, heavenly, ineffable and inexpressible, being indiscernible by bodily eyes. (I 63.2.3)

Such realities are known only to those tried and tested souls who have experience of them. Macarius makes it absolutely clear that when he speaks of the experience of the Spirit, this is to be understood in the most robust of terms. When he speaks of the experience

---

[6] Cf. *Phaedrus* 246cd.
[7] The theme is also found in the *Odes of Solomon*, the *Acts of Thomas*, and the works of Aphrahat the Persian Sage.

of the Spirit as light, for example, this is no analogy. The perfect mystery of Christianity, declaimed by the Apostle Paul, is the experience through divine operation of "the illumination of the heavenly light of the Spirit." "This is not," he clarifies, "a revelation of knowledge and concepts but the eternal illumination of the hypostatic light" (I 58 1.1, 2.1). This constant inner experience of the Spirit has an almost ontological character. Divine grace is permanently rooted in us "like a substance" (II 8.2). The experience and revelation of that grace comes about through cooperation or *synergeia* with the Holy Spirit. Human participation in this work of cooperation consists in ascetic effort and prayer within the context of the sacramental life of the church.

Certain currents within the radical, Spirit-centered Syrian ascetic tradition from which Macarius emerged came to reject the ecclesiastical and sacramental structures of the church as of no use in the quest for the direct apprehension of the gifts of the Spirit. Macarius reacted to this anti-sacramental tendency by insisting that the Holy Spirit acts in and through the church and her sacraments. The Spirit "presides over and participates in the whole liturgy of the holy Church of God" (I 52.2.3). In baptism, we receive the effacement of sins and the "beginning of the life of the Spirit" (I 43.6). Baptism is a pledge, a talent that must be worked with (III 28.3.3), in order that the "life" of the Spirit might be experienced as manifest within us.

This life of the Spirit is frequently spoken of as one of mingling or mixing.[8] Indeed the Spirit so unites him/herself to our natures as to become a *second* or *other* soul within the human person. This "other soul" *is* the "divine and heavenly Spirit hearing, crying, praying, knowing, and doing the will of God" in us. This is an explicit outworking from Rom. 8:26 (see I 63 1.1-4). He also puts the reverse proposition: "without that soul which is the Spirit our soul is dead and useless" (II 30.5). But with this soul, the very life of the Spirit within us, we become double, both created and uncreated (see III 10.3.4).[9] The acquisition of the Spirit entails an intimate and almost organic union whereby the Spirit quite literally abides in us, becoming another soul within us and integrating us into the life of the Trinity.

> When the soul attains spiritual perfection, totally purged of all the passions and perfectly united to and mingled with the Spirit, the Paraclete, in ineffable communion, then the soul is itself vouchsafed to become spirit, being commingled with the Spirit. It then becomes all light, all spirit, all joy, all repose, all gladness, all love, all compassion, all goodness and kindness. It is as though it had been swallowed up in the virtues of the Holy Spirit as a stone in the depths of the sea is surrounded by water. Such people are totally mingled with and embraced by the Spirit, united to the grace of Christ, and assimilated to Christ. (I 13.2.4)

Pneumatic, christocentric, and trinitarian—such is the Macarian vision of the Christian life. As a closing remark, it may be noted that there is nothing individualistic about this vison. Those who are united to the Spirit come to share in the depths of divine compassion:

---

[8] Again, mixing language is a prominent feature of the Syriac Christian tradition. It is also a marked feature of Cappadocian Christology. Macarius's mixing language allows him to express the intimate and utter union of God and the soul without compromising their ontological discontinuity.

[9] The "second soul" theme is also found in Aphrahat the Persian sage. A similar intuition is present in Irenaeus's identification of body, soul, and [Holy] Spirit as constituent of the perfect human being. See *Against the Heresies* 5.9.1.

"burning with the love of the Spirit for all humankind, they take to themselves the sorrow and grief of the whole Adam" (I 13.2.2).

I have chosen to spend a great deal of time on Macarius because I take him to represent simply the fullest and most candid expression of pneumatology that the Eastern Orthodox tradition has to offer. For reasons of space, the remainder of this chapter will be somewhat less detailed, offering rather some "edited highlights" of later pneumatological reflection within that tradition.

The legacy of Macarian pneumatology is patently evident in figures such as Ss. Mark the Monk, Diadochus of Photice, Maximus the Confessor, Symeon the New Theologian, and Gregory Palamas. But of these, only Symeon approaches Macarius in the ardency and immediacy with which he speaks of his own direct experience of the Holy Spirit. Much later Orthodox thought on the Holy Spirit tends to get somewhat waylaid by the endless and often rather arid debate on the *filioque*. As Sergius Bulgakov has wryly observed with pardonable hyperbole: "it is remarkable that this *filioque* debate killed all interest in the theology of the Holy Spirit."[10] In what follows, I shall attempt to avoid getting too bogged down in the intricacies of the *filioque* dispute (dealt with elsewhere in this volume) and endeavor to tease out some of the more positive aspects of the theology of the Holy Spirit as articulated in the later Byzantine tradition.

Maximus the Confessor, a theologian who, we may note, saw in the *filioque* no great impediment to East–West understanding, finds a particular place for the Holy Spirit within his theology of the divine *logoi*—the pre-eternal divine ideas that are manifest within every created thing giving order and coherence to the creation. Our chief purpose in life is to orient ourselves to see and participate in these *logoi*, and, in particular, to conform ourselves to our own particular *logos* in order to approach and be gathered in by the source and ground of the *logoi*—the Logos or Word of God himself. In this deifying process, it is the Holy Spirit who "accords perfection through luminous, simple and complete wisdom to those found worthy of *theosis*, bringing them by all means and ways to the Cause of beings."[11]

The cardinal role of the Holy Spirit within human sanctification and deification is very much a given for the Byzantine tradition. Saint John of Damascus privileges this dimension of the ministry of the Holy Spirit in his precise statement of faith given in his *Exact Exposition of the Orthodox Faith*.

> Likewise we believe also in one Holy Spirit, the Lord and giver of life: who proceeds from the Father and rests in the Son: the object of equal adoration and glorification with the Father and Son, since he is co-essential and co-eternal: the Spirit of God, direct, authoritative, the fountain of wisdom, and life, and holiness: God existing and addressed along with Father and Son: uncreated, full, creative, all-ruling, all-effecting, all-powerful, of infinite power, Lord of all creation and not under any lord: deifying, not deified: filling, not filled: shared in, not sharing in: sanctifying, not sanctified: the intercessor, receiving the supplications of all: in all things like to the Father and Son: proceeding from the Father and communicated through the Son, and participated in by all creation, through himself creating, and investing with essence and sanctifying, and maintaining the universe: having subsistence, existing in its own proper and peculiar

---

[10]*The Comforter*, trans. Boris Jakim (Grand Rapids, MI: Eerdmans, 2004), 130.
[11]*Questions to Thalassius* 63 (PG 90 673CD).

subsistence, inseparable and indivisible from Father and Son, and possessing all the qualities that the Father and Son possess, save that of not being begotten or born.[12]

John insists on procession of the Holy Spirit from the Father alone as to cause but allows for the eternal "rest" of the Holy Spirit in the Son. The communication of the Spirit by the Son represents not merely a temporal but also an eternal dynamic. Within this eternal divine *perichoresis*, it is possible to speak of procession from the Father *through* the Son.[13] This is an insight later taken up by Gregory of Cyprus and St. Gregory Palamas—indeed it lies at the base of what might be called an Orthodox *filioque*—a recognition of the eternal procession of the Spirit from the Father "through" or even "and" the Son but not in respect of causation.[14]

Photius of Constantinople produces in the ninth century a somewhat more straitened account of procession in insisting on procession from the Father alone and ruling out any form of procession from the Son except in respect of the sending of the Spirit to the temporal creation. This monopatrist position represents a rather extreme position that fails to do justice to the theologies of John and Maximus. And while there is in Photius a genuine concern that the Frankish *filioque* downgrades the Son while erasing the distinction between the Son and Father, the unremitting polemic of his *Mystagogy* adds little of positive value to the Orthodox Church's understanding of the person and ministry of the Holy Spirit.

The same cannot be said for St. Symeon the New Theologian (949–1022), that great Byzantine mystic who rivals Macarius in the candour, vividness, and directness of his account of the Holy Spirit. For Symeon, as for Macarius, the vision of God as light stands at the summit of the Christian life and is to be understood as a gift of the Holy Spirit.[15] Our whole life is to be dedicated to the pursuit of this gift. Symeon calls on each and every Christian to seek out the experience of God and to attain "the mystical and truly inexpressible contemplations, the transcendently splendid and unknowable knowledge given by the illumination of the Holy Spirit, by which we mean the invisible visions of the glory and divinity beyond light and transcending knowledge."[16] Such experiences are always profoundly trinitarian in character. Speaking in this context of the "ineffable speech" heard by St. Paul (2 Cor. 12:4), Symeon holds that this speech is the Son of God communicated by God the Father through the mouth of the Holy Spirit; in other words, "this is the Son of God the Father, declared by the Holy Spirit and, by the Spirit's illumination, revealed to those who are worthy."[17] For Symeon, it is a terrible blasphemy to say that we moderns (whether of his eleventh or of our twenty-first century) no longer have access to the direct experience of the Spirit spoken of by the apostles. Much of Symeon's devotion to the Paraclete can be seen in his powerful and para-liturgical prayer of invocation to the Holy Spirit that opens his collection of hymns:

> Come, all-powerful, for unceasingly you create, refashion and change all things by your will alone.

---

[12] *Exact Exposition of the Orthodox Faith* 1.8.
[13] Ibid., 1.12.
[14] See further Marcus Plested, *Orthodox Readings of Aquinas* (Oxford: Oxford University Press, 2012), 37–9.
[15] See, for example, Symeon's *Catechetical Discourse* 22.
[16] *St. Symeon the New Theologian. On the Mystical Life: The Ethical Discourses*, trans. Alexander Golitzin, 3 vols. (Crestwood, NY: St. Vladimir's Seminary Press, 1995), 1:121.
[17] Ibid., 121–2.

Come, invisible, whom none may touch and handle.
Come, for you continue always unmoved, yet at every instant you are wholly in movement; you draw near to us who lie in hell, yet you remain higher than the heavens.
Come, for your Name fills our hearts with longing and is ever on our lips; yet who you are and what your nature is, we cannot say or know.
Come, eternal joy. [. . .]
Come, Alone to the alone, for as you see I am alone: you have separated me from all things and made me to be alone upon the earth.
Come, for you are yourself the desire that is within me, and you have caused me to long after you, the wholly inaccessible.
Come, my breath and my life. Come, the consolation of my humble soul. Come, my joy, my glory, my endless delight.[18]

In the fourteenth century, St. Gregory Palamas produced a remarkably constructive approach to the problem of the *filioque* that finds a place for the Son in the eternal procession of the Spirit without compromising the monarchy of the Father—the Father as the sole source or fount of divinity. But Palamas remains intensely interested in the theology and ministry of the Holy Spirit even when grappling with this thorny issue. His discourse never strays far from the work of the Spirit in the saints, as for instance in his affirmation that "the Holy Spirit is naturally and eternally of the Father and in the Son, and goes forth and is manifest from the Son to the saints."[19] Gregory went on to dedicate much of his life to the defense of the reality of this manifestation of the Spirit in the saints. Like Symeon before him, he emphatically upholds the reality of human vision and experience of God. But Gregory goes beyond Symeon in articulating a clear dogmatic basis for human participation in God affirming that while humans can indeed see and experience God as he reveals himself in his energies or operations, they do not see and comprehend God in his inaccessible and imparticipable essence. The vison of God as light, for example, is to be construed precisely as a vision of God in his self-giving energy or operation. This divine and deifying activity of God is extended to humans by the Father through the Son and in the Spirit. The Spirit in this schema is pre-eminently the divine person who lifts and incorporates human beings into the life of the Holy Trinity.

Orthodox reflection on the Holy Spirit in subsequent centuries tended to a depressing degree to be subsumed within debates surrounding the *filoque*, debates that rarely achieved the constructive creativity evinced by St. Gregory Palamas.[20] But the tradition of experiential Spirit-centered asceticism lived on as witnessed in the Transvolgan elders, the Kollyvades movement, and the monastic revival represented by St. Seraphim of Sarov and the *Optina* elders. The twentieth century saw also something of a revival of Orthodox pneumatology in figures such as Sergius Bulgakov, Vladimir Lossky, Paul Evdokimov, and Dumitru Staniloae—all of whom wrote extensively on the topic. Space does not, alas, permit any very extensive treatment of these inestimable contributions.

---

[18]*Saint Symeon the New Theologian: Hymns of Divine Love*, trans. George Maloney (Denville: Dimension, 1978), 9.
[19]*Apodictic Treatise* 2.71 in Γρηγορίου του Παλαμα συγγράμματα, ed. Panayiotis Chrestou, 5 vols. (Thessalonica, 1962–92), 1:143–4.
[20]Perhaps we may see a partial exception in Maximos Margounios. See further Plested, *Orthodox Readings of Aquinas*, 146–7.

The same may be said of the profoundly pneumatological character of Orthodox liturgy and sacramentology—from the accent placed on the *epiclesis* in the eucharist to the "seal of the gift of the Holy Spirit" granted in holy chrismation and of course the ubiquitous prayer to the Holy Spirit, "O Heavenly King."

This brief survey does not and cannot do justice to the full range and whole depth of Orthodox pneumatology. It will, however, have given some intimation of at least some of the distinctive "highlights" of the Orthodox Christian understanding of and encounter with the Holy Spirit. In particular, I trust it will have drawn attention to the golden chain of experiential pneumatology represented by Macarius, Symeon, and Seraphim.

FOR FURTHER READING

Krivocheine, Basil. *In the Light of Christ: Saint Symeon, the New Theologian (949–1022), Life, Spirituality, Doctrine*. Crestwood, NY: St. Vladimir's Seminary Press, 1986.

Plested, Marcus. *The Macarian Legacy: The Place of Macarius/Symeon in the Eastern Christian Tradition*. Oxford: Oxford University Press, 2004.

Ware, Kallistos. *The Orthodox Way*. Rev. ed. Crestwood, NY: St. Vladimir's Seminary Press, 1995.

Welker, Michael, ed. *The Spirit in Creation and New Creation: Science and Theology in Western and Orthodox Realms*. Grand Rapids, MI: Eerdmans, 2012.

CHAPTER NINETEEN

The Holy Spirit

Lutheran Perspectives

CHERYL M. PETERSON

HISTORICAL DEVELOPMENT OF LUTHERAN PNEUMATOLOGY

Lutherans historically have been more known for their work on the second article of the Creed—Christology and justification—than on the third. Few Lutheran theologians have written dogmatic works on the Holy Spirit. Nineteenth-century theologian Theodore Schmauk reasoned that "inasmuch as the doctrine of the Holy Ghost was not brought into greatest prominence in the controversies of the Lutheran Church, the dogmaticians of the Church did not pay it the attention which they gave to the many other parts of the doctrinal system."[1] Yet the Lutheran tradition has richer resources for contemporary pneumatology than first meets the eye, starting with Martin Luther's own teaching on the Holy Spirit.

For Luther, "the Holy Spirit is God's real, personal presence" and "not a transcendent cause of a new (supernatural) nature" in a believer nor simply a manifestation of divine power.[2] As Regin Prenter notes in his comprehensive study of Luther's pneumatology, Luther rejected the medieval idea of "created grace" infused into the believer's heart, which in turn enabled one to love God and to become "righteous," thereby being justified by God.[3] Instead, Luther defined grace relationally as the personal presence of the Holy Spirit in and with the believer, imparting God's favor and mercy and enabling the believer to trust in God's mercy (through the gift of faith) and to love God and neighbor in return.

The "peculiar function and office" of the Holy Spirit for Luther is to "reveal and glory Christ, to preach him, and to testify to him," specifically "the proclamation of forgiveness of sin, of redemption from death, of comfort, of joy in Christ."[4] This emphasis is seen in Luther's earliest writings, including his lectures on the Psalms (1513–15) and Paul's Epistle to the Romans (1515–16), where Luther relates the work of the Holy Spirit primarily to the faith that justifies the believer.[5] The Holy Spirit's role is to present to

---

[1] Theodore Schmauk, "The Doctrine of the Holy Spirit and Recent Treatments of the Subject," *The Lutheran Church Review* (1901): 64.
[2] Regin Prenter, *Spiritus Creator*, trans. John M. Jensen (Philadelphia, PA: Muhlenberg, 1953), 19.
[3] Ibid., 176.
[4] *LW*, 23:278.
[5] Lois Malcolm, "Luther on the Holy Spirit," in *The Oxford Encyclopedia of Martin Luther*, ed. Derek Nelson and Paul Hinlicky, 3 vols. (Oxford: Oxford University Press, 2017), 2:618–19.

believers "the priceless Christ and all his benefits; to reveal them to us through the gospel and to apply them to the heart, making them ours."[6]

The Spirit works through the preaching and hearing of God's Word to enable believers to come to faith to receive these benefits, as Luther writes in the explanation of the "Third Article" of the Apostles' Creed in *The Small Catechism* (1529): "I believe that by my own understanding or strength I cannot believe in Jesus Christ my Lord or come to him, but instead the Holy Spirit has called me through the gospel, enlightened me with his gifts, made me holy and kept me in the true faith."[7] Heiko Oberman goes so far as to describe the sermon as an "apocalyptic event" for Luther, leading him further to propose that the chief rediscovery of the Reformation was not the sole efficacy of grace or the primacy of Scripture, but the "understanding of the Holy Spirit as the dynamic presence of God."[8]

Luther stressed that the Spirit worked through the external means of the proclaimed Word and the sacrament to create faith and bring renewal. He was critical of those such as Andreas Karlstadt who claimed to have direct, unmediated, and authoritative experiences of the Spirit. "On this basis, they judge, interpret, and twist the Scripture or oral Word according to their pleasure"; against such "Enthusiasts," he writes, "it must be firmly maintained that God gives no one his Spirit or grace apart from the external Word which goes before."[9]

The most extended treatment of the Holy Spirit in the Lutheran Confessions (*BC*, 1580) appears in Luther's explanations of the Apostles' Creed in *The Small* and *Large Catechism*. No other articles or sections specifically are devoted to the Holy Spirit in the other documents of *BC*, including the *Augsburg Confession* (hereafter CA, 1530), but there are numerous references to the Holy Spirit throughout the treatment of topics such as the Trinity, justification, and the relationship of faith to good works.

While Luther and Melanchthon emphasize the vital role of the Spirit in justification and the passivity of the believer in receiving Christ's righteousness, they also point to the role of the Spirit in the "new life" that results from being justified. The Spirit is received as a gift by justified sinners in order to renew and sanctify them, creating in them love toward God and neighbor, and enabling them to respond in good works and righteous living.[10] As CA 20 ("Of Good Works") states, "Moreover because the Holy Spirit is received through faith, consequently hearts are renewed and endowed with new affections, so as to be able to bring forth good works."[11] The authors of the later *Formula of Concord* (hereafter FC, 1577) similarly refer to the Spirit of "rebirth and renewal" (Tit. 3:5) who "takes away our hard and stony hearts and replaces them with new, soft hearts of flesh, that we may walk in his commands (Ezek. 11:[19], et al)."[12]

Luther placed the work of the Holy Spirit in the life of the church as well as in the life of the individual. In *The Large Catechism*, Luther highlights the communal—and transformative—aspects of the new life that Christians receive through Christ by the power

---

[6] Luther, "Pentecost," in *Sermons of Martin Luther*, ed. John Nicholas Lenker, 7 vols. (Grand Rapids, MI: Baker, 1988), 7:333.
[7] Robert Kolb and Timothy J. Wengert, eds., *The Book of Concord: The Confessions of the Evangelical Lutheran Church*, trans. Charles Arand, et al. (Minneapolis, MN: Fortress, 2000), 355; hereafter, *BC*.
[8] Heiko A. Oberman, "Preaching and the Word in the Reformation," *Theology Today* 18, no. 1 (1961): 21.
[9] Luther, *The Smalcald Articles* in *BC*, 322.
[10] *BC*, 566.
[11] CA XX, §29 (Latin text), in *BC*, 57.
[12] *BC*, 549.

of the Holy Spirit. Believers are simultaneously incorporated into the holy community as "a part and member, a participant and co-partner in all the blessings it possesses."[13] This holy community "possesses a variety of gifts, and yet is united in love without sect or schism"; it also grows through fruit produced by the Spirit and through being made holy, which Luther connects to the "full forgiveness of sins," which includes not only individual forgiveness but also the ways that believers "forgive, bear with and aid one another."[14] Because the debates within Lutheranism that led to the FC that had to do with the Holy Spirit focused on the question of justification, this communal aspect of the Spirit's work was not further developed by the second generation of Lutheran theologians.

In responding to the controversy over the relationship of works to faith sparked by George Major, the FC did, however, make a clearer demarcation between the event of justification and sanctification (FC 4) than can be seen in Melanchthon's discussion of justification in *Apology* 4, where he discusses regeneration alongside of God's justifying act with more fluidity. By the seventeenth century, Lutheran dogmaticians sought to further systematize these ideas in their adoption of an *ordo salutis* (order of salvation), that is, an arrangement of the Holy Spirit's work that begins with "faith and justification," after which follow five "consequences of justifying faith": vocation, illumination, conversion and regeneration, mystical union, and renovation.[15] In their scholastic delineation of the stages by which grace is applied to the believer, the more dynamic and personal quality of Luther's pneumatology got lost, or at least overshadowed.

In the late seventeenth and eighteenth centuries, Pietists like Philip Spener and August Hermann Franke were less concerned with the order of salvation than its experience in the lives of believers through new birth and holy living. They emphasized the "working presence of the Holy Spirit, the sealing, the illumination (by virtue of that which the Spirit brings to us from the truth created from the Word), the Spirit's consolation, the loving taste of eternal things."[16] Against charges of "enthusiasm," Spener argued that Pietists do not seek an inner revelation apart from the scriptures or the sacraments; instead, the Spirit hallows and seals God's word within believers.[17] Spener spoke of the "resignation" needed to live the sanctified life, calling Christians to "give ourselves to the Holy Spirit as an empty canvas on which he is to paint" and to "do the works which would come forth through them as the Spirit willed, and not to hinder the Spirit" for the honor of God and the good of the neighbor.[18] Later pietistic movements would become more focused on "empirical righteousness," which in the view of their opponents led to various forms of legalism and moralism.

A number of nineteenth-century Lutheran theologians—Karl Friedrich August Kahnis, Karl Friedrich Nösgen, and Karl von Lechler—published dogmatics on the doctrine of the Holy Spirit in the latter part of the century that broadened the focus of the Spirit's work beyond that of the individual Christian's life. Their contributions included providing exegetical foundations for pneumatology (Kahnis and Lechler) and a history of the doctrine (Nösgen) as well as responding in various ways to Friedrich Schleiermacher and

---

[13]Ibid., 438.
[14]Ibid.
[15]Heinrich Schmid, ed., *The Doctrinal Theology of the Evangelical Lutheran Church*, 3rd ed., trans. Charles A. Hay and Henry E. Jacobs (Minneapolis, MN: Augsburg, 1961), 407–99.
[16]Philip Spener, in *Pietists: Selected Writings*, ed. Peter C. Erb (New York: Paulist, 1983), 69.
[17]Ibid., 71.
[18]Ibid., 85.

Albrecht Ritschl's programs and what they perceived as a decreasing emphasis on the Spirit as the third "person" of the Trinity.[19]

A broader investigation into the person and work of the Holy Spirit would come in the twentieth century, on the heels of Georg Hegel's synthesis and the great theological systems of Karl Barth, Karl Rahner, and Paul Tillich. In particular, the latter half of the twentieth century saw renewed interest in the doctrine of the Holy Spirit, especially as related to the revival of the doctrine of the Trinity. Within this conversation, significant contributions were offered by Lutherans such as Robert W. Jenson and Wolfhart Pannenberg. Starting from Rahner's Rule that the economic Trinity is the immanent Trinity and vice versa, each offers a futurist possibility for theology by exploring the trinitarian personhood of the Holy Spirit within history's eschatological horizon. Pannenberg utilizes the scientific concept of fields of force in proposing "the dynamic of the divine Spirit as a working field linked to time and space" that orients creatures toward God's future.[20] For Jenson, the Spirit is the eschatological reality of God, the goal of God's ways, "God as the Power of God's own and our future."[21] As such, the Spirit is yet "a distinct identity of and in God" who within the triune Godhead works as liberator immanently, freeing the Father for the Son and the Son for the Father, and economically by freeing the Christian community for God and for the world.[22]

Other developments are worth noting. The emerging ecumenical paradigm of "communion ecclesiology," whereby the church's nature is understood in terms of communion with the triune God and among members, offered member churches in the Lutheran World Federation another opportunity to engage pneumatology from a Lutheran perspective within a trinitarian framework.[23] The Lutheran World Federation (LWF) has also engaged pneumatological questions in its engagement of Pentecostal and charismatic Christianity, in both critical and constructive ways. In a 2008 LWF study, theologians raised concerns about forms of neo-Pentecostal spirituality that emphasize human efforts and promise prosperity, which seem to take the focus off of the cross and justification as God's action on behalf of human beings.[24] This followed a 1986 study that explored concerns raised by the charismatic movement within Lutheranism in northern Europe and North America in the 1960s and the 1970s, including the movement's perceived critique of external means of grace and its attempt to base religious certainty on an interior experience of the Spirit.[25] These were followed by a six-year consultation between a group of Lutheran and Pentecostal theologians at the Ecumenical Institute

---

[19]Karl Friedrich August Kahnis, *Die Lehre vom heiligen Geist* (Halle: H.W. Schmidt, 1847); Karl Friedrich Nösgen, *Geschichte der Lehre yom heiligen Geiste*, 2 vols. (Gütersloh: C. Bertelsmann, 1899); Karl von Lechler, *Die Biblische Lehre vom heiligen Geiste* (Gütersloh: C. Bertelsmann, 1899–1904). See also Schmauk, "The Doctrine of the Holy Spirit and Recent Treatments of the Subject."

[20]Wolfhart Pannenberg, *Systematic Theology*, trans. G. Bromiley, 3 vols. (Grand Rapids, MI: Eerdmans, 1994), 2:102.

[21]Robert W. Jenson, *Systematic Theology*, 2 vols. (Oxford: Oxford University Press, 1999), 2:160.

[22]Ibid., 2:173.

[23]Heinrich Holtze, ed., *The Church as Communion: Lutheran Contributions to Ecclesiology* (Geneva: Lutheran World Federation, 1997). The most dominant version grounds the communion of the church in the *perichoretic* communion of the persons of the Trinity, following John Zizioulas's *Being as Communion* (Crestwood, NY: St. Vladimir's Seminary Press, 1985).

[24]Karen Bloomquist, ed., *Lutherans Respond to Pentecostalism* (Minneapolis, MN: Lutheran University Press, 2008).

[25]Carter Lindberg, *Charismatic Renewal and the Lutheran Tradition*, LWF Report 21 (Geneva: Lutheran World Federation, 1985), 35; see also 41–51.

in Strasbourg, France that produced the document "Lutherans and Pentecostals in Dialogue" and an official five-year dialogue commission between classical Pentecostals and Lutherans, which held its first meeting in 2016.[26]

ISSUES IN LUTHERAN PNEUMATOLOGY

An ongoing issue in Lutheran pneumatology concerns the work of the Spirit in the life of the Christian beyond the "essence of the Holy Spirit's activity," which is to "create faith in the sinner."[27] One school of thought, a form of "Radical Lutheranism," is represented by Gerhard Forde, who, in order to protect the chief article of justification from any danger of works righteousness, famously insisted that sanctification is "the art of getting used to justification."[28] However, an increasing number of Lutherans have embraced a more transformative view of sanctification, drawing on Luther's vital understanding of the Spirit as God's real, personal presence. Regin Prenter's monograph on Luther's pneumatology argues that it is possible to affirm holiness from a Lutheran perspective as long as the "chief article," the doctrine of justification, is not contradicted.[29] In a traditional Lutheran understanding, righteousness properly belongs to Christ and so is only the Christian's relationally through faith. However, as Luther wrote, "Christ did not earn only *gratia*, 'grace,' for us, but also *donum*, 'the gift of the Holy Spirit,' so that we might have not only forgiveness of, but also cessation of, sin."[30] Therefore, if, as contemporary Nordic scholarship says, grace is both "gift" as well as "favor," then the believer experiences not only a receptive holiness (including God's mortification of our self-love and self-glorification), but also an "active holiness," whereby the Holy Spirit is working in the Christian life in both interior (Godward) and exterior (humanward) dimensions.[31] For Luther, the believer who is being sanctified by the Holy Spirit "is both passive and active; he is crucified with Christ and he rises with Him to live a new life."[32] The Holy Spirit works in and through believers to bring this renewal.[33]

More recently, Leopoldo Sánchez has shown that the Lutheran emphasis on God's justification of sinners need not eliminate a robust theology of sanctification with a fresh examination of the question through the lens of Spirit Christology.[34] By emphasizing the Spirit's work in sanctifying the humanity of the incarnate Logos in conversation with

---

[26]The team published the document, *Lutherans and Pentecostals in Dialogue* (2010) as a handbook to future dialogue. Available online: http://strasbourginstitute.org/wp-content/uploads/2012/08/Lutherans-and-Pentecostals-in-Dialogue-Text-FINAL.pdf.

[27]See also Jeffrey K. Mann, "Luther and the Holy Spirit: Why Pneumatology Still Matters," *Currents in Theology and Mission* 34, no. 2 (2007): 111.

[28]Gerhard O. Forde, "The Lutheran View," in *Christian Spirituality: Five Views of Sanctification*, ed. Donald L. Alexander (Downers Grove, IL: InterVarsity, 1988), 13. See also Forde, "Radical Lutheranism: Lutheran Identity in America," *Lutheran Quarterly* 1, no. 1 (1987): 5–17.

[29]Regin Prenter, "Holiness in the Lutheran Tradition," in *Man's Concern with Holiness*, ed. Marina Chavchavadze (London: Hodder & Stoughton, 1970), 123.

[30]Luther, "On the Council and the Churches" (1539), in *LW*, 41:113.

[31]Prenter, "Holiness," 126.

[32]Ibid., 144.

[33]See also Cheryl M. Peterson, "A Lutheran Engagement with Wesley on the Work of the Spirit," in *The Holy Spirit and the Christian Life*, ed. Wolfgang Vondey (New York: Palgrave Macmillan, 2014), 93–108.

[34] Leopoldo A. Sánchez M., *Receiver, Bearer, and Giver of God's Spirit: Jesus' Life in the Spirit as a Lens for Theology and Life* (Eugene, OR: Pickwick, 2015) and *Sculptor Spirit: Models of Sanctification from Spirit Christology* (Downers Grove, IL: InterVarsity, 2019).

patristic authors and Martin Chemnitz's classic Lutheran treatment of Christology, Sánchez shows how a Spirit Christology can complement rather than replace a Logos Christology. He further argues that a Spirit Christology which examines the Spirit's role in Jesus's life and mission can provide a theological framework for a "models-based approach to sanctification." He explores five (often complementary) models of sanctification: renewal, dramatic, sacrificial, hospitality, and devotional. Though his work is ecumenical in scope, Sánchez points to the affinities each model has with Martin Luther's portrayal of the Christian life in his catechisms, lectures, and other writings, revealing a richer theology of the sanctified life than is typically ascribed to the Reformer. Through the agency of the Sculptor Spirit, "the Christian life mirrors Christ's own life in the Spirit, a life under the cross."[35]

Already one can see the move to view sanctification as more than an individual matter, as in the scholastic "*ordo salutis*." Paul Hinlicky and Cheryl Peterson have proposed interpreting sanctification in more communal terms. Hinlicky speaks of the Spirit as the agent of new birth, which he interprets sacramentally and communally as "a public transfer of loyalty, which joined gospel believers to the new people 'called out' by God from their previous identities among the nations."[36] Indeed, the Spirit creates a "new eccentric humanity" that "lives outside of itself by faith in God and love of neighbor and hope for the world."[37] The Spirit thus builds up the community with gifts and fruit, enabling it to be the means through which God gives life in a world that is "stigmatized by death."[38]

Peterson likewise situates the sanctifying work of the Holy Spirit in the "holy community," drawing on Luther's explanation of the Third Article of the Apostles' Creed in *The Large Catechism* and connecting it to the mission of the church. As the Spirit brings believers to faith in the gospel, the Spirit also incorporates them into the holy community, as participants and co-partners in its blessings.[39] The primary blessing is the "full forgiveness of sins," a gift received individually by God but also shared with others in relationship in the ways that Christians "forgive, bear with and aid one another."[40] Sanctification, then, is the movement of the Spirit in a community that lives by the promise of forgiveness and reconciliation it has received through Christ. Luther further states that the Holy Spirit will continue granting forgiveness until the last day, "and for this purpose he has appointed a community on earth, through which he speaks and does all of his work."[41] Luther affirms the agency of the Spirit in terms of not only bringing individual believers to faith, but also empowering transformed and reconciled relationships.

Christine Helmer offers another perspective on sanctification, drawing on Luther's catechetical work. She suggests that one can find "two interwoven narratives of Trinitarian glory" in Luther's explanation of the Apostles' Creed in *The Large Catechism*, whereby God is glorified for who God is as well as for what God does. The Spirit's work in bringing the

---

[35] Sánchez, *Sculptor Spirit*, 203.
[36] Paul R. Hinlicky, *Beloved Community: Critical Dogmatics after Christendom* (Grand Rapids, MI: Eerdmans, 2015), 227.
[37] Ibid., 343.
[38] Ibid., 345.
[39] *BC*, 438.
[40] Ibid.
[41] Ibid., 439. See also Peterson, *Who Is the Church? An Ecclesiology for the Twenty-First Century* (Minneapolis, MN: Fortress, 2013).

believer to Christ "renders visible the inner-Trinity, not through the relations of origin, but through the Trinitarian work of incorporating individuals, the church, and ultimately creation into the sight of the Trinity."[42] This leads her to argue that the point of sanctification is not to draw attention to the believer but to Christ and what God has done in Christ for the whole creation. The Spirit thus glorifies Christ, who glorifies the Father, bringing the confession of faith to its goal: glorifying who God is for what God does in order to transform creation.

Helmer is one of several theologians who has shown that Lutheran theology can fruitfully engage the Spirit in ways that connect to the economy of salvation through "glory." Others make the connection by means of gift/giving, communion, *perichoresis*, and—as we saw in Jenson—freedom and liberation. As for the last point: in the first full-length study of Jenson's pneumatology, Roman Catholic James Daryn Henry explores the ways that Jenson's view of the Spirit as "freedom in God's own life" can deepen the grounding of liberation theology, arguing that liberation does not have its basis only in the mission of the Son and the Spirit in the world, but also in the eternal divine life itself as an aspect of *who* God is.[43]

These insights can also deepen the exploration of a mission-focused ecclesiology proposed by Peterson and others, which highlights the role of the Spirit as the agent of God's mission in the world, offering a fuller view of the Spirit's economic work than traditional Lutheran theology has, with its emphasis on the Spirit's work as calling believers to faith and gathering the church around the word and sacraments.[44] Finally, Edmund Schlink speaks of the "double-movement" of the Spirit that also sends God's people *into* the world. "In this double movement of those being called and those being sent by God, the church exists," and in-between these movements, the church has its life as the worshipping assembly.[45]

Another ongoing issue for Lutherans related to the Holy Spirit involves the role that experience plays in the Christian life. One of the Reformers' concerns, as we saw in the debate with Karlstadt, was making one's experience of the Spirit normative for theological claims. As Karl Froelich writes, their critique was aimed at "an intellectual spiritualism, a disdain for the 'letter,' ... and an insistence on the possession of this Spirit as an inward reality apart from all outward 'means.'"[46] Luther himself could be polemical toward "experience" in this way, but he "had a very positive evaluation of the place of experience in the life of the Christian."[47] Luther even says that the understanding of God that the Holy Spirit brings to the believer is not received "from the Holy Spirit without experiencing, proving, and feeling it."[48]

---

[42]Christine Helmer, "Luther's Theology of Glory," *Neue Zeitschrift für systematische Theologie und Religionsphilosophie* 42, no. 3 (2000): 244.
[43]James Daryn Henry, *The Freedom of God: A Study in the Pneumatology of Robert W. Jenson* (Lanham, MD: Rowman & Littlefield, 2018).
[44]See Peterson, *Who Is the Church?*
[45]Edmund Schlink, *Ökumenische Dogmatik: Grundzüge* (Göttingen: Vandenhoeck & Ruprecht, 1983), 566 (my translation).
[46]Karlfried Froelich, "Charismatic Manifestations and the Lutheran Incarnational Stance," in *The Holy Spirit in the Life of the Church: From Biblical Times to the Present*, ed. Paul D. Opsahl (Minneapolis, MN: Augsburg, 1978), 142.
[47]Theodore R. Jungkuntz, "Secularization Theology, Charismatic Renewal, and the Theology of the Cross," *Concordia Theological Monthly* 42, no. 1 (1972): 17. Jungkuntz cites Walter von Loewenich's classic study, *Luther's Theology of the Cross*, trans. Herbert Bouman (Minneapolis, MN: Augsburg, 1976), 86–99.
[48]*LW*, 21:299 and 36:248, both cited in Jungkuntz.

When Lutherans address this question, they tend to focus primarily on the positive experience of being forgiven of their sins or the existential aspect of justification. Luther offers an example in the description of his 1519 "Tower Experience." After meditating and praying on the phrase "the justice (righteousness) of God" in Paul's letter to the Romans, he came to understand that the righteousness of God is itself a gift from God and not something we must accomplish on our own. He writes, "All at once I felt that I had been born again and entered into paradise itself through open gates." He goes on to describe God's presence in terms usually associated with Pentecostal spirituality: "the work of God, that is, what God works in us; *the power of God, by which he makes us powerful*; the wisdom of God, by which he makes us wise; the strength of God, the salvation of God, the *glory of God*."[49]

In their engagement and dialogue with Pentecostalism and charismatic Christians, Lutherans remain cautious about claims that the Spirit works apart from the word and sacraments, that is, through dreams, ecstatic movements, and unmediated mystical experiences. Lutherans also tend to be uneasy about emphasizing the Spirit as an agent of power, victory, and prosperity, fearing this will lead to a "theology of glory." For Lutherans, any glory can only be found in the cross of Christ, to which the Spirit always points. As Helmer puts it, "Apart from the riches hidden in Christ, the 'poor' Spirit knows nothing."[50]

Nigerian Lutheran theologian Ibrahim Bitrus has suggested that while the theology of the cross remains central for Lutherans, suffering and prosperity should be viewed dialectically. In other words, "it is not sufficient to tell people that God suffers with them; God is with us in our suffering, empowering us to change."[51] One path forward for Lutherans is to explore the Holy Spirit as the presence of God experienced in terms of power as well as salvific and sanctifying grace.[52] As Won Yong Ji notes, experience for charismatic Christians primarily involves a "new awareness of the all-powerful presence of God . . . it is 'God Himself,' not merely His dynamism which constitutes gifts."[53]

Along with power, the theological category of the gift can further develop Luther's key insight of the Spirit as the personal presence of God. In a recent work, Gregory Walter interprets Pentecost as an event of God's self-giving, whereby the Spirit itself is given as a measureless gift not only to "empower the apostolic community to remain in Jesus," but also to "share and be Jesus' cross-marked body, and to fulfill the longings of the nations and the groaning of all creation." In this way, Walter argues, Pentecost allows for much more than a discussion of "the gifts of the Spirit" and for the renewal and transformation of creation itself.[54]

---

[49]Luther's Tower Experience; available at http://www.iclnet.org/pub/resources/text/wittenberg/luther/tower.txt (italics mine). For further discussion of this issue, see Peterson, "Theology of the Cross and the Experience of God's Presence: A Lutheran Response to Pentecostal Wonderings," *Dialog: A Journal of Theology* 55, no. 4 (2016): 316–23.

[50]Helmer, "Luther's Theology of Glory," 244.

[51]Ibrahim Bitrus, "The Influence of Neo-Pentecostalism in Nigeria," in *Lutherans Respond to Pentecostalism*, ed. Karen L. Bloomquist (Minneapolis, MN: Lutheran University Press, 2008), 87. See also Peterson, "A Pneumatology of the Cross: The Challenge of Neo-Pentecostalism to Lutheran Theology," *Dialog: A Journal for Theology* 50, no. 2 (2011): 133–42.

[52]See Cheryl M. Peterson, "A Lutheran Exploration of Spiritual Empowerment, Pentecostal-Style," *Lutheran Forum* 51, no. 2 (2017): 47–50.

[53]Won Yong Ji, "The Work of the Holy Spirit and the Charismatic Movements, from Luther's Perspective," *Concordia Journal* 11, no. 6 (1985): 207.

[54]Gregory Walter, *Being Promised: Theology, Gift, and Practice* (Grand Rapids, MI: Eerdmans, 2013), 42–3.

FOR FURTHER READING

Lutherans and Pentecostals in Dialogue. Strasbourg: Institute for Ecumenical Research; Pasadena: David Du Plessis Center for Christian Spirituality; and Zürich: European Pentecostal Charismatic Research Association, 2010. Available at http://strasbourginstitute.org/wp-content/uploads/2012/08/Lutherans-and-Pentecostals-in-Dialogue-Text-FINAL.pdf.

Malcolm, Lois. "Luther on the Holy Spirit." In *The Oxford Encyclopedia of Martin Luther*, edited by Derek Nelson and Paul Hinlicky, 2:618–36. Oxford: Oxford University Press, 2017.

Opsahl, Paul D., ed. *The Holy Spirit in the Life of the Church: From Biblical Times to the Present*. Minneapolis, MN: Augsburg, 1978.

Prenter, Regin. *Spiritus Creator*. Translated by John M. Jensen. Philadelphia, PA: Muhlenberg, 1953.

CHAPTER TWENTY

Reformed Perspectives on the Holy Spirit

SHANNON NICOLE SMYTHE

It is somewhat customary in doctrinal discussions of the Holy Spirit to begin reflections on the person of the Spirit by noting the Spirit's distinct place within the Godhead as a fully divine person of the Trinity. In this way, the decidedly Reformed privileging of the sovereignty of God—expressed soteriologically as *sola gratia, solus Christus,* and *sola fide*—gets worked out pneumatologically, in the first instance, by a strong creedal and confessionally Reformed commitment to the full divinity of the Spirit as a constituent member of the triune God who proceeds from the Father and the Son. Reformed theology has often self-consciously followed in the line of early church theology by emphasizing the Spirit as the bond of love between the Father and the Son, so in expressing the unique work of the Spirit in the economy of salvation, Reformed accounts of the work of the Spirit highlight that "the Spirit constantly leads our attention away from himself to Jesus Christ, so he hides himself, on the one hand, in Christ; and, on the other hand, he hides himself in his operations in the life of the church and the lives of individuals."[1] T. F. Torrance, in his introduction to Calvin's theology, offers the following illustrative insights into this Reformed pneumatological approach:

> The doctrine of the Spirit is the doctrine of the passage of God's mighty creative power from God to humanity, thrusting them out into the world to do the will of God.... The presence of the Spirit means the actualization in the life of the believer or the church on earth of the humanity of Christ, and therefore it means the recreation of human life in all its large and little aspects, the extension of Christ's Kingdom to the ends of the earth and the penetration of his rule into the depths of the individual in their daily lives.[2]

While it is certainly true that the whole of Calvin's pneumatology is both broad and complex, and that Reformed theology in general contains pneumatological dimensions in nearly every topic of theology and doctrinal loci,[3] it is also normative that Reformed

---

[1] Hendrikus Berkhof, *The Doctrine of the Holy Spirit* (Richmond, VA: John Knox, 1964), 10.
[2] Thomas F. Torrance, "Introduction," in *A Calvin Treasury,* ed. William F. Keesecker, 2nd ed. (Louisville, KY: Westminster John Knox, 1992), 21–2.
[3] As Oliver Crisp notes, Reformed theology affirms that "the Spirit is at work everywhere, at all times, in all places and in particular ways in the action of creation, conservation, redemption, and the consummation of all things."

faith, in particular, highlights the Spirit's role both in enlivening Christian life and in empowering ecclesial life and mission. Indeed, a distinctive mark of the Reformed tradition is "its emphasis on the transformation of life" and an understanding of Christian vocation as "the call to participation in God's reconciliation and renewal of the world."[4] For instance, "A Brief Statement of Faith—the Presbyterian Church (USA)," which was adopted in 1991, confesses, "In a broken and fearful world, the Spirit gives us courage to pray without ceasing, to witness among all people to Christ as Lord and Savior, to unmask idolatries in Church and culture, to hear the voices of peoples long silenced, and to work with others for justice, freedom, and peace."[5]

The vocational and missional aspect of Reformed theology is seen most especially as residing within the domain of the Spirit's work in the world, for "the Spirit actually brings men and women to the beginning of a new life, and makes them the determining subjects of that new life in the fellowship of Christ."[6] Furthermore, it is by the power of the Spirit that Jesus enacts and the disciples participate in God's eschatological reign on earth.

It is the task of this essay to delineate these dimensions of Reformed pneumatology as they can be ascertained from the systematic work of four leading representatives of Reformed theology: John Calvin, Jonathan Edwards, Friedrich Schleiermacher, and Karl Barth. The aim is to ascertain several distinctively Reformed emphases on the doctrine of the Holy Spirit within the realm of Christian life and the life and mission of the church. This will open up to a broader conversation regarding Christian and ecclesial vocation from a pneumatological perspective.

THE SPIRIT-LED CHRISTIAN LIFE IN CALVIN AND EDWARDS

John Calvin is well known for his rich reflections on the Holy Spirit. Early in the 1559 edition of the *Institutes*, Calvin addresses both the eternal essence and divinity of the Spirit and Christ's own Spirit-anointing, which was for the purpose that those who belong to him might share in his power. Then, throughout book three, he lays forth all that the Spirit "secretly" brings to pass in the new life of the Christian "by which we come to enjoy Christ and all his benefits."[7] Specifically, Calvin calls the Spirit the "bond by which Christ effectually unites us to himself."[8] It is only by the grace and power of the Spirit that we are made partakers in the salvation wrought by Christ. In other words, the mediating role of the Spirit serves the goal of actualizing our new life in Christ such that the Christian may taste both the favor of God and the "beneficence of Christ."[9] Through the gift of faith, which is "the principal work of the Spirit,"[10] our reception

---

"Uniting Us to God: Toward a Reformed Pneumatology," in *Spirit of God: Christian Renewal in the Community of Faith*, ed. Jeffrey W. Barbeau and Beth Felker Jones (Downers Grove, IL: IVP Academic, 2015), 100.
[4]Daniel L. Migliore, "The Spirit of Reformed Faith and Theology," in *Loving God with Our Minds: The Pastor as Theologian*, ed. Michael Welker and Cynthia A. Jarvis (Grand Rapids, MI: Eerdmans, 2004), 353.
[5]The Office of the General Assembly, Presbyterian Church (U.S.A.), *The Book of Confessions*, study ed. rev. (Louisville, KY: Westminster John Knox, 2017), 424.
[6]Jürgen Moltmann, *The Spirit of Life: A Universal Affirmation* (Minneapolis, MN: Fortress, 1992), 2.
[7]*Institutes*, 1:537.
[8]Ibid., 1:538.
[9]Ibid., 1:539.
[10]Ibid., 1:541.

of Christ brings the double grace of reconciliation with God through justification and sanctification by the Spirit through the cultivation of a Christian life of holiness. The Spirit of God separates individuals "out from the world" and makes "disciples of those who were previously destitute and empty of heavenly doctrine."[11] In this disciple-making task, the Spirit employs the scriptures in order to teach us how to love and practice justice in our lives. As Spirit-formed disciples who love and practice justice, the double grace that the Spirit actualizes in them is worked out both as Spirit-empowered freedom in Christ and Spirit-led prayer. In these ways, the Spirit of adoption brings the gospel of Christ to be truly known in the lives of believers by teaching them how to love God and neighbor freely and empowering in them true communion with God through prayer.

As with Calvin, so in Jonathan Edwards we find that the Spirit has an integral role in the triune God's work of salvation. For Edwards, the Holy Spirit is the great blessing or inheritance purchased for us by Christ's atonement. This gift of the Spirit indwells God's adopted children so that they are disposed to behave toward God as to a father through the sanctifying first fruits of the Spirit active in them. Believers are united to the Spirit of God as a consequence of the work of Christ, the fruit of which is the development of virtuous habits and dispositions in them. The Spirit's work in the believer flows from the Spirit's place in the inner life of the triune God as the disposition of the Father's infinite love of Godself. We neither know and love God out of our own resources, nor do we have in us naturally what is needed for salvation. "Saving grace in man is said to be the new man or a new creature, and corrupt nature the old man."[12] This grace is not produced in a person's heart unless there is something more added to the person's internal principles, "viz. an immediate infusion or operation of the Divine Being upon the soul. Grace must be the immediate work of God and properly a production of his almighty power on the soul."[13]

Edwards draws from his doctrine of the Trinity in highlighting the role of the Holy Spirit in the economy of salvation as it plays out within the heart of a Christian. In the inner life of the triune God, the Son and the Holy Spirit are the Father's disposition perfectly actualized. Since it is fundamental to God's being to communicate himself perpetually as love, the Spirit, as the love of God, proceeds *ad extra*. Hence, this principle of divine love in Christians, although "not properly capable of a definition,"[14] is "the Divine disposition or nature that we are made partakers of . . . for our partaking or communion with God consists in the communion or partaking of the Holy Ghost."[15] The saving grace in the Christian's soul is not only *from* the Spirit but "also partakes of the nature of that Spirit that it is from."[16] Therefore, it is through a Christian's communion with the Holy Spirit that she inhabits various gracious virtues in her life, follows the commandments, and fulfills her Christian duties. As Christ has united her with the Spirit, so this communion is her very participation in the love and beauty within the life of God.

---

[11] Ibid., 1:538.
[12] Jonathan Edwards, "Treatise on Grace," in *The Works of Jonathan Edwards*, ed. Sang Hyun Lee (New Haven, CT: Yale University Press, 2003), 21:160.
[13] Ibid., 21:165.
[14] Ibid., 21:173.
[15] Jonathan Edwards, "An Essay on the Trinity," in *Treatise on Grace and Other Posthumously Published Writings*, ed. Paul Helm (Greenwood, CT: Attice, 1971), 110.
[16] Edwards, "Treatise on Grace," 21:180.

SPIRIT-DRIVEN ECCLESIAL BEING AND MISSION IN SCHLEIERMACHER AND BARTH

Schleiermacher's main thesis on the Holy Spirit is that the Spirit "is the union of the Divine Essence with human nature in the form of the common Spirit (*Gemeingeist*) animating the life in common of believers."[17] To appreciate Schleiermacher's conception of the Spirit's role in the community of faith, it is necessary to recognize that for him redemption consists of the God-consciousness becoming "stimulated and made dominant by the entrance of the living influence of Christ."[18] In redemption, Christ "stands to the totality of believers in exactly the same relation as the divine nature in him does to the human, animating and taking it up into the fellowship of the original life."[19] Redemption takes place through the impact of Christ's lived sinless perfection among his earliest disciples. However, for the community of Christ's followers, there is no longer a direct connection with Christ as there was for the original disciples. Yet our redemption in Christ, which "is now mediated by those who preach him," must somehow really still proceed from Christ and be "essentially his own."[20] Schleiermacher insists that though "the individual influences" of Christ "no longer proceed directly from Christ" in the church, "something divine must exist. This something we call the Being of God in it, and it is this which continues within the Church the communication of the perfection and blessedness of Christ."[21] That activity done within the church which "prolongs the personal action of Christ" and is called the "common spirit of the Christian Church," Schleiermacher recognizes as corresponding "to all that Christ promised by the Holy Spirit."[22]

In that Christ leaves the Spirit as his continuing presence and activity on earth, the Spirit is the mediator of "Christ's new humanity to us, thereby extending Christ's redemptive work to us."[23] But how does the Spirit's mediation work within the church? Schleiermacher notes that it was not until the disciples began to bind and loose sin that Jesus's influence on them was internalized as their own "really spontaneous energetic activity."[24] "Hence, in order for Christ's activity to count as the disciples' own *spontaneous* activity, their activity must influence others—and in order for their activity to count as reproducing *Christ's* activity, it must have *his* influence on them."[25] The influence of Christ on the disciples is the work of the Spirit and the "common spontaneous activity which indwells all and in each is kept right by the influence of all . . . [and which] corresponds to all that Christ promised by the Holy Spirit and to everything that is represented as the Spirit's working."[26] In this way, "the Holy Spirit mediates the new humanity to us through the church's socially mediated norms."[27]

---

[17] Friedrich Schleiermacher, *The Christian Faith*, ed. H. R. Mackintosh and J. S. Stewart (Edinburgh: T & T Clark, 1928), 569.
[18] Ibid., 476.
[19] Ibid., 468.
[20] Ibid., 490–1.
[21] Ibid., 535.
[22] Ibid., 569.
[23] Kevin W. Hector, "The Mediation of Christ's Normative Spirit: A Constructive Reading of Schleiermacher's Pneumatology," *Modern Theology* 24, no. 1 (2008): 2.
[24] Schleiermacher, *The Christian Faith*, 568.
[25] Hector, "The Mediation of Christ's Normative Spirit," 6–7.
[26] Schleiermacher, *The Christian Faith*, 568.
[27] Hector, "The Mediation of Christ's Normative Spirit," 9.

Not unlike Schleiermacher, Barth's pneumatology unfolds in correlation to his construal of the nature and mission of the church. As he sees it, the hope of all people exists in the fact that between the first and final comings of Christ there is the middle time in which Christ comes to us "in the promise of the Spirit. This is His direct and immediate presence and action among and with and in us."[28] It is through the sending of the Spirit that the particularity of the person of Jesus Christ, in his saving work, is made available to all people. The Spirit's relationship to the saving work of reconciliation is both particular, in that the Spirit is the presence and action of Jesus Christ, and universal, in that the promise of the Spirit is present as the hope of all people, both Christians and non-Christians alike.

During this middle time, one of the main works of the Spirit is to form Christ's followers. The Spirit works "first in the community of God,"[29] even as the community as a whole "reaches its consummation" as the Spirit works in the lives of individual members.[30] The Spirit gathers the community in faith, builds it up in love, and sends it out into the world in hope. That the community "has the form of the Spirit means that . . . it is effectively established and gathered by the One who was and who comes, being not only ruled but continually nourished and quickened by Him. That is why it lives always in expectation, and even in imminent expectation."[31] Therefore, the community is called to weigh its present life and action in the balance of the future coming of Jesus. In his reading of the parable of the ten virgins, Barth suggests that the oil of the lamps is the witness of the Spirit in the waiting church.[32] In this way, the Spirit makes us to correspond to our true status as adopted children of God by making us "to be not merely an object in [Christ's] work but a subject in His service."[33] The determination of the elect, for both the individual and the community, is to actively participate in the love, activity, and work of the triune God by sharing in Jesus's own mission. Election involves being active apostles in service to God and correspondence to Jesus. In its apostolic election, the Spirit makes the community of faith to be "from the very first . . . one long calling upon God."[34] Moreover, the Spirit that has been given to the waiting church is always seeking "new dwelling-places and new witnesses."[35] For this reason, the church is instructed to obey the Spirit in order "that its witness makes new dwelling-places and evolves new witnesses."[36] By the empowerment of the Spirit, the church is led not out of the world but right back into it. It does so in faithfulness to its apostolic mission of witnessing to Christ's perfect work of reconciliation to a world still threatened by the powers of darkness.

THE SHAPE OF LIVING IN THE MIDDLE TIME OF THE SPIRIT

What can we determine about a distinctively Reformed contribution to pneumatology from this brief exploration of Calvin, Edwards, Schleiermacher, and Barth on the Spirit's

---

[28] *CD*, IV/3.1, 350.
[29] Ibid., IV/1, 154.
[30] Ibid., II/2, 314.
[31] Ibid., III/2, 505.
[32] See ibid., 506.
[33] Ibid., IV/3.1, 367.
[34] Ibid.
[35] Ibid., III/2, 506.
[36] Ibid.

work in Christian life and the life and mission of the church? The first thing to notice is that the Spirit is the power of salvation unfolded in and through Christian existence. Each of our Reformed representatives is faithful to the witness of the NT in seeing the Spirit as the Spirit of Christ. For Calvin, Christ's Spirit-anointing is for the sake of those who belong to Christ so that they have a share in this power. The Spirit makes disciples of Jesus in ways that radically transform human existence in the world. As they learn to love and practice justice, to partake in Christ's freedom, and to pray as Christ did in the Spirit, so by the Spirit they come to participate in Christ in the variegated realities of their daily existence. Therefore, "being in Christ is a being in the Spirit."[37] Lest we think that the Spirit as the existential power of salvation is somehow a diminishment of the Spirit's unique agency, Edwards's connection between the immanent and economic Trinity provides a vision by which to affirm that the Spirit flows directly out of the Spirit's place in the life of the triune God as God's infinite love of Godself. As God's love is repeated in Christians through new habits and dispositions, they are made to partake in the divine self-repetition of the love and beauty of God, which is the Spirit. In this way, the love made real in their lives is the Spirit living in them (1 Jn 4:12) and hence, their true participation in God's life.

Moving now to Schleiermacher and Barth, we find an interesting discussion regarding how the Spirit works in the ministry and mission of the community of faith. For Barth, the time of the church is the time between the resurrection and *parousia* of Christ. As we saw for Schleiermacher, it is through the church's socially mediated norms that the Spirit facilitates not only Christ's redemptive activity to others, but also the process by which our reception of Christ's redemptive activity becomes internalized as our own activity. In this way, Schleiermacher's pneumatology has the distinction of positing "no gaps between the Spirit's activity and human activity" since for Schleiermacher the "Spirit's personhood is not diminished by being intersubjectively mediated."[38] Moreover, a distinctive element of the Spirit's mediation of Christ's redemptive activity is the way it enables the church to continue to follow Christ in new settings. Within the ministry of the church, Schleiermacher observes that there is to be "a self-identical element, whereby it remains the same amid change, and a mutable element, in which the identity finds expression."[39] As redemption is the process of Christ's activity becoming a Christian's own, so the Spirit's work in the community of faith consists in making their activity that of Christ's own in ever-new situations. Here, the Spirit's work as the socially mediated repetition of Christ's new humanity "is not the supplementation of new occurrences but the movement of the singular occurrence out of the past into new historical moments."[40] The Spirit mediates Christ's saving work in and through the faith community in constantly changing circumstances.

This corroborates nicely with Barth's emphasis that the Spirit given to the church is always seeking new dwelling places and witnesses. The mission of the church is grounded upon its obedience to the ever-moving Spirit, which it must follow back out into the world in service. Indeed, "the spirituality of its existence" consists in the

---

[37] Gerhard Ebeling, *Dogmatik des christlichen Glaubens*, 3 vols. (Tübingen: Mohr, 1979), 3:63. Quoted in David W. Congdon, *The God Who Saves: A Dogmatic Sketch* (Eugene, OR: Cascade, 2016), 139.
[38] Hector, "The Mediation of Christ's Normative Spirit," 16.
[39] *The Christian Faith*, 582.
[40] Congdon, *The God Who Saves*, 143.

entire being and action of the church witnessing "in a sincerely worldly character" that it "belongs" to the world.[41] Insofar as this is the case, the church has been given Christ's Spirit in order that by its obedience to the Spirit there would occur new dwelling places and witnesses to the Spirit. Thus the Spirit makes the church participate in the mission of God in the world by empowering its vocation to witness to God's reconciliation of all things in Christ. As the community of faith lives out its vocation of witness, the "divine life in the Spirit" is actualized in it.[42] Linking this again with Schleiermacher's pneumatology, we find that a second distinctive element of Reformed pneumatology is the Spirit's empowerment of churchly existence to an active witnessing that extends "beyond itself into the world"[43] such that Christ's redemptive activity is taken up in new times and places and then passed on to others in new settings and circumstances.

This is instructive when we recall that the event of the church's pentecostal birth, by which the proclamation of God's saving work comes to each person in their particular cultural idioms even as all flesh is gifted with the poured-out Spirit, disabuses us of the notion of any one culture or location circumscribing the church's identity. Pneumacentric Christian life and ecclesiology in a Reformed key connects the vocation of the Christian and the faith community with the Spirit-empowered ability to witness to the good news of God's kingdom in a multiplicity of cultures and contexts. In that the Christian and the church live into the reality of a Spirit-empowered life and mission, so the history of this middle time is made to be "an act of divine life in the Spirit"[44] where the event of election in Jesus Christ is "inseparable from one's existential participation in it as an apostolic witness."[45]

It should not be surprising that in returning again to the distinctively Reformed emphasis on the transformation of life and on vocation as the call to participation in God's reconciliation of the world, we are brought to another distinctive of Reformed theology, the doctrine of election. What is instructive for our purposes here is to highlight the Spirit as the missing link between the Reformed doctrines of election and vocation. As Edwards highlights that the involvement of humans is crucial for God's self-repetition *ad extra*, so the Spirit is the transformative grace of God's union with humanity. As Katie Cannon notes, "This union is created by God, sustained by the love of Christ, and made continuous, morning by morning, by the Holy Spirit. We have been gripped by God's Spirit, touched by divine love, and redeemed by grace."[46] Both the church and the individual Christian have been elected to the vocation of witness. As this election is lived out in ever new and concretely particular Spirit-empowered repetitions of Christ's redemptive activity, so the co-witness of the Spirit within the human witness takes shape in the world in accord with the self-repetition of the divine love of the triune God.

---

[41]*CD*, IV/3.2, 776.
[42]See Ibid., II/2, 184.
[43]Ibid., IV/3.2, 779.
[44]Ibid., II/2, 184.
[45]David W. Congdon, "*Apokatastasis* and Apostolicity: A Response to Oliver Crisp on the Question of Barth's Universalism," *Scottish Journal of Theology* 67, no. 4 (2014): 466.
[46]Katie Geneva Cannon, "Transformative Grace," in *Feminist and Womanist Essays in Reformed Dogmatics*, ed. Amy Plantinga Pauw and Serene Jones (Louisville, KY: Westminster John Knox, 2006), 151.

FOR FURTHER READING

Kim, JinHyok. *The Spirit of God and the Christian Life: Reconstructing Karl Barth's Pneumatology*. Minneapolis, MN: Fortress, 2014.

van der Kooi, Cornelius. *This Incredibly Benevolent Force: The Holy Spirit in Reformed Theology and Spirituality*. Grand Rapids, MI: Eerdmans, 2018.

Lee, Sang Hyun. "Jonathan Edwards's Dispositional Conception of the Trinity: A Resource for Contemporary Reformed Theology." In *Toward the Future of Reformed Theology: Tasks, Topics, Traditions*, edited by David Willis and Michael Welker, 444–55. Grand Rapids, MI: Eerdmans, 1999.

Moltmann, Jürgen. *The Church in the Power of the Spirit*. Minneapolis, MN: Fortress, 1993.

CHAPTER TWENTY-ONE

The Theology of the Holy Spirit in Anglicanism

EPHRAIM RADNER

Anglicanism has no peculiar theology of the Holy Spirit.[1] The term "pneumatology" is a modern invention, appearing in Latin in the late sixteenth century and in English not until the seventeenth and especially eighteenth centuries. It initially referred to a broader metaphysical and then naturalistic discussion of "spirit" as a nonmaterial (or at best quasi-material) category of being. The term might refer to God-as-Spirit; but it even more often referred to created spiritual matter. The elision of these references, however, is part of the story of pneumatology's modern development, and the term makes its explicit appearance within Anglicanism around 1700. After that point, a convergence of interests turns pneumatology (in a modern sense) into a wider pneumatic vision or philosophy of reality. Only in the 1970s does "pneumatology" consistently refer to or become a specific doctrinal topic.[2] Before the later twentieth century, formal theological discussions of the Holy Spirit—in Anglicanism, but also in much of Protestantism and Catholicism as well—were generally haphazard and *ad hoc*. The Spirit was discussed in the context of the Trinity and of the redeemed human lives of Christians, often in a way that was interchangeable with and unsystematically mingled with discussions of "grace." That there might or should be a systematic theology of the Holy Spirit in particular is a modern preconception.

Anglican theological reflection on the Spirit, through the rise and until the final domination of modern pneumatological concerns, was traditional in its unsystematic interest, perhaps even more so than other Protestant traditions. This was largely because

---

[1] By "Anglicanism," what is meant here is the ecclesial tradition that has grown directly out of the reformed Church of England. This tradition is today embodied in a range of independent Anglican churches, scattered around the world and related to one another either formally, through mechanisms associated with the offices of the Anglican Communion, or in more informal ways, through shared forms of liturgy and devotional practice. There are an estimated 80 million plus Anglicans in the world today. Some figures and resources can be found at http://www.anglicancommunion.org. Some recent statistical material and analysis on the Anglican Communion can be found in David Goodhew, ed., *Growth and Decline in the Anglican Communion: 1980 to the Present* (New York: Routledge, 2017). A still useful overview, if somewhat out of date, is Stephen Neill, *Anglicanism* (London: Mowbray's, 1977). The fullest discussion is given in *The Oxford History of Anglicanism,* four volumes to date (Oxford: Oxford University Press, 2016–).

[2] The history of "pneumatology's" modern invention is traced in Ephraim Radner, *Profound Ignorance: Modern Pneumatology and Its Anti-modern Redemption* (Waco, TX: Baylor University Press, 2019).

the key formative theological instrument in Anglicanism was the Book of Common Prayer (BCP), whose general thrust was decidedly medieval in many important respects. The following essay summarizes aspects of this foundational Prayer Book perspective on the Holy Spirit and then notes several of the developing stages in Anglican attitudes to the Spirit, leading to the general integration of Anglican theology with modern pneumatological interests. This final evolution corresponds to the Prayer Book's own demise as an organizing theological force in Anglicanism and to the recognition of those existential demands that had, in part, fueled the rise of modern pneumatology since the seventeenth century and beyond.[3]

THE BOOK OF COMMON PRAYER

The appearance in 1549 of the first BCP constitutes the formative starting point of Anglican theology. Composed by the Archbishop of Canterbury, Thomas Cranmer (1489–1556), the BCP was imposed by Parliament as the sole form of worship to be used by the English people, and this exclusive usage made it the single most influential document in English church history, both in its positive force and in its role as a lightning rod of opposition. Cranmer, though a man of radical reformation doctrinal commitments in certain respects, tended to use and re-apply texts from the tradition in putting together the BCP, especially the Sarum rites that were dominant in southern England in the late Middle Ages. The majority of the Collects—common prayers associated with the liturgical calendar as well as prayers for special occasions—he simply translated, albeit magnificently, from the medieval store he had received. Whole services, like marriage or ordination, made use of these prayers. Even the scriptural Lectionary, which was so central to the BCP's focus, was, at least in its general form and purpose, something Cranmer inherited.[4]

If there was something deeply innovative in the BCP, at least in practice, it was the articulate sense of Scripture's central, almost exclusive, power in shaping Christian life and in communicating the very grace of God's transforming truth to the Christian people. Cranmer's Lectionary, which laid out biblical readings for daily and Sunday worship, was designed to provide congregations a vernacular reading of the entirety of Scripture—OT and NT and the entire Psalter at several reprises—over the course of a single year. The result was a deliberately scriptural prayer book, immersing worshippers in the biblical words both devotionally and cognitively, with the purpose of inner and outer—spiritual and moral—transformation. As evident in key liturgies like that of holy communion, a central feature and criterion of Christian faithfulness and the work of divine grace was "charity" toward one's "neighbor." "Common prayer" involved the common reading of Scripture in its entirety, bolstered by laws of common liturgical (and hence scriptural) practice that had as their aim the creation and preservation of a "commonwealth," that is, a good society, the British nation itself.

Earlier reformers, like the Bible translator William Tyndale (1494–1536), had held similar views about the ethical fruit of scriptural reading and had explained this in explicitly pneumatic terms: the Spirit, granted to the Christian in conversion and baptism,

---

[3]It is important to note that the term "pneumatology" in this chapter refers to the specifically early modern and modern developments in the discussion of "spirit" and "holy spirit" together.
[4]Online versions of the 1549 BCP and subsequent versions can be found at http://justus.anglican.org/resources/bcp/.

transforms the heart and will to "love the law" for the sake of a charitable common life.[5] The BCP itself, while it does not contradict this articulate focus, instead engages the Holy Spirit (in the nomenclature of "spirit," "ghost," "spiritual," and "ghostly") in a loose—if limited—way which can be placed under four headings. There are regular trinitarian doxological references to the Spirit; references to the Spirit in the context of prayers for repentance and absolution, as an agent of transformation, just as analogously, the Spirit works in baptism and ordination (granting "gifts" in the traditional medieval perspective); the Spirit is particularly linked to the petitioned social virtues of "unity" and "concord"; and finally, the realm of the "spiritual" is contrasted to that of the "flesh" as the location of a divine orientation and relationship.

None of this is extensive or synthesized into a specific "theology." More than the prayers themselves, the BCP assumes that Christians will hear about the Spirit most extensively simply through the in-course lectionary-based ecclesial reading of Scripture. The BCP orders this through regular worship that is shaped by the expected contours of creaturely life—birth, marriage, labor, illness, mutual care, and death—punctuating the round of weeks and years of a human life. The reality of the Holy Spirit is manifested within these God-given limits and does its work to order them into a "spiritual" realm of creaturely faithfulness, whose main forms are given in the life, teachings, death, and resurrection of Jesus, the incarnate Son of God, and whose lived vehicle is in the common life of family, community, and nation. A succinct summary of this vision is given in the BCP's Great Litany.

How pervasive in Anglicanism was the BCP's spare pneumatic vision, ordered on the one hand to a bare scriptural enunciation, and on the other to sustaining the peacefully socially ordered space of common mortality before Christ, such that "charity" in its relational pragmatics seemed the main pneumatic demonstration? The answer is, in a general way, "very pervasive." The vision was reflected in the official sixteenth-century Homilies, to be read in parishes and in official catechisms like Alexander Nowell's (1517–1602), as well as in the more elaborated theology of writers like Richard Hooker (1554–1600) and Lancelot Andrewes (1555–1626). The Homilies mention the Spirit only here and there, with their greatest focus on discussing the fear of death and pneumatic assurance and the authority of the British church versus Rome in assuring a common life of peace.[6] Nowell's Catechism, for all its proto-Puritan accents, orders all its teaching around a deuteronomistic view of the formative role of Scripture in creating and in being commended by the ordered community of family and nation. He notes the Spirit's role in applying scriptural truth, subordinating it mostly to the standard BCP focus on the "mysteries" of Christ.[7] Hooker, often considered England's greatest theologian of the period, stressed the "virtue" or power of the Spirit to use Scripture's bare reading to convert souls and shape over time a charitable social life in which "edification" in Christ

---

[5] Key texts of Tyndale in this regard are his Preface to the New Testament and *The Obedience of a Christian Man*, which can be found in the Parker Society edition of William Tyndale, *Doctrinal Treatises and Introductions to Different Portions of the Holy Scripture* (Cambridge: Cambridge University Press, 1848).

[6] For an accessible nineteenth-century edition, see *The Two Books of Homilies Appointed to be Read in Churches* (Oxford: Oxford University Press, 1859). See in particular I.9, "An exhortation against the fear of death" and II.16, "An Homilie concerning the coming down of the holy Ghost, for Whitsunday."

[7] Alexander Nowell, *A Catechism, Written in Latin: Together with the Same Catechism Translated into English by Tho. Norton, & C.* (Cambridge: The University Press, for the Parker Society, 1853). Key passages can be found on 114–15, 117, 139, 160–7, 170–3, 183–203, and 217–18.

was to be the main criterion of pneumatic discernment.[8] There is finally Andrewes, the great preacher and biblical translator, who has been called one of the most pneumatically centered of the period's Anglican theologians.[9] His long series of Pentecost Day sermons given over several years is an extraordinarily rich set of scriptural meditations. And while, like Hooker, he can be seen as espousing a pneumatically infused idea of human transformation, almost "Eastern" in its parallel to *theosis*, Andrewes will always return to the social and physical limitations of creaturely life as the boundaries for pneumatic manifestation, which occurs necessarily in the corporate church, in its sacraments, and through the gifts of charity, humility, and repentance.[10] This vision remains steady in the parochial formation of the Church of England through the end of the eighteenth century and well into the nineteenth.[11]

PNEUMATOLOGICAL CURRENTS

The forces that slowly moved against this general BCP vision, and converged in various ways, arose from different directions. Many of these, however, shared common motivations drawn from the seventeenth-century moral challenges of coercion, violence, and suffering and the increasingly complex demands of social diversity. While Anglican theologians like Hooker and Andrewes worried over the socially disintegrative threats of privatized or subjective understandings of pneumatic reality, early Puritan challenges to the BCP were less reflective of substantive theological differences with respect to the Spirit than they were founded on concerns about authority and the integrity of institutional office.[12] To be sure, these concerns had, and eventually demonstrated, pneumatic consequences. But apart from their wordiness, early Puritan alternatives to the BCP remained congruent with the latter's general *ad hoc* scriptural and social pneumatism. It was only as the seventeenth century wore on that a truly subjectivist understanding of the Spirit's work came to the fore in the quickly ramifying streams of original Puritan sources.

Hence, John Bunyan's (1628–1688) *Discourse on Prayer* (1662), written while in prison and two-thirds of which is devoted to what it means to "pray with the Spirit," lays out a relentless argument against formal (e.g., BCP) prayers that is bound to a complete theology of interiority, not so far from aspects of Quakerism.[13] Since "external" religious life—churches, offices, prayerbooks, sacraments, catechisms—all mask "hypocrisy," only the deepest work of the Spirit in the heart and will of an individual constitutes true Christian

---

[8]Richard Hooker, *The Works*, ed. The Rev. John Keble; 7th ed. rev. The Very Rev. R. W. Church and The Rev. F. Paget, 2 vols. (Oxford: Clarendon, 1888), vol. 2. Key texts: V. 38.1 (59–60); V. 27:2 (127–8); cf. 22:13 (105); 26:3 (124); V. 59 and 60, esp. 60:2 (255–6); V.22.1 (89); cf. 22:13 (105); 22:10 (99–101); V. 56.10 (252–3).
[9]Nicholas Lossky, *Lancelot Andrewes the Preacher (1555–1626): The Origins of the Mystical Theology of the Church of England*, trans. Andrew Louth (Oxford: Clarendon, 1991).
[10]Lancelot Andrewes, *Ninety-Six Sermons*, 5 vols. (Oxford: John Henry Parker, 1841), 3:107–401.
[11]See, for instance, the parish sermons by William Langford (1745–1814), both on the Creed and on the Litany, in *A Series of Familiar Discourses on the Apostles' Creed, the Lord's Prayer, and the Litany, with a Treatise on Confirmation and the Sacrament* (London: C. and J. Rivington, 1824 [1808]), esp. 93–5.
[12]Cf. the material gathered in Peter Hall, ed., *Documents Illustrative of the Liturgy of the Church of England: Vol. 1, The Puritan Prayer-Book* (Bath: Binns and Goodwin, 1848).
[13]John Bunyan, *A Discourse on Prayer* in *The Works*, 2nd ed. (London: E. Gardner, 1736), 1:443–62. That Quakerism is a certain kind of Puritanism in its understanding of the Spirit was a debated argument of Geoffrey F. Nuttall in his classic *The Holy Spirit in Puritan Faith and Experience* (Chicago: University of Chicago Press, 1992 [1947]).

"affection" and faith. "Sincerity"—Bunyan's greatest criterion of Christian authenticity—must, finally, be found beyond words themselves, and Bunyan will commend wordless praying "in the spirit" through "tears" and "groans." Even the Lord's Prayer falls short of such true pneumatic invocation. On the other hand, the ecumenically minded Puritan Richard Baxter (1615–1691) will take the same principle of pneumatic interiority and immateriality and argue that "sincerity" is ultimately invisible and thus indeterminate. Christians should therefore presume charitably the faith of others—even of pagans—based on visible fruit.[14] Baxter would become a leader in the search for building a church based on simple "fundamentals" of doctrine, leaving such charitable presumption about others to frame a comprehensive church of otherwise diverse opinions. Finally, someone like the congregationalist John Owen (1616–1683), who almost uniquely for another 200 years, applied the term "pneumatology" to discussions of the Holy Spirit in particular, focused on the demonstrative gifts of the Spirit and its sanctifying work to argue for identifying the true (and sincere) church wherever such demonstrations might appear. This proved the justification for a resolutely local and constantly shifting ecclesiology.[15] All of these theologians wrote out of the context of division, civil war, and exclusion.

Some Anglican theologians working in the same context sought to establish ecclesially unifying frameworks based on metaphysical grounds, mostly pneumatic in nature. The so-called "Cambridge Platonist" Ralph Cudworth (1617–1688), for instance, posited a "spiritual" reality shared by Christ with human beings that sanctified, but did so especially through the "conscience" of the individual.[16] The language of truth, for Cudworth, became attached to "pneumatic" holiness that is obediential but also transcendental, couched in the vocabulary of "breath," "fire," upward movement, and "fluttering." God himself was understood as the pinnacle of such rarified energy, which Cudworth identified with the "light." A turn to this interior light, as well as a respect for its integral worth in others, should be the basis for a faithful and unified church and nation. Cudworth's views here shared much with Baxter's. What was distinct was their claim to a pneumatic metaphysical basis. Other theologians, like Cudworth's colleague Henry More (1614–1687), engaged this basis yet further, now in an effort to establish the reality of God against what he saw as a creeping "atheism."[17] More posited a spiritual substance, immaterial yet extensive—"spirit"—that would prove the ground for both natural and supernatural worlds. "Movement at a distance," gravity, and what today we might call "paranormal" events were investigated and experimented with (Newton was a part of this larger set of interests), and "pneumatic" reality was theorized as foundational to the cosmos itself. Cosmic "spirit," to be sure, had already been proposed in the sixteenth century—one

---

[14] See Richard Baxter, *Knowledge and Love Compared*, in *The Practical Works of the Rev. Richard Baxter* (London: Millis, Jowett, and Mills, 1830), 15:9–295, esp. 150–60 and 231–43.

[15] John Owen, *Pneumatologia, or, A Discourse Concerning the Holy Spirit Wherein an Account Is Given of His Name, Nature, Personality, Dispensation, Operations, and Effects [...]* (London: F. Darby, 1676).

[16] On aspects of Cudworth's philosophy, see J. A. Passmore, *Ralph Cudworth: An Interpretation* (Cambridge: Cambridge University Press, 1951). His major metaphysical work was his three-volume *The True Intellectual System of the Universe* (London: Richard Royston, 1678). More accessibly, see "A Sermon Preached before the Honorable House of Commons at Westminster, March 31, 1647," found in the useful selection of the works of Cambridge Platonists, *Cambridge Platonist Spirituality*, ed. Charles Taliaferro and Alison J. Teply (Mahwah, NJ: Paulist, 2004), 55–94.

[17] Henry More, *An Antidote against Atheisme* (London: Daniel, 1653). Also, for a succinct metaphysical discussion, see Henry More, *The Immortality of the Soul* (London: T. Fletcher, 1659), 449–70.

thinks of Paracelsus and Giordano Bruno—but now the category was entering respectable Anglican theology and natural science and was receiving for the first time the designation of "pneumatology." It is important to recognize, however, that one of the motivations for these new theories was specifically moral, as the case of the philosopher Anne Conway's (1631–1679) careful theodicy of suffering makes clear.[18]

ANGLICAN PNEUMATOLOGICAL FERMENT

Within Anglicanism, we see these various interests, driven by the established Church's own difficult place in trying to hold together a now clearly religiously (and a-religiously) fractious populace, come together in the search for a pneumatic faith that could "comprehend" this straining reality of differences. The search in fact continues into the twentieth century, as pneumatology itself becomes a broadly accepted theological framework. In the early eighteenth century, however, this pneumatological perspective is only tentatively embraced by a few. But, precisely because of the Church of England's central social role, upheld in fact by its self-conscious comprehensive liturgical mission, the Anglican contribution to pneumatology in this modern sense is decisive, even as the pneumatological trajectory in question ends by subverting the founding character of Anglicanism's early *ad hoc* and scriptural theology of the Holy Spirit.

We can see this decisive shift in the work of Robert Clayton (1695–1758), a wealthy Irish Anglican and eventual bishop. Clayton set himself to expounding an explicit Arian Christology even while defending what he viewed as the integrity of biblical revelation. Practical Unitarianism of one kind or another was not uncommon among Anglican divines in his era, and observers had no trouble pointing fingers in that regard, blaming the general trend toward "rational religion" as precisely the doorway to a God—spirit or not—in whose being all was synthesized.[19] In Clayton's case, it is interesting that his own Arian argument was based on a larger metaphysical claim regarding "spirit." Clayton's 1750 *Essay On Spirit* (over 15 editions in the next 50 years) has been described as an extreme form of "animism" in its vision of the cosmos as a grand hierarchy of "spirit."[20] Only God is a "pure" Spirit, Clayton argued, without a body, and indivisible. Yet everything else is *also* "spirit" of some degree or another. The Son represents the final pneumatic entity between the rest of creation and God. Clayton offers a range of biblical and antique documentation for his metaphysic and discourses on angels, cherubim, and other spiritual beings in his exposition of the spiritual. Even the "Holy Spirit"—a kind of angel really—is subordinate to the pure Spirit of God and is designated as such in the course of scriptural custom and figuration.[21] To speak of the "Trinity" is permissible, Clayton concludes, as long as one does not confuse a figure of speech for an actual "consubstantial" entity.[22]

Clayton's purpose was to re-establish the need for metaphysical mediation, which in turn would guarantee the need for a (biblical) revelation. His Arianism was a logical cog

---

[18]Anne Conway, *The Principles of the Most Ancient and Modern Philosophy*, trans. and ed. Allison P. Coudert and Taylor Corse (Cambridge: Cambridge University Press, 1996).
[19]Paul Lim, *Mystery Unveiled: The Crisis of the Trinity in Early Modern England* (Oxford: Oxford University Press, 2012).
[20]Robert Clayton, *An Essay on Spirit: Wherein the Doctrine of the Trinity Is Considered in Light of Nature and Reason; as Well as in the Light in Which It was Held by the Ancient Hebrews* (Dublin: J. P. Droz, 1750).
[21]Ibid., chaps. 74, 79, and 108.
[22]Ibid., chap. 149.

in this argument, for it underlined the spiritual hierarchy in its intrinsically *mediated* nature: everything moves up a ladder of pneumatic being, and there must be a special mediator between "pure spirit" (God) and less pure spirits, including human beings. It was Clayton's scripturalism that marked a conceptual shift, for now, like a Trojan Horse; a basically anti-scriptural metaphysic was transposed into the midst of biblical faith, placing many of its created distinctives—bodies, sufferings, struggles, and unresolvable destinies (like Job's)—in tension with a deeper force for pneumatic integration. For Clayton, as for many non-trinitarians like him, a clearly moral religion was the only basis for a peaceful society. Only a world of spirits and hidden reward and punishment can justify such a moral order. Once spirit and ethics become centrally intertwined, however, everything shifts to a practical search to overcome the hierarchies, that is, a search for uniformities rather than distinctions in an effort to overcome lower levels of life and achieve the highest. Ultimately, "bodies" are problematic in this quest, but so are differences of any kind, which exist only as a general mark of distance from true Spirit that will finally become the measure of all things (as they are, in Clayton's theology, for all Christian doctrine).

Clayton's anti-trinitarianism was clearly unorthodox (he died just as heresy charges against him were being lodged). But orthodox Anglicans embraced the pneumatic logic behind it, increasingly using it to justify calls for a more tolerant and inclusive church, for an understanding of a more religiously pluralistic world, and for founding the need for "religion" at all. Wesleyan and Evangelical movements each took hold of aspects of these developing pneumatological tools, especially the more "demonstrative" elements of pneumatic naturalism in both its physical and moral components.[23] While the story is obviously complex, one can see the rise of Christian Romanticism and its embrace of philosophical idealism in the late eighteenth and nineteenth centuries as extensions of the larger logic, driven by similar impulses and engaging both conservative and more liberal theological outlooks. It was Coleridge's role to provide this logic a quite specific vocabulary and order—Spirit speaking to spirit—that proved so influential in modern Anglican theology. He did so primarily by locating the logic of pneumatic ethics now in the center of Anglican interest, that is, the reading of the Bible. *Aids to Reflection* (1825)—which picked up the earlier pneumatic reflections of, among others, Henry More—and then *Confessions of an Inquiring Spirit* (posthumously published in 1840) were the key works here, making their way to America as well. Coleridge used the framework of Kant and other German post-Kantian idealists, mixing it with mystical and political readings of his own, to describe a universe of real "facts" that can only be apprehended through symbolic means. The Bible as such is a supreme gathering of symbolic language for the truth, and its understanding is provided by the divine Spirit engaging the reflective capacities of the human spirit. Coleridge managed to marry a high scripturalism to an interior experientialism, which proved a fertile mix that was taken in many directions.

---

[23]On Wesley, see Richard E. Brantley, *Locke, Wesley, and the Method of English Romanticism* (Gainesville, FL: University of Florida Press, 1984) and Deborah Madden, ed., *"Inward & Outward Health": John Wesley's Holistic Concept of Medical Science, the Environment, and Holy Living* (London: Epworth, 2008). On the Anglican evangelical side, James Hervey (1714–1758) is an influential figure in his biblical naturalism, which fit well with developing pneumatic understandings of nature. His most popular work, *Meditations and Contemplations* (1746–1747), went through numerous editions.

Coleridge was more than typical, however, for he exercised direct influence, if often unsystematic, on a range of subsequent nineteenth-century Anglican thinkers—from Keble and Newman to Maurice and Westcott—as well as on radical liberal critics like Bp. Colenso and finally into what develops in the United States as a peculiar pneumatological culture that directly shapes central aspects of American Anglicanism.[24] Some of his thinking, less directly and ironically (given his own deep distaste for evangelicalism), even flowed into developing strands of affective Protestantism—one recalls Coleridge's positive interest in the charismatic Irvingites[25]—and mixed in with other pneumatic interests within a common culture in which holiness expressions would eventually integrate with full-fledged Pentecostal or charismatic orientations. In any case, the search for the "something else" "behind it all" and the refashioning of scriptural and Christian claims into linguistic symbols that speak to a deeper "religious experience" become, though only gradually, the standard way by which modern religious truth is explained and enunciated until the present. This search is, furthermore, the main way by which modern pneumatological thinking entered into Anglican thinking and finally, after the twentieth centuries' two world wars, became a formative element in much of Western Anglicanism.

THE DECISIVE SHIFT

As idealistic philosophy itself became increasingly adopted and adapted in Britain, the notion of a fundamental metaphysical reality of "spirit" that was also identified with the "absolute" character of God led to various versions of panentheistic theology, like that of Andrew Seth Pringle-Pattison, and although held within relatively firm traditional ecclesial constraints, it eventually poured out beyond them.[26] What largely seems to have turned a set of relatively recondite intellectual currents into a broad theological movement, popularly embraced, was the experience of the First World War and its shattering of just the ecclesial and social confidence that might have held together pneumatic expansiveness with shared social coherence.

After the First World War, Christian writers who had direct experience of the stresses and carnage of the battlefield, sought new avenues of theological sense-making. Among the most influential in his time was Geoffrey Anketell Studdert Kennedy (1883–1929), a celebrated chaplain whose subsequent preaching and writing career (along with political

---

[24] A standard work is still Charles Richard Sanders's classic study, *Coleridge and the Broad Church Movement* (Durham, NC: Duke University Press, 1942). A more recent, if partisan, outline here is Graham Neville's *Coleridge and Liberal Religious Thought: Romanticism, Science and Theological Tradition* (London: I. B. Tauris, 2010). The American line entered into the wider literary and philosophical culture around people like Emerson, but it can be seen as rooted in later nineteenth-century Episcopalian theology, as in the work of William Porcher Dubose, whose *The Reason of Life* (New York: Longmans, Greene & Co, 1911) uses a self-consciously "spiritual" reading of the Logos to provide a thoroughly pneumatological picture of evolutionary progress of pneumaticization through history. On Dubose's vision in its broad liberal reach, see Robert Boak Slocum, *The Theology of William Porcher Dubose: Life, Movement, and Being* (Columbia, SC: University of South Carolina Press, 2000).

[25] See Sue Zemka, *Victorian Testaments: The Bible, Christology, and Literary Authority in Early-Nineteenth-Century British Culture* (Stanford, CA: Stanford University Press, 1997), 13–67, esp. 53–67.

[26] The story is told in Gary Dorrien's *Kantian Reason and Hegelian Spirit: The Idealistic Logic of Modern Theology* (Malden, MA: Wiley-Blackwell, 2012). Chapter 7, "Idealistic Ordering: Lux Mundi, Andrew Seth Pringle-Pattison, Hastings Rashdall, Afred E. Garvie, Alfred North Whitehead, William Temple, and British Idealism" deals with the British, and largely Anglican, context.

activism) included widely read poetry, sermons, and books.[27] Studdert Kennedy was particularly effective, as he spoke directly to younger men returning from the war, in questioning traditional notions of divine sovereignty, and he attempted to replace this with a highly personalistic faith in an evolutionary vision of kenotic love, whose suffering would prove the vehicle for the historic growth of "life" itself. Studdert Kennedy saw himself as an apologist for the continued relevance of the Christian church, but his message was basically anti-institutional, and his identification of a moving "force" within the world—divine "life"—partook of a range of earlier pneumatological categories, even if he himself was philosophically vague about it all. Much more explicit in this vein was the theologian Charles Raven (1885–1964), who came to have a central academic role at Cambridge. Raven had also been through the war and himself had suffered from shellshock. Seeking to found his theological vision on more scientific grounds (and Raven was himself a skilled naturalist), he fastened on the then-popular theories of evolutionary emergentism.[28] His volume *Creator Spirit* proposed a comprehensive pneumatological evolutionary scheme in which creation and its various entities, with human beings at the summit, were all on the way to a pneumaticizing transformation. Jesus stood as both the pinnacle of this evolutionary movement and also as its expressive principle, the figure through whom Spirit worked its way via a form of natural selection (hence the evolutionary *principle* of the Cross) toward a fulfilled spiritual consciousness. Raven's work in some ways paralleled Teilhard de Chardin's (which he knew), though with an explicit pneumatological center, and though refined over the years, it remained true to the pneumatological naturalism of his post–First World War vision.

In both Studdert Kennedy and Raven's cases, pneumatology in its modern instrumental categories functioned as a kind of theodicy that was able to relativize Anglicanism's constraining ecclesial forms. The evolutionary aspect of the Spirit's encompassing movement both explained suffering and promised progress. It could also articulate the limitations of traditional Christian claims and practices, blaming them for their static complicity in human misery. The articulation and wide acceptance of so-called "Spirit Christologies" after the Second World War[29]—emphasizing the human Jesus's pneumaticization rather than his divine incarnation—was in full keeping with this outlook. Indeed, Geoffrey Lampe (1912–1980), one of the key players in this movement, had himself shared experiences in the Second World War similar to Studdert Kennedy's.[30] Some Spirit Christologies were founded on a pneumatic metaphysical monism, but some were driven by nonevolutionary ethical commitments, which saw the Spirit as undergirding all efforts at social amelioration.[31]

---

[27]See, for instance, G. A. Studdert Kennedy, *I Believe: Sermons on the Apostles' Creed* (New York: George H. Doran, 1921), 40–5 and 220–9. See also a recent anthology, with a useful introduction by Kerry Walters: G. A. Studdert Kennedy, *After War, Is Faith Possible? The Life and Message of Geoffrey "Woodbine Willie" Studdert Kennedy* (Eugene, OR: Cascade, 2008).
[28]Charles Raven, *The Creator Spirit: A Survey of Christian Doctrine in the Light of Biology, Psychology, and Mysticism* (Cambridge, MA: Harvard University Press, 1927).
[29]For a useful overview, see Myk Habets, "Spirit Christology: Seeing in Stereo," *Journal of Pentecostal Theology* 11, no. 2 (2003): 199–234.
[30]G. W. H. Lampe, *God as Spirit* (Oxford: Clarendon, 1977).
[31]David N. Power's "The Holy Spirit: Scripture, Tradition, and Interpretation," in *Keeping the Faith: Essays to Mark The Centenary of Lux Mundi*, ed. Geoffrey Wainwright (Philadelphia, PA: Fortress, 1988), 152–78 is interesting because, though written by a Catholic, it is based on a celebrative response to a late nineteenth-century essay by the Anglican Charles Gore.

The latter became a staple of Western Anglican commitments, driven by pragmatic concerns over ministry and mission but funded nonetheless by earlier pneumatological tools. By the 1970s and 1980s, this ethical pneumatology had managed to upend the traditional BCP vision on both its scriptural and creaturely grounds: the new synthetic moral vision tied to the Spirit's life and to its emancipatory mission relied on smoothing out (or eliminating) scriptural and creaturely disjunctions in favor of an integrative social project whose prosecution reflected some of the original worries over theodicy that drove early modern pneumatological concerns. It is mostly in this context that one should read the theological program (as opposed to the experiential significance itself) of the Anglican charismatic renewal that emerged in the United States and Britain in the 1970s and then moved to areas like Singapore, where it remains vibrant. This program traded off of a familiar pneumatological focus on personalized, affective, and often anti-institutional concerns, many of which were tethered to the promise of sublating the normal constraints of mortality. The charismatic movement was, in any case, clustered in a demographic that had missed the last war and was now the full beneficiary of the health transition that itself was buffering common social experience from the constant existential assaults of mortality.[32]

The unsynthesized character of Anglicanism's acceptance of modern pneumatological thinking, however, is important to emphasize. Diverse pneumatological aspects put down roots in various churches and in parts of churches, but this also called out diverse rejections of these theological outlooks, creating a range of ecclesial tensions. It is no surprise that outside the West, for instance, the BCP vision has, at least until recently, maintained a much greater traction.[33] The East African Revival of the 1930s to the 1970s was less pneumatologically than christologically oriented, and it managed to stay integrated within strong BCP church cultures.[34] This was true in other areas where revival happened within relatively resilient Anglican contexts of BCP sensibility, as in Singapore, drawing in a wealth of scriptural pneumaticism without however reordering common life in broad pneumatological directions. Pentecostal and Free Evangelical charismatic movements, however, have influenced African and other non-Western Anglican churches more recently at the same time as impulses toward political liberalization have gained force. The theological ancillaries of these elements have often proved to be in tension with deeper commitments. In fact, though, both these new Pentecostal and politically liberal elements reflect the inroads of modern pneumatology within the broader Anglican Communion. Accompanying these new theological infusions, one sees throughout the Communion

---

[32]Cf. Douglas James Davies, *Mors Britannica: Lifestyle and Death-Style in Britain Today* (Oxford: Oxford University Press, 2015), 166. On the tension in the charismatic movement between mortality and the claim for a healing that might overleap mortality, see the discussion of the death of David Watson, a leader of the Anglican charismatic movement in the UK, in the biography by Teddy Saunders and Hugh Sansom, *David Watson: A Biography* (London: Hodder & Stoughton, 1992) as well as Watson's own *Fear No Evil: A Personal Struggle With Cancer* (London: Hodder & Stoughton, 1984). On the broader theological role of the twentieth-century so-called Health Transition, with its doubling of the life-expectancy rate in places like the UK and North America, see Ephraim Radner, *A Time To Keep: Theology, Mortality and The Shape of a Human Life* (Waco, TX: Baylor University Press, 2016), chap. 2.

[33]See for a limited and already dated overview Miranda K. Hassett, *Anglican Communion in Crisis: How Episcopal Dissidents and the African Allies Are Reshaping Anglicanism* (Princeton, NJ: Princeton University Press, 2007).

[34]Philip Turner, "The Wisdom of the Fathers and the Gospel of Christ: Some Notes on Christian Adaptation in Africa," *Journal of Religion in Africa* 4, no. 1 (1971): 45–68; Kevin Ward and Emma Wild-Wood, eds., *The East African Revival: History and Legacies* (Burlington, VT: Ashgate, 2012).

more and more common elements of BCP worship being left aside, with respect to both order and particular forms of lectionary-based or creedally organized services. Many of these traditional elements are viewed as no longer reflecting the existential character of developing societies, both economically and in terms of health and life-expectancy. The once generally common BCP is disappearing, either through diverse Prayer Book revisions or through simple disuse in favor of local alternatives.[35] It would be wrong to say that Anglicanism's BCP vision no longer exists, but it does so only sporadically and marginally in the West and only under the strains of alternative formative perspectives elsewhere. Where this is leading is not clear. The drastic decline in membership of most Western Anglican churches stands as a new question in the face of pneumatological thinking that has not yet been addressed seriously in a theological way and might end up reorienting modern pneumatology's own assumptions.[36] A proper pneumatology of the church, for instance, would have to be able to explain how, in the Holy Spirit's ordering, the church that is experiencing a pneumatic awakening also suffers tremendous conflict and decline. Whether such a question constitutes a dead-end or a creative spur to modern Anglican pneumatology remains to be seen.

CONCLUSION

The BCP's "theology of the Holy Spirit" was non-pneumatological in a modern sense in that it did not attribute to the Spirit an integrative function, either theologically or experientially. Rather, the BCP located the Holy Spirit only within the encounter of mortal life with its divine Creator as described by Scripture in a straightforward and unsystematized fashion. Everything the scriptures said about the Holy Spirit (as about the Father and the Son) was believed to be utterly true, yet so were the limits of mortal existence within which that truth was received and lived. The very shape of the BCP quite deliberately promoted this understanding of Scripture's truth and mortal life's inescapability. These convictions, furthermore, were bound to another element that shaped Anglican understandings of the Holy Spirit: a powerful social ethic that was the corollary of that fundamental acceptance of created mortality (focused on family, community, and nation) and that defined pneumatic gifts and virtues in terms that furthered and expressed this ethic (humility, charity, order, and "edification"). Ecclesial integrity and coherence thus became criteria for pneumatic authenticity. What counted as pneumatological development in early modernity both occurred around the edges of this fundamental outlook concerning the Holy Spirit and also eventually pushed directly against it in the form of converging strands of Puritan and more radical as well as rationalistic alternatives.

These alternatives often reflected reactions or desired resolutions to what were viewed as problematic aspects of the BCP vision, rooted as it was in static created forms as well as accepted ignorance before the oftentimes intellectually obscure claims of divine truth. Thus, developing modern pneumatological reflection involved a search for intellectual coherence (versus perceived scriptural confusion), release from mortal limitation (versus the acceptance of mortal constraints), individual or personal freedom (versus experienced

---

[35]For a good overview of the history of Prayer Book Revision as well as new directions, see J. Barrington Bates, "Expressing What Christian Believe: Anglican Principles for Liturgical Revision," *Anglican Theological Review* 92, no. 3 (2010): 455–80. Bates offers his own evolutionary pneumatological vision.
[36]See Goodhew, ed., *Growth and Decline in the Anglican Communion*.

social coercion), and, in an almost summarizing way, metaphysical comprehension (versus unintegrated experience). The social and individual disaster of the First World War—along with the cascading sequels of the twentieth century's conflagrations—turned these various quests into a common and unavoidable assault on the plausibility of the BCP's Christian existential framework. That framework now seemed, in its *ad hoc* acceptance of the givens of Scripture and existence, incapable of assimilating unbearable suffering and the wreckage of dissolved social relations. No new theology has taken its place wholescale. Rather, what we see today is the spread and acceptance, without synthesis, of all the various pneumatological alternatives that had gradually been forming since the seventeenth century, even while, of course, more traditional Anglican pneumatic perspectives and experiences carried on in an increasingly desultory fashion, fraying at the seams along with the unraveling of a coherent ecclesial existence. Because Anglicanism itself has been a profoundly ecclesial Christian tradition and because modern pneumatology has itself been motivated by strong anti-ecclesial impulses, Anglicanism and pneumatology often stood toward each other in postures of unease that, today, have failed to relax.

FOR FURTHER READING

The Book of Common Prayer: The Texts of 1549, 1559, 1662. Edited by Brian Cummings. Oxford: Oxford University Press, 2011.

Brantley, Richard E. *Locke, Wesley, and the Method of English Romanticism.* Gainesville, FL: University of Florida Press, 1984.

Brownell, Thomas. *The Family Prayer Book, Or, The Book of Common Prayer . . . Accompanied by a General Commentary.* New Haven, CT: Sidney's Press: 1823.

Clayton, Robert. *An Essay on Spirit: Wherein the Doctrine of the Trinity Is Considered in Light of Nature and Reason; as well as in the Light in Which It was Held by the Ancient Hebrews. . . .* Dublin: J. P. Droz, 1750.

Dorrien, Gary. *Kantian Reason and Hegelian Spirit: The Idealistic Logic of Modern Theology.* Malden, MA: Wiley-Blackwell, 2012.

Lampe, G. W. H. *God as Spirit.* Oxford: Clarendon, 1977.

Lossky, Nicholas. *Lancelot Andrewes the Preacher (1555–1626): The Origins of the Mystical Theology of the Church of England.* Translated by Andrew Louth. Oxford: Clarendon, 1991.

Nuttall, Geoffrey F. *The Holy Spirit in Puritan Faith and Experience.* Chicago: University of Chicago Press, 1992 [1947].

Radner, Ephraim. *Profound Ignorance: Modern Pneumatology and Its Anti-modern Redemption.* Waco, TX: Baylor University Press, 2019.

Raven, Charles. *The Creator Spirit: A Survey of Christian Doctrine in the Light of Biology, Psychology, and Mysticism.* Cambridge, MA: Harvard University Press, 1927.

CHAPTER TWENTY-TWO

The Holy Spirit in Wesleyan Perspective

JASON E. VICKERS

To understand pneumatology from a Wesleyan perspective, it will help to locate the Wesleyan theological tradition within the wider landscape of Christianity. As a form of the Christian religion, Wesleyanism is something of a curiosity. On the one hand, it is easily the foremost living expression of the Pietist revolution in Protestant theology and spirituality.[1] Whatever else Wesleyans are, we are Pietists to the core. With our Pietist forebears and contemporaries, we place a strong emphasis on religious experience and on the transformation of the heart. As a form of Pietism, Wesleyanism is truly "heart religion."[2] On the other hand, Wesleyanism springs from eighteenth-century Anglican soil. So we are also heirs of the great Anglo-Catholic tradition. With our patristic and medieval Catholic forebears and with Reformation and modern-day Anglicans, we have a strong sacramental orientation. One might even say that, contrary to popular misconceptions, Wesleyanism is a hyper-sacramental theological tradition.

In this essay, I will develop an account of pneumatology from a Wesleyan perspective that reflects both the Pietist and Anglican aspects of Wesleyanism. I will begin by discussing the work of the Holy Spirit from a Pietist point of view. I will then pause to note a popular misconception of Pietism, namely, that it is a form of Christianity that rejects mediation. This will set the stage for a discussion of the Anglican aspect of Wesleyan

---

[1] The term "Pietism" is itself a matter of controversy in part because scholars use the term to refer to a wide range of renewal movements within Lutheran, Reformed, and Anglican theological traditions. In this essay, I will be using the term to refer exclusively to the Methodist, Wesleyan Holiness, and Pentecostal branches of the Pietist family tree. For more on the genealogy of Pietism, see Dale Brown, *Understanding Pietism* (Grand Rapids, MI: Eerdmans, 1978); Carter Lindberg, *The Third Reformation: Charismatic Movements and the Lutheran Tradition* (Macon, GA: Mercer University Press, 1983); and F. Ernest Stoeffler, *The Rise of Evangelical Pietism* (Leiden: Brill, 1971). Also, I am well aware that some scholars would question whether present-day Pentecostals should be considered Pietists. My own reading of the history suggests that Pentecostalism is an extension of Pietism in its Methodist and Wesleyan Holiness forms. For more on this, see Randall J. Stephens, "The Holiness/Pentecostal/Charismatic Extension of the Wesleyan Tradition," in *The Cambridge Companion to John Wesley*, ed. Randy L. Maddox and Jason E. Vickers (Cambridge: Cambridge University Press, 2010), 262–81. See also, Donald W. Dayton, *Theological Roots of Pentecostalism* (Grand Rapids, MI: Zondervan, 1987) and Henry H. Knight III, ed., *From Aldersgate to Azusa Street: Wesleyan, Holiness, and Pentecostal Visions of the New Creation* (Eugene, OR: Pickwick, 2010).

[2] See John Wesley, "The Circumcision of the Heart," in *John Wesley's Sermons: A Collection for the Christian Journey*, ed. Kenneth J. Collins and Jason E. Vickers (Nashville, TN: Abingdon, 2013), 591–9.

pneumatology. Finally, I will conclude by suggesting that, in pneumatology, the Pietist and Anglican aspects of Wesleyanism come together in a way that is both highly compelling and unusually generative for the work of ministry in the world.

THE HOLY SPIRIT AND THE TRANSFORMATION OF THE HUMAN HEART: WESLEYANISM'S PIETIST HERITAGE

The Pietist revolution in Protestant theology revolves around one central idea, namely, that there is more to being a Christian than believing rightly or being good. From a Pietist point of view, it is simply not enough to have right beliefs about God or to be a well-mannered and well-regarded member of society. Rather, *becoming* a Christian requires a deeply personal, life-changing encounter with the living God, and *being* a Christian requires an ongoing relationship with the living God. As such, the Christian life is not something that human beings can achieve on our own, either through intellectual assent to the cognitive contents of the Christian faith or through moral earnestness. It requires divine action from beginning to end. If we are to encounter the living God, it is going to require action from God's side.

This brings us to the first work of the Holy Spirit from a Pietist perspective. Before we can come to know and love God, the Holy Spirit must first awaken us to a double truth. First, the Spirit must awaken us to the truth about ourselves, namely, that we are not living the way God intended us to live. For instance, the Spirit must help us see that we are living primarily out of fear rather than freedom and love. Consequently, we spend our lives desiring and pursuing everything under the sun except for the one thing that can truly make us happy, namely, a relationship with the living God that revolves around deep trust and gratitude. Thus the Spirit must help us see that in our obsessive attempts to acquire the things of this world, we are actually ruining the world and destroying the very possibility of our own flourishing. The Spirit must awaken us to the startling reality that we will never experience true joy and happiness if we continue on the path that we are on. And the Spirit must reveal to our minds and our hearts the painful reality that we have deeply disappointed and even offended the living God.

Were awakening only to involve coming to grips with the truth about ourselves, most clear-thinking people would be terrified. Fortunately, the Spirit also awakens us to a fundamental truth about God, namely, that despite our self-absorption and even open rebellion, God desires to set us free from the tyranny of fear so that we can know true happiness and joy that come from placing our trust in almighty God. However, we need to be very careful here. From a Pietist point of view, it is not simply a truth *about* God that the Spirit reveals to our hearts and our minds. Rather, the Spirit enables us to see that the living God is even now approaching—that he is coming toward us—and his name is Jesus Christ.

Having awakened us to the truth about ourselves, the Holy Spirit enables us to repent and to confess Jesus as Lord. The crucial thing to note here is that the Spirit does not simply enable us to confess belief in Jesus as a historical figure from the past who might serve as an inspiration for political revolution today. The Spirit also enables us to discern that the One who lived and died a criminal's death on the cross in the first century is the same One who is now drawing near, not to condemn us but to heal and save us and ultimately to transform us from within. Thus, from a Pietist point of view, confessing

Jesus as personal Lord and savior is not a matter of mere intellectual assent to the proposition "Jesus is Lord"; rather, it is an act of deep personal trust, the chief manifestation of which is a ready willingness to surrender the totality of our lives to the One who is present now. We do not simply become believers; we become followers and disciples who will go wherever the Lord calls us to go and who will do whatever he asks us to do.[3] This act of confession, which is simultaneously an act of submission and surrender, involves such a transformation and alignment of the mind, heart, affections, and will that it is nothing short of a miracle. In other words, it is something that we can only do with the help of the Holy Spirit.

To this point, we have been describing the Spirit's work in awakening, justifying, and regenerating. Once we have placed our trust in Jesus, we believe that the Spirit continues to be at work in our lives, transforming our hearts and minds in ways that bear a growing resemblance to Jesus. We believe that the Spirit works within us to draw us ever more deeply into a dynamic relationship with the risen Lord and to enable us to hear the voice of the Lord and to follow him ever more closely all the days of our lives. This work of God in us radically transforms the way we relate to the world. Instead of relating to the world out of fear (trying to possess and control the world for ourselves), we begin to relate to the world in freedom and love. Instead of treating people as stepladders or doorstoppers, we find ourselves yearning to help and serve people. Instead of viewing people as our enemies, we begin to see all people as our friends. In short, our lives are increasingly characterized by grace, mercy, love, and compassion. All of this is the Spirit's work of sanctification.

We could easily say much more here. For instance, we could talk about the fruit of the Spirit and the Spirit's work in entire sanctification and Christian perfection.[4] However, we have said more than enough to give the reader a sense for how the Pietist aspect of Wesleyanism shapes the way that Wesleyans view the work of the Spirit. In summary, we view the work of the Holy Spirit primarily in terms of the transformation of human lives through a deep, personal encounter with the risen Lord. And this means that, for Wesleyans, pneumatology is inextricably intertwined with Christology and soteriology.

Unfortunately, few forms of Christianity have been more subject to caricature and popular misconceptions than Pietism. For example, in contemporary Christian theology, "Pietism" commonly denotes a form of Protestant Christianity that rejects mediation in favor of the Holy Spirit's direct, unmediated infusion of grace into the human heart. This view of Pietism is shared by critics and advocates alike. For example, Kathryn Tanner, a critic, complains that, for Pietists, the Holy Spirit works "immediately—both instantaneously and directly, *without any obvious mediating forms*—in exceptional

---

[3]The extraordinary participation by Wesleyans and other Pietists in the modern missionary movement is an inspiring testimony to this truth. See Ruth A. Daugherty, *The Missionary Spirit: The History of Mission of the Methodist Protestant Church, 1830–1939* (New York: GBGM Books, 2004); Robert Sledge, *"Five Dollars and Myself": The History of Mission of the Methodist Episcopal Church South, 1845–1939* (New York: GBGM Books, 2005); Linda Gesling, *Mirror and Beacon: The History of Mission of the Methodist Church, 1939–1968* (New York: GBGM Books, 2005); J. Steven O'Malley, *"On the Journey Home": The History of Mission of the Evangelical United Brethren Church, 1946–1968* (New York: GBGM Books, 2003); Robert J. Harman, *From Missions to Mission: The History of Mission of the United Methodist Church, 1968–2000* (New York: GBGM Books, 2005).

[4]For more on entire sanctification and Christian perfection, see John Wesley, *A Plain Account of Christian Perfection*, ed. Randy L. Maddox and Paul Chilcote (Kansas City, MO: Beacon Hill, 2013).

events, rather than in the ordinary run of human affairs, upon the interior depths of individual persons, apart from the operation of their own faculties, in ways that ensure moral probity and infallible certainty of religious insight."[5] Roger Olson, an advocate, agrees, celebrating Pietism as a movement in which the Holy Spirit deepens "individuals' spirituality" and renews church life through an "inward, *unmediated*, transforming experience of God."[6]

While some forms of Pietism may indeed reject mediation, Wesleyans do not. If anything, Wesleyans are hyper-sacramental in orientation and outlook. For starters, we believe that the Holy Spirit enables us to discern and encounter the healing and transforming presence of our risen Lord in the sacraments of baptism and holy eucharist. Likewise, we believe that the Holy Spirit enables us to hear the risen Lord speaking to our hearts through preaching and the reading of Holy Scripture, which is to say, through the ministry of the Word. In other words, Wesleyans are deeply committed to the mediation of divine grace through the ministry of Word and Sacrament.

THE HOLY SPIRIT AND THE SACRAMENTAL LIFE OF THE CHURCH: WESLEYANISM'S ANGLICAN HERITAGE

As noted at the outset, the Wesleyan tradition has deep roots in Anglican soil. John and Charles Wesley were both ordained elders in the Church of England, as was their father before them. Nurtured in Anglican theology and spirituality, the Wesley brothers inscribed the heart and soul of prayer book religion deep within the movement that now bears their name. Like their Anglican forebears, they believed that the Holy Spirit mediates divine grace through the ministry of Word and Sacrament. Let us look at each of these in turn.

With respect to the ministry of the Word, most Wesleyans distinguish between the written and the preached Word, affirming the mediation of God's presence and power to heal and to save through both. For example, John Miley, a nineteenth-century Methodist theologian, offered the following instructions on reading Scripture: "When, therefore, we read the Scriptures, we should remember that God is speaking to us in his own word, as with his own voice, and that while we read we stand in his Divine presence, and should reverence him who speaks." He continues,

> Think you the high-priest would have approached thoughtlessly or carelessly the mercy-seat, upon which, and amid the hovering wings of the cherubim, the Shechinah, or Divine Presence, rested, and from which the Divine oracles were given out by an audible voice? And no more should we come thoughtlessly or carelessly to the reading of God's sacred, living word. While we read, we should reverence him *in whose presence we are*, and whose word we read.[7]

---

[5] Kathryn Tanner, "Workings of the Spirit: Simplicity or Complexity?" in *The Work of the Spirit: Pneumatology and Pentecostalism*, ed. Michael Welker (Grand Rapids, MI: Eerdmans, 2006), 87 (emphasis added).
[6] Roger E. Olson, "Pietism and Pentecostalism: Spiritual Cousins or Competitors?" *Pneuma* 34, no. 3 (2012): 335 (emphasis added).
[7] John Miley, "The Duty of Reverence in Approaching God," in *The Ohio Conference Offering; or Sermons and Sketches of Sermon, on Familiar and Practical Subjects, from The Living and the Dead*, ed. Maxwell P. Gaddis, 3rd ed. (Cincinnati, OH: The Methodist Book Concern, 1854), 218 (emphasis added).

Similarly, Wesleyans routinely refer to the mediation of God's healing presence and transforming power in connection with preaching.[8] For example, Bishops Francis Asbury and Thomas Coke instructed early American Methodist preachers that the purpose of preaching was to bring people to "a *present* Saviour," showing "the willingness of Christ *this moment*" to bless them and to bring "a present salvation *home* to their souls."[9] A few years later, in a letter to his bishop, a nineteenth-century Methodist preacher named Anthony Banning described a visit that he made to a Native American village in Sandusky, Ohio, saying, "Soon after preaching began . . . I truly felt the place awful by reason of the presence of God."[10] Similarly, upon visiting an early Methodist preaching service, a Quaker exclaimed, "It is the Power of God: the Lord is in this place!"[11]

Just as Wesleyans associate God's presence with the written and spoken Word, there is also a long history of locating and affirming God's presence in the sacraments of eucharist and baptism. For example, in the eighteenth century, Charles Wesley stressed that in the eucharist Jesus Christ was "present in his power to heal."[12] In another hymn, he declared, "His presence makes the feast."[13] In the early nineteenth century, Francis Ward described a communion service that took place in a camp meeting in New York, saying, "The Lord spread a table for his people in the wilderness, and hundreds partook of the sacramental bread and wine, the symbols of the Redeemer's passion." He then added, "There they commemorated his dreadful sufferings and covenanted with him anew, and there they received fresh effusions of his love."[14] In the early twentieth century, various members of the Church of God (Cleveland, TN) reported that, in the eucharist, (a) they were "greatly blessed with the presence of the Lord"; (b) "God was there"; (c) "the Holy Ghost manifested Himself"; (d) "Jesus himself was present"; and (e) Jesus "seemed to manifest his presence."[15] Also in the early twentieth century, a member of the Pentecostal Holiness Church testified, "At 3:00 P. M., we had the sacrament, and we can say the presence of the Lord was so very real and near to us."[16]

With respect to the mediation of grace through baptism, one particularly interesting testimony has to do with opposition to infant baptism. Fanny Newell, an early nineteenth-century Methodist, maintained that it was the presence of God at the baptism of her infant son that convinced people to embrace infant baptism, saying,

---

[8]The strong association of the presence and work of the Spirit with preaching can be seen in the way Wesleyans describe preaching. It is not uncommon, for instance, for Wesleyans to use the phrase "Spirit-filled" when describing both preachers and sermons. Similarly, older generations of Wesleyans would sometimes say that a preacher had "the anointing"—a term that was meant to convey that the Holy Spirit was clearly present in his or her preaching.

[9]*The Doctrines and Discipline of the Methodist Episcopal Church, in America* (Philadelphia, 1798), 86 (emphasis original).

[10]Anthony Banning, "Extract of a Letter from Anthony Banning to Bishop M'Kendree," *Methodist Magazine* 3 (April 1820): 155.

[11]As quoted by Lester Ruth, *A Little Heaven Below: Worship at Early Methodist Quarterly Meetings* (Nashville, TN: Kingswood, 2000), 45.

[12]Charles Wesley, *Hymns on the Lord's Supper* (Madison, NJ: The Charles Wesley Society, 1995), 29.

[13]Ibid., 69.

[14]As quoted by Lester Ruth, *Early Methodist Life and Spirituality: A Reader* (Nashville, TN: Kingswood, 2005), 214.

[15]As quoted by Chris E. W. Green, *Toward a Pentecostal Theology of the Lord's Supper: Foretasting the Kingdom* (Cleveland, TN: CPT, 2012), 110–12.

[16]As quoted in ibid., 126.

> At a quarterly meeting held in Cabot, we devoted our son to God in the holy ordinance of baptism. And so manifest was the approbation of that God, to whom we set him apart by this sacred seal, that error stood back, and one of the most rigid said, "Let them who think it their duty to baptize infants do it, and the Lord bless them."

Newell continued,

> A young woman, who had waited to be baptized by immersion on this occasion, rose in a distant part of the crowded assembly, and said with a loud and quick voice, "Let me go to heaven with little children" [and] rushed through the crowd, kneeled down, and was baptized by pouring. This gave such a shock to the people, *and the glory of God was so manifest* that all appeared to be satisfied that God owned the ordinance.[17]

We could easily provide countless other examples of Wesleyans bearing witness to the healing presence and transforming power of God mediated through the ministry of Word and Sacrament.[18] The important thing to note at this stage, however, is how Wesleyans view the role and work of the Holy Spirit in mediation. As some of the testimonies make clear, Wesleyans believe that what is mediated in the ministry of Word and Sacrament is nothing less than the saving presence of our Lord and savior Jesus Christ. It is Christ's healing presence that is mediated through baptism and eucharist, and it is the risen Lord himself who speaks to our hearts through Holy Scripture and preaching. As Pietists, we believe that the presence and work of the Spirit in the mediation of God's redeeming presence takes place primarily in the minds and hearts of the worshippers themselves. The Holy Spirit opens the eyes of our hearts to the healing presence of the Lord in holy communion. And the Holy Spirit enables us to hear the risen Lord speak through preaching and Holy Scripture.[19]

THE HOLY SPIRIT AND EXTRAORDINARY MEANS OF GRACE: WESLEYANISM'S HYPER-SACRAMENTALITY

Wesleyanism represents a dynamic bringing together of Pietism and Anglicanism. On the one hand, the Pietist impulse in Wesleyanism stresses the work of the Holy Spirit within. As such, Wesleyans place a strong emphasis on the interior life, beginning with the Spirit's awakening and illumining activity and continuing in the Spirit's enabling, transforming, and empowering activity. On the other hand, the Anglican impulse stresses the mediation of divine grace in the form of real presence in the sacraments and divine speaking through Scripture and preaching. Therefore, the Spirit's work in the interior life of human beings is not self-referential or self-enclosed; rather, it directs our minds and our hearts to something exterior, namely, the risen Lord who draws near to us in the sacramental life of the church.

But Wesleyanism does not just represent a bringing together of Pietism and Anglicanism with respect to the ministry of Word and Sacrament; it also represents a Pietist adaptation

---

[17] As quoted by Ruth, *Early Methodist Life and Spirituality*, 218–19 (emphasis added).
[18] For more on this, see Jason E. Vickers, "Holiness and Mediation: Pneumatology in Pietist Perspective," *International Journal of Systematic Theology* 16, no. 2 (2014): 192–206.
[19] This does not mean that Wesleyans deny that the Spirit's own presence is mediated through the sacramental life of the church. On the contrary, Wesleyans believe that the fullness of the triune God is present in Word and Sacrament.

of Anglicanism's sacramental orientation to a broader sphere. Rather than restricting the presence of Christ to the *ordinary* means of grace, John Wesley insisted that the Spirit made manifest Christ's presence through *extraordinary* means as well. This adaptation, which can be viewed as an expansion of the doctrine of mediation, was deemed necessary by Wesley on primarily pragmatic grounds. In eighteenth-century England, a growing number of people did not attend church in the first place, which raised the pressing question: Outside the church's sacramental life, how does the Spirit work within the human heart to bring about awakening, illumination, and a recognition of Jesus as Lord?

For Wesley, the answer to this question came from the revival that he was now helping to lead. The English or Wesleyan revival was not taking place primarily in the church's regular services. Rather, it was occurring in fields and other irregular venues. Of particular importance was field preaching, a phenomenon in which people would gather in an outdoor setting to listen to someone preach. From Wesley's perspective, the fact that so many people were being awakened by the Holy Spirit to the truth of the gospel and subsequently enabled to submit their lives to the lordship of Christ suggested that the Lord himself was present and at work in these events. Thus, Wesley came to distinguish ordinary from extraordinary means of grace.[20]

At this stage, we should emphasize that Wesley believed that the Spirit would ultimately lead people to the church, and he stressed the importance of active participation in the ordinary means of grace. For example, he was particularly insistent that the Methodists participate in holy communion as often as possible.[21] But Wesley was also intensely committed to the work of evangelism and missions, and he came to believe that the Holy Spirit made manifest the redeeming presence of Christ in all sorts of extraordinary places and ways as well, ranging from farmers' fields to prison cells.

Far from rejecting mediation, then, Wesleyans tend to embrace what can only be called a kind of hyper-sacramentalism. Across space and time, we have stressed that the Spirit makes manifest to human minds and hearts Christ's redeeming presence both within and beyond the sacramental life of the church. Within the sacramental life of the church, we believe that the Spirit reveals the presence of the risen Lord in the sacraments properly so called (baptism and holy eucharist) and enables us to hear our Lord speak in preaching and through the reading of Holy Scripture. Beyond the sacramental life of the church, we also believe that the Holy Spirit is present and at work in the hearts and minds of unbelievers everywhere, awakening them to the truth of the gospel and enabling them to discern the saving presence of Christ in every corner of God's good creation.

This strong hyper-sacramental orientation is what makes Wesleyanism such a dynamic and compelling movement in the history of Christianity. On the one hand, we affirm that God is present and at work in the ministry of Word and Sacrament and therefore in and through the lives and work of the ordained. On the other hand, we affirm that the Holy Spirit works outside the church and in the lives and work of the laity as well. Thus, we have a long and impressive history of commitment to church and para-church ministries as well as to ordained and lay ministries. Indeed, when it comes to the work of ministry, we Wesleyans are a highly creative and industrious bunch. We are constantly scanning

---

[20] For more on Wesley's understanding of the means of grace, see Karen B. Westerfield Tucker, "Wesley's Emphases on Worship and the Means of Grace," in Maddox and Vickers, *The Cambridge Companion to John Wesley*, 225–44.

[21] John Wesley, "The Duty of Constant Communion," in Collins and Vickers, *John Wesley's Sermons*, 84–93.

both local and global horizons for new places where people need to hear the good news of the gospel. And we enter those places with a quiet confidence that the Holy Spirit is already at work, preparing people for a life-changing encounter with the risen Lord.

FOR FURTHER READING

Cunningham, Joseph W. *John Wesley's Pneumatology: Perceptible Inspiration*. Ashgate Methodist Studies. London: Routledge, 2014.

Dabney, D. Lyle. "Pneumatology in the Methodist Tradition." In *The Oxford Handbook of Methodist Studies*, edited by William J. Abraham and James E. Kirby, 573–86. Oxford: Oxford University Press, 2009.

Jones, Beth Felker. *God the Spirit: Introducing Pneumatology in Wesleyan and Ecumenical Perspective*. Wesleyan Doctrine Series. Eugene, OR: Cascade, 2014.

Knight III, Henry H., ed. *From Aldersgate to Azusa Street: Wesleyan, Holiness, and Pentecostal Visions of the New Creation*. Eugene, OR: Pickwick, 2010.

Starkey, Lycurgus M., Jr. *The Work of the Holy Spirit: A Study in Wesleyan Theology*. Nashville, TN: Abingdon, 1962.

CHAPTER TWENTY-THREE

Quaker Pneumatology

CHERICE BOCK

IS THERE A QUAKER DOCTRINE OF THE HOLY SPIRIT?

The Religious Society of Friends (Quakers) began in 1647 when George Fox, after much soul searching, Bible reading, and years of dissatisfaction with the dead ritualism of the Church of England of his day, experienced a divine encounter. He then traversed the countryside of England, preaching about his direct experience and encouraging others that they, too, had access to God inwardly without need for a priestly mediator or physical sacrament. While this story includes similarities to the beginnings of some other denominations, Fox's encounter was deeply personal and relational. Through it, he felt invited into communion with Christ, and he also felt called to share about his experience with others.

After climbing Pendle Hill in the Lake Country of England in 1652, Fox saw a vision of a "great people to be gathered."[1] Though his spiritual experience was personal, he was called not only to more inward contemplation, but also to gather a community of those who sought similar experiences and to speak out against priests who preached the word of God but did not act is if they knew the enlivening Present Teacher whom Fox had encountered.

In some ways, one could say that all Quaker theology and practice can be boiled down to pneumatology: the heart of the tradition is anchored in the belief that each person has mystical access to the divine, which places all people on an equal plane and requires personal responsibility for seeking that inward connection.

One could also argue that Friends have very little in the way of a systematic doctrine of the Holy Spirit. It is common in historical Quaker writings to see the persons of the Trinity used interchangeably and without concern for separating the work of each person. Brinton states, "Friends, being in general neither Trinitarian nor Unitarian, could almost be called Multiplarian if their vague and ambiguous theology could elicit a name."[2] For example, of the transformative spiritual experience in 1647 mentioned earlier, Fox recorded:

> And when my hopes in [priests] and in all [people] were gone, so that I had nothing outwardly to help me, nor could I tell what to do, then, Oh then, I heard a voice which

---

[1] George Fox, *The Journal of George Fox*, ed. J. L. Nickalls (Philadelphia, PA: Philadelphia Yearly Meeting, 1997 [1694]), 133.
[2] Howard H. Brinton, "The Quaker Doctrine of the Holy Spirit," *Quaker Religious Thought* 1, no. 1 (1959): 5.

said, "There is one, even Christ Jesus, that can speak to thy condition," and when I heard it my heart did leap for joy. Then the Lord did let me see why there was none upon the earth that could speak to my condition, namely, that I might give him all the glory; for all are concluded under sin, and shut up in unbelief as I had been, that Jesus Christ might have the pre-eminence, who enlightens, and gives grace, and faith, and power. Thus, when God doth work who shall let [prevent] it? And this I knew experimentally.[3]

In this description of the experience, Fox mentions "a voice," "Christ Jesus" (and "Jesus Christ"), "the Lord," and "God," but he does not mention the Holy Spirit. He gives credit to the Lord who "could speak to my condition," to Jesus Christ "who enlightens," and to God who "doth work." While it is possible that he thinks of the voice he heard as the voice of the Holy Spirit, he does not name it as such. What was important to him was that he had the experience, he was inwardly transformed, and it was affected through Christ rather than through the priests' instructions or other tactics with which he tried to fill his internal void.

It is also difficult to articulate a Quaker doctrine of the Holy Spirit due to the fact that for at least the last two centuries, not all Quakers have necessarily thought of themselves as Christians, though many do.[4] Therefore, identifying a pneumatology that would be adhered to by all Friends is virtually impossible.

In itself, however, this point says a great deal about Quaker pneumatology: the reason one can call oneself a Quaker without adhering to Christianity is that Friends emphasize personal mystical experience and deemphasize dogma. In some branches of Friends, this spiritual experience might be connected to Jesus or some other god, or it may be expressed in humanist or non-theistic terms. In other branches of Friends, adherence to Christian belief is considered quite central, and Evangelical Friends tend to believe and act in ways similar to other evangelical Christians.

What ties most Friends together is the idea that there is "that of God in every one":[5] the Spirit of God is accessible and recognizable to each human being.[6] Not only is this Spirit accessible, but connection to the Spirit is essential to being a Friend, according to early Quaker theologian Robert Barclay.

> Even if thousands were to be convinced intellectually of the truths that we maintain, if they could not feel this inward life, and their souls did not turn away from unrighteousness, they would add nothing to us. For this is the bond by which we

---

[3] Fox, *Journal*, 11.
[4] The earliest Friends did see themselves as followers of Jesus Christ, as can be ascertained from the name they called themselves, the Religious Society of Friends, referring to the passage in John 15 where Jesus states, "You are my friends if you do what I command you" (Jn 15:14). They thought of their movement as "primitive Christianity revived," a term William Penn used as the title for his 1696 book. Friends today who do not consider themselves Christians argue that early Friends were a product of their time and culture and that although they were naming a spiritual force that cannot be limited to the Christian faith, they used language that was familiar to and acceptable within their cultural context.
[5] While most Friends would generally agree with this idea, some might qualify the use of the term "God," recognizing that every person has something of what we think of as "God" in them but not necessarily agreeing on whether or not that something is an entity external to humanity.
[6] Fox, *Journal*, 263.

become "one spirit with him" (1 Cor. 6:17) and so with one another. Without this no one can worship with us.[7]

The Spirit serves as a lens through which Friends view the world. The Spirit helps interpret the Bible, points out places in the self and the broader community that need transformation, and invites members into relationship with the divine and with one another. Friends attempt to listen to the Spirit individually and collectively when trying to make decisions. While this pneumatology allows for radical freedom in discernment, it also leaves Friends doctrine open to a wide variety of interpretations. Since each person can listen to the Spirit and is encouraged to act on what each hears, every person's interpretation is as valid as another.

Therefore, although there is much emphasis on the Spirit who is present in the midst of the gathered community and who guides meetings for worship and business in the Quaker tradition, this Spirit is not necessarily differentiated from (or identified with) God the Father or Jesus Christ. This entity is often referred to by names other than those generally used in systematic theology, including (but not limited to): "Inner Light," "Pure Wisdom," "the Light of Christ," "the Present Teacher," "the Seed," "the Root," and so forth. Friends do not often discuss the economy of the Trinity but focus mainly on the way they experience the Spirit as active in their lives, recognizing this (for those who are Christians) as the Spirit of the same One who spoke to the Hebrew prophets and became incarnate in Jesus.

Given these difficulties of describing an authoritative Quaker pneumatology, I will define pneumatology from the Friends perspective as "reflection on experience of the Present Spirit." As Roswith Gerloff put it, "Spirituality is pneumatology in action. Pneumatology is spirituality in reflection."[8]

For Friends, theology flows from the interaction between personal and communal experience of the Spirit in worship and meditation and from active engagement with living one's faith in real life. Therefore, Quaker pneumatology is inextricably linked with Quaker practice and reflection on that practice to discern the continued direction of the Spirit.

The rest of this article will explain the Quaker concept of the Inner Light and discuss connections between the personal and communal aspects of Quaker pneumatology. Given the broad spectrum of Quaker belief, I cannot claim to speak for all Quakers. What I can do, however, is to state my own Quaker perspectives, with the recognition that not all Friends will agree with my conclusions.

ONGOING REVELATION AND THE INNER LIGHT

Robert Barclay's (1648–1690) *Apology for the True Christian Divinity as Professed by the People Called Quakers* remains the seminal Quaker theological treatise. Trained at the Roman Catholic Scots College in Paris, Barclay became a Quaker in 1666. He placed emerging Quaker thought and practice in conversation with the Bible and historical

---

[7]Robert Barclay, *Barclay's Apology in Modern English*, ed. D. Freiday (Manasquan, NJ: Hemlock, 1967 [1678]), 255. By this, Barclay does not mean people are not allowed to worship with Friends if they are not participating in this spiritual bond but that this bond (Barclay's original term was "cement") is what occurs when one is truly worshipping with the gathered community.
[8]Roswith Gerloff, "Theory and Practice of the Holy Spirit," *Quaker Religious Thought* 41, no. 2 (1975): 2.

theologians. As pertains to pneumatology, Barclay utilized a trinitarian framework to describe the importance of the Spirit, emphasized ongoing revelation, and developed the Quaker idea of the Inner Light. Of the Trinity, he said:

> The only knowledge of the Father is by the Son
> The only knowledge of the Son is by the Spirit
> God has always revealed [God's] self to [God's] children by the Spirit
> These revelations were formerly the main purpose of faith
> That purpose continues to be the object of faith to this day.[9]

In other words, while the Father and Son are divine persons, the only way we know the Godhead (apart from Jesus's incarnation) is through the Spirit. He posits that the "main purpose of faith" is experience of the Spirit. Nothing else is necessary, although the Bible is helpful in discerning what is of the Spirit and what is not. Barclay is not attempting to downplay the importance of the Bible—in fact, he states that inward revelation will not contradict the Bible—but he emphasizes that without the presence of the Spirit as interpreter, theological doctrines and biblical passages are lifeless. He likens this to a living body compared to a corpse.[10]

According to Barclay, a Christian is one who has the Spirit of Christ. "Who will deny that many illiterate [people] may be saved and that many have been saved?" he queries.[11] All have access to the Spirit and can follow that Spirit regardless of whether they have heard the name of Christ, while some who know the Bible and church teachings only have outward knowledge and "remain altogether ignorant of the inward and unmediated revelations of God's Spirit in the heart."[12]

Barclay worked to describe what it is in the human being that can recognize and connect to the Spirit. He says that all people have access to God, and Friends often use terms such as "Inner Light," "Inward Light," "Light of Christ," or simply "Light" to describe that to which people are connecting. The use of light imagery is a reference to the description of the light that enlightens every person in John 1 and to other imagery regarding enlightenment versus darkness in the biblical witness. Barclay states that this Inner Light is not a part of the human being but is something that we can sense that is outside ourselves. While we can use our brains to reason, and this can help us understand some things about our faith, our rational faculties cannot connect us to the experience of this Inner Light.

He further distinguishes the Inner Light from the conscience because the conscience is marred by sin.[13] Our consciences are connected to our sociocultural norms and values. A Catholic may feel a prick of conscience if eating meat during Lent, or a Jew may feel a prick of conscience if eating shellfish, but others who do not have these cultural assumptions will not be troubled in conscience when engaging in these practices.

To further the analogy of light and explain the difference between the Light and the conscience, Barclay likens the conscience to a candleholder while Christ's Spirit is the flame. A candleholder is a natural location for a light to burn, but it cannot bring light; it

---

[9] Barclay, *Apology*, 23.
[10] Ibid., 40, 32.
[11] Ibid., 22.
[12] Ibid.
[13] Ibid., 92; cf. Tit. 1:15.

can only wait to be lit. Without the light, the candleholder is without purpose, just as our consciences are not of much use to us without the enlivening Spirit. As the candleholder is meaningless except in anticipation of a candle, so also church traditions remain empty without the presence and direction of the Spirit.[14]

EQUAL ACCESS TO THE HOLY SPIRIT

An important aspect of Quaker pneumatology is that since everyone has access to the Inner Light, it creates an egalitarian community. Friends note in biblical passages such as Joel's prophecy recounted in Acts 2:17-18 that God's Spirit would be poured out on all and that they would prophesy (including sons and daughters, young and old, slaves, and men and women). Friends are also inclined to note Gal. 3:26-28, which says that people are baptized in Christ through faith and are one in Christ (including Jew, Greek, slave, free, male, and female). Not only did early Friends read about these outpourings of the Spirit in the Bible, but they themselves experienced people from all walks of life prophesying and sensing the presence of the Spirit in profound ways.

Friends pneumatology was an expression of their faith that they could take the Bible at its word: all had access to the Spirit. This pneumatology was confirmed in their experience, and, simultaneously, their experience opened the scriptures to them so that they could understand the ongoing revelatory nature of the Spirit's presence.

From the beginnings of the Quaker movement, women and men from any class were encouraged to speak, preach, teach, prophesy, write, and travel in ministry as the Spirit prompted and when this leading was confirmed by the gathered community. At the time, these testimonies of inward and personal revelation of the Spirit, the ability for the individual to interpret Scripture via the Holy Spirit, the rights of women and men of various classes, and the ability to receive salvation outside of the church hierarchy were all seen as very threatening to the power structures of the church and state. Friends did not appoint pastors or priests, and they practiced the sacraments spiritually without the need for physical elements or authorized clergy. Each moment was seen as sacramental, and each person was perceived as a vessel through whom the sacred could enter the world.

Barclay said, "Since Christ has provided such a good instructor [the Spirit], why is it necessary to lean so much on the traditions and declarations with which so many Christians have burdened themselves?"[15] Rather than following the traditions of church and society that they saw as empty at best and unjust at worst, Friends read the Bible with the help of the Holy Spirit and felt convicted to act in ways that got them into trouble. These included refusing to tip their hats, to address "superiors" with titles, or to practice other indicators of deference to the class system because we are all one in Christ Jesus. They also refused to swear oaths based on Mt. 5:33-37. Due to these practices and the fact that it was illegal for people to meet for worship outside the Church of England, many in the first generation spent time in jail. During their incarceration, they recognized the horrible conditions of the jails and the unjust conditions (such as poverty) that resulted in many individuals ending up in jails.

Based on these experiences, their sense of leading from the Spirit, and their reading of the Bible's calls to justice for the oppressed, Friends became involved in prison and

---

[14]Ibid., 92–3.
[15]Ibid., 35.

mental health reform, advocated for changing laws that severely disadvantaged the poor, and advocated for laws stipulating freedom of religion. While Friends did not start out as a denomination that emphasized social justice, this became one of the main tenets of the Friends tradition. Friends analyzed Scripture in connection with their own experience and context, allowing the Inner Light to illuminate injustice and to offer courage as they stood up for what they perceived to be truth and justice in the face of persecution.

In the centuries since, Friends became early advocates of the abolition of slavery in the United States and Britain, continued to work toward prison and mental health reform, advocated for women's rights, and felt called to follow literally Jesus's command to be peacemakers. They wanted to live in a way that took away the "occasion for all wars," feeling a deep conviction that came to be called conscientious objection to war.[16] Again, Friends read the Bible with the help of the Holy Spirit, and rather than rationalizing away the passages that command love of enemy and living as peacemakers, they chose to trust that Jesus meant what he said and that the Spirit would help them carry out this work in the world. Since conscientious objection was not originally legal in England or the New World, Friends felt the Inner Light inviting them to live out this testimony and therefore bore the consequences. Eventually, conscientious objection became legal, and many Friends have carried this testimony across the denomination's history.

As Friends seek the Light, search the scriptures, and examine their experiences, many feel the leading of the Spirit to work toward active peacemaking and to actively get in the way of policies and practices that necessitate war. This emphasis on peace also flows out of the belief in the equality of all people to recognize and know God's Spirit; it also stems from a humble conviction that it is God's job to decide who lives and dies. While we can participate in a range of creative solutions and disruptions to ensure that people are not continually oppressed, there is always the hope that each one—even our enemies—will see the Inner Light. By killing enemies or in other ways treating them unjustly, we take away their chance to connect with that Light.

While equality of all people has long been a testimony held by Friends, it is not always practiced well. Friends worked tirelessly on the Underground Railroad and in other ways to eliminate the practice of slavery, but there are very few Friends of color in the United States, Canada, and the United Kingdom. Friends became successful in business and education, and as such, they have tended to be drawn from the white, upper-middle class, educated elite in the northern hemisphere; these are not always open in practice to the Spirit working through those of different class, education, or race than themselves. Since Friends practice can feel fairly intellectual, divorced as it is from physical objects and bodily ritual, it can come across as elitist, open only to those with the intellectual ability and privilege of education to interpret Scripture and tradition in light of scholarship and Friends history. Friends in the United Kingdom, the United States, and Canada tend to be introverted and reserved, as befits a worship practice based around silence, and this can feel constraining to those who experience the Spirit in louder, more active, or more charismatic ways.

On the current scene, Friends are working on issues related to the lingering effects of colonialism, as the numbers of Friends in Latin America and Africa now far exceeds the number of Friends in the United States, Canada, and the United Kingdom, but the power and wealth structures of Friends are slow to follow demographic shifts. Friends are also

---

[16] Fox, *Journal*, 399–400.

divided over the rights of gender and sexual minorities to marry and hold leadership positions. As Friends work through these current areas of disagreement, Quaker pneumatology is being put to the test. Can we all sense the same Spirit, and will that Spirit still draw us together so we become one in Christ? If we spend time discerning and we come to different, deeply held convictions, how do we know who is hearing the Spirit? These are some of the pressing pneumatological questions facing the Friends today.

MYSTICAL AND PROPHETIC, INWARD AND COMMUNAL

At its best moments, Quaker pneumatology holds together both personal, mystical experience of the divine and a call to loving action in communities. This is both a personal and communal experience and works best when practiced in a group. Friends are encouraged to spend time in silent prayer and meditation on their own, to practice listening and being attentive to the Spirit, and to develop holy expectancy. They may sense or hear the Spirit while alone and in turn have a message for themselves personally, another person, their worshipping community, or someone outside their faith community.

Friends are also invited to seek the Spirit together during meetings for worship. Traditionally, this happens through meeting in silence and waiting expectantly for the Spirit to speak to and through the gathered members. In the case of pastoral Friends, all those who gather are still expected to come to worship ready to listen for the movement of the Spirit. While a pastor or group plans the worship elements ahead of time, the planning is to be done through listening to the Spirit, and it is the work of the Spirit, rather than the leaders, that brings vitality to the worship experience.

While the Friends tradition includes a strong mystical and contemplative element, times of personal and communal contemplation are expected to lead to faithful action. Friends practice communion through communing directly with the Present Spirit. Similarly to traditions believing in transubstantiation of the communion elements, Friends believe that the actual presence of God is made manifest through that intentional time of silent communion. While the Spirit is always present and active, Friends work to become attentive to what the Spirit is doing. The moments of communion within the worship service are not the only times to encounter the living God, but the individual carries the Inward Light throughout their days. However, something special happens when Friends gather. Isaac Penington described gathered meetings for worship thus: "They are like a heap of fresh and living coals, warming one another as a great strength, freshness, and vigor of life flows into all."[17]

Due to the emphasis on each person's ability to attend to the Spirit within, it is often assumed that Quakerism is a radically individualistic religion, but that is not the design of the Friends tradition. Instead, the Friends practice of corporate listening means that each person humbly adds their understanding and insight, whether in a meeting for worship or a meeting for business,[18] trusting the gathered community to discern together in a way that is more complete than the individual can alone. Friends recognize that it is all too easy to come to a decision based on logic alone or on unexamined cultural assumptions.

---

[17]Isaac Penington, *Works of Isaac Penington*, 4 vols. (Sherwood: David Hesterton, 1863 [1681]), 4:55.
[18]Commonly called "a meeting for worship with a concern for business."

Therefore, special attention is paid to dissenting voices to see if an individual may be hearing a prophetic word that can help the community live more fully in accordance with the Inner Light.

Contrary to popular opinion, Friends do not seek consensus on a given decision in their business meetings. They do aim to hear the will of the Spirit and seek consensus that the group has articulated their best discernment of the sense of the meeting, that is, the direction the Spirit is leading them. This is not always the same thing as everyone liking the decision. As Friends gather together to discern around business items, each Friend holds a radical responsibility to seek the Inner Light, to speak one's piece of truth as one is called and able, and to submit one's own preferences and opinions to the will of the Present Spirit. This requires an incredible amount of trust, for Friends must trust one another to approach the situation with a similar willingness to let go of personally desired outcomes and to do the difficult work of truly listening to the Spirit speaking in themselves and through each other.

Friends abolished the hierarchy of the priesthood and the divine right of the monarchy, believing in the simple yet frightening idea that God can and does speak to the people. Friends cannot rely on a priest or a political ruler to discern for them, for they have personal responsibility in their own faith journey. Each one can be a prophet, a messenger from God, in connection with the Spirit; therefore, each is called to live a life of radical faithfulness that challenges unjust social and religious situations across time and place. While this can feel scary and vulnerable, and it is a practice that is wide open to error and misuse, the top-down authority of the priesthood and monarchy are replaced with communal fellowship of the gathered body. One is not left alone to discern the will of the Spirit, but one has the benefit of a group of peers and mentors—a body of Christ gathered with the Spirit's Light illuminating each step.

To practice Quaker pneumatology, then, requires conviction and humility, courage and vulnerability, trust and grace. And when the gathering waits expectantly and the Spirit moves in power, the beauty and joy of the experience are indescribable.

To conclude, the Religious Society of Friends is a small denomination that is far from perfect, but it can be seen as part of a long stream of mystical traditions that recognizes and participates in the creative and prophetic power of the divine. In this way, it is connected to all other renewal movements in which the inbreaking power of the Spirit cannot be ignored and truth, depth, wisdom, and love are practiced in fearless and joyful community. Its pneumatology is both radical and ordinary, completely orthodox and utterly prophetic. While Friends are in a sense a denomination, the deeper meaning of the name "Friends" is that we can all be Friends of the Present Teacher as we journey together, lit by the Inner Light.

FOR FURTHER READING

Barclay, Robert. *Barclay's Apology in Modern English*. Edited by D. Freiday. Manasquan, NJ: Hemlock, 1967 (1678).

Fox, George. *The Journal of George Fox*. Edited by J. L. Nickalls. Philadelphia, PA: Philadelphia Yearly Meeting, 1997 (1694).

Gerloff, Roswith. "Theory and Practice of the Holy Spirit." *Quaker Religious Thought* 41, no. 2 (1975): 2–17.

Steere, Douglas V., ed. *Quaker Spirituality: Selected Writings*. Mahwah, NJ: Paulist, 1984.

CHAPTER TWENTY-FOUR

The Holy Spirit and Anticlericalism

J. ALEXANDER SIDER

If there is a standard story about the doctrine of the Holy Spirit in sixteenth-century Anabaptism, it goes like this: The early Anabaptists were wary of the spiritual freedom that was exercised by other radicals; therefore, they thought of the Holy Spirit as working primarily through the mechanism of communal discernment and were suspicious of individuals when they claimed to have been uniquely inspired by God.

As stories go, this is tidy, setting clear boundaries for who counted as Anabaptist and who did not. Unfortunately, it is also question begging because what it meant to be an early Anabaptist was by no means as clear as the story implies. Moreover, there is not much evidence among the earliest Anabaptists for the kind of communal hermeneutics through which contemporary Mennonite theologians have sought to filter and control the doctrine of the Holy Spirit.[1] Instead, the earliest Anabaptists had pneumatologies in which the Holy Spirit enlivened the individual soul, principally in baptism, but also in the discipline of scriptural exegesis. In the following pages, I begin with historical considerations that present the problem of who counted as an Anabaptist in the sixteenth century and then move to a consideration of the doctrine of the Holy Spirit as it shaped baptism and biblical interpretation in first-generation Anabaptism, concentrating on Balthasar Hubmaier. While Hubmaier's example probably cannot be generalized—his theology of baptism differed markedly, for instance, from that of the Swiss Brethren—investigating his pneumatology does create a platform for comparison to other early Anabaptists.[2]

HISTORICAL CONSIDERATIONS: WHO COUNTS?

When considering what sixteenth-century Anabaptists thought about the doctrine of the Holy Spirit, one confronts the following major question: Who is the subject? In other words, who counts as a sixteenth-century "Anabaptist"? As is well-known, sixteenth-century German peasants and townsfolk did not run amok loudly proclaiming themselves

---

[1] Such a position might have developed among some Anabaptists by the late sixteenth century. See C. Arnold Snyder, ed., *Later Writings of the Swiss Anabaptists, 1529–1592* (Kitchener, ON: Pandora, 2017).
[2] A similar, but more extensive, study of early Anabaptist Christology was the focus of John Rempel's *The Lord's Supper in Anabaptism: A Study in the Christology of Balthasar Hubmaier, Pilgram Marpeck, and Dirk Philips* (Scottdale, PA: Herald, 1993).

"Anabaptists"—it was not a term of self-identification. Instead, "Anabaptist" (*Wiedertäufer*, and eventually *Täufer* in German) originated as a derisive term. Like many aspersions, it was cast with little regard for conceptual precision because the point of using the term was not accuracy but "othering." That is to say, the meaning of "Anabaptist" differed not just by user (it meant something different to Luther than it did to Zwingli, for instance), but also by use. Those who called others Anabaptists did not pay terrific attention to whether they meant the same thing by the term today as they had yesterday. The point, in most cases, was not to level a specific charge against a group of people; it was to identify a group of people as "not us" in a derogatory way. In this respect, "Anabaptist" in the sixteenth century resembled a racial or ethnic slur, a fact that was reinforced once Anabaptists began to migrate to Moravia, the Netherlands, Alsace, Poland, North America, Russia, and the Ukraine, all the while cementing a set of distinct ethnic identities.

Since "Anabaptist" was a derisive term, its use did not neatly coincide with specific theological content. Most people who were called Anabaptists not only rejected the practice of infant baptism, but also baptized believers as a public acknowledgement of their confession of faith. Importantly, however, this commonality masks a diversity of rationales and intensity of practice. Many of those who were called Anabaptists practiced believer's baptism by water, but others rejected water baptism entirely. Periodically, some Anabaptists practiced the "community of goods," while many aspired to such community but did not do it, and others had economic practices indistinguishable from those of their non-Anabaptist peers (many of whom also aspired to ideals concerning community). Some of those who were called Anabaptists espoused nonviolence; many, perhaps the majority in the earliest months of the movement, did not. Some of those called Anabaptists were heavily influenced by humanists and favored "plain" interpretation of Scripture, while others continued medieval practices of figural interpretation. Most, if truth be told, were rather inconsistent in their exegetical method. As C. Arnold Snyder put it, the Anabaptists "were an unusually heterogeneous lot, especially in their first generation. Even a sympathetic contemporary observer like the spiritualist Sebastian Franck—who knew individual Anabaptists well—complained that 'almost no one agrees with anyone else in all matters.'"[3]

Because "Anabaptist" originated as a slur, then, it cannot be used to identify a set of people who held similar views or social practices without bringing to bear on that process of identification a set of criteria alien to the contexts in which it was originally used and exclusive of some people who were, in fact, called Anabaptists. This dynamic creates a problem for the study of early Anabaptism: it is impossible to give an accurate summary statement about Anabaptist practices and beliefs. We can, however, investigate individuals and ask how far their influence extended in the sixteenth century. Where pneumatology is concerned, Balthasar Hubmaier makes an excellent test case.

EARLY ANABAPTIST PNEUMATOLOGY: THE CASE OF BALTHASAR HUBMAIER

Hubmaier (1480–1528) was an Anabaptist leader for the final three years of his life, first in Waldshut, near the Swiss border with Germany, and later in Nikolsburg, Moravia.

---

[3] C. Arnold Snyder, *Following in the Footsteps of Christ: The Anabaptist Tradition* (Maryknoll, NY: Orbis, 2004), 17.

Hubmaier is distinguished among early Anabaptist leaders not only for his scholastic education, but also for the extent of his literary output, which ranged from short correspondence to lengthy treatises. Often, his influence on sixteenth-century Anabaptism is regarded as limited, both because his theology differed from the Grebel-Sattler line on the issue of Christian nonviolence and because the faction of Moravian Anabaptists most closely associated with him died out within a year or two of his execution. However, it is likely that Hubmaier's views on the Holy Spirit compare well to those of other early South German and Swiss Anabaptists whose theological positions are less well attested. He was certainly the one among them who offered the closest to a systematic exposition of pneumatology. Yet, even in Hubmaier's writings, the doctrine of the Holy Spirit was not treated as a theological topic in its own right, but rather approached obliquely in discussions of biblical exegesis, baptism, and the church.

Hans-Jürgen Goertz has argued that Hubmaier's theology of Scripture as well as his views on the Holy Spirit should be interpreted in light of the anticlerical situation in which many early Anabaptists found themselves.[4] Broadly speaking, in pre-Reformation Europe, anticlericalism comprised a set of popular movements, literary tropes, and theopolitical positions in which people criticized the authority vested in priests, Religious, and the magisterium of Roman Catholicism, particularly as that authority was represented by wealth and temporal power. Where biblical interpretation was concerned, early Anabaptists adopted strategies from the anticlerical movements of the preceding decades for neutralizing the expertise of priests and Bible scholars. They especially emphasized the hermeneutical perspective that attention had to be paid to the letter of Scripture or the "plain sense" of the text. Often, this hermeneutic has been interpreted as Anabaptists aligning themselves with humanists in rejecting the methods of spiritual exegesis that dominated the Middle Ages.

Sometimes, too, as in cases under the influence of John Howard Yoder, this hermeneutic has been interpreted in the following way: any interpretation of Scripture requires congregational discernment in order to validate that it is actually the Holy Spirit guiding interpretive practice and not merely the opinions or views of one person, no matter how scholarly or authoritative. Yoder pointed to this hermeneutic—which he called "the Rule of Paul," adopting Zwingli's phrasing—in many of his writings, but he clarified the assumptions behind his position in a 1966 paper presented to the Goshen College Biblical Seminary Alumni Association and later published in *The Mennonite Quarterly Review* as "The Hermeneutics of the Anabaptists." There, he wrote:

> Balthasar Hubmaier had not yet become an Anabaptist when . . . he addressed to . . . John Eck a challenge to debate. The key provision in his proposal for the ground rules of the disputation was drawn from 1 Corinthians 14:29. He placed the audience . . . completely within the framework of a congregation gathered for worship, as Paul describes the same. . . . He proposes that before this gathering each party should speak his convictions, and then let the congregation decide who has spoken more nearly according to Scripture.[5]

Yoder also noted that Zwingli was a proponent of communal interpretive practice and concluded that by the time Anabaptism began, the Rule of Paul formed a common

---

[4] Hans-Jürgen Goertz, *The Anabaptists*, trans. Trevor Johnson (London: Routledge, 1996), 51.
[5] John H. Yoder, "The Hermeneutics of the Anabaptists," *The Mennonite Quarterly Review* 41, no. 4 (1967): 301.

conviction among reformers in and around Zurich. When Scripture was interpreted well, in other words, it was because the congregation was empowered by the Holy Spirit to understand the sense of the text. According to Yoder, "This means that the tools of literary analysis do not suffice; that the Spirit is an interpreter of what a text is about only when Christians are gathered in readiness to hear it speak to their current needs and concerns."[6]

For all its contemporary influence, Yoder's view of early Anabaptist hermeneutics is problematic, historically considered. In the writings of figures like Hubmaier, the rejection of scholarly expertise or individual inspiration was by no means thorough or systematic. Moreover, the claim that congregations are the properly inspired interpreting bodies did not appear as a hermeneutical principle in its own right in the early Anabaptist movement; instead, it showed up as a tactic within a larger anticlerical strategy. Snyder explained the connection between Anabaptist spirituality and anticlericalism in this way:

> Anabaptist footage in late medieval reforming sentiments is evident in the common critique of pastors who claim to be preaching the truth, but nevertheless continue to live dissolute and undisciplined lives. Negatively expressed, this attitude may be called anticlerical; positively expressed, the same attitude points to the Anabaptist insistence that inner regeneration and the presence of the Spirit must produce visible, outward good fruits. In the absence of such fruits there was reason to question the presence of the Spirit; and without that Spirit, there could be no true interpretation of the Bible. Thus the necessary reading of the letter by those in possession of the Spirit was tested in Anabaptist hermeneutics by the necessary outer manifestations of inner, spiritual renewal.[7]

In view of anticlericalism, early Anabaptist hermeneutics should be seen as more than a set of comments on proper exegetical method; they were also a tool for divesting their opponents of authority, especially that derived from education or ecclesiastical standing. While Hubmaier's own educational pedigree was excellent, he nonetheless employed this tactic regularly, as early as his comments at the Second Zurich Disputation in October 1523. There, during a discussion of the use of images in the Mass, Hubmaier said that on "all divisive questions and controversies only Scripture, canonized and sanctified by God Himself, should and must be the judge, or heaven and earth must fall."[8] The implication, as in his disputation with Eck, is that Scripture is a clear testimony to the way of Christ that adjudicates practical theological concerns in a publicly accessible way. Scripture is "the plumb line of the bright clear Word of God."[9] While Zwingli initially agreed with Hubmaier's account of the place of Scripture in practical theology, by the end of the disputation, Hubmaier had used his insistence on the primacy of Scripture to undermine Zwingli's authority and promote thoroughgoing iconoclasm.

This fact should not obscure Hubmaier's use of and appreciation for informed exegesis, let alone for exegetical techniques like *lectio divina* derived from late medieval Augustinian spirituality, such as are found in his "Twelve Articles in Prayer Form" and "A Brief Our Father."[10] When the Peasants' War forced Hubmaier out of Waldshut in the

---

[6]Ibid.
[7]C. Arnold Snyder, *Anabaptist History and Theology: An Introduction* (Kitchener, ON: Pandora, 1995), 161.
[8]Wayne Pipkin and John H. Yoder, trans. and eds., *Balthasar Hubmaier: Theologian of Anabaptism* (Scottdale, PA: Herald, 1989), 23.
[9]Ibid., 24.
[10]Ibid., 234–44.

fall of 1525, he was compelled by gout to try to hide in Zurich rather than take refuge farther afield in Basel or Strasbourg.[11] Yet, he was soon discovered and placed under house arrest. Then, after having sufficiently recovered from his illness, he was sent to the Wellenberg, or Wasserturm, a prison for Anabaptists housed in a fortified tower on an island in the Limmat, where he remained until Easter 1526. Although he published them from Nikolsburg the following summer, Hubmaier wrote the "Twelve Articles in Prayer Form" and "A Brief Our Father" while imprisoned and impoverished in Zurich.

The texts are notable in two respects: first, they are nearly devoid of polemic, and second, they employ a periphrastic technique common to late medieval Augustinian spirituality. Hubmaier does not appear to have had many texts or references at his disposal during his imprisonment; thus, he adopted a "confessional" tone rather than carry on arguments with his opponents. However, Pipkin and Yoder are wrong to claim that the writings' "form is original in that the affirmations of the Apostles' Creed are transformed into a prayer and expanded into a description of Christian experience."[12] Instead, the texts fit the structure of *lectio divina* as practiced in devotional medieval Christianity up to the Reformations. Admittedly, most contemporary studies on the persistence of medieval interpretive practices in Reformation-era German sources focus on the *Theologia Germanica*, which, while a text in mystical theology that involves spiritual exegesis, does not generally employ techniques associated with *lectio divina*. Yet, texts like Hubmaier's—periphrastic meditations on the Creeds, the liturgy, and the Lord's Prayer—were staples of medieval spirituality from at least the ninth century forward, and they are often overlooked as sources for understanding medieval hermeneutics precisely because they are so repetitive and pious. That such repetitiveness and piety are part of the point of the discipline is rarely acknowledged. The basic structure of *lectio divina* can be divided into four moments: recitation, meditation, prayer, and contemplation. In traditions deriving from Abelard and Hugh of St. Victor, these steps correspond to the fourfold sense of Scripture common to medieval scholastic exegesis (literal, typological, moral/tropological, and anagogical). The technique helped the reader craft a polysemous interpretive practice that disciplined the soul by attuning it to the workings of the Holy Spirit in Scripture and life. While the final two steps were rarely committed to writing, the Augustinian tradition saw a large number of written examples of the first two steps that were used as a consistent platform for the practices of prayer and contemplation.[13]

In both texts, Hubmaier records a short phrase—for instance, "I believe and confess in the remission of sins," or "Thou who art in heaven"—and then embarks on a meditative paraphrase catalyzed by the recitation. Each text ends with a summary prayer marked by scriptural language (though unreferenced) and an anagogical orientation: "In thee, Father, I hope; let me not be ashamed in eternity," and "Thou dost give and thou dost take, may thy name be praised."[14]

The very existence of these texts shows that Hubmaier was not ill-disposed toward individual inspiration or the illumination of the mind by the Holy Spirit. Their content gives us an impression of what he thought the work of the Holy Spirit in the soul of the

---

[11]Ibid., 161.
[12]Ibid., 234.
[13]Cf. Henri de Lubac, *Medieval Exegesis*, trans. E. M. Macierowski, 3 vols. (Grand Rapids, MI: Eerdmans, 2000), 2:188ff.
[14]Pipkin and Yoder, *Balthasar Hubmaier*, 240, 244.

believer looked like. The issue for him was not that an interpretation is uninspired if it is given individually or by an educated authority. The issue was, rather, that education and ecclesiastical authority were not the keys to biblical interpretation. Instead, the key was enlivening by the Holy Spirit, which in Hubmaier's texts is not mentioned as a function of the congregation or community. When, for instance, pressed to explain the role of Scripture and preaching in the salvation of sinners, Hubmaier insisted that hearing the Word of God as externally preached or encountered in the Bible was of secondary importance to the internal influence of the Holy Spirit on the believer's soul. The transforming and life-giving power of the Holy Spirit, contemplatively encountered, was for Hubmaier what created the capacity to hear the external word well.[15]

Nowhere is Hubmaier's emphasis on the internal influence of the Holy Spirit in greater evidence than in his theology of baptism, which was developed in conversation with and contrast to that of Huldrych Zwingli. The key feature of Zwingli's theology—which he outlined in the 1524 text *Exposition of the Articles* and developed in May 1525 in *Von der Taufe, von der Wiedertaufe, und von der Kindertaufe*—was a sharp distinction between inner and outer baptism. He maintained the distinction on the following two bases: first, because God is transcendent, things like water are not appropriate vehicles for God's action; and second, because water is to the believer as whitewash is to sepulchres, it does not touch what is on the inside. Therefore, Zwingli argued, baptism by the Holy Spirit, or the inner baptism, is independent of the outer baptism, that is, baptism by water. When God acts in the life of the believer, God does so directly and not by means of external agents such as water.

Because Zwingli's theology of baptism did not emphasize the response of faith from the believer, he argued that infant baptism was appropriate. Hubmaier's view differed from Zwingli's, as David Steinmetz has summarized well. According to Steinmetz, "Whereas Zwingli emphasized divine initiative and the freedom of the Holy Spirit, Hubmaier stressed the human response to grace and the freedom of the will."[16] For Hubmaier, unlike Zwingli, when the believer is reconciled with God in the saving act of Jesus Christ, the Holy Spirit communicates with the soul of the believer—this is the inner baptism—and prompts a response, namely, one of confession and penitence, which awakens the believer's faith and leads to her or his acceptance of water baptism.[17] Baptism by water is, in Hubmaier's words,

> nothing other than a public confession and testimony of internal faith and commitment by which the person also testifies outwardly and declares before everyone that he is a sinner. He confesses himself guilty of the same, yet at the same time he wholly believes that Christ has forgiven him his sin through his death and has made him righteous through his resurrection before the face of God our heavenly Father.[18]

Yet, despite describing water baptism as "nothing other" than a public confession, Hubmaier also describes water baptism as one way the believer "breaks out into word and

---

[15] Goertz, *The Anabaptists*, 51.
[16] David C. Steinmetz, *Reformers in the Wings: From Geiler von Kaysersberg to Theodore Beza*, 2nd ed. (Oxford: Oxford, 2001), 143.
[17] Pipkin and Yoder, *Balthasar Hubmaier*, 100.
[18] Ibid.

deed" in response to the inner work of the Holy Spirit on her or his soul.[19] Like Zwingli, Hubmaier thought that the Holy Spirit was transcendent and ubiquitous, working directly in the believer's heart in saving ways. Because of that ubiquity, however, for Hubmaier, water baptism functioned not only as an outward symbol of a prior saving grace, but also as a working out of that grace. In water baptism, the believer "proclaims and magnifies the name and the praise of Christ, so that others might also become sanctified and be saved through him in word and faith, in the same way as he also came to faith and the knowledge of God through other people who preached to him about Christ."[20] The issue at stake for Hubmaier is not merely that water baptism is an outward symbol of inner transformation, though in a post-Wesleyan context it is easy to understand how that view of his theology of baptism has proliferated. Instead, the Holy Spirit acts in the believer's water baptism to bring others to faith by prompting them "to take refuge in the Word of God."[21] In other words, water baptism is itself preaching, a proclamation of the word that people might "hear" externally and that promotes internal transformation in their lives by the power of the Holy Spirit. Apart from that function as, we might say, a *verbum visibile*, which not only points to but also participates in the life-giving work of the Holy Spirit, water baptism is meaningless for Hubmaier.[22]

As with his theology of Scripture, Hubmaier's theology of baptism should be read in light of the anticlerical situation in sixteenth-century Europe. Once this is done, two things become evident. First, Hubmaier's pneumatology is not nearly so distant from that of Müntzer, the Zwickau prophets, Franck, and Schwenkfeld, as is often assumed, because all these people deployed pneumatological claims in the service of anticlerical agendas. Second, the liberatory potential of Hubmaier and other early Anabaptists' pneumatologies comes into view. Their arguments about the Holy Spirit and Scripture or the Holy Spirit and the sacraments were never simply about defining correct practice according to the witness of Scripture. They were also about claiming a measure of social control, particularly by divesting priests or other religious authorities of their power.

It is critical not to view anticlericalism as only or mainly a social-political phenomenon. It was also theological; or perhaps more pointedly, sixteenth-century anticlericalism can best be described as a social-theopolitical phenomenon. Emphasizing anticlericalism as principally social-political without acknowledging the theological dimensions of the social-political is akin to the conservative theological tactic of labeling twentieth-century liberation theologies "Marxist"—it only makes sense given the assumption that there is a properly "theological" discourse that is not "social-political." Indeed, if one examines sixteenth-century Anabaptist historiography of the past forty years, one will find just such an argument being made by the theological curators of contemporary Anabaptist-Mennonite theology against the writings of so-called "secular" and "Marxist" historians. It is in such a context that the story about early Anabaptists' wariness of pneumatologies that emphasized individual inspiration took root. Yet, this set of arguments, too, is about social control. If one can successfully "secularize" the anticlerical situation of the early Anabaptists, then one can dismiss the elements of their pneumatologies that militate against control by the authorities, and one can curate a contemporary Anabaptist-Mennonite theology that

---

[19] Ibid., 101.
[20] Ibid.
[21] Ibid.
[22] Cf. Rempel, *The Lord's Supper in Anabaptism*, 57.

successfully tames the anticlerical impulse by making the community the agent of the Holy Spirit. And, as any of us who have been Mennonite for any amount of time know, the discernment of the community is as effective and forcible an authoritarian tool of suppression for dissent as any teaching magisterium has ever been. That is, however, an argument for another day. Thankfully, the Spirit blows where it will.

FOR FURTHER READING

Goertz, Hans-Jürgen. *The Anabaptists*. Translated by Trevor Johnson. London: Routledge, 1996.

Hubmaier, Balthasar. *Balthasar Hubmaier: Theologian of Anabaptism*. Translated and edited by Wayne Pipkin and John H. Yoder. Scottdale, PA: Herald, 1989.

Snyder, C. Arnold. *Anabaptist History and Theology: An Introduction*. Kitchener, ON: Pandora, 1995.

CHAPTER TWENTY-FIVE

Pentecostal Perspectives in Pneumatology

PETER ALTHOUSE

Over twenty-five years ago now, Barthian theologian John Webster said to me that Pentecostals are in a unique position to make important contributions in the area of pneumatology. He was right. The emphasis Pentecostals place on the experiences of the Spirit and the theological articulations that attempt to make sense of those experiences have provided Pentecostals—and especially a growing body of Pentecostal theologians—with strong interest in developing their pneumatological sensibilities. Pentecostalism emerged as a form of Protestant Christianity at the dawn of the twentieth century that accentuated the activity of the Spirit. The Azusa Street revival in Los Angeles and other Pentecostal centers around the globe engaged in a form of worship that included ecstatic religious phenomena such as "speaking in tongues" (or glossolalia), healing, deliverance from demonic spirits, and the operation of charismatic gifts. These experiences are a central part of Pentecostal worship and everyday spirituality.

While the early stages of the movement witnessed a concerted effort to situate their experiences of the Spirit in "Bible doctrines" and "doctrinal statements," the last fifty years has witnessed a rise of an intellectual or critical tradition in Pentecostalism. The work of these scholars engaged Pentecostalism from within their disciplines and took an ecumenically sensitive stance to other positions while remaining unabashedly Pentecostal in orientation. This faithfulness includes a critical evaluation of their own heritage, a willingness to set correctives when appropriate, and a desire to nourish and expand the theological significance of Pentecostal theological notions.

Pentecostal theologians in particular are re-evaluating the different theological loci from the perspective of pneumatology. On the one hand, a number of scholars have cast the significance of Pentecostalism in terms of spirituality rather than formal theological dogma. Harvard theologian Harvey Cox, for instance, argues that the appeal of Pentecostalism lies in its return to a primal spirituality.[1] Church of God (Cleveland, TN) theologian Steven Land likewise argues that Pentecostalism is best understood as a spirituality that integrates Christ and the Spirit around the fivefold gospel themes of

---

[1] Harvey Cox, *Fire from Heaven: The Rise of Pentecostal Spirituality and the Reshaping of Religion in the Twenty-First Century* (Reading, MA: Addison-Wesley, 1995).

salvation, sanctification, Spirit baptism, healing, and eschatology.[2] On the other hand, the development of a theology of the Spirit has been correlated to the loci of soteriology, ecclesiology, and missiology with related themes of ecumenism and interreligious dialogue. My interest in this chapter is to explicate the latter position. In what follows, I explore the contributions of select Pentecostal theologians and their potential implications for pneumatology. In order to accomplish this task, I highlight the work of Veli-Matti Kärkkäinen, Frank Macchia, and Amos Yong since they stand at the forefront with their creativity when it comes to pneumatology. I will follow with a brief outline of my own contributions to the field.

THE RESURGENCE OF PNEUMATOLOGY IN ECUMENICAL PERSPECTIVE

Fuller Theological Seminary professor Veli-Matti Kärkkäinen has made pneumatology a central focus of his theological work. The scope of Kärkkäinen's concern is to articulate a theological understanding of the Holy Spirit in ecumenical, global, historical, and contextual spheres. Kärkkäinen argues that this "resurgence of pneumatology" since the latter half of the twentieth century is an attempt to address the lacuna of theological implications surrounding pneumatology.[3] He argues that an ecumenical approach from the perspective of pneumatology can make important contributions in ecclesiology (especially in the area of *koinonia*), trinitarian thought, soteriology, and missiology. Pentecostal-charismatic Christianity has an important seat at the table alongside Eastern Orthodoxy, Roman Catholic, and Protestant traditions as Pentecostals work to develop their understanding of their own pneumatological positions.[4] In terms of ecclesiology, Kärkkäinen insists that a Pentecostal pneumatological orientation would help the broader Christian church overcome the tension between "charism" and institution" by seeking to develop a "charismatic structure." The church, claims Kärkkäinen, is a charismatically structured fellowship that necessitates a pneumatological foundation for ecclesiology.[5] "The emergence of charismatic gifts, the release of the whole people of God into ministry by the power of the Spirit, a manifold charismatic testimony by word and deed, a new enthusiasm for evangelism, etc., are but examples of the new sign of life given by the Spirit to the whole church."[6]

The concern for a pneumatological ecclesiology also has a trinitarian focus for Kärkkäinen in which *koinonia* (fellowship) is rooted in the life of the Father, Son, and Holy Spirit. The *koinonia* among divine persons founds the basis for *koinonia* among members of the church. The outpouring of the Spirit at Pentecost is the beginning of the gathering of the messianic community in which the gifts of the Spirit establish a deep

---

[2]Steven J. Land, *Pentecostal Spirituality: A Passion for the Kingdom* (Sheffield: Sheffield Academic Press, 1993); also see Veli-Matti Kärkkäinen, *Pneumatology: The Holy Spirit in Ecumenical, International, and Contextual Perspective* (Grand Rapids, MI: Baker Academic, 2002), 90–1.
[3]Veli-Matti Kärkkäinen, *Toward a Pneumatological Theology: Pentecostal and Ecumenical Perspectives on Ecclesiology, Soteriology, and Theology of Mission*, ed. Amos Yong (Lanham, MD: University Press of America, 2002), 78–9.
[4]Kärkkäinen, *Pneumatology*; idem, *The Holy Spirit: A Guide to Christian Theology* (Louisville, KY: Westminster John Knox, 2012).
[5]Kärkkäinen, *Toward a Pneumatological Theology*, 93.
[6]Ibid., 95.

communion among Christians who participate with God in the upbuilding of the church. This communion is an eschatological reality in which the communion of the church in fellowship with the Father, Son, and Spirit oscillates between the "now" and "not yet" while simultaneously being a historical, visible sign of the work and mission of God in the world.[7] The church therefore is a charismatic fellowship in that the Spirit gives life and power to individuals and, through them, to the church corporately. However, at issue for Pentecostals is that in navigating the tension between charism and structure, they need to work out a theology of church authority and of the relationship between the local and universal structures of the church.[8]

One final comment in this brief exposition of Kärkkäinen's pneumatology is the relationship between pneumatology, eschatology, and mission. Bemoaning the lack of a pneumatological outlook in the theology of missions generally, Kärkkäinen insists that a pneumatological missiology must be rooted in the relationship between the Spirit and the eschaton. "Eschatological expectation finds expression in pneumatic manifestation. . . . The present that is filled with the Spirit can experience the eternal as present (pneumatology); eschatologically, the present that is oriented to the eschaton grasps the eternal as future (eschatology)."[9] Kärkkäinen adds that Jesus Christ is the content of the message of the kingdom and therefore also the expression of God's Spirit. Consequently, the relationship between the future and the present as found in Christ Jesus is already pneumatologically mediated. Jesus is the bearer of the Spirit, is raised from the dead by the Spirit, and is the giver of the Spirit at Pentecost. The Spirit constitutes the church and calls it to missionary service as it looks to the future kingdom when the Spirit will consummate God's salvific work in creation and humanity.[10]

SPIRIT BAPTISM AS THE SPIRIT OF PENTECOST

Frank Macchia has made pneumatology a central focus of his theological work, initially in an effort to develop a theological framework around the "crown jewel" of Pentecostalism, Spirit baptism, through a reworking of justification and Christology. Macchia's major resources in this endeavor are the theologies of Johann and Christoph Blumhardt as well as Karl Barth. The Blumhardts develop a theology of healing: Johann articulates a "Christus Victor" theology in response to the healing deliverance of a woman tormented by spirits, and Christoph highlights the healing of social and cosmological alienation. Macchia connects the "Spirit of Pentecost" to the "kingdom of God" in Johann Blumhardt's theology in order to recognize the presence of the living God in the world. The Spirit represents Christ to the world as the inaugurator of the kingdom and the end for the people of God.[11] Consequently, Christ is present in his kingdom through the mediation of the Spirit of Pentecost. The outpouring of the Spirit of Pentecost is both the inbreaking of the kingdom and the vehicle through which the gifts of the Spirit are expressed in the church. However, drawing on Christoph, Macchia suggests the Spirit of Pentecost is also

---

[7]Ibid., 99–101.
[8]Ibid., 109–12.
[9]Ibid., 222.
[10]Ibid., 226.
[11]Frank D. Macchia, *Spirituality and Social Liberation: The Message of the Blumhardts in the Light of Wuerttemberg Pietism* (Metuchen, NJ: Scarecrow, 1993), 72.

a healing liberation of the ills in society as well as the destructive forces in creation. In other words, Macchia's pneumatology cedes space not only for the outpouring of the Spirit coinciding with the inbreaking of the future kingdom now, but also for social justice responses to dehumanization, social alienation, and creation care as the pneumatological outcome of divine healing.

Macchia views Spirit baptism as the root metaphor for Pentecostal pneumatology that connects Pentecost and kingdom. His early work attempts to articulate Spirit baptism sacramentally as a foretaste of the kingdom breaking into the world in a theophanic, sense-oriented manifestation of the inner reality of the Spirit's presence in the individual but also of the church spreading into the world.[12] He later attempts to redefine Spirit baptism through the lens of sanctification and eschatology in order to "augment the kingdom of God motif with the sanctification theme of participation in, and union with, God."[13] As such, Spirit baptism cannot be restricted to prophetic and charismatic gifting but must be seen as soteriological in scope. The soteriological reworking of Spirit baptism is developed in terms of its trinitarian and ecclesiological ramifications.

Macchia's most recent work furthers his goal of undergirding soteriology with a pneumatology of Spirit baptism.[14] Specifically, Macchia contends that justification is only possible in the fullness of the life of the Spirit. The problem, he argues, is that the Roman Catholic and Protestant positions on justification have come to an impasse. Roman Catholic theology holds the position that justification is an enacted infusion of love through the synergy of cooperative grace that provides the fruit of righteousness.[15] Protestant theology holds the position that justification is a forensic declaration of righteousness in the individual, but in doing so, it ended up confining the Spirit to an afterthought in theology.[16] Macchia insists that justification is found in God's covenantal faithfulness that mediates Christ through the impartation and indwelling of the Spirit. Once again, the indwelling Spirit is viewed through the Pentecostal lens of the infilling of Spirit baptism that overflows with divine love and regenerative power. In this pneumatological turn, Macchia believes he has found the key to unlock the roadblock between Catholic and Protestant stances on justification.

THE PNEUMATOLOGICAL IMAGINATION AND THE THEOLOGY OF RELIGIONS

Amos Yong has established himself as an important Pentecostal theologian as well as theologian of the Spirit. Pneumatology stands at the center of Yong's theological concerns throughout his work and provides a basis upon which he addresses and constructs other theological areas. Yong's initial contribution to the field of the theology of religions is an attempt to flesh out the implications for interfaith dialogue from the starting point of

---

[12] Frank D. Macchia, "Sighs Too Deep for Words: Towards a Theology of Glossolalia," *Journal of Pentecostal Theology* 1 (1992): 47–73; idem, "Tongues as a Sign: Towards a Sacramental Understanding of Pentecostal Experience," *Pneuma: The Journal of the Society for Pentecostal Studies* 15, no. 1 (1993): 61–76.
[13] Frank D. Macchia, *Baptized in the Spirit: A Global Pentecostal Theology* (Grand Rapids, MI: Zondervan, 2006), 42.
[14] Frank D. Macchia, *Justified in the Spirit: Creation, Redemption, and the Triune God* (Grand Rapids, MI: Eerdmans, 2010).
[15] Ibid., chap. 2.
[16] Ibid., chap. 3.

pneumatology.[17] Specifically, he argues that the Pentecostal and charismatic experiences of the Spirit offer a venue in which a pneumatological approach to other religions will complement the dialogues in the Christian theology of religion.[18] The problem in interreligious dialogue, according to Yong, is the christological impasse. The particularity of the incarnate and crucified Christ who mediates salvation stands in tension with the declaration of God's universal love for all people and the whole of creation. Yong asks the question of whether starting with the doctrine of the Spirit might not help develop constructive proposals to discern when the Spirit is present and active in non-Christian religions. He insists that discerning the presence of the Spirit in other religions will offer venues for fruitful points of correspondence. His shifting to a pneumatological framework is premised on the trinitarian distinction between the economy of the Son in the work of redemption and the economy of the Spirit, even as their economies overlap. Moreover, according to Yong, a pneumatological approach is fostered by a Pentecostal spirituality that is rooted in an experiential category that sustains an emphasis on the Spirit.

Yong develops two theological categories in order to flesh out his method: the "pneumatological foundation" and the "pneumatological imagination." He contends that a metaphysical framework can ground the pneumatological interpretation of the religions as well as provide an understanding when the Spirit is present and active. Yong engages pragmatist philosophy and draws on (a) Donald Gelpi's empirical theology and notion of "fallibilistic epistemology," (b) C.S. Peirce's semiotic theory and the notion of "contrite fallibilism" that argues all knowledge is provisional, and (c) Robert Neville's philosophical theology of creation *ex nihilo*.[19] The pneumatological foundation proposed by Yong attempts to account for human experience in a way that is public in nature and potentially universal. A pneumatological foundation is developed in relation to trinitarian metaphysics and the Word-Spirit relationship that attempts to account for divine presence and absence. This leads to his category of the pneumatological imagination as "a way of seeing God, self and world that is inspired by the Pentecostal-charismatic experience of the Spirit."[20] The plethora of Pentecostal and charismatic experiences along with their phenomenological manifestations account for the pneumatological imagination that funds the pneumatological foundation. "Living in the world by way of a pneumatological imagination simply means participating in the fields of force generated by the Spirit's presence and activity."[21]

The pneumatological imagination is a way to account for the presence and activity of the Spirit in the life of the individual, the church, and the world. However, Yong also wants to account for demonic spirits, as this cosmological perspective is central to many forms of Pentecostal-charismatic Christianity and serves as a lens through which Pentecostals view other religions. One of Yong's pneumatological tasks is to account for the demonic spirit(s) in a pneumatological approach to the theology of religions. To do this, Yong employs the category of religious cosmology in which the demonic is extrapolated

---

[17] Amos Yong, *Discerning the Spirit(s): A Pentecostal-Charismatic Contribution to Christian Theology of Religions* (Sheffield: Sheffield Academic Press, 2000), 24–5.
[18] Ibid., 20; also see idem, *Beyond the Impasse: Toward a Pneumatological Theology of Religions* (Grand Rapids, MI: Baker Academic, 2003).
[19] Yong, *Discerning the Spirit(s)*, 98–100.
[20] Ibid., 102.
[21] Ibid., 177.

from the notion of divine absence.²² He rejects a dualistic account that gives demonic spirits ontological status and instead assigns these spirits a cosmological status that is without independent beingness—that is, a real and destructive force field within time and space. A cosmology of spiritual beings, claims Yong, recognizes the unpredictability and uncanniness of human experience that is not easily quantifiable. Yong states, "To name the demonic is to recognize the forces of destruction, sin and death which threaten human life."²³ The demonic spirits are the force fields that neutralize the presence and activity of the Spirit while perpetuating destruction and evil in creation.²⁴ The absence of the divine is recognized as demonic, whereas the presence of the divine is seen as the presence of the Spirit in human experience that extends along personal and social trajectories. Recognizing the difference, for Yong, is the task of spiritual discernment.

Yong's *Spirit-Word-Community* extends the pneumatological imagination to develop a theological hermeneutic and method from a pneumatological starting point.²⁵ Yong revisits the themes of pneumatological foundations and pneumatological imagination and adds pneumatic encounters or intuition. For Yong, pneumatology is a second-order description about the experience of the Spirit, whereas pneumatic encounters are a series of ongoing and pre-theoretical experiences of the Spirit that need thematization in theological reflection and communication. Yong insists the work is a speculative exploration of how pneumatology structures and relates to the world (metaphysics), to the knowing process (epistemology), and to theological hermeneutics and method (i.e., God-self-world in reverse order).²⁶ The pneumatological starting point, claims Yong, is better able to open up to a robust trinitarianism than the christological approaches already proposed. The pneumatological starting point "reconfigures altogether the methodological problematic framed by dialectic precisely because it opens up toward a trinitarian conception. Previous theological methodologies either fail to sustain the dialectical movement or collapse the dialectic altogether because they lack a pneumatological 'engine.'"²⁷ The trialectic of Spirit-Word-Church is a relational one emerging from the pneumatological orientation that propels the back and forth movement of the dialectic opening up toward a trinitarian reconfiguration.²⁸ More could be said, but creativity regarding the pneumatological quest forms the basis for Yong's theological claims.

SPIRIT OF THE LAST DAYS AND THE KENOSIS OF SPIRIT

My own work on Pentecostal pneumatology is an ongoing project that takes its cue from the theology of Jürgen Moltmann and to a lesser extent Karl Barth. This orientation places my work in the contemporary theological framework of Protestant Orthodoxy in dialogue with the developing Pentecostal critical tradition. Initially, I found in Moltmann's

---

[22] Amos Yong, *The Spirit Poured Out on All Flesh: Pentecostalism and the Possibility of Global Theology* (Grand Rapids, MI: Baker Academic, 2005), 253–4.
[23] Yong, *Discerning the Spirit(s)*, 236.
[24] Ibid., 240.
[25] Amos Yong, *Spirit-Word-Community: Theological Hermeneutics in Trinitarian Perspective* (Eugene, OR: Wipf & Stock, 2002), 1.
[26] Ibid., 8.
[27] Ibid., 14.
[28] Ibid.

theology of hope a means to engage in a revision of Pentecostal eschatology in a way that was more in keeping with the Pentecostal emphasis on the activity of the Spirit in the church and the world. Moltmann's theology of hope views the coming advent of the triune God from out of the *novum* of the eschatological future as transformative of the present conditions in order to overcome sin, oppression, and the suffering of creation.[29] Transformation is brought about by the eschatological inbreaking of the kingdom of Christ through the Spirit. The Spirit of God who leads Jesus into his messianic mission becomes the Spirit of Christ in order to fulfill that mission. Christ and the Spirit share in a messianic co-mission in which the particularity of Christ's life, death, and resurrection is universalized through the outpouring of the Spirit. The kingdom that is to come is mediated in the present through experiencing the presence of the Spirit as the Spirit of Christ and as the living energies of the new creation. Through the Spirit, the paschal sufferings of Christ stand in identity with the suffering of creation in order to overcome that suffering so that humanity and all creation is taken up into the life of God.[30]

Since this initial foray, I have begun to construct a Pentecostal pneumatology around the themes of *kenosis*, *charisma*, and Pentecost. Some of this work is published elsewhere.[31] I will briefly sketch an outline of my thoughts on Pentecostal pneumatology. Once again, I found resources in Moltmann who has articulated a theology of Spirit kenosis that if teased out could provide the groundwork for constructing a robust Pentecostal pneumatology. Kenosis is translated into English variously as "emptying," "condescension," or "humiliation," though "divine self-giving" is my preference. Self-giving allows one to see that kenosis is not simply a divine activity in the economy of salvation, but that it is at the very core of the immanent trinitarian God as an expression of divine love. In other words, kenosis is constituent of the very nature of God in the interrelational self-giving of persons one to the other that is expressed outwardly in the economy of salvation to humanity and creation.

For Moltmann, a trinitarian perspective of the Word made flesh, the descent or emptying of God to take on the form of humanity, is constitutive to the kenotic nature of God *in se* as well as the entire activity of God from creation to eschaton. Each of the divine persons of the triune God is kenotically self-giving in the manner appropriate to each one's role and work. Kenosis of Spirit is most revealed in the trinitarian event of the cross. The self-emptying of the Son is at its most profound in Jesus's cry of dereliction of abandonment on the cross. Yet the event is mutual in that while Jesus is abandoned by the Father to godforsakenness for the sake of the world, the Father abandons the Son and becomes sonless. Kenosis of Spirit in the crucifixion is one of mediating the suffering of godforsakenness in order to overcome suffering. "The path the Son takes in his passion is then at the same time the path taken by the Spirit, whose strength will be proven in Jesus' weakness. The Spirit is the transcendent side of Jesus' imminent way of suffering.

---

[29] Peter Althouse, *Spirit of the Last Days: Pentecostal Eschatology in Conversation with Jürgen Moltmann* (London: T & T Clark, 2003).
[30] Ibid., 131–9.
[31] Peter Althouse, "Implications of the Kenosis of the Spirit for a Creational Eschatology: A Pentecostal Engagement with Jürgen Moltmann," in *Creation, Science and Spirit: Pentecostal Forays into the Science-Religion Dialogues*, ed. Amos Yong (Eugene, OR: Pickwick, 2009), 155–72; idem, "Kenosis and the Imago Dei: Contributions of Christology to the Study of Godly Love," *The Science and Theology of Godly Love*, ed. Amos Yong and Matthew Lee (DeKalb, IL: Northern Illinois University Press, 2012), 56–76. See also Stephen T. Pardue, *The Mind of Christ: Humility and the Intellect in Early Christian Theology* (London: Bloomsbury, 2003), 16–17.

The '*condescension*' of the Spirit leads to a progressive *kenosis* of the Spirit, together with Christ."[32] In the moment of abandonment, the life-giving Spirit suffers the death of the Son. In the moment of Jesus's death, he "breathes out" the Spirit and "gives him up."[33] This is the moment of the Spirit's abnegation, the nullification of the Spirit's life-giving work in which the messianic mission of the Son, a mission that the Spirit is fully invested in, comes to nothing.[34] No longer can Jesus cry out, for he is without voice in his dying breath.

What I hope to add to this picture is a discussion that the pouring out of the Spirit at Pentecost (itself an image of loss, emptying, and self-giving) and the charismatic activity of the Spirit in the church (and presence in the world) in which God is experienced as present are possible through the prior act of Spirit kenosis. *Charisma*, which is translated as "gift," is a derivation of the word *charism* and implies self-giving. The charisma of the Spirit is rooted in the foundational gift of eternal life in Christ given by the Father (Rom. 6:23). The charismata of the Spirit flow out of the charisma of God in Christ, as Ernst Käsemann notes: "Other charismata only exist because of the existence of this one charisma to which they are all related, and they only exist where the gift of eternal life is manifested in the eschatological inaugurated dominion of Christ."[35] To extend the argument, the manifestation of charismatic gifts in Pentecostalism is only possible in the prior kenotic, self-giving love of the Spirit, who with the Father and the Son gives to creation and the church entry into the life of God so that we may participate in the eschatological mission of God.

CONCLUSION

This all too brief discussion of the Pentecostal perspective on pneumatology overlooks the contributions of a new generation of Pentecostal scholars, such as Daniela Augustine, Daniel Castelo, Steven Felix-Jaegar, Peter Neumann, Lisa Stephenson, and others. Nor have I included a discussion of pneumatological contributions in the area of biblical studies and biblical theology by scholars such as John Christopher Thomas, Robby Waddell, Martin Mittlestadt, Blaine Charette, and others who analyze Scripture through the lens of the Spirit. My purpose has been to offer an overview of Pentecostal perspectives in pneumatology by Pentecostal scholars who have made pneumatology a substantial portion of their theological investigations.

FOR FURTHER READING

Castelo, Daniel. *Pneumatology: A Guide for the Perplexed*. London: Bloomsbury, 2015.

---

[32] Jürgen Moltmann, *The Spirit of Life: A Universal Affirmation*, trans. Margaret Kohl (Minneapolis, MN: Fortress, 1992), 62.
[33] Ibid.
[34] D. Lyle Dabney, "Naming the Spirit: Towards a Pneumatology of the Cross," in *Starting with the Spirit*, ed. Gordon Preece and Stephen Pickard (Hindmarsh: Australian Theological Forum, 2001), 45. Idem., "*Pneumatologia Crucis*: Reclaiming *Theologia Crucis* for a Theology of the Spirit Today," *Scottish Journal of Theology* 53, no. 4 (2000): 511–24.
[35] Ernst Käsemann, *Essays on New Testament Themes* (Philadelphia, PA: Fortress, 1982), 64.

Kärkkäinen, Veli-Matti. *Toward a Pneumatological Theology: Pentecostal and Ecumenical Perspectives on Ecclesiology, Soteriology, and Theology of Mission*. Edited by Amos Yong. Lanham, MD: University Press of America, 2002.

Macchia, Frank D. *Justified in the Spirit: Creation Redemption, and the Triune God*. Grand Rapids, MI: Eerdmans, 2010.

Yong, Amos. *The Spirit Poured Out on All Flesh: Pentecostalism and the Possibility of Global Theology*. Grand Rapids, MI: Baker Academic, 2005.

CHAPTER TWENTY-SIX

Charismatic Perspectives on the Holy Spirit

ANDREW K. GABRIEL

The charismatic movement spans denominations and church traditions. Given the wide range of Christians who would qualify as charismatic, the pneumatology of charismatic Christians is diverse. Nevertheless, one consistent emphasis coming from the charismatic movement is that after conversion, Christians can and should expect to encounter the Spirit in dramatic ways. After clarifying what is meant by the charismatic movement, this essay surveys various understandings of Spirit baptism found within the movement, outlines some spiritual experiences people within the movement tend to expect, and offers some constructive comments regarding the general emphases within charismatic pneumatology.

CHARISMATIC MOVEMENTS

Aside from the NT church itself, which was able to observe when Christians had received the Spirit (Acts 8:17-18), historical evidence shows that spiritual gifts were regularly present in Christian worship gatherings at least to the middle of the third century.[1] Since that time, Christianity has seen a long history of charismatic or renewal movements that have emphasized that Christians should expect not only to know that the Spirit is a divine person of the Trinity, but also to have intense and dramatic encounters with the Spirit.[2]

For example, in the seventh century, the Spirit was active in the Celtic Church, enabling visions, healing, prophecy, and exorcisms. In the high Middle Ages, one finds groups like the Cathars, Catholic dualists in France who replaced the sacraments with a baptism of fire and the Holy Spirit that was received through the laying on of hands. There are also groups like the Radical Reformers, Anabaptists during the Protestant Reformation of the sixteenth century; many of them emphasized that Christians could encounter the Spirit as powerfully in their day as Christians had in the NT era through experiences of visions, dreams, prophecy, and the "inner word" revealed directly from the Holy Spirit. In

---

[1] Ronald A. N. Kydd, *Charismatic Gifts in the Early Church: An Exploration into the Gifts of the Spirit during the First Three Centuries of the Christian Church* (Peabody, MA: Hendrickson, 1984), 57.
[2] Louis Bouyer refers to these historical movements as "charismatic movements" in his essay "Some Charismatic Movements in the History of the Church," in *Perspectives on Charismatic Renewal*, ed. Edward D. O'Connor (Notre Dame, IN: University of Notre Dame Press, 1975), 113–31.

many respects, the evangelical movement within Protestantism in the eighteenth century also began as a kind of charismatic movement. It perpetuated revival meetings under the preaching of men like Jonathan Edwards and John Wesley. These men saw people in their meetings cry out, faint, and shake as they encountered the Holy Spirit.[3] Many other stories could be told about the presence of charismatic spirituality throughout church history.

When scholars refer to the charismatic movement, however, they are usually referring to instances of contemporary charismatic renewal that have occurred within Christianity since the beginning of the twentieth century and especially after the 1950s and 1960s. In a certain sense, the charismatic movement comes after and out of the classical Pentecostal movement. On several occasions, Pentecostals shared their experience of the Spirit with non-Pentecostals, who subsequently experienced the Spirit in dramatic ways yet remained within their own historical denominations.

As a result of the historical connection between the charismatic and Pentecostal movements, much of what could be said regarding the pneumatological emphases of Pentecostals could also be said of charismatic Christians. Therefore, many scholars speak of a Pentecostal-charismatic movement and include Pentecostalism within their definition of the charismatic movement. For the purposes of this essay, however, the editors of this volume have distinguished classical Pentecostalism from the charismatic movement, the former referring historically to denominational Pentecostalism. This essay, then, represents charismatic perspectives on pneumatology from all other church traditions: the Catholic Church, the Orthodox Church, and Protestantism, including non-denominational and evangelical expressions of neo-Pentecostalism. In total, this includes over 400 million Christians in the world today.[4] Given the theological diversity of charismatic Christians, one could justifiably argue that there is not one charismatic movement within Christianity but many within the church.

CHARISMATIC UNDERSTANDINGS OF SPIRIT BAPTISM

Given the historical connection of the charismatic movement to classical Pentecostalism, the experience of Spirit baptism has had a prominent place in much of the charismatic renewal. There is, however, no one charismatic position regarding Spirit baptism. Nevertheless, most charismatics expect to have a post-conversion experience of Spirit baptism, although the substance, evidence, and outcomes of this experience are usually understood differently from Pentecostals.

Charismatics from a sacramental church tradition generally use the phrase "baptism in the Spirit" to refer to the impartation of the Spirit that comes through sacramental initiation into the church (especially through the sacrament of baptism). At the same

---

[3] See Stanley M. Burgess, *The Holy Spirit: Medieval Roman Catholic and Reformation Traditions* (Peabody, MA: Hendrickson, 1997), 24–5, 134–40 as well as idem., "Evidence of the Spirit: The Medieval and Modern Western Churches," in *Initial Evidence: Historical and Biblical Perspectives on the Pentecostal Doctrine of Spirit Baptism*, ed. Gary B. McGee (Peabody, MA: Hendrickson, 1991), 20–40.

[4] This group consists of Catholic (177 million), Orthodox (4.2 million), Protestant (35 million), and independent (259 million) charismatic Christians. Numbers are current as of 2010, as reported in the *World Christian Database* (Brill, 2011) and by Todd M. Johnson, "Global Pentecostal Demographics," in *Spirit and Power: The Growth and Global Impact of Pentecostalism*, ed. Donald E. Miller, Kimon H. Sargeant, and Richard Flory (Oxford: Oxford University Press, 2013), 320–1.

time, they might also refer to a post-conversion reception of the Spirit as a Spirit baptism. For example, Francis Sullivan, a charismatic Catholic, describes the reception of the Spirit through the sacraments as the *theological* sense of baptism in the Spirit, and post-conversion receptions of the Spirit as the *experiential* sense of baptism in the Spirit. In other words, according to his view, all baptized Christians have been baptized in the Spirit, even if they have not had a perceivable experience of the Spirit. The latter consists of new outpourings (often more than one) of the Spirit or new releases of the Spirit within Christians that make them aware that the Spirit is working within them in new and powerful ways.[5] Sullivan grounds his view through a study of the book of Acts, where he finds that people could "repent and be baptized" (initiation) and yet still expect that they could "receive the gift of the Holy Spirit" (Acts 2:38).

Those from non-sacramental charismatic traditions also affirm that Christians might have a post-conversion experience of Spirit baptism. Larry Hart, a charismatic Baptist, believes Spirit baptism is a biblical metaphor that includes many dimensions of the work of the Spirit. Aside from any contemporary experiences of the Spirit, he argues that when John the Baptist announced that Jesus would baptize believers "with the Holy Spirit and fire" (Lk. 3:16), John indicated that Spirit baptism is "an eschatological reality descriptive of all of Jesus' saving activity."[6] As far as the Christian experience is concerned, Hart reasons that Spirit baptism includes Christian initiation on account of Paul's statement, "For in one Spirit we were all baptized into one body" (1 Cor. 12:13, ESV). Hart contends that Spirit baptism also extends throughout the Christian life as believers experience "renewal by the Holy Spirit" who was "poured out on us generously through Jesus Christ our Savior" (see Tit. 3:5-6). Finally, Hart also incorporates the Pentecostal emphasis regarding Spirit baptism as an experience that empowers believers for mission and ministry, as Jesus emphasized in Acts 1:8: "You will receive power when the Holy Spirit comes on you; and you will be my witnesses."[7] Hart's multi-dimensional explanation of Spirit baptism is charismatic in as much as he believes that Christians have a perennial need for renewal through Spirit baptism and expects Christians can experience Spirit baptism in such a way that it will be accompanied by signs and wonders.

In contrast to denominational Pentecostals, who tend to privilege speaking in tongues as the key indicator that a person has been baptized in the Spirit, charismatics usually view any intense experience of the Spirit as an indicator that a person has experienced Spirit baptism. This might include speaking in tongues, but not necessarily. Other signs might include some other manifestation of the spiritual gifts, such as receiving and engaging in a gift of prophecy or healing.[8] Less dramatic results of Spirit baptism could also serve as ongoing signs of the experience, such as a greater commitment to one's faith, a greater devotion to Christ, an increased desire to share the gospel with others, or an increased desire to praise God.

Charismatic Christians generally view the experience of Spirit baptism, or being filled with the Spirit, as a source of personal renewal. Peter Hocken observes that for those in

---

[5] Francis A. Sullivan, *Charisms and Charismatic Renewal: A Biblical and Theological Study* (Eugene, OR: Wipf & Stock, 2004), 59–75.
[6] Larry Hart, "Spirit Baptism: A Dimensional Charismatic Perspective," in *Perspectives on Spirit Baptism: Five Views*, ed. Chad Owen Brand (Nashville, TN: B & H Academic, 2004), 111–12.
[7] Ibid., 156; see also 107–8.
[8] Henry I. Lederle, "Initial Evidence and the Charismatic Movement: An Ecumenical Appraisal," in McGee, *Initial Evidence*, 131–2.

the charismatic movement, "Being filled with the Holy Spirit is an essential prerequisite for the capacity to praise, for the ability to evangelize, for all ministries of deliverance and the overcoming of evil, and for the exercise of the spiritual gifts." Charismatics often expect that this personal renewal will also have ecclesial impact; Hocken continues, "This power of the Spirit is experienced as a gift of the risen Lord Jesus, flowing from obedience to God's Word and manifested in every form of Christian ministry and service, in Word and in sacrament, in ministries within the body of Christ, and in service to those outside."[9]

EXPECTATION OF SPIRITUAL GIFTS

The charismatic movement derives its name from the Greek word *charismata*, which is translated in English as "gifts" or "spiritual gifts" (1 Cor. 1:7, NIV). It should then come as no surprise that one key feature of the charismatic movement is that it emphasizes that Christians today can expect to encounter all the spiritual gifts listed in the Bible (see especially Romans 12 and 1 Corinthians 12 and 14).

This view was not common among Christians at the turn of the twentieth century. Many conservative Protestants at the time were cessationists. From their reading of church history and biblical texts like 1 Cor. 13:8-10—"tongues . . . will be stilled"—they concluded that God's intention was that the dramatic spiritual gifts, like speaking in tongues and healing, would help establish the early church, only to cease after the apostolic period.[10] Like their conservative counterparts, liberal Christians also believed that the miraculous gifts were not present in the contemporary church. But, unlike their conservative counterparts, liberals denied the reality of *all miracles*, from the resurrection of Christ to speaking in tongues and healing. The Pentecostal and charismatic movements together have had much influence on the church over the last century, and many Christians would now agree that miraculous spiritual gifts do sometimes legitimately occur today.

Charismatic Christians do not just affirm the contemporary existence of all spiritual gifts; they also want to experience them in their own lives. As one Lutheran charismatic writes, "The Holy Spirit is no different today than he was in the days of the early church. . . . The charismatic renewal is sounding this word of hope and faith in the church today: 'Spiritual gifts—*all* of them—are part of God's provision for the church. Let us use them!'"[11] And charismatics emphasize that the gifts are not only given to clergy, but also to all believers to empower their ministry. The dramatic and more controversial gifts of the Spirit are particularly associated with the charismatic movement, especially prophecy, speaking in tongues, and healing.

Charismatic Christians generally emphasize the revelatory nature of the gift of prophecy. While non-charismatics might affirm that prophecy still occurs today, they sometimes understand prophecy as nothing more than the application of Scripture through pastoral preaching. By contrast, J. Rodman Williams, a charismatic Presbyterian, observes that in the NT, the gift of prophecy is exercised as the result of "a revelation" (1 Cor. 14:30).

---

[9]Peter D. Hocken, "Charismatic Movement," in *NIDPCM*, 515.
[10]The most influential cessationist book from the early 1900s was Benjamin B. Warfield, *Counterfeit Miracles* (New York: Charles Scribner's Sons, 1918).
[11]No author listed, "Manifesting Spiritual Gifts," in *Welcome, Holy Spirit: A Study of Charismatic Renewal in the Church*, ed. Larry Christenson (Minneapolis, MN: Augsburg, 1987), 251.

He then contends that "a person prophesies because God has revealed something to him.... This obviously is not a prepared message, for the revelation immediately issues in the spoken prophecy. Spontaneity marks such an occasion and the words are divinely inspired."[12]

On the popular level, charismatics sometimes limit prophecy to instances where an individual claims to make a divinely inspired prediction about the future. This is common in the print and online communications from such sources as *Charisma* magazine. More thoughtful charismatics usually draw on 1 Cor. 14:3-4 to propose that while there may be an element of prediction to prophecy, prophecy takes place more widely "for the purpose of building up and strengthening people, exhorting and encouraging certain actions, and bringing consolation and comfort."[13]

Speaking in tongues is another common spiritual gift practiced by charismatics. While charismatic Christians do not always associate this with the experience of being baptized in the Spirit, many charismatics view speaking in tongues as integral to their spiritual vitality. Dennis Bennett, an Anglican priest whom historians typically point to as the father of the charismatic movement, explains the experience:

> Speaking in tongues, or praying with the Spirit, is what happens when a Christian believer speaks [a language unknown to him or herself] and allows the indwelling Holy Spirit to guide the form of the words uttered. It is not ecstasy, suggestion, hysteria, or hypnosis.... Speaking in tongues is initiated by a simple act of the will, just as speech in any language would be.[14]

Bennett continues by making a distinction between speaking in tongues in private (or praying in tongues) and speaking in tongues in a gathering of believers. He grounds this distinction in Paul's affirmation that "I speak in tongues" in private, which is in contrast to his usual preference to speak in an intelligible language "in the church" (1 Cor. 14:18-19). The former, tongues in private times of prayer, is the most common way that charismatics practice speaking in tongues. This practice is intended for the benefit of the individual praying. By contrast, when the gift of speaking in tongues is practiced in a gathering of believers, it is often followed by someone practicing the gift of interpretation—that is, someone follows the tongues speech by summarizing the content of the message in a language known to those present and for the benefit of all those who have gathered.

Healing is another gift of the Spirit that is often associated with the charismatic movement. In the original Greek language of the NT, the Apostle Paul does not actually refer to a singular gift of healing but to "gifts of healings" (both plural in 1 Corinthians 12). Craig Keener, a charismatic Baptist, suggests, "The plural [healings] probably signifies, as many charismatic commentators suggest, that the Spirit develops in different Christians the faith to pray for different kinds of ailments."[15] And Siegfried Grossman, a German charismatic associated with the Evangelical Free churches, proposes that the plural "gifts" indicates that the person who performs the healing does not receive the gift of healing

---

[12] J. Rodman Williams, *Renewal Theology*, 3 vols. (Grand Rapids, MI: Zondervan, 1990), 2:382.
[13] Ibid., 2:383.
[14] Dennis J. Bennett, "The Gifts of the Holy Spirit," in *The Charismatic Movement*, ed. Michael P. Hamilton (Grand Rapids, MI: Eerdmans, 1975), 18.
[15] Craig S. Keener, *3 Crucial Questions about the Holy Spirit* (Grand Rapids, MI: Baker, 1996), 114.

but rather transmits the gift to the person who receives the healing. In other words, "Each individual healing is a gift of God's grace."[16]

While those in the charismatic movement generally recognize that God also uses doctors to help cure people, this is not what they have in mind regarding gifts of healings. Rather, they believe that these gifts refer to times that God the Holy Spirit miraculously heals a person regardless of any medical intervention. Furthermore, charismatic Christians often teach that when this gift is given, God heals not only out of compassion and for the physical well-being of the person prayed for, but also to draw attention to the truth of the gospel that is often proclaimed along with prayers for healing (cf. Acts 14:3). Therefore, charismatics sometimes refer to the use of healing and other miracles in evangelistic ministry as "power evangelism."[17]

OTHER MANIFESTATIONS OF THE SPIRIT

Aside from claiming to experience gifts of the Spirit that Paul explicitly describes in his letters, many charismatic Christians expect that people may experience the Spirit in additional ways that will affect their bodies. While these experiences are not as common as those described earlier, some charismatics will testify to shaking as they experience the power of the Spirit, experiencing Spirit-inspired crying or laughter, or falling under the power of the Spirit. The latter experience is sometimes referred to as being "slain in the Spirit." This might be similar to how Peter "fell into a trance" and then had a vision from God (Acts 10:10-11) and to how Paul "fell into a trance" one day while praying in the temple (Acts 22:17). On their best days, charismatics recognize that all these experiences can be faked or manufactured, but at the same time, they contend that an authentic experience of the Spirit might lead to involuntary, physical, bodily responses.[18]

A CRITICAL APPRECIATION

The charismatic movement has reminded the church that the Spirit is still present and active in the church as a life-giving stream, not just hidden and idly dwelling within Christians. This emphasis by charismatics is one integral factor that has led to a renewed interest in pneumatology in the last century. In fact, if it were not for the Pentecostal and charismatic movements, it is very possible that the book you are reading would not exist and that the Spirit would still be what theologians have called (as recently as 1985) the "Cinderella of theology."[19]

The challenge for charismatics, especially at the popular level, is to not elevate the value of the dramatic gifts of the Spirit over the less spectacular gifts of the Spirit. Christians must remember that encouraging is just as much a gift of the Spirit (Rom. 12:8)

---

[16]Siegfried Grossman, *Charisma: The Gifts of the Spirit* (Wheaton, IL: Tyndale, 1972), 42.
[17]John Wimber and Kevin Springer, *Power Evangelism: Signs and Wonders Today* (London: Hodder and Stoughton, 1985).
[18]Jack Deere, *Surprised by the Power of the Spirit: A Former Dallas Seminary Professor Discovers that God Speaks and Heals Today* (Grand Rapids, MI: Zondervan, 1993), 91–2, 96–8.
[19]Kilian McDonnell, "A Trinitarian Theology of the Holy Spirit?" *Theological Studies* 46 (1985): 191–3. The idea of the Spirit as the "Cinderella" of theology first came from G. J. Sirks, "The Cinderella of Theology: The Doctrine of the Holy Spirit," *Harvard Theological Review* 50 (1957): 77–89.

as prophecy is and therefore is no less supernatural and no less needed in the church. Likewise, Paul warned the early Corinthian believers who had different gifts of the Spirit not to say to one another, "I don't need you!" (1 Cor. 12:21).

It would be a mistake to think that God has given gifts of the Spirit only to those within the charismatic movement. Although Paul instructs the Corinthians to desire the spiritual gifts, he also indicates that every believer has received a gift of the Spirit when he says that God gives gifts "to each one" for the common good (1 Cor. 12:7) and that the Spirit gives a gift "to each one, just as he determines" (v. 11). Therefore, even though not every Christian participates in the more spectacular gifts of the Spirit, Yves Congar rightly observes that the whole church is charismatic (gifted by the Spirit), not just a particular movement within the church.[20] Furthermore, some theologians argue that all sorts of movements in the church can even be considered Spirit-inspired, communal charisms (gifts) to the church.[21]

Those within the charismatic movement do well when they remember that regardless of what spiritual gifts they have, those who "do not have love" are "only a resounding gong or a clanging cymbal" (1 Cor. 13:1). The wind of the Spirit sometimes blows like a gentle breeze, and people are not always aware of it. But at other times, as the charismatic movement emphasizes, the Spirit blows like a strong wind, shaping its surroundings in visible and unexpected ways.

FOR FURTHER READING

Cartledge, Mark J. *Encountering the Spirit: The Charismatic Tradition*. Maryknoll, NY: Orbis, 2006.

Christenson, Larry, ed. *Welcome Holy Spirit: A Study of Charismatic Renewal in the Church*. Minneapolis, MN: Augsburg, 1987.

Lederle, Henry I. *Treasures Old and New: Interpretations of "Spirit-Baptism" in the Charismatic Renewal Movement*. Peabody, MA: Hendrickson, 1988.

McDonnell, Kilian, ed. *Presence, Power, Praise: Documents on the Charismatic Renewal*. 3 vols. Collegeville, MN: Liturgical, 1980.

---

[20] Yves Congar, *I Believe in the Holy Spirit*, trans. David Smith, 3 vols. (New York: Seabury, 1983), 2:162.
[21] For example, James Pedlar, *Division, Diversity and Unity: A Theology of Ecclesial Charisms*, American University Studies (New York: Peter Lang, 2015).

CHAPTER TWENTY-SEVEN

Perspectives on the "Spirit" in Africa

DANIEL K. DARKO

Pneumatology in Africa is rooted in African cosmologies. As a theological category, the subject can be properly understood only in the broader framework of spirit-cosmology in Christian thought and praxis. It is in the context of spiritual beings that the person and work of the Holy Spirit find its distinctives and significance. In other words, the Holy Spirit is studied, invoked, and embraced against the background of the sub-Saharan African worldview. The Spirit and other spiritual entities are existentially active in daily human affairs. African pneumatology is thus pragmatic. It is molded by and wrapped in the patterns of traditional African spirituality. If there is a "Holy Spirit," then there must be evil spirits that coexist in the spiritual realm, as the saying goes. The conceptual framework and lived experiences in regard to spirit beings have seen no significant change from the earliest Christian thinkers on the Continent to the modern illiterate laity of the African church. It remains true that "the African worldview does not accommodate the Western tendency to separate physical and spiritual, natural and supernatural, personal and social."[1]

North African thinkers of early Christianity contributed to the shaping of ecclesiastical structures and doctrinal formulations in no insignificant ways. A discussion on African pneumatology would typically engage the likes of Clement of Alexandria, Origen, Cyril of Alexandria, or Augustine of Hippo. Some may even deem the treatment insufficient unless it included the pneumatology of Athanasius. Important as these African fathers are, the task in this essay has a limited scope, departing from the forebears of African Christian thought in two ways. The first matter is geography. The early fathers served and practiced mostly in the northern part of Africa, which is predominantly Muslim at the moment. The reference to "Africa" in this work, however, is to sub-Saharan Africa. The vastness of the region under consideration is the reason generalities would take precedence over particularity in the ensuing discussion. The second matter is timeframe. Our focus is not to recount how early Christians developed pneumatology in Africa, but to explore perspectives of the Holy Spirit in contemporary sub-Saharan Africa from the last quarter of the twentieth century to the present.

---

[1] Allan Anderson, "African Initiated Churches of the Spirit and Pneumatology," *Word & World* 23, no. 2 (2003): 179.

This study will be approached with two main focal areas. The first part addresses foundational issues in regard to "missionary" pneumatology as well as indigenous languages, customs, and practices that affect the conception of the Holy Spirit. The second deals with prominent features in the beliefs and practices of pneumatology. Africa is neither monolithic nor a single country. Theological positions and ecclesiastical norms are vast, and this work makes no claim to capture all confessional positions or theological diversity on the Continent. The weakness of a study of this kind is its lack of focus on a particular region. The strength is to provide a broad view with particular attention to common features that may be found in many parts of the continent. The ensuing study is representative and engages scholars from different countries in the quest to provide a fair account of pneumatology in sub-Saharan Africa. The decision to engage African scholars is a deliberate part of the methodology to give the reader a good glimpse of how Africans do theology and justify their church practices.

MISSIONARY PNEUMATOLOGY VS. INDIGENOUS PNEUMATIC EXPERIENCES

Western missionaries to Africa not only pioneered churches but also ran Bible colleges to train local leaders for Christian ministries. Pneumatology in such institutions often took the form of classic Reformed systematic theology or the Arminian frame of the same. African cultures and spirituality appeared to have nothing to contribute to the "sacred" consciousness of the missionary curriculum. Consequently, African sensibilities and practices were undermined or demonized, if not labeled as syncretic. The notion that some spiritual gifts have ceased in operation since the completion of the canon or the maturity of the church is rampant in mission institutions.[2] The missionaries taught what they knew and helped those who concurred to pursue further studies in the efforts to sustain their theological legacies.

Increasingly, there is little to show for missionary success in altering beliefs since the worldviews that inform African concepts of the spirit-world could not be deprogrammed or ostracized from the African consciousness. Missionary institutions, using classic textbooks, often failed to equip students for robust engagement with African customs and sensibilities, especially with regard to the person and work of the Holy Spirit.[3] African spirit-cosmology and spiritual encounters during conversion from paganism leave converts with deep appreciation for the power of the Holy Spirit to redeem and deliver people from satanic strongholds and to protect believers from malevolent forces. The conflict between missionary pneumatology and indigenous experiences is a persistently debated matter.

Pneumatology is not merely a subject to be treated esoterically or as an academic exercise but as constituting real experiences with a powerful spiritual agent that surpasses

---

[2]This author was one such student who learned to pass exams while questioning the value of a course in the African context.
[3]See Marthinus L. Daneel, *Fombidzanu: Ecumenical Movement of Zimbabwean Independent Churches* (Gweru: Mambo Press, 1989), 340. Daneel argues for the need for particular attention to holistic pneumatology in theological education in Africa. Seminaries in Africa continue to use Western textbooks, for the most part. In my particular experience as a student, we used textbooks of scholars advocating for cessationist pneumatology and notions of the spirit-world that were far removed from the context of students in the classes.

all other deities and ancestors. As in ancient Judaism or the Greco-Roman world, Africans believe that spiritual forces empower, enable, and intervene in human affairs to ensure personal and communal well-being. The missionary unrest in what they observe in pagan or indigenous practices may be alleviated by learning African spirituality and locating the Holy Spirit in that framework. Pneumatology wrapped in post-Enlightenment thought-patterns may demonize "grassroots pneumatology" that conceives of an interface of the celestial and terrestrial realms—the physical and metaphysical realities. As Allen Anderson notes,

> The difficulty with Western approaches to "non-Western" religious phenomena—and in this case pneumatological manifestations in Africa—is a dualistic rationalizing that misunderstands a holistic worldview. . . . Theology based on a European model has missed much in biblical pneumatology that speaks directly into the world of Africa—and in fact into the worldview of almost everyone except Western peoples.[4]

Africans tend to resist post-Enlightenment bifurcations of spiritual and material worlds in their approach to pneumatology. The language and referents to the Holy Spirit are rooted in and have powerful cultural resonance. Culture is expressed through language inasmuch as language defines belief systems. Pneumatology in Africa must be understood from the prism of indigenous Africans prior to credible evaluation of its strengths and pitfalls by an outsider. Systematic theology's category of pneumatology borne out of apologetics and structured in modernist frameworks is difficult for Africans to own.

"NO STRANGER IN AFRICAN SPIRITUALITY": LANGUAGE, CULTURE, AND AFRICAN PNEUMATOLOGIES

Language is part of culture, and words have meaning only in context. African culture and religion are hardly distinguishable. Traditional beliefs, religious practices, and consciousness in a community inform reception and expression of Christian beliefs. Two foundational issues deserve particular attention: (a) language and (b) the reality of spiritual powers in the realm where the Holy Spirit takes a dominant role.

Bible translators and local churches use culturally loaded terms to make sense of the person and work of Holy Spirit. These words evoke certain sensibilities or sometimes misguided pneumatologies. Native English speakers with Enlightenment epistemologies may underestimate the importance of language in doctrinal formation, especially pneumatic experiences. For instance, Christians in Africa are familiar with the existence of "good" and "evil" spirits. The Holy Spirit is usually portrayed as a sacred or good spirit, which if misunderstood would be similar to other referents—such as deceased ancestors. Language conjures analogous concepts and invites commensurate theological ideas; the African experience is not unique.

For example, the Akan people of Ghana understand spirit (*sunsum*) not only as the embodiment of the Supreme Being (God), but also as spirits that are active in nature and find residence even in inanimate objects. Coupled with Akan anthropology, in which the

---

[4] Allen Anderson, "Stretching the Definitions? Pneumatology and 'Syncretism' in African Pentecostalism," *Journal of Pentecostal Theology* 10, no. 1 (2001): 102.

spirits of humans (*sunsum*) live beyond bodily existence to remain active in the community as deceased ancestors, it is not remote conceptually to perceive the Holy Spirit in terms of the function of ancestors. Spirit connects humans to God in deep and profound ways similar to shared DNA in modern parlance. "The concept of *sunsum* (spirit) therefore enables one to speak of the Holy Spirit and its relation both to God and nature. This may also enable one to understand the Holy Spirit as cosmic in nature and as divine in being."[5]

Limitations of translation and conceptual transfers open African Christians to several possibilities in regard to the nature of the Holy Spirit. Christianity as a religion of the Bible lends itself to acculturation and appropriation of biblical teachings in the reception culture. Consequently, Africans articulate their experiences with the Holy Spirit in the logic of their understanding of the spirit-world. For example, the Kiswahili people in East and Central Africa use the word *Roho*, which is the generic word for "spirit," to translate "Holy Spirit," thereby opening pneumatology up to a variety of familiar concepts. In Uganda, the Protestant Acholi use *Cwiny Maleng* ("heart," but with broader meaning than in English), whereas the Roman Catholic counterparts of the same people group prefer *Tipu Maleng* ("shadow" or "ancestral spirit") for the Holy Spirit.[6] The theological import of these terms cannot be overstated. The repertoire of terms, concepts of the spirit-world, and experiences with spiritual forces become driving forces in "popular" pneumatology.

An anthropologist recounting an experience with a convert from witchcraft to Christianity in the West African country of Benin helps to shed more light on this phenomenon. He explains how the convert abandoned, destroyed, and found total deliverance from "evil witchcraft." The candidate, however, describes his new standing with God in terms of being "a witch in the Holy Spirit."[7] The convert asserts, "I've seen many things in the Holy Spirit that are much stronger and even go beyond that which I'd seen the *uhoohu* (witchcraft) of man. . . . I am really a witch in the Holy Spirit."[8] Linguistic and conceptual parallels from the local language do not translate well in English to meet the standard of sound theology. Drawing from the terms for "good witchcraft," the work of the Holy Spirit is being interpreted as more powerful witchcraft. The idea is not to undermine the Holy Spirit, but to express an encounter with a more powerful spiritual force, the Holy Spirit.

African scholars construct aspects of pneumatology in the frame of ancestral belief systems. It is believed that deceased ancestors are active and do have significant roles in communities. Custom dictates that the supreme god of creation, patron deities of towns/villages, and ancestors can be invited or invoked in libations during family gatherings to take their place and offer their contributions. These ancestors are apparently good spirits pursuing the interest of the people and ensuring continuity of their legacies.[9] "To be recognized and celebrated as an ancestor, one needs to have left a positive legacy; an ancestor models exemplary character and life-enhancing qualities, skills, or behavior for

---

[5]Robert Owusu Agyarko, "The *Sunsum* of *Onyame*: Akan Perspectives on an Ecological Pneumatology," *Journal of Reformed Theology* 6 (2012): 254.

[6]James Henry Owino Kombo, *Theological Models of the Doctrine of the Holy Spirit: The Trinity, Diversity and Theological Hermeneutics* (Carlise: Langham Global Library, 2016), 112–13.

[7]Jahannes Mers, "'I am a Witch in the Holy Spirit': Rupture and Continuity of Witchcraft Beliefs in African Christianity," *Missiology* 36, no. 2 (2008): 201–18.

[8]Ibid., 203.

[9]See Kwame Bediako, *Jesus and the Gospel in Africa* (Maryknoll, NY: Orbis, 2004), 29–32.

the living community."[10] It is noteworthy that the portrait of the Holy Spirit as analogous to the ancestors does not imply belief in the Holy Spirit as an ancestor. The concept of ancestors simply serves as a comparative referent in describing the Holy Spirit.

A Yuroba scholar (from Nigeria) finds parallels with the Holy Spirit and ancestors in his attempt to make sense of the Trinity. He notes, "Most Yuroba Christians believe that the Holy Spirit is a divine essence who communicates to believers through ecstasy, vision, and dreams."[11] Relative to the Trinity, "the Yuroba people now view God the Father as 'the Great ancestor,' God the Son as the 'Proto-ancestor,' and God the Holy Spirit as 'Grand ancestor.'"[12] The Holy Spirit as the Grand-ancestor functions as an "intermediary"[13] similar to traditional ancestors. Apparently, the Grand-ancestor (Holy Spirit) gives guidance, intercedes, and connects believers with God the Father and Jesus Christ. "As the ancestor *par excellence,* the Holy Spirit is the source of a new life, and the fountainhead of Christian living."[14] As a church practice, it is not unusual for Christ-followers to devote substantial amount of time to praying and inviting the Spirit to preside, protect, and guide proceedings in a worship service.

African pneumatology is interlinked to African cosmology. Pneumatology at the grassroots is grounded in biblical precedence and exhibited in pragmatic overtures. The interface of spiritual and material worlds in this cosmology heightens human sensitivity to the potential deployment of malevolent spirits by adversaries to inflict pain, diseases, death, and so on. The gods, ancestors, and other spiritual means are solicited to safeguard human fate and prosperity. To introduce an unbeliever to the Christian God typically includes the idea that God's power supersedes all other spiritual powers. To talk about salvation is to suggest deliverance from sin, evil, and the control of malevolent forces on the part of this God. To talk about the Holy Spirit is to affirm the presence of God's empowering agent, an ever-present Spirit to guide and avenge those who deploy evil omens against Christ-followers.

BELIEFS AND PRACTICES OF PNEUMATOLOGY IN AFRICA

Pneumatology in Africa is largely shaped by two broad perspectives. The first would be that of Western mission churches or missionary Bible colleges of non-Pentecostal backgrounds that replicate traditional Western ideas and espouse a cessationist pneumatology. Even within this perspective, the mainstream churches such as the Baptists, Anglicans, Presbyterians, Methodists, and Mennonites[15] are increasingly altering their pneumatology and worship services in response to cultural forces and charismatic norms. The second

---

[10] Agbonkhianmeghe E. Orobator, *Theology Brewed in an African Pot* (Maryknoll, NY: Orbis, 2008), 114.
[11] Caleb Oluremi Oladipo, *The Development of the Doctrine of the Holy Spirit in the Yuroba (African) Indigenous Christian Movement* (New York: Peter Lang, 1996), 113.
[12] Ibid., 102.
[13] Ibid., 107.
[14] Ibid.
[15] It is becoming a frequent feature of African church life to find church members lining up for prayer and healing in some of these traditions. For instance, I hear people speaking in tongues regularly in West African Baptist churches during Sunday services. Methodist, Baptist, Presbyterian, and even Christian churches espouse charismatic pneumatology in contradiction to the foundations laid by their missionary pioneers. A weekly evening prayer meeting of a Presbyterian church in Cairo (Egypt) is as vibrant, charismatic, and emphatic of the move of

perspective would be the pneumatology of African-led churches or those that fall under the broader rubric of African Independent/Indigenous Churches (AICs), which are non-dogmatic in their beliefs. These traditions appeal to biblical precedents and patterns in theological reflection and ecclesiastical practices. The cessationist pneumatology promoted by some institutions is being subjected to critical scrutiny in these contexts both for its theological soundness and its relevance to Christianity in Africa. The Holy Spirit is real in African Christian thought, as is the Spirit's power, which is drawn upon and exercised by Christ-followers. I devote the remainder of this work to discuss some representative and prevailing aspects of pneumatology in Africa.

THE HOLY SPIRIT IN THE SOTERIOLOGY OF AFRICA

Salvation is more than enrollment in church membership or a ticket to heaven for most Africans. The religious culture assumes that humans are subject to spiritual forces whose protection and prosperity they require and rely on. Members of clans or tribes cherish their ancestors for what they do in the spiritual realm on their behalf. Apart from that, the African mind cannot ignore the reality of evil powers. To embrace salvation by grace through faith in Jesus Christ is to relinquish allegiance to traditional gods and to denounce the positive role of ancestors. Assurance of salvation in Christ then requires a high degree of certitude in God's power and the Holy Spirit to ward off evil and to empower the individual. Perhaps this kind of change underlies the expectation of the Holy Spirit to serve the role of ancestors.

Moreover, salvation is deliverance from sin. Sin is an antisocial act in the moral framework of Africans. It impairs human relations and negatively impacts the community. This breach of divine order for humanity mars relationship with God as well. The Holy Spirit functions to convict sinners and deliver demon-possessed persons, thereby validating God's ability to save and ward off malevolent forces. The Spirit affirms divine sonship (Rom. 8:16, Gal. 4:6), offers security, and guarantees protection against diabolic forces.[16] The "sealing of the Spirit" (2 Cor. 1:21-22, Eph. 1:13-14) is a spiritual reality with material consequences. The Spirit marks the believer for God's ownership and enhances formation in regeneration (Jn 3:5-6). It is in this vein that the Spirit is said to dominate every aspect of a Christian's life.[17] As one author expresses this perspective, "Our world is becoming increasingly violent and wicked because people are hardening their hearts to the voice of the Holy Spirit."[18] Sin among Christians is thus tantamount to insensitivity to the Holy Spirit.

THE HOLY SPIRIT AS AN EMPOWERING AGENT

The notion of spiritual empowerment is seared in African consciousness. Athletes, businessmen, and even students seek spiritual aid to succeed. Expressions such as the

---

the Holy Spirit as most Pentecostal churches on the continent. These African churches point to real results and to gifts of the Holy Spirit that meet the needs of their congregants and empower members for Christian outreach.
[16]Kwame Bediako, *Jesus and the Gospel in Africa* (Maryknoll, NY: Orbis, 2004), 26–7.
[17]Timothy Palmer, *Christian Theology in an African Context* (Bukuru: African Christian Textbooks, 2015), 115, 118.
[18]Wilbur O'Donovan, *Biblical Christianity in African Perspective* (Carlisle: Paternoster, 1995), 135.

"vigor of God," anointing, the filling of the Spirit, the zeal of the Lord, and the "unction to function" are utilized to explain the work of the Holy Spirit.[19] As one Methodist minister and scholar posits, "My understanding is that the power of God is synonymous with the zeal of God in action, as we see in the work of the Holy Spirit."[20] Old Testament prophets and judges are noted to show how God endows people with the power of the Holy Spirit to perform various functions. Christians anticipate "visitations" of the Holy Spirit or his "manifestation" in worship gatherings. It is not unusual for glossolalia to precede prophetic utterances in AIC or Pentecostal gatherings as the mark of the presence of God in their midst. The "vigor of God" takes the form of divinely enabled inner or physical strength for the weak.

The nature and manifestation of spiritual gifts (Romans 12, 1 Corinthians 12 and 14, Ephesians 4) is one area where African churches depart from the articulation of the doctrine in Western Christian thought. The classic understanding of spiritual gifts to include teachers, evangelists, and administrators is shared by Africans. However, most African churches believe and practice as the norm the miraculous gifts such as divine healing, exorcism, speaking in tongues, giving a word of knowledge, and prophecy. Christ-followers in Africa are perplexed to hear some missionaries express their doubts about satanic powers. Missionaries may be wise to know that African silence may not be equated with persuasion.[21] A common phenomenon in AICs and mission churches today is a renewed emphasis on the power of the Holy Spirit to unleash prophecies, heal, and set people free from strongholds of demonic powers. Hitherto, Pentecostals had emphasized speaking in tongues as evidence of the Holy Spirit in the believer, but that theology has now given way to emphasis on other encounters with the Holy Spirit. One author highlights this dynamic in the following way:

> The Holy Spirit, God's empowering presence, is the one who facilitates the direct character of the encounter. A sense of transformation takes place at the personal and communal levels including a new dynamism in worship inspired by the Holy Spirit. The foremost theological emphasis of Pentecostal charismatic Christianity is therefore transformative encounter with God who is "holy" and who is "spirit."[22]

"Anointing of the Holy Spirit" used to be a distinct parlance in charismatic churches, but it is now widespread in African churches. The charismatic activity in AICs, even in non-Pentecostal denominations, accounts for the widespread use of charismatic jargon and phenomena. Praying for anointing, receiving anointing, anointing water, being anointed of God, or "Holy Ghost anointing" are common expressions in Pentecostal, Baptist, Methodist, and Presbyterian circles, to name a few. The Catholic Charismatic Renewal

---

[19] See J. Kwabena Asamoah-Gyadu, *Jesus Our Immanuel: An Exercise in Homiletic Theology* (Achimota: African Christian Press, 2012), 70–83.

[20] Ibid., 82.

[21] As students in a college where most instructors were American missionaries and the few locals were often called out by students to explain why they could not share their experiences with the missionaries, we were taught cessationist doctrines on the gifts of the Holy Spirit. I knew of only one person who was partly persuaded. The rest studied for the exams and dismissed what was termed the "powerless Christianity" being promoted by the missionaries. We came from Baptist, Presbyterian, Methodist, AIC, Catholic, and Christian Church backgrounds, but our lived experiences could not be compromised by the missionary agenda.

[22] J. Kwabena Asamoah-Gyadu, "Born of Water and the Spirit: Pentecostal/Charismatic Christianity in Africa," in *African Christianity: An African Story*, ed. Ogbu U. Kalu (Trenton, NJ: Africa World Press, 2007), 353.

movement or ECWA (Evangelical Churches of West Africa in Nigeria) may not use these terms, but many of their members participate and embrace this charismatic theology.[23] Anointing "has long been practiced in traditional Africa as part of religious ceremonies confirming someone's spiritual authority, or as a cleansing ritual when commissioning for an assignment, or simply as a medical ritual."[24] Jesus claims at the beginning of his ministry in Nazareth that he is anointed by the Spirit of God to perform a broad range of extraordinary ministries (Lk. 4:18-19). Anointing is the administering of oil to the body accompanied by prayers either for healing and empowerment, or for initiation into a particular office/task. Metaphorically, it denotes the empowering of God to perform ministry functions under the unction of the Holy Spirit. This phenomenon is well attested in both Old and New Testaments. Anointing as a moisturizer or lotion (Ruth 3:3, 2 Sam. 12:20, Amos 6:6; cf. Mk 14:8, Jn 12:3), anointing of an object for sacred use or to sanctify it (Gen. 28:18; Exod. 30:22-29, 40:9-10; Lev. 8:11; Num. 7:1), anointing as divine unction for leadership (1 Sam. 10:1; 1 Kgs 1:39, 19:15-16), and anointing for healing (Isa. 1:6, Lk. 10:34, Rev. 3:18) are all attested in our biblical traditions. Some African churches employ the term "anointing" as a synonym for the enabling of the Holy Spirit via human agency or by means of a substance to effect various positive outcomes.

Another feature of pneumatology in Africa is the notion of "the filling with/of/by the Holy Spirit." The notion of filling a vacuum in a person's life by the agency or with the substance of the Holy Spirit evokes powerful sentiments.

> To be controlled or possessed by a spirit is a common experience in Africa. Most people have witnessed someone under the control of a spirit. When a person is under the control of a spirit, his character and behavior may be dramatically changed. He or she may have unusual physical strength and endurance. The person may speak in a strange language which is not his own language. He or she may speak prophecies or messages from an ancestor or a divinity.[25]

To be filled with or by the Holy Spirit is to be subject to the Spirit. The manifestations may be visible features or audible sounds. Traditionally, a fetish priestess in African Traditional Religion (ATR) may be possessed by a spirit and manifest in ecstasy during ritual performances. However, the Christian experience is mostly in the form of symbolic gestures, speaking in tongues, and prophetic utterances. It is believed that the Holy Spirit also fills those who live in fear with courage to serve ministerial functions (cf. Acts 4:8, 13).

Africans share similarities in culture and beliefs with the ANE (ancient Near East) and the Greco-Roman worlds. As such, while a Western Christian may find beliefs and practices in regard to the Holy Spirit strange, most of these find precedence in biblical texts. For example, some believers in my village area and elsewhere openly share about the gifts of the Holy Spirit that enable them to excel in their trade/profession. Bezalel is often cited as an example of how the Holy Spirit empowers individuals in this regard. As the text reads, "I have filled him with the Spirit of God, with ability and intelligence, with

---

[23] Some mission churches are currently facing theological dilemmas due to emerging charismatic activities in their midst and the growing number of those who refuse to accept a theology that espouses both the diminished influence of demonic powers and the cessation of certain gifts of the Holy Spirit.

[24] Samuel Waje Kunhiyop, *African Christian Theology* (Grand Rapids, MI: Zondervan, 2012), 98.

[25] Wilbur O'Donovan, *Biblical Christianity in African Perspective* (Carlisle: Paternoster, 1995), 142.

knowledge and all craftsmanship, to devise artistic designs, to work in gold, silver, and bronze, in cutting stones for setting, and in carving wood, to work in every craft" (Exod. 31:3-5, ESV).

THE HOLY SPIRIT IN LEADERSHIP

The Holy Spirit is central to Christian leadership, especially in AICs. A dominant feature is that of prophetic leadership. Traditional concepts of leadership have a spiritual dimension. In rural areas, the gathering of sub-chiefs in the palace of a paramount chief reserves an important seat to the priest/priestess of the patron deity. Historically, leaders led in battles, took territories, and promoted the welfare of their constituents with the help of the gods, ancestors, or other spiritual agents. Typically, the seat of a chief/leader in Ghana has a stool name, and a newly appointed leader takes on the name and inherits the spiritual powers accompanying the stool or office. Physical prowess and spiritual powers are intertwined in the role of leaders. Leadership, in this sense, is analogous to biblical leadership, where men and women are called by God and empowered by the Holy Spirit to perform their functions. The African church expects its leaders to be endowed with spiritual authority in their ability to meet the needs of the people.[26]

Pioneers of AICs exercised leadership in the mode of prophets by emphasizing prophetic activities, exorcisms, and healings. Much numerical growth in AICs is due in part to the popular embrace of prophetic leadership. "The AIC's aimed at restoring to the African church the vitality of the presence of the Holy Spirit, which was seen as accounting for the 'dry denominationalism' of the mission churches."[27] Leadership in these traditions is perceived as spiritual mantles to serve and guide the people—as with Moses, Joshua, Elijah, and Elisha. It is African custom to pass on such a leadership mantle with its accompanied spiritual powers to a successor. Christ-followers in Africa seem to find these concepts appealing and worth emulating. Apparently, God endorses this pattern and manifests the power of the Holy Spirit through such leadership.[28] Church leaders do not make comparisons to traditional patterns but to biblical figures.[29]

Prophecy is an important medium by which the Holy Spirit manifests in local churches. Paul admonishes Christ-followers to desire spiritual gifts, and it seems those in Africa hear that as a mandate (1 Cor. 14:3-4). "It is significant in the African church context that the charismatic prophetic leadership of Elijah and Elisha was characterized by frequent recourse to symbolic ritual acts, a feature also common in African churches."[30] It is commonplace that leaders refer to themselves as prophets who provide revelatory

---

[26]African church leaders do not put high premium on theological education, but rather on the ability to exercise the gifts of God in addressing the needs of the people. Sometimes, high-level theological education from Western institutions increases skepticism of one's ability to lead a church.
[27]Asamoah-Gyadu, "Born of Water and the Spirit," in Kalu, *African Christianity*, 341.
[28]Martinus L. Daneel, "Communication and Liberation in African Independent Churches," *Missionalia* 11, no. 1 (1983): 87.
[29]Anderson, "African Initiated Churches of the Spirit and Pneumatology," 181–3. Anderson provides a concise account with references to biblical parallels to show that these practices in African churches are not anymore African than they are Jewish.
[30]Anderson, "Stretching the Definitions?" 108.

messages of encouragement and guidance.[31] Major problems and questionable claims have emerged in the ministry of so-called prophets whose ministries are neither theologically sound nor humanly sensible.

Pneumatic gifts in African thought and praxis may not be orthodox, especially if the yardstick is in the post-Enlightenment mold. Significant areas of discomfort with Western comrades include the distance between African spirit-cosmology and Western theological orthodoxy. There are also cultural analogies with the Hebrew people and early Christ-followers that are not present in Western cultures. Culture and how we appropriate biblical theology underlie potential misgivings, misinterpretation, and harsh criticism from self-appointed arbiters of theological orthodoxy. Biblical pneumatology is broad and complex. Appreciation of shared beliefs as Christians, shared traditions as denominations who practice differently, and even shared joy in the spread of the gospel may harness a genuine quest to understand and also to be understood. Difference must not engineer dissension in the global church.

OTHER ASPECTS OF GRASSROOTS PNEUMATOLOGY IN AFRICA

The work of the Holy Spirit in African churches may be observed in Christian gatherings where musical lyrics, tempo, singing, and dancing are perceived to be energized by the power of the Holy Spirit. Prophecy may occur as the people of God worship, invoke the Holy Spirit, plead the blood of Jesus, or declare the mighty works of God in worship. Some African cultures share the notion of water, wind, and fire as symbols of spiritual activities—as these are found in the OT. Moreover, "the 'spirit' or 'wind' is that which a person receives from God and has in common with him, the personal life force that gives being and life, strength and power, harmonizing a person with the rest of humanity and the universe."[32] In African religions, spiritual power or blessing could be transferred via objects or substances such as water, oil, cola nut, cowry shells, and so on. It is discernible, in some cases, that what is being ascribed to the Holy Spirit is rather a misguided practice borrowed from African traditions. The ability to differentiate between the work of the Holy Spirit and syncretism is an ongoing challenge. However, the default posture of some to read syncretism into unfamiliar pneumatic experiences is often misguided and unfounded.

ABSENTEES IN PNEUMATOLOGY OF AFRICA

A student of pneumatology in Africa may observe rare features or the absence of certain topics that are important in Western thought. First, the Holy Spirit as the third person of the Trinity or the Trinity as a whole gains attention only where parallels are being made to traditional beliefs. The unique African context does not provide impetus for robust discussion on monotheism, polytheism, and the Trinity. Second, little attention is given

---

[31]Nathaniel I. Ndiokwere, *Prophecy and Revolution: The Role of Prophets in the Independent African Churches and in Biblical Tradition* (London: SPCK, 1981), 230–73. Ndiokwere shows that prophetic leadership in African churches draws from OT traditions to enact rituals and offer symbolic gestures that meet traditional sensibilities of African Christians.
[32]Anderson, "African Initiated Churches of the Spirit and Pneumatology," 179.

to the fruit of the Holy Spirit or character formation in the work of the Holy Spirit. Moral failings in churches claiming powerful experiences with the Holy Spirit would benefit from holistic pneumatology. Third, African pneumatology is principally utilitarian in outlook. The person and fellowship of the Holy Spirit seem to give way to the notion that "the Holy Spirit is around only to help me."

The bleary intersection of culture, customs, and traditions in the reception and appropriation of biblical accounts of the Holy Spirit account for what appear to be different emphases. Pneumatology as a theological construct in the West may differ from African viewpoints, not in the soundness of theology but in emphasis and expression. Theology is non-esoteric but experiential and pragmatic in Africa. Christian beliefs are not "bookish," that is, singing from hymn books or reading from lectionaries/missals. It is noteworthy that apart from specific cultural resonances and referents, Christian beliefs and practices in other non-Western contexts overlap significantly with what we find in Africa. The Christian minority in the West may want to acknowledge the shift in the center of gravity in global Christianity from the West to the rest. The context of the fledging first-century church was one in which the center of intellectual activity had shifted from Athens in the classical times to Alexandria. North African leaders would later play important roles in Christianity without resistance. Today, Western Christians may need to consider how to engage Africans constructively in matters of theology and in understanding the work of the Holy Spirit in particular.

Pneumatology in Africa is mostly charismatic and pragmatic yet biblically grounded. Its charismatic outlook must not be equated with naiveté or sensationalism, as some suggest. The church is seeing growth in Africa, but Africa cannot claim to know all in matters of doctrine. Therefore, Africans stand in need of healthy dialogue with Western Christians. May God let his Holy Spirit accord us with knowledge and discernment, as we pray "Come Holy Spirit we need you . . . come with thy strength and power."

FOR FURTHER READING

Asamoah-Gyadu, J. Kwabena. *African Charismatics: Current Developments with Independent Pentecostalism in Ghana*. Leiden: Brill, 2005.

Chike, Chigor. *The Holy Spirit in African Christianity: An Empirical Study*. Milton Keynes: Paternoster, 2016.

Oladipo, Caleb Oluremi. *The Development of the Doctrine of the Holy Spirit in the Yoruba (African) Indigenous Christian Movement*. New York: Peter Lang, 1996.

CHAPTER TWENTY-EIGHT

Toward an Asian Pneumatology

A Reflective Reading

DAVID SANG-EHIL HAN

Constructing an Asian pneumatology requires a discerning reflection on the particularities of cultural grammars of life deeply engraved in the Asian contexts, just as it should bear a faithful witness to the scriptural testimony on how God is and becomes present in the power of the Spirit. The term "Asian," however, presents a number of challenges in this regard. Besides the fact that Asia is geographically expansive, life in Asia is filled with complexities and diversities of various kinds, whether it be religion, culture, ethnicity, or language. Accordingly, the task of constructing a Christian pneumatology with Asian distinctives becomes quite daunting, if not impossible altogether. This particular study is a modest attempt to consider contextual distinctives in Asia with a view toward constructing a Christian theology of the Spirit.

The study provides, first, a broad reading of the particularities of the Asian religious context. Mapping out the contours of the Asian religious context is intended to underscore the "non-Christian" and "multi-religious" realities of life in Asia.[1] Insofar as a Christian theology of the Spirit should address all dimensions of life, not just the "spiritual," a mapping of the Asian religious contexts would have a significant bearing on our discussion in Asian pneumatology. Second, the study will consider a distinctively Asian concept of the spirit, *ch'i*. The concept of *ch'i* allows for the generation of creative possibilities that may revision a holistic view of the person and work of the Spirit. The process would require a discerning reflection in sifting through the pneumatological insights gained. Third, the study will observe significant pneumatological themes and possibilities

---

[1] In the Asian context, one cannot avoid the issues surrounding interfaith dialogues. Referencing the work of S. J. Samantha, *Courage for Dialogue: Ecumenical Issues in Inter-Religious Relationships*, Kirsteen Kim appeals to the "free" and "unbound" agency of the Holy Spirit to help us cross the barriers of people, including religions. Kim then concludes, "The question is not *if* but *where* and *how* the Spirit is present in people of other faiths. . . . In India . . . Hinduism and Christianity [are] as two streams of water having a common source." "The Reconciling Spirit: The Dove with Colour and Strength," *International Review of Mission* 94, no. 372 (2005): 24. The task of theology cannot be, however, a mere matter of discovering or recognizing the points of convergence among different religions; rather, it should yield a creative interpretation of the particularities of the Christian message that opens up a dialogical space to inquire about not only the questions of "where" and "how," but also "if."

that juxtapose dialectically the Asian concept of *ch'i* and a holistic vision of the Spirit. In particular, ecological and ethical concerns will be addressed as being essential to revisioning holistically the person and work of the Spirit. The study casts at its end an Asian pneumatology that stands as a creative and complementary corrective to the Word-centered theologies of the West.

ASIAN RELIGIOUSNESS AND THE SPIRITUAL PRESENCE

Despite the present rise of atheistic secularism in the West, it seems reasonable to conclude that the history of Western civilization has been intricately intertwined with the religious identity of the Christian religion. One may even argue that much of the root grammars of life and culture in the West has been deeply affected and shaped by the history of theological discourse over Christian faith. On the contrary, Christianity is a relatively new religion on Asian soil and has not been privileged as such. The contextual realities in Asia have been shaped, rather, by the presence of multiple religious traditions—for example, Buddhism, Confucianism, Taoism, and Shamanism.[2] As Heup Young Kim explains, "those religions are *ontologically given to our existences*. . . . We do not have an epistemological distance to put them in the subject-object dichotomy."[3] If one's theological speech were to be meaningful in and to the contextual realities of the receiving culture, it cannot ignore the particularities associated with these religious traditions and their grounding and ongoing effects on the grammars of life in the Asian culture.[4] Hence, a theological speech rooted in Christian tradition should engage discerningly and creatively the "depth grammars"—the religiousness—of life in the Asian context.

"Religiousness" in Asia is not only "pluralistic" in form and content, but also "pervasive" in nature. Religion represents not just a "part," but the "depth dimension" of life in the Asian context; that is, religion undergirds all elements needful to sustain and thrive in life. Comparatively speaking, Aloysius Pieris notes that "the West studies all the world religions, whereas *the East simply practices them*. Religion is a department in many a Western university, just as it has been a 'department' in life. Among us *in the East, however, religion is life*."[5] For the Asian context, religion is deeply grounded in and has been pervasively affecting the ordinary practices of life. Accordingly, the multi-religious realities and the depth dimension that religion constitutes in and for life in Asia would have no insignificant bearing to pneumatology.

---

[2]Heup Young Kim, "An Asian Journey Seeking Christian Wholeness: Owning up to Our Own Metaphors (*Theotao*)," in *Asian and Oceanic Christianities in Conversation: Exploring Theological Identities at Home and in Diaspora*, ed. Heup Young Kim, Fumitaka Matsuoka, and Anri Morimoto (Amsterdam: Rodopi, 2011), 31–2.
[3]Ibid., 32.
[4]See Heup Young Kim, *Wang Yang-ming and Karl Barth: A Confucian-Christian Dialogue* (Lanham, MD: University Press of America, 1996). Speaking confessionally, Kim articulates this dilemma in his Korean context: "The more I study Christian theology, the more I become convinced how deeply Confucianism is embedded in my soul and body, my spirituality. Subtly but powerfully, Confucianism still works inside me, as my native religious language. If theology involves the response of one's total being to God, it entails a critical wrestling with this embedded Confucian tradition" (1).
[5]Aloysius Pieris, S.J., *Love Meets Wisdom: A Christian Experience of Buddhism* (Maryknoll, NY: Orbis, 1988), 3 (my italics).

To begin, despite marked disparities among various religious traditions in Asia, they all affirm varying kinds of "cosmic" presence of powers of dynamic vitality that generate and nourish all things that exist in the universe. Even in a "non-theistic" religion such as Buddhism, the cosmic nature of divine presence (or dynamic vitality) is not denied but understood as essential to sustain the ecology of all things in existence.[6] The appeal toward the "cosmic" presence of dynamic vitality inherent in the Asian religious traditions then offers a critique to "anthropocentric" theologies of the West. It pushes us toward constructing an "anthropo-cosmic" vision of the universe wherein the creation (nature) and human beings are considered as essentially coalesced with one another as a harmonized whole.[7] Speaking pneumatologically, the anthropo-cosmic vision that Asian religious traditions proffer stands also as a constructive critique to variegated expressions of the "spiritualizing" tendency in Christian pneumatology that restricts the empowering presence of the Spirit merely to "personal experiences" of human beings. Citing Jürgen Moltmann's insight, Pieris thus argues that a Christian theology of the Spirit should recover its holistic vision that unites the redemptive Spirit of Christ with the Father's *ruach* that hovers over all creation since the inception of time.[8]

The religious traditions of Asia also advocate a "relational view of life." Religious visions aspire individuals to embody responsible living, as particularly evidenced in the Confucian way of promoting moral responsibility.[9] Instead of merely "adjusting" to the world or accepting passively various constraints that the world may impose on an individual, Confucianism embraces the idea of a transcendent vision that encourages one to live responsibly while going through the vicissitudes of life.[10] Individuals become "spiritual" not by "departing from or transcending above our earth, body, family, and community but *by working through them*."[11] The ordinary practices of life in our daily living are not considered to be merely secular, but they become venues in and through which the spiritual presence is understood to be cosmologically decreed. That is, one partakes in a cosmic transformation or lives responsibly to Heaven's Mandate by working it out in continuous cultivation of moral responsibility in concrete situations of earthly life.

The "participatory" motif is just as, if not more, pronounced in Taoism. *Tao*, which means "the Way," is a mysterious and unknowable force in the universe out of which

---

[6]Aloysius Pieris, S.J., "The Holy Spirit and Asia's Religiousness," *Spiritus* 7 (2007): 126–8. Pieris notes, "the Buddhist scriptures do not deny the existence of these gods, but treat them as species of beings that are inferior and subordinate to the humans who have attained Nirvana, such as the Buddha and the Arahans (Saints)" (127). Accordingly, "non-theistic" spirituality in Asian religions (e.g., Buddhism, Jainism, Taoism, and Vedantic Hinduism) is not irreligious in nature but, more accurately, represents "religious this-worldliness." It is therefore clearly distinguishable from the contemporary atheism of the West that is characteristically *secular* and *this-worldly*.

[7]Kok-Weng Chiang and Geoffrey Tan, "A Pneumatological Eco-Theology from an East Asian Confucian Perspective," *Asian Journal of Theology* 26 (2012): 2, 12–16. See also Kim, *Wang Yang-ming and Karl Barth*, 34.

[8]Pieris, "The Holy Spirit and Asia's Religiousness," 130.

[9]Generally speaking, Confucianism may be regarded as a particular ethical system, not necessarily a religion; under the "non-theistic" framework of the aforementioned Asian religions, Confucianism presents a particular way of living life that carries with it certain "religious" connotations. This is especially true if we consider how the "religious" character of Confucianism has historically evolved in and through its interaction with the religions of the West (e.g., Catholicism).

[10]Chiang and Tang, "A Pneumatological Eco-Theology," 15.

[11]Wei-Ming Tu, "The Ecological Turn in New Confucian Humanism: Implications for China and the World," *Daedalus* 130 (2001): 245 (my italics).

everything flows.[12] Resisting the dualistic essentialism of Western theologies and philosophies that distinguish being (logos) from existence (praxis), the concept of *tao* underscores the interwovenness of being and becoming that is readily evidenced in the transformational experiences of life. So, Heup Young Kim articulates:

> As its Chinese word consists of two ideographs, meaning "head" (*t'i*, being) and "vehicle" (*yung*, becoming), *tao* means both the source of being (logos) and the way of cosmic becoming (praxis). Accordingly, *tao* can be reduced neither to being nor to becoming; rather it is the being in becoming or the logos in transformative praxis. *Tao* is not an option or either-or, but embraces the whole of both-and. It does not force one to stay at the crossroad of logos (being) and praxis (becoming), *but actualizes one to participate in a dynamic movement to be united with the cosmic track*.[13]

The Confucian promotion of moral responsibility and the Taoist emphasis on the transformative praxis converge on the point that a transcendent vision (or a cosmological operation of the spiritual presence) is structurally related to and with the struggles experienced in the earthly life. The actualization of the transcendent vision—when it takes place in and through experiencing the rigors of earthly living—finds its tangible expressions when individuals become morally responsible and virtuous in the context of communal life. The religious vision in Asian religions cannot be divorced from tangible demonstrations of "moral responsibility." Furthermore, "moral responsibility" in this regard is not merely an aspect but the fulfillment of what it means to be truly human; in this, the emphasis is placed on the process (or progression) of "becoming."

The "relational" and "participatory" view of life envisaged in the Confucian and Taoist traditions encourages us to revisit constructively what it means to be "spiritual" or "being filled with the Spirit." Given the trajectory of Confucian and Taoist thinking, being full of the Spirit cannot be disassociated from becoming authentically human; rather, without becoming "truly human" (i.e., morally responsible in communal living), it becomes impossible for individuals to claim that they are living under the indwelling and empowering presence of the Spirit. A constructive reflection in this regard may further resonate with the biblical picture of the way of Jesus Christ. Being anointed with the Spirit, Jesus's life was not spared from the harsh realities of earthly living and struggling; it was none other than the Spirit who drove him into the wilderness (Mk 1:12). "Being in the wilderness"—where he was tempted by Satan and was with the wild animals (v. 13)—carried with it a symbolic significance for his life's entire journey that culminated with his suffering and eventual death on the cross; he was made perfect through suffering (Heb. 2:10). The upshot of this was the re-creation of, and the possibility for, all humanity to embrace a true humanity in him. The Spirit-anointed way of life on display in Jesus's earthly journey is now provided to all who would take up and follow. In journeying through the wilderness of life with the self-same Spirit, we learn to participate in the way of Jesus Christ, living responsibly to the vision of God in and through the concrete situations of life.

---

[12] See Herbert Fingarette, *Confucius—The Secular as the Sacred* (New York: Harper & Row, 1972). Fingarette expands the meaning of *tao* to refer to "the right Way of life, the Way of governing, the ideal Way of human existence, the Way of cosmos, the generative-normative Way (Pattern, path, course) of existence" (19).
[13] Kim, *Wang Yang-ming and Karl Barth*, 35–6 (my italics).

Another distinctive way to speak about spirituality or the spiritual presence in Asian religions is to reflect on the residual effects of shamanistic traditions in various aspects of life. Speaking particularly of the Korean context, Younghak Hyun notes that shamanistic rituals and belief systems represent the grassroots spirituality of "Korean consciousness" and are profoundly entangled with both the nation's history of "being oppressed against" and the stories of oppression suffered by *minjung* (i.e., common people).[14] Personally and collectively, Koreans are known to live with the ever-present realities of *han*.[15] *Han* is an unresolved "lump" or "knot" deeply ingrained in an individual, family, community, or nation that, if unattended, can become disruptive or even destructive in variegated spheres of life. As Suk-Mo Ahn helpfully notes, *han* is not an ephemeral feeling or temporal emotion but a complex web of emotions that becomes deeply engraved on the heart of individuals.[16] Collectively, however, *han* also becomes a significant identifier for the accumulated pain and suffering particularized among certain groups in society (e.g., those based on gender or class discriminations), just as it can point to an archetypal (emotive) disposition of all Koreans rooted in their shared history of 5,000 years that is filled with stories of tragedy and victimization. Positively, however, the presence of *han* represents a profound sense of resilience among those who are oppressed as well as an indefatigable reminder of the injustice suffered. Not only that, but if sublimated rightly, *han* can serve as a catalyst to empower individuals, communities, and even nations in their hopeful and persistent aspiration to make all things whole.

In keeping with this trajectory, the shamanistic rituals that a *mudang* (i.e., Korean shaman) performs are believed to bring a peaceful resolution or liberation from variegated instances of *han*, since the purpose of the rituals are to deter any acting out of vengeance by haunting ghosts. Koreans believe that the souls of the victimized are unable to, or may even resist, transition into the next life without provision of an adequate appeasement (which is called *"han-pu-ri"* in Korean) regarding the injustice suffered in their past lives. The appeasement envisioned in this regard entails

---

[14]Younghak Hyun, "Minjung Theology and the Religion of Han," *East Asia Journal of Theology* 3, no. 2 (1985): 357. Given the scope of this paper, the focus has been intentionally limited to the Korean context.

[15]For a detailed discussion on the culture and fabric of *han*, see Sang-Ehil Han's work, *A Revisionist Spirit-Christology in Korean Culture* (Ann Arbor, MI: UMI, 2004), especially chap. 2. See also Jae Hoon Lee, *The Exploration of the Inner Wounds—Han* (Atlanta, GA: Scholars Press, 1994) and Andrew Sung Park, *The Wounded Heart of God: The Asian Concept of Han and the Christian Doctrine of Sin* (Nashville, TN: Abingdon, 1993). Han's work in particular explains *han* in terms of distinctive dimensions (i.e., the personal and the collective dimensions) and different levels (i.e., the original/archetypal and the secondary). With regard to the latter, the archetypal *han* is understood to be deeply hidden, never arriving at final and full resolution, but providing the impetus for being manifested in the secondary *han*. The concept is comparatively similar to the Kierkegaardian concept of *angst*. For Lee, the collective *han* at the archetypal (or unconscious) level is similar to Carl Jung's concept of "collective unconscious" (*The Exploration of the Inner Wounds*, 3–5). Park echoes a similar comparative analysis, but he also notes the difference: "unlike Jung's 'collective unconscious,' however, this *han* does not take over the content of the *han* of a previous generation, but the structure of *han*-memory . . . transmittable to another generation through the framework of ethnic ethos, tradition and culture. . . . That is why we have the variety of racial ethos. . . . Furthermore, Jung's 'collective unconscious' is impersonal, but the collective unconscious *han* is personal, including rational and emotional dimensions accumulated in the ethnic ethos" (*The Wounded Heart of God*, 39). Comparing the concept of *han* with the Christian understanding of sin, Park thus notes: "Sin is not passed on to posterity, but *han* does pass through the channels of human existence and social tradition" (ibid., 80). As such, children inherit the consequential, suffering conditions of an inherited cultural ethos.

[16]Suk-Mo Ahn, "Toward a Local Pastoral Care and Pastoral Theology: The Basis, Model, and Case of Han in Light of Charles Gerkin's Pastoral Hermeneutics" (PhD Diss., Emory University, 1991), 305.

the unveiling of unjust actions that were previously covered up or unresolved. By channeling the spirit(s) of various hierarchy, the shamans help make known the hidden stories of the victimized for the whole community.[17] This act of unveiling in the process of *han-pu-ri* represents both a vindication over injustice as well as a peaceful reconciliation that the power structures of this world are incapable to effectuate. Shamanistic practices and belief systems in Korea are certainly not without perilous consequences.[18] Nonetheless, their appeal to the spirit realm to vindicate the wounds of the victimized and, consequently, to bring a peaceful resolution is a powerful reminder that the world of the spirit—however one conceives it—cannot be thought in disassociation from earthly affairs. In fact, a peaceful resolution or reconciliation of earthly matters can only be ultimately attained by the intervention of power resident in the spirit-world. Constructively cast, this opens a creative possibility to re-examine the intercessory work of the Spirit (Rom. 8:26). In her groanings, the Spirit identifies with human travails and stands as the mediating presence between heaven and earth, bringing reconciliation to earthly troubles.

THE SPIRIT IN THE ASIAN CONTEXT: *YIN, YANG,* AND *CH'I*

Beyond a broad mapping of the spiritual dimension in Asian religions, the process of constructing a distinctively Asian pneumatology would require the deciphering of distinctive attributes associated with the concept *ch'i*. If one were to translate *ch'i* in Western languages and concepts, it would carry the ideas of "wind (air)," "breath," and "spirit" that are known to constitute essential elements in and for life. To this extent, the basic concept of *ch'i* is not dissimilar to the Hebrew concept of the Spirit, that is, *ruach*. Just as the Hebraic understanding of *ruach* (i.e., the Spirit of God) carries the connotation of the "cosmic presence" of God, *ch'i* as a distinctively Asian concept is also understood to be a cosmic life energy attending to all aspects of life in the universe.

Being essential in and for all living creatures, *ch'i* "generates" and "nourishes" life. Characterized as a "movement," *ch'i* is involved not only in originating life, but also in sustaining all things in the universe through its agency of empowerment. It is not inconsequential, therefore, that the Chinese characters for *ch'i* carry the double meaning of "feeding" (giving) and "eating" (receiving) food. As Grace Ji-Sun Kim articulates, *ch'i* is "a vital, dynamic, original power that permeates the entire universe and leads to an ultimate reality. *Ch'i* brings cohesiveness and order as it essentially holds the universe together."[19]

---

[17]Hyun Kyung Chung, "*Han-pu-ri*: Doing Theology from Korean Women's Perspective," *The Ecumenical Review* 40 (1988): 28–9.
[18]*Minjung* theology (i.e., Korean liberationist theology) has been particularly keen on exploring the "social justice" and "liberationist" motif through its constructive reflection on the selective features of shamanistic practices and belief systems in Korea. For a critical review of *minjung* theology's appropriation of shamanistic practices and belief systems, see Han, *A Revisionist Spirit-Christology in Korean Culture*, especially chap. 3.
[19]Grace Ji-Sun Kim, "In Search of a Pneumatology: Chi and Spirit," *Feminist Theology* 18, no. 1 (2009): 121. See also C. S. Song, *Jesus in the Power of the Spirit* (Minneapolis: MN: Augsburg Fortress, 1994), 293. Describing the cosmic presence of *ch'i*, Song quotes, "*Ch'i* fills the space between heaven and earth. Heaven and earth themselves, all things between heaven and earth, are all constituted by *ch'i*. Because of *ch'i*, all things between heaven and earth move, change, and function. It itself moves and moves all things. It is the subject of changes

As *ch'i* functions to originate and empower life in all spheres of the cosmos, the process is understood to be neither linear nor cyclical in nature; it is rather "a continuous pulsation of life and death."[20] Furthermore, the process takes place through the interaction of two vital forces, *yin* and *yang*, that are understood to be dialectically opposed to one another. *Yin*, for example, represents the essence of the earth, whereas *yang* refers to that of heaven. The *yin* and *yang* polarities can be further extended to other oppositional realities such as female/male, negative/positive, quiescence/activity, rest/motion, and death/life.[21]

Although *yin* and *yang* are characteristically oppositional to one another, we should note that they do not exist separately from one another; they are essentially understood to be united. As Veli-Matti Kärkkäinen observes of Jung Young Lee's reflections, "*yin* is not only *yin* but also *yang*; *yang* is not only *yang* but *yin* as well."[22] A good illustration of this in Christian theology is the conception of God in which we affirm both God's transcendence *and* immanence. *Yin* and *yang* are both understood to be necessary, and it is through their interaction with one another in a harmonious unity that a generative and nourishing power of *ch'i* is engendered.

Ch'i is not only a cosmic life-force existing in the universe, but it also exists within the human body. Being external to and existing within the human body, the interpenetrating movement of *ch'i* generates a vital energy needed to ensure the bodily and psychological well-being of a human person.[23] Furthermore, the lack or absence of *ch'i* would lead to various kinds of disruption and disharmony in an individual's life; it can even lead the person to suffer a mental or physical illness. Being the all-pervasive presence of life-force in the universe, *ch'i* is not to be construed as a mere external force to being human. Existing within human beings, it functions to vitalize all that constitutes human persons—body, mind, and spirit.

PNEUMATOLOGICAL THEMES AND POSSIBILITIES

The particularities aforementioned of the Asian context offer intriguing theological possibilities for pneumatology. To begin with, the concept of *ch'i* espouses a holistic view of the universe in which humanity is a part. As a "cosmic" life-force, *ch'i* vitalizes all things existing in the universe, but by existing in human beings, it also nourishes all aspects of human life. In its life-generating and nourishing operations, *ch'i* is indiscriminate of the objects it encounters and empowers. It brings all things that exist in the universe into the process of harmony and unity. That the process takes place through generative interactions of dialectical polarities accentuates the "interrelatedness" between nature

---

and movements and the origin that causes them." *Philosophy of Ch'i*, ed. Onozawa Seiichi, Fukunaga Atsuji, and Yamanoi Yu (Tokyo: Tokyo University Press, 1978), 356 as quoted in Song, *Jesus in the Power of the Spirit*, 293.
[20]Kim, "In Search of a Pneumatology," 122.
[21]Jung Young Lee, *The Trinity in Asian Perspective* (Nashville, TN: Abingdon, 1996), 25.
[22]Veli-Matti Kärkkäinen, *The Trinity: Global Perspectives* (Louisville, KY: Westminster John Knox Press, 2007), 319.
[23]Song, *Jesus in the Power of the Spirit*, 293. Kim notes that for the Chinese, the disciplines such as Chi Kung and Tai Chi can lead to experience *ch'i* bodily—"a tingling sensation, a feeling of physical fulness and ultimately as a palpable circulation of energy in the body" ("In Search of a Pneumatology," 124). Thinking holistically about the life-giving energy that *ch'i* generates, the healing it brings is also believed to address other dimensions (e.g., mind, emotions, and psychological well-being) of being human, including the spiritual dimension.

(impersonal/inanimate) and human beings (personal/animate). That is, as dialectical polarities, these actually require one another in order for life as a whole to be generative and nourishing. Disruption or lack of harmonious unity precipitates malfunction and affliction for all involved.[24] If the insights of the Asian understanding of *ch'i* were to be taken constructively, they offer a critique of anthropocentric tendencies in Christian pneumatologies of the West.[25] The Asian concept of *ch'i* helps us envisage the work of the Spirit in which the ecological concerns in nature and the redemption of humanity are understood to be essentially intertwined with one another. The Spirit who redeems humans and makes their lives whole is the self-same Spirit who generates and nourishes life in the whole creation. Thinking in a similar vein, Moltmann views pneumatology as the theological thread that weaves ecological theology and cosmic Christology.

> The new approaches to an "ecological theology," "cosmic Christology", and the rediscovery of the body, start from the Hebraic understanding of the divine Spirit and presuppose that the redeeming Spirit of Christ and the creative and life-giving Spirit of God are one and the same. So experience of the life-giving Spirit in the faith of the heart and in the sociality of love leads of itself beyond the limits of the church to the rediscovery of the same Spirit in nature, in plants, in animals, and in the ecosystems of the earth.[26]

It should also be noted that *ch'i* as a pneumatological concept is primarily focused on "movement" and "change." *Ch'i* as an animating life-force generated through the "interaction" between *yin* and *yang* is not a "substance," nor does it have a particular form. The presence of *ch'i* is either felt or experienced. As such, *ch'i* can be described only in terms of a *movement* or *change* that the process of the *yin-yang* interaction generates. Carrying primarily the idea of "movement" or "change," the concept of *ch'i* prompts and gives prominence to a participatory way of conceiving a Christian doctrine of the Spirit. Experiencing the Spirit that effects a "movement" or "change" in an individual would not be viewed merely as an "application" of the Spirit's power, nor would such experience be considered as temporary or episodic in nature. Instead, experiencing the Spirit anticipates the process of holistic transformation in which individuals are brought into a journey of ever-deepening fellowship with the Spirit. The Spirit then becomes the

---

[24]Song, *Jesus in the Power of the Spirit*, 293–4.
[25]Taking seriously the Asian insights of *ch'i* in constructing a Christian doctrine of the Spirit is not without fundamental issues and problems. As Kirsteen Kim notes, theological attempts in this direction often espouse a hybrid approach between the concept of *ch'i* and the Christian understanding of the Spirit and ignore in the process that the presence of different cultures and religions in Asia would disallow a unified theological vision. See Kim, "Review of *The Holy Spirit, Chi, and the Other: A Model of Global and Intercultural Pneumatology*," *Pneuma* 35 (2013): 112. Simon Chan in his review of Moltmann's *The Spirit of Life* echoes a similar concern when he notes that in the Asian religious context, "the personal identity of the Holy Spirit has to be defined against a host of other spirits as part of the day to day life, struggle and witness of the church. In such a context, one cannot simply assume that any religious experience . . . can be uncritically attributed to the cosmic Spirit." Chan, "An Asian Review," *Journal of Pentecostal Theology* 4 (1994): 40. Insights from the Asian concept of *ch'i* in this present study are not intended to obscure the diversity among pneumatologies in the East nor to subsume different spirits with various names under the one and self-same spirit; instead, the insights drawn are to serve as a catalyst to trigger creative and deeper explorations within the worlds of scriptural witnesses and Christian traditions in order to offer a distinctive Christian pneumatology that can account for contextual realities of the ordinary practices of life in Asia.
[26]Jürgen Moltmann, *The Spirit of Life: A Universal Affirmation* (Minneapolis, MN: Fortress, 2001), 9–10.

ever-present agency of "creative becoming" for individuals. Furthermore, in the process of becoming (or experiencing the life-generating work of the Spirit), the "movement" or "change" individuals experience becomes simultaneously the process of being identified with the person of the Spirit.[27] That is, in experiencing the Spirit, we are drawn into the life-generating work of the Spirit and become active participants of it. We take on in our living the life-generating and life-nourishing characteristics of the Spirit, resisting the allurement of the spirit of stagnation, dominance, and control.

Although the movement or change that *ch'i* effects intends to be positive (i.e., generation or nourishment in and for life), it is intriguing to note that such a positive effect is understood to be yielded only through a dynamic interaction between the two oppositional elements, that is, *yin* and *yang*. Moreover, the interaction does not envision or call for an eventual downfall or demise of one or the other because without the presence of both elements, *ch'i* would not be generated. In the Asian concept of the spirit, then, the emphasis is placed on the idea of holding opposites in a dialectical correlation.

The idea of holding two opposites dialectically can be creatively construed in developing a holistic pneumatology "from below." One can envisage, for instance, the biblical picture of the liberating Spirit on the one hand and the image of the groaning Spirit on the other. A dialectical juxtaposition of these oppositional images of the Spirit helps us understand that the liberating work of the Spirit cannot be detached from the Spirit's identification with the travails of the creation. Likewise, the intercessory groanings of the Spirit have in view the ultimate reality of liberation for the creation.

Interestingly, however, as Kirsteen Kim notes, the classical paradigm of the West has long emphasized the "priestly" aspect of the Spirit's reconciling work, wherein the Spirit is portrayed primarily as the agent who provides access to the Father through Jesus Christ (Eph. 2:18). In this paradigm, the Spirit is imaged as "hovering over" the whole creation from above in consummating her work of reconciliation. In contrast, the contextual realities in Asia demand that we take seriously the "spirit-world" paradigm, emphasizing the "prophetic" role of the reconciling work of the Spirit. In this paradigm, the liberating work of the Spirit is understood as rising up from below.[28] In constructing a theology of the Spirit in the Korean context, Jong Chun Park follows the spirit-world paradigm and advocates the image of the Spirit as the "crawling" God. For Park, the Mother Spirit "crawls" in the midst of her children, joining in their groanings for liberation.[29] The Spirit's crawling in the midst of human travails and the creation's groanings has liberating effects in which courage to resist realities of suffering leads to a vibrant hope for the new creation and renews the rhythms of life in the present. Being identified with this Spirit of God is to participate in her groanings and to experience the liberating power of the Spirit. Herein, the Spirit drives us to Jesus Christ and his way of life, wherein the power to heal, as Moltmann claims, is the power of his suffering.[30]

---

[27] Lee, "Trinity as Embrace of Yin-Yang," 316–17. Reflecting on the interaction between *yin* and *yang*, Lee challenges the substance-based theologies of the West and advocates a "theology of change." For Lee, change is not a mere function of being but is "the very source of becoming and the reality of being" (317). The scope of this study would not allow us to discuss this in further detail, but it is worth noting that the *yin* and *yang* way of thinking encourages us to view change as "primary" instead of it being merely derivative or a function of being.
[28] Kim, "The Reconciling Spirit," 26.
[29] Jong Chun Park, *Crawl with God, Dance in the Spirit: A Creative Formation of Korean Theology of the Spirit* (Nashville, TN: Abingdon, 1998), 10–12.
[30] Moltmann, *The Spirit of Life*, 191.

CONCLUSION

Constructing an Asian pneumatology is a challenging task if one were to take seriously the variegated complexities and diversities rooted in the Asian context. First, a constructive and discerning reflection is necessary with regard to the fact that the age-old religious traditions are deeply grounded in the grammars of life in Asia. The upshot of this reflective process would be a revisionist pneumatology that can both complement and critique Christian pneumatologies rooted in the Western milieu. Second, an Asian pneumatology seems to be closely aligned with the cosmic view of the Spirit's presence. Consequently, instead of being anthropocentric, an Asian revisionist pneumatology would call for the anthropo-cosmic vision in which ethical concerns for social justice and reconciliation, for instance, are not disassociated from ecological concerns for creation care. Third, an Asian pneumatology is rooted in the "spirit-world" paradigm wherein a heavenly vision and earthly living are intimately intertwined with one another. This is particularly thematized in the stories of *han* in Korean culture. The "spirit-world" paradigm further helps revision the reconciling work of the Spirit in which the present reality of suffering is conjoined with, and hence reinterpreted by, an empowering vision of hope for the new creation. Fourth, an Asian pneumatology seems to take on a sanctificationist approach with its promotion of participation in the work of the Spirit. Being filled with the Spirit is to be unequivocally identified with the Spirit's groanings in matters of earthly travails. In this, the anointed (or, Spirit-filled) way of Jesus Christ stands as the paragon of life. Fifth, in reflecting constructively on the religious narratives in Asia, it seems interesting to note that the Spirit stands as the interlocutor between a heavenly vision and earthly living, whereas the history of the Christian religion has often tended to identify Jesus Christ exclusively as the point of contact between God and humanity. In light of this trajectory, constructing an Asian pneumatology may therefore present a creative possibility to revision the Word-centered theologies of the West, reconstructing a Christian theology with the Spirit at the center.

FOR FURTHER READING

Han, Sang-Ehil. *A Revisionist Spirit-Christology in Korean Culture*. Ann Arbor, MI: UMI, 2004.

Hyun, Younghak. "Minjung Theology and the Religion of Han." *The East Asia Journal of Theology* 3, no. 2 (1985): 354–9.

Kim, Grace Ji-Sun. "In Search of a Pneumatology: Chi and Spirit." *Feminist Theology* 18, no. 1 (2009): 117–32.

Kim, Heup Young. *Wang-Yang-Ming and Karl Barth: A Confucian-Christian Dialogue*. Lanham, MD: University Press of America, 1996.

Song, C. S. *Jesus in the Power of the Spirit*. Minneapolis, MN: Augsburg Fortress, 1994.

CHAPTER TWENTY-NINE

Spirit of Integration and Solidarity

Asian American Pneumatologies

DANIEL D. LEE

From migration and interculturality to marginality and solidarity, various themes enliven Asian American theology generally and pneumatology more specifically. As the most diverse and complex racial category in the United States, Asian America poses unique challenges to the task of "contextual" theology.[1] Because of this contextual complexity and plurality, Asian American theologians themselves vary widely in their situational understanding as well as their methodological approaches. This complexity results in both a conceptual fecundity as well as a diffusion, or even fragmentation, of what falls under this category of Asian American theology. However, I will argue for *integration* of these seemingly divergent themes as one of the key pneumatological contributions from the Asian American context. The Spirit of God is the One who holds together the disparate aspects of Asian America, revealing truth about the powers and principalities at play, bringing healing and restoration to the places of unseen and inarticulate pain, and integrating whole selves toward union with Christ and with others through Christ, all for the purposes of God's kingdom work.

Before this constructive proposal, I will begin with a broad framing of what Asian America means using a heuristic tool that deconstructs the contextual matrix of every expression of Asian America as the intersection of Asian heritage, migration, American culture, and racialization. Through this heuristic apparatus, we will be able to reveal the often-implicit presuppositions about contextual definitions and their related methodologies. Second, I present three Asian American pneumatologies as envisioned by Amos Yong, Anselm Min, and Grace Ji-Sun Kim, each organized around the theme of migration, solidarity, and Asian heritage, respectively. Finally, I will present my own pneumatology oriented toward a Spirit of integration who brings together the disparate parts of fragmented Asian American selves and communities.

---

[1] I am indebted in this piece to Amos Yong and Kirsteen Kim for their invaluable comments and insights. I am assuming that all theology is contextual, although Eurocentric theology has been afforded a kind of implicit normativity with a hegemonic force, which has also made it more vulnerable to cultural captivity. I reiterate this point to clarify how I am using the idea of theological contextuality.

HYBRIDIC INTERSECTIONS OF ASIAN AMERICA

Before proceeding with any discussion of these theological themes, we must begin with a clear understanding of the substance and boundaries of Asian America. Depending on what segment or definition of Asian America is assumed by an Asian American theologian, the pressing issues identified and engaged in their work will follow suit.

Of course, every context is dynamic and internally complex as well as porous to external influences. Kathryn Tanner avers how the postmodern critique reveals the ways in which modern conceptions of culture were too simplistic and essentialistic.[2] However, the task of contextual theology often assumes a form of "strategic essentialism," as Gayatri Chakravorty Spivak articulates, in order to collectively identify a common concern to address theologically.[3] This contextual concern functions as a *unifying theme* gathering the myriad of individual and sub-segment experiences under a common denomination. The Asian American context struggles with identifying a unifying theme.

We might think of the black context as defined by the question of race, particularly of blackness according to James Cone.[4] The Hispanic context might still be organized under its shared colonial history and mestizo existence.[5] Even in their contestations about reductive homogenizations and intersectionality, these themes for the black and Hispanic community still possess enough experiential capital and collective saliency to fund a constructive theological discussion.[6] However, the issue of a unifying theme becomes quite problematic for the Asian American context. As the most diverse and complex of the racial groups in the United States, Asian America does not have simple common themes under which to gather its "heterogeneity, hybridity, [and] multiplicity."[7]

Seeking to unpack this complicated context, we can begin with the demographics of Asian Americans consisting of over sixty different ethnic heritages. Even if we narrow down our scope to the six largest ethnic groups (Chinese, Filipino, Indian, Vietnamese, Korean, and Japanese), these groups share no common religious or cultural heritage, language, or colonial history. In terms of racialization, while "yellow" often serves as a shorthand for Asian Americans, this description ignores the "brown" third (Filipino Americans, Indian Americans, and others). In this regard, there are historical and phenotypical reasons why Filipino Americans are regularly grouped with Hispanics.[8] Also, some Indian Americans register as black enough to experience similar racist harassment.

Early Asian American theologies, like the beginnings of Asian American studies, used East Asian heritage as a template, which led to an "ethnic monopolizing" of the whole context. Thus, these early works identified with the cultural heritage of Confucianism and cast similar racialized experiences as "yellow" and so ambivalently between black and

---

[2]Kathryn Tanner, *Theories of Culture* (Minneapolis, MN: Fortress, 1997), 40–56.
[3]Gayatri Chakravorty Spivak, *In Other Worlds* (New York: Routledge, 1988), 205.
[4]James Cone, *A Black Theology of Liberation* (Maryknoll, NY: Orbis, 1970).
[5]Justo L. González, *Mañana: Christian Theology from a Hispanic Perspective* (Nashville, TN: Abingdon, 1990).
[6]For a critique of ontological blackness, see Victor Anderson, *Beyond Ontological Blackness: An Essay on African American Religious and Cultural Criticism* (New York: Continuum, 1995) and J. Kameron Carter, *Race: A Theological Account* (Oxford: Oxford University Press, 2008).
[7]Lisa Lowe, "Heterogeneity, Hybridity, Multiplicity: Marking Asian American Differences," *Diaspora: A Journal of Transnational Studies* 1, no. 1 (Spring 1991): 24–44.
[8]Anthony Christian Ocampo, *The Latinos of Asia: How Filipino Americans Break the Rules of Race* (Stanford, CA: Stanford University Press, 2016).

white.[9] Taking up the full heterogeneous Asian American category, these kinds of narrow (mis)representations and ethnic monopolizations must be avoided, even as the political significance of the "Asian American" racial grouping is retained.[10] Indeed, the term "Asian American" was developed to engender positive political and activist identity in reaction to the racist and colonialist "Oriental" identifier.[11]

Given the problem of the elusive unifying theme for the Asian American context, there are two kinds of methodological responses. One is to adopt an ethnic-specific framing such as Japanese American theology, Filipino American theology, and so on, with its corresponding unifying or at least salient theme(s). The other is to take the political and activist approach, leading to a public theology focused on social location and structural pressures as the unifying theme. While both responses have their relative merits, what is needed is an intersectional or polycentric approach, rejecting the idea of a unifying theme while still accepting the need for a panethnic coalition for political resistance against racism and imperialism. Elsewhere, I have described Asian America as the intersection and interaction of four themes, namely (a) Asian religious and cultural heritage, (b) migration experience, (c) American culture, and (d) racialization. Collectively, I call this heuristic matrix the "Asian American Quadrilateral."[12] Each of these categories serves as a portal to enter the Asian American experience, while none of them can, in and of themselves, grasp the whole without the danger of hermeneutical reduction or distortion. The four themes can also function as a typology of sorts to interpret the methodology of various Asian American theologies.

Given the limits of this chapter, the deep intricacies of the Asian American context cannot be explored further. However, keeping these various methodological approaches and categories in mind will protect us from crude stereotypes or other theoretical infelicities. With this basic and interpretative reminder, we can now appreciate the place and role of at least three different approaches to Asian American pneumatology.

SPIRIT OF CULTURAL REDEMPTION, SOLIDARITY, AND LIFE FORCE

Among Asian American theologians, Amos Yong, Anselm Min, and Grace Ji-Sun Kim stand out for developing creative pneumatologies, although they vary significantly from each other in method, concern, and proposal.

Self-identifying as a Pentecostal and evangelical, Malaysian Chinese American theologian Amos Yong utilizes his pent-evangelical imagination for a theology that "draws from Asian traditions and patterns of thought."[13] Yong formulates the Asian American context diasporically in general, stressing the global migration of Asians, including within the United States. Thus, his discussion moves from the concerns of Asian Pentecostal

---

[9]Peter C. Phan and Jung Young Lee, eds., *Journeys at the Margin: Toward an Autobiographical Theology in American-Asian Perspective* (Collegeville, MN: Liturgical, 1999).

[10]Yen Le Espiritu, *Asian American Panethnicity: Bridging Institutions and Identities* (Philadelphia, PA: Temple University Press, 1992).

[11]Karen L. Ishizuka, *Serve the People: Making Asian America in the Long Sixties* (New York: Verso, 2016), 3.

[12]Daniel D. Lee, *Double Particularity: Karl Barth, Contextuality, and Asian American Theology* (Minneapolis, MN: Fortress, 2017), 45–51.

[13]Amos Yong, *The Future of Evangelical Theology: Soundings from the Asian American Diaspora* (Downers Grove, IL: InterVarsity, 2014), 135.

theologians to Asian Americans. The outpouring of the Spirit on Pentecost upon all flesh undergirds his pent-evangelical imagination. For Yong, pneumatology serves primarily as an imagination and method to fund the possibility and reality of a global theology, including Asian and Asian American theologies.[14]

The miracle of tongues in the second chapter of Acts proclaims that all languages "can indeed be vehicles of the gospel and can declare the wonders of God."[15] Yong understands the divine redemption of human language to include linguistic, cultural, and religious dimensions. In discerning this redemption, there must be "a dialectical trialogue" involving the interpretation of the biblical text, the current work of the Spirit, and various contexts. Moreover, this pneumatological affirmation should be understood as not only permission or invitation, but also a command and requirement for the global movement of the gospel.

Enabled by a biblical mandate, Yong's affirmation of the Spirit's redemption of Asian language, culture, and religions offers a methodological basis for constructively and critically drawing from these resources. This inclusion of Asian religions, which is not often included in evangelical contextualization discussions, is an especially important development because of the deep enmeshment of Asian culture and religions.[16] Yong envisions these Asian resources to distinctively and primarily fund Asian American theology as it engages themes like migration, racism, politics, and so on.

Engaging Yong's core argument, we can ask if his Asian American context is distinguished enough from the Asian one. Yong clearly recognizes that the history and experience of Asian Americans as a racial minority is integral to this context.[17] However, this reality of racialization does not play a methodologically significant role here. Are the over 170 years of Asian American history and experience not also rich material for theological reflection? His diasporic or "global" thinking might lead to downplaying the difference between Asians and Asian Americans. Asian Americans have long suffered from racist stereotypes of being "perpetual foreigners" who can never become truly American. Fortunately, elsewhere Yong expands his pent-evangelical imagination to include the interconnection between the Spirit's outpouring to mutuality and solidarity across linguistic, ethnic, and economic lines in the process of developing a *perpetual foreigner* hermeneutic that is critically diasporic and anti-imperial.[18]

Whereas Yong spotlights pneumatological recovery of Asian heritage, Korean American Catholic theologian Anselm Min underscores the Spirit of fellowship and solidarity as healing the division arising from differences in nationality, culture, religion, ethnicity, gender, class, and language and guiding the world to live together without doing violence to each other. Min proposes what he believes is a way to address the concerns of our divided globalized context through a new post-liberation framework of "solidarity of

---

[14] See more reflection on this connection to global theology in Amos Yong, *The Spirit Poured Out on All Flesh: Pentecostalism and the Possibility of Global Theology* (Grands Rapids, MI: Baker, 2005).
[15] Yong, *The Future of Evangelical Theology*, 136.
[16] See Nadeau on how Asian religions can persist culturally even without religious dimensions. Randall L. Nadeau, *Asian Religions: A Cultural Perspective* (Malden, MA: Wiley-Blackwell, 2014). On a separate note, the field of theology and culture also generally ignores religions as part of culture.
[17] Yong, *The Future of Evangelical Theology*, 121.
[18] See Amos Yong, "American Political Theology in a Post Age: A Perpetual Foreigner and Pentecostal Stance," in *Faith and Resistance in the Age of Trump*, ed. Miguel A. De La Torre (Maryknoll, NY: Orbis, 2017), 107–14.

others," meaning that "there is no privileged perspective, that all are others to one another, that we as others to one another are equally responsible."[19]

Previously, Jung Young Lee with his concept of marginality and Sang Hyun Lee's framing of liminality also sought to move beyond liberation as a paradigm to address the struggle of racial minorities.[20] These works were particular to the Asian American racial experience, although the wider implications were clear. The scope of Min's work, however, is much more expansive, covering all axes of identity and oppression in a globalized and pluralistic world. Thus, Min writes more implicitly as an Asian American posing questions that are relevant to, but also beyond, the Asian American context. This posture beyond the Asian American context is a methodological move driven by the conviction that "the time has come for the oppressed group to enter into a more self-conscious, systematic solidarity."[21] With this movement beyond liberation theologies, Min proposes his "solidarity of others" paradigm. There are two aspects of this paradigm: the Holy Spirit and its "power of self-transcendence for communion and solidarity," and the body of Christ as its "ruling metaphor."[22]

This pneumatological aspect is developed on two levels. First, following Augustine, Min recognizes the Holy Spirit as the "self-effacing, selfless God whose selfhood or personhood seems to lie in transcending herself to empower others likewise to transcend themselves in communion with others."[23] Importantly, the Spirit creates communion and solidarity without erasing the particularities of individuals. Second and correspondingly, human praxis in line with this Spirit should adopt (among other points) a *concrete social* metaphysics that can account for our economic, political, and cultural relational matrix, rather than a *substantialist* or *I-Thou interpersonal* metaphysics with its accompanying limitations. This concrete social metaphysics in turn can guide and fund political praxis.

The ways that Min sublates human differences with solidarity without totality à la Levinas are laudable.[24] They not only stimulate academic discourse, but also guide ecclesial praxis. As a paradigm to move beyond particular ethnic theologies, this idea of solidarity mirrors Gary Okihiro's project of recalling ethnic studies back to its origin in the Third World Liberation Front of 1968 with its agenda of subjectivity and collective liberation of oppressed peoples around the world.[25] While Min's call for oppressed groups to enter into a more organized solidarity can be wholeheartedly affirmed, this collective vision would not supersede the tasks of theology for particular ethnic or racial communities like

---

[19] Anselm Kyongsuk Min, *The Solidarity of Others in a Divided World: A Postmodern Theology after Postmodernism* (London: T & T Clark, 2004), 82.

[20] Jung Young Lee, *Marginality: The Key to Multicultural Theology* (Minneapolis, MN: Fortress, 1995) and Sang Hyun Lee, *From A Liminal Place: An Asian American Theology* (Minneapolis, MN: Fortress, 2010). While both Lee and Lee are Korean American, this theme of marginality/liminality has relevance more broadly. Thus, Vietnamese American Catholic theologian Peter Phan picks up the issue of marginality in his work as well. See Peter C. Phan, *Christianity with an Asian Face: Asian American Theology in the Making* (Maryknoll, NY: Orbis, 2003).

[21] Min, *Solidarity of Others in a Divided World*, 134.

[22] Ibid., 121, 150.

[23] Ibid., 118.

[24] In a sustained engagement, Min assesses that Levinas in critiquing totality moves one-sidedly toward infinity of the other. Moving beyond Levinas, Min offers the triple dialectic of totality, infinity, and solidarity for authentic human community. Ibid., 23–6.

[25] Gary Y. Okihiro, *Third World Studies: Theorizing Liberation* (Durham, NC: Duke University Press, 2016).

the Asian American community. Just as theology is a self-reflective exercise of the church, the multiplicity of churches requires equally diverse theologies.

On a critical note, Min's Augustinian line of reasoning together with his use of the feminine pronoun for the Holy Spirit raises concerns about patriarchy especially in the Asian American context. Feminist theologians point out how the Augustinian notion of a selfless "bond of love" can marginalize the Spirit, converging with the experience of women in church and society.[26] Similarly, the Spirit's feminine traits often fall prey to stereotypical and patriarchal definitions.[27] Thus, when Min asserts that the "three divine persons are not all equal in every aspect" while stressing the self-effacement of the Spirit, his proposal can misfire for Asian Americans who are also dealing with the Asian cultural heritage of patriarchy.[28]

Our third Asian American pneumatology exhibit includes key elements of the first two. Korean American mainline Presbyterian theologian Grace Ji-Sun Kim, working out of a postcolonial feminist methodology, focuses on the patterns of domination and subordination supported by Western theology, constructing a pneumatology of hybridity using the Eastern concept of *Chi*.[29] *Chi*, which is the Chinese term, represents life substance and energy with philosophical, health, and ecological features. Kim's key move is to argue that the concept of *Chi* can be "found to be similar to or largely the same" as the Christian doctrine of the Holy Spirit.[30] She argues that this commonality can open dialogue and bring greater understanding between the East and West. Kim believes the main hindrance to this way of thinking is Christocentricity, with its particularity that rejects this similarity between the Eastern concepts of God and Christianity. More specifically, the problem is the *filioque* clause that tethers the Holy Spirit to Christ, obscuring the inclusive interreligious point of contact.

Kim brings together a wide number of sources and approaches that we see in Yong and Min as well as her postcolonial insights. Akin to Min's conceptualization of the Spirit as relationality or solidarity, Kim wants to see the Spirit as the in-between God of liminality and hybridity while still affirming the personhood of the Spirit. *Chi*'s mind-body integration and its immanent presence in all things are enlisted to break down toxic dualisms and binary thinking and bring about communion and embrace of the other. Kim's theological fecundity arises out of this deconstruction of dualistic modes of thinking and the resulting pneumatological corporeality via *Chi* as life-force, where race,

---

[26] See Elizabeth Johnson, *She Who Is: The Mystery of God in Feminist Theological Discourse*, tenth anniversary edition (New York: Crossroad, 2003), 130; Gavin D'Costa, *Sexing the Trinity: Gender, Culture and the Divine* (London, SCM, 2000), 11–16.
[27] Johnson, *She Who Is*, 148.
[28] Min, *Solidarity of Others in a Divided World*, 123.
[29] A prolific author, Kim has also written three pneumatological volumes: *The Holy Spirit, Chi, and the Other: A Model of Global and Intercultural Pneumatology* (New York: Palgrave Macmillan, 2011); *Colonialism, Han, and the Transformative Spirit* (New York: Palgrave Macmillan, 2013); *Embracing the Other: The Transformative Spirit of Love* (Grand Rapids, MI: Eerdmans, 2015). For the purpose of our discussion, I will focus on the first volume only, which serves as a generative work for the other two books. We should note that Kim's work serves as one example among others that connects *Chi* and the Holy Spirit. See, for example, Koo Dong Yun, *The Holy Spirit and Ch'i (Qi): A Chiological Approach to Pneumatology* (Eugene, OR: Pickwick, 2012) and Hyo-Dong Lee, *Spirit, Qi, and the Multitude: A Comparative Theology for the Democracy of Creation* (New York: Fordham University Press, 2014). Yun and Lee are oriented more toward the Asian context than the Asian American one.
[30] Kim, *Holy Spirit, Chi, and the Other*, 60.

gender, ecology, and sociopolitical oppression can all be seamlessly covered under the work of the Spirit.

While affirming the creative moves in Kim's work, one could ask: Is what occurs in Kim's pluralistic theological project an eclipsing of Christ in Christianity in favor of the Spirit for the sake of interreligious dialogue and fellowship?[31] Living with a peaceful and hospitable posture in a pluralistic world does not necessitate the loss of theological concreteness, as we see in the work of Anselm Min. While strategic, Kim's rhetoric of East versus West as well as a general homogenizing of "the East" might weaken her agenda. Also, her dependence on these generalized categories could be interpreted as still functioning within an Orientalist framework.

TOWARD A SPIRIT OF INTEGRATION FOR FRAGMENTED SELVES AND COMMUNITIES

Asian cultural and religious heritage and the pressing concerns of liberation and solidarity in our globalized and pluralistic world are indeed salient issues for the Asian American experience. Rather than the sociopolitical level of the previous discussion, in this section I propose a psychological entry to Asian American pneumatology, particularly the work of the Holy Spirit in relation to the trauma-induced identity and process of personal integration as a complement to broader sociological concerns.[32] Then moving from the personal to communal and structural realms, I will gesture toward the Spirit's empowerment for the work of solidarity and justice.

Various concepts are used to define and understand the hybridity and multiplicity of Asian American identity: biculturalism, code switching, double consciousness, and enculturation/acculturation are some examples.[33] These conceptions of identity do not adequately address the challenge of self-integration, of owning various aspects of self together in divine shalom. For example, biculturality might be a description of adroitly code switching back and forth while still lacking the consciousness of the systemic forces that necessitate the need for this skill. As a sociopolitical expression of oppression and survival under white normativity, this so-called biculturality reflects fragmentation or even balkanization of various unacceptable selves.

Within this racial-cultural rubric, bicultural competence could be interpreted negatively as a trauma-induced double self. In Kevin Nadal's concept of microaggressive trauma, everyday indignities, slights, and insults over time add up to manifest trauma-like symptoms.[34] In trying to interpret a possibly dichotomized life, categories of trauma could

---

[31]In Kim's Sophia Christology, the concept of global wisdom functions much like Spirit-*Chi* so that the concreteness of Jesus Christ is again marginalized. Thus, for Kim, the issue seems not Christocentricity, but Christ. Grace Ji-Sun Kim, *The Grace of Sophia: A Korean North American Women's Christology* (Eugene, OR: Wipf & Stock, 2002).

[32]This section draws from my presentation on the fragmented self in Asian American identity and the process of integration. Daniel D. Lee, *Trauma-Induced Double Self and Asian American Identity*, poster presented at the annual convention of Asian American Psychological Association (AAPA) Annual Convention, San Francisco, CA, 2018.

[33]See for example, T. LaFromboise, H. L. K. Colman, and J. Gerton, "Psychological Impact of Biculturalism: Evidence and Theory," *Psychological Bulletin* 114 (1993): 395–412.

[34]Kevin L. Nadal, *Microaggressions and Traumatic Stress: Theory, Research, and Clinical Treatment* (Washington DC: American Psychological Association, 2018).

offer a new perspective with fresh insights. Referring to children who have suffered abuse or trauma for a long period of time, Judith Herman observes that "when it is impossible to avoid the reality of the abuse, the child must construct some system of meaning that justifies it."[35] These children create a double self—a good, pure, perfect, overachieving self untainted by abuse, which balances out the dirty, bad self. Along with creating a perfectionist self that is "a superb performer . . . an academic achiever, a model of social conformity," "fragmentation becomes the central principle of personality organization."[36] The concept of double self explains Asian American self-hatred and self-blaming in regards to racial-ethnic identity, along with the overachieving and perfectionistic tendency toward becoming an honorary white or model minority. As a survival or success strategy, one might adopt a bifurcation where the private/communal (*Gemeinschaft*) Asian self is operating at home and within ethnic circles, while the public/societal (*Gesellschaft*) "American" self is presented to the white-normative world outside.[37]

Trauma studies also gives us the concepts of intrusion and constriction.[38] Intrusion here means that every microaggression carries the accumulated weight of all those prior past incidents. This intrusion disrupts life by constricting it, causing one to avoid places and situations where one might be exposed to the risk of microaggressions. However, since these everyday incidents are ubiquitous, physical constriction to safe spaces is difficult, although many Asian Americans might avoid going to rural areas, the Midwest, or the South. More commonly, this constriction occurs in terms of creating a constricted self for the public—a redacted or truncated self more presentable and less visible. This self-editing where the unpresentable Asian parts are repressed when in unsafe contexts might be positively considered as code switching or biculturality. The so-called bicultural competence within this framework is a pathological acquiescing of the two selves, both located separately within their respective worlds.

For many Asian Americans, this discernment of self-editing becomes a skill required for everyday life—unconscious and almost second nature. Furthermore, after years of such practice, the deformed or truncated self becomes one's own self-understanding, leading to dissociation from one's body or a fragmentation of the self into pieces. Moreover, even as almost second nature, this constant self-redaction or selective repression as a "continually active process" can be taxing, draining well-being and creativity.[39] The idea of a double self presents the possibility of such exhausting dissociation even when Asian Americans might express high levels of bicultural competence, albeit dichotomized.

Whereas Anselm Min and Grace Kim have theorized the Spirit's power and works for relating to the other, I propose that this same Spirit brings about an *intra*personal reconciliation. The Spirit as the integrator of our fragmented self can be understood in three aspects.

---

[35] Judith Herman, *Trauma and Recovery: The Aftermath of Violence–From Domestic Abuse to Political Terror* (New York: Basic, 1992), 103.
[36] Ibid., 105, 107.
[37] See how Hurh and Kim use the categories of *Gemeinschaft* and *Gesellschaft* to analyze racial pressures and ethnic affiliation; Won Moo Hurh and Kwang Chung Kim, "The Religious Participation of Korean Immigrants in the United States," *Journal for the Scientific Study of Religion* 29, no. 1 (1990): 19–34.
[38] Herman, *Trauma and Recovery*, 37, 42.
[39] Sigmund Freud understood repression as an unconscious and yet still active process. See Stephen Frosh, *A Brief Introduction to Psychoanalytic Theory* (New York: Palgrave Macmillan, 2012), 59.

First, the Spirit of God is the One who holds together the disparate aspects of Asian American selves. The Apostle Paul uses the body as an analogy for the macrocosm of society and the church, all the while interrogating and subverting assumptions about honor and status (1 Cor. 12:12-25).[40] What has been considered honorable is not truly worthy of that status, and the seemingly inferior members are in reality indispensable ("our ugly parts have greater beauty, while our beautiful parts have no need" in Martin's rendering of verse 23).[41] The Spirit that brings all these members together as one brings about "an actual reversal of the normal, 'this-worldly' attribution of honor and status."[42]

Taking the body analogy psychologically for the fragmented Asian American self, one can say that the Spirit's work reassigns status and honor to the various aspects of the polycentric identity. The immigrant status or being phenotypically Asian—considered ugly in the sight of a white-normative world—could be held in honor. Meanwhile, what is taken as beautiful—the presentable, white-assimilated self—should be evaluated more soberly. What is especially cogent in this work of the Spirit is that all aspects of Asian American identity are gathered and held together in Christ. The Holy Spirit integrates the Asian American self with its body, cultural heritage, and family lineage, which all suffered disconnection and dissociation because of racial trauma. Of course, this gathering and holding together does not mean the dispensing of the strategic code switching that is necessary to navigate the world in its fallenness. However, the Spirit's presence and work pervade and operate at a deeper level. This relating and communing of the disparate aspects of the self can be expressed as the perichoretic work of the Spirit, keeping in union the apparently disparate and contradictory.

Second, the Spirit of God helps express the unarticulated pains and hurts that come from these redacted parts of Asian American selves.[43] The Holy Spirit is the One who "searches everything" (1 Cor. 2:10) and "guides us to all the truth" (Jn 16:13, Rom. 8:26-27). With trauma, while the body might remember and keep score, the explicit identification of pain often remains hidden and unnamed.[44] With microaggressive trauma that is essentially accumulative, there will not be one single incident but rather a thousand subtle ones that the self has erased in order to survive. In other words, since the racial microaggressions that create the fragmented self are essentially invisible, they can manifest as a frustrating and mentally sapping experience of internal conflict. In this place, the Spirit reveals the hidden nature of the pain and reveals the truth of social and structural powers of oppression.[45] The connection between flesh and language at the pentecostal outpouring is evocative of how the Holy Spirit empowers the embodied and linguistic articulation. The work of naming the reality of racial microaggressions and trauma as well as the broader forces of colonialism and imperialism in that vein is a pneumatological

---

[40]I am indebted to Martin's work on the Greco-Roman backdrop of Paul's body analogy. See Dale B. Martin, *The Corinthian Body* (New Haven, CT: Yale University Press, 1995).
[41]Ibid., 95.
[42]Ibid., 96.
[43]While my concern is narrower with the idea of a fragmented self, I draw inspiration from Rambo's innovative pneumatology envisioning the Spirit as the persisting and remaining divine presence, post-trauma. Shelly Rambo, *Spirit and Trauma: A Theology of Remaining* (Louisville, KY: Westminster John Knox, 2010), 111–41.
[44]Van der Kolk's works underscores how the body knows more than the mind regarding trauma. Bessel van der Kolk, *The Body Keeps the Score: Brain, Mind, and the Body in the Healing of Trauma* (New York: Penguin, 2014).
[45]Rambo, *Spirit and Trauma*, 123–5.

work of opening the mouths of the oppressed to cry out, making both pain and healing intelligible.

Third, the Spirit integrates self in union with Christ and, through Christ, with each other. On this point, I affirm the themes of solidarity and communion with others in our globalized pluralistic world that Min and Kim present, especially Min's idea of the body of Christ as its "ruling metaphor." What is desperately needed in our divided and pluralistic world is a reimagining of our religious particularity, such as our Christocentricity, acknowledging the violent confusions and co-opting of the past in light of the present work of God in the world and the church. This reimagining follows the mysterious work of the Spirit who transgresses the confessional boundaries of the church as Yong and Kim explore with their interreligious moves.

The Spirit's inner work of gathering, uniting, and healing the self extends to Asian American communities that also collectively can be fragmented.[46] The similar dynamics of redaction and dissociation could also be ecclesially manifested as well, even often theologically enabled.[47] Incorporating the personal and the communal, the Spirit's movement continues with the outer work of gathering, uniting, and healing our fragmented and divided world. While these inner and outer works might be understood as in tension or even conflict, they are united in the Spirit who brings all things together in Christ as the Spirit of participation. To use missional terminology, centrifugal integration of the self and centripetal solidarity with others are both the work of the same Spirit.[48]

As Asian American theologians take up the burning questions of the Asian American church and community, they will not only serve this particular faith community, but also through and from them contribute to and stimulate the global church. This chapter was presented as a brief taste of what this diverse community's pneumatological reflections have to offer.

FOR FURTHER READING

Kim, Grace Ji-Sun. *The Holy Spirit, Chi, and the Other: A Model of Global and Intercultural Pneumatology*. New York: Palgrave Macmillan, 2011.

Lee, Jung Young. *The Trinity in Asian Perspective*. Nashville, TN: Abingdon, 1996.

Min, Anselm Kyongsuk. *The Solidarity of Others in a Divided World: A Postmodern Theology after Postmodernism*. London: T & T Clark, 2004.

Park, Andrew Sung. *Triune Atonement: Christ's Healing for Sinners, Victims, and the Whole Creation*. Louisville, KY: Westminster John Knox, 2009.

Yong, Amos. *The Future of Evangelical Theology: Soundings from the Asian American Diaspora*. Downers Grove, IL: InterVarsity, 2014.

---

[46]My proposal could be understood as seeking to construct a narrative of cultural trauma for Asian Americans as a way of making sense of our experience. See Jeffrey C. Alexander, et al., *Cultural Trauma and Collective Identity* (Berkeley, CA: University of California Press, 2004).

[47]Some of the Asian American evangelical churches seeking to be multiethnic for the purpose of inclusivity while denying their Asian Americanness could be understood as "fragmented" and suffering dissociation. See Russell Jeung, *Faithful Generations: Race and New Asian American Churches* (New Brunswick, NJ: Rutgers University Press, 2005).

[48]Michael J. Gorman, *Becoming the Gospel: Paul, Participation, and Mission* (Grand Rapids, MI: Eerdmans, 2015), 37.

CHAPTER THIRTY

The Spirit in the Colonial Difference

A Story of Pneumatology in the American Global South

OSCAR GARCÍA-JOHNSON

This article finds its place in this collection just after I have finished writing *Spirit Outside the Gate*.[1] All too fresh still, my first thought was that I am confronted with the risk of repeating myself, for most of what I wanted to say about the subject of pneumatology in the American Global South (the Americas and its global diaspora) I said already in *Spirit Outside the Gate*. On second thought, how could one feel satisfied with the work barely begun on a subject that theological and missiological studies have neglected for five centuries, which is the case of the Holy Spirit in the context of the Americas? Inevitably, whatever I say theologically in this article about the Holy Spirit will be linked to this book. At the same time, it is new to readers and myself. Thus, the best approach is for me to provide readers with a sort of bridge logbook that might serve them as officers of the watch while navigating the Spirit's limitless geography.

THE STORY OF (THE SPIRIT IN) THE COLONIAL DIFFERENCE

This article rests on the following assertion: the story of the Spirit in the lands and peoples of the Americas can be told best from the colonial difference, which stands interstitially in the canonical imagination of the Americas,[2] that is, from the subaltern side of history and faith before and beyond colonial modernity and the canonical imagination of the West. Since historiography is the natural horizon of epistemology, border historiography is a more appropriate tool than Eurocentered historiographies for unfolding the theological stories in the Global South that are routinely negated or omitted by Westernized

---

[1] *Spirit Outside the Gate: Decolonial Pneumatologies of the South* (Downers Grove, IL: InterVarsity, 2019).
[2] "The canonical imagination of the Americas" refers to an independent and prolific *locus* of pneumatological knowledge that does not oppose the canonical imagination of the West as a form of self-constitution (anti-Western) but exists prior to and beyond and transverses—even enriches—the traditions of the West in the context of the American Global South. See ibid., chap. 9.

theological scholarship. It has taken a long time to recognize and act on this proposition, but works in this direction are beginning to blossom.[3]

In *The Story of Latino Protestants in the United States*, the Protestant historian and theologian Juan F. Martínez frames historiography (history, migration, religious faith, and sociocultural identity) in a way that accounts for the "totality" and complexity of the Protestant stories of the peoples of the Americas, more particularly in the United States.[4] Their Protestant trajectory is constructed as "subaltern readings" of peoples representing a "counternarrative history." Martínez's framing challenges Occidentalized modern dichotomies and theoretical apparatuses normally used to build inaccurate (and oppressive) images of Latino/Hispanic identities and history, be that in the United States, Latin America, or the global diaspora. Hence, religious, cultural, geopolitical, and linguistic essentialisms are typically challenged. For instance, we see that Latinas[5] are not by default Catholic, Spanish-speakers, immigrants to the United States, undocumented, poor, or uneducated. Protestant Latinxs (better known as *evangélicos*) are not all Republican or conservative in the white evangelical way. And Latino immigrants do not assume only one patriotic narrative simply because they migrated to a foreign land. Building on Juan Driver and Justo González's historiographic perspectives, Martínez marks his approach by envisioning Latina Protestants as a community in historic pilgrimage, in a migration from the periphery. In transnational and transoccidental[6] style, Martínez escapes the narrative traps of colonial modernity when telling the story of Latino Protestants in the United States, traps such as Eurocentric (male) whiteness, the nation state, individualism, neoliberal economics, monoculturalism, Enlightenment rationality, and mainline denominationalism. Remarkably, the fifth theme informing his historiography is "the work of the Holy Spirit," which he posits as an implicit framework of his historiographical approach.

---

[3]Since the 1960s, the founders of the philosophy of liberation, especially Enrique Dussel, attempted a Latinamericanist framing for church history. *Historia de la Iglesia en América Latina: Coloniaje y Liberación* (Barcelona: Nova Terra, 1974). More recently, a transmodern/postcolonial effort followed. Hans-Jürgen Prien, ed., *Religiosidad e Historiografía: La Irrupción del Pluralismo Religioso en América Latina y Su Elaboración Metódica en la Historiografía* (Frankfurt am Main: Vervuert-Iberoamericana, 1998). In the Protestant wing (beyond Jean-Pierre Bastian, who remains within Western/modern presuppositions, although with a Latinamericanist emphasis), the prominent Protestant historian and theologian Justo L. González transitioned from (initially) consensus historical (Western) theology to contextual, non-Eurocentered historiography. *Mapas para la Historia Futura de la Iglesia* (Barcelona: Kairos, 2001) and idem. and Ordina González, *Nuestra Fe: A Latin American Church History Sourcebook* (Nashville, TN: Abingdon, 2014). But it is not until very recently with works such as Michael Jiménez's *Remembering Lived Lives* (Eugene, OR: Wipf & Stock, 2017) and Juan F. Martínez's *The Story of Latino Protestants in the United States* (Grand Rapids, MI: Eerdmans, 2018) that we see a new genre of non-Westernized/transmodern/de(post)colonial Protestant historiography begin to flourish.
[4]Martínez, *Latino Protestants in the United States*, 28–30, 216–20.
[5]Acknowledging the fact that one name does not suffice when describing the fluidity, complexity, intersectionality, multi-locality, and ambiguity of Latinos and Latinas across the Americas (the United States included), we will use several names interchangeably, all referring to the subaltern Latina community. It goes without saying that the latest attempt to include an oft-neglected group (that is, "emerging diasporic generations") is "Latinx," which of course, like the others (Latina, Latino, Latino/a, Latina/o, Hispanic, etc.) does not do justice to the cultural and social diversality of the signified community.
[6]Transoccidentality, among other things, is a decolonial imaginary that envisions the *imago Dei* decolonized-resurrected in Christ's Spirit. It is conceived as a place of epistemic freedom saturated by ontological and pluriversal complexity, where inter(intra)subaltern dialogue replaces dominant Western colonial monologue. Hence, it is a border space of human imagination at the erasures of imperiality/modernity/Occidentalism. See García-Johnson, *Spirit Outside the Gate*, chap. 3.

I concur with Martínez that the Holy Spirit constitutes a permeating presence, a ubiquitous *compañero/a* (companion) of the people of faith in their five centuries of Christian itinerary in the American Global South. As a consequence, this presentation situates itself in the Latinx diaspora (third space) and, more precisely, in the colonial difference, and from there it addresses the American Global South (Latin America, the Latinx Caribbean, and the Latinx diaspora). We ask, what does it mean epistemologically, theologically, and ecclesiologically to be in mission with the "Spirit of Life" (Moltmann), the "Wild Child of the Trinity" (Maldonado Pérez), and the "Decolonial Healer of the Americas" (García-Johnson)?[7] In other words, what does it mean epistemically to tradition the Holy Spirit and her life-giving patterns and healing agenda? What does it mean culturally, theologically, politically, and otherwise to discover oneself in the enabling and healing ecology of the Spirit, particularly when one's land, sense of peoplehood, and view of historical realization carry the marks of an unhealed wound—a wound inflicted, on the one hand, by the complicity of a civilizing Christian mission and, on the other hand, by a handful of Euro-American colonial and neocolonial powers whose occidentalizing global designs enabled them to introduce themselves as the agents of God bringing the gospel, sociopolitical order, and historical salvation to "primitive and barbaric" communities in need of civilizing support?

These are the kinds of questions informing *Spirit Outside the Gate*. And to answer them, one needs to strategically stand at a distance (delinked as much as possible) from the colonial matrix of power giving life to the visions and ambitions of the civilizing imperial agents and their rhetoric of salvation. It is no longer a matter of trying to position oneself methodologically behind, under, above, or even against the Western self-imagined deific authority, historical entitlement, and apostolic mandate over the land and people of the American continents (and the rest of the world). But instead, what is required to counterbalance this Eurocentric overemphasis is a bold repositioning of oneself prior to, within the interstitial spaces, and beyond the epistemic walls built across the centuries to simulate and historicize a representation of a developed Western self over and against imagined barbaric personae of the natives and hybrids of the American Global South. Regrettably, occidentalizing representations of Jesus Christ (Christologies) stand in between these two anthropological imaginaries. The goal is to build a pneumatologically healing path, that is, an account of the Holy Spirit among the peoples of the American Global South in their own terms.

OUTSIDE THE GATES OF WOUNDING CHRISTOLOGIES

The Council of Chalcedon (451) has been used as the "worldwide" reference for Christology throughout Christian history. Its confession has become the ground upon which normative christological discourses have been ascribed, debated, and revised. Chalcedonian Christology (a binary belonging to a particular context) has become the hermeneutical condition of Western Christology and, by extension, to Christology everywhere in the world. How can one speak of Jesus Christ before and beyond Chalcedonian Christology

---

[7]Jürgen Moltmann, *The Spirit of Life: A Universal Affirmation*, trans. Margaret Kohl (Minneapolis, MN: Fortress, 1992); Loida I. Martell-Otero, Zaida Maldonado Pérez, and Elizabeth Conde-Frazier, *Latina Evangélicas: A Theological Survey from the Margins* (Eugene, OR: Cascade, 2013), chap. 2; García-Johnson, *Spirit Outside the Gate*.

and its Western global traditioning without receiving condemnation? This impossible task led me to challenge the popular idea that Jesus Christ is the same as (subsumed in) Western Christology. This, of course, does not deny that Western Christology and its various global permutations (Western traditioning) have a hold on the historical witness to Jesus Christ. But equally true is the fact that God's wider revelatory presence in the world is not a captive of Western Christology, and in many instances, we can argue, God has stood against the predatory abuses of Western christological representations in the world. Needless to say, Western critical traditions have pushed back against these abuses. But now we are facing a global "revision" in ways that such Western critical traditions no longer stand at the center of the revision. We give substance to this claim by assessing how Western Christologies have been used in alliance with economic, political, and cultural forms of imperialism in colonial territories and more recently in neocolonial projects. This is particularly the case with the American Global South.

The untangling of Western categories in christological imaginations is a necessary exercise in epistemic constructions and theological discourse since, throughout the Americas, these have been rational instruments of the wounding dialects spoken by coloniality, modernity, and Occidentalism. Moreover, this untangling may only be achieved through a venture into pneumatology—via an indigenous pneumatological imagination—and a corresponding "containment" of Christology as we know it in the South—deeply embedded by the colonial wound of the Conquest and the colonial matrix of power. To be clear, this containment is not of Jesus Christ per se, whose incarnational reality and trinitarian character remains within the domain of the Holy Spirit's embodied imagination in the American Global South. In fact, it is this incarnational imagination of the Spirit of Jesus Christ in the Global South that has the potential to heal Latin America's christological colonial wound—through a critical analysis of the omission and reductionism inflicted upon Western Christology but also through the signaling of the emergence of a truly liberating-decolonial pneumatology.

I have assessed the impact of the conquest and colonial order upon christological imaginations in the Americas as well as the modern making of Latin American Christology since the period of the political independence of Latin America.[8] First, I provide an account of the intersectionality of the colonial matrix of power and the rhetoric of salvation as the birthplace of a christological imagination in the Americas. In other words, the Iberian Christ imposed upon the land and the peoples of Latin America was ubiquitous and instrumental in the construction of a colonial/imperial logic that sanctified and justified expansionism (appropriation of lands), violent evangelization, displacement, colonial order, and an economic and spiritual conquest. It must be noted that the implications of such logic forged a series of concrete, traumatic, and dehumanizing experiences—such as God-mandated suffering, monarchical paternalism in the midst of orphanhood, and the commodification of bodies and land as disposable elements at the service of "God and Gold"—all of this with concrete and historical consequences. Nonetheless, we point to the realities of vicarious aesthetics of survival in the midst of the conquest as generating an indianization of Christology, particularly through the medium of colonial art. This is most present in painting, sculptures, and songs that witness to a Christ-rooted faith received, transmitted, and transformed by the originating cultures of the Americas. Two clear examples include *La Última Cena* by Peruvian Quechua painter Marco Zapata

---

[8] See *Spirit Outside the Gate*, chap. 7.

(1700s) and Nahua approaches to Christianity as a continuation of their own religion with the opportunity to redefine and reject the meaning of an imposed Christology.

Finally, through Leonardo Boff's analysis of the invasions of the Americas and the corresponding implications for christological imaginations in the Americas, I frame the developments of modern Christologies in the Americas. Projects such as panamericanism (1900s), the doctrine of development (1930s–1960s), and market capitalism (1970s–present) emerged as enterprises that presented subsequent attempts at colonial civilizing projects. We note that Latin American Christologies that emerged respectively in these periods (a) continued utilizing Eurocentered assumptions ("historical Jesus" versus "Christ of faith"); (b) supplanted Iberian Christology with Americanized Christologies resulting in denying the "way of the cross" as biblical praxis; and (c) launched three main theological experiments to attempt an independent christological discourse in the Americas (integral mission Christology, liberation Christology, and US Latino/a Christology). We come to the conclusion that although most christological developments attempted to untangle the problem of Iberian Christology in the Americas and were committed to their context at multiple levels, they did so without sufficient success due to limited decolonial methods and imaginations susceptible to cultural and epistemic critiques. Inescapably, the pneumatological deficiency of Western Christologies has also become the pneumatological deficiency of the Christologies of the American Global South.

THE PNEUMATOLOGICAL DIFFERENCE

I attempt to remedy this pneumatological deficiency in the particular context of the American Global South and hopefully with benefits for Western Christologies at large.[9] To argue transoccidentally in favor of a pneumatological difference, three subjects must be elaborated: (1) the Spirit as the first word of theology in the West, (2) the Spirit as the primal experience and praxis of God in the Global South, and (3) the Spirit as the epistemic horizon in the transoccidental difference of the American Global South. These three elaborations sustain our claim that pneumatology is an amniotic and nurturing factor for identifying God in the Americas. Furthermore, the pneumatological difference represents a new beginning for the Christian understanding of the world and its pluriversal character. The possibility of acknowledging this pneumatological difference is a gift of our time to us, and the acknowledgement and embodiment of this difference in our discourses constitute our mandate.

In dialogue with Lyle Dabney, Catherine Keller, and Jürgen Moltmann, I reroute theology by articulating the "Spirit as the first word of theology" as a way to unstrap Western theology from the objectivizing and unitive logic of colonial modernity. Dabney's theological proposition of a "first theology"—one that begins with the notion that we are "otherwise engaged in the Spirit" from the start—pairs with the effort to shape a theological imagination that acknowledges the conditions of pneumatology as an amniotic, nurturing factor for discerning God's wider revelatory presence in the Americas before, across, and beyond the West. Keller reminds us that "both Christology and pneumatology have functioned within mainstream theology since Nicea-Chalcedon as the exceptional moments of immanence that prove the rule of the transcendence—'the

---

[9] Ibid., chap. 8.

rule of the Father.'"[10] Alternatively, within the West, Moltmann, "by defining 'vitality' as 'love of life' . . . directs it to the ends of Christian ethics."[11] Clearly the West has a point of contact here with the Majority World, and in particular with Latina global theology. If life itself constitutes a *locus theologicus* of the Spirit of God, then pneumatology—ethically grounded as an expression of good (decolonized) living (*buen vivir*), vitality, and love of life—is a theological theme that needs to inform a new theological beginning for the American Global South.

As important theological voices in the West have begun to acknowledge the pneumatological difference or shift in Christianity, scholars from the Global South are beginning to offer theological interpretations not just of theological data but of their domestic experience and committed praxis of God's presence and work. In the context of the Americas, for instance, the experience of the Spirit as embodied in the renewal movements and as examined by Latin American critical thinking has become an object of serious study. Two different sources give voice to the pneumatological activity in the Americas: Latino global Pentecostalism and Latin American liberation pneumatology. To put it in perspective, what Western theologians such as Moltmann and Dabney have come to understand through academic study as a generative discourse that reroutes many centuries of theological elaboration is a theology of the Spirit of life or first theology, which our Pentecostal brothers and sisters from the Americas know through the worship service in practice. These Latino/a sisters and brothers, all the way from the revivals in Chile (1903–1909) to Los Angeles (1906–1910) until today, comprehend pneumatological theology through worship as the most fundamental experience of God, where the Spirit mediates knowledge, communion, and mission, and where God and his gospel are received, obeyed, and proclaimed in the power of the Spirit of God. The rerouting of theology by way of pneumatology in the Global South is not only theoretical (a proposal), but also praxiological (a witness).

At the other end of the spectrum, Latin American liberation theologians are also elaborating a pneumatological turn in liberation discourse. Among others, Víctor Codina wants to emphasize the pneumatological basis of the liberationist project by pointing to the fact that at its genesis the Spirit of God was present and pressing for a liberative trajectory "out of" the poor in the Americas. That is, "the Holy Spirit works in history through the victims of history, that is, the poor. The Holy Spirit works, thus, from below, not from above, from the oppressed people."[12] Again, in the context of the Americas, as in the case of the renewal movements, discourse follows experience and praxis. Rerouting implies re-experiencing and re-acting critically to the new conditions of life while attentive to the wisdom of the received traditions and, above all, following the guidance of the Holy Spirit here and now and among us. In doing pneumatology in the Americas, a remarkable difference from Western pneumatological approaches such as that of Moltmann and Dabney is Codina's commitment to "begin from the spiritual experience, from mystagogy, before launching evangelization and catechesis." This experience in the

---

[10]Catherine Keller, "Pneumatic Nudges: The Theology of Moltmann, Feminism, and the Future," in *The Future of Theology: Essays in Honor of Jürgen Moltmann*, ed. Miroslav Volf, Carmen Krieg, and Thomas Dörken-Kucharz (Grand Rapids, MI: Eerdmans, 1996), 145.
[11]Ibid., 146.
[12]Victor Codina, *El Espíritu del Señor Actúa desde Abajo* (Maliaño: Sal Terrae, 2015), Kindle loc. 2867. All quotations are my personal translations.

context of an impoverished continent, argues Codina, "necessarily guides us to opting for the poor, and many times is born from within that very context. Hence, mysticism turns into prophecy and liberating praxis."[13]

Transoccidentalism as a critical epistemology can be used theologically as an imaginary where the epistemic codes of human identity organize at the border of the regime of imperiality/coloniality/Western modernity/Occidentalism.[14] This means that doing pneumatology from the transoccidental difference implies decolonizing Christian epistemology by "engaging in knowledge making and transformation at the edge, in and of, the disciplines."[15] But concretely speaking, where is the (transoccidental) pneumatological difference to be identified? We can find it in life itself, as Moltmann cleverly affirms: "God in, with, and beneath each everyday experience of the world,"[16] which is mirrored in the biblical imaginary when we look for it. Life in the American Global South is filled with memories and traditions, experiences and rituals, and wounds and hopes. Again, in the American Global South, life is the very ground of pneumatology, and hope in the Spirit is its redemptive horizon, however historically unrealized. Because of this reality, the Spirit works with multiple canons in the American Global South—from ancestral traditions to received traditions to emerging traditions—all of which overlap at the theology of continuity in creation (as the beginning) and re-creation through the discontinuity of sin and death (as its end), to put it in Dabney's terms.[17]

DECOLONIAL PNEUMATOLOGIES OF THE SOUTH

I further develop decolonial (border) pneumatology as a contribution of the South.[18] Decolonial pneumatology attempts to pave the way for a different discourse, one situated at the border of predominant paradigms and disciplines related to the Spirit and oriented toward decolonial healing. Decolonial pneumatology, to further clarify, does not intend to treat the Spirit as a subject of study as if "the Spirit" is "something" we can know and explain and predict by means of our intellectual apparatus (history, rationality, relationality, temporality, spatiality, historiography, ethnography, etc.). Decolonial (border) pneumatology is about border people of faith engaged with and enabled by the "Spirit Outside the Gate" at the border of life and death, oppression and justice, Orthodoxy and heterodoxy, poverty and affluence, the West and the non-West, the Uncreated Invisible and the created visible, hopelessness and utopia. I have proposed the Spirit as a "decolonial healer" as the most obvious of all pneumatological entryways. Admittedly incomplete and incipient, this elaboration may trigger constructive criticism and invite others to join in with enthusiasm as we seek to recover and reclassify theological and cultural meanings in

---

[13]Ibid., Kindle loc. 3070.
[14]See *Spirit Outside of the Gate*, chaps. 2 and 9.
[15]Walter Mignolo, "Decolonizing Western Epistemology/Building Decolonial Epistemology," in *Decolonizing Epistemologies: Latina/o Theology and Philosophy*, ed. Ada María Isasi-Díaz and Eduardo Mendieta (New York: Fordham University Press, 2012), 42.
[16]Moltmann, *The Spirit of Life*, 34.
[17]D. Lyle Dabney, "Otherwise Engaged in the Spirit: A First Theology for a Twenty-First Century," in *The Future of Theology: Essays in Honor of Jürgen Moltmann*, ed. Miroslav Volf, Carmen Krieg, and Thomas Dörken-Kucharz (Grand Rapids, MI: Eerdmans, 1996), 154–63.
[18]See *Spirit Outside the Gate*, chap. 10.

the Global South—a pending scholarly task now being formulated by the yet-to-be fields of transoccidental studies and Latinx global studies.

Decolonial pneumatology can give theological substance to "traditioning communities"[19] in the Americas that, just as in the West, have a hold on the historical presence of the Spirit in their midst—a story of the Spirit in the American Global South, if you will. *Spirit Outside the Gate* shows how the Spirit may be identified as a continuing life-giving and decolonial healer in three theologically neglected groups: Original Americans, Afro-Latin Americans (Afro-Latinxs), and immigrant communities, particularly Latina women. It goes without saying that my approach may easily apply to other neglected groups in the American Global South who also share modern-colonial-imperial subjugations, such as Muslims, Jews, the poor, people with disabilities, and so forth. With respect to the Original Americans, I conclude that the "Spirit Outside the Gate" is a nomad and decolonial healer who abides *not in time* but among the Original American people in their stories, songs, prayers, ceremonies—all rooted deeply in Grandmother, the earth, as "their ways of life revere" creation and the Creator, believing that their stories will ultimately heal and "win over the immigrant conquerors and transform them."[20] With respect to the Afro-Latinos/as, in the context of Yoruba-Christian spiritualities, the "Spirit Outside the Gate" may be understood as a "guide for life representing the Jesus who died, [as] . . . the ancestors in traditional Yoruba religion guide the living relatives after death."[21] In the same breath, the "Spirit Outside the Gate" corresponds to the Trance-Spirit that fills them with holy knowledge, with purpose, prophecy, cultural and racial worth, and makes them dance, sing, shout, and move up the ladder of social, economic, and educational advancement against the systematic assault on their social mobility by world-systems designed to keep them at the bottom of the social order. Lastly, with respect to Latina (immigrant) women, we present a constellation of expressions traditioned as *abuelitas-madres-comadres-tias* pneumatologies, nurturing Latina theological imagination and enabling them to create identity, community, and public life anew. In short, the "Spirit Outside the Gate" legitimizes Latina women suppressed by patriarchal, racist, and ecclesial structures, and it functions as a decolonial healer of the Latina woman commonly treated as *sata* (mongrel, mutt) and *sobraja* (leftover) by the oppressive and patriarchal world designs surrounding her—the Spirit redeems her as *santa* (holy woman).[22]

FOR FURTHER READING

Boff, Leonardo. *Come, Holy Spirit: Inner Fire, Giver of Life, and Comforter of the Poor*. Translated by Margaret Wilde. Maryknoll, NY: Orbis, 2015.

Codina, Víctor. *Creo en el Espíritu Santo: Pneumatología Narrativa, Presencia Teológica*. Maliaño: Sal Terrae, 1994.

---

[19] "Traditioning communities" alludes to the fact that the theological frontiers of indigenous and Afro-Latinx communities in the Americas have been porous, nomadic, and pluriversal, thereby showing epistemic *mestizajes* that facilitate the transit of multiple religious traditions and the territorialization of different beliefs without essentializing (fusion). See *Spirit Outside the Gate*, chap. 9.

[20] George E. Tinker, *Spirit and Resistance: Political Theology and American Indian Liberation* (Minneapolis, MN: Fortress, 2004), Kindle loc. 1638–40.

[21] Samuel Cruz, *Masked Africanisms: Puerto Rican Pentecostalism* (Dubuque, IA: Kendall Hunt, 2005), 64.

[22] See Martell-Otero, Pérez, and Conde-Frazier, *Latina Evangélicas*.

Cruz, Samuel. *Masked Africanisms: Puerto Rican Pentecostalism*. Dubuque, IA: Kendall Hunt, 2005.
García-Johnson, Oscar. *The Mestizo/a Community of the Spirit: Toward a Postmodern Latino/a Ecclesiology*. Eugene, OR: Pickwick, 2009.
Martell-Odero, Loida I., Zaida Maldonado Pérez, and Elizabeth Conde-Frazier. *Latina Evangélicas: A Theological Survey from the Margins*. Eugene, OR: Cascade, 2013.
Medina, Néstor. *Christianity, Empire, and the Spirit: (Re)Configuring Faith and the Cultural*. Leiden: Brill, 2018.

CHAPTER THIRTY-ONE

Black Theologians of the Spirit

FREDERICK L. WARE

In the contemporary black theological movement that began in the 1960s, two African American theologians, Albert B. Cleage Jr. and James H. Cone, would become the first to expound the long-held notion of liberation and empowerment by the Spirit in the black experience in the United States.[1] Their theology of the Spirit is constructed from deep reflection on the faith born in response to the divine presence amidst the existential crisis of dehumanization and oppression.[2]

One of their interlocutors, Charles H. Long, described the crisis and subsequent faith response in this way:

> To whom does one pray from the bowels of a slave ship? to the gods of Africa? to the gods of the masters of the slave vessels? to the gods of an unknown and foreign land of enslavement? To whom does one pray? From the perspective of religious experience, this was the beginning of African American religion and culture. In the forced silence of oppression, in the half-articulate moans of desperation, in the rebellions against enslavement—from this cataclysm another world emerged.[3]

The Spirit is not only an opening to another world, one that is independently real and absolutely just, but also the mainspring of social transformation and human flourishing in this world. According to Cleage and Cone, the divine Spirit, who for Christians is the Holy Spirit, is God's presence and work in oppressed peoples' struggle for liberation, freedom, and justice.

THE HOLY SPIRIT IN BLACK LIBERATION THEOLOGY

Albert Cleage's earliest construction of pneumatology, as is true of his conceptualization of black liberation theology, is founded upon black Christian nationalism. In the first

---

[1] Albert Cleage describes his theological work as that of a practitioner or activist whose principal audience is black people and Cone's contribution as that of a professional academician who makes black theology intelligible to non-black audiences; see *Black Christian Nationalism: New Directions for the Black Church* (Detroit: Luxor, 1980 [1972]), xvii. In spite of this difference between audiences, their perspectives are very similar.
[2] Charles Long names this emphasis on Spirit and the spirituality emerging from it as "soul-stuff." "African American Religion in the United States of America: An Interpretative Essay," *Nova Religio* 7, no. 1 (2003): 21.
[3] "Passage and Prayer: The Origin of Religion in the Atlantic World," in *The Courage to Hope: From Black Suffering to Human Redemption*, ed. Quinton Hosford Dixie and Cornel West (Boston, MA: Beacon, 1999), 17.

and third articles of the Black Christian Nationalist Creed, the Holy Spirit is described as God's work of liberation apparent in oppressed peoples' resistance to injustice and their fight—even violently—for freedom and justice.[4] This phenomenon of liberation is present—or as Cleage would say, born anew—in every generation of humankind. According to Cleage, by way of general revelation, God as the supreme and ruling power in the universe is known or knowable to all persons and therefore has many names. In whichever manner people name God, they may discern that the God of the universe is also the chief arbiter in moral matters.

Cleage makes a shift from a christocentric pneumatology to a metaphysical pneumatology. Cleage initially described the Spirit as God's work of liberation in terms of Christology centered on the Black Messiah. As a Black Christian Nationalist, Cleage makes the assertion that Jesus, the Black Messiah, was sent by God to liberate the black Israelites and subsequently invites others to join him in the struggle against oppression and the building of a free black nation.[5] That Jesus and his fellow Israelites are black means for Cleage that they are non-white, having no ancestry among the white peoples of Europe.

According to D. Kimathi Nelson, who worked with Cleage for several decades and later succeeded him as leader of the Shrines of the Black Madonna, Cleage grew in his theological perspective to become a "revolutionary mystic."[6] In Cleage's shift to a metaphysical pneumatology, God—who is spirit—is cosmic energy and creative intelligence. He theorized that religious experience, that is, the individual's intentional encounter with God, is the beginning of social change. The Spirit is this energy and intelligence pervading the universe and exercising influence within the network of forces for which God provides order. In humans' worship of God as Spirit, they access the supreme power and knowledge in the universe and thereby gain wisdom and courage for personal and social change.

From his end, over the entire course of the black theological movement, James Cone maintained and never wavered from a christocentric pneumatology. According to Cone, "The divine Spirit is not a metaphysical entity but rather the power of Jesus, who breaks into the lives of the people giving them a new song to sing as confirmation of God's presence with them in historical struggle."[7] The Holy Spirit is the Spirit of God and of Christ, as God was and is working in Christ, and as Christ is present in the lives of believers. Cone affirms God as Trinity, the Father and Son (Christ) working through the Holy Spirit to impact human lives.[8] Dwight Hopkins, a former student of Cone, has extended Cone's trinitarian thought to a triadic pneumatology of the Spirit of God as the Spirit of liberation wherein God is the Spirit for us, Jesus the Spirit with us, and human purpose the Spirit in us.[9]

---

[4] Cleage, *Black Christian Nationalism*, xiii.
[5] Ibid., 250.
[6] "The Theological Journey of Albert B. Cleage, Jr.: Reflections from Jaramogi's Protégé and Successor," in *Albert Cleage, Jr. and the Black Madonna and Child*, ed. Jawanza Eric Clark (New York: Palgrave Macmillan, 2017), 22.
[7] James H. Cone, *Speaking the Truth: Ecumenism, Liberation, and Black Theology* (Grand Rapids, MI: Eerdmans, 1986), 18.
[8] See James H. Cone, *Black Theology and Black Power* (New York: Seabury, 1969), 56–7.
[9] See Dwight N. Hopkins, *Down, Up, and Over: Slave Religion and Black Theology* (Minneapolis, MN: Fortress, 2000); also note Peter Hodgson, "The Spirit and Religious Pluralism," *Horizons* 31, no. 1 (2004): 22–39 for a nuanced model of religious pluralism that identifies spirit as the essential feature of religions of any kind.

Though from different perspectives, Albert Cleage and James Cone are in essential agreement that for black Christians, the Holy Spirit is generally God working to liberate the poor and oppressed throughout the world and specifically God working to unite, empower, and free black people. According to Cone, the Holy Spirit is the Spirit of God and of Christ at work in the lives of believers and non-believers to accomplish God's purposes for all humans in the world.[10] Simply stated, the Holy Spirit is God working in the world. Cleage says, "The Holy Spirit is the revolutionary power which comes to an exploited people as they struggle to escape from powerlessness and to end the institutional oppression forced upon them by an enemy."[11] For African Americans, this enemy is white people who, as a racial group, have control over America's social institutions.[12] The only appropriate response to this enemy and monopoly on power is resistance, which Cleage will say comes in many forms and is expressed in the rage, courage, and resolute determination of black people to be free.[13]

For black people, believers and non-believers alike, the experience of the Spirit and responses to the presence of Spirit have occurred in the contexts of their struggle for freedom and justice. They know the Spirit by how the divine presence, a waymaking power, operates in their history through events not attributable solely to their efforts.[14] In the case of believers, in their experiences of worship, they acquire (a) a sense of there being a transcendent or ultimate reality, (b) insight into the limitations of oppression, and (c) hope regarding the coming transformation of the world.[15]

REFLECTIONS ON THE DAY OF PENTECOST

Albert Cleage, more so than James Cone, turns to Acts 2, the story of the descent of the Holy Spirit on the Day of Pentecost, in order to offer further interpretation of the role of the Holy Spirit in black liberation. According to Cleage, the narrative is both historical and symbolic. On the one hand, the story is an interpretation of a historical event, the birth (maybe rebirth) of the black nation that Jesus sought to build.[16] On the other hand, the story is a paradigm for the unity of the black nation. The story is symbolic of a new sense of unity among a small group of black Israelites who were ready to move into areas of risk and sacrifice for building the black nation. With regard to the miracle of tongues related by the story, Cleage says that through many languages, the Spirit communicates the same message: "the story of the Black Messiah calling men to [join him in the] struggle against oppression."[17] Persons may not know the languages of others but, with the help of

---

According to Hodgson, it is Spirit, not the symbols God or Christ, by which we can compare religions and discern what the divine is doing in and through these religions.
[10] Cone, *Black Theology and Black Power*, 56–7.
[11] Cleage, *Black Christian Nationalism*, 249.
[12] Ibid., 81–2, 84–5, 93.
[13] Ibid., 251–2.
[14] In African American religious thought, God is often depicted as the waymaker who creates out of nothing or makes from existing circumstances a way—an opportunity or alternative—for persons to move forward in life when they reach what appears to be an impasse. God makes possible life's furtherance and fulfillment no matter what kinds of economic, social, and political conditions under which persons must live.
[15] James H. Cone, *God of the Oppressed* (New York: Seabury, 1975), 141–6.
[16] Albert B. Cleage, *The Black Messiah* (New York: Sheed and Ward, 1968), 237.
[17] Cleage, *Black Christian Nationalism*, 250.

the Spirit, they can understand that others are speaking about the experience of suffering and uttering a desire for liberation.[18]

Contrary to what most Christian theologians will say about the Day of Pentecost marking the birth of the church, Cleage will argue that this event is the start of a movement. Jesus, the Black Messiah, was building a movement, not a church that would become a mere social institution among several others.[19] For Cleage, the church is not insignificant; the church is very important. The church is a basis for unity and a location from which to work for social change.[20] On the Day of Pentecost, the Spirit unified Jesus's followers and, as Cleage points out, will do the same for black people today.[21] Cleage's hope is that the unity in the black church will spread throughout the black population.

THE SPIRIT'S WORK IN BLACK UNITY

Albert Cleage emphasizes the formation of community as a major work of the Spirit. The Spirit accomplishes this work of creating community by first enabling persons to overcome the selfishness and estrangement associated with individualism which, for both society and the church, is a problem.[22] Under the myth of individualism, persons fail to discern their connection and responsibilities to others and to recognize that the highest quality of life requires recognition of the priority of the common good. According to Cleage, individualism is a distortion of the gospel message about salvation that has been perpetuated by the Western church and the slave Christianity that whites gave to black people.[23] Cleage claims that the focus of Christianity is on group, society, and community—not individuals per se.[24] He says that believers feel the Holy Spirit as a people, not as solitary individuals.[25] By virtue of their belonging to a group—that is, the black church or black nation—the Spirit of God initiates encounter.

The person's encounter with God in the Spirit is key to overcoming individualism. According to Cleage, among the "processes by which the individual is able to overcome his individualism and become part of a group [are] . . . the sudden Pentecostal experience which occurs unexpectedly when the walls of individualism have been eroded quietly through sustained, deeply emotional group experiences over an extended period of time."[26] This encounter with the divine, according to James Cone, conveys truth. God is a symbol, a word that "opens up depths of reality in the world."[27] In particular, that which is gained in the human-divine encounter is truth about the connection between historical struggle and ultimate reality. This spiritual experience gives meaning and purpose to history. The person is made aware of a cause in life beyond his or her individual pursuits. The cause of

---

[18]Ibid., 250–1.
[19]Cleage, *The Black Messiah*, 44–5.
[20]Ibid., 20.
[21]Ibid., 237–9.
[22]Ibid., 107.
[23]Ibid., 43 and Cleage, *Black Christian Nationalism*, 32.
[24]Cleage, *The Black Messiah*, 43.
[25]Cleage, *Black Christian Nationalism*, 251.
[26]Ibid., 72–3; see also 211.The other processes are (1) the confrontations, criticisms, and mutual love that occur as a result of a person belonging to a group and (2) the affective experience of an African religious ceremony of initiation into the group.
[27]James H. Cone, *A Black Theology of Liberation* (Maryknoll, NY: Orbis, 1990 [1970]), 57.

justice is a greater cause because the quality of life which they seek is unattainable and, if it seems achieved, is of short duration without the stability and peace provided by justice. This larger struggle for justice is not pointless. It is, in Cleage's words, something that is sacred by virtue of the fact that liberation, freedom, and justice are God's work.[28]

Second, the Spirit brings persons into solidarity, uniting them in a shared pursuit of freedom. This achievement of solidarity is no simple matter. There are several challenges to realizing black unity. In one of Cleage's written prayers, he asks for God's presence in the Spirit and the Spirit's work of rendering a sense of community among black people.[29] The unity sought is not some type of conformity. Rather, this is a unity within diversity. Cleage recognizes that African Americans are not a monolith; they fight for freedom in different ways but can be—and at certain times in history have been—united in this common struggle against oppression. Any successes experienced are because of their unity. Their becoming a community is a birth in and through the Spirit.[30]

This black unity that Cleage envisions encompassing the entire African American population begins in the Holy Spirit's work of gathering believers in the church. In the context of the black experience in America, the black church is a basis for black unity.[31] In James Cone's systematic theology, the Christian church, with the black church being its most authentic expression, is proclaimer of God's liberation, participant in the struggle for liberation, and a model of the freedom promised by God to all humankind.[32] Cleage claims that from the unity accomplished by the Spirit, blacks are empowered to change the world.[33] Moreover, the Holy Spirit not only unites black people, but also brings them into solidarity with peoples everywhere in the world who are oppressed.[34]

DIVINE INTERVENTIONISM, HUMAN AGENCY, AND THE BLACK NATION

Albert Cleage and James Cone's pneumatologies do not presuppose or provide warrant for an interventionist perspective that places the burden and work of liberation solely on God. The work of liberation is human work that is divinely inspired, guided, and sustained unto completion. As Cleage says, persons are doomed if they adopt the belief that God is going to take care of everything.[35]

According to Cleage, God inspires and partners with us in order to build. African Americans are "participating" in the freedom that God will bring eventually and fully to the world.[36] The work of building the black nation involves, for example, the Freedom Now Party led by Cleage, rallying black persons to vote into elected offices other blacks as their representatives. Other works for building the black nation and for which Cleage appeals to God for the Spirit's help include: takeover and development of black schools, social and political organization of black neighborhoods, and nurturing relationships

---

[28]Cleage, *Black Christian Nationalism*, 9.
[29]Cleage, *The Black Messiah*, 21.
[30]Cleage, *Black Christian Nationalism*, 75.
[31]Cleage, *The Black Messiah*, 20.
[32]Cone, *A Black Theology of Liberation*, 130–2.
[33]Cleage, *The Black Messiah*, 240.
[34]Cleage, *Black Christian Nationalism*, 251.
[35]Cleage, *The Black Messiah*, 79.
[36]Ibid., 132, 142.

between black elders and black youths. Additional works for building the black nation are the following: reorganization of the black church for the transformation of black communities, training persons for leadership roles in black communities, fostering business development and economic cooperation, teaching communalism and exposing the dangers of individualism, and proclaiming a message that salvation as survival on earth in the here-and-now is as important as life in the hereafter.[37]

Whereas Cleage emphasizes the concept of the black nation, Cone emphasizes the concept of black power. According to Cone, black power is God's Spirit working in the world to liberate the poor and oppressed. Cone sees the work of God as involving more than the mere building of a black nation. He sees God revealing and inviting all persons to enter the new humanity in Jesus Christ—a genuine and humane community defined by love, justice, and peace.[38] For African Americans in the 1960s and in the following decades, awareness of this new humanity has been raised by the black power movement. Cone notes that black power advocates define it as "black people taking the dominant role in determining the black-white relationship in American society."[39] Cone defines black power as "complete emancipation of black people from white oppression by whatever means black people deem necessary."[40] These means may include "selective buying, boycotting, marching, or even rebellion."[41] Black power is thus the quest of blacks to be human and to determine their own destiny apart from the people who are oppressing them.

SANCTIFICATION, SALVATION, AND SPIRITUAL GIFTS

Among James Cone's many contributions to black liberation theology is his explanation of the role of the Holy Spirit in sanctification and salvation. According to Cone, the Holy Spirit is at work in salvation as well as influencing persons' responses to it. Cone defines sanctification as Christian living and worship in the experience of salvation.[42]

According to Cone, black religion grounds salvation in history and eschatological vision. Salvation is viewed eschatologically, that is, over the grand sweep of time (the past and present) and with anticipation of its completion. The believers' sight of God's future leads them to feelings of discontent with current injustices and motivates them to work for the realization of justice in the world. At any given moment, believers are made aware that their struggle for justice is God's struggle also. They believe that the present and near future will give way to God's design of freedom and justice. Cone says, "To be sanctified is to be liberated—that is, politically engaged in the struggle for freedom."[43] This liberation, this sense of being liberated or freed, is "the power of God's Spirit invading the lives of the people."[44] The Spirit enables persons to affirm and to live in light of a future that is

---

[37] Cleage, *Black Christian Nationalism*, 62–3.
[38] Cone, *God of the Oppressed*, 176 and *For My People: Black Theology and the Black Church* (Maryknoll, NY: Orbis, 1984), 174.
[39] Cone, *Black Theology and Black Power*, 1.
[40] Ibid., 6.
[41] Ibid.
[42] Cone, *Speaking the Truth*, 32.
[43] Ibid., 33.
[44] Ibid., 20.

not only yet to come, but also not always obvious based on observations of the past and present.

It is likely that Cleage and Cone do not regard 1 Corinthians 12, Paul's discussion of the gifts of the Spirit, as a definitive list of the *charismata*. For the black church or black nation, the Spirit bequeaths many gifts. Included among these gifts are the shout and, as discussed earlier, insight into what God is doing in human history. The black church, as an eschatological community, "[believes] that the Spirit of Jesus is coming to visit them in the worship service each time two or three are gathered in his name and to bestow upon them a new vision of their humanity."[45] When black Christians gather for worship, they shout, communicating in their speech and bodily movements their awareness of God's presence and affirmation of their humanity. Cleage says that the shout (during worship) is an eschatological sign of God's affirmation of black people's humanity and establishment of justice.[46] Cone says, "To shout is to 'get happy.' It happens in the moment of conversion and in each renewal of that experience in the worshipping community. Shouting is one's response to the movement of the Spirit as one encounters her presence in the worship service."[47] This joy is a reaction of the people to the visitation of God's Spirit who discloses and reaffirms their new identity while living in a society that views them marginally and then pejoratively.

BLACK LIBERATION THEOLOGY AND AFROPENTECOSTAL THEOLOGY

Though the Spirit is important in black religious experience, pneumatology is not a central category in black theology.[48] This omission is egregious, considering the growth and revitalization of African American churches that has occurred in light of the Pentecostal movement. Pentecostalism is the fastest growing form of Christianity in the world, not to mention its extension and influence among black churches in the United States, Africa, the Caribbean, South America, and the United Kingdom. If not Pentecostal in terms of doctrine, African American churches are often Pentecostal in terms of worship and religious practices.

Critical of what he sees as the worst in Pentecostalism, Cleage says that the gift of the Holy Spirit is "wasted" with fascination with tongues speaking (glossolalia), enjoyment of ecstasy and the shout, being together but not organized for impactful social action, spiritualizing social problems in a manner that obstructs identification of the enemy and social institutions that perpetuate oppression, and honoring persons for heroic deeds in the struggle for justice but not taking responsibility to become personally involved in this struggle.[49] Cleage suspects that the enthusiastic worship in Pentecostal churches may distort the shout in a manner that provides support for escapism and an individualistic view of salvation. Cleage declares that the Holy Spirit is given for empowerment for work

---

[45] Ibid., 18–19.
[46] Cleage, *The Black Messiah*, 6.
[47] Cone, *Speaking the Truth*, 26.
[48] In *Is God a White Racist?* (Boston: Beacon, 1998 [1973]), William R. Jones argued that the central category of black theology is theodicy, whereas in *Redemption in Black Theology* (Valley Forge, PA: Judson, 1979), Olin P. Moyd argued that the central category is eschatology.
[49] Cleage, *Black Christian Nationalism*, 254, 256–7.

in the world, not personal enjoyment of ecstasy and warm feelings of togetherness.[50] He believes that the touch of the Holy Spirit requires nothing less than a response of social action.

Similarly, Cone is critical of an individualistic notion of sanctification. He says that the limitation of the Spirit's work to "private moments of ecstasy or with individual purification from sin" is a distorted and "impoverished" view of the work of God's Spirit in the believer.[51] According to Cone, salvation is God's work happening within history, not just personal spiritual experiences. He says,

> The working of God's Spirit in the life of the believer means an involvement in the world where men are suffering. When the Spirit of God gets hold of a man, he is made a new creature, a creature prepared to move head-on into the evils of this world, ready to die for God. That is why the Holy Spirit is the *power* of God, for it means continuation of God's work for which Christ died.[52]

As Cleage would say, the building of the black nation requires that African Americans make sacrifices for it, as Jesus did.[53]

For the black liberation theologians in the tradition of Cleage and Cone as well as the black Pentecostal theologians who are deeply concerned about liberation, there are challenges. The questions are many. How will black churches reconstruct the notions of race and ethnicity in such a way as to promote black solidarity without compromise of the Christian principle of universal community? If black churches are not reflective of universal community, then how might they—while allowing the Holy Spirit to lead—reorganize for freedom, equality, justice, and inclusion? These questions seem to be variants of a single question about the Spirit-filled black church in a world characterized by diversity and complicated by pluralism. Cleage and Cone offer answers.

FOR FURTHER READING

Buhring, Kurt. "The Spirit of Resistance: Dwight N. Hopkins's Trinitarian Framework." *Black Theology* 10, no. 2 (2012): 184–94.

Hopkins, Dwight N. *Down, Up, and Over: Slave Religion and Black Theology*. Minneapolis, MN: Fortress, 2000.

Roberts, J. Deotis. "The Holy Spirit and Liberation: A Black Perspective." *Mid-Stream* 24, no. 4 (1985): 398–410.

Williams, Eric Lewis. *More Than Tongues Can Tell: Significations in Black Pentecostal Thought*. PhD diss., University of Edinburgh, 2015.

---

[50] Ibid., 259.
[51] Cone, *Black Theology and Black Power*, 58.
[52] Ibid.
[53] Cleage, *The Black Messiah*, 9.

CHAPTER THIRTY-TWO

Latinx Perspectives

DANIEL CASTELO

In their suggestive volume, Zaida Maldonado Pérez, Loida I. Martell-Otero, and Elizabeth Conde-Frazier refer to the Holy Spirit as "the Wild Child."[1] This is a unique way to think of the Spirit, and by being unique, it may be off-putting or difficult to accommodate for those who have other metaphorical inclinations. Although they readily tend to use relational imagery for theological topics, these authors are not in any sense diminishing the identity and role of the Spirit by using the language of "child"; rather, the metaphorical force of this language is registered by the modifier "wild," which when conjoined to the imagery of a child has the impact of suggesting one who acts fearlessly, spiritedly, and spontaneously. A "wild child" typically causes a scene by throwing conventionality out the door in a memorable way; a "wild child" stirs things up.[2]

What makes this imagery appropriate and insightful for pneumatology? The answer to this question can be reflective not only of the perspective at work in the volume by these *Latina Evangélicas* (evangelical Latinas), but also of the overall orientation of a Latinx perspective[3] on the person and work of the Holy Spirit. In particular, this essay will stress the Spirit's "wildness," for this feature of the presence and work of the Holy Spirit resonates with a marginalized people group in a sociopolitical reality in which they find themselves.

---

[1] See Zaida Maldonado Pérez, Loida I. Martell-Otero, and Elizabeth Conde-Frazier, *Latina Evangélicas: A Theological Survey from the Margins* (Eugene: Cascade, 2013), chap. 2.
[2] Ibid., 14.
[3] One of the ongoing discussions in this field is the precise nomenclature to use. Variants include "Hispanic Theology," "Latino Theology," "Latino/a Theology," "Latin@ theology," "Latinx Theology," and others. Each option has its advantages and disadvantages, including varying capacities to account for all the diversity that is inherently at work under these headings (including Iberian, Amerindian, and African heritages). Other matters at work are referencing significant migratory patterns (Mexican, Puerto Rican, Cuban, and the range of Central American countries) as well as people who have long-standing claims to regions (such as the early settlers in the American Southwest). Although all these modifiers and their noun forms continue to be used in the field, in this chapter the choice has been made in favor of "Latinx Theology" as a title for the following reasons: the phrase (a) reflects an emerging option that has the potential to be standardized and this because (b) it resists the inherent gender binary reflective in Spanish (the female "a" and the masculine "o") while (c) retaining this root in a neologism for the predominantly English-speaking, American context. Put another way, the modifier "Latinx" is and is not English and Spanish; in a way, it is its own, unique "thing," which is appropriate given that the theological movement (which began in earnest in the 1970s) attempts to highlight something "emergent" and "new." Despite these advantages, this article will switch terms within the chapter itself since one option has not become standardized (and it is questionable that one will be in the foreseeable future).

"WILDLY" RECALLING HISTORY

In a chapter he titles "The Significance of a Minority Perspective," esteemed historical theologian Justo González remarks that one should not pass over theological perspectives that deviate from the established norm since common views, "precisely because they are common, involve a prejudice that is difficult for us to see," while noting that "a seemingly more biased view will help us discover that prejudice."[4] Several features of this statement are worth elaborating. Just on the surface of the claim, the assumption is that common views will deem alternative views "biased." This is a strategy of marginalization since implied by this viewpoint is that what is common is somehow "bias-free." But an interaction undertaken in good faith with alternative, "more biased" views should expose prejudice in common views as well. After all, theological views, whatever their shape, have prejudices and biases; the deeper we can press into them, the clearer we can understand both ourselves and others. The challenge, of course, is how to press deeply into them so as to expose those biases, and for González, such work must involve interlocutors who represent truly different alternatives.

One might think that this work of exposing prejudices and biases is strictly intellectual, cognitive work. It is not. When one thinks of the many cases in which Jesus Christ appears on the scene in the NT, not all turned to him in faith. We may infer that they did not do so because of biases operating at deep registers, ones that go beyond the intellectual. In fact, we see an interesting dynamic when some examples are put forth. On the one hand, some cases show Jesus outrightly rejected by the crowds, including those in his hometown who knew him all too well (Mt. 13:54-57) and the prestigious and powerful temple priests and elders (see the many scenarios in Matthew 21–22); on the other hand, one finds instances in which people apparently recognize him immediately for who he is and in turn respond fittingly on account of that awareness (the cases of Simeon and Anna in Luke 2 are pertinent examples). The difference between these two kinds of responses is not based on intellection; rather, it is based on ranges of spiritual perception. Some people harbor biases and prejudices that are exceedingly idolatrous and human-centered, whereas those who respond fittingly to Jesus do so propelled by a "bias of the Spirit." When Jesus and others throughout Scripture repeatedly reference empirical language such as having or not having "ears to hear" (Deut. 29:4, Jer. 5:21, Ezek. 12:2, Mt. 11:15, Mk 4:23, Lk. 14:35), they are not speaking of a naturalized empiricism, but of a kind of "spiritualized" empiricism in which the presence of the Spirit bears witness to the truth of the gospel and the purposes of God. Martell-Otero, Maldonado Pérez, and Conde-Frazier speak of this as *la presencia de Dios que se puede sentir* (the presence of God that can be felt).[5]

These differences are noticeable not simply in responses to Jesus, but also on a host of other matters, including recalling history faithfully and earnestly. To take up this last point pneumatologically, the Spirit is the One who makes it possible for believers to re-member, to "put together again," their collective narratives in a way that is biased toward the truth and so the purposes of God. This overall point is important for Latinx theological perspectives because Hispanics on the American scene cannot participate in what González calls "myths of innocence." When Americans speak of their founding as a country and raise cases of purity and valor (the Puritans on the Mayflower, the expedition of Lewis and

---

[4] González, *Mañana* (Nashville, TN: Abingdon, 1990), 21.
[5] Martell-Otero, Maldonado Pérez, and Conde-Frazier, *Latina Evangélicas*, 21.

Clark, and so on) as well as the genius of the founding fathers (Thomas Jefferson, James Madison, and others), these narratives have the effect of whitewashing what is a bloody history replete with revolution, conquest, and displacement. Vague expressions such as "manifest destiny" and "conquering the West" are often used without recognizing the blatant and disastrous impact surrounding them. One of those people groups lost in this casting of history is the Latinx population of this region. Their background, interestingly, predates English settlements in the early colonial era (and, of course, both were predated by Native Americans). "Nineteen years before the British founded their first colony in the land that Sir Walter Raleigh called Virginia, the Spanish based in Cuba founded a city that still exists in Saint Augustine, Florida. And twelve years before the Pilgrims landed on Plymouth Rock, the Spanish founded the city of Santa Fe, New Mexico."[6] Such facts are not meant to say that the Spanish colonists somehow have a greater right to "own" the land than the British colonists do; rather these observations and other indicators (including the present-day names of so many cities, states, and geographical markers that have a Spanish background) point to how the story of the United States has been Anglicized and so purified not simply of diversity but also of contestation and conflict.

The difficulty of hearing this alternative—albeit true—history is reflective of a strategic narrative. As González continues, "The reason why [the United States] has refused to hear the truth in its own history is that as long as it is innocent of such truth, it does not have to deal with the injustices that lie at the heart of its power and its social order."[7] Those with privilege and power do not care to account for this history because it calls into question why they have privilege and power in the first place. But those who do not benefit from such history and its ensuing arrangements are not able to simply bypass it as if it were insignificant; for them, it is exceedingly consequential for their daily lives across generations.

Related to this challenge of recounting history well, the "Wild Child" who is the Spirit is the One who can embolden the telling of difficult stories and in turn convict the hearts of those who do not wish to hear them. These matters are not abstractions or far-removed concerns for Latinxs; quite the contrary, they are pending, ongoing issues, as demonstrated in such crises as children being separated from their mothers and locked in cages on the US-Mexican border, all in the name of protecting arrangements that have conveniently been forgotten to have been established through violence, annexation, and displacement. The words prompted by the Spirit through Jeremiah's witness still ring true today: "Thus says the LORD: Act with justice and righteousness, and deliver from the hand of the oppressor anyone who has been robbed. And do no wrong or violence to the alien, the orphan, and the widow, or shed innocent blood in this place" (Jer. 22:3). Acting with justice and righteousness involves recounting the histories of misdeeds, suffering, and violence. The whitewashing of history through "myths of innocence" only exacerbates the conditions for current-day oppression and injustice. Spirit-empowered agents of memory, ones led by the Spirit to remember the teachings of Jesus (Jn 14:26), are needed to tell bravely the stories that common accounts conveniently forget. Although such work always comes at a cost, it is nevertheless vital work in which truth is at stake.

---

[6]González, *Mañana*, 31. For more on this history, see Carrie Gibson, *El Norte: The Epic and Forgotten Story of Hispanic North America* (New York: Atlantic Monthly, 2019) and Robert Goodwin, *América* (London: Bloomsbury, 2019).
[7]González, *Mañana*, 39.

THE SPIRIT OF LIVING "IN-BETWEEN"

In many ways, the Latinx experience is one of hyphenation or of living "in-between" identities. As to the first expression, if the hyphen is used grammatically in such cases, then it would be at work in identifiers such as "Cuban-American," "Guatemalan-American," "Peruvian-American," and so on.[8] In saying that the Latinx experience is one of hyphenation, one points to the dynamic, liminal space of the hyphen. This space is not inconsequential, as if the true action points are the words before and after it; rather, the space of the hyphen is an existential reality for many in the Latinx population; it is a place in which each of the surrounding words is not quite accurate to describe who they are and the significance of their experiences. For example, people who identify as "Mexican" may never fit into certain people's understandings of what that ethnic identity represents; some may even think that they are not "Mexican enough" because of preconceived notions of what that designation means. And yet, in their daily lives in the United States, these individuals may very well become racialized as persons of color and thereby be "othered" so that they suffer from the long-standing struggles of this country with white supremacy and racism; from that latter vantage point, they would not fit in the United States either, given this country's "Anglicized majority."[9] One could say, then, that these people of the hyphen live as perpetual "misfits."[10] The "in-between" space of the hyphen is the place out of which they struggle with and define their identities.

This experience of living "within the hyphen" and "in-between" is one that can be correlated dogmatically with the doctrine of the Holy Spirit. The case has been made that the Spirit is the "Cinderella of Theology," often neglected and forgotten.[11] Part of this neglect inevitably has to do with the Spirit being a kind of "misfit" to the theological enterprise and the worldviews that support this work in any given intellectual world. As a result, the Spirit is often ignored or depersonalized, features with which Latinxs can relate given their own experience.[12] Time and time again, the Spirit demonstrates an identity of being the God of "in-between" spaces. For instance, the Creation-creator gap is a space in which the Spirit of God sweeps over the face of the deep (Gen. 1:2); the Spirit also inhabits this Creator-creation gap by being the One who comes over Mary in the conception of Jesus (Lk. 1:35). The Spirit is the prophetic Spirit who inspires the prophets to foretell the coming of the Messiah (many instances possible here, but the cases of Isa. 11:1-5 and the Suffering Servant Songs stand out). The Spirit is poured out

---

[8] In the case of many style guides, the hyphen in these kinds of designations has been increasingly dropped over the last few decades, which overall represents a welcome modification.

[9] This Anglicized or English-speaking majority is a construct itself, sometimes denominated via the term "whiteness." For a history of this concept, see Nell Irvin Painter, *The History of White People* (New York: W. W. Norton, 2010).

[10] For a more sustained reflection on this reality, see Fernando F. Segovia, "Two Places and No Place on Which to Stand," in *Mestizo Christianity: Theology from the Latino Perspective*, ed. Arturo J. Bañuelas (Maryknoll, NY: Orbis, 1995), 28–43.

[11] See G. J. Sirks, "The Cinderella of Theology: The Doctrine of the Holy Spirit," *Harvard Theological Review* 50, no. 2 (1957): 77–89.

[12] Samuel Solivan has picked up this last point; he writes, "The depersonalization of the Holy Spirit is important to Hispanic American pneumatology because the relationship of the Spirit to persons, in this case Latinas and Latinos who daily experience treatment as nonpersons, can provide a transformative model of personhood and self-esteem." "The Holy Spirit—Personalization and the Affirmation of Diversity," in *Teología en Conjunto*, ed. José David Rodríguez and Loida I. Martell-Otero (Louisville, KY: Westminster John Knox, 1997), 53.

upon both sons and daughters and male and female slaves (Joel 2:28-29), suggesting that the Spirit stands within the gaps of social stratification. The Spirit stands in the space between life and death by being the Spirit of resurrection (Rom. 1:4). The Spirit is promised to be both with us and in us (Jn 14:17), thus occupying the space between the inner self and everything beyond it. The Spirit is the eschatological Spirit, standing in between the "already" announced kingdom and the "not yet" consummation of that kingdom in the time to come. In short, these and many more examples show that the Spirit is "God in the hyphen" or "God of the in-between spaces,"[13] making the Spirit a true Paraclete/Comforter for those who find themselves labeled as "misfits."

The Spirit is a "Wild Child" here since the Spirit dignifies the experience of those who are given this "misfit" status by showing experientially and in power that these who apparently belong "nowhere" are indeed temples of the Holy Spirit. This confirmation problematizes the "misfit" label itself and the arrangements that make it possible. Just because an identity does not "fit" preconceived notions or categories does not make it any less valuable. In fact, this "lack of fit" can occasion important—and maybe even necessary—change that results from a nonconformist perspective. As the ancients have said, "like tends to like," thereby sustaining not simply broad, mythical narratives but cultural hegemonies and systemic power arrangements as well. The divine "Wild Child" stresses the possibility of a space upon which to stand that does not "fit"—a space that can be holy when it bears witness against instances of injustice and trauma that perpetuate poverty and discrimination at a systemic, structural level. The Spirit is not tribalistic or partisan; rather, the Spirit is *radically for all creatures* in that this One is the life-giving Spirit of God. By being for all creatures, the Spirit validates and dignifies voices that have over time learned to invalidate their voice and experience. What the Spirit does in this case is nothing short of a kind of sanctification and healing so that the marginalized and the voiceless "learn to trust themselves, the gifts of God, and the power of their personhood" as they discern the work of the Spirit in their lives and through their agency.[14]

"WILD" SOLIDARITY

Néstor Medina has remarked that "one would be hard pressed to find any substantial work dealing explicitly with the work and nature of the Spirit in Latina/o theology."[15] That is not to say that Latinxs have not said anything about the Spirit, but this gap of a sustained treatment does point to the prominence of other theological topics that have undergone significant development within the movement of US Hispanic theology. Two of these cases are Christology and Mariology. In the case of Christology, Latinx theologians have often appealed to Christ as the Liberator, the One who suffers rejection and accomplishes the work of healing and salvation. If reference is made to the Spirit in these proposals, it is often one that suggests a kind of subordination (at least in emphasis); such patterns are quite prominent in broader theological discussions. The other topic is Mariology,

---

[13]This imagery is not unusual in pneumatology, as it has been used in other contexts, including Christian mission; for the latter, see John V. Taylor, *The Go-Between God: The Holy Spirit and the Christian Mission* (London: SCM, 1972).
[14]Martell-Otero, Maldonado Pérez, and Conde-Frazier, *Latina Evangélicas*, 26–7.
[15]Néstor Medina, "Theological Musings toward a Latina/o Pneumatology," in *The Wiley Blackwell Companion to Latino/a Theology*, ed. Orlando O. Espín (Malden, MA: Wiley-Blackwell, 2015), 173.

especially in devotion to the Lady of Guadalupe. In various Catholic Latinx proposals, themes that are often connected to the Holy Spirit in other settings are elaborated in terms of the Guadalupe.[16] Despite these emphases taking center stage, however, much needs to be said with regard to Latinx pneumatology, especially with the growing ranks of Latinx Pentecostals and other *evangélicos/as*.

A first point of order in this effort is to reclaim the language of pneumatology as not simply important theologically, but in some ways even central. This requires a "flipping" or "twist" of what typically traffics as theologically conventional. Often the Spirit is considered at the end of any systematic elaboration. Even creedally, the Spirit occupies the space of the "Third Article." Several gestures to make this "flip" or "twist" have happened as of late, including the movement known as "Third Article Theology."[17] These gestures suggest that rather than ending with the Spirit, one ought to *begin* the theological task with the Spirit. Of course, such a move would reconfigure many customary progressions in theological elaboration. For instance, in Christology, one could follow the prompt of Clark Pinnock ("Let us see what results from viewing Christ as an aspect of the Spirit's mission, instead of (as is more usual) viewing Spirit as a function of Christ's"[18]) and allow it to shape how one thinks of Jesus's messiahship, birth, ministry, teachings, passion, death, resurrection, and ascension. The "twist" or "flip" would be exceedingly generative.

For Latinx Christians, this "flip" or "twist" would have ramifications for their starting point to the theological task, namely the concrete experiences of their daily living, which is sometimes labeled *lo cotidiano* (daily or quotidian living). For any number of Latinx theologians, "lo cotidiano functions as locus theologicus. In other words, ordinary living is privileged as source, provides content, particularizes context, and marks the spaces and place(s) from which Latin@'s *do* theology."[19] This is markedly a gesture toward embodiment, praxis, and concreteness, and one over and against abstraction/speculation. How would a robust emphasis on the divine "Wild Child" influence how one elaborates *lo cotidiano*?

Medina offers some "musings" worth noting. In particular, he lifts up a series of terms that together comprise a constructive pneumatological approach to *lo cotidiano*. The first term he mentions is *convivencia*. This term is an existential notion that most basically "points to the *act* of living and sharing life with someone(s) within the context of the larger community."[20] Basic to *convivencia* is another term in Latinx theology, namely *en conjunto*. Both *convivencia* and *en conjunto* point to the way Latinxs think first and foremost in terms of relationality; they are shaped and formed in the context of relationship. This relational aspect, of course, is among others in a community, but the added dimension of church and spirituality suggests relationship *coram Deo* (before

---

[16]Medina points to two scholars who undertake these kinds of emphasis, Orlando Espín and Neomi De Anda; see "Theological Musings toward a Latina/o Pneumatology," 178–80.

[17]See Myk Habets, ed., *Third Article Theology: A Pneumatological Dogmatics* (Minneapolis, MN: Fortress, 2016) for a programmatic collection of essays. For more on this point from a Latinx perspective, see Daniel Castelo, "*Diakrisis* always *en Conjunto*: First Theology Understood from a Latino/a Context," in *Constructive Pneumatological Hermeneutics in Pentecostal Christianity*, ed. Kenneth J. Archer and L. William Oliverio, Jr. (New York: Palgrave Macmillan, 2016), 197–209.

[18]*Flame of Love: A Theology of the Holy Spirit* (Downers Grove, IL: InterVarsity, 1996).

[19]Carmen M. Nanko-Fernández, "Lo Cotidiano as Locus Theologicus," in Espín, *Wiley Blackwell Companion to Latino/a Theology*, 15 (emphasis original).

[20]Medina, "Theological Musings toward a Latina/o Pneumatology," 181.

God). When connected, the relationship with God and one another is a spiritually rich, synergistic unfolding in which living and sharing life in the Spirit is itself life-giving and sustaining.

Convivencia oftentimes "has historically been understood within the context" of another term, namely *sobre-vivencia*.[21] This term involves "overcoming" what is for many in the Latinx community a reality of living in *lo cotidiano*: "incredible odds in the midst of violence, discrimination, lack of opportunities, systemic exclusion/marginalization, and so on."[22] One of the important aspects of stressing *lo cotidiano* as a *locus theologicus* is that it quickly raises the viability of theologizing within circumstances of struggle, pain, oppression, and marginalization. This *locus* cuts to the quick as to how theologizing can help one live life "in the Spirit" when so much is pointing otherwise. The Spirit who helps us in our weakness (Rom. 8:26) is the One who empowers believers to face life, and to do so with hope while resisting despair. *Sobre-vivencia* suggests that Christians worship an "overcoming Spirit."

Finally, the themes of *convivencia* and *sobre-vivencia* point in Medina's proposals to *acompañamiento* (accompaniment). *Acompañamiento* has been a theme highlighted by Latinx theologians,[23] but Medina stresses its inevitable pneumatological dimensions. The Holy Spirit is the Christian God who lives where people live, faces what people face, and joins people in their struggles. Walking according to the Spirit (Romans 8) also implies that the Spirit walks with us. Such is a remarkable claim since this Spirit is the One who not only brought the world to be, but who also anointed and empowered Jesus in his ministry—the Spirit who made Jesus "the Christ" is the One who accompanies us. The *acompañamiento* of the Spirit highlights concretely the promise of Jesus that he would not leave his disciples orphaned (Jn 14:18).

When these three terms—*convivencia, sobre-vivencia*, and *acompañamiento*—are taken together, we see how the Spirit offers us a "wild" form of solidarity, one that expands radically the promises of Jesus. The Holy Spirit is "God with us" in all circumstances and moments of our lives, that is, in the realities of *lo cotidiano*. This kind of pneumatological vision truly is a hopeful and inspiring one.

CONCLUSION

A recurrent situation I encounter among students and clergy alike is a reticence about the person and work of the Spirit. But this reticence may not simply be linguistic; it may also involve a kind of disinclination or reluctance "to not even go there." Why? My sneaking suspicion is that many believers know implicitly that the Spirit is a disruptor, a catalyst for change, an agent who unsettles and challenges—in short, a "Wild Child." Those who are comfortable with the status quo may prefer not to be troubled, but for the poor, disenfranchised, and marginalized, their hope rests on the potential for change. As those who perpetually have their histories forgotten, their identities labeled as insufficient, and their status "othered" by wider forces, Latinxs embrace precisely the disruptive and

---

[21] Ibid.
[22] Ibid.
[23] See Robert S. Goizueta, *Caminemos con Jesús: Toward a Hispanic/Latino Theology of Accompaniment* (Maryknoll, NY: Orbis, 1999) and Sammy Alfaro, *Divino Compañero: Toward a Hispanic Pentecostal Christology* (Eugene, OR: Pickwick, 2010).

transformative dimensions of the Spirit's presence. The heart of their epicletic prayer is ultimately Marian: "Come, liberating Spirit; come, sanctifying Spirit; come, wild Person of the Trinity; *heme aquí* (here am I); let it be with me and those around me according to your word" (cf. Lk. 1:38).

FOR FURTHER READING

Medina, Néstor. "Theological Musings toward a Latina/o Pneumatology." In *The Wiley Blackwell Companion to Latino/a Theology*, edited by Orlando O. Espín, 173–90. Malden, MA: Wiley-Blackwell, 2015.
Nanko-Fernández, Carmen. *Theologizing en Espanglish*. Maryknoll, NY: Orbis, 2010.
Solivan, Samuel. *The Spirit, Pathos and Liberation*. Sheffield: Sheffield Academic Press, 1998.
Villafañe, Eldin. *The Liberating Spirit*. Grand Rapids, MI: Eerdmans, 1993.

CHAPTER THIRTY-THREE

Where the Wind Blows

Pneumatology in Feminist Perspective

LISA P. STEPHENSON

With the resurgence of pneumatology occurring simultaneously with feminist theology's emergence as an academic discipline, one might easily assume that feminist theology would not experience the eclipse of the Spirit with which the Western theological tradition has been accused. Yet, surprisingly, the doctrine of the Spirit has also experienced neglect among feminist theologians. Feminist spirituality notwithstanding, feminist systematic reflections on the Spirit are few and far between. And, in light of the recent gains made in the broader Western theological tradition in this area, the paucity among feminist theology is even more glaring.[1] On the one hand, it is not without warranted trepidation that feminists tread lightly in the waters of pneumatology. The historical construction of this doctrine contains untold patriarchal baggage that feminists must excise in order for them to find pneumatology life-giving rather than oppressive.[2] On the other hand, even though this is the case, the lack of sustained feminist reflection on the Spirit still seems odd, given that feminists strive to overcome latent patriarchal stumbling blocks embedded within theology.

Several feminists have offered their own reasons as to why there is a dearth of feminist pneumatology, though the rationales given are not altogether convincing. Nicola Slee suggests that the absence of pneumatological reflection in feminist theology can be accounted for in that feminists are more interested in lived experience than abstract speculation.[3] Practical commitment is valued over systematic treatises. Yet, while lived experience is certainly privileged among feminists, it does not suffice for an adequate explanation when this reasoning does not hold true for them with respect to other doctrines, including that of Christology or a theology of God the Father. Others, like Sallie McFague, find traditional Christian pneumatology (i.e., the Spirit as the re-creation

---

[1] Many feminist works that are offered as surveys of Christian doctrine frequently either subsume pneumatology under other loci (e.g., ecclesiology or spirituality) or neglect it altogether. For examples, see Rosemary Radford Ruether, *Sexism and God-Talk: Toward a Feminist Theology* (Boston: Beacon, 1983); Catherine Mowry LaCugna, ed., *Freeing Theology: The Essentials of Theology in Feminist Perspective* (New York: HarperCollins, 1993); Natalie K. Watson, *Feminist Theology* (Grand Rapids, MI: Eerdmans, 2003).
[2] Mary Grey, "Where Does the Wild Goose Fly To? Seeking a New Theology of Spirit for Feminist Theology," *New Blackfriars* 72 (1991): 90–1; Helen Bergin, "Feminist Pneumatology," *Colloquium* 42, no. 2 (2010): 189–91.
[3] Nicola Slee, "The Holy Spirit and Spirituality," in *The Cambridge Companion to Feminist Theology*, ed. Susan Frank Parsons (Cambridge: Cambridge University Press, 2002), 172.

of life available only through Christ) to be too narrow and exclusive. In contrast, these feminists want to broaden their understanding of Spirit to mean the life-giving breath that animates all things.[4] Yet, again, this preference seems less than convincing. Feminist theology at large deals with an exclusive "God the Father" and "God the Son," so why not also with an exclusive "God the Spirit"? Moreover, must these two perspectives be mutually opposed to one another? Can they not come together in a creative interplay? Anne Claar Thomasson-Rosingh surmises that a further explanation might be found in that feminists simply deem a critique of traditional pneumatology unnecessary. If this is true, then inherent in this assumption is the belief either that pneumatology is by its very nature already feminist, or that the critiques of the Father and Son are sufficient enough. If the former, one underestimates the pervasiveness of patriarchal thinking within Christianity. If the latter, one underestimates the importance of the Spirit within Christianity. Thomasson-Rosingh aptly notes, "It seems as if feminist theology, at least as far as sustained systematic critique is concerned, has followed the patriarchal agenda of preference for the 'Father' and the 'Son' and still has to investigate further the meaning of Spirit."[5]

The few feminists who are turning their attention to pneumatology are doing so in ways that react to and critique some of the trenchant hierarchical dualisms that have plagued Western thought: transcendent/immanent, spirit/matter, mind/body, male/female, patriarchy/mutuality. In using pneumatology to undercut these dualisms, feminists employ the Spirit through means that bring God nearer, permeate matter, affirm bodies and embodiment, empower females, and privilege mutuality over patriarchy. The approaches feminists adopt to accomplish this task vary, but feminist pneumatology offers a different way of viewing God, the world, and ourselves. In this essay, therefore, I will survey the various contours of feminist pneumatology by offering representative examples and suggest a way forward that has not yet been developed among feminists but holds promise for feminist pneumatology in the future.

THE SPIRIT AS "SHE"?

A pressing theological issue for feminists has always been that of God-language. "The way in which we speak about God is of fundamental importance, for our language about God both reflects and shapes our most fundamental convictions about the nature of truth, our human and cosmic destiny, and our own human nature, since we affirm we are made 'in the image of God.'"[6] Consequently, feminists have engaged in a widespread attack on patriarchal God-language, which one can understand as the exclusive, literal, and oppressive use of male images to name God. While feminists have devoted considerable theological energy into critiquing the patriarchal constructions of God as Father and Son, some have also devoted their attention to the way in which the Spirit is named.

---

[4] Sallie McFague, "Holy Spirit," in *Dictionary of Feminist Theologies*, ed. Letty M. Russell and J. Shannon Clarkson (Louisville, KY: Westminster John Knox, 1996), 146–7; idem., *The Body of God: An Ecological Theology* (Minneapolis, MN: Fortress, 1993), 141–50.

[5] Anne Claar Thomasson-Rosingh, *Searching for the Holy Spirit: Feminist Theology and Traditional Doctrine* (New York: Routledge, 2015), 3–4.

[6] Nicola Slee, *Faith and Feminism: An Introduction to Christian Feminist Theology* (London: Darton, Longman and Todd, 2003), 23.

At first glance, one might assume that a simple and beneficial connection is to refer to the Spirit as "she" and posit her as the divine feminine alongside the Father and Son.[7] This move seems warranted by the female imagery Scripture uses to depict the Spirit as the One who "births" new life in creation, the incarnation, and new creation, as well as the historical precedent set in early Semitic and Syrian traditions which referred to the Spirit as "she."[8] However, while there are a few like Alwyn Marriage who think this is a useful relationship to develop and thus do so, the more widespread opinion among feminists is that it is problematic to identify the Spirit as *the* female person of the Godhead, regardless of well-meaning intentions.[9]

The first concern with identifying the Spirit as the divine feminine is that the inherent logic utilized to justify this association is flawed. That is, those who maintain the Spirit as the divine feminine warrant this move on the basis of noting the similarity between the characteristics attributed to the person and work of the Spirit with those traditionally associated with being a woman (e.g., mothering, affectivity, and intimacy). However, this rationale inherently reinforces the stereotypes of "masculine" and "feminine." It takes an anthropological dualism—noted repeatedly by feminists to be problematic—and divinizes it, thus legitimizing it. Moreover, positing the Spirit as the divine feminine also has the effect of restricting one's conception of the Spirit, as well as that of the Father and Son. For example, if one depicts the Spirit as comforting, then this seems to ignore the fiery metaphors associated with the Spirit; and if comforting is most associated with the Spirit, then what does this imply about the persons of the Father and the Son? Is the act of comforting mutually exclusive to the Father and the Son?[10]

A second concern arises when one considers the way in which pneumatology has functioned historically, especially in the West, within trinitarian models. At best, the tradition is inclined to depict a subordination of the Spirit, at worst a neglect. While this observation is not unique to feminists as many others share it, what feminists note is that when this subordinated and neglected God becomes a "she," this serves to reinforce women's own historical subordination and neglect. In fact, some conclude that it may be precisely because the Spirit is spoken of in metaphors of female resonance that the theological energies devoted to pneumatology have lagged behind those devoted to the Father and the Son.[11] Resonating with this observation, Slee says, "The hiddenness, anonymity, and invisibility of women is mirrored and reflected in the facelessness and namelessness of the Spirit in Christian worship, theology, and life."[12]

These concerns, of course, do not preclude using female God-language or referring to the Spirit as "she," but they do prescribe the way in which one must approach this task.

---

[7]This is what several male theologians have done. See Yves Congar, *I Believe in the Holy Spirit*, 3 vols. (New York: Seabury, 1983), 3:155–64; Donald L. Gelpi, S.J., *The Divine Mother: A Trinitarian Theology of the Holy Spirit* (Lanham, MD: University Press of America, 1984), 215–38; Leonardo Boff, O.F.M., *The Maternal Face of God: The Feminine and Its Religious Expressions* (San Francisco, CA: Harper & Row, 1987), 80–103; Jürgen Moltmann, *The Spirit of Life: A Universal Affirmation* (Minneapolis, MN: Fortress, 1992), 157–60.
[8]Slee, "The Holy Spirit and Spirituality," 182.
[9]Alwyn Marriage, *Life-Giving Spirit: Responding to the Feminine in God* (London: SPCK, 1989).
[10]See Sarah Coakley, "'Femininity' and the Holy Spirit?" in *Mirror to the Church: Reflections on Sexism*, ed. Monica Furlong (London: SPCK, 1988), 124–35; Elizabeth A. Johnson, *She Who Is: The Mystery of God in Feminist Discourse* (New York: Crossroad, 1992), 50–4; Slee, *Faith and Feminism*, 23–30.
[11]Johnson, *She Who Is*, 128–31.
[12]Slee, *Faith and Feminism*, 73–5; idem., "The Holy Spirit and Spirituality," 172.

Johnson argues that one may use female experience as a source for speaking about God—including the Spirit—but it must be done in such a way that female imagery is used as an equivalent divine symbol that expresses the fullness of the divine, not just an expression of some dimension.[13] For example, Johnson herself proposes that Woman Wisdom, Sophia, is an appropriate female image of the Spirit because here Sophia is not an aspect of God, but God. Johnson develops this further and maintains that this Spirit-Sophia may also be named "friend," which she finds to be a more captivating variant of the traditional pneumatological metaphors of "love" and "gift" because it implies a relationship that is characterized by mutual trust and responsibility, engagement in common interests, and inclusivity toward others. Johnson describes the Spirit as the friend "par excellence" because "the Spirit not only makes human beings friends of God but herself befriends the world."[14] Johnson also suggests that women's experience of being a sister, mother, or grandmother has the potential to specify further this pneumatological model of friend.[15]

THE SPIRIT, DIVINE IMMANENCE, AND EMBODIMENT

A large portion of feminist pneumatology is characterized by a focus on divine immanence, in which the Spirit of God is present and at work in the world through matter, bodies, and women. Elizabeth Johnson faults classical theism for depicting God as the Supreme Being who made and rules all things but is unrelated to it and unaffected by it. This view elevates divine transcendence at the expense of divine immanence. Disagreeing with this perspective, Johnson highlights the Spirit as the living God present and active throughout the world. She maintains that the historical world serves as a potential sacrament of divine presence and activity, including the natural world, personal and interpersonal experiences, and macro systems. As such, the experience of the holy is not limited to religious events (e.g., church, word, sacrament, and prayer), but permeates the whole world. The Spirit's field of play is unlimited. Accordingly, Johnson highlights two particular actions of the Spirit in the world. The Spirit vivifies all of creation, since it is the Spirit who is the creative power that brings the world into existence and continues to sustain it. The Spirit also renews and empowers because brokenness and sin affect creation. From personal renewal to social, political, and even cosmic renewal, the Spirit is the source of transforming energy among all creatures. Thus, when the presence and activity of the Spirit is located in the world, God is not just transcendent but also immanent; matter is no longer divorced from Spirit but is an intrinsic part of creation in and through which the Spirit works; bodies, as products of the Spirit's vivifying and renewing work, are holy, including those of women.[16]

---

[13] Johnson, *She Who Is*, 42–57.
[14] Ibid., 145.
[15] Ibid., 141–6. Sallie McFague also utilizes the metaphor of "friend" to speak about God. However, while McFague's use of this metaphor stands alongside that of "mother" and "lover," she does not intend for this functional "trinity" to correlate with an ontological one. Therefore, McFague's model of God as friend is not equivalent to Johnson's. See Sallie McFague, *Models of God: Theology for an Ecological, Nuclear Age* (Philadelphia, PA: Fortress, 1987), 224.
[16] Johnson, *She Who Is*, 124–8, 133–9; idem., *Women, Earth, and Creator Spirit* (New York: Paulist, 1993), 41–4, 57–60. For other feminist writings that focus on the work of the Spirit in the world, see the following: Chung Hyun Kyung, "Come, Holy Spirit—Renew the Whole creation" in *Signs of the Spirit*, ed. Michael Kinnamon

A corollary to this focus on divine immanence is an emphasis on embodiment. Rebecca Button Prichard utilizes the five senses as a hermeneutical scheme to organize the pneumatological images she finds in Scripture and tradition. She intentionally focuses on a somatic metaphorical structure in order to intersect pneumatology with the created world and bodily existence. With this lens, Prichard brings to the fore the multifaceted ways in which the Spirit makes creation her home. Through speech, one learns to listen for the Spirit everywhere because boundaries of institutions, privilege, or sex do not constrain her. One can hear the Spirit in the words of the faithful, but not always in the words of the orthodox. One can hear her in the mighty wind and in the still small voice. Her words bring life but not always comfort. And her words enable one's own that come to fruition in action. Through vision, one can see the work of the Spirit in creation as well as human nature. The Spirit is responsible for the greening of the earth by means of giving life, renewing, refreshing, healing, restoring, and reconciling. Through taste, and more particularly the images of hunger and thirst, one can observe the interconnection between bodily and spiritual desires. It is the Spirit that satisfies one's hunger and sanctifies one's tastes. It is also the Spirit that helps one to maintain the delicate balance between feasting and fasting, safeguarding one from overindulgence and unnecessary deprivation. Through touch, one can know the Spirit as the fire of God. As such, the Spirit is a comfort and a caution as she both warms, welcomes, leads, and guides but also burns, refines, and consumes. When one kindles this fire in her own hearth and heart, one is a conduit for God's passion and compassion. Finally, through smell, one can sense the distinctive scent of the Spirit that permeates all of creation. The Spirit's perfume is full of life. Ever present to humanity, the Spirit also enables one to discern the aromatic distinctions of others: fair or foul, life or death.[17]

Similar to Prichard's use of embodiment to reflect on the Spirit—especially her use of speech—Andrea Hollingsworth posits the Spirit as the divine voice. As such, this voice requires lungs, vocal cords, and lips in order to be heard. It cannot exist as an immaterial entity but requires embodiment. Specifically, this embodiment takes form among women as the divine voice enables women to find their own voices. Moreover, the Spirit as divine voice affirms relationality and diversity. With respect to the former, in order for one to speak, others must give ear. The vocal exchange is dependent upon those speaking *and* those listening. In this sense, the divine voice is not identified with one interlocutor or the other, but is mediated in and through the interlocutory process itself. With respect to the latter, the Spirit as divine voice also affirms diversity, as the sound of the Spirit does not just emerge from one mouth or language, but from many. The Spirit's voice is polyvocal.[18]

Another feminist who focuses on the Spirit and embodiment is Thomasson-Rosingh, and she approaches it from a sexual perspective. She claims that:

> the experience of the Spirit and the experience of sexual ecstasy are very similar. The pleasure of becoming one with a fellow human is similar to the happiness of becoming one with God. . . . If the line on which sexuality and spirituality are opposites becomes a circle, sexuality and spirituality will become neighbors. This idea of the similarity of

---

(Geneva: World Council of Churches, 1991), 37–47; McFague, *The Body of God*, 141–50; Susan Rakoczy, "Living Life to the Full: The Spirit and Eco-Feminist Spirituality," *Scriptura* 111 (2012:3): 395–407.

[17]Rebecca Button Prichard, *Sensing the Spirit* (St. Louis, MO: Chalice, 1999).

[18]Andrea Hollingsworth, "Spirit and Voice: Toward a Feminist Pentecostal Pneumatology," *Pneuma* 29 (2007): 189–213. Cf. Grey, "Where Does the Wild Goose Fly To?" 93–5.

intercourse and being filled by the Spirit makes the sexual experience and the body an epiphany of pneumatology.[19]

Thus, viewing sexuality through the lens of pneumatology might make it become more "holy ground" requiring careful attention and silence. Conversely, viewing pneumatology through the lens of sexuality might make the Spirit more fun, concrete, and earthed as well as grounded in relationship in a different way.[20]

THE SPIRIT AND HOUSEHOLD STRUCTURES

Some feminist pneumatology examines the ways in which the Spirit inspires and empowers new "households" of living that reject patriarchal privilege. Nancy Victorin-Vangerud is concerned with the way the patriarchal family model has influenced Christian theology and communities and how persons have used pneumatology to sustain and enforce this reality. She maintains that as the model of the human family has transformed over time, so too must the theological model of God (as the triune family) and the theological models of community (as a spiritual family). Central to all this change is a new understanding of the Spirit. In order to construct this new understanding, Victorin-Vangerud utilizes feminist maternal resources to reconfigure Spirit-language, which seeks to promote proper trust and mutual recognition while avoiding poisonous pedagogy (i.e., practices that teach others to repress their own needs and desires at the expense of conformity).[21] Employing this lens, she analyses three contemporary pneumatologies espoused by male theologians and refines them so that the distorted relational models do not continue. She shifts Jürgen Moltmann's pneumatology from one of self-surrender to self-commitment, Michael Welker's from self-withdrawal to self-assertion, and Colin Gunton's from self-giving to self-care. She then turns to the gentile Pentecost to demonstrate the connection between the Spirit and mutual recognition. In this event, in which the Spirit is poured out on the gentiles, dignity and mutuality are given to those who were without. The unity that emerges is not at the expense of assimilation or subordination, but the differences are preserved as the Spirit facilitates a diversity in unity. This transformation from an economy of domination to one of mutual recognition can only come about as possibilities for conflict are faced, and new fruit of the Spirit—including anger—are allowed to be displayed and recognized as the work of the Spirit, too.[22]

Thomasson-Rosingh also notes the promise of the gifts of the Spirit for a feminist pneumatology. Like Victorin-Vangerud, she understands that some have used these gifts to build the hierarchy of patriarchy, but she maintains that they are ultimately tools that are too valuable to let go and are essential for building a community of the Spirit. Thomasson-Rosingh does not view the lists of gifts found in Scripture as static and unchanging, but contextual. The Spirit gives them in specific circumstances, to specific communities and individuals, for specific purposes. Consequently, this contextual nature invites Thomasson-Rosingh to explore what gifts are present today in communities of

---

[19] Thomasson-Rosingh, *Searching for the Holy Spirit*, 150–1.
[20] Ibid., 151.
[21] It is "feminist" in that it is concerned with the abuse of male power over women; it is "maternal" in that it is concerned with the abuse of power by mothers over children. See Victorin-Vangerud, *The Raging Hearth: Spirit in the Household of God* (St. Louis, MO: Chalice, 2000), 89–115.
[22] Victorin-Vangerud, *The Raging Hearth*, 143–64, 187–212.

the Spirit. She does not provide an exhaustive list but highlights six. The first gift is discernment, which enables persons and communities to find and value other gifts. The second gift is language, the purpose of which is inclusion; Spirit-language is meant to serve as an invitation, crossing borders and eliminating them. The third gift is insight, which is indispensable to communities of the Spirit that need to be able to find their way. The fourth gift is prophecy, which is dangerous because it uproots, calls for change, warns, and discerns the future based on the current course of action. The fifth gift is healing, which includes the body, emotions, and relationships. As such, the gift of healing serves as a magnet in the community of the Spirit, creating a desirable place for others to want to be. The sixth gift is miracles, which function to bring hope. Miracles are open doors where there had before only been dead ends.[23]

A FURTHER FORAY FOR FEMINIST PNEUMATOLOGY

Characteristic of all the feminist pneumatologies noted earlier is an approach that makes the Spirit the subject of study rather than the method. On the one hand, there is nothing atypical about this tactic, as it is one that characterizes most pneumatologies, whether feminist or not. On the other hand, feminists may unwittingly be perpetuating a patriarchal framework even as they attempt to undermine it. That is, in terms of method, feminist theology has continued to subscribe to the patriarchal agenda of preference for the Father and Son.[24] Feminists have well recognized the subordination of the Spirit to the Father and Son as a theological *topic* but have not yet acknowledged the subordination of the Spirit to the Father and Son as a theological *approach*. In order for feminists to remove the vestiges of patriarchy completely from pneumatology, feminists must not only change the subject of the conversation but the framework as well.

This method of doing theology is emerging among a handful of other scholars and is termed a "third article theology."[25] As such, it is defined as a "conscious and considered approach to conceiving of theology and witnessing to God's self-revelation in Word and works, from the perspective of the Spirit where questions of pneumatology set the agenda and control the trajectory of the dogmatic enterprise, rather than pneumatology being the sole focus."[26] A third article theology looks *through* the Spirit, not only *at* the Spirit. Whereas those employing this methodology have made great gains in truly bringing pneumatology to the fore, it has not yet been an approach that feminists have adopted. However, a third article theology holds great promise for feminist pneumatology. If, as

---

[23]Thomasson-Rosingh, *Searching for the Holy Spirit*, 139–48.
[24]For example, Thomasson-Rosingh has critiqued Victorin-Vangerud's pneumatology in *The Raging Hearth* for being too christocentric. The pneumatologies of Moltmann, Welker, and Gunton that Victorin-Vangerud examines are christocentric, which results in her own feminist transformation of them to continue to be christocentric. And, then, when Victorin-Vangerud devotes a whole chapter to feminist pneumatology itself, two-thirds of it is concerned with feminist Christology. Commenting on this, Thomasson-Rosingh says, "Why, even in pneumatology, is the Son more important than the Spirit? I think this might be because the Son reinstates a safe and familiar patriarchal framework" (*Searching for the Holy Spirit*, 48). Johnson begins to make the methodological move toward adopting a pneumatological approach in *She Who Is* when she subverts the traditional order of the Trinity and begins with the Spirit. However, she fails to sustain this pneumatological approach in the following chapters in her treatment of Jesus-Sophia and Mother-Sophia.
[25]It has been designated such in reference to the third clause of the Nicene Creed.
[26]Myk Habets, "Prolegomenon: On Starting with the Spirit," in *Third Article Theology: A Pneumatological Dogmatics*, ed. idem. (Minneapolis, MN: Fortress, 2016), 3.

some have suggested, the neglect of the Spirit and the marginalization of women have a symbolic affinity that goes hand in hand, then what better way to heighten and reaffirm the Spirit's subjectivity—and, in turn, women's subjectivity—than privileging the Spirit as the hermeneutical lens through which to read all other doctrines? Here, I offer a brief example of the way in which a feminist third article theology could be employed.[27]

One feminist way of dealing with theological anthropology is to affirm women's equal being and worth through the theological symbols of *imago Dei* and *imago Christi*.[28] However, these approaches represent a theo-logical and christological method, respectively, leaving out a pneumatological method altogether. In order to construct anthropology from a feminist third article perspective, one can read these two theological symbols through a pneumatological lens as well as propose a pneumatological approach wherein the Spirit comprises its own theological symbol, *imago Spiritus*, to complement the first two.

With respect to the *imago Dei*, Gen. 1:26-27 serves as the foundational text in which the narrative declares both male and female are made in the image of God. In order to understand how the Spirit helps to constitute the *imago Dei*, one must look at Gen. 1:2, wherein before creation becomes a reality, the *ruach Elohim* is hovering over the face of the deep like a mother bird hovering over her egg.[29] Thus, presupposed in the act of creation is not just the word of God that brings forth life, but the Spirit that readies the chaos for the word. The word is spoken in the Spirit, similar to the way in which breath brings forth words. Creation begins with the Spirit and, consequently, the *imago Dei* begins with the Spirit.

With respect to the *imago Christi*, Gal. 3:26-28 serves as the foundational text in which the baptized become christomorphic and Christ's identity replaces former divisions and inequalities. This is not to suggest that one exists in sexual similarity to Jesus, but that one lives a life that is consistent with Jesus's compassionate and liberating life in the world by taking on his characteristics, virtues, and intentions. In order to understand how the Spirit helps to constitute the *imago Christi*, one must recognize that this christomorphic identity is not possible without the presence of the Spirit. That is, throughout the NT, the Spirit plays an integral role in the birth, life, death, and resurrection of Jesus. From beginning to end, Christ's mission is integrally intertwined with the Spirit's. Therefore, if the Spirit is essential to the life of Christ, the Spirit is also essential to forming persons into the *imago Christi*. It is only possible to image Christ through the power and presence of the Spirit.

With respect to the *imago Spiritus*, Lk. 24:49 and Acts 1:4-5, 2:1-41 serve as the foundational texts in which Spirit baptism functions analogously to the way water baptism functions in Galatians on three accounts. First, both symbols utilize the metaphorical imagery of "putting on" (*enduo*). In Galatians, it is a putting on of Christ (Gal. 3:27), and in Luke-Acts it is a putting on of the Spirit (Lk. 24:49, Acts 1:8). Second, both symbols herald and effect the emergence of the new creation. In Galatians this is understood by means of an Adam Christology, and in Luke-Acts this is understood by means of

---

[27] For a more detailed account of a feminist third article approach, see Lisa P. Stephenson, *Dismantling the Dualisms for American Pentecostal Women in Ministry: A Feminist-Pneumatological Approach* (Leiden: Brill, 2012), 115–35, 167–90; idem., "A Feminist Pentecostal Theological Anthropology: North America and Beyond," *Pneuma* 35, no. 1 (2013): 35–47.

[28] Johnson, *She Who Is*, 69–75.

[29] Ibid., 82–6.

the restoration of Israel. Third, both symbols necessitate certain ethical imperatives that require that this new identity be lived out within the community. Former identities are rendered meaningless, and a new form of praxis is expected (Gal. 3:28; also Acts 8:4-39; 10–11). As a result, Luke-Acts offers this third symbol of *imago Spiritus*, which privileges the Spirit in its anthropological proposals and can thus serve as a further way of asserting women's equal being and worth that stands alongside that of the *imago Dei* and the *imago Christi*.

CONCLUSION

Feminists have made several worthwhile contributions to contemporary pneumatology. From their critiques and proposals concerning God-language, to the ways in which they highlight the Spirit's presence and work in the world, to their proposals for household restructuring—feminist theology is bringing fresh and needful insights about the Spirit of God. And because pneumatology has been neglected for so long and only recently is experiencing a renewed emphasis of theological attention, feminists stand at an opportune moment in time in which they can be a part of the conversation and formation of a doctrine that, in many respects, is still at the ground stages of development. But this can only happen if feminists finally turn their full attention to the Spirit and recognize there is much more work to be done, both in terms of content and method. It is time for feminists to heed the call of the Spirit, venture out, and see where the path may lead.

FOR FURTHER READING

Johnson, Elizabeth A. *She Who Is: The Mystery of God in Feminist Discourse*. New York: Crossroad, 1992.

Prichard, Rebecca Button. *Sensing the Spirit: The Holy Spirit in Feminist Perspective*. St. Louis, MO: Chalice, 1999.

Stephenson, Lisa P. *Dismantling the Dualisms for American Pentecostal Women in Ministry: A Feminist-Pneumatological Approach*. Leiden: Brill, 2012.

Thomasson-Rosingh, Anne Claar. *Searching for the Holy Spirit: Feminist Theology and Traditional Doctrine*. New York: Routledge, 2015.

Victorin-Vangerud, Nancy M. *The Raging Hearth: Spirit in the Household of God*. St. Louis, MO: Chalice, 2000.

CHAPTER THIRTY-FOUR

Pneumatology and the Canonical Heritage

MARK E. POWELL

For many Christians today, the Holy Spirit is associated with the individual and with spectacular gifts and manifestations. This popular assumption, however, is far too narrow. The Holy Spirit works through the individual Christian, but whatever the Spirit does through the individual is set in the context of the church and God's mission through the church. The Spirit is related to spectacular gifts and manifestations, but more often the Spirit works through the mundane—even messy—aspects of ecclesial life. In other words, pneumatology and ecclesiology are closely related. It is significant that in the Nicene Creed, the church and regular means of grace like baptism are addressed under the article on the Holy Spirit.

Irenaeus, following the Apostle Paul, affirms the Spirit's work through the church and through regular means of grace. "'For in the Church' it is said [1 Cor. 12:28], 'God has set apostles, prophets, teachers,' and all the other means through which the Spirit works. . . . For where the Church is, there is the Spirit of God; and where the Spirit of God is, there is the Church, and every kind of grace."[1] For Irenaeus, the Spirit and the church are intimately related, and the Spirit works through a number of regular means, including church leaders, Scripture, and the rule of faith. This abundance of resources that the Spirit gives and that, over time, the church identifies as being effectual for spiritual formation is the church's canonical heritage.

DEFINING THE CANONICAL HERITAGE

The term "canonical heritage" was coined and popularized by William J. Abraham in *Canon and Criterion in Christian Theology*.[2] Both Catholics and Protestants usually reserve the term "canon" for Scripture and view Scripture as a criterion for religious, and sometimes all, beliefs. Abraham calls for a broader conception of canon both in terms of content and function. In terms of content, Abraham returns to the earlier use of the term

---

[1] Irenaeus, *Against Heresies*, 3.24.1.
[2] William J. Abraham, *Canon and Criterion in Christian Theology: From the Fathers to Feminism* (Oxford: Clarendon, 1997), see especially chap. 2.

in the first millennium, where "canon" was applied to far more than just Scripture.³ The church "possesses a canonical heritage of persons, practices, and materials" that includes canons of Scripture, doctrine, saints, teachers, liturgy, sacraments, bishops, councils, ecclesial regulations, icons, and more.⁴ In terms of function, Abraham argues that the church's canonical heritage is better located in the arena of soteriology than epistemology. No doubt Christians appeal to the canonical heritage in theological debates, and the exact nature of such appeals and broader issues in religious epistemology deserve careful attention.⁵ Abraham, however, emphasizes the many ways the Spirit uses the canonical heritage for spiritual formation.

Clearly, Abraham operates with a generous disposition toward the church's canonical heritage. He is less interested in defining the exact contents of the canonical heritage and more interested in its soteriological function. For instance, Protestants typically exclude the Apocrypha from the canon of Scripture, but the soteriological function of Scripture—that is, its role in bringing people to salvation and spiritual maturity—is similar for Catholic, Orthodox, and Protestant Christians. Even Christian traditions that contest parts of the canonical heritage such as formal creeds, the episcopacy, and saints still confess their faith in hymns, have church leaders who exercise authority, and recognize men and women, both living and dead, as exemplars of the faith. Further, there is some degree of overlap in the purposes of the canons, so if one canon is missing or misused, other canons can compensate.

THE GIFT OF THE CANONICAL HERITAGE

The mere existence of the many resources in the church's canonical heritage raises important questions that are best explored in light of pneumatology. Where did the canonical heritage come from, and how does it function in the life of the church? Regarding its origin, the canonical heritage is best conceived as the Spirit's gift to the church. The generosity of the Holy Spirit is emphasized by the Apostle Paul, who speaks of the Spirit as the giver of spiritual gifts (1 Corinthians 12), and by the Nicene Creed, which identifies the Spirit as the "life-giving one." Just as the Spirit gives life and spiritual gifts, so the canonical heritage is best conceived as another example of the Spirit's generosity. Some items of the canonical heritage, such as the sacraments of baptism and the eucharist, appear as early as Pentecost. Most of the canonical heritage, however, emerged from a long and often informal process. Historically, Christians have viewed the emergence of the canonical heritage not as a coincidence but as the result of the Spirit's work.

Consider the canon of the New Testament. The NT documents were written during the first century, and the first lists of the twenty-seven-book canon appear in the fourth century. In addition to the process of writing and canonization, there were the

---

³For a concise presentation of the broad use of "canon" in the early church, see Hermann Wolfgang Beyer, "κανών," in *TDNT*, III:596–602. See especially section C, "κανών in the Christian Church."

⁴William J. Abraham, Jason E. Vickers, and Natalie B. Van Kirk, eds., *Canonical Theism: A Proposal for Theology and the Church* (Grand Rapids, MI: Eerdmans, 2008), 2. Abraham presents his vision of the canonical heritage in Theses IX-XVI (2–3).

⁵Abraham raises concerns about conceiving ecclesial canons as epistemic criteria in *Canon and Criterion* and presents his vision of religious epistemology in *Crossing the Threshold of Divine Revelation* (Grand Rapids, MI: Eerdmans, 2006). Several authors, including myself, explore issues at the intersection of ecclesial canons and epistemology in *Canonical Theism*, Part II.

transmission of oral tradition and the collecting and editing of sources, especially in the Synoptic Gospels and Acts (see Lk. 1:1-4). This entire process of orally passing on the gospel, writing the NT documents, and canonizing the NT is the Spirit's work through the church to preserve the apostolic witness.[6]

The emergence of the canon of doctrine—that is, the early rules of faith, baptismal confessions, and creeds—is another example of the lengthy and informal process of canonization. The rules of faith and baptismal confessions were written by various authors living throughout the Roman Empire, yet they possess similarities in content and organizational structure. Some of these early faith statements highlight the Father and Son only, but more often they emphasize and are organized around the headings of Father, Son, and Holy Spirit. Even formal creeds like the Nicene Creed (or the Niceno-Constantinopolitan Creed), which is traditionally attributed to the Second Ecumenical Council in 381, emerged from technical theological debates and even political pressure from numerous sides.[7] Nonetheless, creeds like the Nicene and Apostles' Creed continue to receive widespread ecumenical acceptance today and are affirmed either explicitly or implicitly by Catholics, Orthodox, and most Protestant Christians. The canon of doctrine, like the rest of the canonical heritage, is best conceived as the Spirit's gift to the church.

THE CANONICAL HERITAGE AS A MEANS OF GRACE

What, then, about the soteriological function or purpose of the canonical heritage? Why has the Spirit given the canonical heritage to the church? The Spirit may use the canonical heritage in numerous ways, but the Spirit clearly uses it (a) to reveal God, (b) to sanctify and heal Christians, and (c) to equip Christians for God's mission through the church. The following discussion, which is intended to be representative rather than comprehensive, takes each of these functions in turn, starting with how the canonical heritage reveals God.

Revealing God

Christians have always esteemed Scripture among the church's canons because of the unique way it reveals God and gives witness to the apostolic faith. John affirms, "No one has ever seen God. It is God the only Son, who is close to the Father's heart, who has made him known" (Jn 1:18). Jesus is the highpoint of divine revelation, and John records the teachings and signs of Jesus so that people may know God and have life through the Son (14:6, 20:31). Paul emphasizes that his message is not "from a human source, nor was I taught it, but I received it through a revelation of Jesus Christ" (Gal. 1:12). Similarly, the Nicene Creed, following the witness of the biblical authors, recognizes the Holy Spirit as "the one who spoke through the prophets" (see also 2 Pet. 1:20-21, 1 Thess. 2:13).

---

[6]For standard accounts of the development of the NT canon, see Bruce M. Metzger, *The Canon of the New Testament: Its Origin, Development, and Significance* (Oxford: Clarendon, 1987) and Harry Y. Gamble, *The New Testament Canon: Its Making and Meaning* (Philadelphia, PA: Fortress, 1985).

[7]Recent and influential presentations of this history are found in Lewis Ayres, *Nicea and Its Legacy: An Approach to Fourth-Century Trinitarian Theology* (Oxford: Oxford University Press, 2004) and Khaled Anatolios, *Retrieving Nicaea: The Development and Meaning of Trinitarian Doctrine* (Grand Rapids, MI: Baker Academic, 2011), especially chaps. 1–2.

The canon of Scripture has a unique role in revealing God, but the church's other canons are important here as well. The canon of doctrine—which includes early rules of faith, baptismal confessions, and formal creeds—emerged alongside the canon of Scripture beginning in the second century. Early Christians were well aware of the fact that one could possess the canon of Scripture and fail to grasp the Christian vision of God. This trinitarian vision of God receives classic articulation in the Nicene Creed (381) and important clarification in the Chalcedonian definition (451) and is affirmed, explicitly and implicitly, throughout the canonical heritage.[8] The canon of doctrine clearly articulates the Christian vision of God and, in particular, the Holy Spirit. The Spirit, who is worthy of praise together with the Father and the Son, is the presence and power of the one true God.

The items of the canonical heritage play unique roles in proclaiming and preserving the revelation of God. For instance, sacraments such as baptism and the Lord's Supper are symbolic actions that bear witness to the saving work of Jesus. John of Damascus speaks of the icons as "books of the illiterate . . . teaching without the use of words those who gaze upon them."[9] Church leaders, through the use of executive authority, protect the teaching of the faith, and teachers expound upon and clarify the faith. The items of the canonical heritage proclaim the Christian faith in their own unique way, but ideally, they work together to present the inexhaustible mystery of God.

Sanctification and Healing

The canonical heritage is the Spirit's instrument for sanctification and healing in the lives of believers. Christian salvation includes reconciliation with God and inclusion in the church, but it also involves the long process of transforming one's thoughts and desires. The Holy Spirit is traditionally associated with the work of sanctification, and the Spirit works through the canonical heritage to accomplish profound spiritual healing. The canon of Scripture, through which the Spirit speaks, is "living and active" and "able to judge the thoughts and intentions of the heart" (Heb. 4:12). The sacraments are important here as well. Through faith and baptism, Christians receive the indwelling of the Spirit and the forgiveness of sins. In the eucharist Christians regularly renew their covenant commitment with God and, filled with the Spirit, commune with God through the risen Lord. Early Christians spoke of the eucharist as food for spiritual healing: Cyprian of Carthage calls the eucharist "the food of health, or salvation," and Ignatius of Antioch describes it as "the medicine of immortality" so that "we should live forever in Jesus Christ."[10] Scripture and the sacraments are rich with meaning, and throughout history the Spirit has used these items of the canonical heritage to transform believers' lives.

Related to Scripture and the sacraments, regular participation in worship and the liturgy is formative. Consider the ancient Christian practice of singing "psalms and hymns and spiritual songs" (Eph. 5:20). In *Confessions*, Augustine speaks of the influence of the singing at the church in Milan soon after his conversion.

---

[8] William Abraham calls this trinitarian vision of God, which is rooted in the church's canonical heritage, "canonical theism."

[9] John of Damascus, *On the Divine Images*, trans. David Anderson (Crestwood, NY: St. Vladimir's Seminary Press, 2002), 39.

[10] Cyprian of Carthage, *On the Lord's Prayer*, 18 and Ignatius, *Letter to the Ephesians*, 20.2.

> How I wept during your hymns and songs! I was deeply moved by the music of the sweet chants of your Church. The sounds flowed into my ears and the truth was distilled into my heart. This caused feelings of devotion to overflow. Tears ran, and it was good for me to have that experience.[11]

In her recent autobiography, Anne Lamont shares how the singing of a humble church meeting near San Francisco, California, began the process of her conversion from alcoholism, drug addiction, antagonism to the Christian faith, and despair.

> There was no sense of performance or judgment, only that the music was breath and food. Something inside me that was stiff and rotting would feel soft and tender. Somehow the singing wore down all the boundaries and distinctions that kept me so isolated. Sitting there, standing with them to sing, sometimes so shaky and sick that I felt like I might tip over, I felt bigger than myself, like I was being taken care of, tricked into coming back to life.[12]

The Spirit uses the liturgy and its many parts—the reading of Scripture, the eucharist, singing, prayer, the recitation of the creed, the giving of monetary resources, the benediction, and more—to bring profound healing to people who are spiritually sick and dying.

Similarly, John of Damascus, in his defense of the icons, testifies to their power in "sanctifying the sight" and counteracting distorted thoughts.

> Suppose I have few books, or little leisure for reading, but walk into the spiritual hospital—that is to say, a church—with my soul choking from the prickles of thorny thoughts, and thus afflicted I see before me the brilliance of the icon. I am refreshed as if in a verdant meadow, and thus my soul is led to glorify God. I marvel at the martyr's endurance, at the crown he won, and inflamed with burning zeal I fall down to worship God through His martyr, and so receive salvation.[13]

John emphasizes the language of healing and transformation. For John, the church is a "spiritual hospital," and the icons, as well as the lives of the saints, are instruments of spiritual healing. Even in Christian traditions that have traditionally opposed icons and the saints, there is strong interest in icons like Andrei Rublev's *The Old Testament Trinity*, religious artwork like Matthias Grünewald's Isenheim Altarpiece, and spiritual biographies of saints old and new, Catholic and Protestant.[14] Further, ethicists stress that growth in virtue requires a community of faith and tangible expressions of Christian living. To grow in Christian virtue, or "the fruit of the Spirit" (Gal. 5:22-23), one must see the Christian virtues embodied by others. Throughout the history of the church, the

---

[11] Augustine, *Confessions*, trans. Henry Chadwick (Oxford: Oxford University Press, 1991), 164.
[12] Anne Lamont, *Traveling Mercies: Some Thoughts on Faith* (New York: Pantheon, 1999), 48. Additionally, Darryl Tippens offers a beautiful reflection on the power of congregational singing in *Pilgrim Heart: The Way of Jesus in Everyday Life* (Abilene, TX: Leafwood, 2006), chap. 12.
[13] John of Damascus, *On the Divine Images*, 39.
[14] Several books on the Trinity published since the late twentieth century have Rublev's icon on the cover. The Reformed theologian Karl Barth often discussed *The Crucifixion* from Grünewald's Isenheim Altarpiece. And spiritual biographies, such as Eric Metaxes's volumes on Protestant leaders like Dietrich Bonhoeffer, Charles Colson, Martin Luther, William Wilberforce, and others, are best-sellers.

Spirit has used the lives of saints—both living and dead, famous and obscure—to draw Christians closer to God and to produce the fruit of the Spirit.

Equipping for Mission

The Spirit uses the canonical heritage to equip the church to participate in God's mission in the world. Scripture is "inspired by God and is useful for teaching, for reproof, for correction, and for training in righteousness, so that everyone who belongs to God may be proficient, equipped for every good work" (2 Tim. 3:16-17). The Greek word *theopneustos*, here translated "inspired," literally means "God-breathed." Throughout Scripture, the breath of God, or Spirit of God, is associated with creation and the gift of life (Gen. 1:2, 2:7; Ps. 33:6, 104:30; Ezek. 37:1-14). Scripture as "God-breathed" is brought into being and made alive by the Holy Spirit. As such, it is the Spirit's instrument for equipping the church "for every good work." As Robert W. Wall affirms, "'inspiration' envisions a God who is continually enlivening the congregation that uses Scripture in 'teaching, correction, reproof, and training,' as the medium through which the Spirit of the resurrected Christ conveys God's life-giving power to those who humbly receive it."[15]

Early creeds, like the Nicene and Apostles' Creed, not only serve as confessions of orthodoxy, but also as outlines for teaching the Christian faith in evangelism and catechesis. This is especially so in situations, both ancient and contemporary, where printed Bibles are scarce or not available in one's native language. The creeds are easily memorized and present an outline of central Christian beliefs. Or consider the liturgy, which often ends with a benediction that includes both a blessing and a charge. As Christians leave worship and time in God's presence, they are empowered by the Spirit to serve in the world.

The episcopacy, or authorized leadership in the church, plays a crucial function in equipping and serving the church. At issue is not the precise form of ecclesiastical structure, whether episcopal, presbyterian, or congregational, but the crucial role ecclesial leaders play. William Abraham contends, "The church needs holy overseers who will give themselves body and soul to the care of the faithful across space and time. We need living, breathing agents of the Spirit who humbly and firmly exercise their ministry as a gift to the church as a whole."[16] For those who worry about the historical and contemporary abuses of authority, Abraham's advice is simple:

> we need more and less powerful bishops, not less and more powerful bishops. Bishops should be close to the ground, should be deeply involved in local congregations, and should know their local environments intimately. They should be elected as fitting agents of the Holy Spirit; and they should fulfill their ministry in fear and trembling and in humble dependence on the Holy Spirit.[17]

The abuse of authority is a real issue, but as has already been noted, the Spirit uses the canons of the church, when missing or misused, to compensate for one another. Abuses of episcopal authority have been and can be checked by appeals to Scripture and other canons. An emphasis on the soteriological function of the episcopacy also helps protect

---

[15]Robert W. Wall, "A Theological Morphology of the Bible: A Prescription for 'Spiritually Disabled' Students," in *Immersed in the Life of God: The Healing Resources of the Christian Faith*, ed. Paul L. Gavrilyuk, Douglas M. Koskela, and Jason E. Vickers (Grand Rapids, MI: Eerdmans, 2008), 59.
[16]"Handing on the Teaching of the Apostles," in Abraham, Vickers, and Van Kirk, *Canonical Theism*, 58.
[17]Ibid., 58–9.

against abuses. Nevertheless, ecclesial authorities are indispensable for the life of the church. Like the rest of the church's canons, when the episcopacy performs at its best and in humble submission to God, it is the Spirit's instrument for equipping the church for service.

CONCLUDING OBSERVATIONS

These examples are representative, and there is some overlap in the categories of revealing God, sanctifying believers, and equipping for mission, but these examples are suggestive of the many ways the Spirit uses the canonical heritage for spiritual formation. In conclusion, we will consider important implications of stressing the soteriological function of the canonical heritage.

First, during a time of uncertainty, when the Western church faces a decline in members and influence, the canonical heritage reminds us of the abundance of spiritual resources that the Spirit has given the church. We certainly need to be open to prophetic and innovative proposals for church renewal, but we also need to have humility before the Spirit and confidence in the resources the Spirit has provided.[18] The Spirit has already given the church a canon of "living and active" Scripture; a canon of doctrine that emphasizes the trinitarian vision of God and God's work of creation and redemption; sacraments that, when received in faith and repentance, impart the indwelling of the Spirit, forgiveness of sins, and spiritual nourishment; formal and informal liturgical practices that, for millennia, have brought people into the presence of God; leaders, teachers, and saints who serve the church, exemplify the faith, and help Christians grow in virtue; icons that present the faith in striking images; and many other resources. These numerous resources are diverse, readily available, and spiritually profound. They touch the whole person and bring healing to broken and dying lives. Any proposal for renewal that traffics in gimmicks and despair and that disregards the canonical heritage and the Spirit's work through these proven means of grace should be received with caution or rejected outright.

Second, emphasizing the soteriological function of the canonical heritage could lead to ecumenical rapprochement as well as mutual critique on the contested elements of the canonical heritage. For instance, some Protestants have historically opposed the canons of saints and icons because they are not authorized by the NT, but the concern with these canons runs much deeper. John Calvin, an exemplar of this tradition, rightly worried that saints and icons easily lead to "superstition and idolatry."[19] Catholic and Orthodox teachers, however, also recognize the potential abuses of these canons and seek to clearly distinguish the worship given to God alone and the honor given to saints and icons. In other words, the Protestant concern is a real one, is addressed in the best of Catholic and Orthodox reflection and practice, and has led to needed reform when saints and icons were misused. At the same time, Catholic and Orthodox Christians are right to challenge attempts to completely eradicate the canons of saints and icons. Icons, visual images, spiritual biographies, and lived examples of faith have had a significant

---

[18] Jason E. Vickers explores this theme in more detail in *Minding the Good Ground: A Theology for Church Renewal* (Waco, TX: Baylor University Press, 2011), especially 61–3, 91–6.

[19] John Calvin, "On the Necessity of Reforming the Church," in *Calvin: Theological Treatises*, ed. J. K. S. Reid (Philadelphia, PA: Westminster, 1954), 183–216.

impact even on the most iconoclastic of Christians. Furthermore, during a time when people are inundated with violent and sexually provocative images as well as reluctant and questionable role models, there is a real need for the spiritual healing that icons and saints provide. Focusing on the soteriological function of the canonical heritage allows for renewed discussion and appreciation of the contested elements of the canonical heritage.

The Spirit's work through the canonical heritage reminds us of the importance of the church and regular, material means of grace. Most certainly the Spirit "blows where it chooses" (Jn 3:8) and can work apart from the church and the canonical heritage. But pneumatology and ecclesiology are closely related. The church truly is the temple of the Holy Spirit (1 Cor. 3:16, 2 Cor. 6:16), and the Spirit has equipped the church with abundant resources to fulfill its purpose until the coming of our Lord.

FOR FURTHER READING

Abraham, William J. *Canon and Criterion in Christian Theology: From the Fathers to Feminism.* Oxford: Clarendon, 1997.

Abraham, William J., Jason E. Vickers, and Natalie B. Van Kirk, eds. *Canonical Theism: A Proposal for Theology and the Church.* Grand Rapids, MI: Eerdmans, 2008.

Gavrilyuk, Paul L., Douglas M. Koskela, and Jason E. Vickers, eds. *Immersed in the Life of God: The Healing Resources of the Christian Faith.* Grand Rapids, MI: Eerdmans, 2008.

CHAPTER THIRTY-FIVE

Discernment

DOUGLAS M. KOSKELA

In one sense, the topic of discernment occupies a unique space in pneumatological discourse. It is unique because discernment is ostensibly something that human beings do rather than an explicit aspect of the person and work of the Holy Spirit. In another sense, however, the topic brings us right to the heart of pneumatology. It is a weighty claim when someone asserts that the Holy Spirit has spoken or moved in a particular way. When such a claim is made, the importance of careful reflection on the Holy Spirit becomes abundantly clear. Indeed, the stakes are high whether or not the claim is authentic. If the Spirit truly is moving and the community of faith fails to perceive it—through incredulity, inattentiveness, or outright fear—then the church fails to live into its calling in that instance. If the claim does not reflect the genuine guidance of the Holy Spirit but is accepted by the community as such, then the consequences can be disastrous. The work of discernment is therefore necessary for the church, and it is work that is notoriously challenging.

Two Johannine texts nicely frame the conversation. In Jn 16:13, Jesus tells his disciples, "When the Spirit of truth comes, he will guide you into all the truth; for he will not speak on his own, but will speak whatever he hears, and he will declare to you the things that are to come." Yet we find in 1 Jn 4:1 a cautionary note: "Beloved, do not believe every spirit, but test the spirits to see whether they are from God; for many false prophets have gone out into the world." In the first passage, Jesus identifies the Spirit as the One who will guide the fellowship of believers into truth. The community of faith can thus expect that the Spirit will be at work in their midst and that it is possible for them to comprehend where God is leading them. Yet the second passage makes it clear that not every claim about the Holy Spirit's leading is genuine. In some cases, people who believe they sense the movement of the Spirit may simply be mistaken. This can occur, for example, when one confuses one's own desires with the will of God. In other cases, as the reference to false prophets in 1 John suggests, outright deception or manipulation may be involved. Either way, the church's confidence in the Spirit as its guide into truth does not entail the naïve and uncritical reception of all claims to the Spirit's movement. The healthy practice of spiritual discernment enables the community of faith to avoid two great pneumatological errors: attempting to silence the Holy Spirit and legitimizing false claims to the Spirit's leading.

CONTEXTS OF DISCERNMENT

There are numerous settings in which the language of discernment arises in the Christian life at both the personal and communal level. We often speak of vocational discernment, for example, in which people or communities aim to understand the nature of God's calling for their lives. We engage in moral discernment whereby we reflect on the ways our theological convictions find concrete expression in the decisions and actions of day-to-day life. Pastoral discernment is often necessary in the course of the ordained ministry, such as when a pastor prayerfully considers how to minister to someone struggling with repeated patterns of sin. At the congregational level, churches need doxological discernment when considering changes to forms of worship. Or, at a broader level, denominational bodies occasionally encounter situations that require doctrinal discernment—perhaps considering a proposal to revise the denominational statement of belief.

From another angle, we might categorize the various contexts of discernment into two basic groups. These two categories can be distinguished by the object of discernment: Are we aiming to discern a course of action, such as what to do or teach? Or are we trying to discern the legitimacy of a purported word or movement of the Holy Spirit to see if it is genuinely from God—that is, testing the spirits, as suggested in the 1 John text? In the first category, a person or community is approaching a new season or decision point, and thus they are seeking God's leading as to how they might move forward faithfully. For instance, a congregation may begin a conversation about its mission statement in order to shape its priorities for the coming years. Or to take another example, a college sophomore needing to select a major may engage in a period of vocational discernment. In these instances, what is being sought is guidance from God. In the second category, there is a claim to guidance from God already on the table. Someone believes that the Holy Spirit has already spoken, and what is being sought is a conclusion as to the legitimacy of that belief. In other words, the task is to discern between true and false appeals to the Spirit's movement. An example of this sort of discernment occurs when a person proposes a new direction for a congregation, appealing to the leading of the Holy Spirit in making the case. Another instance is when someone senses a clear call to pastoral ministry. That person's community will engage in a period of examining that calling, both in informal ways (prayer and conversation with the pastor and others who know the person well) and in formal ways (interviews with the board of ordained ministry). These examples enable us to see an important difference between our two categories. In the first cases, the process of discernment is initiated by the circumstances or needs of the person or community. In the latter cases, it is the perception of God's initiative that prompts the discernment of the community.

While much of what follows will apply to the first category, our primary focus will be on the latter category. This is appropriate for a volume on pneumatology for two reasons. A first reason is that the second category of discernment is prompted by an explicitly pneumatological claim. A person or group believes that the Holy Spirit is at work, and thus the community of faith sets forth to test the spirits. When genuine, such instances are initiated by God rather than our agendas; thus, the emphasis is on the agency of the Holy Spirit. Second, in the first category of discernment, the focus is on the particular person or community—its gifts, its history, and the circumstances that led it to appeal to the Holy Spirit for guidance. But in the second category, the focus is on the person and work of the Holy Spirit. Does this particular claim reflect what we know of the Spirit? Does it align with how the Holy Spirit has moved in the past? It is a process that requires, in other words, a pneumatologically informed response. This is not to say that the particulars of the circumstances will be unimportant in the second category. A genuine word of God for one person or community at a certain time may be the wrong word for another. But in discerning between true and false claims to the Spirit's movement, pneumatological considerations take priority over self-reflection.

GUIDELINES FOR DISCERNMENT

While the context of discernment might involve the particular circumstances of a person or a community, the process of discernment is always communal. This is true in two respects. First, it is rarely (if ever) wise for a person to attempt to discern the genuine movement of the Spirit on one's own, even if the sense of the Spirit's guidance addresses one's own life. The capacity for self-deception is always present, particularly when someone perceives that the Spirit is moving in the very direction that reflects one's own desires. Granted, communities are also capable of self-deception, and there are indeed instances in which the genuine leading of God meets initial communal resistance. Still, seeking the prayerful, attentive involvement of trusted others is a mark of wisdom when one senses God's leading, particularly when the consequences of self-deception are significant. The experience and spiritual insight of other believers enable both the recognition of potential confusion and the affirmation of the authentic leading of the Holy Spirit. The second reason that discernment is always a communal act is that we rely on signposts of the church through the ages throughout the process. Even when the community of faith senses the Spirit leading it in new directions, the witness of Scripture and the Christian tradition provides the means of confirming that it is indeed the Spirit at work. This leads naturally to a consideration of the guidelines by which the community engages in discernment.

A first and essential criterion of discernment is christological. The Holy Spirit points to Jesus and continues to connect us to the work of the incarnate Son. While there is a characteristic elusiveness to the movement of the Spirit,[1] the life and work of Jesus provide a concrete means for recognizing where and how the Spirit is at work. As the great French Dominican theologian Yves Congar put it, christological reference is "the essential condition for the soundness of any pneumatology."[2] Elsewhere, Congar expressed this idea in the form of a maxim: "If I were to draw but one conclusion from the whole of my work on the Holy Spirit, I would express it in these words: no christology without pneumatology and no pneumatology without christology."[3] If an appeal is made to the Spirit's movement in a direction that leads us away from divine revelation in and through Jesus, then something has gone deeply wrong. Thus, a crucial starting point for discernment of the Holy Spirit is christological attentiveness.

Indeed, both of the Johannine passages identified earlier point us in this direction. After affirming that testing the spirits is necessary because many false prophets have gone out into the world, 1 Jn 4:2 continues: "By this you know the Spirit of God: every spirit that confesses that Jesus Christ has come in the flesh is from God, and every spirit that does not confess Jesus is not from God." The pressing issue in this context appears to be some form of docetism that was threatening the theological unity of the community. In response, the text points to the confession of Jesus in faithfulness to the apostolic witness as the basis for discernment. The reference to a particular doctrinal conviction—"that Jesus Christ has come in the flesh"—is notable for our purposes. Vague appeals to Jesus that neglect the apostolic teaching about the significance of his life and work do not provide a sufficient check against false prophecy. In the Johannine vision, a thin Christology will not support faithful discernment.

---

[1] We see this, for example, in Jesus's description of the Spirit in his conversation with Nicodemus in Jn 3:8.
[2] Yves Congar, *I Believe in the Holy Spirit*, trans. David Smith, 3 vols. (New York: Crossroad, 1997), 1:167.
[3] Yves Congar, *The Word and the Spirit*, trans. David Smith (San Francisco, CA: Harper & Row, 1986), 1.

The essential connection between Christ and the Spirit is also reflected throughout the John 16 text. Jesus identifies himself as the one who will send the Spirit who will guide them into truth (v. 7). Moreover, Jesus suggests that the Spirit will "prove the world wrong about sin . . . because they do not believe in me." And even when the Spirit comes to guide the disciples, the Spirit will do so by pointing to the Son. Referring to the Spirit of truth, Jesus says in verse 14, "he will glorify me, because he will take what is mine and declare it to you." Throughout this passage, it is clear that the Spirit is not on a new or unique mission. Rather, the Spirit is continuing the mission given by the Father and instantiated in the incarnate Son. While the Holy Spirit will be the disciples' guide after Jesus goes to the Father, the Spirit's illuminating work among them is not focused self-referentially. It is focused christologically, and thus they should not trust any claim to the Spirit's guidance that directs them elsewhere.

While Christology thus provides a first and necessary test for the authentic discernment of the Holy Spirit, it will not be decisive in every instance. It is likely that this criterion will be most helpful in situations of large-scale doctrinal or moral discernment at the conciliar or denominational level. It is less likely to enable much progress in discernment in more specific circumstances of vocational or pastoral discernment. This is not at all because Christology is unimportant at the local or personal level. Rather, it is because the alternatives at issue may be fully compatible with the apostolic witness to Jesus. That is, there is little or nothing in the Christian confession of the person and work of Jesus that would indicate whether a congregation should remove the organ from its sanctuary. Or, to use another example, suppose someone strongly feels the guidance of the Holy Spirit to move to another country to begin a new ministry. However, Christian friends and family members who know him best are concerned about his motivation and question his cross-cultural sensitivity. Both he and his circle of discernment may share a very similar christological vision and yet disagree over the wisest course of action in such a case. While reflecting christologically on claims to the Spirit's guidance is therefore necessary, it is not always sufficient to bring a process of discernment to a satisfactory conclusion.

A second guideline for discernment is the theological and pastoral witness of the church over time. When the community of faith enters into a time of discernment, it does not start from scratch or proceed without guidance from the past. It has a whole host of treasures that have been graciously given by the Holy Spirit—Scripture, creeds, sacraments, and the like. This "canonical heritage," as noted in Powell's article in this volume, should not be conceived as a collection of epistemological tools so much as means of immersion into the life of God.[4] These gifts point to and connect people with the God who is at work for their salvation. Furthermore, they chart the many ways that the church has given expression to God's salvific action throughout time and space. The significance of these materials for discernment is that they offer, to use a legal image, a vast array of case precedent. If we want to know whether a claim to the Spirit's guidance in the present is genuine, we neglect this witness to the Spirit's guidance in the past only at our peril. I want to emphasize that the primary purpose of the canonical materials is not to help us make decisions; rather, it is to draw us ever more into the life of God. Yet

---

[4] For a collection of essays on the nature and function of the canonical heritage, see William J. Abraham, Jason E. Vickers, and Natalie B. Van Kirk, eds., *Canonical Theism: A Proposal for Theology and the Church* (Grand Rapids, MI: Eerdmans, 2008).

to aim to discern the movement of this God without attention to such treasures is sheer folly.

This is not to say, of course, that every instance of discernment can be settled by appealing to the canonical heritage (a qualification we also saw with the christological principle). Nor does it mean that Christian communities have always discerned rightly in the past. Prophetic correction is often needed as the Spirit works through specific persons to shed light on essentials that have been neglected or forgotten. Indeed, this can be a difficult word to hear, and it is often resisted. Cynthia M. Campbell writes, "The prophetic voice has a way of being disruptive and challenging, and is as difficult when the news is good as when it is bad. The problem with prophets is that they speak a word of the Lord from beyond our immediate confines. They bring a message that challenges our current operating assumptions."[5] Embracing the canonical treasures of the church does not for a moment mean that the prophetic impulse is stifled. On the contrary, true prophets both draw from and call the community back to these means of grace. By drawing us to God, Scripture and the Christian tradition orient the prophet to speak God's word faithfully and dispose the community to receive that word humbly. Indeed, only a community immersed in such riches is in a position to distinguish true from false prophecy.

If the second guideline emphasizes diachronic connection to the Christian community, a third guideline focuses on synchronic connection to fellow believers. It is crucial in any process of discernment to involve members of the community who are in a particular position to recognize the authentic movement of the Spirit. Such people fall into either or both of two categories. First, "the discernment of spirits" is identified by Paul as a particular gift of the Spirit in 1 Corinthians 12:10. This would suggest that some people are endowed with particular spiritual insight that can serve the church in times of discernment. Such a gift is not attained through study or moral exertion but rather given freely by the Holy Spirit for the building up of the church. "To each is given the manifestation of the Spirit for the common good," as Paul puts it in verse 6. Clearly, then, spiritual gifts such as this one are not meant to be kept private or used only for discernment in one's own life. Rather, the community of faith welcomes the generosity of the Spirit and draws on the insight of those with the gift of discernment when testing the spirits.

Second, those who are spiritually mature can offer wisdom and experience that have been cultivated by "a long obedience in the same direction."[6] Whether or not one is particularly endowed with the gift of spiritual discernment, a lifetime of faithful discipleship can prepare one to distinguish between the voice of God and misleading voices. There is considerable attention given in the NT to the theme of spiritual maturity as a key to discernment. Ephesians 4:14-15 warns: "We must no longer be children, tossed to and fro and blown about by every wind of doctrine, by people's trickery, by their craftiness in deceitful scheming. But speaking the truth in love, we must grow up in every way into him who is the head, into Christ." In Heb. 5:14, the mature are

---

[5]Cynthia M. Campbell, "We Believe in the Holy Spirit, Who Has Spoken through the Prophets," in *Fire & Wind: The Holy Spirit in the Church Today*, ed. Joseph D. Small (Louisville, KY: Geneva, 2002), 44.
[6]The phrase is Friedrich Nietzsche's, but it was Eugene H. Peterson who borrowed it for use as an image of faithful discipleship. See *A Long Obedience in the Same Direction: Discipleship in an Instant Society,* 2nd ed. (Downers Grove, IL: InterVarsity, 2000).

described as "those whose faculties have been trained by practice to distinguish good from evil." And Paul's prayer for the church at Philippi in Phil. 1:9-10 is instructive: "And this is my prayer, that your love may overflow more and more with knowledge and full insight to help you to determine what is best, so that in the day of Christ you may be pure and blameless." While the gift of spiritual discernment is given especially to some, the NT witness would lead us to expect that any mature Christian has developed a capacity to speak into the process in a fruitful way. Over a lifetime of immersion in worship and the spiritual disciplines, one comes to recognize the voice of God. In times of discerning whether an appeal to the Holy Spirit's guidance is genuine, such wisdom is an essential resource. In fact, without forgetting the first two guidelines, it is often the case that this third guideline is the most decisive in more personal cases of vocational or pastoral discernment. The particulars of a situation can vary greatly, and there is no flow chart or algorithm that leads to genuine spiritual discernment. But the prayerful counsel of seasoned believers can orient a community to God in a way that enables it to move forward faithfully and wisely. And once we recognize the importance of this sort of orientation toward God, we are naturally led to a consideration of the posture of discernment.

THE POSTURE OF DISCERNMENT

The bulk of attention in discussions of spiritual discernment is often given to process and criteria. We want to know the proper steps to take in order to distinguish between true and false prophecy. And indeed, as the forgoing comments have suggested, there are essential guidelines that the community of faith should always keep in mind when testing the spirits. Yet the obsession with process runs the risk of overshadowing something far more fundamental in the realm of discernment, namely, our disposition toward God. Even a good process for spiritual discernment is not particularly fruitful if the discerning community is not rightly oriented in relation to God. There is no substitute for an appropriate spiritual posture when discerning the Holy Spirit. With this in mind, we turn to three main considerations: prayerful attentiveness, humility, and the expectation of renewal.

We noted at the outset that discernment is, on the face of it, a human activity. Yet it is also the case that the Holy Spirit is doubly involved in it—both as the source of the word or movement to be discerned and as the One who enables God's people to engage in discernment. As we have seen, the Holy Spirit points us to Christ, has guided the church throughout the ages in and through the canonical heritage, has generously gifted some with the particular charism of discernment of spirits, and is at work in the lives of maturing believers to enable their capacity for discernment. One thing should be clear throughout this discussion: God wants to get through to us. Keeping that in mind will give us our bearings in the midst of the epistemological and spiritual challenges of false prophecy. If indeed we are addressed by a God who speaks and desires to be heard, then our attention should be entirely devoted to that God with anticipation. The community whose life is bathed in prayer and who looks to God with trust is in a position to sense the Spirit's movement in its midst. While we are rightly cautious about the very real danger of false claims to the Spirit's movement, we must not allow skepticism to undermine our confidence in God's capacity to speak and be heard. A posture of prayerful attentiveness is thus appropriate for a discerning community.

While skepticism poses one danger to discernment, arrogance poses quite another danger. Excessive confidence in one's own wisdom can inhibit spiritual clarity. In that light, humility is also essential in discerning the authentic movement of the Holy Spirit. From the vast biblical witness to the value of humility in enabling spiritual sight, we might point to the exhortation in 1 Pet. 3:8 to have "a tender heart" and "a humble mind." While we might expect humility to be exclusively an attribute of the heart, this text pairs humility with the mind. The implication is that pride is a danger that attends our pursuit of knowledge, and thus those who are seeking to discern truly must maintain a humble mind. The threat posed by arrogance is made particularly clear in 1 Timothy 6:3-5. In that text, those who contest the sound words of Jesus and the teaching that is in accordance with godliness—roughly parallel to our first two guidelines for discernment—are "conceited, understanding nothing" and have "a morbid craving for controversy and disputes about words." Similarly, 2 Cor. 10:5 references "every proud obstacle raised up against the knowledge of God." The connection of humility and true prophecy also appears in other early Christian literature. Frances Young points to the *Shepherd of Hermas* as a key example in this regard. Drawing out the vision of the *Shepherd*, Young writes: "The true prophet speaks 'as the Lord wills,' never receiving remuneration and humbly living a good and simple life. The one who only seems to have the Spirit exalts himself, wants the first seat, is bold and talkative, lives among luxury and delusions, and only prophesies for reward."[7] The emphasis on humility in these texts points to two conclusions. First, in assessing claims to the Spirit's guidance, the community must consider the posture of the one making the claim. Conceit is a telltale sign of false prophecy, while humility is an indicator of one whose attention is on the Holy Spirit as the church's guide. Second, humility on the part of those evaluating the claim—that is, on the part of those engaging in discernment—puts the community in a position to listen faithfully. Since genuine discernment comes from the Spirit rather than human knowledge (1 Cor. 2:6-16), those who are testing the spirits place their trust in God rather than their own ingenuity.

Finally, it is worth remembering that spiritual discernment is not an end in itself. A word from God is given to a community of faith in order that the community might become more fully what God intended it to be. Thus, the posture of discernment must also include an expectation of what God aims to do in the midst of the community. The guidance of the Holy Spirit does not bolster the agenda that the church has set for itself; rather, the Holy Spirit leads the church toward renewal. In reflecting on OT prophetic texts, Michael Welker notes that prophetic speech in God's Spirit was aimed at Israel's renewal: "The act of making possible the recognition of evil spirits and lying spirits aims at a regeneration, a renewal of the life held captive by these spirits. It envisages a new reality, renewed from its own roots."[8] In the same way, the church in the present draws on the enabling power of the Holy Spirit to discern faithfully the movement of that same Spirit. As the resources of the Christian tradition are recalled and reactivated by God's guidance, the fresh wind of the Spirit brings new life to the community of faith. Trusting in God's provision for humble, attentive, and prayerful minds, the body of believers moves forward in confident anticipation of what lies ahead.

---

[7]Frances Young, *God's Presence: A Contemporary Recapitulation of Early Christianity* (Cambridge: Cambridge University Press, 2013), 275.
[8]Michael Welker, *God the Spirit*, trans. John F. Hoffmeyer (Minneapolis, MN: Fortress, 1994), 96.

FOR FURTHER READING

Congar, Yves. *The Word and the Spirit*. Translated by David Smith. San Francisco, CA: Harper & Row, 1986.

Farnham, Suzanne G., et al. *Listening Hearts: Discerning Call in Community*. Rev. ed. Harrisburg, PA: Morehouse, 1991.

Small, Joseph, ed. *Fire & Wind: The Holy Spirit in the Church Today*. Louisville, KY: Geneva, 2002.

Young, Frances. *God's Presence: A Contemporary Recapitulation of Early Christianity*. Cambridge: Cambridge University Press, 2013.

CHAPTER THIRTY-SIX

Mysticism and Renewal

DANIEL CASTELO

At the end of 1 Corinthians 3, Paul speaks of Christian leadership, of how the Corinthians should not boast, since all belong to them, they belong to Christ, and Christ belongs to God (vv. 21-23). In other words, they should not be driven by the "cult of personality," be it Paul, Apollos, Cephas/Peter, or someone else. The implication here is that Christian ministry involves belonging to God and not exorbitantly adhering to or identifying with another human being, however significant the person is in the church. At the start of 1 Corinthians 4, Paul shares a very broad claim about Christian ministry so as to clarify this leveling effect of all belonging to God: "Think of us in this way, as servants of Christ and stewards of God's mysteries." The first phrase is understandable enough, should one be acquainted with Christian language over some time; one easily finds the language of "disciples," "servants," and one could even say "slaves" of Christ in Scripture as well as in Christian settings. But the last phrase, "stewards of God's mysteries," is much less common. The first word is fiduciary in nature: these "stewards" (*oikonomoi*) are entrusted with managing and guarding a "household." As part of this household metaphor, Paul mentions "mysteries" (*mustēria*). What is the referent of the latter term?

Interestingly, Paul uses this language on several occasions in this epistle (2:7, 13:2, 14:2) but also throughout his literary corpus. The term "mysteries" comes loaded with connotations stemming from a pagan background, but as is the case with so many terms in the Bible, the language is employed by Paul to signify something specifically Christian—be it an account of Israel's hardening (Rom. 15:25), knowledge (Rom. 13:2), God's wisdom (1 Cor. 2:7), glossolalia (1 Cor. 14:2), eschatology (1 Cor. 15:51), the gospel (Rom. 16:25, Eph. 6:19), lawlessness (2 Thess. 2:7), the faith (1 Tim. 3:9), the message of Christ Jesus (1 Tim. 3:16), Christ's church (Eph. 5:32), and, most prominently, Christ himself (Eph. 1:9, 3:3-4, 5:32; Col. 1:26, 27, 2:2, 4:3). Given this textual evidence and its prominence in Paul's writings, one could say that in a Pauline idiom the term "mysteries" broadly refers to the person, message, and work of Christ. Christian ministers are to steward and care for this precious heritage of who Christ is, what he has done, and what he has said; these cases—Christ's person, Christ's work, and Christ's teaching—can be described fittingly in Paul's mind as "mysteries." In this sense, Christians qua Christians traffic in holy mysteries; Christianity is a mystery-laden, or mystical, tradition.

Surveying this textual evidence may appear tedious on first blush, but the effort is to some degree necessary since the language of "mysticism" in English comes loaded with a variety of connotations. Some people hear the language of "mysticism" as a sociological category, given that it is used to describe features of various religions or religiosity in general; others associate the language with cults or "New Age" spiritualities. My sense is that most Christians in the contemporary English-speaking world would not be inclined to say that Christianity is a mystical religion, despite all the earlier verses serving as a counter-witness.

The avoidance of this language, though, is not simply lamentable on the basis of scriptural (specifically Pauline) patterns; this inattention also represents a missed opportunity to account for features of the theological enterprise and the Christian life that run counter to conventional forms of thinking this side of the European Enlightenments. These features are exceedingly pneumatological ones, and as a result, their identification and use may serve not simply the work of claiming past voices and themes, but they also may factor in the process of revitalizing and renewing Christian witness in an age of pluralism, secularism, and diminishing religious devotion in the Global North. The case to be made in this chapter is that in Christianity, mysticism and renewal go hand in hand as features of the Spirit's active work in the world.

RECLAIMING THE LANGUAGE OF MYSTICISM

In addition to the reservations outlined earlier, Christians may also worry about the experiential connotations associated with mysticism. These worries can have at least the following features. First, mysticism carries with it the association of intensely privatized, individualistic experience(s). One assumes that if a person has a "mystical experience," that experience is publicly inaccessible, making it difficult to relate as well as to evaluate. As a result, these kinds of experiences are deemed by some as problematic in that there is little that one can do with them once they are shared. One cannot say that another person's mystical experience is blatantly "wrong" when the criteria for such a determination are not clear. These last points lead to a second reservation: mystical experiences seem to be at day's end "irrational"—they simply do not make sense, given the plausibility structures we prominently rely on so as to order the world and to live in it. Privatization and irrationality, then, prove to be two important deterrents to Christians appropriating the language of mysticism for their faith.

As to the first point, one should note that mysticism and privatization need not go hand in hand. Notice the scriptural passages with which we began this chapter: Paul says that ministers should be "stewards of God's mysteries," a phrase that indicates at least that (a) these mysteries are in some sense "public" given that they are managed and cared for by ministers of the gospel, and (b) these mysteries belong to God and not individuals per se. On both points, the push is outward (toward exteriority), not inward (toward interiority). One can infer from this contrast, then, that perhaps the connotation of individual, private experiences for the language of mysticism is not all there is to account for within Christian discourse related to the theme. The history of Christian mysticism, in fact, suggests precisely that point.

Mark McIntosh indicates that in English settings a turning point for matters related to spirituality and mysticism was the twelfth century; at this time,

> *spiritualitas* . . . came to be used not only in its early sense, as the power of God animating Christian life, but as whatever "pertains to the soul as contrasted with the body"; and this new connotation lies behind "those conceptions of spirituality which willy-nilly used it as the reason for giving the physical world and especially the human body a largely negative role in what they conceived of as authentic Christian life."[1]

---

[1] Mark I. McIntosh, *Mystical Theology* (Malden, MA: Blackwell, 1998), 7, with partial quotes from Bernard McGinn, "The Letter and the Spirit: Spirituality as an Academic Discipline," *Christian Spirituality Bulletin* 1,

This development is not altogether surprising in that Christianity has often had to wrestle with quasi-gnostic tendencies in its history, but the push to interiority and individualization is also something markedly detectable in the latter stages of the Middle Ages, features that would only be more fully pronounced in modernity. This shift represents a clear momentum in the direction of more anthropocentric forms of endeavoring, ones that emphasize ascetical and existential features of what McIntosh calls "the mechanics of the spiritual quest."[2] Exemplars of this tendency are sometimes said to be Teresa of Ávila and Madame Guyon because the push in these and other proposals is in the direction of going ever deeper into the human self. The point to stress here is not the limits of one historical figure or another but rather the broad shifts that occur in the West related to worldviews and social imaginaries.

One could argue that in prior epochs this anthropocentric momentum was not always as pronounced as it came to be in modernity. Rather than a world that was increasingly depicted as closed and self-contained, prior accounts sometimes offered the view that the world was open, that change and transformation were possible from the outside.[3] This in turn had significant implications for how Christians envisioned God's participation in the world. With a more open-ended approach to reality, Christians could imagine a kind of participatory ontology, one in which the self grows more authentic and true to itself by engaging in something other than itself. This vision relies on a take of reality that has God's presence as available and discernable in everyday happenings. Dogmatically, this vision would be thoroughly pneumatological, since the Spirit would be the One in whom Christians "live, move, and have their being" and since this One is not far but very much close to the creation and so the community of faith (see Acts 17:27-28).

As to the second point—that mystical experiences are irrational because they do not fit our typical plausibility structures for what makes sense and how things cohere—much rides on what is deemed "rational." Happenings are deemed "rational" when they fit a collective set of judgments promulgated by a social arrangement at a given point in time. Therefore, everything denominated as "rational" by a twenty-first-century north-transatlantic context will not be so for a first-century Mediterranean context. Just the very distinction that some make between "faith" and "reason" suggests a constructed independence of two terms that would not necessarily hold when other eras and worldviews are referenced; in fact, the distinction may not even hold when ruggedly pressed on its own within the contemporary setting. Therefore, the casting of mystical experiences or of mysticism generally as irrational relies on a number of predeterminations and assumptions, some of which may not hold up when scrutinized, especially from a particular Christian point of view.

Although not an easy topic to broach, it nevertheless is important to state: Christianity's account of what is "reasonable" is an affront to many contemporary cultural and intellectual sensibilities and proposals in the north transatlantic. One can say that Christians operate out of a "rationality of the Spirit" as distinguished from other kinds, including what are generally deemed "hard" rationalities. To highlight this point for the present, Christians believe the God of their confession has spoken *and speaks*, that this One has revealed God's very self

---

no. 2 (1993): 3.
[2]McIntosh, *Mystical Theology*, 8.
[3]Works that press into these shifts are sundry, but one that is important for its diagnostic acumen is Charles Taylor, *A Secular Age* (Cambridge, MA: Belknap, 2007).

and is presently self-disclosing, that this One has worked in the world and *is presently at work*. Those claims may be softened or even ignored through any number of strategies, including deism, cessationism, dispensationalism, inerrancy, or others. The appeal of these alternatives is significant for many, since at day's end what is being entertained by such remarks is quite radical and difficult to fathom, namely that God's Spirit not only has been at work in the world in the past but also is active *here and now*. As difficult as this admission is on a conceptual level, it bears repeating that the invitation to conversion is not simply one of assent; it is one of worldly nonconformity with an eye to conversion and transformation, of having our "minds renewed" (Rom. 12:2) through an encounter with the living God. Ultimately, then, mysticism within Christianity denotes *the real and presently available possibility of encountering YHWH/Trinity in a powerful, life-altering way and in turn living in a way that recognizes YHWH/Trinity as the One who ultimately matters*.

Securing the connection between mysticism and the phenomenological dynamics of encounter is important for relaying the significance of this understanding. In fact, Christian mystics from throughout Christian antiquity have repeatedly done so in order to communicate the character and impact of their experiences. One such quality is immediacy. Andrew Louth remarks that mysticism is a "search for and experience of immediacy with God. The mystic is not content to know *about* God, he longs for union with God."[4] The idea of encounter conveys the idea of immediacy or accessibility of the one being met. A second characteristic of the dynamics of encounter would be address. In encounters, parties address one another, and in doing so, names are often revealed and utilized. One thinks of the many different mystical encounters narrated in Scripture, from Moses at the burning bush in Exodus 3 to Paul's Damascus Road experience in Acts 9. In these cases, YHWH/Jesus addresses the persons, and the persons learn the name of the one addressing them. This dynamic has been popularized in English theological circles via the work of Jewish theologian Martin Buber when he speaks of the interplay in the "I-Thou" encounter.[5] In short, encounters are deeply personal. A third dynamic of encounter worth pointing out that is already embedded in what has been said so far is the kind of knowledge that ensues from it. Rather than descriptive or somehow distanced or removed, the knowledge derived from encounters is personal and direct. These features of immediacy and address lead to a very specific kind of knowledge, one analogously illustrated in a secular sense by Michael Polanyi's *Personal Knowledge*. All these aspects of encounter—immediacy, address, and personal-intimate knowledge—are very much pneumatological ones for Christians, especially (but not exclusively) this side of Christ's ascension. Whether one appeals to the Johannine picture of the Spirit being requested by Jesus to be "another Paraclete" to the disciples who will be with and in them and who will be the Spirit of truth who recalls to their memory the teachings of Jesus, the Lukan picture of the Spirit anointing and empowering the disciples and those who would engage in ministry throughout the Mediterranean to Jew and gentile alike, or the Pauline picture of the Spirit being deeply embedded in believers' selves so that the Spirit bears witness to their spirit and groans with sighs too deep for words—the theological purchase is comparable: the Spirit is key to our understanding of, participating in, and relating to the God of Christian worship. In other words, the Spirit is central to stewarding God's mysteries.

---

[4] *The Origins of the Christian Mystical Tradition* (Oxford: Clarendon, 1981), xv (emphasis original).
[5] See for instance Martin Buber, *I and Thou* (New York: Touchstone, 1996).

MYSTICISM NOT FOR ITS OWN SAKE

If the language of mysticism is claimed by Christians in a way that recognizes the possibilities mentioned earlier, then its thrust should be clear: not inward into the depths of the self alone, but outward in mission and service to the world. Of course, the self is involved, but not singularly so. The encounter with the living God is meant to change not simply individuals, but also circumstances. The examples of Moses and Paul cited earlier as well as many prophetic call narratives point to the way mystical encounters have wide, social consequences. A word that can help keep these two poles together, the inward and the outward, is transformation. The term implies change that makes a difference. As Elaine Heath remarks,

> Christian mysticism is about the holy transformation of the mystic by God, so that the mystic becomes instrumental in the holy transformation of God's people. This transformation always results in missional action in the world. The idea that mysticism is private and removed from the rugged world of ministry is simply false. All the Old Testament prophets were mystics. Their visions, dreams, and other experiences of God were for the express purpose of calling God's people back to their missional vocation.[6]

As significant as these claims are, however, the notion of transformation is plagued by very real, practical questions. Can change really happen in this life? Is transformation possible?

Many forces in our lived experience press us to think that transformation in this life is not possible. The saying goes, "the more things change, the more they stay the same." Systems are typically inertial despite concerted and sustained efforts to change them. Human vices are readily apparent and predictable, and they seem to appear at every generational turn. Ours is a jaded culture, unable or unwilling to believe in something beyond itself for fear of disappointment and of falling prey to naiveté. Christians can easily succumb to these tendencies as they go on to suffer pain, disappointment, and loss. It may appear to be the safer (and so wiser) option to not hope and so not be disappointed than it is to hope and then be disappointed.

A number of counterarguments could be raised to the naysayers of the possibility of transformation. These can be registered on a number of fronts, including the frontiers of science, neuroscience, and others.[7] Theologically, Christians must remain open to the possibility of transformation in that they hold on to the incarnation, not simply on the ground that *God* became flesh but that God became *flesh*. In other words, the incarnation had effects not simply at the soteriological level, but at the creaturely level as well. Summarily put, *the created realm was impacted by the Son's incarnation; it was reconstituted or remade at a basic level.* This point is implied by the broad Athanasian argument that the Son, who created humanity, assumed humanity so that humanity could become God(like), an act that can only inspire awe.[8] It is an argument also at work in Irenaeus when he speaks of the maturation and perfection of humanity taking place over time and after the event of the Son's incarnation, which is a recapitulation of

---

[6] Elaine A. Heath, *The Mystic Way of Evangelism* (Grand Rapids, MI: Baker Academic, 2008), 15.
[7] For explorations into these and other fields, see Oliver Davies, *Theology of Transformation* (Oxford: Oxford University Press, 2013).
[8] See St. Athanasius, *On the Incarnation*, trans. A Religious of C.S.M.V. (Crestwood, NY: St. Vladimir's Seminary Press, 2002), 93 (§54).

humanity that, yes, is backward-looking but also forward-directing: "the Word of God, our Lord Jesus Christ . . . did, through his transcendent love, become what we are, that He might bring us to be even what He is Himself."[9] Otherwise put, as Christ's disciples, we are called to participate into a new humanity, one that of course has resonances with humanity as we typically (and perhaps jadedly) know it, but that also has an openness to possibility—a kind of possibility available to those who live and walk according to the Spirit (see Romans 8). What is being envisioned here is a kind of change enacted by the transformative presence and work of the Spirit through a synergistic interplay of the Spirit working in us so as to conform us to the mind of Christ (see 1 Corinthians 2).

What does this new humanity look like? It is characterized by the many gifts of the Spirit listed throughout Scripture. Whether the options are drawn from Isaiah 11, Romans 12, 1 Corinthians 12; Ephesians 4, or some other list, the collective push is in the direction of a detectably different way of living where sacrifice is more prevalent than self-seeking, where love is more prominent than hate, where compassion is more of a first-response than aggression. Stewarding these mysteries, then, means growing in conformity to and participating in them, not primarily with the self's individual edification as a goal but with the end of the empowerment of the church's witness in the world. This kind of Spirit-prompted change and power is ultimately what will drive the establishment of God's kingdom on earth; it is what will sustain witnesses and martyrs in their testimony to the truth and justice the world so desperately needs to hear and see.

CONCLUSION

In the Christian circles in which I was raised, an evangelistic strategy that was sometimes talked about was the aim of converting the "worst sinner in town." The idea behind this approach was that if an exceedingly well-known scoundrel came to faith, the floodgates of salvific possibility would open for the rest of the community. If God could do something with that person, it was remarked, then surely the power of God would be made real in the eyes of an onlooking community. The change would be such that people would find it attractive and desirable. In our current situation, plenty of people yearn for a kind of metaphysical density; they desire to ground their existence upon something greater than themselves. But that desire can only be kindled and fanned when it meets something deep and meaningful. Churches are often striving to grow and to adapt so as to meet this desire for something deep and meaningful. No strategy or mechanism, however, can take the place of a mystical encounter with the living God, that is, the Spirit who in turn transforms and makes a difference in people's lives.

As essential as this mystical encounter is, it happens to be a delicate matter. Cases within Scripture point to how people can work against the Spirit's purposes; these instances can fall under the heading of "sins against the Spirit."[10] Renewal is far from automatic. This point is especially hard for contexts of privilege to heed. Power and privilege prompt the desire for control and manipulation. As an archetype of this scenario, one recalls the case of the rich young man (Matthew 19) who had legitimate questions and was

---

[9]*Against Heresies*, 5.Preface; ANF, 1:526.
[10]This makeshift category includes "blaspheming" (Mt. 12:31-32), "lying" (Acts 5:1-11), "resisting/opposing" (Acts 7:51), "grieving" (Eph. 4:30), "quenching" (1 Thess. 5:19-21), and "insulting/outraging" the Spirit (Heb. 10:26-29).

extensively engaged in conversation with Jesus, but who ultimately refused to follow Jesus when confronted with the challenge of giving up his possessions. This encounter with the summit of Christian mysteries, the Son of God in the flesh, ended as a grief-filled and heart-breaking failure. Renewal is not something that we as humans achieve, but it is predicated upon renunciation; it involves making space and being hospitable toward the Spirit's transformative presence and work. In light of this dynamic, then, one must be continuously confronted by the following questions: Whom do we love, and why? What do we desire, and why? The answers to these should serve as an indicator of how we are living into the charge of being "stewards of God's mysteries."

FOR FURTHER READING

von Balthasar, Hans Urs. *Word and Redemption: Essays in Theology 2*. New York: Herder and Herder, 1965.

Boyer, Steven D., and Christopher A. Hall. *The Mystery of God: Theology for Knowing the Unknowable*. Grand Rapids, MI: Baker Academic, 2012.

McIntosh, Mark I. *Mystical Theology*. Malden, MA: Blackwell, 1998.

CHAPTER THIRTY-SEVEN

Anointing and Power

CHRIS E.W. GREEN

Pentecostals often refer to "anointing" (sometimes "unction") and "power," and they do so in a mode peculiar enough to warrant careful reflection.[1] This way of speaking about the Spirit and the Spirit's work is rich with theological promise. In what follows, I will attempt to trace the shape of the metaphor as used by Pentecostals and to identify its roots in Scripture and the Christian tradition. I will also work to tease out the implications of this metaphor for pneumatology in particular and Christian doctrine and practice in general.[2]

TRACING THE SHAPE OF THE METAPHOR

It is difficult, if not quite impossible, to define the phrase "anointing and power" as Pentecostals use it. But it indicates, among other things, unusual "affectiveness" and effectiveness. These terms, as Pentecostals use them, seem to be paired so that one can stand for the other. Ministers are described as anointed, as are songs, sermons, prayers, testimonies, services, and even moments within services. An anointed song, for example, stands out from other songs by virtue of its performative vitality and affective energy. And an anointed sermon is one that is exceptionally moving, powerful, and effective. At times, "anointing" is almost synonymous with gifting or charism: a minister who has "an anointing" is known for a certain authority, passion, and dynamism.[3]

Typical usage suggests that we should distinguish between "*the* anointing," which is another name for the Holy Spirit, and "*an* anointing," which refers to a particular work of the Spirit on a person, during an event, or for a particular moment. The aim of the minister and the congregation in every worship service is to "flow in the anointing," which is another way of saying "yield to the Spirit." In brief, Pentecostals use "anointing and power" to name a special work of the Spirit as it is experienced in the worshipping community, a work that demonstrably "comes and goes" according to a nexus of factors, including the secret ordering of divine providence, the greatness of human need, and the intensity of believers' desire and readiness for a "move of God."

---

[1] I am using the term "Pentecostals" in an encompassing way for classical and neo-Pentecostals as well as charismatics.
[2] Thanks to Danielle Larson, Phil Harris, and Robb Blackaby for their help with drafts of this paper.
[3] See "Anointing with Oil" in *NIDPCM*.

A few examples taken more or less at random from Pentecostal publications should make the point. First, in December 1907, the leader of the Azusa Street meetings, William Seymour, wrote to *The Bridegroom's Messenger* to testify of his experiences:

> We find people all around in these little missions full of darkness, Churches [sic] full of darkness, and when this wonderful and precious gospel is preached under the anointing of the Holy Ghost, darkness is dispelled and Christ is seen, for He is that great light.[4]

Second, the January 1936 edition of *Latter Rain Evangel* published the following note about Marie Burgess, the associate pastor of Glad Tidings Tabernacle in New York City and a founder of the turn-of-the-century prayer movement in Zion, Illinois: "Her heart caught the fire, and opening her whole being to the truth she received the Baptism of the Holy Spirit and also a definite call to Gospel work. There came with this Baptism a mighty anointing for service and a vision of a lost world."[5]

Third, in a summer edition of the 1968 *Pentecostal Evangel*, Walter Beuttler submitted a relatively lengthy article on spiritual gifts in which he observed,

> The ability to "prove all things" necessitates spiritual discernment. This comes from the anointing of the Spirit, "The anointing which ye have received . . . teacheth you of all things" (1 John 2:27). What damage has been done by spiritually incompetent leadership! Spiritual things are spiritually discerned. The heavier the leader's anointing, the keener is his discernment, and the greater his certainty.[6]

Fourth, in 2002 Oral Roberts shared some of his "ministry secrets" with *Charisma* magazine's "Ministry Today" website. One of those secrets he named as "the explosiveness of the anointing," a secret he said he learned from his mother.

> She was a woman of few words, but the anointing she had through her closeness to Jesus caused her words to penetrate one's soul quickly. In my ministry I have tried to make every word count. I have tried not to preach until I knew I had the anointing. When I have succeeded in doing this, God has done great things.[7]

Fifth, and finally, Ray H. Hughes Sr., one-time head of the National Association of Evangelicals (NAE) and three-time presiding bishop of the Church of God (Cleveland, TN), insisted on the closest relationship between Jesus and the Spirit, and so between the minister and the anointing. Citing Acts 10:38, he concludes, "When Christ was anointed with power, He went about doing good. The anointing motivated, actuated, and propelled Him to do good. Likewise, when the anointing comes upon us, we will be constrained to go."[8]

---

[4]*The Bridegroom's Messenger* 1.5 (January 1, 1908), 2. Although it is not evident in this citation, Seymour frequently distinguished between "the anointing that abides," which he took to be a second work of grace, and "the baptism of the Holy Ghost," which he took as a third work of grace. In this, Seymour was following his teacher, Charles Fox Parham; see Daniel Castelo, *Pentecostalism as a Christian Mystical Tradition* (Grand Rapids, MI: Eerdmans, 2017), 143.
[5]*The Latter Rain Evangel* 27.4 (January 1936), 12.
[6]*The Pentecostal Evangel* 28.17 (May 1968), 3.
[7]Available online: http://ministrytodaymag.com/index.php/features/6289-secrets-i-have-learned; accessed July 2, 2017.
[8]*Classic Pentecostal Sermon Library, Vol. 6: Ray H. Hughes, Sr.* (Cleveland, TN: Pathway, 2011), 131.

FINDING THE ROOTS OF THE METAPHOR

No doubt, the Pentecostal use of the metaphor has precedent in Wesleyan Holiness revivalist usage. And the practice of anointing with oil for healing and ordination has shaped the use of the metaphor extensively as well.[9] But the deepest roots of this metaphor are biblical—specifically as drawn from passages in the King James Version.

Pentecostals engage more or less all the texts that refer to anointing, including stories of prophets anointing kings and priests (e.g., Moses anointing Aaron and his sons or Samuel anointing David), the Levitical directions for the anointing rites, the mandate for imposition of hands for healing (Jas 5:14), and poetic allusions to anointing (especially Psalm 133). 1 John 2:27 ("the anointing you have received of him abideth in you"), Isa. 10:27 ("the yoke shall be destroyed because of the anointing"), and Acts 10:38 deserve special attention because of their prominence in Pentecostal speech and imagination. The latter in particular is arguably the *locus classicus* of the anointing metaphor for the Pentecostal movement as a whole.

In this last passage, which records Peter's address to Cornelius's household, the apostle declares that "God anointed Jesus of Nazareth with the Holy Ghost and with power: who went about doing good, and healing all that were oppressed of the devil; for God was with him." Holy Spirit, power, anointing, the presence of God, healing, and deliverance—these realities, as Pentecostals understand them, are so tightly interrelated that each term implies all the others. Where the Spirit is, healing and deliverance are sure to happen. Where healing and deliverance are happening, it is only because the anointing, the presence and power of God, is at work.

HONORING THE PROMISE OF THE METAPHOR

Pentecostals use the metaphor of "anointing and power" in a variety of ways. The characteristic use is deeply trinitarian, even if Pentecostals by and large have not noticed that it is or articulated how and why it matters. By following Scripture in referring to the Spirit as "the anointing" and Jesus as "the anointed one," Pentecostals are affirming the tightest possible interrelationship between Christ and the Spirit. In effect, the intelligible use of the anointing metaphor requires us to acknowledge that Christ cannot be known apart from who the Spirit is, and that the Spirit cannot be known apart from what Christ does. In other words, Christology must be thoroughly pneumatological, and pneumatology must be thoroughly christological.

This account of the Spirit's relation to Christ is closely related to Gregory of Nyssa's understanding as he lays it out in the concluding paragraph of his *On the Holy Trinity*:

> the Divine Scripture says that the Holy Spirit is the unction of the Only-Begotten, interpreting the dignity of the Spirit by a transference of the terms commonly used in this world. For as, in ancient days, in those who were advanced to kingship, the token of this dignity was the unction which was applied to them, and when this took place there was thenceforth a change from private and humble estate to the superiority of rule, and he who was deemed worthy of this grace received after his anointing another

---

[9]In the churches of my youth, one of our evangelists would *drink* the olive oil used for the altar service as a sign of his passion for the anointing to fall on him.

name, being called, instead of an ordinary man, the Anointed of the Lord: for this reason, that the dignity of the Holy Spirit might be more clearly shown to men, He was called by the Scripture the sign of the Kingdom, and Unction, whereby we are taught that the Holy Spirit shares in the glory and kingdom of the Only-begotten Son of God.[10]

The logic is relatively straightforward: we know Christ as king and the nature of his kingdom because we recognize the Spirit as the sign. If Christ is the king, it is the kingly Spirit who makes him so. It is this same logic that Pentecostals imply—if never explicitly acknowledge—in their account of Christ as the Spirit-anointed one.

Second, there is also embedded in the Pentecostal use of the anointing metaphor a robust doctrine of participation. The Spirit and Christ are so closely related, so intimate, and so at-one that for a believer to be intimate with one is the same as being intimate with the other. To be close to Jesus is necessarily to be close to the Spirit; to be close to the Spirit is necessarily to be close to Jesus. To be allied with the Anointed One is to be baptized in his anointing; to be "anointed" is to be baptized into Christ.

This way of thinking also resonates strongly with the pneumatology of St. Irenaeus—among other church fathers—who describes Christ's anointing as the medium or effector of salvation: "the Spirit of God descended on him . . . that we, receiving from the abundance of his anointing, might be saved."[11] Jesus, in such an account, is not only the exemplar of the Spirit-filled life, but also the mediator. Believers are not only living Jesus's Spirit-filled life after him, but are also living it in and with him. All of that is made possible by the Spirit who acted upon Christ so that he could act upon us as well.

Third, the Pentecostal use of the metaphor emphasizes the identity of the Spirit's person and work: "the anointing" (that is, the person of the Spirit) effects "an anointing" (that is, the work of the Spirit) for Christ and the various members of his body. In this way, the metaphor strongly affirms the divinity of the Spirit because only of God, who is "simple," can we say that person and work are strictly identical.[12] Similarly, the metaphor indicates "the anointing" does what only God can do, which, again, is an argument for the Spirit's divinity, an argument that is remarkably close to the key argument St. Basil makes in *On the Holy Spirit*.

Fourth, the Pentecostal use of the metaphor focuses attention on the event of gospel-proclamation and in particular the events of intercessory prayer and preaching as they take place in the life of the congregation. It indicates that there is a "something more," an excess of possibility, that is present when believers are gathered together for worship or scattered for witness that is not there when believers are alone.

Fifth, the Pentecostal use of the metaphor also forces our attention onto the Spirit's power to change lives and circumstances. The Spirit's influence is understood to be not

---

[10]Gregory of Nyssa, *On the Holy Trinity*, available at http://www.newadvent.org/ fathers/2904.htm, accessed March 20, 2019.

[11]*Against Heresies* 3.9.3. See also Anthony Briggman, "The Holy Spirit as the Unction of Christ in Irenaeus," *Journal of Theological Studies* 61, no. 1 (2010): 188.

[12]See Stephen R. Holmes, "Something Much Too Plain To Say: Towards a Defense of the Doctrine of Divine Simplicity," *Neue Zeitschrift für Systematische Theologie und Religionsphilosophie* 43, no. 1 (2001): 137–54; see also Stephen R. Holmes, "The Attributes of God," in *The Oxford Handbook of Systematic Theology*, ed. John Webster, Kathryn Tanner, and Iain Torrance (Oxford: Oxford University Press, 2007), 54–71.

merely intellectual or affective but immediately and personally transformative. The Spirit speaks and acts; the Spirit reveals and awakens; and the Spirit heals and delivers. And this, again, resonates with the broader tradition, both historically and ecumenically.

Many examples could be given, but perhaps it is enough simply to cite Irenaeus again: "we also hear of many in the church who possess prophetic gifts, and who through the Spirit speak all kinds of languages and bring to light for the good of all the hidden things of creatures and declare the mysteries of God. . . . They are spiritual because they partake of the Spirit."[13]

Sixth, the metaphor, at least as Pentecostals typically use it, underscores the radically democratic nature of the body's ministry. Adults as well as children, men as well as women, the spiritually immature as well as the mature, the "lost" and "lukewarm" as well as the saved and "on fire"—anyone in the congregation might be anointed for this or that event at any time.

INSTEAD OF A CONCLUSION: RE-VISIONING THE METAPHOR

In all these and perhaps other ways as well, the Pentecostal use of the anointing metaphor holds promise for pneumatology specifically and for Christian doctrine and practice generally. But there are also problems inherent in the use of the metaphor that need to be addressed.

First and foundationally, while it is true that Pentecostalism as a mystical tradition has made room for the supra-rational in part through the non-reflective nature of Pentecostal praxis,[14] it is nonetheless appropriate and even necessary for theologians within and without the movement to think carefully about the anointing metaphor and its uses. To this point in the tradition's history, Pentecostals are by and large unaware of the rich promise of the metaphor, which means that they use it naively and sentimentally rather than knowingly and wisely. Tragically, most of the theology embedded in Pentecostal spirituality remains unconsidered and so unarticulated, and this state is malignant, threatening to disease the entire tradition.

Second, too many Pentecostals think of the anointing in functionalist and individualistic terms, as if the Spirit's power is something that "comes and goes," something that individuals come "under" for a time before it "lifts." But for Christ, there is no "lifting" of the anointing. The Spirit abides in Christ. The Spirit rests on Christ.[15] And Christ does not move in and out of his calling. He never shirks his "active solidarity with the state and fate" of creatures.[16] As a result, our participation with Christ in the Spirit is not occasional or sporadic but is widely and deeply continuous and continuing. Anyone who is in Christ, anyone who is in communion with the Father, anyone in whom the Spirit dwells, is necessarily "anointed"—whether that reality is experienced at any given time in any particular way or not.

---

[13]*Against Heresies* 5.6.1.
[14]See Castelo, *Pentecostalism as a Christian Mystical Tradition*, 122.
[15]See Eugene F. Rogers, Jr., *After the Spirit: A Constructive Pneumatology from Resources Outside the Modern West* (Grand Rapids, MI: Eerdmans, 2005).
[16]Karl Barth, CD III/2, 210.

The Spirit's power is not sporadic, even if our experiences seem random or occasional. Does this mean that the Spirit does not give special graces for particular moments? No, of course not. But it does mean that we should not see those graces as somehow more the work of the Spirit than other, hidden graces that fill our lives because of the presence of the Spirit. The anointing is ever-present, manifesting the gifts that are needed as they become necessary.

Third, Pentecostals are often at risk of thinking much too narrowly about experience. And they are at risk of trusting too completely in the individual's and/or the congregation's ability to discern what is and is not a work of God. These temptations come at least in part from assuming that the marks of effectiveness are obvious and that they appear immediately. It also comes from thinking that a minister's energetic conviction or intense affect are sure signs of the Spirit's presence and so are proofs of that minister's good character. In truth, however, any number of dramatic phenomena may be mistaken as signs of the Spirit's power. Besides, the infinite Spirit is inexhaustibly creative: no work of the Spirit is the same as any other work done before or after that moment. Discerning the Spirit, therefore, is not about intuitively recognizing this or that phenomenon; instead, discerning the Spirit is about ascertaining the fruit of the Spirit's presence in the character of the community's shared life. Where the Spirit has been at work, love, joy, peace, patience, kindness, meekness, temperance, and self-control are in blossom. Any spirituality that does not issue in those marks of character cannot be the Spirit's doing.

Fourth, Pentecostals often think of the anointing's power as an overwhelming force, a violent energy that overcomes all obstacles. But divine power has no opposition as God has no opposites. God's power is the power to create, which by definition does not and cannot violate creatures because it is the very source of that creatureliness itself. God cannot do violence any more than God can lie. God fulfills. Only demons possess. The "anointing," therefore, cannot violate the personhood of the believer or overwhelm their personality. And that means that a minister who claims to become a different person "under the anointing" is losing touch with the integrative sanctification God means to work in the lives of all people.[17] Instead, the surest sign of the Spirit's work is the deep, lasting integration and wholeness of persons-in-community.

Fifth and finally, just as power should not be thought in conflictual terms, the anointing must not be understood as a thing—not as a force and not even as a person (at least in the everyday sense of the word). "The anointing" is simply God the Spirit being personally present and active as only God can—not as an object of desire but as the source, guide, and goal of desire that makes everything that is what it is. Once this is understood, it becomes obvious that we do not have a relation to the Spirit that is other than our relationship to Christ, for our very relatedness to Christ is determined by the Spirit. Loving Christ, we are caught up in the Spirit of his Father, absorbed in God's own adoration and delight in God. The anointed life, therefore, is a Trinity-saturated life—a life baptized in the love that God gives to God and so pours out on all creation.

---

[17] Chillingly, I once heard a Pentecostal preacher say, "I like who I am under the anointing."

FOR FURTHER READING

Gabriel, Andrew K. *The Lord Is the Spirit*. Eugene, OR: Pickwick, 2014.

Kärkkäinen, Veli-Matti. *Spirit and Salvation: A Constructive Christian Theology for the Pluralistic World, Vol. 4*. Grand Rapids, MI: Eerdmans, 2016.

Wenk, Matthias. *Community-Forming Power*. London: Bloomsbury, 2004.

Yong, Amos. *Mission after Pentecost*. Grand Rapids, MI: Baker Academic, 2019.

Yong, Amos. *Spirit of Love*. Waco, TX: Baylor University Press, 2012.

CONTRIBUTORS

Margaret B. Adam, PhD, is Visiting Tutor at St. Stephen's House, University of Oxford.

Peter Althouse, PhD, is Adjunct Professor of Philosophy, Florida Southern College.

Daniela C. Augustine, DTh, is Reader in World Christianity and Pentecostal Studies, University of Birmingham (UK).

Cherice Bock, PhD cand., is Adjunct Professor of Ecotheology at Portland Seminary, George Fox University.

Daniel Castelo, PhD, is Professor of Dogmatic and Constructive Theology, Seattle Pacific University and Seminary.

Marc Cortez, PhD, is Professor of Theology, Wheaton College.

Daniel K. Darko, PhD, is Professor of New Testament, Gordon College.

Andrew K. Gabriel, PhD, is Vice President of Academics and Associate Professor of Theology, Horizon College and Seminary.

Oscar García-Johnson, PhD, is Assistant Provost for the Center for the Study of Hispanic Church and Community and Associate Professor of Theology and Latino/a Studies, Fuller Theological Seminary.

Chris E. W. Green, DMin, PhD, is Professor of Theology, Southeastern University.

Nijay K. Gupta, PhD, is Associate Professor of New Testament, Portland Seminary, George Fox University.

David Sang-Ehil Han, PhD, is Dean, Vice President for Academics, and Professor of Theology and Pentecostal Spirituality, Pentecostal Theological Seminary.

Laura C. S. Holmes, PhD, is Associate Professor of New Testament, Seattle Pacific University and Seminary.

Douglas M. Koskela, PhD, is Professor of Theology, Seattle Pacific University and Seminary.

Jackson Lashier, PhD, is Associate Professor of Religion, Southwestern College.

Daniel D. Lee, PhD, is Assistant Provost for the Center for Asian American Theology and Ministry and Assistant Professor of Theology and Asian American Ministry, Fuller Theological Seminary.

J. J. Johnson Leese, PhD, is Assistant Professor of Christian Scripture, Seattle Pacific University and Seminary.

Matthew Levering, PhD, is James N. and Mary D. Perry, Jr. Chair of Theology, Mundelein Seminary, University of Saint Mary of the Lake.

John R. (Jack) Levison, PhD, is the W. J. A. Power Professor of Old Testament Interpretation and Biblical Hebrew, Perkins School of Theology, Southern Methodist University.

D. Stephen Long, PhD, is the Cary M. Maguire University Professor of Ethics, Southern Methodist University.

Kenneth M. Loyer, PhD, a United Methodist pastor, has taught theology and Methodist studies at four schools.

Lee Roy Martin, DTh, is Professor of Old Testament and Biblical Languages, Pentecostal Theological Seminary.

David R. Nienhuis, PhD, is Professor of New Testament Studies, Seattle Pacific University and Seminary.

Cheryl M. Peterson, PhD, is Trinity Endowed Chair in Mission and Ministry, Professor of Systematic Theology and Associate Dean for Academics, Trinity Lutheran Seminary at Capital University.

Marcus Plested, DPhil, is Henri de Lubac Chair and Professor of Greek Patristic and Byzantine Theology, Marquette University.

Mark E. Powell, PhD, is Professor of Theology, Harding School of Theology.

Ephraim Radner, PhD, is Professor of Historical Theology, Wycliffe College, University of Toronto.

J. Alexander Sider, PhD, is Professor of Religion, Bluffton University.

Shannon Nicole Smythe, PhD, is a minister of Word and Sacrament in the Presbyterian Church (USA).

Lisa P. Stephenson, PhD, is Professor of Systematic Theology, Lee University.

Jason E. Vickers, PhD, is Professor of Theology, Asbury Theological Seminary.

Wolfgang Vondey, PhD, is Professor of Christian Theology and Pentecostal Studies and Director of the Centre for Pentecostal and Charismatic Studies, University of Birmingham.

Robert W. Wall, ThD, is the Paul T. Walls Professor of Scripture and Wesleyan Studies, Seattle Pacific University and Seminary.

Frederick L. Ware, PhD, is Associate Dean for Academic Affairs and Associate Professor of Theology, Howard University School of Divinity.

Thomas G. Weinandy, O.F.M., Cap., is a former member of the Vatican's International Theological Commission, Capuchin College, Washington, DC.

AUTHOR INDEX

Aalders, G. Ch. 146
Abraham, W. J. 337–8, 340, 342, 348
Agyarko, R. O. 272
Ahn, S. 285
Albertz, R. 75, 87
Alexander, D. L. 201
Alexander of Alexandria 157
Alfaro, S. 325
Ambrose of Milan 173, 181–2
Anatolios, K. 339
Anderson, A. 269, 271, 277–8
Anderson, D. 168, 340
Anderson, V. 292
Andrewes, L. 217–18
Aphrahat the Persian 191–2
Aquinas, Thomas 66, 105, 134, 166, 175, 180, 183–4, 194–5
Arand, C. 198
Archer, Jr., G. L. 85
Archer, K. J. 324
Arendt, H. 131
Aristotle 17
Arius 156–7, 163, 166
Arrington, F. A. 76
Artson, B. S. 112
Asamoah-Gyadu, J. K. 275, 277
Asbury, F. 231
Asterius 157
Athanasius 128, 152, 156–61, 167–72, 180, 269, 357
Atsuji, F. 287
Augustine 47, 58, 136–7, 144–6, 148–9, 166, 172–5, 182–3, 269, 295, 340–1
Ayres, L. 155–7, 160, 163–4, 174, 339

von Balthasar, H. U. 187
Banning, A. 231
Bañuelas, A. J. 322
Barbeau, J. W. 123, 208
Barbour, I. 112, 114
Barclay, R. 236–9
Barnes, M. R. 152–3, 170

Barr, J. 146–7
Barrett, C. K. 7, 9–10, 13
Barth, K. 2, 86, 115, 200, 208, 210–14, 251, 253, 256, 282–4, 293, 341, 365
Bartholomew I 121, 126–7, 131
Basil of Caesarea 63, 135, 137, 152, 159–63, 167–71, 182–3, 364
Bastian, J. 302
Bates, J. B. 225
Bauckham, R. 50–1
Baumgartner, W. 75
Baxter, R. 219
Beck, T. D. 19
Bediako, K. 272, 274
Beeley, C. A. 71–2, 160, 171
Behr, J. 153–4, 169
Beker, J. C. 21, 23
Benedict XVI (Joseph Ratzinger) 71, 144
Bennema, C. 10
Bennett, D. 265
Benson, A. 79
Bergin, H. 327
Berkhof, H. 207
Berthold, G. C. 172
Berthold, H. 190
Bettenson, H. 144, 173
Beuttler, W. 362
Beyer, H. W. 338
Bitrus, I. 204
Black, C. C. 13
Blenkinsopp, J. 84
Bloomquist, K. L. 200, 204
Blumhardt, C. 253
Blumhardt, J. 253
Bobrinskoy, B. 165
Boff, L. 305, 329
Boulnois, M. 172
Bouman, H. 203
Bouyer, L. 187, 261
Boyd, C. 67
Brand, C. O. 263
Brantley, R. E. 221

Brinton, H. H.   235
Briggman, A.   152, 364
Brown, D.   227
Brown, R. E.   43, 57
Bruce, F. F.   25
Brueggemann, W.   76, 79
Bruno, G.   220
Buber, M.   356
Bulgakov, S.   128–9, 193, 195
Bunyan, J.   218–19
Burgess, M.   362
Burgess, S. M.   262
Burke, T. J.   76
Butterworth, G. W.   154

Calvin, J.   85, 137–8, 207–9, 211–12, 343
Campbell, C. M.   349
Cannon, K. G.   213
Cantalamessa, R.   58
Carroll, J. T.   10
Carson, D. A.   122
Carter, J. K.   292
Castelo, D.   29, 146, 258, 362, 365
Chadwick, H.   341
Chan, S.   288
de Chardin, T.   223
Charette, B.   258
Chavchavadze, M.   201
Chemnitz, M.   202
Chiang, K.   283
Chilcote, P.   229
Chrestou, P.   195
Christenson, L.   264
Chung, H. K.   286, 330
Church, R. W.   218
Clark, J. E.   312
Clarkson, J. S.   328
Clayton, P.   118
Clayton, R.   220–1
Cleage, A. B.   311–18
Clement of Alexandria   41, 269
Clendenin, D. B.   121, 125, 129–30
Clines, D. J. A.   146
Coakley, S.   329
Codina, V.   306–8
Cohen, I. B.   114
Coke, T.   231
Coleridge, S. T.   221–2
Collins, K. J.   227, 233
Collins, R.   94
Colman, H. L. K.   297
Conde-Frazier, E.   303, 308–9, 319–20, 323

Cone, J. H.   292, 311–14, 316–18
Congar, Y.   2, 69, 165, 173, 181, 185, 267, 329, 347
Congdon, D. W.   212–13
Conway, A.   220
Cooper, L. E.   84
Corbon, J.   187
Corse, T.   220
Coudert, A. P.   220
Cox, H.   251
Cranmer, T.   216
Crisp, O.   207, 213
Crossan, J. D.   122
Cruz, S.   308–9
Cudworth, R.   219
Curtis, E. M.   146
Cyprian of Carthage   340
Cyril of Alexandria   167, 171–2, 269
Cyril of Jerusalem   156–8

Dabney, L.   146, 258, 305–7
Daley, B.   170
Daneel, M. L.   270, 277
Daugherty, R. A.   229
Davidson, R.   146
Davies, B.   72
Davies, D. J.   224
Davies, O.   357
Davis, J. J.   117
Davis, S. T.   68, 70
Dayton, D. W.   227
D'Costa, G.   296
De Anda, N.   324
Deasley, A. R. G.   7
Deere, J.   266
Deferrari, R. J.   182
De La Torre, M. A.   294
DelCogliano, M.   157, 159
Denzinger, H.   166, 171, 177
Desprez, V.   190
Diadochus of Photice   193
Dick, M. B.   148
Didymus the Blind   152, 159–62, 182
Dionysius of Alexandria   163
Dixie, Q. H.   311
Dobbs, B. J. T.   114–15
Donovan, A.   115
Dörken-Kurcharz, T.   306–7
Dorrien, G.   222
Dörries, H.   190
Doutreleau, L.   152
Doyle, M. T.   186

Driver, J. 302
Dubose, W. P. 222
Dunn, J. D. G. 7, 18–19, 22–3
Dussel, E. 302

Ebeling, G. 212
Eck, J. 245–6
Edwards, D. 115, 119, 140
Edwards, J. 208–9, 211, 213, 262
Einstein, A. 115, 117
Ellington, S. 75, 87
Elowsky, J. C. 172
Emery, G. 175, 183
Ephrem the Syrian 190
Erb, P. C. 199
Espín, O. 323–4
Espiritu, Y. L. 293
Eusebius 26, 46
Eusebius of Nicomedia 156
Evans, E. 154
Evdokimov, P. 195
Even-Shoshan, A. 75

Faraday, M. 116
Faur, J. 148
Fedotov, G. 189
Fee, G. D. 19–23, 80
Felix-Jaeger, S. 258
Fingarette, H. 284
Firth, D. G. 76, 78
Flory, R. 262
Foley, E. 130
Forde, G. 201
Fox, G. 235–6, 240
France, R. T. 12
Franke, A. H. 199
Fredericks, G. 80
Freedman, D. N. 75
Freiday, D. 237
Freud, S. 298
Froelich, K. 203
Frosh, S. 298
Furlong, M. 329

Gaddis, M. P. 230
Gamble, H. Y. 339
Garrigou-Lagrange, R. 186
Gavrilyuk, P. L. 342
Gebhardt, E. 190
Geivett, R. D. 68, 70
Gelpi, D. 255, 329
Gerber, C. T. 144

Gerloff, R. 237
Gerton, J. 297
Gesling, L. 229
Gibson, C. 321
Goertz, H. 245, 248
Goizueta, R. S. 325
Goldberg, L. 85
Goldingay, J. 76–9, 85
Golitzin, A. 194
González, J. L. 292, 302, 320–1
González, O. 302
Goodhew, D. 215, 225
Goodwin, R. 321
Gore, A. 223
Green, C. E. W. 127, 231
Green, J. B. 8, 10–11, 14
Green, M. 76
Greenspahn, F. E. 78
Greenspoon, L. J. 84–5
Gregory of Cyprus 194
Gregory of Nazianzus (the Theologian, Nazianzen) 152, 160–3, 167, 170–1, 175, 183, 190
Gregory of Nyssa (Nyssen) 152, 160–4, 167, 169–71, 190, 363–4
Gregory Palamas 193–5
Grey, M. 327, 331
Grossman, S. 265–6
Gunton, C. 59, 143, 332–3

Habets, M. 111, 146, 178, 223, 324, 333
Hall, P. 218
Hamilton, M. P. 265
Hamilton, V. P. 146
Hamlin, E. J. 80
Hanson, P. D. 84–5
Hanson, R. P. C. 151
Harman, R. J. 229
Harrington, D. J. 122
Harris, R. L. 85
Harrison, G. 187
Hart, L. 263
Hassett, M. K. 224
Haught, J. F. 112, 114
Hay, C. A. 199
Heath, E. A. 357
Hector, K. W. 210, 212
Helm, P. 209
Helmer, C. 202–4
Hendel, K. 141
Henry, J. D. 203
Herman, J. 298

Herring, S. L. 147–8
Hervey, J. 221
Heynen, W. 146
Hilary of Poitiers 173
Hildebrand, S. 161
Hildebrandt, W. 75–8
Hildegard of Bingen 135, 141
Hill, C. E. 41
Hill, E. 137, 174, 182
Hill, W. 23
Hill, W. J. 175
Hinlicky, P. 197, 202
Hippolytus 155
Hocken, P. 263–4
Hodgson, P. 312–13
Hoffmeyer, J. F. 351
Hollingsworth, A. 331
Holmes, S. R. 364
Holtze, H. 200
Hooker, M. D. 9
Hooker, R. 217–18
Hopkins, D. 312
Horn, F. W. 75, 81, 86
Horton, M. S. 147
Horton, S. M. 76, 78
Hossfeld, F. L. 81
Hotchkiss, V. 177
Hovorum, C. 114
Hubmaier, B. 243–50
Hughes, R. H. 362
Hünermann, P. 166, 171, 177
Hurh, W. M. 298
Hutchingson, J. E. 112
Hyun, Y. 285

Ignatius 340
Irenaeus 15, 41, 135–6, 138–40, 151–6, 158, 161, 164–5, 192, 337, 357, 364–5
Isasi-Díaz, A. M. 307
Ishizuka, K. L. 293

Jacobs, H. E. 199
Jacobsen, D. 29
Jakim, B. 193
Jammer, M. 116
Jarvis, C. A. 208
Jenni, E. 75
Jensen, J. M. 197
Jenson, R. W. 127, 200, 203
Jerome 173
Jervell, J. 29, 52

Ji, W. Y. 204
Jiménez, M. 302
John Chrysostom 25
John of Damascus 193, 340–1
John Paul II 178, 187
Johnson, C. V. 130
Johnson, E. A. 141, 296, 329–30, 333–5
Johnson, L. T. 56, 62
Johnson, T. 245
Johnson, T. M. 262
Jones, B. F. 123, 208
Jones, J. 184
Jones, S. 213
Jones, W. R. 317
Jung, C. 285
Jungkuntz, T. R. 203
Jungmann, J. A. 185

Kahnis, K. F. A. 199–200
Kaku, M. 117
Kalu, O. U. 275, 277
Kant, I. 221–2
Kärkkäinen, V. 251, 257, 285, 364
Karlstadt, A. 198, 203
Käsemann, E. 258
Keating, D. A. 172
Keble, J. 218, 222
Keener, C. 30, 265
Keesecker, W. F. 207
Keller, C. 305–6
Kelly, J. N. D. 151, 166, 176
Kim, G. J. 286–7, 291, 293, 296–8, 300
Kim, H. Y. 282–4
Kim, K. 281, 288–9
Kim, K. C. 298
Kinghorn, K. 70
Kinnamon, M. 330
Klostermann, E. 190
Knierim, R. 135
Knight, H. H. 227
Kombo, J. H. O. 272
Kohl, M. 258, 303
Köhler, L. 75
Kolb, R. 198
van der Kolk, B. 299
Koskela, D. M. 342
Krieg, C. 306–7
Kroeger, M. 190
Kunhiyop, S. W. 276
Kutsko, J. F. 147
Kydd, R. A. N. 261

AUTHOR INDEX

LaCugna, C. M. 327
LaFromboise, T. 297
Lamont, A. 341
Lampe, G. W. H. 223
Land, S. J. 29, 251–2
Langford, W. 218
von Lechler, K. 199–200
Leclercq, J. 75
Lederle, H. I. 263
Lee, H. 296
Lee, J. H. 285
Lee, J. Y. 287, 289, 293, 295
Lee, M. 257
Lee, S. H. 209, 295
Lenker, J. N. 198
Levering, M. 175
Levinas, E. 295
Levison, J. R. 14, 17, 46, 51
Lienhard, J. T. 157
Lim, P. 220
Lindberg, C. 200, 227
Lints, R. 147
von Loewenich, W. 203
Long, C. H. 311
Lossky, N. 218
Lossky, V. 122, 128, 195
Louth, A. 114, 157, 218, 356
Lowe, L. 292
de Lubac, H. 247
Luther, M. 141, 197–9, 201–5, 244, 341
Lyons, G. 7, 9–10

Macarius 190–4, 196
McCabe, H. 72
Macchia, F. D. 48, 51, 146, 252–4
MacDonald, P. S. 112
McDonnell, K. 266–7
McDowell, C. L. 147–8
McFague, S. 141–2, 327–8, 330–1
McGee, G. B. 262–3
McGinn, B. 354
Macierowski, E. M. 247
McIntosh, M. 354–5
Mackey, H. B. 187
McMullin, E. 114
Madden, D. 221
Maddox, R. L. 227, 229, 233
Malcolm, L. 197
Maldonado Pérez, Z. 303, 319–20, 323
Maloney, G. 195
Mann, J. K. 201
Manning, R. R. 137

Manzone, A. 172
Marcellus of Ancyra 157, 163
Marcus, J. 9–10, 13
Maré, L. P. 81
Mark the Monk 193
Marriage, A. 329
Marriott, G. L. 190
Martell-Otero, L. I. 303, 308–9, 319–20, 322–3
Martin, D. B. 299
Martin, L. R. 96
Martínez, J. M. 302–3
Matsuoka, F. 282
Maximos Margounios 195
Maximus the Confessor 122, 176, 193–4
Maxwell, D. R. 172
Maxwell, J. C. 116
Medina, N. 323–6
Melanchthon, P. 198–9
Mendieta, E. 307
Mers, J. 272
Metzger, B. M. 339
Meyendorff, J. 121, 130
Middleton, J. R. 147
Migliore, D. L. 208
Mignolo, W. 307
Miley, J. 230
Miller, D. E. 262
Miller, J. M. 187
Min, A. K. 291, 293–8, 300
Mittlestadt, M. 258
Moessner, D. P. 26
Moloney, F. J. 122
Moltmann, J. 12, 86, 115, 119, 123, 133, 140, 208, 256–8, 283, 288–9, 303, 305–7, 329, 332–3
Montague, G. T. 76
Moody, D. 76–7
More, H. 219, 221
Morimoto, A. 282
Moser, P. K. 68, 70
Motyer, J. A. 85
Moyd, O. P. 317
Murphy, F. A. 183
Murphy, N. 117

Nadal, K. L. 297
Nadeau, R. L. 294
Nanko-Fernández, C. M. 324
Ndiokwere, N. I. 278
Neill, S. 215
Nelson, D. K. 312

Nelson, D. R. 197
Neve, L. 76-7
Neville, G. 222
Neville, R. 255
Newell, F. 231-2
Newton, I. 114-17, 219
Nicholson, E. W. 76
Nickalls, J. L. 235
Nienhuis, D. 49
Nösgen, K. F. 199-200
Novatian 154
Nowell, R. 217
Nuttall, G. F. 218

Oberman, H. 198
Ocampo, A. C. 292
O'Connell, M. J. 187
O'Connor, E. D. 261
O'Donovan, W. 274, 276
Okihiro, G. 295
Oladipo, C. O. 273
Oliverio, L. W. 324
Olson, R. 230
O'Malley, J. S. 229
O'Murchu, D. 112
Opsahl, P. D. 203
Origen 154-5, 159, 163, 166, 168, 269
Orobator, A. E. 273
Ostdiek, G. 130
Ouspensky, L. 125
Owen, J. 138, 219

Paget, F. 218
Painter, N. I. 322
Palin, J. 128
Palmer, T. 274
Pannenberg, W. 115-17, 200
Paracelsus 220
Pardue, S. T. 257
Parham, C. F. 362
Park, A. S. 285
Park, J. C. 289
Parsons, S. F. 327
Passmore, J. A. 219
Pauw, A. P. 213
Peacocke, A. 117
Pedlar, J. 267
Peirce, C. S. 255
Pelikan, J. 1, 177
Penington, I. 241
Penn, W. 236
Perkins, L. 75

Peterson, E. H. 349
Phan, P. C. 293, 295
Photius of Constantinople 176-7, 194
Pickard, S. 146, 258
Pieris, A. 282-3
Pinches, C. 67
Pinnock, C. H. 139-40, 324
Pipkin, W. 246-8
Plato 191
Plutarch 17
Polanyi, M. 356
Polkinghorne, J. 116-17, 119, 139
Power, D. N. 223
Poythress, V. S. 118
Preece, G. 146, 258
Prenter, R. 197, 201
Prichard, R. B. 331
Prien, H. 302
Pringle-Pattison, A. S. 222
Pseudo-Dionysius 184

Quash, B. 60

Radde-Gallwitz, A. 157
Rahner, K. 115, 200
Rakoczy, S. 331
Rambo, S. 299
Raven, C. 223
Rea, J. 76, 78
de Régnon, T. 173
Reid, J. K. S. 343
Reinhard, K. L. 144
Rempel, J. 243, 249
Ritschl, A. 200
Roberts, O. 362
Rodríguez, J. D. 322
Rogers, E. F. 365
Rolt, C. E. 184
Rousseau, A. 152
Rublev, A. 341
Ruether, R. R. 327
Russell, L. M. 328
Russell, R. J. 117
Ruth, L. 231-2

de Sales, F. 187
Samantha, S. J. 281
Sambursky, S. 115
Sánchez, L. A. 201-2
Sanders, C. R. 222
Sansom, H. 224
Santmire, P. 136

AUTHOR INDEX

Sargeant, K. H. 262
Saunders, N. 116
Saunders, T. 224
Scheeben, M. J. 185–6
Schleiermacher, F. 199, 208, 210–13
Schlink, E. 203
Schloss, J. 118
Schmauk, T. 197, 200
Schmemann, A. 123, 125–8
Schmid, H. 199
Schreiner, T. R. 27
Schüle, A. 148
Segovia, F. F. 322
Seiichi, O. 287
Seneca 17
Seraphim of Sarov 121, 189, 195–6
Seymour, W. 362
Shapland, G. R. B. 167
Shelton, R. L. 7
Shults, F. L. 119
Siecienski, A. E. 165, 176
Simpson, Z. 118
Sirks, G. J. 266, 322
Sledge, R. 229
Slee, N. 327–9
Slocum, R. B. 222
Small, J. D. 349
Smith, D. 69, 185, 267, 347
Smith, G. 85–6
Smith, J. K. A. 29, 119–20, 124, 130–1
Snyder, C. A. 243–4, 246
Solivan, S. 322
Song, C. S. 286–6
Soskice, J. 60
Southgate, C. 139
Spener, P. 199
Spivak, G. C. 292
Springer, K. 266
Staats, R. 190
Staniloae, D. 122–4, 195
Steinmetz, D. 248
Stelan, R. 17
Stenmark, M. 112
Stephens, R. J. 227
Stephenson, L. 258
Stoeffler, F. E. 227
Stronstad, R. 84, 129
Strothmann, W. 190
Studdert Kennedy, G. A. 222–3
Sullivan, F. 263
Swete, H. B. 174
Symeon the New Theologian 185, 193–6

Talbot, M. R. 147
Taliaferro, C. 219
Tan, G. 283
Tanner, J. P. 80
Tanner, K. 229–30, 292, 364
Tanner, N. P. 182
Taylor, C. 355
Taylor, J. B. 84
Taylor, J. V. 323
Teply, A. J. 219
Tertullian 41, 46, 154–6, 166, 172–3
Theodoret 164
Theophilus of Antioch 151–2
Thiselton, A. C. 7, 70, 76
Thomas, J. C. 48, 51, 258
Thomas, W. H. G. 76
Thomasson-Rosingh, A. C. 328, 331–3
Tillich, P. 200
Timpe, K. 67
Tinker, G. E. 308
Tippens, D. 341
Torrance, I. 364
Torrance, T. F. 115, 207
Treiyer, E. 52
Tu, W. 283
Tucker, K. B. W. 233
Tuell, S. S. 84
Turner, M. 80
Turner, P. 224
Twelftree, G. H. 19
Tyndale, W. 216–17

Uhlein, G. 141

Van Kirk, N. B. 338, 342, 348
Vasilijevic, M. 130
Vickers, J. E. 338, 342–4, 348
Victorin-Vangerud, N. 332–3
Volf, M. 306–7
Vollert, C. J. 186
Vondey, W. 201

Waddell, R. 258
Wainwright, G. viii, 59, 223
Wall, R. W. 342
Wallace, M. I. 119
Walls, J. L. 70
Walter, G. 204
Walters, K. 223
Waltke, B. K. 85
Ward, F. 231
Ward, K. 224

Ward, M. 60
Ware, K. 196
Warfield, B. B. 264
Warrington, K. 76, 78
Watson, D. 224
Watson, N. K. 327
Webster, J. 251, 364
Wegner, P. D. 76, 78
Welker, M. 18, 77, 79, 90, 112, 114, 117–18, 196, 208, 230, 332–3, 351
Wengert, T. J. 198
Wesley, C. 190, 230–1
Wesley, J. 3, 105, 107–8, 190, 201, 221, 227, 229–30, 233–4, 262
West, C. 311
Westermann, C. 75, 87
Whapham, T. J. 115–16
White, J. L. 134
Whitman, A. 114
Wickham, L. 170
Wildberger, H. 85
Wild-Wood, E. 224

Williams, D. T. 75, 143, 146
Williams, F. 160, 170
Williams, J. R. 264–5
Williams, R. 156
Wimber, J. 266
Wolff, H. W. 79
Wright, C. J. H. 76
Wright, S. J. 127

Yoder, J. H. 245–8
Yong, A. 75, 112–13, 119–20, 252, 254–7, 291, 293–4, 296, 300
Young, F. 351–2
Yu, Y. 287
Yun, K. D. 296

Zemka, S. 222
Zenger, E. 81
Zernov, N. 128
Zimmerli, W. 84–5
Zizioulas, J. 200
Zwingli, H. 244–6, 248–9

SCRIPTURE INDEX

Gen.		29:21	98	40:9-10	276
1	14, 58, 136, 147	31:11	12	40:34-35	57
		31:13	12	40:35	8, 57
1–2	12, 146	37:5-11	97		
1–3	148	39:6	97	Lev.	
1:1	133	39:23	97	8:11	276
1:1-2	103	40:1-23	97	11:44-45	130
1:1-3	138	41:38	82, 96	12:4	98
1:2	3, 9, 17, 48, 86, 128, 139, 143, 147, 189, 322, 334, 342	41:39	82, 96	12:6	98
		42:25	98	20:8	80
		Exod.		Num.	
		2:23	78	6:5	98
		3	356	7:1	276
1:4	103	3:1-15	60	11:10-30	129
1:10	103, 139	3:8	77	11:17	80
1:12	103, 139	3:12	77	11:17-25	77
1:18	103, 139	8:15	75	11:25-29	9, 83
1:20	145	8:17	98	11:29	98
1:21	103, 139	10:13	77	12:13	84
1:24	145	10:19	77	24:1-3	90
1:25	103, 139	14:13	92	24:2-9	83
1:26-28	136, 334	14:21	77	24:2	98
1:31	103, 139	15:2	76	27:18	82
2	148	15:26	84		
2:4–3:24	139, 147	19:5	103	Deut.	
2:7	9, 45, 52, 86–7, 127–9, 133, 138–9, 144–7, 342	25:1–31:11	98	1:13-15	82
		25:8-9	57	4:1	95
		28:3	82, 98–9	4:5	95
		30:22-29	276	6	187
		31:2-6	99	6:13	59
		31:3	9, 82	6:16	59
		31:3-5	277	8:3	59
2:19	139	31:18	80	9:10	75, 80
3	103	34	22	11:19	95
3:1-12	103	34:6-7	79	13:1-5	39
3:13-24	103	34:29-35	22	16:18-19	82
6:3	87	35:4-33	98	20:2-4	92
7:22	86	35:30-35	82, 99	29:4	320
8:11	134	35:31	82, 99	34:9	82
12:1-3	103	35:34	99		
21:19	98	35:35	99	Josh.	
25:24	98	36:1-2	82	3:15	98
28:18	276	36:8	98		

Judg.

2:11-19	77
2:16	78
2:18	78
3:9	78
3:9-10	78
3:9-12	90
3:10	90, 98
3:11	82
3:15	78
3:30	82
3:31	78
4:5	82
5:31	82
6	182
6:34	9, 78, 90, 91, 98, 134
8:28	82
11:29	9, 78, 90
12:3	78
12:7	82
13:5	78
13:25	78
14:6	9, 17, 78, 89, 90, 98
14:16	89
14:19	78, 90
15:13	89
15:14	78, 90
16:31	82

Ruth

3:3	276

1 Sam.

10:1	276
10:1-13	89
10:6	9, 98
10:10	13
11:6-7	90
16:1	98
16:13	9, 81, 98
16:14	81
17:47	92
18:12	81
25:10	91

2 Sam.

1:18	95
12:20	276
22:16	77
22:35	95

1 Kgs

1:39	276
8:10	98
8:15	98
18:12	13, 83
19:8-13	60
19:15-16	276

2 Kgs

2:9	56, 83
2:15-16	83
3:9-12	83
17–25	34

1 Chron.

12:16-18	91
12:17	91
12:18	83, 91
25:1	92
25:7	95

2 Chron.

6:4	98
15:1	91
15:8	91
20:14	83, 91
20:15-17	92
20:18-19	92
20:20-23	92
20:27-28	92
24:20	83, 91
24:20-22	93

Ezra

5:2	83
7:10	95

Neh.

9:19	77
9:20	77

Est.

1:5	98

Job

12:7-9	137
27:3	87
32:8	75
33:4	86, 134, 146
34:13-15	134
34:14-15	87, 143
38:4-7	123
38–41	139

Ps.

2	159
2:7	10, 154
8	136, 137
8:8	75
18:35	95
19	137
19:1	137
29	137
33:6	143, 146, 153, 156, 158, 342
34:1	184
51:1-5	81
51:10	81
51:11	20, 80, 147
65	137
90:4	8
103:30	158
104	137, 139
104:27-30	139
104:28-30	87
104:29-30	75, 87, 134
104:30	143, 147
106:21	76
110	10
116:10	20
133	363
137	57
139	111
139:7	138, 147
139:7-8	35
147:3	85

Prov.

8:14	94
20:26	82

Isa.

1–39	97
1:6	276
3:25	94
5:11-13	94
6:1	98
7:4	94
8:10	94
8:12-13	94
9:7	85
10:3	94

SCRIPTURE INDEX

10:13	94	61	96	43	83
10:24	94	61:1	14, 59, 79, 83, 85	43:7	57
10:27	363			44:4	98
10:33-34	93	61:1-3	95	47:9	84
11	86, 95, 96, 101	63:10	81		
		63:10-11	20, 80	Dan.	
11:1-4	95	63:11	77	1:4	100
11:1-5	85, 93, 322	63:14	77	1:17	100
		64:1	13	1:20	100
11:1-9	94	65:14	95	2:31	101
11:2	98	65:17	96	3:22	101
11:3-5	97			4:8	100
11:4	79	Jer.		4:9	100
16:3	94	2:13	134	4:18	100
19:14	17	5:21	320	5:11-12	100
19:20	95	14:8	76	5:11	82
22:22	85	16:18	98	5:12	100
29:10	17	17:13	134	5:14	100–1
29:14	94	22:3	321	6:3-4	101
30:33	75	23:5	85	6:3	100
32:15	84	23:24	98	7:13	50
33:5-6	94	23:25-28	39	7:19	101
33:7	95	25:12	98		
40:7-10	79	30:9	85	Hos.	
40–42	79	33:15-22	85	3:5	85
42	96	44:25	98	11:1	13
42:1	10, 85			13:4	76
42:1-4	12, 94	Ezek.			
42:1-7	95	2:2	83	Joel	
42:2	95	3:14	83	2:28	86
42:5	87	8:3	13	2:28-29	14, 19, 84, 104, 323
42:6	102	11:5	84		
43:3	76	11:19	198		
44:3	19	12:2	320	2:28-32	4, 79
44:3-4	84	34:23-24	85	2:29-31	144
44–55	102	36:17	80	3:1-19	79
46:7	95	36:20	80	3:17	57
46:13	102	36:23	81	3:20-21	79
48:16	83	36:26-27	98		
49:6	102	36:26-31	81	Amos	
50	96	37:1-14	9, 84, 85, 342	4:13	157
50:4-5	95			4:14	159
53:3	102	37:5	87	6:6	276
53:7	28	37:6	84	9:11	85
55:3	85	37:9	87		
56:3-8	96	37:9-10	84	Mic.	
56–59	96	37:10	87	3:1	97
59:1-2	103	37:11	87	3:5-8	97
59:3	104	37:14	84, 87	3:8	83
59:6-8	104	37:24-28	85	6:8	97
59:11	104	39:28-29	86, 104		
59:12-16	104	39:29	19	Hab.	
59:21	86	40:34-35	98	2:14	98

SCRIPTURE INDEX

Hag.		26:63	13	1:1-4	339
2:2-13	83	27:40	13	1:15	8, 55
2:5	77, 147	27:43	13	1:17	56
		27:54	13	1:18	57
Zech.		28	182	1:35	8–10, 12, 56, 57, 322
2:10	57	28:17	25		
4:6-9	83	28:18-20	107		
7:12	83	28:19	8, 11–13, 61	1:38	129, 326
10:2	39			1:41	8, 10
12:7-10	79	28:20	61	1:45	10
12:9	79			1:52-53	10
13:1	79	Mk		1:67	8, 10
		1:8	8–10	1:76	10
Mt.		1:10	8–9, 11, 58	2	320
1:18	8, 11, 56			2:24	10
1:20	8, 11–12	1:12	8–9, 13, 59, 138, 284	2:25-27	8, 10, 14
1:21	56			2:25-35	102
1:23	13			2:28-32	102
2:15	12–13	1:12-13	10–11	3:16	8–10, 25, 263
3:11-12	134	1:21	10		
3:11	8, 9, 25	1:21-27	11	3:21-22	129
3:16	8–11, 13, 58, 134	1:27	10	3:22	8, 9, 11, 58
		1:34	13		
3:17	12–13	1:39	13	4:1	8, 59
4:1-11	10–11	2:7	182	4:1-13	10, 11, 14
4:1	8, 13, 59	3:15	13	4:14	8, 11, 59
4:3	13	3:22	13	4:16	14
4:6	13	3:29	8	4:16-18	28
5:33-37	239	3:29-30	11	4:16-19	11, 12, 14
8:29	13	4:23	320	4:18	8
10:20	8, 11, 173	6:3	34	4:18-19	276
11:13	10	6:13	13	6:19	173
11:15	320	8:27–9:1	13	7:38	60
12:18	8, 12	8:28	10	9:19	10
12:28	8, 12	8:31-32	13	9:20	43
12:31-32	8, 358	9:7	60	9:33	60
12:32	11	9:31	13	9:34	8
13:54-57	320	10:33-34	13	9:35	60
13:55	34	11:32	10	10:21	8, 14
14:5	10	12:36	8, 10	10:34	276
14:33	13	13:11	8, 11–12, 60	11:13	8, 14
16:16	13			11:20	12, 75
17:5	13, 60	14:3	60	12:8	11
19	358	14:8	60, 276	12:9-10	11
19:19-20	60	14:22-25	61, 107	12:10	8, 11
21:26	10	14:32-42	13	12:11	11
21–22	320	14:58	59	12:11-12	60
22:43	8, 10	16:9-20	12	12:12	11
25:14-30	124			14:35	320
26:7	60	Lk.		16:16	10
26:12	60	1–2	14	20:6	10
26:26-29	61, 107	1:1	55, 60	21:15	11

22:14-20	107	8:26-29	45	17:23	49	
22:15-20	61	8:31-32	46	18:21	61	
22:53	61	8:42	160	19:34-35	38	
24:16	32	8:42-43	45	20:19-23	45	
24:31	32	11:50-51	60	20:21-23	52	
24:31-32	28	12:3	60, 276	20:22	45, 62, 145, 148, 173	
24:38	31	12:16	166			
24:39	31	12:23	44			
24:44-49	25, 28, 47	12:47-50	45	20:31	47, 339	
24:45	28, 32	13–17	44	21:24	41, 43	
24:49	8, 14, 25, 32, 334	13:1-20	61	21:24-25	47	
		13:31-33	44			
24:50-53	62	14–16	37, 105	Acts		
		14–17	42, 59	1:1	46	
Jn		14:5	44	1:1-2	62	
1	156, 159, 238	14:6	44, 339	1:1-3	138	
		14:15	45, 59	1:3	32	
1:1	122	14:15-17	105	1:4-5	334	
1:3	156, 159	14:16	5, 44	1:5-8	28	
1:14	45, 57, 129	14:16-17	44–5	1:8	8–9, 14, 25, 27, 34, 47, 129, 263, 334	
		14:17	4, 43, 323			
1:17	45	14:18-21	45			
1:18	57, 339	14:18	325			
1:29	43, 46	14:25-26	11, 44			
1:29-34	45	14:26	32, 45–7, 59–60, 105, 173, 321	1:8-11	62	
1:32	43, 58			1:14	14	
1:34	43			1:16	28	
2:19	59			1:21-22	27	
3:1-21	22	14:27	105	1–2	45	
3:3	35	15	236	2	4, 25, 294, 313	
3:5-6	35, 274	15:13-15	44			
3:5-8	43–4, 48	15:14	236	2:1-4	134	
3:6-8	134	15:26	43, 45, 47, 57, 159–62, 168, 170–3, 179	2:1-41	104, 334	
3:8	344, 347			2:3	52	
3:11-21	43			2:4	29–30	
3:16	46, 130			2:5	29, 129	
3:31-36	43			2:6	129	
3:32-35	45			2:14-36	9	
3:35	174	15:26-27	44, 59	2:17	30	
4:10	174	16	348	2:17-18	239	
4:14	134	16:5-15	59–60	2:17-21	14	
4:23-24	43	16:7-11	44	2:19	30, 52	
4:24	22, 111, 155	16:7	187	2:36	29–31	
		16:8-11	46	2:37-47	62	
6:63	138	16:12-15	44	2:37	174	
6:69	37	16:13	43, 45, 299, 345	2:38	27, 29	
7:16-18	45			2:42	27, 31	
7:37-38	44, 53	16:15	167	2:44-45	28	
7:37-39	134	16:16	45, 46	3:6	52	
7:38	45	17	61	3:10	32	
7:38-39	43, 85	17:4	44	3:16	52	
7:39	44–5	17:17	45	3:17	31	

3:19	31	9:41-42	27	24:31-32	28
4:1-22	11	10–11	335	24:45	28
4:5-13	32	10:10-11	266	28:1	32
4:7	52	10:19	28	28:25	28
4:8	27, 29, 276	10:34-44	29	28:31	29
		10:38	362–3		
4:8-12	9, 26	10:44	28	Rom.	
4:10-12	52	11:17	28	1:4	18, 323
4:13	27, 32, 276	11:24	29	1:8	18
		11:27-30	28	1:19-20	137
4:23-31	30, 52	12:14	32	3:23	104
4:25	28	13:2	28	5:5	18, 20, 40, 105, 174
4:29-31	29	13:9	27, 29		
4:30	30	13:9-12	9		
4:31	9, 27, 29, 30	13:17	52	6:3-4	106
		14:1-2	52	6:23	258
4:32-35	28	14:3	27, 29, 266	7:6	18, 19
4:32-37	62			8:1-5	40
4:32-35:16	27	14:14-18	28	8:2-9	18
4:36-35:11	28	14:27–15:29	28	8:2	19
5:1-11	358	15:7-11	29	8:4	20
5:12	27	15:9	28, 31	8:5-6	20
5:12-16	26, 29	15:20	28, 31	8:9	18, 22
5:32	11, 27, 28	15:26	105, 171	8:10-11	19
6:1-6	28	15:28	31	8:14-16	179
6:2	31	15:29	28	8:14	18, 20
6:3	30	16:6-7	28	8:15	19, 173
6:4	29	16:7	22, 29	8:15-16	18
6:5	9, 29	16:8	105	8:16	274
6:8	30, 52	16:10	26	8:18-23	142
6:10	9	16:13	105	8:19-23	140
7:1-56	11	16:15	105	8:19	142
7:38-44	28	16:16	17	8:21-23	142
7:51	11, 358	17:1-9	28	8:22-23	144
7:51-53	27	17:6	29	8:26	192, 286, 325
7:55	9, 29	17:16-34	137		
8:1	34	17:22	28	8:26-27	18, 22, 299
8:4-39	335	17:24-29	28		
8:13	29	17:27-28	355	9:1	18, 20
8:14-16	28	17:30	31	12:2	356
8:14-19	29	18	31	12:5	108
8:17-18	261	18:26	29	12:6-8	35
8:20	174	19	30	12:8	266
8:29	28	19:1-7	31	13:2	353
8:32-35	28	19:5-6	29	14:17	18–20
8:39-40	29	19:8	29	15:13	18, 20–1
9	356	19:26	28	15:16	18–20
9:1-19	40	20:18-35	27	15:18-21	19
9:17	29	20:23	28	15:19	18
9:27	29	21:11	28	15:25	353
9:29	29	21:25	28	15:30	22
9:34-35	27	22:17	266	16:25	353

SCRIPTURE INDEX

1 Cor.		2 Cor.			1:13-14	274
1:2	20	1:21-22	274		1:17	21
1:7	264	1:22	52		2:18	289
1:22	21	2:13	18		3:3-4	353
1:24	155	3:2	127		3:8	39
2:6-16	40, 351	3:3	18		4	275, 358
2:7	353	3:6	22		4:3-6	40
2:10	18, 134, 299	3:8	22		4:7-13	35
		3:13	20		4:14-15	349
2:11	18, 22	3:15	22		4:30	18, 52, 358
2:12	18	3:17	5, 18, 22, 171		5:20	340
2:13	18, 21				5:23	108
3:16	344	3:18	20, 128		5:32	353
4:21	18	4:7	20		6:19	353
6:11	20	4:13	20			
6:17	237	4:14	21		Phil.	
6:19	18–20, 134	5:5	21		1:9-10	350
		5:17-21	105		1:19	22
7:34	18	6:6	18		1:27	18, 22
11:1	27	6:16	344		2:1	22, 40
11:23-26	106	7:1	18		3:3	18, 22
12	264	7:13	18		4:18	18
12:1-11	21	10:5	351			
12:3	18, 20, 40, 49, 69, 185	12:4	194		Col.	
		13:13	18, 20, 23		1:5	35
		15:28	122		1:18	108
12:4	21				1:26	353
12:4-11	35, 40	Gal.				
12:7	21, 267	1:12	339		1 Thess.	
12:8	22	2:2	39		1:5	20
12:9	84	2:7-9	42		1:5-6	18, 20
12:10	18	2:9	33		2:13	339
12:12-25	299	3:2	19		4:8	20
12:12	21	3:5	19		4:13-15:11	21
12:13	263	3:14	19		4:18	18
12:21	267	3:26-28	239, 334		5:19-21	358
12:27	108	3:28	335		5:23	20
12:28	337	4:6-7	179			
13:1	267	4:6	173, 274		2 Thess.	
13:8-10	264	5:16-18	20		2:7	353
14	264	5:22	20, 105			
14:2	353	5:22-23	35, 341		1 Tim.	
14:3-4	265, 277	5:22-25	40		2:5-6	104
14:14-15	18	5:25	20		3:9	353
14:18-19	265	6:1	17		3:16	353
14:30	264	6:18	18		5:12	157
15:8-9	39				6:3-5	351
15:28	122, 141	Eph.				
15:45	125, 145, 148	1:9	353		2 Tim.	
		1:10	134		2:15	35
15:51	353	1:13	18, 35, 52, 68		3:16-17	342
16:18	18					

Reference	Page(s)
Tit.	
1:15	238
3:5	198
3:5-6	263
Heb.	
2:5-9	62
2:10	284
4:12	340
5:14	349
6:4	158
7:27	107
10:26-29	358
12:1	125
Jas	
1:1-4	34
1:5-8	35
1:8-11	34
1:12	35
1:13-15	34
1:16-19	35
1:21	35
1:22	127
1:22-27	35
2:1-26	35
2:2-7	34
2:8	35
2:21	35
2:25	35
3:1-12	35
3:14-16	34
3:17	35
4:1-4	34
4:1-10	49
4:2-3	35
4:5-7	49
4:8	34, 35
4:11-17	35
5:1-6	34
5:9	35
5:11	35
5:13-18	35
5:14	363
5:17	35
1 Pet.	
1:1	35
1:2	36
1:3	35
1:6	36
1:6-9	35
1:7	36
1:10-12	36
1:11	22
1:13	35
1:13-16	36
1:21	36
1:23-25	36
2:5	36
2:9	36
2:11-12	35
2:21	36
3:8	351
3:18-22	107
4:12-14	36
5:10	36
2 Pet.	
1:4	2, 37
1:8	37
1:11	37
1:16	36
1:18	37
1:20-21	339
1:21	37, 49
2:1	37, 38
2:1-3	36
2:4-10	37
2:10-22	39
2:15-16	37
2:21	37
3:2	36
3:5-7	37
3:11	37
3:13	37
3:16	37
1 Jn	
1:1	37, 48–9
1:1-4	46
1:4	47
2:1	5, 45
2:2	45
2:4-6	38
2:12-28	49
2:18-27	48
2:19	37
2:20	37, 46, 48
2:22	48
2:24	38
2:27	37, 46, 48, 362–3
2:28	49
2:28-33:10	43
2:29-33:1	49
3:3-10	49
3:11	38
3:14	38
3:17	38
3:23	49
3:23-24	48
3:24	38, 49, 68
4:1	38, 49, 345
4:1-6	37, 47–9, 52
4:2	38, 49, 69, 347
4:6	38, 43, 45, 48
4:7-8	38
4:9-10	49
4:12	212
4:13	38, 68
4:14-15	49
4:16	174
4:23-24	43
5:1-5	49
5:6	45
5:6-8	38
5:13	49
2 Jn	
5-6	38
7	38
9	38
3 Jn	
5-10	38
Jude	
1	34
3	38–9
4	38
8	38–9
10–16	39
17	38
19	39
20–24	39
Rev.	
1:2	50–1
1:4	50
1:10	50

1:13	50	3:18	276	14:1-2	52
2–3	50–1	3:22	50	14:4	52
2:7	50	4:2	50	16:12-16	51
2:11	50	11:5	52	17:3	50
2:17	50	12:12	51	21:4-5	67
2:29	50	13:1-8	52	21:10	50, 144
3:6	50	13:10	52	22:1-2	53
3:13	50	13:11-18	51, 52	22:17	3, 53, 187

www.ingramcontent.com/pod-product-compliance
Lightning Source LLC
Chambersburg PA
CBHW080533300426
44111CB00017B/2710